MW00535412

# Lessons from East Asia

## STUDIES IN INTERNATIONAL TRADE POLICY

# Lessons from East Asia

Edited by Danny M. Leipziger

*Ann Arbor*

THE UNIVERSITY OF MICHIGAN PRESS

2000   1999   1998   1997      4   3   2   1

*A CIP catalog record for this book is available from the British Library.*

Library of Congress Cataloging-in-Publicaton Data

Lessons from East Asia / edited by Danny M. Leipziger.
      p.   cm. — (Studies in international trade policy)
   Includes index.
   ISBN 0-472-10679-1 (cloth)
    1. East Asia—Economic policy.   2. Asia, Southeastern—Economic policy.   3. Economic development.   I. Leipziger, Danny M.
   II. Series.
HC460.5.L47   1996
338.95—dc20                                         96-35267
                                                         CIP

## STUDIES IN INTERNATIONAL TRADE POLICY

# Contents

    *Maxwell J. Fry*

11. Common Foundations of East Asian Success                 541
    *Peter A. Petri*

    Contributors                                             569

    Index                                                    571

# Preface

This compilation of case studies and cross-country essays focuses on the role of public policy in the experience of the East Asian economies. Much has been written on the theme of successful development in the region. What hopefully distinguishes this volume is that the country case studies have been coauthored by local researchers, all with strong policy experience, as well as by World Bank economists. The essays, originally produced as part of the World Bank's major effort in studying the East Asian success story, known as the *East Asian Miracle* work,[1] were reviewed by an international panel of experts at a conference at the East West Center in Hawaii, and they benefited from the views of numerous country experts.

I have organized the book to parallel the research design. Part 1 includes the case studies for the first generation of rapidly developing East Asian economies—the tigers—while part 2 incorporates the later generation success stories—the cubs—plus the Philippines, a country only now beginning to show significant progress. Part 3 includes cross-country essays on public investment, foreign direct investment, and cross-country patterns to synthesize the lessons learned and propose actions for other development aspirants to pursue.

A major theme running through the volume is regional learning and regional contagion.[2] Beginning with the model and experience of Japan, and continuing with the impressive achievements of countries originally considered unviable in the 1950s and 1960s, like Korea and Taiwan, regional policy lessons permeated borders easily. The 1980s brought further lessons and flows of capital to the second generation of rapid industrializers. And the 1990s have

1. World Bank, *The East Asian Miracle* (Washington, D.C., and New York: Oxford University Press, 1993); D. Leipziger and V. Thomas, *The Lessons of East Asia: An Overview of Country Experience* (Washington, D.C.: World Bank, 1993).

2. On the important role of Japan, see K. Yamamura and Y. Yasuba, eds., *The Political Economy of Japan* (Stanford: Stanford University Press, 1987); H. K. Kim, "The Japanese Civil Service and Economic Development," in *The Japanese Civil Service and Economic Development,* ed. H. K. Kim et al. (Oxford: Clarendon Press, 1995); K. Yamamura, "The Role of Government in Japan's Catch-up Industrialization," EDI Working Paper 93–28 (Washington, D.C.: World Bank, 1993); and M. Kagami, T*he Voice of East Asia: Development Implications for Latin America* (Tokyo: Institute of Developing Economics, 1995).

seen regional contagion benefit new aspirants like Vietnam.[3] Clearly, however, the transferability of lessons depends on the institutional framework in which policy is formulated, the consistency of policy, and the quality of implementation. The aspects of development are emphasized in this volume.

It is noteworthy that in the East Asian country experience the time horizon of both public policy and private sector actions appears to be longer than elsewhere; put differently, governments and other economic agents appear prepared to invest for the long haul. Second, the level of cooperation—call it planning, coordination, or simply institutionalized understandings—seems distinctly higher in East Asia between the public and private sectors. Third, the concept of competition, which underlies global markets, seems more easily internalized in the region, to the point that cooperation, coordination, and competition can be integrated in the formulation of public policy.

The economics profession has expended a lot of energy trying to find the root causes of East Asia's economic success.[4] Pack and Page (1993) focus on the process of accumulation, total factor productivity, and export expansion. Other commentators have focused on the importance of initial conditions (Rodrik 1994, 1995), the key role of human capital formulation (Birdsall and Sabot 1993), and the role of capital augmentation rather than technical progress in explaining East Asia's success (Kim and Lau 1994). Yet others, like Wade (1990, 1993) and Haggard (1993), point out that mainstream economics places excessive emphasis on the export promotion story and provides inadequate attention to the governance story. We hope to add to our store of knowledge in this area via the country studies approach.

A key area of debate continues to be the role of industrial policies in the performance of East Asian economies. Much has been written on this topic;[5]

---

3. See D. M. Leipziger, *Awakening the Market: Vietnam's Economic Transition* (Washington, D.C.: World Bank, 1992); D. Dollar, "Vietnam: Successes and Failures of Macroeconomic Stabilization," in *The Challenge of Reform in Indonesia*, ed. B. Ljunggren (Cambridge: Harvard Institute for International Development, 1993); and World Bank, *Transition to the Market* (Washington, D.C.: World Bank, 1993).

4. See H. Pack and J. Page, "Accumulation, Exports and Growth in the High Performing Asian Economies," 1993, mimeo; Overseas Development Council, *Miracle or Design? Lessons from the East Asian Experience* (Washington, D.C.: Overseas Development Council, 1994); D. Rodrik, "Initial Conditions: The Importance of Equality and Education," in Overseas Development Council, *Miracle or Design*, 15–54; D. Rodrik, "Getting Interventions Right: How South Korea and Taiwan Grew Rich," *Economic Policy* (April 1995: 69–121; N. Birdsall and R. Sabot, "Virtuous Circle: Human Capital Growth and Equity in East Asia," 1993, mimeo, World Bank; J. Kim and Lau, "The Sources of Economic Growth of the East Asian Newly Industrialized Countries," *Journal of Japanese and International Economics* 8 (1994): 235–71; S. Haggard, "Politics and Institutions in the World Bank's East Asia," in Overseas Development Council, *Miracle or Design*, 84–104; and R. Wade, "Selective Industrial Policies in East Asia: Is the East Asian Miracle Right?" in Overseas Development Council, *Miracle or Design*, 57–80.

5. For a smattering of opinions, see A. Amsden, *Asia's Next Giant: South Korea and Late Industrialization* (New York: Oxford University Press, 1989); R. Komiya, M. Okuno, and K.

however, very little consensus has emerged, in part due to the selective nature of the investigation. Looking at Korea, one gets a distinctly different set of lessons than one gets from Singapore, and even in Korea much depends on when the judgment is made. The story gets even more complex when one includes the second generation NICs (newly industrializing countries) because we can now assess, for example, the rather mixed record of Malaysia and the virtual non-existence of industrial policies in Thailand. The inclusion of eight East Asian economies allows for a broader account of the effectiveness and importance of industrial policies.

These essays therefore aim to fill two major gaps—the paucity of country-specific work on the institutional side of development policy and the failure to explain the mixed record of industrial policies in East Asia. These areas are highlighted in all the case studies, and the lessons are synthesized in the introductory essay by Leipziger and Thomas.

The research effort reflected in this volume owes a number of significant debts. As research director for the East Asia Country Studies Project at the World Bank, I received substantial support from Lawrence Summers, Nancy Birdsall, John Page, Gautam Kaji, Callisto Madavo, Marianne Haug, and Vinod Thomas. Participants at the Honolulu conference in November 1992 included Duck-Soo Han, Hal Hill, Chalmers Johnson, Wolfgang Kasper, Hyung-ki Kim, Paul Kreisberg, Chung H. Lee, Manuel Montes, Seiji Naja, Takashi Nohara, John Page, Tambunlerthchai Somsak, Wanda Tseng, Wing Thye Woo, Ippei Yamazawa, and Zainal Aznam Yusof. Research assistance was provided by Jason Brown and John Normand. The manuscript was prepared by Bernadette Infante-Wells, Amy Beth Curry, and Diane Leslie Bouvet.

While the initial work was completed as part of the World Bank's investigation of East Asia's success, the views expressed in this book are those of the authors alone and do not necessarily reflect those of the World Bank.

With the challenge of development still ahead of many nations, it is hoped that this volume may shed some deeper light on the record of East Asian success. To those students and future policymakers who may read this volume, the message is that through enlightened policies, strong commitment, and vigorous and consistent implementation much can be done.

Danny M. Leipziger

Suzumura, *Industrial Policy of Japan* (New York: Academic Press, 1989); D. Leipziger and P. Petri, in *The Balance between Industry and Agriculture in Economic Development,* ed. J. G. Williamson and V. R. Panchamukhi (New York: St. Martin's Press, 1989); R. Wade, *Governing the Market* (Princeton: Princeton University Press, 1990); D. Leipziger and P. Petri, "Korean Industrial Policy," in *Korea's Political Economy,* ed. L. C. Cho and Y. H. Kim (Boulder: Westview Press, 1994); D. Leipziger, ed., *Korea: Transition to Maturity,* New York: Pergamon, 1988; and World Bank, "Korea: Managing the Industrial Transition," 1987, Washington, D.C.: World Bank.

# An Overview of East Asian Experience

*Danny M. Leipziger and Vinod Thomas*

The success of East Asian development is legendary. No other group of developing countries has done as well in fostering growth, reducing poverty, integrating with world markets, or raising standards of living. Over the past 25 years, per capita incomes have almost quadrupled. Absolute poverty has fallen by about two-thirds on average, population growth rates have declined rapidly, and health and education levels have improved markedly. The first set of success stories, the Asian tigers, has led to a second generation of rapidly industrializing, fast-growing economies. And now China has started a new engine of regional growth.

Though often spoken of as a single group, the East Asian countries are, in fact, remarkably diverse. The region includes some of the richest and poorest developing countries, some of the most populous and some with small populations, those with a store of natural resources and those with virtually none. Moreover, despite its steady growth, East Asia is still grappling with serious challenges, including environmental degradation, infrastructural bottlenecks, and poverty. But, if there is a single firm lesson to be drawn from the region in the past few decades, it is that difficult challenges have a history of being met.

## The Search for Country Lessons

Why have the different economies of East Asia been so successful? To shed light on this question, the World Bank studied several countries in the region, complementing other approaches and cross-country analyses.[1] The analyses were conducted by teams that included local experts as well as World Bank economists. The task was daunting, but it has added to our knowledge and provided glimpses into why East Asia has been so successful.

---

1. The Country Lessons Project includes case studies of Hong Kong, Korea, Singapore, Malaysia, Thailand, and Indonesia. See also World Bank, *The East Asian Miracle: Economic Growth and Public Policy* (Washington, D.C.: World Bank, 1993); and World Bank, *World Development Report, 1991* (Washington, D.C.: World Bank, 1991).

The country studies show the diversity of the East Asian phenomenon, with tremendous variation across the countries and over time. No one formula or standard prescription has been decisive. Several compelling factors do, however, emerge as major contributors.

Importantly, policy approaches adopted by East Asian economies were not uniform. The first generation of newly industrialized economies (NIEs), Korea, Singapore, and Taiwan, China, chose a good deal of state intervention, as Japan did earlier. Hong Kong was an exception for the most part. Among the second generation of successful East Asians, Indonesia and Malaysia had little success with their early interventions, and they have turned less interventionist over the past dozen years as their economic performance has improved markedly. Other recent NIEs, like Thailand and coastal China,[2] in many respects are avoiding interventionist industrial policies.

These differences notwithstanding, it could not be pure coincidence that the fastest-growing economies in recent decades are concentrated in East Asia. Indeed, the country studies found that, behind the substantial country variations, there are significant common features that policymakers elsewhere might take to heart.

A country's development prospects are influenced by three sets of factors: *endowments, policies,* and *institutions,* which are set out in the Development Checklist (see appendix). The checklist is illustrative and must be interpreted with caution since the categorizations are at times subjective and subject to the time period considered. Nevertheless, in order to see patterns that are shared among East Asian economies, it is a potentially useful exercise. It dispels the notion that all East Asian countries shared identical features; quite to the contrary, it highlights considerable diversity. It also manages to draw a strong distinction between many of the characteristics common to first-generation, in contrast to second-generation, NIEs.

The traditional focus of economists has been on policies, which turn out to be crucial to the East Asian experience. Regional success has also been analyzed by other social scientists who have emphasized the quality of policy making, leadership, nationhood, cohesion, and the role of the state.[3] The review of these more intangible features is motivated by the observation that policies similar to those undertaken elsewhere have proven to be more productive in East Asia; similarly, in some cases government interventions have not had the

---

2. China clearly pursued very interventionist policies until the late 1970s. The country has been adopting market reforms gradually since then, with spectacular results. In view of its special circumstances, China is not a central part of this discussion.

3. See, for example, S. Haggard, *Pathways from the Periphery: The Politics of Growth in the Newly Industrializing Countries* (Ithaca: Cornell University Press, 1990); C. Johnson, *MITI and the Japanese Miracle* (Stanford: Stanford University Press, 1987); and E. Vogel, *The Four Little Dragons: The Spread of Industrialization in East Asia* (Cambridge: Harvard University Press, 1991).

dire consequences that many would have predicted. Clearly one must distinguish between policy interventions and policy distortions, between distortions affecting particular markets and those affecting the economy as a whole, and between pervasive and nonpervasive distortions.

Turning to the three aforementioned features, the country studies found that none of the initial four NIEs—Korea; Taiwan, China; Singapore; or Hong Kong—was endowed generously with natural resources. (The later NIEs—Indonesia, Malaysia, and Thailand—were richer in natural endowments.) For the initial NIEs, the only resource was people, in the form of a relatively well-educated labor force. For these first-generation NIEs, economic development was a matter of survival and therefore of national urgency. They met the challenge by forcefully committing themselves to becoming exporters in global markets.

Common to East Asia's success were policies for macroeconomic stability, human resource investments, and outward orientation—quite different from what happened in most other developing regions. Because these economies to a large extent took international prices as an ultimate guide to domestic resource allocation, macroeconomic stability was seen as central to the maintenance of competition. In addition, a number of regimes had a strong aversion to inflation. Some societies, or segments thereof, also exhibited an inclination toward human capital investments, which augmented public policy with high household investments. And it was not just the design and selection of policies; it was also implementation. By any standard, implementation of policies was East Asia's forte.

At the core of development success in East Asia has been pragmatic policy making—meaning, most importantly, the relative absence of ideology and the willingness to repudiate failed policies. Thus, polices have been reversed swiftly if experience showed that they were ineffective, as with the abandonment of the flirtation with selective industrial policies in Malaysia and Indonesia in the early 1980s, the curtailment in 1979–80 of the heavy and chemical industry drive in Korea, and the abandonment of Singapore's high-wage policy in 1985. The strong policy response of Indonesia to macroeconomic instability and Thailand's exchange rate management in the mid-1980s are other cases in point of timely and effective policy actions.

Bureaucracies can facilitate reform or they can prevent it. In many successful East Asian industrializers, bureaucracies were agents of development. Put differently, East Asia's technocrats have generally been part of the political mandate for reform. In Singapore, bureaucrats and party officials worked hand in glove for the national agenda. In Indonesia and Malaysia, the political leadership allowed technocrats substantial freedom to manage the economy. In Thailand, the bureaucracy provided continuity when political processes faltered, and in both Korea and Taiwan, China, core economic ministries were key to government efforts to develop the economy. The means differed, but the institutions were influential in hastening economic development.

Korea, Singapore, and Taiwan, China, the fastest postwar industrializers, are credited with "visionary" leadership and efficient bureaucracies. They also achieved national consensus on development goals and had a centralized political apparatus to implement their fairly interventionist strategies. Many observers tend to view each of these features as major, if not decisive, causes of success. Indeed, East Asia's achievements have cast a glow over the region that often transforms every initial policy and institutional condition into a positive contributor to success.

This conclusion would be too simplistic and misleading. After all, in many other countries centralized power has been accompanied by poor policies. Similarly, numerous countries have had either visionary leadership, a strong bureaucracy, or concerted government interventions associated with poor results. Conversely, during successful episodes, some of these features were absent in many other country settings. It would seem that each of these factors may not, by itself, be necessary—and certainly not sufficient—for success, and some may have been costly even if overall success was achieved. But with hindsight these NIEs seem to have benefited from a combination of sociopolitical features that accompanied their superior economic policies.

It should be emphasized that there were some big policy mistakes in East Asia—in industrial policy, financial policy, and the absence of sufficiently forward-looking environmental policies. And, as a result, the region now faces serious challenges in sustaining rapid development. Yet, the question is why past mistakes did not cause the kind of damage that is so apparent in other countries, and, further, how these mistakes were recognized and corrected. It is these issues that offer the most valuable lessons for new market entrants like Vietnam or perennial aspirants like the Philippines. What is it about the quality of decision making, and the ability to turn decisions into action, that has led to the outstanding record?

One strong conclusion is that macroeconomic discipline, outward orientation, and human resource investments—and political stability—were common features that paid off in the successful East Asian economies. But the actions associated with success in the first-generation NIEs involved more intervention than did those in the second generation, an important finding in light of the greater relevance of the latter experience in the current international environment. East Asia, therefore, makes a case neither for a laissez-faire approach to economic policy making, nor for placing a heavy hand on the tiller. The crucial factor was the way that governments supported markets in helping to unleash entrepreneurship.

The second strong conclusion is that, contrary to the recent fashion worldwide, one of the key ingredients in East Asia's success was active government.

It was not more government that had a positive effect; it was better government. East Asia thus offers a contrast to widespread episodes of policy failure. Development economics lacks an adequate theory of why good government policy is pursued by some and not others, an approach combining economics, political organization, and technocratic decision making.[4] While the region offers no universal paradigm in this respect, it does provide some useful lessons in successful policy making.

## Making the Most of Initial Conditions

Asked in the early 1950s to name the success stories of the next 30 years, only a seer would have chosen Hong Kong, Korea, Singapore, or Taiwan, China. All were lacking in natural resources. All had ratios of arable land to population that were so low that meeting basic consumption needs was questionable. The two largest economies, Korea and Taiwan, China, were heavily dependent on food aid from the United States. The story of early East Asian success is much less one of favorable initial conditions than of the countries turning adversity into opportunities.

All four had only one resource: *an adaptable and disciplined labor force.* From around 1960, the major distinction between these four countries and most low-income countries lay in human resource development. In secondary education, for example, East Asian economies (except Indonesia and Thailand) exceeded the average of other developing countries by many multiples. They combined this high level of education with imported technology and returning expatriates to produce rapid productivity growth.[5] Korea, Taiwan, China, and Singapore produced spectacular gains in tertiary education in one generation.[6]

A second initial factor was that *national vulnerability* created the necessity of economic success. Korea was a divided country, competing in a cold war environment with a more industrialized neighbor; Taiwan, China also felt compelled to assert its economic independence; Singapore was a city-state thrust into a competitive environment and attempting to reach nationhood; and Hong Kong was a market outpost for China. This political imperative, combined with the work discipline of societies in Korea, Singapore, and Taiwan,

---

4. A. Fishlow, "Review of Handbook of Development Economics," *Journal of Economic Literature* 29 (December 1991): 1728–37.

5. A. Bhattacharya and J. Page, Jr., "Adjustment, Investment, and Growth in High Performing Asian Economies," mimeo, 1992.

6. N. Birdsall and R. Sabot, eds., "Virtuous Circles: Human Capital Growth and Equity in East Asia," background paper for *The East Asian Miracle,* World Bank, Policy Research Department, 1993. See also R. Barro and J. Lee, "International Comparisons of Educational Attainment," paper presented at the conference How Do National Policies Affect Long-Run Growth? World Bank, Washington, D.C., February 1993.

China, seems to have turned weak initial conditions into advantages to an extent seldom seen elsewhere.

A third "initial condition" was the relative *equality of income* in the first generation NIEs. This factor was more of a change brought about by policy than an inheritance. Most other low- and middle-income countries were not able to achieve similar equality of income or assets. Large land reform schemes in both Korea and Taiwan, China eradicated the landholding classes and made wage income the major source of advancement. Public housing investments in Singapore and Hong Kong were early priorities of governments bent on maintaining a national consensus on development policies.

Fourth, governments embraced *export development.* This was not dictated by ideology but by realism. Their small size and low incomes dictated that external markets would provide the major source of revenue. Singapore's leaders are fond of noting that their economy was too small to change international markets, so they decided to change their own economy.

Finally, export drives required *domestic entrepreneurship,* which some societies possessed but which did not always seem to exist. In Singapore, publicly owned corporations, behaving commercially, took the lead. In Korea, government had to foster the creation of firms, encouraging their growth and laying the foundation for the modern-day *chaebul* or conglomerate. Using the Japanese model of *zaibatsu* and the general trading company, the Korean government was able to compensate for the apparent lack of entrepreneurship. East Asian economies have done exceedingly well in monitoring each other's success and, when necessary, borrowing one another's institutions.

## External Circumstances

The original "East Asian miracle" was postwar Japan, which shared some similar conditions with the early NIEs, Korea and Taiwan, China. With little in the way of physical assets, all three began their development with the desire to accumulate capital in their first decade of development. Korea and Taiwan, China initially were critically dependent on foreign aid. It accounted for as much as 50 percent of fixed investment in some of the early years. For Korea over a period of three decades (1946–76), the United States alone provided more than 500 current dollars per capita in economic and military assistance. For Taiwan, China aid was $425 per person. Once the growth engine was sparked, however, high domestic savings rates took over and maintained the process of accumulation.

Export development in the early NIEs was helped by the expanding U.S. market of the 1960s and 1970s, and the model was Japan. This was particularly true of Korea, which was most inclined to compete directly in large industries like steel, shipbuilding, and automobiles. Taiwan, China relied more on a range of smaller firms in most sectors,[7] while Hong Kong and Singapore were en-trepôt exporters. Within two decades, the "tigers" were firmly established, to the envy of other economies.

The East Asian story was not one of favorable external conditions pro-ducing the region's outstanding performance. Most other regions faced simi-lar external conditions. But the East Asians committed themselves, almost from the outset, to becoming players in the global scene. With rather similar endowments, Korea and Taiwan, China followed the Japanese lead, attempting to acquire state of the art technology and inputs. Much of Korea's imitative strategy evolved as a reaction to Japanese dominance spurred by a desire for economic independence. Its work ethic, as seen in its 55-hour average work week, was motivated by a national drive to succeed.

The success of the second generation of NIEs in the 1980s cannot be pri-marily attributed to favorable external conditions either. Malaysia, Thailand, and Indonesia were resource rich but did not excel until manufactured exports were developed. Importantly, these second-generation NIEs laid the foundation for their surge with stable macroeconomic policies and political stability. These factors plus low labor costs appealed to foreign investors—those facing higher costs at home, such as Japan in the first instance, but later including Taiwan, China and Korea. Japanese-led foreign investment followed American and regional Chinese capital in the southern tier, providing the transfer of technol-ogy that the first-generation NIEs struggled to acquire. This allowed the Asian "cubs" to penetrate the U.S. market, especially during the 1980s. Coupled with aggressive exchange-rate policies following the Plaza Accord in 1985, they acquired a strong position as exporters. Malaysia and Thailand became about the fastest-growing economies in the world in the second half of the 1980s.

There were exceptions to all this. The Philippines failed to respond to the challenge, despite its rich endowment of human capital and its access to foreign aid and credit. Myanmar, Vietnam, Laos, North Korea, and Mongolia, for vari-ous reasons, have not done well in recent decades. Commentators point to the Philippines' deeply rooted structure of oligopoly and the sizable inequalities in income and wealth as causes for the relatively poor performance. These factors, combined with a relatively weak bureaucracy, it is argued, allowed the elite to engage in rent-seeking activities at the expense of development objectives. The Philippines stands out as a country that did not achieve an export vision.

Elsewhere, however, there was an outbreak of "regional contagion," a factor we consider important for the region's success. Foreign direct invest-ment (FDI) inspired the transfer of financing and know-how in the later NIEs. In 1991, after Mexico and China, Malaysia, Thailand, Indonesia, and Korea

7. C. Dahlman and O. Sananikone, "Taiwan China: Policies and Distribution for Rapid Growth," mimeo, World Bank, 1993.

were the third, fifth, seventh, and eighth largest recipients of FDI among developing countries. They accounted for almost a quarter of total flows to developing countries. Adding China raises the proportion to more than a third. In Malaysia, FDI accounts for 20 percent of gross domestic investment. The figure is not much lower in the southern Chinese provinces, where the world's fastest growth is being recorded in the 1990s.

## Macroeconomic Policies

Perhaps the factor most consistently present in the successful East Asian economies was a sound macroeconomic policy framework. This was characterized by fiscal discipline, adequate incentives for saving and investment, and an outward-oriented trade policy. Originally imposed by bilateral donors as a condition for continued assistance in the early NIEs, these policies were quickly internalized and became tenets of development policy.

### Fiscal Discipline

One of the most striking lessons from East Asia is the consistent presence of macroeconomic stability.[8] East Asia's governments exercised macroeconomic discipline, ensuring that the fiscal and external deficits were generally kept under control. Prudent foreign borrowing helped the avoidance of debt crises, which set back progress elsewhere in the developing world in the 1980s. Macroeconomic stability gave predictable and credible signals to savers and investors about prices and returns, which in turn encouraged risk taking, investments, and growth.

Over the past quarter of a century, the fiscal deficit and the current account deficit in developing East Asia were less than half the average for other developing countries, and high-income East Asia had surpluses. Exchange rates for East Asian developing economies were seldom overvalued, in contrast to the situation in other developing countries. Interest rates were generally positive in real terms, while in the rest of the developing world they tended to be negative. By and large, East Asia managed to keep inflation in single digits.

From time to time, macroeconomic difficulties did occur, but they were swiftly contained to ensure that deficits never got seriously out of control. For example, Korea's inflation rate hovered around 20 percent in the late 1970s as a result of the Central Bank's financing of heavy and chemical industries and the government's purchase of food grains. But stability was restored, as civil ser-

---

8. W. Max Corden, "Seven Asian Miracle Economies: Overview of Macroeconomic Policies," background paper for *The East Asian Miracle,* World Bank, Policy Research Department, 1993.

vice salaries were contained, rice purchase prices restrained, and state spending eventually frozen (in 1983). Indonesia's public sector deficit exceeded 4 percent of GDP in 1986 as oil prices declined and terms of trade deteriorated. But the government made sharp budget cuts in 1987–88, and by 1989 the deficit was down to 1.3 percent of GDP. Malaysia's fiscal deficit approached 20 percent of GDP during 1981–82 as expenditures outpaced revenues, which were hurt by terms of trade shocks. But the government quickly squeezed spending, bringing the deficit down to about 10 percent of GDP in 1984 and 5 percent in 1987, while at the same time using domestic, noninflationary sources of financing.

The contribution of macroeconomic stability to growth came not only from low and stable deficits but from the composition and quality of public finances. Public investment as a proportion of GDP in East Asia was similar to that in other developing countries, though it was higher in Malaysia, Taiwan, China, and Singapore. But public consumption was lower than average. The share of wages and salaries in government expenditure has varied considerably, ranging from 15 percent in Korea over the past two decades to 30 percent in Malaysia. During periods of general restraint, the East Asian economies managed to protect crucial investments, as shown, for example, by the continuing reviews of public expenditure in Indonesia and Korea.

Macroeconomic stability has been supported at times by law, which serves also to underscore the governments' commitment to providing a secure and predictable commercial environment. Indonesia and Thailand have balanced budget laws. In Taiwan, China before 1987, a law limited the value of outstanding government bonds to no more than 40 percent of the central government's annual budget. Stability in Indonesia has been aided by an open capital account, which, combined with the desire to avoid inflation, served as a check on monetary expansion. Finally, the personal distaste for high inflation on the part of political leaders, for example, in Korea, Malaysia, and Singapore, kept macroeconomic stability high on the policy agenda.

Underlying this macroeconomic record has been a high degree of pragmatism and flexibility, in the sense that governments had few ideological objections to needed policy corrections. Thailand and Indonesia engineered major depreciations of their exchange rates in the mid-1980s. Malaysia and Korea reversed their costly targeting of heavy industries when these proved to be a fiscal drain and threatened growth.

### Investments: More and Better

Investment shares (in GDP) in East Asia rose sharply over the past quarter of a century, rising from somewhat higher figures than in other developing regions to some 50 percent higher. Private investment rose to be two-thirds higher in the successful East Asian economy compared with other developing regions. Private investment was encouraged by a generally supportive macroeconomic environment and by leading public sector infrastructure investments. The lack of high tariffs on imported capital goods was also helpful in raising private investment.

Public investment shares in East Asia, on average, have been similar to those in other regions. While cross-country comparisons may well underestimate total "public" investment in those NIEs where public or quasi-public entities played dominant roles, it is more the efficiency of public investment than its size that distinguishes it from performance in other developing countries. East Asia's total factor productivity growth (TFPG) was three to six times (depending on the measures) greater than the developing country average. This efficiency would seem to be largely a result of the region's policy and institutional frameworks. The rate of return on World Bank's projects was higher in East Asia than elsewhere. In the period 1974–92, projects had an average 18 percent rate of return in East Asia, compared with about 16 percent in the rest of the developing world.

Analysis of national rates of return on investment does show that those who have industrialized rapidly are more efficient users of capital.[9] The question is whether this is due to better project selection, swifter implementation, and/or better capture of externalities. Evidence tends to indicate that all three factors were at work. NIEs are, of course, often caught in a virtuous cycle with respect to project selection, particularly as far as scale is concerned. Rapid growth tends to validate ex post somewhat risky initial investment conditions. A case in point was the Seoul-Pusan highway in Korea or the scale of production of China Steel in Taiwan, China. Implementation records can be inferred from the experience of the World Bank in its projects, where East Asia's success in implementation is superior. Most interesting is the conclusion that the use of five-year plans and coordination mechanisms to convey information between government and the private sector have both served to enhance the level and quality of private investments, particularly in the early NIEs.[10]

Many of the gains associated with capital accumulation depend on the productivity of labor. The educational status of the population was in general higher in East Asia in the 1960s than in other developing regions. Educational investments thereafter were also higher, leading to universal primary education and widely available secondary education. As fertility rates fell in the 1970s, educational expenditures per child increased. Various indicators suggest that the quality of education is also high in the region compared with elsewhere. In-

---

9. World Bank, *The East Asia Miracle.*

10. E. Campos, "Institutions and Public Policy," issues paper for *The East Asia Miracle,* World Bank, 1993.

dicative of the desire to increase human capital is the high proportion of those investments made by private households. In Korea, an equal share of GDP was spent by the private and public sectors. High-quality labor, as seen in Korea or Singapore, for example, has aided industrial flexibility, increased economic efficiency, and produced greater equity.

East Asia's investment performance has been aided by rapidly increasing savings shares (in GDP) as well as external capital flows. Domestic resource mobilization is a regional strength, fostered by high private savings as well as fiscal prudence, which generated increasing public savings. Savings shares are now more than 50 percent higher on average than in other developing countries. Although savings propensities may be dominated by income gains, demographics, and the like, East Asian experience points to low inflation and generally higher real interest rates than elsewhere. This alone does not explain the region's prodigious savings, however. There seems to be a natural drive to save, as seen in curb market savings and cooperative savings clubs, which were prominent in the first-generation NIEs. Governments helped transform these informal into formal savings by fostering institutions such as postal savings accounts and generally excluding savings from taxation. Mandatory savings schemes were also favored by some. Given the high rates of return on invested capital, encouraging savings in the high growth of East Asia has not been a problem and has led to a virtuous savings-income cycle.

## Outward Orientation and an Export Push

East Asia's success in international trade and investment is well documented.[11] The region's developing countries expanded their exports more than twice as fast as the average for other developing countries, tripling their share of exports in GDP over the past quarter of a century. Their share of foreign direct investment to the developing countries rose from about 16 percent in 1970 to over 33 percent in 1990. The flow of trade and investments was crucial to the transfer of technology and the gains in efficiency and productivity. Thus, exports fueled growth to an extraordinary degree.[12]

That much may be beyond dispute; the nature of the underlying policies is not. The question remains how much free trade and how much intervention

---

11. A. O. Krueger, ed., *Export-Oriented Development Strategies: The Success of Five Newly Industrializing Countries* (Boulder: Westview Press, 1985); L. Westphal, "Industrial Policy in an Export-Propelled Economy: Lessons from South Korea's Experience," *Journal of Economic Perspectives* (summer 1990): 41–59.

12. B. Balassa, "The Lessons of East Asian Development: An Overview," *Economic Development and Cultural Change* 36 (1988): 273–90; H. Pack and J. Page, "Accumulation, Exports, and Growth in the High Performing Asian Economies," paper presented at the Carnegie-Rochester Conference on Public Policy, April 1993.

took place in East Asia. This raises the important distinction between free trade and neutrality of incentives. Depending on its nature, an intervention can have different effects on incentives. Sometimes it is market distorting, sometimes not.

Recent evidence on the relative prices for exports, imports, and domestic goods suggests a remarkable degree of neutrality in East Asia. In other words, local prices of traded goods on average departed much less from world prices than in other developing regions, even as there were substantial variations for some individual items and for some countries in East Asia. Prices of traded goods for the East Asian economies were generally closer to world prices than elsewhere.[13]

Nevertheless, outward orientation should not be equated with import openness. Especially in the 1960s and 1970s, several economies exhibited moderate import protection. While such protection in East Asia was usually offset by export incentives, as late as the mid-1980s, the effective protection rate for manufacturing was nearly 30 percent in Korea, 50 percent in Thailand, and 70 percent in Indonesia. By the end of the decade, however, these rates had declined substantially, to the benefit of exports and the economy.

One key difference in the earlier (1960–80) period was that in East Asia economic policies ensured that import protection did not produce the antiexport bias that it did elsewhere. This distinction can be traced to the region's general unwillingness to allow the exchange rate to become overvalued and the fact that exporters were given access to offsetting incentives (e.g., duty exemption, free access to foreign exchange, and free trade zones), which favored exports. There was also effective institutional support for exports (especially in Korea, Taiwan, China, and Singapore) as well as considerable labor market flexibility. The effects of successful government support are typified by the assistance that led Malaysia to start growing palm oil—it now ranks as the world's largest producer, with half the acreage under public control—and the Pohang Steel Complex in Korea, which became a global leader, again in public hands.

A favorable domestic climate for FDI was another key difference. Foreign capital was welcomed, whether in the form of wholly owned subsidiaries of multinationals, joint ventures, or licensers. Malaysia and Thailand made dramatic shifts in favor of FDI in the 1980s; today China is doing the same, with similarly impressive results. Malaysia again illustrates the point about government support: many multinationals in electronics invested in the country in

13. V. Thomas and Y. Wang, "Government Policies and Productivity Growth: Is East Asia an Exception?" (this volume); S. Bhalla, "Free Societies, Free Markets, and Social Welfare," mimeo, July 15, 1993; D. Dollar, "Outward Oriented Developing Economics Really Do Grow More Rapidly: Evidence From 95 LDCs, 1976–85," *Economic Development and Cultural Change* 40, no. 3 (1992) 523–44.

response to active government encouragement. Today Malaysia is the developing world's leading exporter of semiconductors and the third-largest producer (after Japan and the United States).

## Selective Industrial Policy

The term *industrial policy* has many meanings. In the East Asian context, it has been used synonymously with deliberate attempts to change a country's industrial structure, usually to encourage the growth of capital intensive industries. The industrial policy debate was rich, initially pitting the neoclassical economists against a small group of interventionists. Today, with the success of East Asian economies, *industrial policy* is no longer a dirty phrase to most economists. Indeed, numerous elegant reasons have been advanced in support of market intervention, ranging from classic externalities to information gaps[14] and strategic trade advantages.[15] The debate has turned to the role of government in guiding markets[16] or deliberately underpricing capital to achieve rapid industrialization.[17] These discussions cannot be divorced from the more general role of government in coordinating investment decisions and supporting infant industries with the ultimate aim of penetrating world markets. The most forceful examples of selective industrial policy are Japan and Korea. These are very important, but they only tell part of the story of East Asia's success.

### The Korea Story[18]

Korea pursued an industrial policy, by which we mean the comprehensive use of public instruments to industrialize, at least from the start of the Third Republic under President Park Chung Hee. However, during the 1961–71 period this policy was sectorally neutral. Manufactured exports were promoted through a familiar range of policies, but the government was satisfied to capitalize on Korea's comparative advantage in labor-intensive manufactures. Beginning in 1971, however, the government began a coordinated campaign, known as the heavy and chemical industry (HCI) drive, to build up six designated industries.

---

14. J. Stiglitz, "Markets, Market Failures and Development," *American Economic Review Papers and Proceedings* (May 1989): 197–203.

15. P. Krugman, ed., *Rethinking International Trade* (Cambridge: MIT Press, 1990).

16. Robert Wade, *Governing the Market: Economic Theory and the Role of Government in East Asian Industrialization* (Princeton: Princeton University Press, 1990).

17. A. Amsden, *Asia's Next Giant: South Korea and Late Industrialization* (New York: Oxford University Press, 1989).

18. World Bank, *Korea: Managing the Industrial Transition,* 2 vols. (Washington, D.C.: World Bank, 1987); K. Kim and D. Leipziger, "Korea: A Case of Government-Led Development" (this volume).

It increased protection and provided many incentives to certain firms whose actions were carefully controlled.

The most important measure was heavily subsidized credit. What distinguished this industrial intervention was not only its thoroughness but also its premise that firms in steel, shipbuilding, machinery, electronics, petrochemicals, and metals would achieve internationally competitive levels within a decade. In this respect, Korean intervention differed from the policy pronouncements in Brazil or India and many other import-substituting countries. Success was measured by export performance, and eventually all subsidies were expected to be withdrawn. The nature of the policy is clear, although it has at various times been judged both a failure and a success. For our purposes, it is enough to say that Korea did alter its industrial structure dramatically, and in most of the targeted industries it succeeded in penetrating international markets. But the issue is not whether technical efficiency was achieved but whether it was achieved profitably. The country study concludes that it was on balance successful but that its long-term costs are usually understated. Specifically, the socialized nature of risk bearing and the tight controls on the financial system in Korea led to many publicly managed bailouts of industry. Today, the financial sector is still not free of the shackles of directed credits or their costs, as borne by commercial banks, government banks, and the Central Bank itself.[19]

Faced with considerable macroeconomic difficulty in the period 1979–80, largely as a result of the second oil shock, Korea abandoned the HCI drive. Over the next decade the government stopped trying to pick winners; it liberalized trade and it loosened its grip on the financial sector. Some Korean economists argue that Taiwan, China outperformed Korea without undertaking the costly HCI drive.[20] Others say that the interventions were largely successful in accelerating the process of dynamic comparative advantage, and that were it not for the oil shock the period would have been an unqualified success. This evidence is reviewed in the Korea case study. No other rapid industrializer intervened quite so heavily, although the new literature on Taiwan, China shows an effort to direct the industrial efforts of entrepreneurs.[21]

19. D. Leipziger and P. Petri, *Korean Industrial Policy: Legacy of the Past and Directions for the Future* (Washington, D.C.: World Bank, 1993); J. H. Kim, "Korea's Recent Experiences with Industrial Restructuring in Response to Trade Friction," mimeo, Korea Development Institute, 1990; S. W. Nam, "Institutional Reform of the Korean Financial System," mimeo, Korea Development Institute, 1990; S. W. Nam, "Korea's Financial Policy and Its Consequences," mimeo, Korea Development Institute, 1991.

20. Yoo, J. H., "The Industrial Policy of the 1970s and the Evolution of the Manufacturing Sector in Korea," Working Papers No. 9017 (Seoul: Korea Development Institute, 1990).

21. See Wade, *Governing the Market.*

## The Singapore Story[22]

The government of Singapore had few qualms about intervening to supplement market forces and bring about desired industrial change. Clearly the size and malleability of the economy made control easier, but Singapore also developed institutions that made it possible. Singapore has been aptly described as a corporate state because the distinction between government and business—indeed, between the political leadership and the bureaucracy—is murky. The first key to Singapore's industrial strategy was an accurate assessment of national resources, followed by clear industrial goals and a real understanding of the relationships and ingredients needed to achieve them. Without capital, technology, or entrepreneurs, Singapore put its industrialization squarely on the shoulders of multinational corporations and foreign direct investment. In order to attract FDI, it invested heavily in education and technical skills and in the infrastructure that multinational corporations (MNCs) value. Where necessary, it used government linked companies (GLCs) to push its development agenda, although these GLCs were run on a commercial basis.

As part of a city-state with a re-export economy, Singapore's first generation of leaders built its industrial strategy around labor policy. Singapore's First Five Year Plan stressed technical education, school building, and family planning. The political agenda included the 1967 Employment Act, which established national employment regulations and clearly delineated worker benefits to attract foreign investors, and the 1968 Industrial Relations Act, which pioneered three-year collective bargaining agreements. The National Wage Council, established in 1972, was a tripartite forum (business-government-labor) that made wage recommendations based on productivity gains and the cost of living. As in Korea, wages were a policy tool used to ensure competitiveness. Balancing these labor market interventions were social policies (such as housing) to improve living standards and a major public role in education and training.

In addition to encouraging foreign investors, the government decided in the late 1970s to promote higher-technology, higher-value-added industries. It instituted a high-wage policy in an attempt to move quickly out of traditional labor-intensive manufactures. Although this policy did stimulate investment in electronics, machinery, pharmaceuticals, and precision products, by 1985 Singapore was experiencing its first severe recession. Rather than nominally devalue the currency, the government opted to reduce labor costs through a large reduction in employer contributions to the Central Provident Fund. The implicit 12 percent wage cut was possible because the union movement was

---

22. T. Soon and S. Tan, "Singapore: Public Policy and Economic Development" (this volume).

allied with government and the political leadership. In effect, the government tried to position its labor force to make it attractive to multinationals, adjusting its price, augmenting its skills, and tinkering with financial incentives to change its trade pattern and stay ahead of its competitors in East Asia.

## The Taiwan, China Story[23]

A glance at Taiwan, China's history could suggest that the country's initial conditions—the economic infrastructure from Japanese colonialism, entrepreneurial talent from mainland China, and U.S. aid—were unique. But Taiwan, China's rapid industrialization owed much more to domestic policies. In addition to the early success of land reform in bringing about remarkable equity of income and wealth, policies for macroeconomic stability, domestic investments, and industrial development were highly effective.

After the import-substitution phase of 1953–57, the government promoted exports during the period 1958–72. It gradually reduced import protection and offset antiexport bias by providing free trade status and other incentives for exporters. It also set export targets and supported the development of labor intensive industries. Economic growth between 1963 and 1972 averaged nearly 12 percent a year.

For various economic and political reasons, the 1970s saw the emergence of a more self-reliant strategy with large investments in infrastructure, industrial upgrading, and further import substitution. Public enterprises were used as a means of industrial policy, especially for a big push in heavy and chemical industries. Some of these state enterprises, for example, the China Steel Corporation, performed remarkably well by any standard, but many were outright failures. Economic performance, though robust overall, revealed strains, especially in competitiveness. In the 1980s, the policy was switched to place a greater emphasis on liberalization and further export development. The results were striking. The economy generated massive payment surpluses and the means to invest elsewhere in the region on a scale rivaling that of Japan.

## The Hong Kong Story[24]

In the early 1950s, Hong Kong embarked on its export drive, a decade before the other early NIEs. It has always been different from the other three, particularly in the small and noninterventionist role of its government. For most of the past 40 years, Hong Kong's economic and productivity growth have been the

---

23. Dahlman and Sananikone, "Taiwan China: Policies and Institutions for Rapid Growth (this volume).

24. See Chau (this volume).

highest in the region. Industrialization was initiated by migrant industrialists, largely from Shanghai, but fostered by local merchant entrepreneurs. Small enterprises flourished, supported by a government dedicated to stability and "positive nonintervention."

Hong Kong's continued prosperity in the past dozen years has been built on its links with southern mainland China—and vice versa. During this period, China doubled average incomes faster than any other country on record. The growth of Guangdong Province, adjacent to Hong Kong, where millions of migrant workers from other provinces come to work, has been phenomenal. Today the province aspires to be the fifth "tiger," and it has achieved this through free market policies rather than state intervention.

## The Malaysia Story[25]

Over the term of its Fourth Five Year Plan (1981–85), Malaysia pursued import substitution with renewed vigor. Its models were Japan and Korea: hence the Look East Policy, which was launched in 1981, and the decision to bring in Korean advisers to help pick and produce industrial winners. The government created a holding company, the Heavy Industries Corporation of Malaysia (HICOM). It was charged with creating a nucleus of critical industries, including basic metals, machinery and equipment, automobiles, building materials, pulp and paper, and petrochemicals. The public sector's investment in HICOM from 1981 to 1986 was intended to reach 6 to 8 billion ringgits, a sum equal to the national development budget.

The symbol of this selective industrial policy (IP) was the Proton Saga, a car whose production was heavily subsidized by both the Malaysian government and its Japanese partner, Mitsubishi. Unlike Korea's HCI push, which aimed to achieve international competitiveness, HICOM industries, although monitored by government, were under no such compulsion. They lost money, suffered from poor management and excess capacity, and required government bailouts. Between 1981 and 1985, the number of nonfinancial public enterprises rose from 498 to 702, while the percentage that was profitable fell from 62 to 55 percent. Faced with mounting deficits, the government changed its policy and began a major program of privatization.

The lessons can be summarized as follows. First, IP was aimed at internal industrial objectives, such as changes in ownership and employment patterns, rather than the achievement of international levels of efficiency or export targets. For this reason, in part, the system of rewards and penalties could not be ruthlessly applied. Second, no clear overall goals were established whereby

---

25. I. Salleh and S. Meyanathan, "Malaysia: Growth, Equity, and Structural Transformation" (this volume).

infant industries could be judged. Third, insufficient domestic competition was fostered to create incentives to perform, and state-owned enterprise (SOE) monitoring systems were inadequate. Fourth, the selection of industries was based too heavily on traditional import-substitution criteria and insufficiently on global marketing concerns.

## The Thailand Story[26]

Thailand has had fairly consistent and rapid growth since 1955. It has emphasized private sector development, outward orientation, and macroeconomic stability. However, in the 1960s and 1970s, the government made various efforts to protect and promote domestic industry. Compared with Korea or Taiwan, China, these were not highly coordinated. The general thrust of policy since then has been to allow free markets rather than to intervene in them. Even when selective interventions were contemplated, as with the Eastern Seaboard Program (a regional development scheme), they were eventually curtailed.

Within this overall picture, import substitution policies in the 1970s favored capital intensive industries. Industry's share of GDP rose substantially in the 1970s, while its share of the labor force showed little increase. Balance of payments problems and concern with the pattern of industrialization prompted a shift in the early 1980s to export development and import liberalization. Effective protection for manufacturing was reduced by the mid 1980s, though it was much higher than in Korea and Malaysia. Any antiexport bias, however, was vigorously offset by exchange rate policy, export incentives, and the promotion of FDI by the Board of Investments. A halfhearted attempt at capital-intensive industrial promotion was pursued in the Eastern Seaboard project; however, in the end its more costly and inefficient elements were curtailed.

On balance, sectoral interventions had only mild effects on overall performance. The government's interventions were poorly coordinated, the private sector was robust, and Japanese investment was heavy. As a result, Thailand avoided costly industrial adventures while maintaining basic macroeconomic stability. It could, of course, be argued that more effective intervention could have raised growth rates further, but that presumes a state apparatus that Thailand did not possess.

## The Indonesia Story[27]

In much the same way that Korea pursued its capital-intensive HCI drive in the 1970s, Indonesia tried to create its own dynamic comparative advantage in the

---

26. S. Christensen, D. Dollar, A. Siamwalla, and P. Vichyanond, "Thailand: The Institutional and Political Underpinnings of Growth" (this volume).

27. A. Bhattacharya and M. Pangestu, "Indonesia: Development Transformation and the Role of Public Policy" (this volume).

early 1980s. Led by a blueprint known as the Investment Policy List, industrial entry was directly controlled, capacity limits set, local content requirements enforced, and foreign investment discouraged. Behind high trade barriers, local industry, mostly in the form of state-owned companies, attempted to move into "upstream activities," produce more "value added" outputs, and protect itself against the terms of trade losses it suffered in the post–oil boom years. This foray into steel, plastics, and petrochemicals, helped by subsidized credits and trade protection, was a failure.

The Indonesian experience suggests that capital-intensive industrial transformation cannot easily be imposed. Indeed, it is not even necessary for late industrializers. Between 1985 and 1988, the government changed course. It reduced its share in the industrial sector from 43 to 23 percent (1989). Industrial concentration (four-firm ratio) fell from 54 percent on average to 32 percent. Trade was dramatically liberalized, and foreign investment was actively encouraged. The results were remarkable. Despite a cumulative terms-of-trade drop of over 40 percent between 1986 and 1988, the productivity of land, labor, and capital grew strongly in 1988–91, GDP grew at an average 7.1 percent a year, and nonoil exports boomed. Indonesia, impoverished in the 1960s, an oil economy in 1970s, and an inefficient spender in the early 1980s, has now become another East Asian dynamo. It has done so through traditional outward-oriented policies and an abandonment of selective industrial policies.

## The Philippines Story

Judging by its factor endowments—both natural and human resources—and by its position in East Asia in the early 1960s, the Philippines was the best bet to succeed. Apart from resources, it boasted a unique relationship with the United States and a well-educated labor force. It had the head start on its neighbors in terms of savings, incipient manufacturing, and even some necessary institutions. Nevertheless, the country has consistently underperformed, losing ground first to the tigers, and then to the cubs. Indeed, in the last few years a modest economic turnaround has taken place, but with ground having been lost for at least two decades the Philippines still has a long way to travel to join its more successful neighbors.

Much of the problem can legitimately be blamed on poor policies, although political instability in the late 1980s and early 1990s contributed considerably to a lack of confidence in the country by both international investors and domestic savers. But perhaps as much to blame as faulty policy was the pervasive inefficiency and failures of governance that distinguish the Philippines from many of its neighboring countries. Compared to the best performers, the country comes up short in responding to crises (often deferring such needed steps as oil price increases) and being able to tackle difficult issues. Its high public debt became an albatross, and its industrial sector, despite ample incentives, never reached international levels of efficiency.

Some will claim that the political constraints in the Philippines are mostly to blame; however, the country is not unique in having had one-party rule, excessively concentrated wealth, and a rent-seeking private sector. Still, despite ample models of success, the necessary political and social consensus eluded the Philippines for many years. While the country didn't always do badly in economic policy formulation, its economy was for most of the 1960–90 period characterized by low total factor productivity, low labor absorption in manufacturing, a continued heavy dependence on agriculture, excessive foreign borrowing for unproductive purposes, and macroeconomic instability as the country moved from one crisis to another.

It is clear, for example, that its development strategy represented an accommodation of an unsustainable growth strategy and a mortgaging of the country's future growth. Despite able technocrats, policy making was highly politicized. The executive, even in the post-Marcos era when corruption was reduced, could not maneuver successfully among the politicized judiciary and the Congress. A social compact never emerged, and the country with the best preconditions and prospects became the outlier among rapidly growing East Asian economies, at least until very recently.

The story of the Philippines stands in sharp contrast to the successful sagas of the region. Its record of policy selection and implementation is not strong, and as a result it has the worst growth record of the countries under review. Policy fundamentals improved only slowly and took a heavy toll on growth. Deferring necessary adjustment and borrowing heavily and unwisely has cost the Philippines dearly in terms of foregone income. It is possible that the combination of hard-won gains on the macroeconomic side, increased political stability, regional contagion, and a national realization that few options remain will finally propel the Philippines to its rightful place among East Asian economies.

## The Diversity in Industrial Policy

East Asia's industrial policies showed great diversity. Not all governments intervened heavily, and not all interventions were successful. In the first-generation NIEs, the record points to the potential rewards of socializing risk under an industrial policy. But the risks of such an approach are equally important and are illustrated by the failures of such a policy approach in Malaysia and Indonesia. Moreover, the success of Thailand, Hong Kong, and recently the coastal provinces of China show the merits of avoiding unbridled industrial activism. Countries entertaining an activist industrial policy need to weigh both the risks and the potential gains of this gamble.

Where there were successes, they were based on export development. Governments provided not merely protection for a local industry (as was the case in many other countries) but support of many kinds for export competitiveness. It was crucial that: (1) government guided but did not override the decisions of firms, (2) international price signals were used to gauge efficiency and success, and (3) firms were offered support in exchange for specific performance requirements.

More generally the conditions under which selective industrial policy can work are not usually found. In addition to the capacity to select potential winners linked to exports, the success of the policy depends, first, on the ability of society to place efficiency and public interest above rent seeking and, second, on the pragmatism and flexibility of policy making to reverse failed policies.

Indeed, if these preconditions can be found, it can be argued that they offer the potential for effective government action short of selective industrial intervention. In any event, some of the earlier intervention policies are probably not replicable today, given (1) a less receptive trading environment for export subsidies, (2) more open capital markets, and (3) freer labor markets. Instead, an augmented view of public policy, which we advocate, places emphasis on government's role in supporting investments, particularly in infrastructure and labor skills, international marketing, and technology acquisition. What has separated successful industrializers from unsuccessful ones is whether international efficiency was achieved. This yardstick can be either imposed by government as a quid pro quo for time-bound support or implicitly imposed by foreign investors. Evidence of the 1980s from Thailand, Malaysia, Indonesia, and China tends to show that the second-generation NIEs have relied on foreign investment to provide this discipline.

### Policy Making

Common to successful government interventions was the pragmatism and flexibility to change course as needed. What characteristic of policy making can be associated with such a pattern? In East Asia, it seems that governments are repeatedly able to distance themselves from past policies that have either failed or are no longer useful. This flexibility should not be mistaken for good luck. Rather, more often it was associated with problems or crises leading to change, as is indicated by the following examples.

Korea's pragmatism and policy flexibility is revealing.[28] The end of the heavy-handed HCI interventions, under which the bulk of industrial credit was absorbed by large, capital-intensive industries, was prompted by the second oil

28. World Bank, Korea; Il Sakong, *Korea in the World Economy* (Washington, D.C.: Institute for International Economics, 1993).

shock. In 1980, the economy went into recession. The government opted for macroeconomic stabilization, and the fiscal drain of HCI was no longer afford-able. Trade liberalization was begun in earnest. Credit allocation once more favored exporters, commercial banks were privatized, and troubled HCI indus-tries were put under new management. Incentives to encourage R&D and technological upgrading were put in place, and interventions were limited to strategic bailouts rather than picking winners.[29]

In 1967, Indonesia was not only poor (per capita income of $50 with 60 percent of its population living in absolute poverty) but it was also indis-tinguishable from many other inward-oriented developing countries that were awash with licensing restrictions and protection. Hyperinflation produced the Balanced Budget Amendment in 1967 and a new dedication to controlling inflation. But, despite significant macroeconomic reforms during the 1967–73 period, after the first oil boom the country's inward orientation was encouraged by heavy-handed selective intervention. By 1985, some 28 percent of import categories required licenses, there was a large current-account deficit, and a debt-service ratio of 40 percent. Faced with a deteriorating macroeconomic situation, the government changed course, with a major devaluation and sharp macroeconomic adjustments. It gradually liberalized trade so that the effective rate of protection on capital goods industries fell by 50 percent between 1987 and 1990.

Countries with oil resources, such as Indonesia and Malaysia, at first re-acted to their surpluses predictably, by spending more. However, within five years of the second oil shock, both had cut their fiscal deficits and adjusted their exchange rates in order to compete in the increasingly tough regional manufac-turing sector. Though macroeconomic policies were far from flawless, they were subject to scrutiny and revision. And when industrial policies conflicted with prudent macroeconomic policy the former were adjusted or abandoned.

A striking example of policy change is the increasing role of market eco-nomics in the southern provinces of China. These "experiments" have been largely successful—in fact, the volume of trade between Guangdong and Hong Kong is now almost the size of the Hong Kong's GDP. The success of China's Special Economic Zones (SEZs) in Guangdong and Fujian is due to the ease with which capital and technology are admitted, the flexibility of wages, the freedom to import materials and remit foreign exchange, and the changing role of the state in emphasizing infrastructure provision in the SEZs to attract for-eign investment.[30]

29. D. M. Leipziger, "Industrial Restructuring in Korea," *World Development* 16, no. 1 (1988): 121–36.

30. J. Brown, "Economic Development in Southern China. The Role of the State and the Market," mimeo, World Bank, 1993.

## Bureaucracy

In most East Asian countries, selection for the bureaucracy is an honor, and government has been able to pick its officials from prestigious universities. In Korea, Seoul National University graduates fed the bureaucracy, with the best of them going to the core economic ministries. A Confucian level of status ordinarily reserved for scholars also placed bureaucrats in a preferred position.[31] Overseas training often furthered the career prospects of government officials, and ministers frequently vied for the best-trained technocrats. Central banks also managed to attract highly skilled staff. So did research institutes, which (particularly in Korea) were strongly affiliated with the government. Fellows of the prestigious Korea Development Institute were more highly paid than ministers were, and generous financial incentives were offered to returning foreign-trained experts by the Ministry of Science and Technology's research arm. Indeed, the "reverse brain-drain" was a major factor in upgrading the skills of the Korean bureaucracy.

One of the roles of research institutes has been to digest experience from foreign sources. Copying the successful actions of others is considered part of prudent policy. This search for policy lessons and advice extends also to international organizations such as the World Bank, the advice of which is sought if not always followed. Although both the Bank and Korean authorities enjoy noting that the Bank opposed automobile industry expansion in the mid-1970s, it is more telling that the Bank's work on trade liberalization and energy pricing actively supported government reforms.

East Asia's bureaucracies have emphasized managerial organization and functional responsibilities. Governments have centered their efforts on core economic ministries. A pioneer was Korea's Economic Planning Board, but similar core ministries exist throughout Asia. Their role is to formulate and coordinate economic policy. How did these technocrats in East Asia succeed where other well-trained bureaucrats failed? Country experiences provide some important clues.

Organizationally, economic teams in Indonesia and Korea were coordinated and led by a single, clearly identified, "economic czar,"—a coordinating minister for economic, industrial, and financial affairs in Indonesia and the deputy prime minister and minister of the economic planning board (EPB) in Korea. In Korea, the EPB has traditionally contained both the planning apparatus responsible for successive five year plans and the budget function that finances those plans. Economic policy coordination was equally strong, if not quite so ministerially prominent, in Malaysia. There, the Economic Planning Unit (EPU) reports directly to the prime minister, which is also what happens

---

31. B. N. Song, *The Rise of Korean Economy* (Oxford: Oxford University Press, 1990).

with Singapore's Economic Development Board. Thailand's National Economic and Social Development Board (NESDB) performed a similar coordinating task in forging a consensus on development goals.

Nevertheless, there is variation in the roles of economic ministries. Malaysia's EPU is unusual for both its small size and its mandate, and Thailand's NESDB is distinguished by the unique way in which it achieves consensus. In both countries one may argue that the central bank's role was critical, and that the strong voice of finance ministries on macromanagement usually dominated economic policy making. In Thailand, the action of the technocrats in devaluing the baht in 1984 is seen by many as the critical action that restored the credibility of macroeconomic management and laid the basis for Thailand's financial and industrial surge later in the decade. In Malaysia, the voices of prudence in the Ministry of Finance and Bank Negara kept inflation low for decades, despite variation in industrial policies.

Among planning ministries, those in Korea and Singapore stand out, in part for their ability to implement decisions. The quality of implementation depends on a clear identification by government officials with the goals being pursued. In Korea, monitoring of key economic variables (notably exports) was an obsession, and it permeated the bureaucracy. The extra export effort of the "final 100 days" of each year was legendary. Plan targets, although in some sense indicative, were usually exceeded, and public officials were held accountable for their achievement. Performance evaluation and monitoring systems have become models for the management of public enterprises as well.[32]

Singapore's economic policy apparatus has been different but no less effective. The Economic Development Board (EDB), established in 1961, was able to coordinate policy, offer incentives to foreign investors, acquire land, create industrial estates to attract multinational corporations, and take equity stakes in corporations. Beginning with the five year plan, the EDB was charged with ending bottlenecks, creating new programs, and spearheading Singapore's development drive. In the process, it created the Jurong Industrial Estate, began a joint-venture shipyard project with Japan, offered incentives to investors under the 1961 Pioneer Industries Ordinance (which deferred 90 percent of the corporate profits tax for a period of 15 years for export industries), and promoted exports via the Economic Incentives Bill of 1967. As Singapore's economic objectives matured, it played a prominent role in establishing a Joint Industry Training Scheme with the participation of foreign companies and in attracting foreign investors to Singapore.

The role of technocrats in Indonesia is similar to that in Korea or Singapore. Indonesia's leadership delegated economic policy to a group of sen-

---

32. M. Shirley and J. Nellis, *Public Enterprise Reform: The Lessons of Experience* (Washington, D.C.: World Bank, 1991).

ior officials. This alliance has served both parties well, as it combined pragmatic leadership with capable implementation. In Korea, President Park quickly formed an alliance with the technocrats he needed to implement his vision of Korean development, relying on engineers to design his industrialization strategy and on economists to secure financing. In Singapore, the distinction between political affiliation and technocratic position has often been blurred; People's Action Party goals and national economic goals were the same.

## Leadership

The East Asian state has a record of maintaining political and economic stability and pursuing long-term development goals. The first-generation NIEs quickly developed enough consensus on development goals and a sufficiently broad distribution of benefits to push the economic agenda forward. How was this accomplished? While we do not have the analytic tools to definitively answer this question, country experiences provide useful insights.

In Taiwan, China and Korea, land was a scarce asset, and both regimes were prescient in redistributing land to small farmers. These rural constituencies are still conservative, progovernment supporters. By contrast, land reform has eluded countries such as the Philippines, and the uneven distribution of income has perpetuated poverty and alienation. Korea managed, over the 1965–85 period, to close the gap between urban and rural incomes. Special rural development programs such as the Saemaul Movement, agricultural price supports, and a relatively large rural investment program were prominent features of Korean development. In Singapore, early support and trust were built on the housing policies led by the Housing and Development Board. Through its efforts, begun during the First Five Year Plan, public housing construction was one of the plan's top priorities. As a result, owner-occupied housing rose from less than 10 percent in 1970 to 80 percent in 1980.

In these countries, the notion of shared sacrifice can be seen in anticonsumption campaigns, long hours for workers and managers, and the virtual absence of capital flight. The corollary of shared return is also seen in the dramatic increases in wages in the first-generation NIEs and the unprecedented gains in social indicators, to the point where absolute poverty has been virtually eliminated.

The role of the state in the second-generation NIEs—Malaysia, Indonesia, and Thailand—is far less uniform. The clarity of equity objectives was perhaps most visible in Malaysia's New Economic Policy, a two-decade plan (1970–90) to reorder the distribution of income and wealth in favor of the Bumiputera (Malay) majority. This goal of raising the incomes of the Malay majority served to unite the Muslim population and may have been responsible for keeping interracial peace. The government's other emphasis on education and agricultural advance did yield high returns and can be credited with bringing the percentage of people in absolute poverty down to single digits.

In Thailand, there was initially no strong, equitable, growth strategy in place. Indeed, there was no consensus for a particular set of development objectives. The country's success came later, largely as a result of prudent macroeconomic policies, the beneficent role of foreign investment, and the contagion factor. Observers credit the relatively conservative bureaucracy with steering a steady course amid political vacillation and upheavals and the monarchy with maintaining social stability and a sense of nationhood.[33]

Observers have also attributed some of the economic success to the concentration of political power in the East Asian economies. In Korea, Taiwan, China, Indonesia, and Singapore, to varying degrees, the state held enormous power, dissent was largely absent, and bureaucrats had a relatively free hand in pushing reforms. The greater equality of income in these economies may also have aided reforms by limiting the differences among winners and losers, but the absence of outright opposition to policies decided at the top is said to have expedited economic reforms. In fact, former Prime Minister Lee Kwan Yew of Singapore has questioned the compatibility of purely democratic models with rapid development.[34]

Clearly, however, the equating of political control and economic success is far too simplistic and misleading. Authoritarianism has not been in short supply in the developing world; yet in the majority of these regimes the economic policies and results have been disastrous. The East Asian experience shows superior performance under a variety of different political situations. Both authoritarian and participatory institutional mechanisms in East Asia managed to achieve features favorable to rapid growth—reducing uncertainty, improving economic incentives, limiting economic controls, providing adequate support services, and often providing a strategic vision. All this shows the merit not of political control but of the ability to use political and institutional features to achieve development objectives. The pragmatism of government meant—with the benefit of hindsight—that when it intervened to speed development the probability of failure was much lower there than elsewhere.

### Conclusions

The evidence from East Asia rejects forcefully the notion of any single, decisive, sociopolitical cause of economic success. Instead, it points to a combination of tangible factors consistently associated with progress. None of the

---

33. See Christensen, et al., "Thailand."

34. Excerpt from "The Proven Path to Economic Growth," speech by the Hon. Lee Kwan Yew, Manila, November 19, 1992, transcript.

East Asian countries succeeded unless it had three attributes: outward orientation, macroeconomic stability, and investments in people. And these countries were not always blessed with this triad. They developed institutions and policies that delivered it.

It is our view that any country that achieves successful performance in these policy inputs will be rewarded on the output side. But was that enough to produce the remarkable growth of East Asia? Reformers in other countries are noticing that similar actions on these three fronts have produced much greater payoffs in East Asia than in their own countries.

## Getting Higher Payoffs

First, there is something to be learned from East Asia's style of policy making, which translates policies on paper into actions. Many of the features associated with such effectiveness—consensus building, policy flexibility, and pragmatism—can potentially be replicated. Most clearly, countries not only need to develop a mandate for development, but strategies need to be continually reassessed. Mechanisms of formulating development plans in East Asia served to inform and coordinate the activities of economic agents, and annual management plans served to monitor performance of the public and private sectors and signal the need for policy revisions. East Asia managed to develop business-government relations that allowed such revisions to take place in a mutually beneficial manner.

Second, East Asia is getting a greater payoff for its actions because of regional contagion. The proximity to other successful countries provides a special advantage. In particular, Japan has played a strong leadership role in transferring technology and ideas around the region. At first glance, this advantage may not seem replicable, but that conclusion may well be wrong. With the revolution in communications, geographical proximity is less relevant than it was, and other growth centers are likely to emerge. Increasingly, outward orientation and sound domestic policies enable a country to share technologies and ideas from around the world. Another advantage of regional contagion is that there are proximate comparators for economic performance, which is useful if public policies are openly scrutinized.

Third, does a state need to go further than adopting the fundamentals of strong economic management? The country studies leave no doubt that government intervention in picking winners was prominent in some East Asian countries. The evidence also suggests that some others in the region did equally well without government direction or because such directions failed and were abandoned. In other regions where governments have tried to pick winners, the failure rate has been even higher.[35] In the worldwide context, the

---

35. World Bank, *World Development Report,* 1991.

issue boils down to probabilities: picking winners leads to high rewards in a small percentage of cases where the experiment is successful and to disastrous results in a large percentage of failures.

## Early versus Later NIEs

As seen in the Development Checklist (appendix), political stability, efficient bureaucracies, macroeconomic stability, export drive, and human resource investment were common features across most successful East Asian economies. But, with the exception of Hong Kong, the first-generation NIEs had some systematic differences from the second-generation NIEs.

The first-generation NIEs generally had a more forceful state role in industrialization. Starting with visionary leadership and supported by strong economic ministries, they "went for broke," acquired technology feverishly, and invested heavily in upgrading labor skills. A few used directed credit as part of their strategies, relying on state enterprises when private firms were lacking. What lowered the downside risk of these policies was strong macroeconomic discipline and the use of international price signals as a guide to performance. Macroeconomic discipline meant that countries abandoned imprudent policies when stability was at risk. The use of international prices helped them to measure infant industry performance.

The second-generation NIEs differed considerably from the first in terms of initial conditions and, to some extent, political institutions. The availability of resources in Thailand, Malaysia, and Indonesia allowed for a more relaxed pace of development. More reliant on foreign investment than aid, the second-generation NIEs did not have to follow such an aggressive policy of acquiring technology. Where selective industrial policies were attempted, they largely failed. Yet regional contagion, low wages, and strong fundamentals fostered export industries. Liberalization and reforms removed the public sector from inefficient activities in Malaysia and Indonesia, and even in Thailand state enterprise reform is now a priority. Open capital accounts contrasted with the financial controls used in Japan and Korea in earlier decades.

## The Question of Replicability

Much intellectual energy has been devoted to deciding the right degree of government involvement in industrial policy. This may not be the central question, however. What is clear from the combined experience of East Asia over the past three decades is that certain common features dominate, and they involve some fundamental public policies. Countries may choose "supplemental policies" in an effort to achieve a "growth overdrive,"[36] but these idiosyncratic policies are hard (if not impossible) to replicate.

---

36. P. Petri. "Common Foundations of East Asian Success" (this volume).

More importantly, there are few cases, if any, in which countries that pursued the "core policies" have not succeeded. Put differently, governments that have adopted the essential policies—stable economic management, investment in human capital, and export drive—have been able to entertain the option of a larger role for government in industrialization policy. Whether such interventions would succeed has depended primarily on the policy objective itself and secondarily on the institutional capacity to execute it. Unless these policies are continuously reassessed (and, if necessary, reversed), they stand little chance of success. Moreover, they are neither essential to nor sufficient for rapid growth, as the evidence of the second-generation NIEs demonstrates.

The big question for policymakers is why such diversity of experience in East Asia has produced uniformly good results. The first answer is that success actually has not been universal. The Philippines, for example, was not able to combine enough positive factors from among macrostability, strong technocratic bureaucracy, export competitiveness, political stability, and policy consistency. Equally puzzling is why other countries, such as India, even during periods featuring macroeconomic and political stability and perhaps a talented bureaucracy, have not done equally well. In some, bureaucracies were impediments to private entrepreneurship rather than instruments of change. In others, policy was ideologically determined and not critically reassessed for its effectiveness. And, in yet others, no social consensus existed by which a national development strategy could be forged and implemented.

The diversity of experience within East Asia suggests that universal and sweeping prescriptions are not possible and country-specific circumstances will dominate. Yet, the body of East Asian evidence points to the dominant contribution of stable and competitive economic policies to unleash private entrepreneurship. More often than not, the key to the policy-making process was the positive role of government in charting a development course, creating a longer-term vision shared among key participants, and fashioning an institutional framework for nonideological and effective policy implementation.

APPENDIX

*(see following page)*

*(see following page)*

**Development Checklist**

|  | Early NIEs | | | | Late NIEs | | | |
|---|---|---|---|---|---|---|---|---|
|  | Korea | Taiwan, China | Singapore | Hong Kong | Thailand | Malaysia | Indonesia | Philippines |
| **Initial Endowments** | | | | | | | | |
| Natural resources | Low | Low | Low | Low | High | High | High | High |
| Human capital | High | High | Med | Med | Low | Low | Low | High |
| Foreign aid | High | High | Low | Low | Low | Low | Low | High |
| **Policies** | | | | | | | | |
| Macro stability | Yes | Yes | Yes | Yes | Yes | Yes | Yes | No |
| Export drive | Yes | Yes | Yes | No | Some | Some | Some | Some |
| Human resource investment | Yes | Yes | Yes | Yes | Some | Yes | Some | Some |
| Import openness | Limited | Yes | Yes | Yes | Yes | Yes | Limited | Limited |
| Selective industrial policies | Yes | Some | Some | No | No | Some | Some | Some |
| Directed credit | Yes | Some | No | No | No | Some | No | No |
| State-owned enterprises | Some | Some | Yes | No | Some | Yes | Some | Some |
| **Institutions** | | | | | | | | |
| Central Economic Ministry | Yes | Yes | Yes | No | No | No | No | No |
| Strong bureaucracy | Yes | Yes | Yes | Yes | Moderate | Moderate | Moderate | No |
| Political stability | Yes | Yes | Yes | Yes | Moderate | Yes | Yes | Moderate/No |
| "Visionary" leadership | Yes | Yes | Yes | No | No | Yes | Moderate | No |
| **Outcomes (compared with the rest of the developing world)** | | | | | | | | |
| Growth in the 1960s | High | High | High | High | Moderate | Average | Average | Average |
| Growth in the 1970s | High | High | High | High | Moderate | Moderate | Moderate | Average/Low |
| Growth in the 1980s | High | High | High | High | High | High | High | Low |
| Growth in the 1990s | High | High | High | High | High | High | High | Moderate |

**Selected Macroeconomic Indicators of Development**

| | Population (1993) millions | GNP per Capita (constant 1990 prices) | | | | Average Annual Growth Rate of GNP per Capita (%) | | | Average Annual Inflation Rate | | | Average Annual Central Budget Surplus/(Deficit) as % of GDP | |
|---|---|---|---|---|---|---|---|---|---|---|---|---|---|
| | | 1960 | 1970 | 1980 | 1993 | 1960–69 | 1970–79 | 1980–93 | 1960–69 | 1970–79 | 1980–93 | 1970–79 | 1980–93 |
| Hong Kong | 5.8 | 2,160 | 4,144 | 7,867 | 15,235 | 7.0 | 7.4 | 5.4 | 2.4 | 9.2 | 7.9 | .7 | 2.1 |
| Taiwan | 21.1 | 1,071 | 2,012 | 4,201 | 9,102 | 5.2 | 9.2 | 10 | 2.8 | 10.2 | 3.3 | 1.4 | (2.4) |
| Korea | 44.1 | 860 | 1,475 | 2,809 | 7,438 | 5.8 | 7.2 | 8.2 | 17.5 | 19.5 | 6.3 | (1.0) | .05 |
| Singapore | 2.8 | 1,973 | 3,740 | 7,611 | 16,340 | 6.7 | 6.9 | 6.1 | 1.1 | 5.9 | 2.5 | 1.4 | 6.0 |
| Malaysia | 19.2 | 740 | 1,040 | 1,743 | 3,022 | 3.4 | 5.2 | 3.5 | -0.3 | 7.3 | 2.2 | (6.7) | (4.0) |
| Thailand | 58.1 | 337 | 578 | 857 | 1,867 | 4.9 | 4.6 | 6.4 | 1.8 | 9.2 | 4.3 | (2.2) | (1.6) |
| Indonesia | 187.2 | 195 | 243 | 407 | 687 | 2.4 | 5.3 | 4.2 | 19.5 | 21.5 | 8.5 | (2.9) | (1.0) |
| Philippines | 64.8 | 475 | 564 | 779 | 699 | 2.1 | 3.4 | -0.6 | 5.8 | 13.3 | 13.6 | (2.1) | (2.6) |

| | Exports as Percentage of GDP | | | | Gross Domestic Savings as a Percentage of GDP | | | | Investment as a Percentage of GDP | | | |
|---|---|---|---|---|---|---|---|---|---|---|---|---|
| | 1960s | 1970s | 1980s | 1993 | 1960s | 1970s | 1980s | 1993 | 1960s | 1970s | 1980s | 1993 |
| Hong Kong | 68 | 78 | 106 | 202 | 31 | 32 | 34 | 37 | 33 | 28 | 28 | 27 |
| Taiwan | 14 | 35 | 49 | 56 | 14 | 27 | 31 | 28 | 17 | 26 | 23 | 26 |
| Korea | 5 | 21 | 35 | 40 | 9 | 22 | 31 | 35 | 18 | 28 | 30 | 34 |
| Singapore | 115 | 122 | 166 | 223 | 8 | 35 | 42 | 50 | 20 | 40 | 43 | 44 |
| Malaysia | 48 | 47 | 55 | 73 | 25 | 29 | 33 | 41 | 15 | 24 | 31 | 36 |
| Thailand | 16 | 19 | 25 | 42 | 22 | 26 | 26 | 35 | 23 | 17 | 25 | 37 |
| Indonesia | 25 | 36 | 24 | 24 | 7 | 19 | 33 | 34 | 10 | 19 | 29 | 35 |
| Philippines | 19 | 18 | 25 | 34 | 17 | 21 | 20 | 14 | 20 | 26 | 21 | 24 |

*Sources:* World Bank, International Monetary Fund, Directorate-General of Budget, Accounting and Statistics (Taiwan, China), various years.

**Selected Social Indicators of Development**

| | Average Annual Population Growth Rate (%) | | | | Adult Illiteracy | | Life Expectancy at Birth | | Percentage of Age Group Enrolled[a] | | | | | | Infant Mortality per 1,000 Live Births | |
| | | | | | | | | | Primary | | Secondary | | Tertiary | | | |
| | 1960s | 1970s | 1980s | 1993 | 1960 | 1990 | 1960 | 1993 | 1960 | 1992 | 1960 | 1992 | 1960 | 1992 | 1970 | 1992 |
|---|---|---|---|---|---|---|---|---|---|---|---|---|---|---|---|---|
| Hong Kong | 2.8 | 2.3 | 1.4 | .6 | 29 | <5 | 63 | 79 | 91 | 108 | 24 | 75 | 4 | 20 | 15 | 6 |
| Taiwan | 3.1 | 2.0 | 1.4 | .9 | 46 | 6 | 64 | 74 | 67 | 1.3 | 37 | na | na | na | 24 | 4 |
| Korea | 2.5 | 1.8 | 1.2 | 1.0 | 29 | <5 | 53 | 71 | 94 | 105 | 27 | 90 | 5 | 42 | 51 | 13 |
| Singapore | 2.6 | 1.6 | 1.2 | 1.0 | 31[b] | <5 | 63 | 75 | 112 | 107 | 32 | 70[c] | 6 | 8[d] | 14 | 5 |
| Malaysia | 2.9 | 2.4 | 2.5 | 2.5 | 77 | 22 | 52 | 71 | 96 | 93 | 19 | 58 | 1 | 7 | 45 | 13 |
| Thailand | 3.0 | 2.7 | 1.7 | 1.7 | 32 | 7 | 49 | 69 | 136 | 97 | 8 | 33 | 2 | 19 | 73 | 26 |
| Indonesia | 2.2 | 2.3 | 1.7 | 1.7 | 53 | 23 | 40 | 63 | 67 | 115 | 6 | 38 | 1[e] | 10 | 118 | 66 |
| Philippines | 3.1 | 2.6 | 2.3 | 2.2 | 28 | 10 | 49 | 67 | 95 | 109 | 26 | 74 | 13 | 28 | 66 | 40 |

*Source:* World Bank.

[a] Enrollment rates are estimates of the ratio of children of all ages enrolled in school to the country's population of school-age children within a given cohort. For some countries the enroll-ment ratio may exceed 100 percent because some pupils are younger or older than the country's standard age for primary, secondary, or tertiary school. Late entry into school as well as repetition may also influence these ratios.

[b] 1970.
[c] 1991.
[d] 1990.
[e] 1965.

# Part 1
# The Tigers of East Asia

CHAPTER 1

# Hong Kong: A Unique Case of Development

*Leung Chuen Chau*

## I. Introduction

Hong Kong embarked on its export-led industrialization in the early 1950s, 10 years before any of the other East Asian NIEs. At the time, the economic outlook was not optimistic. With no natural resources or agriculture to fall back on, Hong Kong was not eligible for aid due to its status as a colony. Industrialization was a must, but affluent markets were thousands of miles away. Yet, after more than three decades of rapid growth, it has emerged as the richest economy in Asia after Japan. Section I looks at various facets of its economic achievements and identifies the main sources of its growth.

Four Asian economies, South Korea, Taiwan, Hong Kong, and Singapore, are often referred to collectively as the "tigers" or "little dragons" on the grounds that they share a common cultural heritage and have followed a common development strategy. While the role of the cultural factor is controversial, they certainly did not share a common development strategy. As is discussed in section II, Hong Kong is particularly different because its government chose to play a small and passive role.

Section III looks at Hong Kong's phases of economic development, each with its own leading-edge activities and patterns of growth. From this, we deduce a Hong Kong model of growth. Specifically, we argue that the rapid growth was driven by a class of merchant entrepreneur who specialized in finding and exploiting price discrepancies.

In the context of this model, section IV evaluates the role of policies and institutions. We conclude that local institutions and the policy mix were particularly conducive to commerce-based development. Government housing policies have also contributed, in an unintended and most unexpected manner, to rapid growth.

### Defining Success

Between mid-1949 and mid-1954, half a million refugees from mainland China settled in Hong Kong, increasing the population by 27 percent. Entrepôt trade, which was Hong Kong's lifeblood, flourished in those years, as Hong Kong became the only contact between China and the nonsocialist world. But in 1951, following China's entry into the Korean conflict, the United Nations imposed an embargo on trade between China and the Western world. Entrepôt trade in Hong Kong came to a standstill. Hong Kong had to reshape its economy. With its long heritage of trading, virtually no farming because of its small area and hilly terrain, an abundant supply of labor, and a small domestic market, labor-intensive manufacturing producing for export was the obvious way out. Four legendary decades followed. More and more less-developed countries (LDCs), in Asia and elsewhere, pursued export-oriented industrialization after the1960s. Economic growth slowed down markedly in the West after 1973, and there was an increase in protectionism. But Hong Kong kept growing as fast as ever.

## Economic and Social Progress

Growth rates of per capita income are extremely high by any standard (see table 1.1). In 1961–81, economic growth in Hong Kong was faster than in any other Asian country and much faster than that of Western industrialized countries (Chen 1984, 5–7); Hong Kong's growth rate also tops the list of countries

**TABLE 1.1.   Growth Rates of Key Indicators in Hong Kong**

|  | 1953–60 | 1959–73 | 1973–82 | 1982–91 |
|---|---|---|---|---|
| Population | 4.5 | 2.4 | 2.4 | 1.0 |
| Labor force |  | 3.1[a] | 4.5[a] | 1.3 |
| Employment |  | 2.6[a] | 4.5[a] | 1.5 |
|    Manufacturing employment | 7.7 | 8.7 | 3.1[a] | −2.6 |
| GDP | 9.4 | 9.2[b] | 9.6 | 6.2 |
| Per capita GDP | 6.2 | 6.8[b] | 7.0 | 5.1 |
| Wages for manufacturing workers |  | 6.8 | 2.3 | 1.0 |
| Retail prices | 0.1 |  |  |  |
| Consumer prices |  | 4.2[c] | 10.1 | 7.9 |
| Private consumption |  | 9.4[b] | 9.7 | 6.6 |
| Government consumption expenditures |  | 8.1[b] | 11.1 | 5.0 |
| Gross investment |  | 9.5[b] | 8.9 | 4.4 |
| Domestic exports |  | 13.2 | 8.2 | 6.8 |
| Re-exports |  |  | 15.1 | 22.6 |
| Domestic demand |  | 9.3[b] | 10.4 | 5.7 |
| Electricity production | 13.4 | 14.1 |  |  |

*Sources:* Riedel 1974, 17–9, 98; Lin, Mok, and Ho 1980, 5–6; Census and Statistics Department, *Monthly Digest of Statistics, Annual Digest of Statistics,* various issues; Economic Service Branch, Government Secretariat, *Economic Prospects,* various issues.

[a] Between years of census.
[b] After 1961.
[c] 1964–72.

covered in a recent study by Syrquin and Chenery (1989, 39–41). Only in the 1980s, with political uncertainties at home, did the growth rate slip behind that of other countries in the region. But the economy is extremely resilient. It has never contracted since 1952, and only once has the growth rate stayed under 6 percent for two consecutive years. Characteristically, a year of slow growth was followed by years of robust expansion. Unemployment was eliminated by the end of 1950s. At the time of the March 1961 census, it stood at 1.7 percent. After that it was never a serious problem. Since 1987, there has been a serious labor shortage, with the unemployment rate below 2 percent. Furthermore, this rapid growth with full employment was achieved, until recent years, with relatively stable prices. During the first 30 years there were only two spurts of high inflation—1973–74 and 1979–81—and both were caused largely by external oil shocks. These years aside, the rate of inflation averaged less than 5 percent a year from 1961 to 1980. The supply of food and wage goods from China at stable, administered prices and the widespread provision of public housing contributed greatly to this price stability.

With a 6 percent growth rate averaged over the entire period, per capita income in Hong Kong doubled every 12 years and quadrupled in one generation. According to a United Nations Development Program (UNDP) study, per capita GDP in Hong Kong, adjusted for purchasing-power parity, was the seventh highest among 173 countries in 1991. In Asia, it was second only to Japan (UNDP 1994, 129–31). As both direct and indirect taxes in Hong Kong are considerably lower than in the richer countries in the sample, Hong Kong residents are even better off in terms of disposable income. Coupled with a high savings rate and unabated appreciation of its real estate, it has become a wealthy city.

As for the distribution of income, the available evidence suggests a marked widening in income dispersion during the first decade of industrialization followed by a large reduction between 1961 and 1971 (see table 1.2). Since then, the degree of inequality in the distribution of household income has remained essentially unchanged. The Gini coefficient is currently higher than in most countries of the region. However, the average size of household fell from 4.5 in 1971 to 3.4 in 1991, and household size became more strongly correlated with income in later years. If household income is adjusted for size, there would be some reduction in inequality for 1981 and 1991. Furthermore, proportionately more immigrants from China entered Hong Kong during 1970s and 1980s than in the 1960s. Most of them were unskilled people from rural areas who found employment in low-paying jobs. Their presence lowered the income share of the poorest quintile, thus contributing to greater inequality, although they themselves were much better off than before.[1]

---

1. A detailed analysis and documentation of these developments are found in Chau 1994.

**TABLE 1.2. Distribution of Household Income in Hong Kong**

| Type of Household | Percentage of Recipients | Mean Income ($) | Shares of Quintile Groups (%) | | | | | Gini Coefficient | Maximum equalization (%) | Median Income/ GDP per Capita (%) |
|---|---|---|---|---|---|---|---|---|---|---|
| | | | I | II | III | IV | V | | | |
| 1957 | | 365 | 5.7 | 9.7 | 11.7 | 16.7 | 56.2 | 0.48 | | |
| 1966 Land household | 98.2 | 709 | 4.7 | 8.4 | 12.3 | 16.6 | 58.0 | 0.49 | 37.5 | 33.8 |
| 1971 All households | 100.0 | 1,039 | 5.6 | 10.1 | 13.6 | 19.3 | 51.4 | 0.44 | 32.0 | 36.2 |
| 1976 Land household | 99.1 | 2,026 | 5.3 | 10.0 | 14.2 | 20.4 | 50.1 | 0.43 | 31.3 | 33.7 |
| 1981 All households | 100.0 | 4,042 | 4.6 | 10.1 | 14.7 | 22.7 | 47.9 | 0.43 | 31.0 | 38.1 |
| 1986 All households | 100.0 | 7,304 | 5.0 | 10.0 | 14.3 | 20.9 | 49.8 | 0.44 | 31.4 | 36.9 |
| 1991 All households | 100.0 | 13,998 | 4.7 | 9.6 | 14.5 | 22.1 | 49.0 | 0.43 | 31.4 | |
| With data from Household Expenditure Survey | | | | | | | | | | |
| 1963–64 | | 683 | 4.4 | 8.9 | 12.2 | 17.8 | 56.7 | 0.50 | | |
| 1973–74 | | 1,930 | 4.1 | 10.9 | 15.9 | 22.1 | 47.0 | 0.42 | | |
| 1979–80 | | 4,574 | 6.2 | 10.9 | 15.1 | 21.3 | 46.5 | 0.40 | | |

*Sources:* Chow, S.C., et al. 1981; Census and Statistics Department, 1971a, 1971b, 1976, 1982, 1986, 1991b.

A more direct measure of the spread of well-being and the presence of trickle-down effects is the level and pattern of consumption by lower-income groups. Among residents of public housing estates and manual workers there was a marked improvement in the standard of living, both absolutely and relatively, from the mid-1960s to 1980. They were spending proportionately less on food, and yet their per capita food consumption rose from about two-thirds of the national average in 1963–64 to 20 percent above the overall average in 1979–80.

Another measure of well-being is government expenditure on social services, which increased rapidly after the mid-1970s. As a percentage of GDP, it rose from about 5 percent in the early 1970s to 7 percent in recent years. This has resulted in rapid social progress, as is shown in the appendix table A1.2. Over a brief span of 25 to 30 years, the infant mortality rate was cut by 80 percent, and life expectancy is now longer than in many Western countries. No less revealing, among those aged 15 to 19 in the labor force, the proportion of girls was significantly more than 50 percent in 1976, but the difference was eliminated by 1981 and reversed by 1986. It is likely that the earlier gender discrimination was practiced by low-income households out of economic necessity; its disappearance is a sign of increased affluence and enlightenment.

## Sources of Growth

The expansion of manufacturing was the driving force of the economy in the early years (see table 1.3). The manufacturing sector's share of the labor force was crudely estimated at about 36 percent in 1954, with half of this share employed in traditional handicrafts (Szczepanik 1958, 161). This share went up steadily and peaked in 1971, accounting for almost half of the working population, a proportion seldom found in other cities. By this time, most of the cottage industries had disappeared. In that year, the sector contributed 30 percent of Hong Kong's GDP. From then on, its relative importance has steadily declined. Manufacturing employment, cyclically adjusted, began to decline absolutely around 1987. From 1980 on, more and more manufacturing activities were relocated across the border in Guangdong Province in China. An estimated three million Chinese laborers are currently working for Hong Kong manufacturers.

Hong Kong has always had a very open economy. Founded by traders a century and a half ago, it remains essentially a city of merchants. Some 75 percent of its manufactured products are sold overseas. In the 1960s and 1970s, commodity trade was about 150 percent of GDP and fairly stable. In recent years, with outward processing and the revival of entrepôt trade, the ratio has gone above 230 percent. Typically, the top four industries have accounted for more than 70 percent of total exports (see table 1.4). All of them are labor-

**TABLE 1.3.  Output and Employment Structure in Hong Kong**

| | Percentage Distribution of GDP Current Factor Cost by Economic Activity | | | Percentage Distribution of Working Population by Industry | | | | |
|---|---|---|---|---|---|---|---|---|
| | 1970 | 1980 | 1989 | 1954 | 1961 | 1971 | 1981 | 1991 |
| 1. Agriculture and fishing | 2.0 | 0.8 | 0.3 | 8.4 | 7.3 | 3.9 | 2.0 | |
| 2. Mining and quarrying | 0.2 | 0.2 | 0.0 | | 0.7 | 0.3 | 0.1 | |
| 3. Manufacturing | 30.9 | 23.8 | 18.9 | 35.8 | 43.0 | 47.0 | 41.2 | 28.2 |
| 4. Electricity, gas, and water | 2.0 | 1.3 | 2.3 | | 1.1 | 0.6 | 0.6 | |
| 5. Construction | 4.2 | 6.7 | 5.3 | | 4.9 | 5.4 | 7.7 | 6.9 |
| 6. Wholesale, retail, and import-export trades, restaurants, and hotels | 19.6 | 20.4 | 24.0 | 25.1 | 14.4 | 16.2 | 19.2 | 22.5 |
| 7. Transport, storage, and communications | 7.6 | 7.5 | 8.9 | | 7.3 | 7.4 | 7.5 | 9.8 |
| 8. Financing, insurance, real estate, and business services | 14.9 | 22.8 | 19.8 | | 1.6 | 2.7 | 4.8 | 10.6 |
| 9. Community, social, and personal services | 18.0 | 12.5 | 14.6 | | 18.3 | 15.0 | 15.6 | 19.9 |
| 10. Activities not adequately defined | 0.6 | | | | 1.4 | 1.5 | 1.3 | 2.1 |
| 11. Ownership of premises | | 9.6 | 10.9 | | | | | |
| 12. Nominal sector (imputed bank service charge) | | -5.6 | -5.0 | | | | | |
| GDP at factor cost | 100.0 | 100.0 | 100.0 | | 100.0 | 100.0 | 100.0 | 100.0 |

*Sources*: Census and Statistics Department 1981, 35; *Estimates of GDP, 1966–87* 1988, 26; *Gross Domestic Product, Quarterly Estimates, and Revised Annual Estimates* 1991, 31; Sczcpanik 1958, 161; *Census Report*, various issues.

intensive, light-industry activities. Clothing, for example, has long been the mainstay of Hong Kong's exports, its share changing little over the years. This is most unusual for a product sold in fiercely competitive international markets and subject to all kinds of trade restrictions. Likewise, market concentration is high, with more than 60 percent of exports going to the top five markets. Particularly dominating is the United States, which has always accounted for about a third of the total.

Apart from rapid industrialization, the most notable trend revealed in table 1.3 is the phenomenal growth of the finance and business sector in the 1970s and 1980s. Its employment share quadrupled over the period. The takeoff of financial services started in the late 1960s and gathered momentum in the 1970s, so it conveniently took up the slack left by the slowdown in manufacturing growth. Expansion in the 1970s was a spinoff of worldwide development of the financial industry (which ushered in the globalization of capital markets) and innovative changes in financial services made possible by new electronic and telecommunications technology. Hong Kong was able to benefit because it had many attractions of its own: political stability, no exchange controls, a stable currency fully backed by international reserve assets, a well-defined and well-administered legal system, a noninterventionist government with low taxation, and a geographic location midway between New York and London.

In the 1980s, the financial sector received a big boost from the reforms and open door policy in China. Major banks competed to establish a foothold on this doorstep of China. The number of banks in Hong Kong grew from 74 in 1977 to 165 in 1989, of which 134 were foreign banks. There were also 238 deposit-taking companies and 158 representative offices of foreign banks. These provide a full range of financial services domestically and offshore. By 1991, Hong Kong had become the second largest financial center in the Asia-Pacific region in terms of loan syndication, fund management, gold trading, and stock market capitalization (Jao 1991, 166–67). For local business, the mature financial sector helps to stimulate savings, attract capital, and allocate investible funds. Between 1975 and 1989, bank loans to manufacturing increased 30-fold and for real estate 53-fold. In addition to outside capital, foreign banks can help to further overseas business connections and transmit managerial knowledge and market and technological information.

Tourism is big business in Hong Kong. In 1991, there were more than six million visitor arrivals. These people stayed in 31,000 hotel rooms and spent an average of U.S.$820 each. The industry has contributed between 5 and 7 percent of Hong Kong's GDP in recent years (Yang 1990, 401). Being labor intensive, it has created many jobs. It is also a big customer for Hong Kong's transport and communications facilities. The industry began its sustained growth in the 1960s. Between 1961 and 1980, tourist arrivals grew at 13 percent

**TABLE 1.4. Structure of Domestic Exports from Hong Kong**

| | Percentage Share of Major Industries in Domestic Exports | | | | | | | Distribution of Domestic Exports by Major Markets | | | | | |
| --- | --- | --- | --- | --- | --- | --- | --- | --- | --- | --- | --- | --- | --- |
| Year | Clothing | Textiles | Plastic Products | Electronic Products | Footwear | Watches and Clocks | Electrical Appliances | U.S. | U.K. | West Germany | Australia | Japan | China |
| 1959 | 34.8 | 18.1 | 7.0 | | 4.3 | | | 27.7 | 21.9 | 6.6 | 2.6 | 2.7 | 0.9 |
| 1964 | 36.6 | 16.0 | 11.0 | 2.4 | 3.9 | | | | | | | | |
| 1970 | 35.1 | 10.3 | 11.3 | 9.5 | 2.4 | | | | | | | | |
| 1974 | 38.2 | 11.9 | 9.1 | 12.0 | 1.4 | 2.2 | | 32.4 | 12.1 | 10.7 | 5.7 | 4.6 | 0.4 |
| 1980 | 34.1 | 6.7 | 7.9 | 13.9 | 0.9 | 9.6 | 2.9 | 33.2 | 10.0 | 10.8 | 2.9 | 3.4 | 2.4 |
| 1985 | 34.6 | 6.0 | 8.2 | 20.8 | | 7.4 | 3.5 | 44.4 | 6.6 | 6.2 | | 3.4 | 11.7 |
| 1990 | 39.4 | 7.5 | 3.6 | 25.9 | | 8.5 | 1.5 | 29.4 | 6.0 | 8.0 | | 5.3 | 21.0 |

*Sources:* Census and Statistics Department; *Hong Kong Review of Overseas Trade*, various issues.

annually. Visitors were attracted by Hong Kong's reputation as a "shoppers' paradise," a result of low taxation, free port status, large volume, its concentration of good food, and Shanghaiese tailors who could deliver a custom-made suit in 20 hours. More important, with China closed to tourism, Hong Kong became its proxy. In the 1980s, the open door policy of China helped to sustain this momentum. Particularly after 1987, the large number of Taiwanese visiting China have passed through Hong Kong, to comply with their government's policy. Also, with spreading affluence, southern China itself has become an important source of tourists for Hong Kong.

As table 1.1 showed, the growth of exports slowed down markedly after 1973. Thus, domestic demand has done more than its share in maintaining the momentum of growth. Consider first private consumption, which in the early 1970s accounted for 61 percent of GDP, about a third more than exports. It has increased at a considerably faster rate than has GDP. It has also become more stable. The components registering the greatest gain in the 1970s and 1980s were furniture and furnishings, rent and housing, clothing, recreation, and other services. All of them have very high domestic value-added contents. Gross investment increased at a slower rate than did GDP. It is not clear how out-processing has affected this statistic. At any rate, investment in machinery and equipment has a high import content. That is obviously not true of construction. Table 1.3 shows a sharp jump in the proportion of workers employed in construction between 1971 and 1981. The proportion fell moderately in 1991 but remained well above that in 1971. Wage rates increased much faster in this sector than for the rest of the economy. Property prices went through two prolonged booms: from 1975 to 1981, with a five-fold increase in housing prices (compared with a 72 percent increase in consumer prices); and from 1985 to 1992, when housing prices rose 5.4 times (compared with a 79 percent increase in consumer prices). The wealth effect produced by these booms is not directly reflected in the national income statistics, but its incidence contributed to the buoyancy of the economy. Government expenditures and public and private investment in infrastructure also registered higher than average growth from 1970s onward.

External Circumstances

During the 1950s and 1960s, Western countries enjoyed a long period of sustained growth. This, along with trade liberalization, provided ready markets for Hong Kong's exports. Until the mid-1960s, Hong Kong faced little competition from other nations in the region, which were often plagued by turmoil or political uncertainty. Periodic unrest in Southeast Asia led to capital flight, and a great proportion of that capital ended up in Hong Kong.

Politics and policies in China were by far the strongest external influence on Hong Kong. After 1951, China adopted a closed door policy. Emigration to Hong Kong was largely stopped, so Hong Kong was spared the disruption of massive rural-urban migration that has affected many cities in developing countries. From then, until the late 1960s, China provided Hong Kong with a steady supply of foodstuffs, consumer goods, and construction materials at stable and relatively low prices. As I pointed out in an earlier study:

> Thus, instead of having to contend with an inelastic domestic supply of foodstuffs and increasingly expensive imported food, as the rapidly growing urban centers in developing countries typically face, Hong Kong was blessed with a perfectly elastic supply of foodstuffs from the vast rural hinterland of China . . . at administered stable prices. (Chau 1983, 196–97)

After 1972, China began to raise its export prices but much less than world prices (Chau 1983, 195).[2] China's adoption of economic reform and an open door policy in the late 1970s led to an era of integration that has benefited both economies tremendously. Bilateral trade increased at an annual rate of about 40 percent in the 1980s. Entrepôt trade involving China reemerged as a valuable source of income and growth. Increasingly, China was a big market for Hong Kong's own exports, and in 1985 it became the number one trading partner. The Pearl River Delta has become the workshop for Hong Kong's manufacturers, greatly increasing the scale and profitability of many enterprises. Hong Kong has also acted as the middleman for foreign investment in China, including syndicated loans. This has spurred the growth of finance and business services. Since early 1993, the shares of major enterprises in China were offered for subscription in Hong Kong and listed on the stock exchange. At the same time, as a result of rapid growth in recent years, many of China's enterprises have invested in all sectors of the Hong Kong economy.

## II.  Public Policy and Economic Structure

Hong Kong is noted for three main features: an open economy, small government, and nonintervention. The last one, in particular, is considered to be most unusual for an economy of Hong Kong's size. Nonintervention was particularly remarkable in the 1950s and 1960s, but it has remained a tenet of government policy. Philip Haddon-Cave, who was Hong Kong's financial sec-

---

2. This outcome may not have been intentional. It was China's national policy before 1978 to freeze its wages and price levels.

retary from 1971 to 1981, coined the term *positive noninterventionism* to characterize the government's attitude toward the economy.

> This involves taking the view that, in the great majority of circumstances it is futile and damaging to the growth rate of the economy for attempts to be made to plan the allocation of resources available to the private sector and to frustrate the operation of market forces which, in an open economy, are difficult enough to predict, let alone to control. (1984, xiv)

As a corollary, companies have to pay for their own mismanagement and mistakes, and consumers have to pay the full cost of publicly provided services. The word *positive* means that the government will not reject every proposal for intervention as a matter of principle but has a strong bias against intervening.

The primary role of government is therefore to provide the public services and economic infrastructure that only the government can sensibly provide. Social responsibility to the needy is accepted, but the work ethic must not be weakened by social policies and redistributive fiscal policies (Haddon-Cave 1984, xv). The public sector must be kept as small as possible, to leave more resources to the private sector to react to volatile trading conditions (xvi). To this end, the government tries to stick to a certain guideline for its expenditure/GDP ratio. Another objective is to minimize price distortions. Finally, the government is committed to a balanced budget, not year by year but over the course of a business cycle.

In general, policymakers after Haddon-Cave have upheld these principles. They have made no attempt to guide the direction of Hong Kong's industrial development, despite considerable pressure in the early 1980s for the government to take a more active role. There has been little change in tax rates in the 1980s. The relative size of the public sector, which was rising in 1970s, has stabilized. Since 1985, the budget has regularly been in surplus.

## The Macro Environment

The government's stance of noninterventionism finds its best expression in Hong Kong's macroeconomic setting. Most of the time the authorities have had no means or intention of pursuing a discretionary monetary policy. They have eschewed a countercyclical budgetary policy. There is practically no marketable public debt.

*Monetary System.* There is no central bank in Hong Kong. The currency is issued by two major private banks. Before 1972, the Hong Kong dollar was linked to sterling at a fixed rate of exchange, and all notes were fully backed by sterling assets. This arrangement produced an automatic adjustment process, on classical gold standard lines. A balance of payments deficit caused contraction of the domestic money supply, falling prices, and rising exports, which restored the external balance. There was no room for monetary policy. All things considered, the system worked reasonably well.

The sterling exchange standard came to an end in mid-1972, when sterling began to float. For two years or so, the Hong Kong currency was pegged to the U.S. dollar. The link did not last, as the dollar itself became unstable. The Hong Kong dollar was floated in November 1974. For the first time, the authorities could pursue monetary policy to maintain internal economic stability. They made some attempts to influence the growth of credit but lacked the instruments for effective credit control. As foreign currency–denominated certificates of deposit were designated as liquid assets, the government lost control of credit expansion. It had no public debt instruments with which to intervene directly in the money market. And the fixing of lending rates was in the hands of the Association of Banks, in which the government was not even represented (Youngson 1982, 130–31). From 1977 on, the economy was plagued by excessive credit expansion, a falling exchange rate, and rising inflation. In the words of Jao: "In those years, monetary policy adhered to neither rule nor discretion; it succeeded in controlling neither the price of the money (exchange rate) nor the quantity of money" (1988, 44).

Political events intervened. In July 1982, the British and Chinese governments began to negotiate over the future of Hong Kong. The progress of that negotiation swayed the mood of the territory. The Hong Kong dollar was sold heavily following the second quarter of 1983. The decline turned into a rout on September 23 and 24, when the exchange rate fell 15 percent against the U.S. dollar. On October 15, the Hong Kong dollar was linked to the U.S. dollar at a fixed exchange rate of U.S.$1 = H.K.$7.8. The link has persisted until today, and discretionary monetary policy was once again removed from Hong Kong.

*Budget and Fiscal Policy.* Tax rates in Hong Kong are low, simple, and stable. Individuals pay taxes on their salaries on a sliding scale, but the total tax burden is restricted to a standard rate that has varied between 15 and 17.5 percent in the postwar years. Property income and profits of unincorporated businesses are taxed at the same standard rate. Corporate profits are taxed at a marginally higher rate. Indirect taxes are few and well concealed from ordinary consumers. In all, total tax revenue has amounted to about 11 percent of GDP in recent years. The government also receives sizable nontax revenue, primarily from land sales, which has amounted to more than 70 percent of tax revenue since the 1970s. As a ratio of GDP, public expenditure was very stable from the mid-1960s to early 1970s, between 11 and 12 percent. Then the ratio began to rise rapidly, reaching 17 percent in 1986–87. Due to the relative price effect (Ho

1988, 19), the ratio at constant prices was much more stable, rising only from 13 to about 16 percent. On the whole, the ratio is considerably lower than in other Asian NIEs. On the other hand, as Hong Kong needs to spend little on defense, proportionately more can be devoted to other services. The share of social services—education, health, housing, and welfare—in total expenditures has also been increasing, reaching 45 percent in recent years.

Unlike most other countries, a budgetary surplus has been the rule in Hong Kong. From 1946 to 1990, only seven deficits were recorded. These were the results of highly unfavorable internal or external circumstances. Significantly, there was no difference in budgetary balance before and after 1958, the year in which the British government allowed Hong Kong to decide its own budget. A balanced budget has been a guiding principle for the government. This was made explicit by Haddon-Cave (1984, xviii). Quite unlike other countries, government departments have tended to overestimate their expenditures and underestimate their revenues. With hardly an exception, the realized surplus has turned out to be larger than the budgeted one (or the realized deficit smaller).[3] At times, the unplanned surplus became embarrassingly large. In recent years, the accumulated surplus has amounted to about 80 percent of annual expenditures.

Given the budgetary procedure and the sources of revenue, surpluses tended to rise in periods of boom and fall in slowdowns or slumps. Most governments would have considered this a compliment. But the Hong Kong government went to great lengths to dissociate itself from such Keynesianism. The official position, as pointed out by Cowperthwaite, who was financial secretary before Haddon-Cave, is that Hong Kong has the most open economy in the world and a large part of any increase in expenditures will be leaked through increased imports. Countercyclical budgetary policy will, therefore, be ineffectual (Riedel 1974, 137).

Industry and Trade

A notable feature of Hong Kong's manufacturing is the predominance of small enterprises. In 1955, soon after the start of export-led industrialization, average employment per firm stood at 45, which was small by any standard. But the average size fell by more than half by 1975 and continued to fall (see table 1.5). Although the drop after 1980 might have reflected out-processing, the trend was firmly established. Small enterprises were able to more than hold their ground during decades of rapid growth, continuous structural adjustment,

---

3. For 1982–83, the budgeted and realized surpluses were, respectively, HK 5.1 and 20 billion. As of March 31, 1993, the accumulated financial surplus stood at HK 119.6 billion, and total expenditures for that financial year were 109 billion.

and modernization. This seems to defy both conventional economic wisdom and Marxist dynamics (Lin, Mok, and Ho 1980, 94–97).

A systematic analysis of the competitive strength of small businesses is beyond the scope of this essay. Here we shall only sketch their operation. Typically, they began as spinoffs of existing enterprises after employees had gained expertise in the design, production, or marketing of the products concerned. Most of them managed to launch their businesses without using bank credit, relying instead on extended family and friends (Lin, Mok, and Ho 1980, 96). There is little government bureaucracy to cope with in starting a business, renting premises, and hiring workers. Depending on the nature of the business, small firms market their output through two main channels. They may work as subcontractors for larger firms or they may sell their products to overseas buyers through the multitude of import-export firms. Understandably, the fatality rate of these small concerns is high, as they do not have adequate resources to weather adverse changes in trading conditions. But the costs of both starting and winding up a business are very low in Hong Kong.

Import and export trade is a large part of the Hong Kong economy. In 1988, for example, almost 300,000 people were engaged in it, some 11 percent of the working population. Given the size structure of manufacturing firms, it is perhaps less of a surprise to find that the import-export business is also dominated by small firms. In 1988, the average number of employees per import-export firm was 5.3. Eighty-seven percent of the firms had fewer than nine employees, and more than half had fewer than four (*Annual Digest of Statistics* 1990, 72). Many of these small firms consist of the owners, assisted by clerical help and a messenger, while others are husband and wife teams. Again, entry and exit is easy. Usually, these owners are highly specialized in a market and product line and know some overseas buyers personally. When the buyers are in town with their shopping lists, the traders arrange for factory sales staff to meet the buyers at their offices. As the traders are on personal terms with both parties, it is easier for them to complete the deal. The small traders are informal, flex-

TABLE 1.5.   Hong Kong Manufacturing Establishments and Employment

| Year | Number of Establishments | Number Employed | Average Employment |
|---|---|---|---|
| 1950 | 1,478 | 81,718 | 55 |
| 1960 | 5,346 | 218,405 | 41 |
| 1970 | 16,507 | 549,178 | 33 |
| 1980 | 45,409 | 892,140 | 20 |
| 1990 | 49,087 | 730,217 | 15 |

*Source:* Industry Department, Trade Development Council.

ible, and capable of meeting the special needs of small buyers, particularly those from countries with complicated trade and foreign exchange restrictions. The small traders help to attract small overseas buyers to Hong Kong, and these, in turn, are the lifeblood of many small manufacturing concerns.

The government has played an increasing role in boosting trade activities. Its Trade Department handles bilateral and multilateral commercial relations with Hong Kong's trading partners. Trade promotion is largely coordinated by the Trade Development Council, established in 1966 as a statutory body. It operates 33 offices throughout the world, organizes regular trade fairs and provides up-to-date trade and economic information to local and overseas businesspeople. Support also comes from the government-owned Hong Kong Export Credit Insurance Corporation and a number of trade and industrial organizations.

## Banking, Finance, and Business Services

It is generally recognized that Hong Kong's smooth move into export-oriented industrialization owed much to the market connections and long-established services involved in its entrepôt trade. Trade credit, insurance, shipping and stevedore services, and warehousing were well established. So were various infrastructures such as telecommunications and airport and port facilities. Since those early days, all these supports have expanded considerably. For example, the container port now handles more containers than any other port in the world. Though short of space, ultramodern technology and good management have made it extremely efficient. It takes 12 hours or less to load and unload a ship. All the piers and berths are privately owned. These facilities, along with strong financial backing, made Hong Kong's merchant fleet the second largest in the world in the early 1980s.

Before the 1970s, the financial system was simple and relatively primitive. Commercial banks were well developed as a legacy of the entrepôt past, and their assets were growing at a faster rate than was national income. But there were no other specialized financial institutions such as investment banks. In 1965, when information on the distribution of bank loans became available, less than 20 percent of bank loans were extended to manufacturing industry. How much of this financing was available for fixed investment is not clear (Riedel 1974, 109, 124). Small firms, in particular, could not obtain long- or medium-term bank credit. The stock market was not active, with manufacturing poorly represented on it. Savers had few instruments from which to choose.

After 1970, the situation changed rapidly. The number of commercial banks increased sharply. Most of the newcomers were foreign banks, which brought in foreign capital and financial innovations. Between 1971 and 1989, loans and advances for use in Hong Kong increased 51-fold. Increasingly the stock exchange became a channel for financing expansion. Today, large firms can also obtain financing by issuing bonds and commercial paper. Small firms can easily obtain bank credits by pledging their plant and equipment (or residential property) as collateral. For savers, there is now a host of financial products from which to choose, denominated in all the major currencies.

### Labor Market

The industrial labor market in Hong Kong is the closest embodiment of a neoclassical competitive market found anywhere. Constraints on market forces, like labor laws, government intervention, unionism, monopsonistic employers, and inertia, are conspicuous by their absence.

In the 1960s and 1970s, almost half the labor force was engaged in manufacturing. It remains the largest employer in Hong Kong. Most of these workers, particularly during the heyday of industrialization, are relatively young and unskilled or semiskilled. About 45 percent of them are females. In short, there is a large number of relatively homogeneous and mobile workers. Similarly, there is a large number of employers, most of them small enterprises. Both sides are highly rational or income maximizing. There is no separation of management and ownership among firms. Information is readily available and travels quickly in a small place with highly developed mass media and telecommunications. Labor unions are weak and generally ineffective. There are no entry barriers between industries. The preconditions for atomistic competition are in place. Labor legislation for industrial workers on such matters as hours of work, rest days, sick and maternity leave, severance payments, and long-service payments made their appearance only after 1968. They are lenient by international standards. For example, before the long-service payment ordinance came into effect in November 1991, an employer needed to give just a month's notice, or a month's pay in lieu of notice, to terminate employment for most workers. There are no minimum wage laws.

Manual workers are not hired with a contract. There is little job security: "In Hong Kong's competitive economy geared to exports, lay-off and redundancy are an ever-present shadow over the life of the working class" (England and Rear 1980, 238). On the other hand, workers will not hesitate to quit for a better job—to "fire the boss," as the saying goes. It is common to pay workers by daily rate or piece rate, but their overall package often consists of basic wages and bonus, fringe benefits, and allowances for food and transport. Although basic wages tend to be fairly stable, in the short run for a given grade of labor—which may give an impression of wage rigidity—employers can easily adjust fringe benefits when taking on new workers. The "putting-out" system (in which part of the work is farmed out to persons working at home) and subcontracting give additional flexibility to employers. The prevailing view is that relatively unobstructed market mechanisms are at work in determining wages and employment (England and Rear 1980, 176; Lin, Mok, and Ho 1980, 91–92; Riedel 1974, 76; Chau 1988a). Market performance bears witness to this verdict. Wages are known to be flexible both upward and downward. Excessive unemployment tends to be quickly eliminated.

## The Property Market

The housing and property market is an anomaly in Hong Kong, perhaps in the world. Unlike the rest of the economy, government participation and intervention is extensive and visible. While most goods and services are relatively cheap, private housing in Hong Kong has always been expensive, and increasingly so. It is one of the few things that people in Hong Kong queue up to buy.

All land in Hong Kong is "Crownland," owned by the government. All property is therefore leasehold. In the older part of the city, leases used to run for 999 years from the time of leasing. New leases are generally for a much shorter duration. The significant point is that the government has always monopolized the supply of undeveloped land (much of which it obtained through reclamation from the sea), for which it enjoys exclusive rights. It releases land for development in an orderly fashion, according to the perceived needs of the economy. The amount of land to be released for various purposes in a financial year will be publicized a year or so in advance. This land is allocated by public auction. The lessee of each piece of land is obliged to develop it within a stipulated period so as to prevent land hoarding. Some land for specialized purposes is leased by a special treaty negotiated directly between the government and the applicant.

At the end of the World War II, much of the housing stock in Hong Kong was destroyed or damaged. With massive inflows of people, a severe housing shortage developed. In response, rent control was imposed on all prewar housing. That control is still in effect, though all but a few of the prewar structures have long since vanished. In 1970, rent control was imposed on domestic housing completed after the war. Though the ordinance was introduced as a short-run measure, with a life of two years, it was consistently renewed, revised, or replaced so that the control is still in effect today. It is the stated and sincere intention of the administration to end the controls as soon as circumstances allow. For this reason, newly completed domestic housing is exempted from control.

However, it is public housing that has the greatest impact on Hong Kong property. At present, more households live in public than in private housing. Most households are in rented public housing, but the percentage in "home ownership estates" is rising. The Hong Kong government takes pride in being the "largest landlord in the world." The public housing program started out as a resettlement scheme. In late 1953, a series of shantytown fires left 60,000 people homeless. In 1954, the government decided to rehouse them in permanent structures that it would build. Called resettlement estates, they were high-rise and very basic shacks but at rents affordable to the very poor. Since then, thousands of these units have been built to accommodate squatters who have lost their homes to fire, flood, or government clearance programs. In the early 1960s, a means-tested public housing program was created. But, as in the resettlement program, there is no income restriction for continued occupancy, so the mobility rate is very low. Standards have been steadily improved since the early 1970s and are now on a par with middle-income private housing.

Although half of the population live in public housing, and another 10 to 20 percent live on rent-controlled premises, the residential housing market remains highly active, prosperous, and profitable for those engaged in it. There have been three main price booms: 1970–73, 1976–81, and 1990–94. In each case residential housing prices increased by threefold or more. Such booms were always accompanied by rampant speculation. Over the decades, the appreciation of property prices has far outstripped the rate of inflation. At today's prices, housing in Hong Kong is probably the second most expensive in the world, after Tokyo. In the summer of 1992, in an effort to cool the overheated property market and discourage speculation, banks were instructed to limit their mortgages on the purchase of residential premises to 70 percent of the property price. Prices and rents for nonresidential property have risen as well but at a more moderate pace. Speculation is less common, so the market is less active.

### Flows of Funds

The postwar growth of Hong Kong was never inhibited to any noticeable degree by a lack of investible funds. The high domestic savings rate, facilitated by low taxation and the absence of any crowding out by government borrowing, certainly helped. But the uninterrupted inflow of outside funds was a much more important factor.

Hong Kong has long been an entrepôt for funds as well as of commodities. From the late nineteenth century on, most of the substantive remittances from overseas Chinese to their homeland have been channeled through Hong Kong. This helped to support a community of local banks, money changers, bullion dealers, and moneylenders. In early postwar years, Hong Kong also became the haven for flight capital from mainland China as well as the Chinese communities in Southeast Asia. From 1946 on, a steady flow of capital moved in, partly due to pent-up remittances of the war years. After civil war broke out in China and political and racial tensions flared up in Southeast Asia, the flow became a torrent. It contributed to booms in banking, the bullion trade, the stock market, and real estate. At a time when rice and sugar were still under ration, the financial sector was bustling. The number of banks, for example, doubled in 1946 and redoubled the next year. These capital inflows contributed greatly to the smooth and rapid reconstruction and rehabilitation of the Hong Kong economy.

What attracted these funds to Hong Kong was not investment returns. There were few investment opportunities other than real estate and speculation in currency and bullion. Many of them ended up as deposits in banks. The magnet was a stable and convertible currency, fully backed by sterling, a well-developed and reliable banking system, low taxation, and a functioning legal system for the protection of property rights. Most important, there was no restriction on the movement of funds in and out of Hong Kong. No questions were asked and no official records kept. For the same reason, information to ascertain their size is hard to come by. Szczepanik calculated that, for the period 1947–55, invisible earnings and capital inflows averaged 40 percent of the national income (1958, 142). The flows from China stopped soon after 1950, but overseas Chinese communities, in the region as well in North America and Australia, remained the dominant sources of outside capital for Hong Kong. After industrialization got under way, the pull factor of high returns augmented the push factor of instability at sources for capital inflows. Wealthy Chinese families in the region siphoned off part of their fortunes, along with some family members, to do business in Hong Kong. They all had close-knit networks of relatives and clansmen in Hong Kong and blended smoothly into the local community. The sources and uses of these funds are practically impossible to ascertain. But these families were active in all sectors, and their total impact was great. At this early stage of industrialization, reliance on outside capital was great, and direct foreign investment was still to make a significant impact.

Direct foreign investment (DFI) was insignificant during the initial phase of Hong Kong's industrialization. In the 1950s, such investment was mostly directed toward extracting natural resources that did not exist in Hong Kong. According to a 1960 survey by the Industry and Commerce Department, there were only 27 foreign enterprises engaged in manufacturing. Their total investment, including joint ventures, amounted to a mere U.S.$133 million. It was only after the 1960s, when the local industrial base was firmly established, that large numbers of foreign firms moved in to manufacture labor-intensive garments and electronic products. From 1970 on, the Industrial Department has carried out annual surveys on foreign enterprises in manufacturing. Total value of DFI increased two and a half times between 1971 and 1980, and it increased by another 340 percent over the following decade (Mok 1933, 133, 193), thereby gaining in relative importance. However, the overall weight of DFI remained moderate, as is attested in table 1.6.

This is in sharp contrast to the situation in Singapore, where the shares of foreign-owned firms in manufacturing in 1980 for employment and gross output were, respectively, 58 and 74 percent (Soon and Tan 1996). But the impact of foreign direct investment on Hong Kong's industrialization is much greater than these weights would suggest. Foreign firms were vital in the transfer of technology, managerial know-how, and new products. They also provided valuable on-the-job training for local employees. For example, in the 1970s, when wage costs in Hong Kong were no longer competitive, these firms were the first to move into such skill- and capital-intensive industries as chemicals, electrical appliances, watches and clocks, and printing (Lin, Mok, and Ho 1980, 133). Thus, while industrialization in Hong Kong was initiated by indigenous entrepreneurs (including refugees from the mainland), its subsequent upgrading and diversification owed much to direct foreign investment.

The growth of foreign investment in manufacturing during the 1980s also underrates the overall increase in FDI. In this decade, along with the general restructuring of the local economy, the emphasis of FDI also shifted gradually toward the tertiary sector. The bulk of investment from Japan and the United States was increasingly placed in banking and other financial services, trade, and communications.

Also in the 1980s, the flows of funds in and out of Hong Kong became much more complicated. While foreign direct investment as well as portfolio investment continued to expand rapidly, outward investments by local firms became substantial. Most investment went to China, first for out-processing, then for other purposes. But considerable outward investment was also directed to other countries in the region, particularly to Indonesia and Thailand. In addition, as an emerging financial center Hong Kong also played a key role in channelling outside funds to these destinations. To complicate matters further, flight capital also left Hong Kong in droves after 1982, spurred by political uncertainty in connection with the return of sovereignty to China in 1997. Under this circumstance, even the direction of the net flow, let alone its magnitude, has become a topic for debate. The general impression was that Hong Kong had suffered from a significant outflow of capital during most of the 1980s. But the research team of the Hong Kong Bank concluded, after reviewing all relevant information, that, although "there was a net inflow of

TABLE 1.6.  Share of DFI in Hong Kong Manufacturing (percentage)

|  | 1973 | 1978 | 1981 | 1984 | 1989 |
|---|---|---|---|---|---|
| Employment | 11.0 | 10.5 | 10.0 | 9.8 | 12.7 |
| Gross output | 12.9 | 16.2 | | | 18.8[a] |

Sources: Ho and Chau (1988) Hongkong Bank 1991.
[a] Share of domestic exports.

funds up to 1983, and . . . there may have been some outflow in the period 1984 to 1988 . . . it seems unlikely to have been large" (*Hongkong Bank Economic Report*, November 1990, 1).

## III.  The Nature of Growth and Public Policy

Economic growth in Hong Kong since the early 1950s can conveniently be analyzed in three distinct phases (see fig. 1.1).

### Industrialization

This phase ran from the early 1950s to the early 1970s and contained two sub-phases: 1953–60 and the 1960s. Industrialization in the earlier period was narrowly based, mostly on textiles and clothing. These industries were initiated by external forces, through "the virtually wholesale transfer of capital, machinery, skills, market connections, and entrepreneurial capabilities from Shanghai and other parts of China" (SRI International 1989, 7). After the entrepôt trade was derailed by the U.N. embargo, more resources were put at their disposal. Unemployment was estimated at 150,000, or 15 percent of the labor force, in mid-1954. This represented a virtually unlimited supply of workers at very low wages for the manufacturers. External circumstances were also favorable. Markets in developing countries had an insatiable demand for cheap textiles. Goods of higher quality could enter industrialized countries unobstructed. There was little need for industrialists to do anything else, so very little diversification occurred in the 1950s.

By the late 1950s, an increasing number of local businessmen were moving into manufacturing. Most of them had a trading background and knew little about manufacturing. They were ready to venture into any field that promised a profit. Several failed, but enough of them succeeded to diversify the industrial base. Many new industries and new products made their appearance in the 1960s, particularly plastic flowers, toys, wig products, machinery, and electronics products. Employment growth accelerated in the first half of 1960s (Riedel 1974, 93). Industrial wages, which had been stagnant until 1959, started to rise. Export growth jumped to 12 percent a year in 1961–65 and 20 per cent in 1966–70. Two new industrial towns, Tsuen Wan and Kwun Tong, were developed during this decade. Product diversification was accompanied by drastic changes in the pattern of trade. In 1957, less than a quarter of domestic products were sold to North America and Western Europe; by 1969, their share had reached 75 percent.

Practically all the manufactured exports from Hong Kong during this period were light industry, labor-intensive, consumer products: "Hong Kong finds its comparative advantage in exporting unskilled-labor-intensive

| | 1947-1952 | 1952-1970 | 1970-1982 | 1981-1990s |
|---|---|---|---|---|
| Changing environment | • Post war recovery | • Cut off of China trade<br>• Growth of U.S. and European markets | • Competition from NICS and other low-cost countries<br>• Trade protectionism | • Reemergence of entrepot trade<br>• Increasing international competition<br>• Growing economic links with South China |
| Economic structure | • Entrepot trade and services | • Textiles<br>• Clothing<br>• Consumer electronics<br>• Plastics | • Clothing/textiles<br>• Diversified consumer manufacturing<br>• Financial and business services | • Entrepot trade services<br>• Financial and business services<br>• Fashion apparel and textiles<br>• Diversified consumer manufacturing<br>• Tourism |
| Economic Foundations | • Excellent port<br>• Experienced international trade sector<br>• Extensive shipping and trade links | • Transfer of capital and skills from Shanghai<br>• Low-cost labor | • Low-cost labor<br>• Responsive physical infrastructure (e.g., housing, transportation) | • Quality workforce<br>• Accessible technology<br>• Open and stable legal and regulatory system<br>• Forward-looking physical infrastructure |
| Economic strategy | • Exploit shipping and trading advantages | • Labor-intensive industrialization | • Export-oriented industrial diversification | • Move to higher-value-added manufacturing<br>• Strengthen entrepot services<br>• Build new economic links with China |

Fig. 1.1  Evolution of the Hong Kong economy. (From SRI International, Building Prosperity: A *Five-Part Economic Strategy for Hong Kong's Future* [Hong Kong: Hong Kong Economic Survey, 1989].)

manufactured goods . . ." (Riedel 1974, 34). Most of these products were extremely flexible, as the wig industry showed. Responding to a swing of fashion favoring wigs and other hairpieces in the mid-1960s, the export value of "wigs and false beards" went up from U.S.\$71 million in 1966 to a peak of \$937 million in 1970, when it accounted for 7.6 percent of domestic exports. Its decline was just as dramatic. By 1973, its export value had dropped to \$104 million, and it soon disappeared from the trade statistics. This ability of Hong Kong's manufacturers to shift into those products enjoying strong demand is widely credited as a main cause of rapid export growth. The study by Lin, Mok, and Ho reveals that this "commodity mix effect" accounted for 56 percent of the export growth between 1964 and 1974 (1980, 123–24).

## Broad-based Development

The general environment for Hong Kong's exports became less favorable in the 1970s. After 1973, the West entered a period of slow growth, and, partly as a result, protectionism mounted. With a restricted market, competition from Korea, Taiwan, and other newly industrializing countries intensified. Wages in Hong Kong were much higher than those in Korea and Taiwan. The response was industrial diversification. The relative weight of textiles and clothing fell, while that of toys, clocks, and watches rose. Within each category of goods there was a steady process of trading up to higher-value-added products and wider product ranges (SRI International 1989, 9). Foreign direct investment played a big role in this diversification and modernization. In the 1960s, it had been largely confined to electronics; now foreign companies invested heavily in watches and clocks, electrical appliances, chemicals, printing, and food processing. Still, export growth slowed from 13.2 percent a year in the 1960s to about 8 percent in the 1970s.

During the 1970s, Hong Kong managed to develop from a financial backwater into one of the major financial centers of the world, an achievement that has been compared to the success of industrialization during the previous decade and a half (Jao 1984, 167). In 1971, Hong Kong's financial sector was comprised of commercial banks specializing in retail banking services. By 1980, there were more foreign bank offices in Hong Kong than in any city other than New York and London. In 1981, the category of finance, insurance, and property contributed more to GDP than manufacturing did. This change brought in capital and supported excellent transport and telecommunications facilities. They made Hong Kong an ideal choice as the regional headquarters for multinational companies and boosted the growth of tourism and business travel.

During 1972–81, domestic demand grew at an annual rate of 10.7 percent compared with 8.9 percent for domestic exports. In the second half of the period, there was a noticeable rise in the propensity to consume. Between 1977 and 1981, consumption grew at an average rate of 14 percent per year compared with 10.7 percent for GDP as a whole. The correlation between income growth and consumption growth weakened for several reasons: increased household net worth and growing confidence; entry into the labor force of the baby boom generation, which had grown up in relative affluence and security; the spread of consumerism; aggressive marketing; and the proliferation of new products. Better educated and informed, with more discretionary income at its disposal, the population's appetite for high-quality goods was growing. The trend toward nuclear households and more working women led to the commercialization of work that had once been done in the home, including food preparation, laundry, dressmaking, and child care. High incomes, high profits, and windfall gains from property and stock market booms fed conspicuous consumption. Retail outlets sprang up to meet all tastes and budgets: shopping arcades, department stores, supermarkets, fast food chains, specialty shops, boutiques, hair salons, and gourmet restaurants. Manufacturers began to turn their attention to the home market. A Hong Kong identity and a sense of belonging was building. A local culture took shape, expressed in literature, pop music, mass media, and, most important of all, the local film industry. From the 1970s on, locally produced films gradually replaced foreign films and have gone on to become successful exports.

The increase in consumption propensity was not at the expense of investment. Gross domestic capital formation grew at an average rate of 12.3 percent a year in 1972–81 (appendix, table A1.1), compared with about 10 percent during the previous decade. Part of this faster growth was driven by construction, with developers turning out huge housing complexes, complete with shopping and recreation facilities. Property development and construction have come to be known in popular writing as one of four "pillars" of the Hong Kong economy, along with manufacturing, finance, and tourism.

## The China–Hong Kong Economic Nexus

The 1978 economic reforms in China ushered in a new era for the economic growth of Hong Kong. Essentially, the reforms involved the release of private enterprise, first in the countryside and then in cities; the substitution of market mechanisms for planning and control; and an open door policy. In spite of several retrenchments, the reform program has brought about sustained growth and spreading affluence. During the 1980s, GDP growth averaged 10.1 percent a year, with even faster growth in southern and coastal China. In Guangdong Province, adjacent to Hong Kong, growth and transformation have been spectacular. In the Pearl River Delta, for example, it is estimated that income growth has averaged more than 20 percent a year in the past few years (Chen and Ho 1993, 27). Millions of migrant workers from other provinces now work in Guangdong in the factories, on the farms (local farmers have deserted them for nonfarm jobs), and in services. About three million more have settled in the two Special Economic Zones (SEZs) of Shenzhen and Zhuhai. Half a dozen market towns have been elevated by the central government into cities, each with more than a million people. In 1979, Shenzhen, a town of fewer than 100,000 people on the border of Hong Kong, created the first SEZ as part of the open door policy. By 1991, it had grown to a metropolis of two million people, complete with glossy highrise buildings and traffic jams ("The South China Miracle," *The Economist,* October 5, 1991). Today, the province openly aspires to be the fifth "tiger," after Korea, Taiwan, Hong Kong, and Singapore.

Hong Kong was instrumental in bringing about the economic miracle in South China through massive injections of enterprise, capital, and know-how. It also acted as middleman for investment from other sources, particularly Taiwan and Korea. In the process, Hong Kong has done very well for itself. First, as China's only major commercial gateway to the West since 1949, it stood to benefit handsomely from its open door policy. Re-exports to China increased 38-fold in just three years, from 1978 to 1981 (table 1.7a). A practically unlimited supply of labor was put at the disposal of Hong Kong manufacturers at Chinese wages. And, as southern China became more affluent, the people there looked to Hong Kong for upmarket goods and services. Just as Hong Kong was "instant China" to the West in the 1950s and 1960s (R. Hughes 1968, 50), so it is now "instant West" to mainland Chinese, with rich dividends to the Hong Kong economy in both cases.

The first major move was into outward processing. Wages for skilled and semiskilled workers in Guangdong were (and still are) about a tenth of their equivalent in Hong Kong, and factory space costs were even smaller. From 1980 on, manufacturers in Hong Kong, large and small, began to relocate their operations across the border, with the Hong Kong side specializing in "front office operations"—marketing, finance, design, packaging, and quality control. This greatly enhanced the competitiveness of Hong Kong's exports. Many small operators who had only a handful of workers before the switch now own plants on the mainland with hundreds of workers. It is generally estimated that in 1992 some three million mainland laborers worked directly for Hong Kong entrepreneurs.

At the same time, entrepôt trade has reemerged as a major activity. In the 1980s, re-exports grew at an annual rate of 20 percent or more, and most of this growth resulted from trade with China. Part of this expansion reflected the spread of out-processing, so statistically it displaced domestic exports, explaining their slow growth after 1984. But genuine re-exports of raw materials, capital goods, and consumer durables to China were also expanding

**TABLE 1.7A. Hong Kong's Imports from China**

| Year | Imports from China (U.S.$m) | Annual Growth Rate | Percentage of China's Total Exports | Percentage of HK's Total Imports | Imports for Re-export (U.S.$m) | Annual Growth Rate | Percentage of HK's Total Imports | Percentage of HK's Total Re-exports |
|------|------|------|------|------|------|------|------|------|
| 1960 | 207 | — | 11.2 | 20.2 | — | — | — | — |
| 1966 | 487 | — | 20.5 | 27.4 | 94 | — | 5.3 | 29.1 |
| 1970 | 470 | — | 20.8 | 16.1 | 97 | — | 3.3 | 20.2 |
| 1975 | 1,383 | — | 19.0 | 20.3 | 300 | — | 4.4 | 21.3 |
| 1981 | 5,276 | — | 24.0 | 21.5 | 1,951 | — | 8.0 | 26.2 |
| 1985 | 7,568 | 6.1 | 27.7 | 25.5 | 3,778 | 23.6 | 12.7 | 28.0 |
| 1989 | 25,215 | 29.9 | 48.0 | 34.9 | 20,517 | 43.3 | 28.4 | 54.3 |

*Sources*: Hong Kong data, 1948–60: Census and Statistics Department, various years; Chinese data, 1950–79: State Statistical Bureau, various issues; Chinese data after 1981: General Administration of Customs.

**TABLE 1.7B. Hong Kong's Exports to China**

| Year | Exports to China (U.S.$m) | Annual Growth Rate | Percentage of China's Total Imports | Percentage of HK's Total Exports | Re-exports (U.S.$m) | Annual Growth Rate | Percentage of HK's Total Exports | Percentage of HK's Total Re-exports |
|------|------|------|------|------|------|------|------|------|
| 1960 | 21 | — | 1.1 | 3.1 | 19 | — | 2.8 | 10.0 |
| 1965 | 13 | — | 0.6 | 1.1 | 10 | — | 0.8 | 3.6 |
| 1970 | 11 | — | 0.5 | 0.4 | 6 | — | 0.2 | 1.2 |
| 1975 | 33 | — | 0.5 | 0.6 | 28 | — | 0.5 | 2.0 |
| 1981 | 1,961 | — | 8.9 | 9.0 | 1,438 | — | 6.6 | 19.3 |
| 1985 | 7,857 | 56.1 | 18.6 | 26.0 | 5,907 | 64.5 | 19.5 | 43.7 |
| 1989 | 18,816 | 10.5 | 31.8 | 25.7 | 13,268 | 9.1 | 18.1 | 29.9 |

*Sources:* Hong Kong data, 1948–60: Census and Statistics Department, various years; Chinese data, 1950–79: State Statistical Bureau, various issues; Chinese data after 1981: General Administration of Customs.

very rapidly. In value terms, they increased 34-fold between 1980 and 1991 (table 1.7b).

China is the largest market for exports of services from Hong Kong. China has become a big buyer of Hong Kong machinery for textiles, plastics, and electronics, all of which involve considerable training and after-sale services (Sung 1991, 118). At the same time, China has become by far the most important destination for Hong Kong tourists and vacationers. This exchange of visits helps to promote Hong Kong products. In recent years, Hong Kong based companies began to set up specialty shops, department stores, and supermarkets in big cities all over China.

From the beginning, Hong Kong has been China's largest financier. Three-fifths of all foreign investment in China came from Hong Kong (*Washington Economic Report*, March 3, 1993, 3). But the flows of capital have not always been one way, especially in recent years. From early 1982 to mid-1985, when political uncertainty led to capital outflows and monetary crises in Hong Kong, the Chinese government injected large amounts of capital into the territory (Sung 1991, 95). In recent years, China has accumulated foreign reserves, and its banking system has been a net creditor to Hong Kong's banks since mid-1988. Total net claims stood at HK$52 billion in the third quarter of 1992, or some 6 percent of total bank credits. From 1990 onward, Chinese enterprises have invested heavily in Hong Kong property and equity, which has boosted confidence and liquidity.

There is little doubt that the continuing prosperity of Hong Kong since 1986 has been built on these economic links with China. It was recently estimated by Hseuh and Woo that up to 25 percent of Hong Kong's national income came from the "China trade" (1992). This economic integration is now taking new directions. Large corporations in Hong Kong have begun to invest in infrastructure developments like subways, port facilities, and housing complexes, not only in Guangdong but in Beijing, Shanghai, Chongqing, and other big cities. At the same time, state and provincial enterprises in China are queuing up for a listing on Hong Kong's stock exchange. Increasingly, businessmen and academics are thinking in terms of a southern China growth triangle, which includes Hong Kong, Taiwan, and the four SEZs in southern China.

When China introduced economic reform in the late 1970s and opened its door to the West, any city in Hong Kong's position stood to benefit handsomely. Still, the success in economic relations was beyond expectations and cannot be taken for granted. One should not minimize the complexity of doing business in and with a communist country. Success required great resilience in responding to the changing and growing needs of the Chinese economy for trade, services, technology, and capital. Political risks were added to business risks. Hong Kong was hit by a political crisis in connection with

China's decision, in 1982, to regain sovereignty over Hong Kong in mid-1997.[4] To the businessmen, the temptation to move out has been strong. Indeed, for a few years after 1984, when the Joint Declaration between the Chinese and the British governments was signed, it was not clear whether business was running to, or away from, China or whether the economic viability of Hong Kong could survive the brain drain and capital outflows. But the economy has not only survived; it has prospered. And the emigrants are returning.

## IV.  Modeling Hong Kong's Economic Growth

### Culture and Institutions: An Eclectic Model

The economic success of Hong Kong, Singapore, Korea, and Taiwan from the 1960s onward was unparalleled among developing countries. To explain and generalize their growth experiences, researchers looked for common features. The obvious one is their outward-looking development strategy. Given their small size, however, there was little alternative. Their success has also been attributed to a common cultural heritage, the so-called Chinese factor and Confucian ethic.[5] This argument stresses the adaptiveness and flexibility of businessmen, their work ethic, respect for authority among workers, thrift, the emphasis on education, and the role of family in the formation and operation of business. In addition, all four economies had governments that were credited with providing political stability and a consistent, progrowth policy and environment.

Such arguments have met strong criticism. To the critics, the Chinese factor is neither necessary nor sufficient for economic growth (Balassa 1988, S274–76). Others excluded these factors from consideration because they are not subject to policy action (Kuznets 1988, S35). All that is required, for Asia or elsewhere, is correct policy and a business environment favorable to growth. In the words of Balassa (1988, S288):

> The neutrality and stability of the incentive system, together with limited government interventions, well-functioned labor and capital markets, and reliance on private capital, . . . have been the main ingredients of successful economic performance in East Asia.

The problem with this market-plus-incentive view is that it makes growth seem too easy and too accessible. As Chen put it: "If successful economic

---

4. Richard Hughes wrote a book in 1968, at the time of China's Cultural Revolution, prophetically entitled Hong Kong: Borrowed Place—Borrowed Time.

5. According to Berger latter-day, or "vulgar," Confucianism preaches the following virtues: work ethics and self-discipline, hierarchy and obedience, respect for scholarship, familism, thrift, flexibility, and adaptability (Chen 1988, 25).

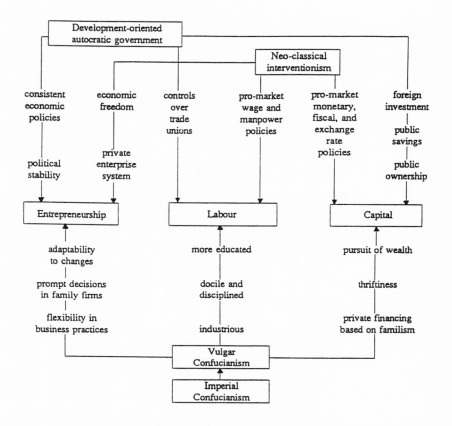

**Fig. 1.2. An NIC model under E01. (From E. K. Y. Chen, "The Economics and Non-economics of Asia's Four Little Dragons: An Inaugural Lecture,"** *Supplement to the Gazette* **[University of Hong Kong] 35 [1] [March 21]: 27.)**

development is as simple a matter as export-orientation and getting the prices right, there would have been very few low income countries left today" (1988, 25). In other words, the responsiveness of the public to economic incentives and the effectiveness of the response cannot be taken for granted. Chen went on to synthesize economic, cultural, and political considerations into an eclectic model to explain the economic growth of the four economies. The main thread of this argument is presented in figure 1.2. Essentially, an autocratic government provides political and policy stability and maintains a well-functioning labor and capital market, reining in the labor unions if necessary. Confucian ethics will motivate people as well as define interpersonal relationships (between family members, business partners, employers and workers, and in business transactions) in a manner conducive to efficiency. Both autocratic government and Confucian values help to boost savings. As Confucianism is also conducive to autocratic government, it is indeed the pivotal force in the model. However, this configuration of cultural and institutional forces serves only the production of labor-intensive, light manufactured goods for which scale economies and technological transformations are not particularly important.

Chen's model is a good summary of the state of the art explanation of economic growth in the four Asian NIEs. But it has real weaknesses. The model does not explain the performance of nonindustrial sectors, and growth in all four countries has been broad based (H. Hughes 1989, 132). The model makes no allowance for the significant differences among the four economies: degree of government intervention, industrialization strategy, industrial structure, and monetary and fiscal policy. For example, as pointed out by Hughes, policymakers in Korea and Taiwan had a strong mercantilist bias toward trade surpluses, and consumption was suppressed in Singapore but not in Hong Kong (1989, 132–35).

## A Hong Kong Development Model

Hong Kong was founded 150 years ago by traders. For the next 100 years, it remained a city of merchants, with entrepôt trade as its main economic base. Then, from 1951 on, external events changed the base to export-oriented manufacturing. Industrialization was initiated by migrant industrialists, largely from Shanghai. But the spread of industrialization, the initiation of a self-sustaining process of industrial development, was the work of local businessmen. Most of them had a background in trading. Though they took on new roles, they have maintained a merchant's mentality and have operated much like traders. We shall refer to them as "merchant entrepreneurs."

A merchant aims at securing income or wealth by the exchange rather than the production of goods. His sole purpose is to make a profit. He does not have an interest in the goods he handles. If he holds on to a commodity, it is only because he expects to sell it for a higher price later. His success is measured solely by the amount of profit made. He is, by nature, a maximizer. But he can also explore new markets and search out new products or sources of supplies. Often this search is initiated by, in the words of Kirzner, "a discovery of price discrepancies." Guided by this hunch, he may have to search high and low for missing links between inputs, output, and markets, bring together different groups of people, and commit his own capital. He will then have to assume risks. He becomes an entrepreneur. Specifically, he performs one or more of the three main types of entrepreneurial activities identified by Kirzner (1984, 52):

> Arbitrage: acting upon the discovery of a present discrepancy between the prices at which a given item can be bought and sold
> Speculation: an arbitrage across time
> Innovative activity: the creation of an output, method of production, or organization not hitherto in use

Thus, the process may involve fabricating or manufacturing. But if he has no interest in the commodity itself, or in the wants it satisfies, or if the discovery excites him solely because of its profit potential, so that when the undertaking ceases to bring in supernormal profits he will not hesitate to dump the project, then he is what I call a merchant entrepreneur.

Given this attitude and motivation, the merchant entrepreneur has certain personal and behavioral characteristics. He is likely to be a nonspecialist. Professional training will only dull his capacity for discovery.[6] He is ever alert to business opportunities. Often he is working on several projects at the same time. As Kizner observed: "To recognize that opportunity A exists need not preclude simultaneously recognizing that opportunity B exists" (1980, 13). He is prone to make quick decisions and act promptly, for otherwise his profits will be eroded by imitators. For this purpose, he must be good at problem solving, so he is likely to be flexible and adaptive. He takes shortcuts. All of these, in turn, will have implications for the way he organizes and operates his business. He will prefer family business or partnership for the sake of quick decisions and secrecy. In his dealing with others, he is prone to informal, oral agreements based on trust. Therefore, personal relationships and personal contacts are highly valued. As a manufacturer, he will prefer products that are not capital intensive, have a short gestation period, and are not too sophisticated. Partly this is dictated by the limited resources he can command in a family business but more because, as a merchant, he does not like to make long-term commitments.

These qualities can be contrasted with those of an industrialist. The task of an industrialist is to produce. He competes on the strength of the quality of his product or on cost effectiveness. He takes pride in his product. He prefers to market it under his brand name. He differentiates his product and tries to cultivate consumer loyalty. Market share is a major objective but business survival is most important. These were the attitudes of the immigrant industrialists from Shanghai who initiated modern industry in Hong Kong. Some of them managed to bring the machinery and raw materials that they had ordered for their Shanghai operations. They started out with big factories and modern machinery (Riedel 1974, 26). There was no searching or trial and error. They were doing what they knew best. Even today, the modern textile industry is still in

---

6. It is more likely for entrepreneurial talent to come from the homes of factory owners than from the children of professionals, civil servants, or executives employed by large corporations.

the hands of their successors, who are a pillar of Hong Kong's manufacturing industry.

The merchant entrepreneurs, on the other hand, were people like those portrayed in a 1968 survey by *The Economist* (October 19, 1968, xix). With resources from a family rice trading business, the young brothers branched into manufacturing. In the late 1950s, they started making rubber sandals, though "they knew next to nothing about them." The venture went well for a while, then started to falter due to import restrictions and was abandoned. Then they heard that there were profits in plastic dolls and decided to try their hand with them. Again, they "knew nothing whatever about the techniques involved." They went overseas to find out. With bits and pieces of the required machinery and production techniques obtained from various sources, and through improvisation and experimentation, they tried to fill the gap in the production process. Meanwhile, they blithely produced plastic flowers. They started making and exporting dolls in 1963, mostly marketed under the labels of leading manufacturers abroad. By 1968, they were doing so well that their main concern was other "unscrupulous Hong Kong manufacturers" pirating their products. A similar story was told by Hughes about the start of the plastic flowers industry (1968, 25).

Even when Hong Kong's industrial structure became more diverse, the basic approach of the merchant entrepreneur remained. Producers in Hong Kong are still known for their flexibility, adaptiveness, and focus on short-run profits. Writing in 1986, Sung noted: "The competitive edge of Hong Kong manufacturing lies in its flexibility and resilience. Hong Kong is successful in the export of products characterized by frequent changes in design . . ." (164).

The success of merchant entrepreneurs is not confined to manufacturing. An excellent example is the late shipping magnate, Y. K. Pao.[7] He came to Hong Kong from Shanghai as a young man. He chose shipping, not because he knew anything about it but because his experience in China predisposed him toward mobile assets that could escape confiscation. A man of modest means, he charmed his way to a bank loan for the purchase of his first ship. His subsequent success was due primarily to the niche he found in financing. He ordered ships from Japanese yards at low cost, taking advantage of the export subsidy of the Japanese government. The ships were immediately leased to Japanese shipping firms on long-term contracts. With these contracts he obtained bank loans to finance the purchase of those ships. In this way he was able to add to his fleet with little of his own money and at low risk. He discovered and exploited an important price discrepancy. He also knew when to leave the business. In the 1970s, he correctly sensed the coming shipping glut and shifted his interest to property, with even greater success. The two other big shipowners in

7. This description of Y. K. Pao's success is taken from Wilson 1990, 135–39.

Hong Kong were less fortunate. They were hit hard by the shipping slump of the 1980s. Significantly, both of them had backgrounds in shipping before they came to Hong Kong and considered shipping their careers.

It is in the property and the equity markets that the mentality of traders finds its fullest expression. What concerns a trader is not the value of the commodity, as he has no intention of holding on to it; what matters is whether someone will pay a still higher price for it. To the dismay of economists and policymakers, Hong Kong's property prices have several times been pushed far beyond their sustainable level, to be followed by an inevitable bust. As for the stock market in Hong Kong, people with modest means speculate in it. They are reflecting a social ethos, a commercial culture that has three elements. The first is a pecuniary standard in which money is seen as the main, if not the sole, measure of success and accomplishment. The rich are admired and respected; getting rich is the goal in life of most people.[8] The second element is an alertness to profit opportunity. For many, to get rich is not just an idle dream but a perceived possibility. They keep their ears and eyes open for opportunities of advancement. They save and invest themselves. The third element is a belief that trading is the quickest and surest route to wealth. The important thing is to be one's own boss. Speculation may be a good way to get the seed money.

With the economic reforms and open door policy in China in the late 1970s, the merchant entrepreneurs in Hong Kong had a field day—"like fishes in water," as the Chinese saying goes. The reforms released a torrent of energy and initiative. They also created numerous price discrepancies. No other group of businessmen could have been better equipped to handle the situation than the merchant entrepreneurs of Hong Kong. In China, many of the institutions required for the smooth functioning of a market economy, including the legal framework, were not yet in place. Infrastructures were inadequate or not well coordinated. Subsidiary services were lacking. The functionaries from Guangdong, though they spoke the same dialect as did the businessmen of Hong Kong, had a different way of doing business. To bridge all these gaps, the qualities of a local merchant entrepreneur are highly valuable: business acumen, flexibility, adaptiveness, and a readiness to take risks. Many deals would be informal and oral, so personal trust and connections were of vital importance.

This Hong Kong culture is not found in the other Asian NIEs, and it helps to account for other misunderstandings about the economy. For example, the extremely weak unionism in this highly industrialized economy greatly sur-

---

8. The craving for wealth is unabashed and undisguised. When people meet on Lunar New Year's Day, they greet each other with the words "may you make a lot of money," much like people elsewhere exchange "Merry Christmas."

prises many visiting economists.[9] But, if workers accept that labor is a tradable commodity like any other, and if they believe in upward mobility, then the urge to organize or be organized will be weak. Second, Hong Kong's great income inequality is consistent with a population of risk takers. Third, both local and visiting economists have been amazed that, whereas "late comers" like Korea and Taiwan had shifted to more capital- and technology-intensive products by the late 1970s, Hong Kong industries continued to specialize in labor-intensive products produced in very small enterprises (Chen 1984, 28; Krause 1988, S50). This ceases to be surprising when we know how the merchant entrepreneurs operate.[10]

## The Role of Government and Institutions

In the beginning, Hong Kong's government was not equipped or predisposed to lead or plan economic growth. Then the economy did so well that there seemed to be no need for much government involvement. But private enterprise does not function in a vacuum. It depends on the existence of accommodating institutions, supporting infrastructure, a healthy and educated labor force, and certain rules, many of which only the government can provide. We shall consider what these preconditions are, for private enterprise in general and the brand of commercial enterprise that flourished in Hong Kong in particular, to reveal the visible and invisible hand of the Hong Kong government.

### An Environment Conducive to Private Enterprise

Hong Kong has been described as a center of grassroots capitalism (Krause 1988, S49). To this end, respect for property rights and low taxes are most important, so that everyone, local and foreign, has free and equal access to all markets. Information should be freely and cheaply disseminated and accessible to all parties. Prices must not be distorted—high taxes distort choice by penalizing work (as against leisure) and risk taking. Low transaction costs are particularly important for a trade-oriented economy with many small enterprises. They include low costs of entry, exit, business transactions, and the making and enforcing of contracts. The availability of credit to small enterprises is vital and includes trade credit and short-term funds as well as long-term finance. Finally, good infrastructure is helpful for all business. Because of

---

9. For example, Turner, who was in Hong Kong in 1976–77 to make an extensive study of labor organization and relations, considered the low level of unionism as remarkable and puzzling (1980, 18–19, 84). Youngson also considered the absence of anxiety or even discussion about labor-management relations to be one of Hong Kong's "most remarkable features" (1982, 152).

10. Kraus explained this as the result of an elastic supply of labor (1988, S50). But wages in Hong Kong were on a par with those in Singapore and much higher than those in Taiwan and Korea.

its large capital requirement and long gestation period, its absence is the main obstacle to growth in many cities.

Underneath the government's policy of noninterventionism is a strong progrowth stance. The government believes that intervention will only lower the growth rate (Peeble 1986, 30). It refused to make taxes more progressive on the grounds that this would erode the incentive to invest (Riedel 1974, 142–43). Noninterventionism entails minimum regulation, a free port, free exchange and flows of capital, and free enterprise in general. Unlike other economies in the region, there has been no policy reversal in Hong Kong. This predictability and continuity in the economic environment greatly reduced uncertainty. On the positive side, the government has preserved social and political stability. It has maintained an effective and efficient civil administration and an independent legal system that enforces British laws. Property rights are clearly defined and conscientiously protected. An Independent Commission Against Corruption was established in 1974, reporting directly to the governor of Hong Kong, which proved to be very effective in eliminating the corruption of civil servants. Later, the authority of the commission was extended to the private sector. It has reduced the cost of doing business and is particularly beneficial to less-well-connected small businessmen and foreign businessmen not accustomed to the art of bribery.

### Infrastructure and Resource Development
These can be discussed under four headings (Sung 1984, 156–57).

*Infrastructure and Institutional Support.* The government invests directly in roads, railways, subways, airports, and waterworks. Given the high population density and unfavorable terrain, it has done a good job in keeping traffic moving in the urban area. The efficient container terminals were privately owned and operated, but their development was planned by the government. All other utilities, like public transport, gas and electricity, telephone, and telegraph, are provided by private enterprises. Most of them operate under franchise with pricing under legislative control. In general, they provide adequate services at reasonable prices and make good profits.

Trade and industrial production received important supports from such government-financed bodies as the Trade Development Council, the Export Credit Insurance Corporation, and the Hong Kong Productivity Council, which were established in the 1960s. More specific supports for industry were introduced in the 1980s.

*Land.* Land is scarce in Hong Kong, so most factories are in high-rise buildings. In the 1960s, two industrial townships were developed. Massive public housing estates guaranteed an adequate supply of workers to these outlying areas. After 1978, the government began to provide land on special terms to high-technology firms that could not be accommodated in traditional factories. Two industrial estates have since been established to provide sites and services at concessional terms for purpose-built factories to accommodate modern industries.

*Human Capital.* The public provision of health and educational services has been steadily upgraded. Nine-year compulsory education was instituted in 1978. Tertiary education expanded rapidly. The government also organized industry-specific training, financed by industry levies. From the 1980s on, more emphasis was placed on technical training. A second polytechnic school and the third University of Science and Technology were established.

*Capital.* Except for the short-lived Loans to Small Scale Industry Scheme, the government did not arrange financing for the private sector. But its policy of low taxes resulted in abundant savings and an ample supply of loanable funds for private investors. Second, instead of competing with the private sector for credit, as is common elsewhere, the conservative fiscal policy brought about sizable budgetary surpluses year after year. Third, as the government did not have firm control over credit expansion, the supply of bank credit could be quite elastic, so a boom in one sector did not crowd out another sector. In recent years, the government also made concerted efforts to attract foreign investment so as to speed up technological transfers.

## The Promotion of Industrial Diversification

From the early days there were intermittent calls for the government to be more active in assisting industrial diversification. The recession of 1974–75 made such arguments more persuasive. An Advisory Committee on Diversification published its report in December 1979. It was a major landmark in the government's changing commitment to industrial development. From that date, the government did make more concerted efforts in technical training, industrial support services, and financing research and development. Since the Hong Kong economy is increasingly being integrated with the Chinese economy, it is probably not an exaggeration to say that the report was out of date as soon as it was published (Chen and Li 1988, 137).

## Financial Regulation

From the 1970s onward, the financial system in Hong Kong grew rapidly in size and complexity. The existing regulatory framework and expertise were not adequate for supervising its operations. Though some economists and observers had called attention to loopholes in the Banking Ordinance in the late 1970s, the government was slow to respond. At the same time, the monetary authorities failed to exercise effective control over credit expansion during the floating rate regime of 1974–83 (Jao 1988, 59). As a result of such negligence, a banking crisis occurred in the early 1980s. Between 1983 and 1986, several major local banks and some deposit-taking companies became insolvent. The government bailed out the failed banks in an effort to restore confidence in the banking system amid an atmosphere of political uncertainty. It revised the Banking

Ordinance in 1986 to provide for more effective supervision. Subsequently, new or revised regulatory frameworks were introduced to oversee operations in other segments of the financial market, like the stock and futures markets. Jao argues that "policy errors, negligence or incompetence on the part of the financial and regulatory authorities" were influential causes of the 1983–86 banking crisis (1988, 59). Thus, the government can claim little credit for the expansion of the financial sector.

## V.   Recent Developments

Notable transitions took place in Hong Kong in 1992. With the arrival of a new governor of Hong Kong in mid-1992, who sought to introduce democratic reforms over the strong objections of the Chinese government, Sino-British relations took a sharp turn for the worse. At the time of writing, the two governments are still talking across each other. The island is likewise divided in its alliance. The economy had lifted itself from the 1989–90 downturn and resumed a stable and sustainable growth.

On July 9, 1992, Chris Patten stepped ashore to be sworn in as the twenty-eighth, and purportly the last, British governor of Hong Kong. Unlike all his predecessors, who were either civil servants or seasoned diplomats, Patten is a career politician. As the former chairman of the Conservative Party and a close associate of British prime minister John Major, he is also a heavyweight in British politics. His personal style is also refreshingly different. He is visible and accessible. Soon after his arrival, he visited some of the most populated low-income neighbourhoods and was at ease with the crowd. He delighted in meeting the press and appearing on the electronic media. His eloquence and charm won him a very high popularity rating.

But the Chinese authority in charge of Hong Kong affairs had been apprehensive over future relations with the British ever since Patten's predecessor, David Wilson, was unceremoniously retired in late 1991. Wilson was a diplomat and Chinese specialist who could confer with Chinese officials in their own langauge. He was on good terms with the Chinese government. It was widely speculated that Wilson was removed because he was deemed too soft and accommodating to the Chinese. Thus, Patten's appointment was greeted with suspicion. His outspoken, unorthodox, and at times undiplomatic manner did not mitigate Chinese apprehensions. Confrontation came sooner than expected. On October 7, Patten unveiled his package of constitutional reforms designed to increase the weight of direct election in the Legislative Council. The Basic Law, which will be the constitution for the Hong Kong Special Adminstrative Region after 1997, provides for a 60-member legislature, with 20 directly elected seats and the rest filled by functional constituencies and an election committee. By changing the composition of those constituencies and the election committee, the governor's proposal would result in the popular election of 39 legislators.

The local response to Patten's proposed reform was generally favorable, particularly after he explained his proposals in a series of unprecedented town hall meetings. The Chinese government, however, came out strongly against the proposed changes. They branded the proposal a violation of the Basic Law, the Sino-British Joint Declaration, and letters of understanding exchanged between the foreign ministers of the two countries in early 1990. Patten did not relent. The British government rallied behind him, and he also solicited support from other Western nations. This did not bode well with the Chinese. Confrontation escalated. The top echelon of the Chinese government added its voice in denouncing the British's "three violations." Patten gazetted his electoral bill in March 1993. Lu Ping, head of China's Hong Kong and Macau Affairs Office, immediately threatened to set up his own "stove," meaning that China would form its own apparatus to handle the transition of June 1997. On April 13, the two sides dramatically agreed to convene talks on electoral arrangements. After rounds of Sino-British talks, negotiations broke down in 1994. Patten's electoral reforms were passed into law at the Legislative Council on June 30. Meanwhile, even as the talks were in progress, China had made good its threat to set up a "second stove." It is known as a preliminary working committee for the future Preparatory Committee of the Special Adminstrative Region, with 27 mainland officials and 30 Hong Kong citizens as members and the foreign minister of China as chairman. This working group was formally inaugurated on July 16, 1993. At the same time, a large number of Hong Kong Affairs advisers were appointed by Beijing to help with the transition. The two sides have gone their separate ways.

By this time, much of the initial enthusiasm for Patten's constitutional reforms had cooled, as witnessed by poor turnouts in various local elections. The preconditions for sustained democratic movements do not exist. Lacking are a grassroots comprehension and demand for democracy, a tradition of related civic education in school, democratic practice in decision making in the workplace and in government, and a crop of dedicated politicians, educators, and advocates to promote the course. This aside, for a political movement to take root, it must have a clear-cut objective of mass appeal, like liberty, human rights, basic needs, the repeal of discrimination, and law and order. All of these are already available to the people of Hong Kong. Advocates of constitutional reform argue that a democratically elected legislature can better safeguard what we have after 1997. It is like selling political insurance. To the optimist, such insurance is hardly necessary. To the pessimist, it is totally inadequate. Last, but not least, there is deference to China's stance on this issue. The economic well-being of Hong Kong is increasingly tied to its links with the Chinese economy.

It is important to note that this governmental squabble had little impact on the general health of the economy. The stock market seemed to be the only segment that was significantly affected. The Hang Seng Index went through a roller-coaster course in late 1992 and early 1993. By late 1993, it, too, showed remarkable resilence in the face of political uncertainty.

The economy was booming, as can be gauged from the aggregates in table 1.8. The overall growth rate, particularly on the per capita term, may look pale by historical standards. But with outward processing and investment gathering momentum, GDP becomes less and less relevant as an indicator of well-being. In the absence of a GNP measure, private consumption may serve as a surrogate. The annual rise of consumption was substantially above that of the previous decade. A very tight labor market, dating from 1987, prevailed, and the unemployment rate rarely rose above 2 percent. And this despite the accelerated out-processing of manufacturing operations, reflected in the sharp fall in manufacturing employment. The rate of capital formation was also high, reflecting not only prosperity but a return of confidence. A high rate of inflation emerged as a by-product.

For 1992 and 1993, the Organization for Economic Cooperation and Development (OECD) nations, which had been major markets for Hong Kong's exports, were in an economic doldrum, and the impetus of growth came mainly from the booming Chinese economy and further integration of the "growth triangle" of southern China, Hong Kong, and Taiwan. The Chinese economy was

**TABLE 1.8.   Growth Rates of Key Indicators, 1992–94**

|                           | 1982–91 | 1992  | 1993  | 1994  |
|---------------------------|---------|-------|-------|-------|
| Population                | 1.0     | 1.0   | 1.8   | 2.4   |
| Labor force               | 1.3     | 0.0   | 2.3   | 2.5   |
| Employment                | 1.5     | −0.7  | 2.2   | 2.7   |
| Manufacturing employment  | −2.6    | −13.2 | −12.1 | −14.3 |
| GDP                       | 6.2     | 5.3   | 5.5   | 5.5   |
| Per capita GDP            | 5.1     | 4.3   | 3.6   | 3.0   |
| Consumer prices           | 7.9     | 9.4   | 8.5   | 8.1   |
| Private consumption       | 6.6     | 8.3   | 7.2   | 7.8   |
| Government                |         |       |       |       |
| consumption exports       | 5.0     | 7.4   | 2.2   | 3.9   |
| Gross investment          | 4.4     | 9.6   | 5.5   | 13.1  |
| Domestic exports          | 6.8     | 0.3   | −5.1  | −2.3  |
| Re-exports                | 22.6    | 28.2  | 19.8  | 13.9  |
| Exports of services       | 9.1     | 11.0  | 8.1   | 7.5   |
| Imports of services       | 10.8    | 7.0   | 7.0   | 7.7   |
| Imports of goods          | 13.6    | 22.3  | 12.8  | 14.1  |

*Sources:* Hong Kong Government Secretariat (1994a and 1994b) 1994, 45, 51; *Hong Kong Monthly Digest of Statistics* September 1994, 2, and January 1995, 2; press coverage of the budget Speech by the Financial secretary to the Legislative Council.

growing at a hefty rate of over 13 percent for 1992–93. In spite of a much-publicized austerity program to cool it, the growth for 1994 was still in excess of 10 percent. The growth in southern China was considerably faster. The impetus of growth was trade and investment, which benefited the Hong Kong economy handsomely. Another key contributing factor to Hong Kong's prosperity was the reduction of interest rates in the United States prior to 1994. As the Hong Kong dollar is pegged to U.S. currency, interest rates in Hong Kong had to follow suit in spite of a fully employed local economy. The trade surplus of China and the influx of funds attracted to the region as a whole added to Hong Kong's liquidity, producing a superboom in the stock and real estate markets. The Hang Seng Index rose by 115 percent in 1993. Prices for large flats had risen by 58 percent from their level in early 1993 when they peaked in early April of 1994. Public spending on infrastructure and growing trade within the region also helped to sustain the growth momentum.

## VI.  Policy Conclusions

By any standard, the Hong Kong government has chosen to play a limited role in shaping the goals and strategies of development and regulating and supervising the operations of private enterprises. The policy mix of a limited but effective government, a well-administered legal system, free enterprise, and an open economy has been unusually effective in promoting economic growth. By the late 1960s, the overall business climate was so favorable that private capital participated in infrastructure development, and the government could devote its resources to public goods and services. All the preconditions for private enterprises to flourish were in place. Self-sustaining growth was set in motion. Not surprisingly, many observers conclude that the government has had little influence on Hong Kong's prosperity. But we should not just equate limited action with negligible contribution. Specifically, in cases in which a market solution is feasible and effective, or when the government cannot claim comparative advantage over private enterprises, nonintervention is a wise policy choice. It was not necessary for the local government to play an active part during Hong Kong's industrial drive mainly because the institutional framework, important infrastructures, including the apparatus for world trade, and an initial supply of capital to accommodate private enterprise were already in place. In general, such preconditions do not exist among developing nations, and active government participation will be necessary to provide them.

Hong Kong was blessed with a succession of favorable external circumstances but these were not indispensable for sustained growth. Importantly, Hong Kong managed to achieve satisfactory growth under unfavorable circumstances, particularly a continuous state of political uncertainty.[11] Entrepre-

---

11.  Hong Kong Island and southern Kowloon were ceded to Britain by the Ch'ing Dynasty. The territory north of Boundary Street in Kowloon, which makes up more than 80 percent of the

neurship must take the credit for this. Under a system of nonintervention and free enterprise, entrepreneurial activities are the key agents that translate positive preconditions and opportunities into success. And the growth process of Hong Kong involved a large number of entrepreneurs running a myriad of large and small business in all sectors of the economy. Their numbers, dedication, business acumen, and versatility have never failed to impress observers from outside. With rising affluence, the state did have to face the issue of income inequality if social harmony was to endure. To its credit, the government managed to strike the right balance between growth and equity. It chose to redress inequality by working on the expenditure side through transfers in kind. The basic needs of all but a few were provided for through an extensive public housing program and a comprehensive education system. Along with rising opportunities, upward mobility is now a reality for all. This was achieved without raising the very low tax rates or incurring public debts. It has, indeed, been an extraordinary achievement.

APPENDIX

**TABLE A1.1.  Average Growth Rates in Real Terms of Components of Expenditures on the Gross Domestic Product, 1972–81 (percentage)**

| | Average Annual Growth Rates | |
| --- | --- | --- |
| | 10 years 1972–81 | 5 years 1977–81 |
| Private consumption expenditures | 9.9 | 13.3 |
| Government consumption expenditures | 11.1 | 13.5 |
| Gross domestic fixed capital formation | 12.3 | 18.0 |
| Total exports of goods | 10.9 | 13.6 |
| Domestic exports | 8.9 | 10.0 |
| Re-exports | 16.9 | 24.1 |
| Imports of goods | 10.3 | 15.0 |
| GDP | 10.1 | 10.7 |
| Per capita GDP | 7.5 | 7.4 |
| Real income | 10.0 | 10.2 |
| Per capita real income | 7.3 | 7.0 |
| GDP deflator | 9.0 | 9.4 |
| Consumer prices | 9.6 | 10.8 |

total area of Hong Kong, was leased under another treaty for 99 years in 1898. The Chinese government made it clear, from the beginning, that it did not recognize those treaties and pledged to regain sovereignty "when the time was right."

**TABLE A1.1.**—*Continued*

| | Average Annual Growth Rates | |
|---|---|---|
| | 10 years 1981–91 | 5 years 1986–91 |
| Private consumption expenditures | 6.6 | 7.1 |
| Government consumption expenditures | 5.0 | 5.7 |
| Gross domestic fixed capital formation | 4.4 | 8.6 |
| Total exports of goods | 14.6 | 18.7 |
| Domestic exports | 6.8 | 6.1 |
| Re-exports | 22.6 | 29.9 |
| Imports of goods | 13.6 | 19.2 |
| GDP | 6.2 | 6.4 |
| Per capita GDP | 5.1 | 5.6 |
| Real income | 6.3 | 6.5 |
| Per capita real income | 5.2 | 5.6 |
| GDP deflator | 7.8 | 9.2 |
| Consumer prices | 7.9 | 8.9 |

*Sources:* Hong Kong Government Secretariat (1982) and (1992).

**TABLE A1.2. Welfare Indicators for Hong Kong**

| | 1961 | 1966 | 1971 | 1976 | 1981 | 1986 | 1991 |
|---|---|---|---|---|---|---|---|
| Infant mortality rate (per 1,000 live births) | 37.7 | 24.9 | 18.4 | 14.3 | 9.7 | — | 7[a] |
| Expectation of life at birth | | | | | | | |
| Male | — | — | 67.4 | 69.6 | 71.9 | — | 77[a] |
| Female | — | — | 75.0 | 76.4 | 77.6 | — | — |
| Hospital beds per 1,000 population | 3.1 | 3.7 | 4.1 | 4.3 | 4.2 | 4.4 | 4.5 |
| Population living in inadequate housing (%) | 78.0 | — | 54.3 | 45.7 | 38.5 | — | — |
| Households sharing living quarters with other households (%) | — | — | 33.2 | 26.1 | 24.6 | 14.9 | 8.5 |
| School attendance ratio by age and sex | | | | | | | |
| 6–11 Male | 86.7 | — | 95.5 | 98.1 | 98.5 | 99.5 | 99.8 |
| Female | 80.0 | — | 94.4 | 97.8 | 98.5 | 99.5 | 99.8 |
| 12–14 Male | 80.0 | — | 89.8 | 90.1 | 92.0 | — | — |
| Female | 79.0 | — | 80.2 | 84.5 | 92.1 | 92.2 | 91.8 |
| 15–16 Male | — | — | 63.9 | 70.7 | 72.4 | 94.5 | 95.6 |
| Female | — | — | 51.1 | 61.7 | 75.1 | — | — |
| 17–18 Male | — | — | 42.4 | 46.2 | 44.9 | 53.9 | 54.3 |
| Female | — | — | 35.2 | 41.2 | 45.0 | 58.3 | 62.7 |
| Private consumption at constant prices from national income account (%) | | | | | | | |
| Foodstuffs | — | 34.0 | 28.1 | 25.5 | 19.8 | 17.4 | 15.3 |
| Clothing and other personal effects | — | 13.0 | 20.2 | 13.6 | 18.5 | 20.4 | 21.7 |

*(continued)*

**TABLE A1.2.**—*Continued*

|  | 1961 | 1966 | 1971 | 1976 | 1981 | 1986 | 1991 |
|---|---|---|---|---|---|---|---|
| Furniture, furnishings, and household equipment | — | 5.1 | 4.8 | 6.2 | 10.4 | 12.3 | 13.1 |
| Average hours of work per week of employees |  |  |  |  |  |  |  |
| Male | — | — | 57.5 | 53.0 | 52.0 | — | — |
| Female | — | — | 53.3 | 49.6 | 47.6 |  |  |
| Median hours of work per week of employees |  |  |  |  |  |  |  |
| Male | — | — | — | 51 | 50 | 48 | — |
| Female | — | — | — | 48 | 47 | 45 | — |

*Source:* Data from UNDP *Human Development Report* and World Bank *Social Indicators of Development*, various years.

<sup>a</sup> 1988.

REFERENCES

Balassa, B. 1988. "The Lessons of East Asian Development: An Overview." *Economic Development and Cultural Change* 36 (3), supplement (April): S273–90.

Census and Statistics Department. Various issues. *Annual Digest of Statistics.* Hong Kong: Census and Statistics Department.

Census and Statistics Department. Various issues. *Hong Kong Statistics.* Hong Kong: Census and Statistics Department.

Census and Statistics Department. Various issues. *Hong Kong Review of Overseas Trade.* Hong Kong: Census and Statistics Department.

Census and Statistics Department. 1971a. Census Circular no. 5/71 (October). Unpublished.

Census and Statistics Department. 1971b. *Hong Kong Population and Housing Census, 1971 Main Report.* Hong Kong: Census and Statistics Department. Pp. 207–9.

Census and Statistics Department. 1976. *Hong Kong By-Census 1976, Basic Tables.* Hong Kong: Census and Statistics Department. Pp. 50–51.

Census and Statistics Department. 1981. *Estimates of Gross Domestic Product 1966–1979. Hong Kong: Census and Statistics Department.* P. 35.

Census and Statistics Department. 1982. *Hong Kong 1981 Census, Basic Tables.* Hong Kong: Census and Statistics Department. Pp. 42–43.

Census and Statistics Department. 1986. *Hong Kong 1986 By-Census, Main Report.* Hong Kong: Census and Statistics Department. 1:50, 2:114–15.

Census and Statistics Department. 1988. *Estimates of Gross Domestic Product 1966–1987.* Hong Kong: Census and Statistics Department. P. 26.

Census and Statistics Department. 1991a. *1991 Census, Summary Results.* Hong Kong: Census and Statistics Department. P. 60.

Census and Statistics Department. 1991b. *Gross Domestic Product, Quarterly Estimates and Revised Annual Estimates.* Hong Kong: Census and Statistics Department. P. 31.

Chau, L. C. 1983. "Imports of Consumer Goods from China and the Economic Growth of Hong Kong." In *China and Hong Kong: The Economic Nexus,* edited by A. J. Youngson. Hong Kong: Oxford University Press.

Chau, L. C. 1988a. "Labour and Labour Market." In Ho and Chau 1988. Pp. 169–89.

Chau, L. C. 1988b. "Public Housing." In Ho and Chau 1988. Pp. 243–56.

Chau, L. C. 1994. "Economic Growth and Income Distribution in Hong Kong." In *Twenty-Five Years of Social and Economic Development in Hong Kong,* edited by B. K. P. Leung and T. Y. C. Wong. Hong Kong: Centre of Asian Studies, University of Hong Kong. Pp. 489–532.

Chen, E. K. Y. 1984. "The Economic Setting." In Lethbridge 1984. Pp. 1–51.

Chen, E. K. Y. 1988. "The Economics and Non-economics of Asia's Four Little Dragons: An Inaugural Lecture." *Supplement to the Gazette* (University of Hong Kong) 35 (1) (March 21).

Chen, E. K. Y., and A. Ho. 1993. "Southern China Growth Triangle, An Over-view." Paper prepared for the ADB Conference on Study of Growth Triangles, Manila, Philippines, February 24–26.

Chen, E. K. Y., and K. W. Li. 1988. "Industry." In Ho and Chau 1988. Pp. 113–39.

Chow, S. C., et al. 1981. "Laissez faire, Growth and Equity—Hong Kong." *Economic Journal* 47 (June).

England, J., and J. Rear. 1980. *Industrial Relations and Law in Hong Kong.* Hong Kong: Oxford University Press.

General Adminisration of Customs. 1989. *Chinese Customs Statistics.* Beijing: General Administration of Customs of the People's Republic of China.

Haddon-Cave, P. 1984. "The Marking of Some Aspects of Public Policy in Hong Kong." In Lethbridge 1984. Pp. xiii–xx.

Ho, H. C. Y. 1988. "Public Finance." In Ho and Chau 1988. Pp. 17–42.

Ho, H. C. Y. 1992. "Real Property Taxation in Hong Kong." In *Real Property and Land as Tax Base for Development,* edited by I. M. Ofori. Taoyuan, Taiwan: Land Reform Training Institute.

Ho, H. C. Y. and L. C. Chau, eds. 1988. *The Economic System of Hong Kong.* Hong Kong: Asian Research Service.

Hong Kong Government Secretariat. 1982. *Economic Prospects.* Pp. 40–41.

Hong Kong Government Secretariat. 1982. *Economic Prospects.* Pp. 48–49.

Hong Kong Government Secretariat. 1994a. *Economic Prospects.* March. Pp. 45, 51.

Hong Kong Government Secretariat. 1994b. *Hong Kong Monthly Digest of Statistics.* September. P. 2.

Hong Kong Government Secretariat. 1995. "Budget Speech by the Financial Secretary to the Legislative Council." January. Transcript.

Hughes, H. 1989. "Catching Up: The Asian Newly Industrializing Economies in the 1990s." *Asian Development Review* 7 (2): 128–44.

Hughes, R. 1968. *Hong Kong: Borrowed Place—Borrowed Time.* New York: Frederick A. Praeger.

Jao, Y. C. 1984. "The Financial Structure." In Lethbridge 1984. Pp. 124–79.

Jao, Y. C. 1988. "Monetary System and Banking Structure." In Ho and Chau 1988. Pp. 43–85.

Jao, Y. C. 1991. "Monetary System and Banking Structure." In Sung and Lee 1991. Pp. 153–68.

Kirzner, I. M. 1980. "The Primacy of Entrepreneurial Discovery." In Institute of Economic Affairs, *Prime Mover of Progress.* Pp. 3–26. London: Institute of Economic Affairs.

Kirzner, I. M. 1984. "The Entrepreneurial Process." In *The Environment for Entrepreneurship,* edited by C. A. Kent. Lexington, Mass.: D. C. Heath. Pp. 41–58.

Kraus, L. B. 1988. "Hong Kong and Singapore: Twins or Kissing Cousins?" *Economic Development and Cultural Change* 36 (3), supplement (April): S45–S66.

Kuznets, P. W. 1988. "An East Asian Model of Economic Development: Japan, Tawian, and South Korea." *Economic Development and Cultural Change* 36 (3), supplement (April): S11–S43.

Lethbridge, D., ed. 1984. *The Business Environment in Hong Kong.* Hong Kong: Oxford University Press.

Lin, T. B., V. Mok, and Y. P. Ho. 1980. *Manufactured Exports and Employment in Hong Kong.* Hong Kong: Chinese University Press.

Peebles, G. 1986. "Hong Kong's Success: What Can We Learn?" *Economic Review* (March): 29–34.

Riedel, J. 1974. *The Industrialization of Hong Kong.* Tubingen: J. C. B. Mohr (Paul Siebeck).

Soon, Teck-Wong, and C. Suan Tan. (In this volume.)

SRI International. 1989. *Building Prosperity: A Five-Part Economic Strategy for Hong Kong's Future.* Hong Kong: Hong Kong Economic Survey.

State Statistical Bureau. Various issues. *China Statistical Yearbook.* Beijing: State Statistical Bureau of the People's Republic of China.

Sung, Y. W. 1984. "The Hong Kong Development Model and Its Future Evolution: Neoclassical Economics in a Chinese Society." In *Economic Development in Chinese Societies: Models and Experiences,* edited by J. C. Jao et al. Hong Kong: Hong Kong University Press.

Sung, Y. W. 1991. *The China–Hong Kong Connection,* Cambridge: Cambridge University Press.

Sung, Y. W. and M. K. Lee, eds. 1991. *The Other Hong Kong Report,* 1991. Hong Kong: Chinese University Press.

Syrquin, M., and H. B. Chenery. 1989. *Pattern of Development: 1950 to 1983.* World Bank Discussion Paper 41. Washington, D.C.: World Bank.

Szczepanik, Edward. 1958. *The Economic Growth of Hong Kong.* London: Oxford University Press.

Turner, H. A. et al. 1980. *The Last Colony: But Whose?* Cambridge: Cambridge University Press.

United Nations. Various issues. *Human Development Report.* New York: United Nations.

UNDP [United Nations Development Programme]. 1994. *Human Development Report,* 1994. New York: Oxford University Press.

Wilson, D. 1990. *Hong Kong.* London: Unwin Hyman.

World Bank. Various Issues. *Social Indicators of Development.* Washington: World Bank.

World Bank. 1991. *World Development Report,* 1991. New York: Oxford University Press.

Youngson, A. J. 1982. *Hong Kong, Economic Growth and Policy.* Hong Kong: Oxford University Press.

CHAPTER 2

# Taiwan, China: Policies and Institutions for Rapid Growth

*Carl J. Dahlman and Ousa Sananikone*

## Introduction

In the short history of nations that were created from the decline of colonial empires in the twentieth century, the rapid and sustained economic development of Taiwan, China over the past 40 years stands as one of the great success stories of the post–World War II era. Within the span of one generation, this small island was able to transform itself from a war-torn colony into one of the world's most dynamic economies. It has achieved exceptionally and persistently high rates of economic growth, averaging 9 percent per year between 1960 and 1990, and its population has enjoyed consistently rising incomes reaching nearly U.S.$11,000 per year in 1993. In addition, it has the distinction of holding the world's largest foreign exchange reserves, totaling U.S.$88 billion in 1993, and over the last decade has emerged as one of the world's largest net exporters of capital. What makes this economic success all the more remarkable, however, is the striking paradox between Taiwan's status as the world's twelfth-largest trading nation and its diplomatic nonexistence for the past 25 years.

This essay examines how Taiwan achieved this economic transformation, focusing on the role of the government in its rapid economic growth. It takes a comprehensive approach to understanding Taiwan's development experience, exploring the dynamic interplay of policy and nonpolicy factors alike. The essay is organized as follows. Section I highlights several performance indicators and identifies the main characteristics of Taiwan's economic performance. Section II reviews the set of historical, social, political, and economic conditions that initially favored Taiwan's early industrialization. Section III traces the different stages of economic development, examines the policy responses taken, and evaluates their economic outcomes. Section IV analyzes the structure of governance and institutions and examines the ways in which they supported and facilitated the implementation of public policies. Section V traces the evolution of the private sector from the end of World War II and explores the evolving relationship between the public and private sectors. Section VI addresses the central objective of this paper and analyzes the nature, motivation, and impact of selective government intervention in the areas of industrial and trade policy, financial markets, and human capital and labor. The newly added section VII reviews recent trends and developments over the last two years and their current or likely impact on Taiwan's economic growth. Finally, section VIII suggests some lessons for other developing countries.

## I. Indicators of Successful Economic Performance

The successful performance of the Taiwanese economy over the past 40 years is evidenced by a number of striking indicators.

*Very Rapid Growth with Equity.* The Taiwanese economy has recorded exceptionally high rates of economic growth over the past 30 years. Between 1960 and 1990, gross domestic product (GDP) grew at an average annual growth of 9 percent, far higher than that of most developing and industrialized countries (table 2.1) over the same period. More importantly, rapid economic

**TABLE 2.1.   Gross Domestic Product for Taiwan and Selected Economies**

| Country | Per Capita GNP 1993 (U.S.$) | Per Capita Income Average Annual Growth Rate (%) | | |
| --- | --- | --- | --- | --- |
| | | 1965–90 | 1965–80 | 1980–90 |
| Asian newly industrializing economies | | | | |
| Taiwan (China) | 10,600 | 7.0 | 9.7 | 7.7 |
| China | 490 | 5.8 | 6.8 | 9.5 |
| Korea | 7,660 | 7.1 | 9.9 | 9.7 |
| Hong Kong | 18,060 | 6.2 | 8.6 | 7.1 |
| Singapore | 19,850 | 6.5 | 10.0 | 6.4 |
| Malaysia | 3,140 | 4.0 | 7.4 | 5.2 |
| Indonesia | 740 | 4.5 | 7.0 | 5.5 |
| Thailand | 2,110 | 4.4 | 7.3 | 7.2 |
| Others | | | | |
| Brazil | 2,930 | 3.3 | 9.0 | 2.7 |
| Mexico | 3,610 | 2.8 | 6.5 | 1.0 |
| India | 300 | 1.9 | 3.6 | 5.3 |
| Japan | 31,490 | 4.1 | 6.4 | 4.1 |
| Germany | 23,560 | 2.4 | 3.3 | 2.1 |
| United States | 24,740 | 1.7 | 2.7 | 3.4 |

*Sources: World Development Report, 1995* (World Bank, 1995); *Taiwan Statistical Data Book,* 1994.

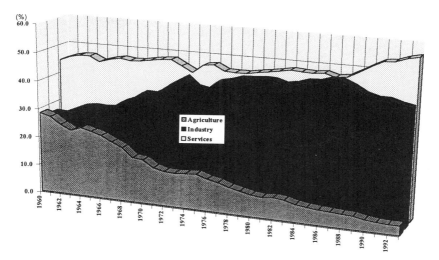

**Fig. 2.1. Structure of production, 1960–93. (From** *Taiwan Statistical Data Book* **1994.)**

growth was accompanied by a similarly dramatic rise in income, thanks in large part to successful agricultural and industrial policies that benefited the majority of the population. Between 1960 and 1993, per capita income increased nearly seventyfold from U.S.$154 to U.S.$11,000.

*Rapid Structural Transformation in Production and Trade.* Rapid industrialization has produced a dramatic change in Taiwan's production structure, transforming it very quickly from a primary into a secondary economy (fig. 2.1). Over the past 30 years, the share of agriculture in GDP has decreased continuously, from 28.5 percent in 1960 to only 3.5 percent in 1993, while industry's share conversely grew from 26.9 to 40.6 percent after rising to a peak of 47 percent in the mid-1980s. Meanwhile, the share of services has risen steadily over the same period from 44.6 to 55.9 percent. This transformation in the structure of production is reflected in the composition of Taiwanese exports: in 1960, agricultural and processed agricultural products accounted for 67 percent of the total value of exports, whereas industrial products provided only 32.3 percent. In 1993, the share of industrial products in total exports was 95.9 percent (fig. 2.2).

*Impressive Export Performance.* Export orientation has been the engine of Taiwan's economic growth, providing the foundation for economic takeoff in the 1960s. The country's reliance on exports is reflected in the increasing share of exports as a percentage of GNP, which grew from 9.55 percent in 1960 to nearly 40 percent in 1993 (fig. 2.3). Exports growth has been sluggish in the last two years due to the slow pace of the international economic recovery and

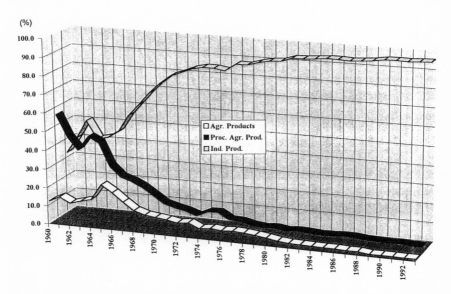

Fig. 2.2.   Composition of exports, 1960–93. (From *Taiwan Statistical Yearbook,* 1994.)

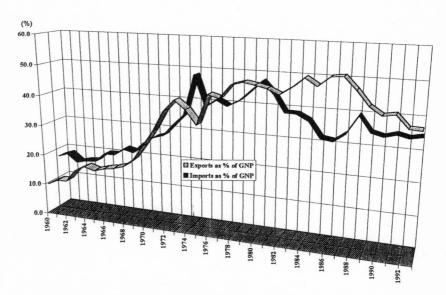

Fig. 2.3.   Exports and Imports as a percentage of GNP, 1960–93. (From *Taiwan Statistical Data Book,* 1994.)

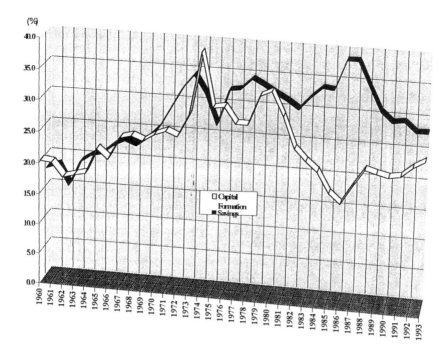

**Fig. 2.4. Savings and capital formation as a percentage of GNP, 1960–93. (From *Taiwan Statistical Data Book,* 1994.)**

weak external demand. However, between 1965 and 1980, Taiwanese exports grew at a spectacular rate of 20 percent per year—the second-highest export growth rate in the world after that of South Korea. In 1993, Taiwan was the twelfth-largest trading nation in the world, with merchandise trade totaling U.S.$151 billion.

*Macroeconomic and Political Stability.* Macroeconomic and political stability have been two principal conditions enabling sustainable growth in Taiwan. With the exception of the 1973–74 oil crisis and the recessionary period of 1980–81, the Taiwnese economy has never experienced a major economic depression or recession. Consumer prices have increased at an average annual rate of 3.2 percent in the past 20 years, and unemployment has never exceeded 3 percent. Apart from low inflation and virtually full employment, highly disciplined macroeconomic management has also accounted for large budget and trade surpluses almost uninterrupted since the mid-1960s.

*Capital Accumulation.* A high growth rate of capital formation has been a crucial factor behind Taiwan's rapid economic growth (fig. 2.4). High rates of investment were initially due to massive U.S. aid from 1950 to 1968, followed by large investment inflows from the United States, Japan, and overseas Chinese starting in the 1960s. In addition, Taiwan has recorded extremely high savings rates—among the highest in the world—with gross national savings averaging about 30 percent of GNP over the past 30 years. As a result, it has a capital-rich economy whose needs, unlike those of most developing countries, have more to do with access to markets and technology than to capital: in 1993, Taiwan had the world's largest foreign exchange reserves, at U.S.$88 billion. In the last decade, it has emerged as the fifth-largest exporter of capital in the world.

*Very High Total Factor Productivity Growth.* High rates of investments in physical and human capital alone do not fully explain Taiwan's rapid economic growth. A striking feature of Taiwan's growth is that it was based in large part on dramatic increases in productivity. In the manufacturing sector, increases in total factor productivity[1] accounted from 56 to 42 percent of growth in value added (table 2.2). The fact that such a large percentage of growth is accounted by an increase in the productivity of factors of production over and above increases in the factors themselves is typical of the high-performing East Asian economies.[2]

*Effective Strategy for Productivity Improvement.* Productivity growth in turn depends on the ability to utilize resources efficiently and an environment that is conducive to improved performance. Taiwan's rapid economic growth has been made possible in large part by an industrial strategy that emphasized and promoted the transfer, absorption, and diffusion of technological progress, leading to improved productivity growth. The transfer of foreign technology

TABLE 2.2.   **Growth Rates of Input, Output, and Total Factor Productivity in Manufacturing**

| Years | Value added | Labor | Capital | A | A/VA |
|-------|-------------|-------|---------|-----|------|
| 1952–61 | 12.1 | 2.7 | 8.7 | 6.8 | 0.56 |
| 1961–76 | 14.7 | 7.8 | 9.9 | 5.9 | 0.40 |
| 1976–89 | 9.7 | 4.3 | 6.7 | 4.7 | 0.48 |
| 1961–89 | 12.4 | 6.2 | 8.4 | 5.2 | 0.42 |

*Source:* Howard Pack, "The Role of Industrial Policy in Taiwan's Development," mimeo, April 1992.
*Note:* TFP is calculated using average factor shares from the national accounts for each subperiod.

---

1. Total factor productivity is a measure of how much of the growth in value added is not accounted for by the growth in labor and capital.
2. See John Page, Jr., and Peter Petri, "Productivity Change and Strategic Growth Policy in the East Asian Miracle" (World Bank, mimeo, 1993), for a discussion of the concept of TFP and cross-country comparisons.

and technical know-how through foreign direct investment, imports of capital goods, technology licensing, subcontracting, reverse engineering, and overseas education and training has enabled local enterprises to upgrade the structure of production, expand the range of goods and services produced, increase opportunities for trade, and on the whole enhance international competitiveness.

*A Flexible Industrial Structure.* Unlike Japan and South Korea, where industry is dominated by giant conglomerates, Taiwan's industrial structure is characterized by the preponderance of independent-minded small and medium enterprises. This flexible structure has enabled the economy to respond quickly to market changes, allowing entrepreneurs to move in and out of product lines and seek out different market niches relatively easily.

*A Pragmatic Approach to Economic Development.* The Taiwanese government has pursued a highly flexible and pragmatic approach to economic development. In contrast to the government's rigid political and ideological stance, economic policies have been surprisingly devoid of ideological content and are constantly adjusted to meet the changing needs of the domestic, regional, and international environment.

*Integration into the World Economy Despite Diplomatic Isolation.* Taiwan's integration in the world economy is all the more impressive in the context of its diplomatic isolation. Indeed, the disparity between the former and the latter attests to the flexibility of economic policies and the spirit of pragmatism and resilience of the Taiwanese people themselves. Taiwan's economic success has rested on a continuous strategy of global integration using not only trade but also other critical linkages such as inward and outward foreign investment, alliances with foreign firms, and overseas studies.

## II. Initial Conditions

Taiwan, China is a small island occupying an area of 13,800 square miles, roughly equal to the size of the Netherlands. It lies just 100 miles off the southeast coast of China, from which it is separated by the Taiwan Straits. With a population of 20.9 million and a density of 1,452 persons per square kilometers, it is one of the most densely populated areas of the world. Only one-quarter of the land is arable, the rest consisting of rugged mountains. There are very few natural resources.

Although occupied long ago by Chinese immigrants, Taiwan was not incorporated into the Chinese empire until the seventeenth century under the Ming Dynasty. Following its defeat in the Sino-Japanese War, China ceded the island to Japan in 1895 but reacquired it in 1945 at the end of World War II. In the aftermath of the Communist victory in China in 1949, the Nationalist forces of General Chiang Kai-shek retreated to Taiwan, where they established a government in exile and imposed an authoritarian regime on the native islander population. Between 1949 and 1951, more than 1.5 million people from various provinces and regions of China emigrated to Taiwan.

Like the other original Asian "tigers" (Hong Kong, Singapore, and South Korea), Taiwan benefited from a number of historical, economic, and cultural factors that gave its postwar economic development a significant head start. Key among these were the positive aspects of the Japanese colonial legacy, the initial injection of administrative and entrepreneurial talent from mainland China, the role of U.S. economic assistance, and the impact of Confucian ethics.

*The Japanese Colonial Legacy.* During its 50 years of occupation (1895–1945), Japan invested considerable effort in developing the Taiwanese economy to serve Japan's economic needs. In the process, it built a sound economic infrastructure that provided the foundation for Taiwan's postwar reconstruction. This included a solid physical infrastructure in the form of roads, railways, and harbors; an extensive agricultural infrastructure that included village cooperatives, agricultural research centers, and large-scale irrigation; and a strong industrial infrastructure consisting primarily of food processing but also some heavy industries. Furthermore, the Japanese colonial administration established a primary education system that left Taiwan with one of the highest literacy rates in Asia after World War II.

*The Impact of Initial Immigration from Mainland China.* The influx of refugees from mainland China during the 1949–51 exodus played a crucial role in Taiwan's rapid industrialization. It provided a sophisticated, ready-made elite of educated and skilled professionals, consisting of bureaucrats, teachers, engineers, and businessmen, who quickly filled the administrative and technical void left by the Japanese. As in Hong Kong, local skills were enhanced by the immigration of successful textile and flour-milling industrialists from Shanghai and Shandong, who quickly reestablished their businesses and accelerated Taiwan's industrialization process. Between 1949 and 1951, Taiwan's population increased by nearly two million people, or one-fourth of its initial size.

*The Role of U.S. Aid.* The United States played an important role in Taiwan's economic takeoff. Following the outbreak of the Korean War in 1950 and its commitment to support the Chinese Nationalist government, the United States became a major player in the Taiwanese economy. From 1949 until its termination in 1968, U.S. aid totaled U.S.$4.1 billion, of which $1.7 billion consisted of direct economic aid and $2.4 billion of military assistance. During the 1950s, U.S. aid equaled about 6 percent of GNP and nearly 40 percent of gross investment in Taiwan. The overall impact of U.S. aid was to strengthen the foundation of the Taiwanese economy by alleviating the heavy defense burden, developing infrastructure, and helping get crucial policy reforms adopted.

*The Impact of Confucian Ethics.* Last, Taiwan's economic success cannot be fully understood outside the framework of its social and cultural heritage.

Although these cannot be measured quantitatively and are often considered a trite and hackneyed theme, several cultural factors account for the success of entrepreneurship in Taiwan: the traditional emphasis on values such as hard work, education, thrift, discipline, and the unity of family. Nevertheless, Confucian ethics by themselves do not explain Taiwan's spectacular economic performance. Rather, one must view Taiwan's economic development as the fortuitous convergence of traditional values and a policy regime that provided stability and economic incentives for growth.

## III. Phases of Economic Development: Public Policies and Economic Outcomes

Taiwan's economic and industrial development since 1949 can be divided into five phases. This section analyzes each stage of development, focusing on the public policies adopted and their economic outcomes.

### Land Reform and Reconstruction (1949–52)

When the Nationalists took over Taiwan in 1949, economic prospects for the island did not seem very bright. Much of the physical infrastructure had been destroyed during World War II, and the postwar evacuation of the Japanese had left a large vacuum in capital, management, and technical expertise. The loss of the Japanese and Chinese markets, the influx of nearly two million refugees from China, and military tensions with the mainland resulted in economic stagnation, runaway inflation, severe shortages of goods and services, and threatened social and political instability.

*Policy Response.* The new government decided to focus on providing growth incentives in the agricultural sector, which at the time accounted for 60 percent of the work force. The focus on agriculture was deemed all the more critical because the existing land tenure system prevented effective resource utilization. The majority of farmers did not own the land they cultivated and paid rents that accounted for at least 50 percent and often as high as 75 percent of annual yield. Hence, tenant farmers had few incentives to increase production, a situation that resulted in low agricultural output and growing discontent in rural areas.

Against this background, land reform was undertaken in three gradual stages: reduction of rent, sale of public land to tenant farmers, and the Land to the Tiller Program, which placed a limit of 2.9 hectares on current land ownership and transferred the rest to the government. Under this third phase, large landowners were required to sell excess land to the government in exchange for which they received commodity certificates and stocks in state-owned enterprises that were scheduled to be transferred to the private sector.[3] The cumulative objectives of these reforms were to eliminate the traditional land tenure system, raise productivity, improve rural standards of living, and enhance social and political stability.

*Economic Outcomes.* Land reform had a dramatic impact on Taiwan's economic, social, and political landscape. Landownership gave farmers a powerful incentive to increase agricultural output, which grew at an average annual rate of 10 percent during 1947–53.[4]

Land reform was instrumental in transferring resources from the agricultural sector to the nascent industrial sector. In fact, the development credo of this period was "developing agriculture by means of industry, and fostering industry by virtue of agriculture." As former landowners turned their newly acquired stocks into capital with which to start new, nonagricultural enterprises, they became in effect Taiwan's first industrialists, managing the transition from an agricultural to an industrial, more commercially oriented economy. Agriculture provided raw materials for the food processing industry, and foreign exchange earnings from agricultural exports were used to import machinery, equipment, and industrial raw materials. With increased farm income and a higher standard of living for farmers, the rural sector grew as a domestic market for manufacturers. Moreover, rural savings helped finance industrial development, which in turn absorbed surplus agricultural labor.

One of the greatest achievements of land reform was a radical and remarkably equitable redistribution of wealth. As much as 13 percent of Taiwan's GDP is estimated to have been redistributed under the Land to the Tiller Act in 1952. As a result of this and other policies, Taiwan is one of the few developing countries in the world to have simultaneously achieved rapid economic growth *and* equitable income distribution.[5]

In retrospect, the success of land reform was almost ensured by a combination of historical circumstances and skillful policies. The first factor was the exogenous status of the newly implanted mainlander government vis-à-vis the native Taiwanese population. Since they had no ties with the local Taiwanese and were not beholden to local interest groups, the Kuomintang had much more political room in which to maneuver in promoting and implementing land reform policies.

---

3. These were among the Japanese industrial assets that were nationalized by the Chinese government in 1945. The state-owned enterprises were in the cement, paper and pulp, and mining industries.

4. Erik Thorbecke, "Agricultural Development," in *Economic Growth and Structural Change in Taiwan: The Postwar Experience of the Republic of China,* edited by Walter Galenson (Ithaca: Cornell University Press, 1979), 144.

5. In addition to land reform, other factors contributing to income equalization in Taiwan were the emphasis on education and balanced growth, a decentralized industrialization strategy, labor-intensive industrialization that absorbed surplus agricultural labor and provided full employment at competitive wages, and the role of small and medium enterprises.

A second factor contributing to the success of land reform was the integrated fashion in which agricultural development was planned, coordinated, and implemented. Agricultural policy was carried out by the Joint Committee for Rural Reconstruction (JCRR), an independent, U.S.-funded supraministerial agency that was able to implement policies quickly and effectively. The provision of a comprehensive support infrastructure inherited from Japan in the form of farmers associations, research centers, and extension services further contributed to agricultural development. The intensive use of technology in agriculture, including modern production techniques such as extensive irrigation, the adoption of power tillers, widespread use of fertilizers, and multiple cropping, also brought a dramatic increase in and diversification of agricultural output.

A third factor contributing to the success of land reform was the implementation of agricultural pricing policies that transferred resources from agriculture to the rest of the economy. The government controlled both the supply and the price of rice through various compulsory rice collections. By purchasing rice at below-market prices, it thus collected a "hidden" rice tax that provided a large source of revenues for the public sector. The most important source of revenues for the government rice collection system, however, was the rice for fertilizer barter program. During the 1950s and 1960s, the government was the sole source of chemical fertilizers in Taiwan and controlled all fertilizer production, imports, and supplies. About 70 to 80 percent of fertilizers were allocated to rice production and distributed to rice farmers. Through the rice for fertilizer barter, the state made huge profits. Agricultural pricing policy also contributed to product diversification by guaranteeing prices for nonrice crops such as sugarcane, asparagus, corn, and mushrooms.

Fourth, from a broad political perspective, land reform was successful because it offered incentives to different groups. It enhanced the status of disfranchised tenant farmers, and by the same token conferred a certain degree of legitimacy on the government in the eyes of the majority of the Taiwanese population. Wealthy landowners—the group most adversely affected by the reform—were given incentives that carefully reintegrated them into the economic system while neutralizing them as a potential political threat to the regime. In this regard, the Nationalist government proved to be quite adept in using land reform to reshape Taiwanese society to suit its economic and political objectives.

## Import-Substitution Industrialization (1953–57)

During most of the colonial period, the Taiwanese economy functioned as an agricultural appendage to Japan, while the latter, in turn, supplied Taiwan with manufactured consumer goods. In the 1930s, Japanese manufacturers established some basic industries in Taiwan, consisting mostly of food processing but also of cement, chemicals, pulp and paper, fertilizers, and metallurgy. The rupture of colonial trade with Japan in 1945, quickly followed by the break with China in 1949, deprived the Taiwanese economy of its major trading partners and created a lack of foreign exchange and severe shortages of imported consumer goods. Prices rose fivefold annually between 1946 and 1948 before jumping nearly 30-fold in early 1949. This hyperinflation was mainly due to large loans for postwar rehabilitation and reconstruction, huge government expenditures, and high levels of inflation on the mainland.

Economic survival and national security were paramount priorities for the government from the early to mid-1950s on. Apart from the pressure to feed and employ the growing population, the Kuomintang faced a threat of invasion (whether real or imagined) from China and needed to stabilize the new regime. Although postwar efforts focused on agriculture, the government was equally committed to developing industry not only as the base for economic self-sufficiency but to support the anticipated recovery of the mainland.

*Policy Response.* Faced with these imperatives, the government's first priority was price stability. The Nationalists' strong commitment to fight inflation must be understood in the context of their mainland experience. During the 1940s, Kuomintang leaders had freely resorted to inflationary mechanisms such as unlimited increases in the money supply and budget deficits to finance their military campaigns. The result was hyperinflation, leading to peasants' revolts against the Kuomintang that contributed to the party's eventual defeat by the Communists. This experience with inflation on the mainland and its disastrous consequences for the Kuomintang taught the Nationalists a bitter lesson that they would not soon forget: political stability is predicated first and foremost on price stability.

To induce price stabilization, the government adopted high interest rates on savings deposits at a rate higher than inflation. In 1950, the Bank of Taiwan offered 7 percent interest on one-month savings deposits, compounding to an annual rate of 125 percent. By June of that year, total time and savings deposits in the banking system rose from NT$6 million in March 1950 to $28 million. Besides leading to a huge increase in private savings, which was used to finance industrial development and other critical investments, the major impact of high interest rates on deposits was a dramatic decline in inflation. The rate of inflation subsequently fell from 3,400 percent in 1949 to 66 percent in 1950, 23 percent in 1952, and 9 percent in 1953.[6]

To promote industrial self-sufficiency, the government adopted a policy of labor-intensive import substitution, using a combination of trade and exchange

---

6. Alvin Hsieh and Tain-jy Chen, "The Role of Foreign Capital in the Economic Development of Taiwan." Conference Proceedings Series, no. 7, July 22–27, 1987. Taipei: Chung-hua Institution for Economic Research, p. 442.

rate policies to encourage domestic industries to produce consumer goods. Extensive quantitative restrictions (QRs) and high tariff rates were placed on imports, sealing many of Taiwan's consumer goods markets from foreign competition. Between 1948 and 1955, the average nominal tariff rate for all imports more than doubled, rising from 20 to nearly 45 percent.[7] Tariff rates as high as 151 to 165 percent were applicable to nearly 4 percent of all import items. Ad valorem duties exceeding 45 percent were levied on nearly a third of all importable items, while tariffs of 15 percent or less were imposed on only 16 percent of all importable items.[8] In addition, nearly one-half of importable commodities were under strict quota restrictions, further protecting domestic industries from foreign competition.[9]

In 1949, the government introduced the "new Taiwan dollar" (NT$) at an initially undervalued exchange rate of NT$5 per U.S. dollar in an effort to keep import prices high (fig. 2.5).[10] Meanwhile, it maintained a multiple exchange rate system that encouraged imports through lower rates and penalized exports through higher rates. Within imports, lower exchange rates were applied to capital equipment and raw materials than to other goods.

To take advantage of Taiwan's abundant labor, the government promoted labor-intensive, light manufacturing industries through special incentives and subsidies. Since Taiwan enjoyed some comparative advantage in textiles with the arrival of industrialists from Shanghai and Shandong, emphasis was placed on the textile sector. A combination of protective measures and government subsidies were used to promote the development of the textile industry. These included high tariffs and QRs on imports of yarn and finished products and restrictions on the entry of new producers to prevent excessive competition. In addition, the government established an "entrustment" scheme whereby it supplied raw materials and provided working capital to textile entrepreneurs and purchased all the yarn produced, thereby assuming all the risks for textile manufacturers.

During this period, the government invested heavily in infrastructure as a base for industrial development by expanding the transportation and power networks that had been built by the Japanese. U.S. aid financed 49 percent of

---

7. Samuel P. S. Ho, *Economic Development of Taiwan, 1860–1970,* (New Haven: Yale University Press, 1978), 191.

8. Chi Ming Hou, "Strategies for Industrial Development," *Industry of Free China* (October 1987): 9.

9. After 1951, imports were classified in four categories: permissible, controlled, suspended, and prohibited. The permissible category included essential capital equipment, raw materials, and essential consumer goods. Of the approximately 500 groups of commodities classified during the 1950s, 55 percent were in the permissible category and 5 percent in the prohibited category (see Ho, *Economic Development,* 191).

10. However, because devaluations did not keep up with the rate of inflation, it became overvalued by 1953. This can be seen in the real exchange rate, with respect to the dollar, as computed in figure 2.5.

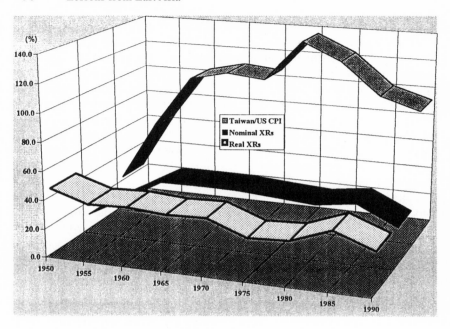

**Fig. 2.5.  Nominal and real exchange rates with respect to the U.S. dollar and the consumer price index, 1950–90. (From *Taiwan Statistical Yearbook,* 1994.)**

public enterprise investment in infrastructure, especially electricity, transportation, and communications.[11] The government also established market support institutions such as the China Productivity Center and the Food Industry Research and Development Institute to provide technical assistance to industrial entrepreneurs.

*Economic Outcome.* The impact of import substitution was a dynamic growth of industrial output in selected industries during the 1950s. Import substitution is estimated to have created as much as one-third of manufacturing growth between 1955 and 1960.[12] Trade and exchange controls were largely successful: the share of consumer goods in total imports fell from 19.9 to 6.6 percent between 1952 and 1957. In retrospect, import substitution prepared the way for export growth by fostering private sector development, albeit in a controlled way, in key industries. Protected from foreign competition, domestic consumer goods industries such as textiles, apparel, wood and leather products,

---

11. Ibid.

12. Robert Wade, *Governing the Market: Economic Theory and the Role of the Government in East Asian Industrialization* (Princeton: Princeton University Press, 1991), 84.

and bicycles developed very rapidly. The effects of import substitution were most notable in the textiles sector, which grew at an annual rate of 54.9 percent between 1949 and 1954.[13] Production of cotton yarn and woolen yarn went up by more than 200 and 400 percent, respectively, between 1951 and 1954.[14] By mid-1953, Taiwan had become more than self-sufficient in yarn and cotton. The government's response at this point was to end the system of support and encourage vertical integration and economies of scale. Low-interest credit was made available to existing firms to expand production, while the government continued to limit the entry of new firms. By the mid-1950s, the domestic market was saturated, resulting in bitter price wars and bankruptcy for many firms. Import substitution rapidly shifted to other industries such as plastics, flour milling, and bicycles.

Import substitution laid the base for industrialization in Taiwan by channelling resources from the agricultural to the industrial sector. By the end of the 1950s, industrial production had doubled, while agriculture's share of domestic production continued to fall. However, import substitution also exacted high economic costs, which accumulated over time. Among the negative consequences of import substitution was the fact that it penalized exports and discouraged traditional export industries such as sugar, rice, and processed agricultural products.[15] Moreover, by promoting the import of intermediate and capital goods and raw materials through lower exchange rates, import substitution encouraged imports, contributing to a trade deficit that eventually amounted to some 40 percent of total imports (this deficit was largely financed by U.S. aid). Finally, import substitution placed the burden of subsidies on consumers, while producers were protected from external competition and enjoyed high prices in the domestic market.

### Export Promotion (1958–72)

The phase of import substitution reached its limit in a relatively short period as the small domestic market became saturated with local goods, particularly textiles, paper, and plastics. The combined effect of slow exports and high levels of capital goods and raw materials imports led to a persistent trade deficit, reaching U.S.$78 million in 1955 or roughly 4 percent of GNP (at current prices). As inflation and unemployment began to rise, overall growth declined from 9 percent in the early 1950s to 6.5 percent in the mid-1950s.

*Policy Response.* The government was faced at this point with a choice of either going into a secondary stage of import substitution or promoting growth

---

13. Ho, *Economic Development,* 188.
14. Wade, *Governing the Market,* 76.
15. Ibid.

through exports of light manufacturing goods, in which Taiwan already had a comparative advantage. On one hand, security minded leaders advocated continued state control of industrial development, particularly investments in defense-related heavy industries. On the other hand, economic bureaucrats, supported by U.S. advisers, pushed for export orientation and private sector development. With the looming specter of the termination of U.S. aid in 1965 and in anticipation of the need to obtain foreign exchange on its own, the government made the decision to shift to a policy of outward orientation and export promotion.

Between 1958 and 1962, the government adopted several far-reaching policies aimed at promoting exports, investment, and industrialization in general. The most important of these was the 1959 Nineteen-Point Program of Economic and Financial Reform, which addressed virtually every component of economic, fiscal, and trade policies. Its objective was to promote private sector development by improving the investment climate, liberalizing administrative controls on industry and trade, and strengthening export promotion efforts. The Nineteen-Point Program laid the foundation for Taiwan's economic takeoff in the 1960s and 1970s and set a precedent for future efforts to liberalize government policies.

First, the multiple exchange rate system was gradually dismantled in 1958 and replaced in 1961 with a unified and undervalued exchange rate that maintained its real rate versus the U.S. dollar through 1972. This was intended to liberalize trade controls (fig. 2.5).[16] Second, the effective rate of protection on various items was lowered to stimulate competition and promote greater economic efficiency: tariffs and import controls were gradually reduced, especially for imports of materials and equipment to be used for exports. Third, export-oriented industries were given a host of incentives, including rebates of customs duties on imported raw materials, exemption from business and stamp taxes, a lower taxable income base, improved access to imported raw materials and capital goods, and assistance with export promotion and market research. Starting in 1957, the Bank of Taiwan offered low-interest export loans at 10 points below commercial rates then available to private sector enterprises for general business purposes.[17] Finally, beginning in 1958, the government adopted high real interest rates on savings deposits to encourage private savings.

16. In fact, the government had allowed exporters to get a higher exchange rate as early as 1955. Between 1952 and 1954, the new Taiwan dollar was unrealistically overvalued, with a basic exchange rate of NT$15 per U.S. dollar (see app., table A2.1). In 1955, the government allowed exporters a higher exchange rate through exchange surrender certificates (ESCs), which were given to exporters. In 1961, a single uniform exchange rate system was introduced at NT$40 per U.S. dollar, a rate that was maintained until 1973.

17. Government export loans were offered at 6 percent per year for those payable in foreign currency and 11 percent per year for those payable in local currency, compared with 19.8 percent (secured) and 22.32 percent (unsecured) in commercial banks.

While the degree of state intervention in the orientation of private firms nowhere approached that found in South Korea in the 1960s, evidence suggests that in the early 1960s the Taiwanese government required certain industries to export a set percentage of their output. For example, beginning in 1964, new cement factories were required to export 100 percent of their production.[18] Furthermore, firms were limited by the small domestic market and were therefore forced to export in order to expand.

In addition to the Nineteen-Point Program, another important measure that had a catalytic impact on private sector development was the adoption of the Statutes for the Encouragement of Investment in 1960. Designed to attract local as well as foreign investment, the statutes offered a wide range of incentives to domestic and foreign firms alike, including a five-year tax holiday for approved export-oriented enterprises, 100 percent equity ownership, free remittance of all profits and interest earnings, repatriation of capital, accelerated depreciation, exemption from import duties, and preferential land sites. To further stimulate domestic industry, local content requirements were placed on foreign firms and later expanded to cover local producers as well. Under this regulation, producers were required to increase their local content from 10 to 40 percent annually, with a maximum of 70 percent of the product value.

Another key measure was the enactment of the Statute for the Establishment and Management of Export-Processing Zones (EPZs) in 1965, which was designed to attract investment in export-oriented, labor-intensive industries in special economic zones. Combining the advantages of an industrial estate with those of a free port, EPZs offered complete exemption from customs duties and commodity and sales taxes and provided other incentives for export-oriented firms to set up in the zones. In the early 1970s, relatively high value-added industries such as precision machinery, electronics, electrical machinery, optical equipment, and plastics were given priority in the zones.

An interesting feature of Taiwan's industrial policy as it moved away from import substitution was the dualistic policy followed by the government. Increased market orientation was limited generally to the export sector, while the domestic market remained sheltered behind high import tariffs. As during the import substitution phase, consumers continued to bear the burden of import duties while domestic entrepreneurs were protected from competition from imports. During this period, high import tariffs and nontariff protectionist measures were partly responsible for the rapid growth of industries such as chemical fertilizers, basic metals, plastics, and automobiles.

---

18. Yu-kang Mao and Chi Schive, "Agricultural and Industrial Development of the Republic of China on Taiwan," in *Reference Papers on Economic Development and Prospects of the Republic of China,* compiled by the Board of Foreign Trade. Taipei: Ministry of Economic Affairs (1991), 53–56.

During this phase of industrial development, the government started a tradition of external consultation that would continue for many decades. In 1958, the Stanford Research Institute (SRI) was commissioned to identify which Taiwanese industries should be developed. Based on Taiwan's comparative advantage in low-cost labor and existing technical capabilities, SRI suggested the development of plastics, synthetic fibers, and various electronic components. Subsequently, key products targeted for export promotion included apparel, consumer electronics, and home appliances such as television sets, transistor radios, refrigerators, watches, and clocks.

*Economic Outcome.* The impact of these policy measures on the Taiwanese economy was nothing short of dramatic. Gross national product grew at an average annual rate of 11 percent between 1963 and 1972. Exports, which had increased by 11.6 percent annually between 1953 and 1962, grew at a rate of 28 percent annually between 1963 and 1972. In terms of value, exports jumped from U.S.$123 million in 1955 to $450 in 1965 and $2.9 billion in 1972.

Export expansion was accompanied by a dramatic change in the structure of production as industry became the dominant sector in the economy and agriculture's share conversely decreased. This shift in the structure of production was also reflected in the composition of exports. In the early 1950s, Taiwanese exports consisted largely of agricultural and processed agricultural products, with industrial products accounting for less than 10 percent of total exports. After the adoption of export promotion policies, the share of industrial products in total exports went up to 50 percent in 1962 and 83 percent in 1972.

What made this dynamic growth in production possible was the enthusiastic private sector response to the incentives provided by the government. Spurred by the liberalized trade regime, domestic manufacturers moved enthusiastically into the world market. From 1960 to 1972, private manufacturing output grew by as much as 19.5 percent annually. Reflecting growing private sector participation in the economy, private industry's share of total manufacturing output rose from 53 percent in 1958 to 86 percent in 1972 (fig. 2.6).

The success of Taiwan's export promotion strategy was facilitated, to a considerable extent, by the open global economic system prevailing during the 1960s and early 1970s. As Western Europe, the United States, and Japan reached new levels of affluence, demand for consumer goods increased significantly. In addition, low prices for energy and other raw materials helped keep production costs relatively low. Tariff barriers in industrialized countries were also relatively low at the time. Beginning with textiles, then food processing, and moving on to electronics, machinery, and synthetic fibers, Taiwanese manufacturers were able to produce consumer goods at prices that were competitive on the world market. One of the secrets of Taiwan's economic success was its use of its comparative advantage in different ways. To industrial countries with high labor costs it exported low-end, inexpensive, manufactured

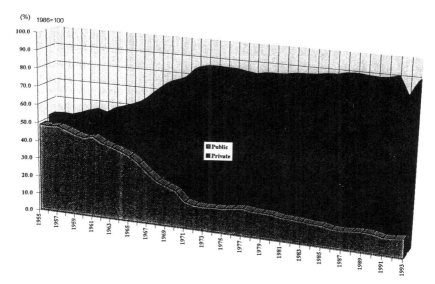

Fig. 2.6. **Distribution of public and private ownership in manufacturing, 1955–93. (From *Taiwan Statistical Data Book,* 1994.)**

products, while it exported relatively capital- and skill-intensive goods to less-developed countries with lower technology levels.

Beyond increased foreign exchange earnings, the impact of outward orientation conferred several positive externalities. The exposure to world markets forced Taiwanese firms to become more competitive by having to constantly upgrade their products, diversify product mixes for different markets, use more advanced technology, and adopt more efficient methods of production and management. Export orientation also marked the beginning of Taiwan's strategy of global integration as the domestic economy developed critical linkages to the world economy through trade and foreign investment. For example, subcontracting arrangements between local manufacturers and foreign buyers such as Sears, J. C. Penney and K-Mart, played a crucial role in transferring technical know-how to local entrepreneurs and building trade channels.

Direct foreign investment (DFI) played a catalytic role in Taiwan's industrialization during this period. DFI gradually replaced U.S. aid as foreign investors flocked in, lured by Taiwan's cheap labor, hard work ethics, sound infrastructure, and relative political and economic stability. Although DFI only amounted to 6 percent of gross capital formation in the 1960s, it contributed much more to manufacturing growth as nearly 80 percent of total DFI went into manufacturing. More importantly, DFI created linkage effects through technology and skill transfer in various sectors of Taiwanese industry, leading to dramatic improvements in the quality of production and to the diversification of industries. Local workers employed by foreign firms quickly acquired new skills. Once they had mastered production technologies, many left the foreign firms that employed them to start their own companies, thereby disseminating new technology and new skills to domestic industry.

Most of the DFI was in export-oriented light industries such as textiles and garments, particularly in export-processing zones that operated under virtually free-trade conditions. In 1965, around 20 percent of total exports were attributable to foreign firms. EPZs played an important role in the growth of Taiwanese exports in the 1960s, accounting for 10 percent of total exports by 1970. Since they were primarily based on labor-intensive industries, EPZs also created large opportunities for employment—by the end of 1973, EPZs employed close to 80,000 workers. More importantly, however, EPZs provided backward linkage effects by increasing local purchases and stimulating domestic production.

One of the most important impacts of labor-intensive industrialization was a more equitable income distribution. Essentially, everyone could enjoy the fruits of their own labor as long as they were willing to work hard. Denied any economic role under the Japanese occupation, the Taiwanese population responded in full force to the new incentives provided by the government—the result was literally a sea of entrepreneurs in the early 1960s. Much as land reform gave rise to a new class of industrialists, export promotion policies created a new, much larger bourgeoisie whose energy was focused on achieving economic prosperity, leaving them little inclination to interfere in political affairs.

In retrospect, the transition from import substitution to export promotion was by far the most catalytic policy change in Taiwan's economic development. It marked the shift from a relatively closed economy to an open economic system, exposing it to the forces of international competition and technological change. It released the pent-up dynamism of the private sector and oriented its focus outward, thereby integrating Taiwan into the world economy. It also represented the beginning of a partial liberalization of the economy in the sense that the state let the market rule while guiding it through selectively provided incentives.

## Industrial Consolidation and New Export Growth (1973–80)

As the 1970s progressed, however, Taiwan's export-led economic growth no longer seemed sustainable without another radical shift in direction. Internal as well as external challenges threatened economic growth. Internally, the rapid manufacturing increases of the 1960s had strained the physical infrastructure, clogging the transportation, electricity, and communications systems.

More critically, the light manufacturing industries that had provided the main-springs of Taiwan's export success in the 1960s were now facing competition from lower-wage producers in the world market.

There were profound external setbacks as well. China's reemergence as a key economic and political player on the world stage increasingly led to Taiwan's diplomatic isolation, as the latter suffered the humiliation of being forced out of key international organizations. In 1971, the United Nations voted to expel Taiwan and seat the People's Republic of China as the sole legitimate government from China. By 1980, Taiwan was forced out of the World Bank and the International Monetary Fund. As foreign investors rushed to the newly opened Chinese market, international confidence in the viability of the Taiwanese economy declined.

The 1973–74 oil crisis had dramatic repercussions on the Taiwanese economy. Real GNP grew by only 1.2 percent in 1974, compared to a double-digit average of 10 percent during the 1960s and early 1970s. For the first time since 1970, the economy registered a trade deficit. This economic downturn was not only the result of oil price increases but of increases in the prices of other commodities and intermediate goods that were critical to the Taiwanese economy, from food to capital equipment. Oil price increases created massive inflation, reaching 47 percent in 1974. Exports declined in real terms by 7 percent per year during 1973–74, as the percentage of exports in the GNP fell from 42 percent from 1973 to 35 percent in 1975.

*Policy Response.* Beginning in 1973, the government quickly moved to establish a more self-reliant development strategy based on industrial consolidation and renewed export growth. This time, it turned to the U.S. management firm of Arthur D. Little to find a way out of the economic crisis. Based on an analysis of Taiwan's economic needs and industrial capabilities at the time, Arthur D. Little recommended heavy investments in infrastructure, industrial upgrading, and secondary import substitution. These recommendations were incorporated into the Sixth Four-Year Economic Development Plan (1972–76).

First, the government adopted two short-term stabilization measures to counter inflation. These involved raising interest rates very sharply and raising oil and other commodity prices as a "shock treatment," accompanied by longer-term actions that reduced taxes.

Second, the government shifted to an industrial strategy that called for the development of capital-intensive, heavy, and petrochemical industries. The objective was to increase domestic production of intermediates needed for the rapid expansion of export industries. This was in effect a secondary phase of import substitution: although dependence on exports remained, many imported intermediates and capital goods were gradually replaced by domestically produced goods such as iron and steel, machine tools, and electrical machinery.

Third, as a means of revitalizing the economy and removing bottenecks to expansion, the government launched 10 major public sector projects at a total cost of U.S.$8 billion. These consisted of six infrastructure projects (highways, railroads, airports, and harbors), three heavy and petrochemical industries, and the construction of several nuclear power plants designed to reduce Taiwan's dependence on imported fuel.

*Economic Outcome.* The Taiwanese economy recovered from the first oil shock relatively quickly thanks in large part to the swiftness of policy actions and the basic resilience of the economy. After a brief period of adjustment during 1974–75, the economy by and large resumed its pre–oil crisis momentum in the latter half of the 1970s. Growth rates returned to more than 10 percent, and inflation fell back to an annual rate of 3 percent. Thanks to the continued growth of exports, the balance of payments deficit that was incurred in 1974–75 moved again into surplus in 1976. When the second oil price shock hit in 1979, followed by world recession, their impact on the Taiwanese economy was relatively mild.

The public sector was the prime beneficiary of government policies during this stage of economic development, in large part because the bulk of restructuring projects could not be undertaken by the private sector. The trend in public sector growth in the 1970s was evident in increased spending on higher education and vocational training, investments in science and technology infrastructure, and large infrastructure projects. As a result, the steady downward trend in the share of government in manufacturing production that had prevailed since the early 1960s suffered a temporary reversal during the 1974–80 period, going back to as high as 15.8 percent in 1977 (app., table A.2.2).

This was primarily because secondary import substitution required large investments in technology- and capital-intensive industries with scale economies, investments the predominantly small-scale private sector did not have the resources to undertake. For this reason, the government used public enterprises much more actively to undertake the big push in heavy and chemical industries. When private investment was not forthcoming, the government established large public enterprises in steel, shipbuilding, and automobiles in the 1970s. To some extent, the rationale for using the public sector to guide industrial policy was reinforced by the government's ideological distrust of big business and its arms-length relations with the Taiwanese private sector.

Public enterprise performances have varied across sectors. Some performed quite profitably. China Steel Corporation, for example, became one of the world's most profitable steel companies. Nevertheless, there were examples of blatant failures, such as the government's ventures into shipbuilding and automobiles in the 1970s. In contrast, public research institutions established during this period to service the needs of industry have fared remarkably well. Key among these are the Electronics Research and Service Organization

(ERSO) and the Information Industry Institute (III), which has played a leading role in the development of Taiwan's information industry, from developing core technologies and new products to transferring the results to industry.[19]

In retrospect, the 1970s represented the first difficult stage of Taiwan's maturation process as it moved from a relatively underdeveloped country taking advantage of the open world economy to a more advanced industrializing country having to adjust to a drastically different international environment. The second stage of adjustment was to come in the next decade.

### High-Technology Industrialization (1981–present)

As it entered its fourth decade, Taiwan confronted an increasingly complex and challenging domestic and international environment, which threatened its economic development. As export growth slackened and domestic demand increased, the double-digit growth of the early 1970s sputtered to just below 7 percent as the decade ended. With Taiwanese labor moving into more technology-intensive industries, manufacturing wages rose faster than productivity gains, undercutting the country's long-standing comparative advantage as a haven of cheap labor. Rising wages, in turn, forced labor-intensive industries to relocate production to other parts of Asia, which offered cheap and abundant labor (for example, wages in China are one-tenth those in Taiwan). This situation was further exacerbated by labor shortages resulting from a gradual shift from manufacturing to service industries. Taiwan's continued integration into the world economy revealed further structural weaknesses and deficiencies, particularly in the financial sector, where government control and the sector's own antiquated structure could not keep up with the demands of an increasingly open international financial system.

At the same time, the world economy presented a much more competitive and protectionist environment. The large trade surpluses accumulated by Taiwan led to growing protectionism on the part of major trading partners. This came mainly in the form of high tariff barriers in areas such apparel, leather goods, and electronics—all areas of Taiwan's comparative advantage. In addition, since the mid-1980s, Taiwanese exports have experienced a gradual loss of competitiveness as a result of rising wages and the appreciation of the new Taiwan dollar (particularly between 1985 and 1989 when the exchange rate went from NT\$40 to \$26 per U.S. dollar). In effect, Taiwanese manufacturers are finding themselves squeezed between competition from Asia's newly industrializing economies in traditional, labor-intensive manufacturing, on one hand, and high-technology products from industrialized countries on the other.

---

19. See Carl Dahlman and Ousa Sananikone, "Technology Strategy in Taiwan: Exploiting Foreign Linkages and Investing in Local Capability," World Bank, December 1990, mimeo.

*Policy Response.* Faced once again with a slackening economy, uncertain oil prices, and keen competition from newly industrializing and developed countries alike, the Taiwanese government responded, once again, by restructuring the economy to meet the challenges of the new international environment. Since the 1980s, the government has set its priority on the development of high-technology industries as a means of enhancing the economy's competitiveness in world markets. Under the Eighth Four-Year Development Plan (1982–86), the government targeted a number of strategic industries for development, namely, the information, machinery, precision instruments, biotechnology, electro-optics, and environmental technology industries, on the basis of their technology intensiveness, low pollution levels, low energy consumption, high-value products, and high market potential.

It must be noted that this emphasis on technology development was neither new nor sudden. In fact, the government had made a priority of industrial technology development starting in the 1950s when it established the National Science Council. Operating under the direct supervision of the prime minister, the council is responsible for formulating national science and technology development plans, which are integrated into the four-year economic development plans. To enhance industrial competitiveness, R&D institutes were set up in strategic areas of industry. The creation of the Industrial Technology Research Institute (ITRI) in 1973 was a landmark in setting up Taiwan's science and technology infrastructure.[20] These efforts to deepen national R&D capability in strategic sectors were reinforced, in the 1980s, with fiscal and financial incentives for R&D activities in high-tech industries, including financial incentives for education and training.[21]

The shift to a high-technology economy has necessitated the close coordination of industrial, financial, science and technology, and human resources policies. In 1984, the Statute for the Encouragement of Investment was amended to provide tax incentives for manufacturers who allocate a percentage of their revenues to R&D. Significant incentives were given to firms to improve production techniques and product diversification: investors in strategic industries received low-interest loans, the right to retain earnings of up to 200 percent of paid-in capital, and the right to defer the start of a five-year income tax holiday for up to four years. The government also encouraged the establishment of venture-capital firms to promote high-tech ventures and technical upgrading. The push for high technology was epitomized in the establishment of the Hsinchu Science-Based Industrial Park in 1980 as an incubator for the

---

20. ITRI's work is divided among eight research institutes: electronics, mechanical engineering, chemical engineering, materials, energy and mining, electro-optics, pollution control, and standards and measures (see Dahlman and Sananikone, *Technology Stategy*).

21. Wade, *Governing the Market*, 98.

nation's high-tech firms. Modeled after California's Silicon Valley, the park offers proximity to two well-known universities, access to research institutes and labs, and a host of fiscal and financial incentives designed to attract investment in high-technology industries.

The government's push for high-technology industrialization was complemented by a parallel restructuring in the area of human resource development. University curricula were revised in order to strengthen technology-related disciplines such as science, mathematics, engineering, and computers. At the same time, the government began a concerted effort to recruit technical manpower from abroad by offering competitive salaries and other incentives to Taiwanese citizens who were studying and working abroad. In the last decade, the number of Taiwanese graduate engineering students in U.S. universities who returned to Taiwan has increased from barely a trickle in the mid-1980s to 1,000 in 1993, thereby creating a reverse "brain drain." Altogether, almost half of the 150 companies established in the Hsinchu Park were started by Taiwanese engineers who had returned from the United States. Following a slow start, the park generated nearly U.S.$5 billion in sales in 1993 and has pushed Taiwan into the ranks of major high-tech producers. It accounts, for example, for half of the world market in scanners and monitors, about 30 percent of the market in network cards and terminals, and about 10 percent of the personal computer market.[22]

Finally, to strengthen the foundation for long-term economic growth, the government invested in 14 new infrastructure projects in 1985, including expansion of the energy, telecommunications, and transportation networks and development of water resources and national parks. The Sixth National Development Plan (1991–96) calls for expending U.S.$330 billion in public sector projects, including regional industrial development and expansion of transportation and communications networks, and bringing an average annual increase of 186 percent to government spending on public investment.[23]

In broad terms, the government's approach to economic development since the 1980s has been to pursue a strategy of increasing liberalization and internationalization. In 1987, foreign exchange controls were lifted on all trade-related transactions. Spurred by large trade surpluses, the new Taiwan dollar appreciated from NT$36–40 per U.S. dollar in the early 1980s to NT$28 in 1988. Foreign exchange rates were further liberalized in 1989 to bring market forces into full play, and the exchange rate appreciated to NT$26 per U.S. dollar. Foreign exchange liberalization opened the door for Taiwanese overseas investment, leading to huge outflows of Taiwanese investment in Southeast Asia totaling U.S.$12 billion between 1987 and 1992. Moreover, import con-

22. *New York Times,* July 19, 1994.
23. *Asia 1991 Yearbook.* 1991. Hong Kong: Far Eastern Economic Review. 226.

trols have been relaxed and customs tariffs drastically reduced over the past several years. In 1989, regulatory controls on bank loan rates and deposit rates were abolished. Since then, interest rates have been gradually liberalized. Measures were taken to strengthen domestic financial competition and raise the quality of financial services. The government's strategy is to encourage the further expansion and diversification of export markets through trade and strategic alliances with foreign firms. Its current efforts at liberalization and internationalization are also intended to promote Taiwan as a regional center of transshipment, warehousing, commerce, and finance (presumably as an alternative to Hong Kong after 1997).

*Economic Outcome.* While it is much too early to assess the definitive impact of these policies, some changes can be observed in the structure of Taiwanese production and exports. In the last several years, a growing number of small, high-technology firms have been producing increasingly sophisticated and higher-value-added products, while the share of the labor-intensive, low-tech industries has steadily declined. During the 1982–92 period, manufacturing industry moved away from low-value-added sectors, as evidenced by the following statistics: (1) while the output of heavy industry grew by 150.1 percent, light industrial output rose by only 48.8 percent; and (2) in 1992, only 8.5 percent of factories were producing textiles, 6.8 percent were processing food, and 4.7 percent were manufacturing wood products, down from 11.6, 11.5, and 7.9 percent, respectively.[24]

A similar shift away from low-value-added products can be observed in exports. In 1992, the share of highly technology-intensive products in total exports was nearly 30 percent, up from 18.4 percent in 1986. Conversely, products with high labor intensity accounted for 38.8 percent of total exports in 1993, down from 41 percent in 1990 and 47 percent in 1986.[25]

Despite these advances, the shift to high-tech industrialization has yet to produce the modernization envisaged by the government for several reasons. First, the rapid rate of technological change and increasing protectionism in industrialized countries have made it difficult for Taiwanese firms to gain access to the kind of cutting-edge technologies necessary for the kind of breakthrough industries that the government favors. Second, most of the small and medium enterprises that make up Taiwanese industry are not in a position to subsidize the R&D and skill training that are necessary to make the shift to high technology. Third, some of the targeted strategic industries, such as electronics, are dominated by rapid technological change and are costly to undertake. As a result, many Taiwanese producers are still very much in the business of assem-

---

24. *Oxford Analytica,* March 14, 1994. Oxford: Oxford Analytica.

25. Chi Schive, *Taiwan's Economic Role in East Asia* (Washington, D.C.: Center for Strategic and International Studies, 1995), 12.

bling components and computer peripherals, and most high-tech inputs are still being imported.

## IV. Governance and Institutions

In order to be successfully implemented, economic policies require strong, effective institutions that are able to achieve the priorities expressed by the top political and economic leadership as well as a dynamic and supportive private sector response. This section examines how the structure and operation of government supported the effective implementation of economic policies.

### The Mainland Government Heritage

Before examining the structure and operation of government in Taiwan, it is helpful to identify the nonpolicy factors or conditions that have contributed to effective state intervention in the economy.

First, the crisis conditions that prevailed in postwar Taiwan—rampant inflation, depleted savings, foreign trade deficits, the social and economic pressures of nearly two million refugees from China, and a weak private sector—both facilitated and necessitated a strong government role in the economy.

Second, the circumstances of the Nationalists' arrival on Taiwan favored the establishment of a dominant one-party state and enabled the government to operate with the autonomy and authority needed for effective intervention. Coupled with the absence of a unified local opposition, the Nationalists' "outsider" status vis-à-vis Taiwanese society effectively cleared the path for the Kuomintang to take full control of political and economic affairs.

Third, the Kuomintang's governing ideology called for the government to assume a leading role in the economy. Based on Nationalist leader Sun Yat-sen's "Three Principles" of nationalism, equality, and welfare, this ideology combined primary reliance on markets with a socialist orientation with respect to social issues. In addition, the Kuomintang's commitment to equity and welfare was reinforced by the lessons of its mainland defeat and justified from the outset a strong role for the government through policies designed to promote social and economic growth.

Fourth, a host of external factors over time provided the rationale for strong government involvement in Taiwan's economic affairs. During the 1950s and 1960s, the ever-present threat of Communist China acted as a strong bond that united state and society in the common task of building a strong economy. The series of external shocks that followed in the 1970s and 1980s—diplomatic isolation, the world oil crises, loss of international competitiveness, and rising protectionism on the part of major trading partners—further reinforced the rationale for cooperating with the state in an uncertain world economy.

Finally, the contribution of cultural tradition to a strong, autocratic government cannot be ignored. The paternalistic relationship between state and society in Confucian culture has enabled the state to operate with wide authority in Taiwan. It can be argued that, from the 1950s until the late 1970s, Taiwanese society was more or less acquiescent with state policies as long as the government successfully delivered economic prosperity and efficient services and that only since the 1980s has the private sector become more politically vocal and demanding.

While these factors in themselves do not make effective government policies or guarantee their successful implementation, the combination of these historical, ideological, social, and cultural circumstances created an environment in which the interaction between government and society, as well as within the government itself, enabled institutions to implement policy effectively.

### Key Policymakers

The success of economic policies in Taiwan owes much to the stability, cohesiveness, and quality of the top political and economic leadership. During the first three decades of Taiwan's postwar development, economic policy making was dominated by a small group of technocrats with a strong commitment to economic growth and public service. Indeed, from the early 1950s until the mid-1980s, no more than a handful of men had decision-making authority over economic policy—including fiscal, monetary, financial, industrial, and trade policy.

A combination of shared experiences, common educational background, and long-standing relationships as colleagues in the economic policy-making structure created an unusually strong bond among top government officials, which in turn helped in the development of a broad consensus among them on the general goals of economic development. All were middle-class mainlanders with university-level education, some of it acquired overseas, primarily in the United States and Western Europe. All had worked their way up the government service ladder in a variety of posts, hence reflecting Taiwan's true meritocratic system. And all were known for their moral integrity, deep commitment to public service, and loyalty to the Kuomintang.

An interesting characteristic of key Taiwanese policymakers during the postwar era was their orientation toward practical results rather than ideological or political goals. Their relatively pragmatic style of economic management may owe something to the fact that a number of them were trained not in economics or business but in engineering and science. For example, C. K. Yen, who held the positions of minister of finance, governor of the Bank of Taiwan, provincial governor, prime minister, and briefly president of the Republic over a period of three decades, began his career as a chemist and mathematician. K. Y. Yin, the economic "czar" throughout the 1950s, was an electrical engineer, as was Y. S. Sun, who held the economic affairs portfolio before serving as prime minister from 1978 to 1984. K. T. Li, minister of economic affairs and finance for more than a decade and now special adviser to the president, was trained as a physicist in Great Britain.

For the most part, top policymakers believed in the principle of a free economy combined with various degrees and types of state intervention. In their view, the government should play a leading role to accelerate economic development and only when "enough people with leadership qualities have been fostered, [should] the leadership in economic development naturally be transferred from the state to society."[26] This thinking in many ways reflects the traditional Confucian concept of government, which holds that the state, much like a parent, "knows best" and is therefore justified in assuming a leadership role.

## The Economic Bureaucracy

Taiwan has a meritocratic system that is reflected in a highly committed and well-qualified civil service. The bureaucracy of core economic agencies is recruited through the highly competitive civil service examination, which is the responsibility of the Examination Yuan, one of the five branches of government. Because of the honor and prestige with which public service is regarded, many university graduates go directly into government service or public enterprises. While government salaries used to be low, they are now considered generally competitive with those offered in the private sector.

An interesting feature of the economic bureaucracy in Taiwan is that, until the last decade, there was very little inflow or outflow (even postretirement) of personnel to and from the private sector. However, many top government officials have previous working experience in state-owned enterprises before they enter government service. Although there is no direct evidence of it, it could be argued that weak and distant ties between public officials and private industry diminished the opportunity for corruption and nepotism and contributed to a more efficient government.

Much of the bureaucracy of core economic agencies consists of a brain trust of young, mostly Western-educated individuals known for their pragmatic approach to policy formulation and implementation. A look at Taiwan's core

---

26. Chien-kuo Pang, *The State and Economic Transformation: The Taiwan Case* (New York: Garland Publishing, 1992), 97.

economic agencies shows a predominance of economists and engineers. For example, the Industrial Development Bureau of the Ministry of Economic Affairs is dominated by engineers, while the latter are outnumbered by economists in the Council for Economic Development and Planning. The staff of the influential Sectoral Planning Division consists almost entirely of engineers. While it is difficult to ascertain the extent to which this engineering background made a difference, it has probably contributed to the flexible, pragmatic, "can-do" attitude of Taiwanese policymakers.

## Institutional Innovations

A distinctive feature of Taiwan's economic bureaucracy was the establishment of supraministerial and independent or semi-independent organs to implement specific aspects of economic policy. These pilot agencies played an important role in Taiwan's economic development, particularly during the early period of reconstruction. Their financial and bureaucratic autonomy gave them the authority to bypass many bureaucratic bottlenecks and carry out policies quickly and effectively. Although these institutions have been restructured many times over the last 40 years, some of them remain very influential. One such key institution was the Joint U.S.-Taiwanese Commission for Rural Reconstruction (JCRR). Created in 1948 to promote agricultural and rural development through the use of U.S. aid, the JCRR played an instrumental role in the success of land reform and agricultural development in Taiwan.

Another such institution was the Council on U.S. Aid (CUSA), which was established in 1948 to administer U.S. aid to the Nationalist government on mainland China. CUSA was one of the first institutions created under the Marshall Plan principle, which required the establishment of a host-country counterpart to the local U.S. aid mission. Organizationally, CUSA operated as a semiautonomous entity rather than under the jurisdiction of line ministries, a status that greatly enhanced its ability to act decisively in coordinating development policies. CUSA was reorganized several times through the years and is now the Council for Economic Planning and Development (CEPD), the leading economic planning agency.

A third institution is the current Industrial Development Board (IDB), the key government agency responsible for industrial development policy and one of the main bureaus of the Ministry of Economic Affairs. IDB first emerged in the early 1950s as the Industrial Development Commission of the Economic Stabilization Board, which had responsibility for industrial development in Taiwan. Like other pilot agencies, it operated outside the regular machinery of line ministries and was fairly independent. One of the reasons IDB has consistently functioned with a high degree of coherence and effectiveness may be the fact that it oversees trade and foreign investment policies as well as domestic industrial policy, which has allowed it to coordinate policies on both the domestic and international fronts.

Because of the wide power and authority given to these independent agencies, economic bureaucrats were able to implement policies without much resistance from the rest of the civilian administration. Moreover, the financial autonomy of these agencies during the early period of reconstruction enabled them to recruit qualified individuals with higher salaries.

## Other Special Institutional Arrangements

Other special arrangements in the economic policy-making structure have also facilitated effective policy implementation in Taiwan. First, the agencies concerned with industrial policy—the IDB and the CEPD—have benefited from the direct involvement of the president and the prime minister, who in a number of instances used to head one or more of the core economic agencies. As a result, industrial issues have always received strong consideration in the formulation of macroeconomic policies.

Second, as mentioned earlier, the inclusion of both trade and industrial policies within the IDB has given it wide authority and power, especially in an economy where international trade has such important linkages with domestic production. It has also contributed to greater coherence in policy formulation and implementation than would have been the case if these had been handled by separate agencies.

Third, in terms of personnel, top decision makers in industrial policy generally reached their positions only after long experience in several agencies and public enterprises, during which time they built close relationships with a stable core of like-minded colleagues. These ties proved helpful in overcoming the difficulties of horizontal communication across ministries, agencies, and commissions, and they provide a basis for consensus on the broad objectives of industrial policy.

Fourth, the feature of overlapping and sequential memberships—for example, between the cabinet and other key economic agencies within the state—further reinforces this basis for coordination.[27] The overlap of officers in the top echelons of the economic bureaucracy contributed to removing the barriers that separated these organizations and reduced conflicts between the various agencies.[28]

---

27. Wade, *Governing the Market*, 225.
28. Pang, *The State and Economic Transformation*, 59.

## V.  Public-Private Sector Relations

### The Private Sector

This section traces the evolution of the private sector in Taiwan and the changing relationship between the public and the private sectors. Prior to 1949, the indigenous private sector in Taiwan was weak and undeveloped. During the Japanese occupation, key industries were controlled by the Japanese. Upon the Nationalists' arrival in 1949, the new government nationalized Japanese assets, which constituted a dominant portion of all industries in Taiwan. Thus, the Taiwanese economy during the early 1950s was characterized by a relatively large public sector and a small-scale private sector.

*Local Capitalists.* The mid-1950s saw the emergence of a new generation of industrial capitalists in Taiwan. As described in section III, land reform enabled former landowners to cash in their stocks in state-owned enterprises and shift their investment from agriculture to the industrial sector, thus becoming Taiwan's first industrialists. The main beneficiaries of this scheme were the wealthy Taiwanese landowning families who had accumulated shares in state enterprises as compensation for compulsorily purchased land. In 1954, the government began to transfer these firms to private ownership.

Government assistance programs during the import substitution period were also instrumental in launching a number of entrepreneurs. Among the best-known beneficiaries of these programs are Wu San-lien, who established the Taiwan Textile Corporation, and Y. C. Wang, a Taiwanese lumberyard owner who manufactured polyvinyl chloride in a plant financed by the U.S. Agency for International Development (USAID) and later established Formosa Plastics, one of Taiwan's most successful conglomerates. By taking advantage of government-granted subsidies and raw materials for the textiles and plastics industries, they were able to develop their businesses into successful and diversified conglomerates.

A new, much larger wave of local entrepreneurs emerged in the 1960s in response to export incentives. Taking advantage of the open world market and the financial and fiscal opportunities offered by the government, tens of thousands of entrepreneurs invested in small- and medium-sized firms.

*Mainland Industrialists.* The Taiwanese private sector received a considerable boost from the arrival of mainland industrialists in the wake of the 1949 exodus. Many were wealthy businessmen who had owned successful textile and flour milling industries in Shanghai and Shandong and had close connections with the Nationalist Party. They were the main beneficiaries of the government's USAID-sponsored program to promote industrial development, and they successfully reestablished their businesses and expertise, contributing to the development of the textiles and flour milling industries in Taiwan.

*Overseas Chinese.* Overseas Chinese have played a very special role in Taiwan's economic development. Conscious of its delicate status vis-à-vis China, the Taiwanese government has actively courted the support of the estimated 28 million ethnic Chinese living overseas. Besides conferring ideological legitimacy on the government, many overseas Chinese serve as the eyes, ears, and hands of the Taiwanese economy in world markets. Initially, overseas Chinese served as important marketing channels for Taiwanese manufacturers, using the local ethnic Chinese network to market Taiwanese products. In the 1960s and 1970s, overseas Chinese were also an important source of foreign investment in Taiwan. In the last decade, however, overseas Chinese have assumed a new importance as a critical source of brain power for Taiwan's high-tech drive. As mentioned in section III, a large number of overseas Taiwanese have decided to go back to Taiwan to set up high-tech firms or work in government research institutions, bringing with them valuable technical expertise acquired from leading firms such as AT&T, IBM, and Texas Instruments. The extended overseas Chinese network also provides a valuable source of market information for local manufacturers, and as such they are an important part of the government's strategy of encouraging alliances between domestic and foreign firms as a means of obtaining access to more advanced technology and new markets.[29]

## Relations between the Public and the Private Sectors

In contrast to Japan and Korea, the public and the private sectors in Taiwan have not enjoyed a particularly close interaction due to the lack of historical and social ties between the Nationalist government and the islander population. The cleavage between the public and private sectors in Taiwan can be traced back to the Nationalists' resolve to create a greater distance between the government and the private sector and not be beholden to private influence. Still stung from their defeat by the Communists, the Nationalists were concerned that wealth accumulation in the hands of a few urban industrialists would lead to the large disparities in income that could provide justification for popular discontent and criticism of the regime. Thus, upon arriving in Taiwan, the regime already nurtured a strong antibusiness bias, which was partly based on the fear that big business would accumulate too much power, possibly weakening the authority of the government and threatening its ability to implement policies successfully.

As a result, the relationship between the public and the private sectors in Taiwan was marked, until recently, by a formality and distance uncharacteristic of other East Asian countries. For example, economic policymakers in Taiwan

---

29. See Dahlman and Sananikone, *Technology Strategy,* 1990.

were not allowed to engage in their own businesses for fear of conveying the perception of corruption. It was not until 1981 that the cabinet finally included members with a private sector background, and the same was true for key economic policy-making agencies such as the Advisory Council to the CEPD and the Central Standing Committee. Weak public-private sector relations made bargaining with private groups particularly difficult, and as a result the government relied primarily on the network of state enterprises and public research and service organizations to guide industrial policy.

Over the past 40 years, relations between the public and the private sectors have evolved considerably and redefined the role of the government in the market. Initially, the government pursued economic objectives by using the state to effect private sector compliance with state policies through a combination of incorporation and repression. Partly because of its exogenous status and partly because it was concerned that native Taiwanese would exert too much influence on economic policies, the government kept control of the political and economic administration in the hands of a small group of mainlanders. Yet it also recognized that preventing dissent alone was not a viable strategy for a population that was 80 percent native Taiwanese and only 20 percent mainlanders. Consequently, the government attempted to win the active support of the islander population by assimilating it into the regime. It accomplished this essentially by incorporating Taiwanese into the economic life of Taiwan, while disallowing, until quite recently, their participation and influence in the political arena. The main policy instruments used were, first, land reform, which gave disfranchised tenant farmers and large landowners a new stake in the economy, and second, export promotion, which channeled the energy of the Taiwanese population into the economic sphere by providing wide incentives. Thus, economic development and prosperity have been the government's primary means of ensuring support from the private sector.

With the passage of time, however, and the coming of age of a new generation of Taiwanese who were born on the island after 1949 and grew up under the Nationalist government, the distance between the private and the public sectors has attenuated significantly. More importantly, economic prosperity is no longer a sufficient means of social consensus building. In the last decade, Taiwanese politics has been dominated by the struggle between a Kuomintang old guard upholding old-style authoritarianism and a Taiwanese society demanding greater participation in the political process. In many respects, these political changes stem directly from Taiwan's economic success. Higher living standards, exposure to foreign ideas, and education have created rising expectations and increased public demand for a better quality of life, including greater political participation, better environmental and consumer protection, and greater government accountability. Increasingly there are calls for greater social spending in areas such as health insurance, pension schemes, and education. Since the mid-1980s, the government has responded to the shifting structure of Taiwanese society by allowing more participatory policies. Since martial law was lifted in 1987, Taiwan has gained the basic elements of a democracy—legal opposition parties, the right to organize political demonstrations, freedom of the press, and a broader electoral process. Taiwan's much-anticipated first direct presidential election in 1996 marks the culmination of Taiwan's changing political process.

## VI.  The Role of Government Intervention
## in Taiwan's Economic Development

The preceding sections have attempted to provide a brief overview of the different stages, policy responses, and economic outcomes in the development of the Taiwanese economy, with consideration given to the initial conditions and special characteristics of governance, institutions, and public-private sector interaction that may have facilitated or supported effective government intervention in the economy. This section will address the central objective of this essay—the role of government intervention in industrial and trade policy, financial policy, and human capital and labor markets—by revisiting Taiwan's economic development from this functional perspective.

### Industrial and Trade Policy

As documented in section III and supported by a number of studies, most notably Robert Wade's highly acclaimed study of the role of the government in East Asian industrialization,[30] the government has intervened actively and frequently in Taiwan's economic development. Intervention has not involved extremely large amounts of government spending primarily because the government has intervened selectively and adjusted its intervention over time (table 2.3).

In evaluating the success of the government's selective intervention, two issues need to be addressed.[31] The first is the extent to which selective intervention actually led firms to invest in the promoted sectors. The second is the degree to which these sectors were the right ones to promote. As both the sectors promoted and the instruments used have varied over time, it is necessary to distinguish the selective intervention policies that were used during each phase of economic development.

During the land reform and reconstruction period (1949–52), the government promoted the agricultural sector through land reform and the provision of

---

30. Wade, *Governing the Market.*
31. Howard Pack, "The Role of Industrial Policy in Taiwan's Industrial Development," mimeo, 1992.

agricultural extension services. However, it taxed the agricultural sector by keeping agricultural prices low and through the rice for fertilizer barter program. It also redirected resources to a new, nonagricultural, entrepreneurial class and promoted industrialization by transferring the bulk of formerly Japanese-owned industries to the private sector. During the import substitution period (1953–58), the government encouraged the development of import substituting industries such as textiles, including cotton and synthetic fibers, by using the multiple exchange rate system and import controls. It is arguable that during these first two phases of Taiwan's economic development, selective government intervention made a significant impact on industrial development because the instruments used were direct, specific, and powerful.

In the third period (1958–72), the government shifted to more functional support for export-oriented industries through fiscal and financial incentives

**TABLE 2.3.    Shifting Focus and Instruments of Selective Intervention over Time**

| Period | Promoted Sectors | Main Instruments |
| --- | --- | --- |
| Land reform and reconstruction (1949–52) | Agriculture fertilizers, other basic industries, cement | Land reform and agricultural extension, public ownership, transfer of Japanese-owned assets to expropriated landowners |
| Import substitution (1953–57) | Textiles, other consumer goods | Tariff protection and nontariff barriers, multiple exchange rates |
| Export promotion (1958–72) | Exporting sectors, especially apparel, consumer electronics, refrigerators, watches and clocks | Rebates on import duties, tax reductions and exemptions, subsidized loans, export processing zones, undervalued exchange rate, attracting foreign investment, export market information |
| | Chemicals, fertilizers, basic metals, automobiles | Tariff protection and nontariff barriers |
| Industrial consolidation (1973–1980) | Petrochemicals, steel, nuclear power, shipbuilding, automobiles | Direct public ownership and trade protection |
| | Machine tools, electrical machinery, consumer electronics, automation industry | Tariff protection and nontariff barriers, consolidation of ITRI, expansion of China Productivity Center with Automation Task Force |
| High-tech. modernization (1981–present) | Information industries, machinery, precision instruments, biotechnology, electro-optics, environmental technology | Tax rebates and exemptions, low-interest loans, equity and venture capital, import duty rebates, Science-Based Industrial Park, R&D subsidies, brand development subsidies |

generally and by using a unified and undervalued exchange rate (fig. 2.5). However, it also targeted some specific industries for exports and encouraged export-oriented foreign investment. At the same time, protection of domestic production was not entirely eliminated, although it was lowered somewhat. Rather, duty-drawback systems and schemes such as export processing zones were used to put exporters on a more advantageous footing in the export market, while the domestic market continued to be protected. The government also promoted some export-related intermediary industries, and a few import substituting industries such as automobiles. It is clear that there was a very successful response to the export promotion strategy, but without additional information than is currently available it is difficult to measure the extent to which targeted export industries responded to specific incentives over and above their general response to the functional support the government provided to exports in general.

During the industrial consolidation period (1973–80), the government actually increased protection to promote secondary import substitution and created new public enterprises to implement its policy of secondary import substitution in heavy industry. There was also growth in some of the other capital goods industries promoted, but it is not clear how important the role of government was in enticing them to set up and expand.

During the current high-tech modernization period (1986–present), the government has promoted high-technology industrialization by targeting the development of "strategic" industries such as biotechnology, information, materials, production automation, and electro-optics. It must be noted, however, that, while the government has played an active role in targeting various industrial sectors for growth, state intervention has been more suggestive than mandatory, providing incentives or disincentives rather than direct fiats. As in the case of the industrial consolidation phase, it is difficult to determine how important the special incentives were in promoting targeted industries. One way of measuring the impact of government intervention in the industrial consolidation and high-tech periods is to compare the share of value added of the broad industrial sectors in Taiwan with the "normal" shares that would be expected of an economy with its per capita income using a Chenery-Syrquin type of regression of the structure of industry at different levels of development.[32] Such a comparison was conducted by Howard Pack in "The Role of Industrial Policy in Taiwan's Development," and table 2.4 is computed based on his results. Chemicals and rubber, which were heavily promoted during the consolidation stage, indeed show a greater than expected share, but surprisingly

32. Hollis B. Chenery and Moshe Syrquin, "Typical Patterns of Transformation," in *Industrialization and Growth: A Comparative Study,* edited by H. Chenery, S. Robinson, and M. Syrquin (New York: Oxford University Press, 1986).

the shares of metal products and machinery and electrical equipment (which typically would encompass the high-tech sectors) are low compared with expected values. On the other hand, textiles and clothing, and especially "others" (primarily light manufactures), stand out with their greater than expected shares. These two sectors represent the labor-intensive sectors that were promoted during the initial export promotion stage.[33]

Another way of evaluating the impact of selective government intervention on industry, and of addressing the issue of whether these were the right sectors to promote, is to look at the evolution of the sectoral structure of manufacturing production and the characteristics of these sectors in Taiwan, including their rate of total productivity growth. This was also done by Pack, and his results are reproduced in table 2.5.

From this table, it is possible to observe that, except for apparel, the sectors demonstrating the fastest growth are essentially those that were promoted during the heavy industry consolidation and high-tech phases—electrical equipment (which includes electronics) and heavy industry. However, despite their rapid growth, the aggregate of these sectors did not grow as fast as it did in other countries because the total share of these sectors was below that predicted by the Chenery-Syrquin regression (table 2.4). According to Pack, the three sectors that grew most rapidly (apparel, electrical equipment, and metal products) were not particularly high in technology, as suggested by their characteristics in terms of wages, value added per worker, or capital to labor ratio. His conclusion is that industrial policy was not effective in inducing

**TABLE 2.4.  Comparison of the Sectoral Structure of Value Added in Taiwan with the Structure Predicted by Chenery-Syrquin Regressions**

|  | 1986 Normal | 1986 Taiwan | Taiwan/Normal |
|---|---|---|---|
| Food and beverages | .17 | .11 | .40 |
| Textiles and clothing | .13 | .16 | 1.23 |
| Wood and wood products | .04 | .03 | .75 |
| Paper and printing | .07 | .04 | .57 |
| Chemicals and rubber | .17 | .23 | 1.35 |
| Nonmetallic minerals | .05 | .03 | .40 |
| Basic metals | .08 | .06 | .75 |
| Metal products and machinery and electrical equipment | .27 | .18 | .67 |
| Other | .02 | .13 | 6.50 |

Source: Pack, "The Role of Industrial Policy," table 5.

33. It should be noted that these structural comparisons have been made at a very high level of aggregation and that a more detailed comparison might show different results.

high-technology sectors to grow and did not focus on industrial sectors exhibiting higher total factor productivity growth (TFP). While this is correct, we propose a slightly broader interpretation of industrial policy. The main difference in our interpretation is that we do not narrow government selectivity to the promotion of high-tech sectors, since the shift to high-tech industrialization only came about a little more than 10 years ago, and its impact is therefore, to some extent, still too premature to assess. During earlier periods, particularly during the initial export promotion phase, the government promoted more labor-intensive sectors, which did grow very fast and demonstrated high rates of TFP. Noting that there is a positive correlation between the high-growth sectors and the estimated rates of TFP growth,[34] we suggest that, in general, the sectors promoted by the government did exhibit significant growth and higher rates of TFP growth. Looking back to the early 1950s, when the government explicitly promoted productivity increases in the agricultural sector and promoted the textiles sector (which has maintained good TFP performance even in later periods), we would argue that by and large the government has intervened quite successfully, although there have been some examples of poor perfor-

**TABLE 2.5. The Evolution of Sectors and Their Characteristics**

| Sector | VA 86/66 | N86/66 | Average W | VA/N | K/L | A* |
|---|---|---|---|---|---|---|
| Apparel | 2.67 | 1.14 | 0.90 | 1.00 | 0.31 | 10.5 |
| Electrical equipment | 2.60 | 1.59 | 0.87 | 0.77 | 0.75 | 7.1 |
| Metal products | 2.50 | 1.80 | 0.86 | 0.66 | 0.65 | 4.4 |
| Basic metals | 2.00 | 1.16 | 1.28 | 2.07 | 3.99 | 7.2 |
| Transportation equipment | 1.50 | 1.59 | 1.13 | 1.30 | 1.23 | 2.7 |
| Precision instruments | 1.40 | 1.63 | 0.89 | 0.98 | 0.43 | 11.0 |
| Chemical products | 1.10 | 1.16 | 1.39 | 1.83 | 2.13 | 3.3 |
| Rubber | 1.00 | 0.92 | 1.05 | 0.60 | 0.68 | 6.3 |
| Machinery | 1.00 | 0.84 | 0.97 | 0.70 | 0.77 | 6.7 |
| Plastics | 0.98 | 10.00 | 0.62 | 0.52 | — | 0.0 |
| Paper and pulp products | 0.80 | 0.95 | 0.99 | 0.98 | 1.16 | 2.3 |
| Wood products | 0.75 | 0.69 | 0.85 | 0.63 | 0.58 | 0.3 |
| Textiles | 0.67 | 0.56 | 1.07 | 0.76 | 1.05 | 7.6 |
| Petroleum products | 0.63 | 0.69 | 1.43 | 7.95 | 7.85 | 0.0 |
| Nonmetallic minerals | 0.43 | 0.74 | 0.93 | 0.76 | 1.46 | 2.4 |
| Food, beverages | 0.38 | 0.48 | 1.07 | 1.91 | 1.64 | 2.0 |

*Source:* Pack, "The Role of Industrial Policy," table 3.

*Note:* VA = value added; N = number of workers; W = wages; VA/N = value added per worker; K/L = capital-to-labor ratio; A* = technology parameter.

34. Pack regressed the percentage of change in value added shown in table 2.5 against the estimated rates of TFP growth A* and found a positive correlation significant at the .01 level.

mance, such as, for example, in the automobile sector. In addition, we would emphasize that the sectors promoted varied according to the stage of economic development, and that, overall, the sectors promoted appeared to have made economic sense given the state of the economy during each stage.

Looking at Taiwan's postwar economy as a whole, the most important government intervention was the switch to export-oriented industrialization in the late 1950s and the strong functional support given to exports. This appears to have been accomplished primarily through the use of an undervalued exchange rate (fig. 2.5), duty drawbacks and other mechanisms that gave exporters access to inputs at world market prices, and the allocation of export credit. Government intervention also included extensive investments in export-related physical infrastructure (ports, airports, internal road transport, and export processing zones) and export-promotion institutions such as the China External Trade Council (CETRA).

The emphasis on exports and developing foreign linkages has also been instrumental in raising TFP. There have been three factors at play in this context. First, Taiwanese firms have had to produce at world levels of cost and quality. Second, operating in foreign markets has forced producers to scan the market continuously for more advanced products and technology. Third, local producers and exporters acquire a tremendous amount of technological and market information by trading in world markets—this includes design, technical specifications, and technical assistance from foreign buyers, traders, suppliers, or foreign venture partners.[35]

In addition, the government invested heavily in technological infrastructure as part of its export and productivity increasing drive. Initially, these efforts focused on norms, standards, quality control, and industrial extension service institutes such as the China Productivity Center. In the 1970s and 1980s, these were expanded to research institutes such as the Industrial Technology Research Institute and to technical training and engineering. Later, the government included specific infrastructures to promote high-technology research and development such as the establishment of the Science-Based Industrial Park in Hsinshu.[36]

## The Financial Sector

The Taiwanese government has used the the financial sector actively as a means of fostering and guiding industrial development. This section examines the basic characteristics of the financial sector in Taiwan. The financial sector

---

35. For a discussion of the technological externalities deriving from outward orientation, see Howard Pack, "Exports and Productivity Growth: The Case of Taiwan," mimeo, 1992.

36. For a discussion of Taiwan's technology strategy, see Dahlman and Sananikone *Technology Strategy,* 1990.

has been characterized by high savings and investment, the preponderance of loan-based financing, a dominance of government-owned banks, controlled interest rates, directed credit, and a large and active curb market.

*High Savings and Investment.* One of the most striking characteristics of Taiwan's economic development has been its high savings rates. Between 1953 to 1980, the ratio of gross savings to GNP increased from 14 to 32 percent. The ratio of investment to GNP rose in line with the increase in the savings ratio until 1981 when the share of domestic investment started to fall even though the savings rate remained high (fig. 2.4).

What were the factors underlying the high rate of savings? First, through virtually all of the postwar period, there has been a positive real interest rate on savings as a result of high nominal interest rates and low inflation (table 2.6). Second, the rapid growth of income and relative equal income distribution have facilitated savings. Third, the traditional frugality of the Chinese and the desire to provide against uncertainty, combined with Taiwan's relatively weak social security and pension system, also contributed to a high savings rate. Fourth, because consumer lending was repressed for a very long time, consumers needed to save in order to be able to make large purchases such as automobiles and housing.

Fifth, state-owned enterprises and government institutions also contributed to savings (app., table A2.4). These two sectors accounted for about 50 percent of gross national savings in 1960, 30 percent in 1970, 31 percent in 1980, and 27 percent in 1988. This has been possible because the government has run a fiscal surplus for most years since the mid-1960s. At the end of 1990, net national borrowing was just 2.3 percent of GNP, and all of that debt was domestic. Sixth, the government has provided tax incentives for savings. Between 1960 and 1980, the Statute for the Encouragement of Investment provided income tax exemptions for interest from two-year or longer-term deposits. In addition, since 1965, the interest from postal passbook accounts has been exempted from income tax. Also, between 1981 and 1990, combined interest and dividend income of up to NT$360,000 was exempted from income tax. Finally, a considerable portion of household savings consists of "forced" savings by the owners of small and medium enterprises because of the discrimination in access to formal credit markets (see subsection 6).[37]

*The Preponderance of Loan-Based Financing.* Due to the absence of other financial instruments, the financial sector in Taiwan has been heavily biased toward bank-based financing. Between 1961 and 1981 and 1986 and 1988, the ratio of bank loans to GDP grew from 32 to 82 percent (table 2.6).[38]

---

37. Paul C. H. Chiu, "Money and Financial Markets: The Domestic Perspective," in *Taiwan: From Developing to Mature Economy,* edited by Gus Ranis (Boulder: Westview Press, 1992).

38. Bank deposits to GDP, however, grew faster, increasing their share from 33 to 130 percent over the same period and leading to a fall in the ratio of loans to deposits in the 1980s.

On the other hand, the market value of listed stocks as a percentage of GDP remained below 15 percent of GDP through 1985, until the big boom in the stock market. Government and corporate bond financing remained very small, reaching a maximum of less then 7 percent in 1986–88.[39]

*State-Dominated Banking Sector.* The banking sector in Taiwan consists of six groups: The Central Bank, domestic banks, local branches of foreign banks, and three other types of local deposit-taking banks (medium-scale business banks, credit cooperatives, and the credit departments of the farmers' and fishermen's associations).[40]

Most of the central banking functions were delegated to the Bank of Taiwan from 1949 until July 1961, when the Central Bank of China (CBC) was reactivated. The basic objectives of the CBC have been to stabilize the value of the currency, promote financial stability, and provide guidance to banking institutions. Its instruments have included the rediscount rate, required reserve ratios, the exchange rate, open market operations, and selective credit controls (including control of interest rates, maximum loan ratios on collaterals, size of the down payment, and duration of bank credit for productive investment). In

**TABLE 2.6.   Key Indicators of Financial Deepening, 1961–88**

|  | 1961–65 | 1966–70 | 1971–75 | 1976–80 | 1981–85 | 1986–88 |
|---|---|---|---|---|---|---|
| Wholesale price index (% change) | 2.11 | 1.89 | 12.57 | 8.88 | 0.83 | −2.72 |
| Interest rate on one-year deposits | 11.78 | 9.30 | 10.90 | 10.95 | 9.80 | 5.20 |
| Real return on one-year deposits | 9.67 | 7.90 | −1.67 | 2.07 | 8.97 | 7.92 |
| Banking loans (L)/GDP (%) | 32.33 | 40.85 | 51.69 | 67.13 | 76.73 | 81.92 |
| Banking deposits (D)/GDP (%) | 32.90 | 41.35 | 52.05 | 67.21 | 83.27 | 130.23 |
| L/D (%) | 98.98 | 98.76 | 99.08 | 100.10 | 94.28 | 62.81 |
| Gross capital formation (K)/GDP (%) | 19.49 | 24.19 | 30.10 | 30.71 | 23.96 | 20.45 |
| Gross national savings (S)/GDP (%) | 18.71 | 23.37 | 30.68 | 32.88 | 32.34 | 37.99 |
| K/S (%) | 104.78 | 103.55 | 98.84 | 93.50 | 74.67 | 54.24 |
| AL/AK (%) | 27.39 | 27.63 | 40.19 | 40.13 | 37.83 | 63.12 |
| AD/AS (%) | 32.05 | 27.48 | 37.60 | 37.79 | 46.75 | 67.22 |
| Market value of listed stocks/GDP (%) | 15.93 | 8.29 | 12.00 | 14.61 | 14.01 | 52.99 |
| Government & corporate bonds outstanding/GDP (%) | 1.99 | 4.44 | 2.84 | 3.05 | 4.43 | 6.76 |

*Source:* Kuo-hsing Chang, "Financial Institutions and Deepening in Taiwan, ROC," in "The Central Bank of China and the Financial Market," mimeo, 1990.

*Note:* Statistics in the table are averages of the end-of-year percentage figures.

---

39. Chang Kuo-hsing. 1990. "Financial Institutions and Deepening in Taiwan, ROC," in *The Central Bank of China and the Financial Market,* mimeo. 19.

40. Nonbanking institutions consist of the Postal Savings System, investment and trust companies, and insurance companies. Only the Postal Savings System will be covered here, as it is a key source of capturing funds for medium- and long-term lending.

addition, the CBC has also pursued selective promotion of some economic activities. For example, to promote exports, the government established in 1974 a special financing facility to provide credit for commercial banks for working capital loans to export industries. This facility provided credit at a rate that has generally been the lowest discount rate and lower than bank deposit rates (see also subsection 5 for the differential between general lending rates and lending rates for exports).[41]

The domestic banks accounted for 42 percent of total assets of financial institutions (app., table A2.5). Twelve of the 16 domestic banks are government owned,[42] and they account for the largest share of total assets of the domestic banks.[43]

Until the 1980s, foreign banks played a very limited role in Taiwan, reflecting the degree of protection given to the domestic banking sector. Even as late as December 1988, their assets accounted for only 2 percent of the total assets of financial institutions in Taiwan (app., table A2.5). Initially, foreign banks were authorized to handle foreign exchange transactions and pre-export loans with borrowings from abroad. They could also accept local currency demand deposits up to 12.5 times their paid-in capital up to a maximum of NT$1 billion. In 1989, foreign banks were allowed to conduct the same operations as domestic banks were. As of October 1989, foreign banks had established 38 branch operations in Taiwan.[44]

Local deposit-taking banks include small- and medium-sized business banks,[45] credit cooperative associations, and credit departments of farmers' and fishermen's associations. In 1988, these accounted altogether for 16 percent of total assets, 18 percent of deposits, and 25 percent of the loans of all financial institutions.

While not a banking institution, the Postal Savings System (PSS) is a critical component of the financial system because it is a key source of funds for the banking sector. Established in China in 1930, the Postal Savings System did not begin operating in Taiwan until 1962. The PSS accepts savings deposits and handles local and overseas remittances but does not extend loans.

---

41. Chiu, "Money and Financial Markets," 22.

42. According to Wade, the four private banks were privatized in the wake of the U.N. de-recognition in 1971 in order to enable Taiwan to establish overseas branches of domestic banks without running into the diplomatic problems involved in asking other countries to host a government-owned bank from a nonrecognized country.

43. Chang (1990), 23.

44. Ibid., 25–26.

45. There are eight medium-sized banks in Taiwan. These evolved from mutual loans and savings companies that originated in the old, private, mutual credit unions. The largest is the Medium Business Bank of Taiwan, owned by the provincial government. Medium-sized banks play an important role in financing small, local businesses. They are not allowed to conduct banking business outside their respective regions.

It has been very important in mobilizing savings in rural and newly developed areas, drawing on some 1,200 post offices and 400 postal agencies around the country. The collected savings are redeposited with the CBC and with the three specialized domestic banks (Bank of Communications, Farmers Bank of China, and Land Bank of Taiwan) and the Medium Business Bank of Taiwan. They are then channeled into loan funds that are used to finance investment projects at preferential interest rates. In 1988, the PSS accounted for 10.4 percent of all assets of the financial system, second only to the CBC (app., table A2.5).[46]

The government's control of the financial system was strengthened by the fact that the foreign capital account of Taiwan was closed until July 1987. In 1987, each person or company was allowed to make outward remittances of up to U.S.$5 million a year and inward remittances of up to U.S.$50,000 a year. These limits have been adjusted since then, and both have been adjusted to U.S.$3 million since July 1990.[47]

*Controlled Interest Rates.* While the government managed the economy so that it paid positive interest rates on savings, it tightly controlled those savings rates and the rates at which banks could make different types of loans. Until 1975, the government controlled the absolute levels of all rates. Lending rates in the formal credit market were half or even one-third the level of those in the informal or curb market and were thus, in a way, preferential. After 1975, the government started to liberalize its control on rates in the following sequence.

July 1975   Banks were allowed flexibility in loan pricing within narrow margins set by the government.

1980   The "Essentials of Interest Rate Adjustment" liberalized rates on negotiable certificates of deposit and bank debentures, discounts on bills of exchange, and on lending foreign currency loans.

1982   Deregulation of supply of market funds: The Central Bank announced that increments in postal savings deposits from April 1982 onward should be redeposited with the four designated specialized banks rather than the Central Bank.

1985   Banks were allowed to set their own prime rates rather than follow minimum and maximum rates set by the Central Bank.

1986–89   Various steps were undertaken to liberalize ceilings on deposit rates, culminating in full liberalization in July, except that no interest could be paid on checking accounts.

46. Chang, "Financial Institutions and Deepening." 27–30.
47. Chiu, "Money and Financial Markets," 173.

1992–95    Competition in the domestic banking sector was enhanced
with new private banks. Foreign banks were allowed to
set up branches in Taiwan with no restrictions on foreign
ownership, and foreigners were allowed to own
Taiwanese stock. The New Taiwan dollar bond was issued.

The government's control over the banks also included strict lending procedures and collateral requirements and strong accountability. According to
one study, "[t]hree quarters of more of what they lend must be secured by collateral, generally in fixed assets. . . . Because Bank officials have been held
personally responsible for every penny of 'the state's money' by government
auditors, they have taken few risks."[48]

*Directed Credit.* Government ownership of banks has enabled it to direct
credit allocation. Four of the government-owned banks have developed specializations over time as part of the government's effort to direct credit toward
specific sectors. Initially set up as a commercial bank, the Bank of Communications is now chartered as a development bank with the mandate to upgrade
domestic industries and foster the development of strategic industries. The
Farmers' Bank of China finances agricultural development and rural construction. The Land Bank of Taiwan extends loans for agricultural purposes.
The Export-Import Bank of China provides risk finance for export activities,
including guarantees to exporters of plant and equipment and overseas construction projects, export insurance, country risk surveys, and credit investigations. These specialized banks mainly extend medium-term (one to seven
years) and long-term loans (beyond seven years) with the redeposits they receive from the Postal Savings System. More generally, according to Wade:

> During the 1950s and early 1960s, the banks received credit allocation
> targets for rather broadly defined sectors, supplemented by more detailed
> case-by-case instructions from planners. By the mid-1960s the banks
> were receiving lists of six to 12 industries to which priority attention
> should be given. These lists were drawn up by the planning agency, with
> the Ministries of Finance and Economic Affairs and the central bank
> having opportunities to suggest modifications. During the 1970s the banks
> themselves began to participate more in drafting the lists. Each bank was
> required to select five of six areas it wished to focus upon for the coming
> year. With the increased participation of the banks came more open ac
> knowledgement of . . . credit targeting. For example, the 1973 Annual
> Report of the Bank of Communications says, "The government has di-

48. Tyler Biggs, "Heterogeneous Firms and Efficient Financial Intermediation in Taiwan,"
in *Markets in Developing Countries: Parallel, Fragmented, and Black* (San Francisco: International Center for Economic Growth, 1992), 175.

rected the different banking institutions to provide special credit facilities for different industries." The 1974 Annual Report states, "The government has promoted a system of lead banking." To comply with this policy the Bank has done its best to satisfy the credit demands of the 21 important firms that it has been made responsible for guiding.[49]

Evidence suggests that there was a mild bias in lending toward exporters, heavy industry, and large firms (table 2.7). The bias toward exporters is evident in the fact that, although export industries accounted for roughly 40 percent of output or valued added,[50] they received more than their share of borrowing by exporters throughout the 1974–86 period. In addition, exporters received a

TABLE 2.7.   Access to Domestic Borrowing by Manufacturing Sector in Taiwan, 1974–86 (percentage)

|  | 1974–77 | 1978–82 | 1983–85 | 1986 |
|---|---|---|---|---|
| Total manufacturing[a] | 63.9 | 48.3 | 38.2 | 31.1 |
| Export industry[b] | 34.4 | 23.9 | 20.5 | 18.4 |
| Domestic industry[c] | 29.5 | 24.3 | 17.7 | 12.7 |
| Share of domestic minus export | −4.9 | 0.4 | −2.8 | −5.7 |
| Heavy industry[d] | 33.8 | 29.0 | 22.5 | 18.3 |
| Light industry[e] | 30.2 | 19.1 | 15.7 | 12.8 |
| Light minus heavy industry | −3.6 | −9.9 | −6.8 | −5.5 |
| Large manufacturing enterprises | 49.5 | 32.9 | 24.8 | 19.8 |
| Small and medium manufacturing enterprises[f] | 14.4 | 15.3 | 13.4 | 11.3 |
| Small minus large enterprises | −35.1 | −17.6 | −11.4 | −8.5 |

*Source:* Biggs, "Heterogeneous Firms," 177, based on *Financial Statistics Monthly,* various issues, and *Flow of Funds in Taiwan District, 1965–1985* (Taipei: *Economic Research Department, Central Bank of China,* ROC, Taipei, various years).

[a] Includes public and private manufacturing enterprises. The decline in manufacturing loans is mirrored by a similar increase in mortgage-based loans to individuals.

[b] Export industries are classified as textiles and apparel, wood products, metal products, export food processing, and miscellaneous manufacturing on the bases of sales-export ratios (20 percent of sales).

[c] Domestic industries are classified as domestic food processing, paper and publishing, chemicals and chemical products, and transportation equipment.

[d] Heavy industries are classified as chemicals and chemical products, nonmetallic mineral products, basic metals, metal products and petroleum, and transportation equipment.

[e] Light industries are those not classified as heavy.

[f] Based on Small and Medium Business Administration. These figures include industry, agroindustry, commerce, and services. We use the administration's percentages to estimate the totals for manufacturing enterprises. Small and medium-sized enterprises are those with less than 300 employees.

49. Wade, *Governing the Market,* 166–67.
50. Calculations for share of exporters and of heavy industry are based on the 1986 industrial census.

preferential rate that was two to six percentage points lower than the average rate on unsecured loans through the 1970s, although these rates gradually converged in the 1980s. The bias toward heavy industry is evident in that, although heavy industry accounted for only around 34 percent of output and value added, more than half the lending to manufacturing went to heavy industry during the 1974–86 period. Finally, the bias against small and medium enterprises (SMEs) is demonstrated by the fact that, even though these accounted for 50 percent of value added in the 1970s and early 1980s, they received only a quarter of the loans to manufacturing in the 1974–77 period, and about a third thereafter.

However, in spite of the bias toward large enterprises, it does not appear that public enterprises, which are generally large, received a disproportionate share of loans. A comparison of the shares of public enterprises in total domestic output with their shares in loans by demand deposit-taking banks suggests that their share of loans was roughly proportional to their share of domestic output, except for the 1961–65 period, when it was higher, and the 1986–88 period, when it was lower (app., table A2.6). During the latter period, there was a relative decrease in borrowing from government-owned enterprises. The fall in oil prices and the appreciation of the new Taiwan dollar reduced the cost of imported oil to the government-owned China Petroleum Corporation and the Taiwan Power Company, reducing their borrowing needs.[51]

*The Large and Active Curb Market.* Why, then, did the financial sector in Taiwan function so well in meeting the needs of the private sector despite a government-controlled financial sector and the lack of other financial instruments? A key reason was the existence of an informal curb market that functioned in parallel to the formal financial sector. Between 1970 and 1980, Taiwan's curb market developed rapidly, accounting for approximately 30 percent of financial assets, roughly as much as financing from formal financial intermediaries.[52]

The most important instrument of the curb market was the postdated check. This was a particularly popular instrument in the Taiwanese context because the Negotiable Instruments Law enacted in 1950 made it a criminal offense to fail to honor a postdated check. In fact, it was the banks themselves—and not the curb market lenders—that initiated criminal prosecution for bad checks.[53] During the 1960s, and through 1974, the differential between short-term bank loans and loans against postdated checks was about 10 percentage points (app., table A2.7). The differential jumped to 15 points in 1974 and widened to as much as 20 points through the early 1980s as the economy

51. Chiu, "Money and Financial Markets," 166.
52. Biggs, "Heterogeneous Firms," table 10.5, 183.
53. Ibid., 182. The criminal offense was abolished in 1987.

adjusted to the effects of the second oil shock and credit tightened.[54] Even in 1986, the year before the criminal penalty for using postdated checks was abolished, the differential was 18 percentage points.

An important feature of the curb market is that it consisted mostly of lending between parties who had prior information about each other as a result of commercial interactions (i.e., between suppliers, subcontractors, equipment leasers, or members of the same subsector) or personal connections (through family or friendship). The curb market functioned as an important complement to the formal market for several reasons.[55] First, it complemented the formal credit market by providing a "small loan" function that consisted of providing credit more efficiently to SMEs than formal financial intermediaries could. This was possible because the informal credit market was based on intermediaries who had access to information about the riskiness or soundness of SME borrowers and could therefore make superior allocative decisions at lower costs than the formal market could. Another important aspect of the curb market was that it facilitated entry and exit by enabling entrepreneurs to start businesses with almost no assets and to rent or lease equipment with borrowed funds. Second, the high interest rates offered in the curb market helped to mobilize savings for productive investments. Third, the curb market also provided a "safety valve" function by accommodating borrowers squeezed out by lower-return projects because of government credit rationing. Thus, borrowers who received low-interest credit from formal institutions could relend the money through the curb market if it offered a higher rate of return than that of their project. The curb market therefore provided a way of reallocating credit from less to more profitable uses. Finally, many of the transactions in the curb market facilitated business dealings because they linked finance with production and reduced uncertainty.

Thus, although the government tightly regulated the formal financial system by repressing formal lending rates and directing credit, the system worked quite well. There appears to have been three main reasons for this. First, by and large, credit seems to have been directed toward areas that made some economic sense. This is particularly true in the case of the general allocation of credit toward export-oriented enterprises. Second, the existence of an active curb market allowed credit reallocation toward high-productivity uses and thus acted as a safety valve for gross misallocations of formal credit. Third, the degree of subsidies implicit in much of the directed credit does not appear to have been very large, as overall the banking sector has been profitable and the government has generally run fiscal surpluses.

---

54. The real difference in the rates was actually smaller since the real interest rates of credit obtained through the formal financial system was increased by bank practices such as requiring the recipient to hold part of the loan amount in checking or other accounts at the bank.

55. These arguments are developed in Biggs, "Heterogeneous Firms," 189–95.

## Human Capital and Labor Markets

*Investments in Education.* As an island nation with few natural resources, Taiwan recognized very early in its development that its most valuable assets were its people, and it has invested heavily in human capital to support economic development. Human resources development in Taiwan has benefited from the fortuitous convergence of a strong cultural orientation toward learning and the government's commitment to education as a means of accelerating economic growth.

In 1990, educational expenditures accounted for 20 percent of total government spending and 6.6 percent of GNP, placing Taiwan well ahead of developed countries such as Japan and West Germany. Private sector investment in education has increased considerably in the past 20 years as Taiwanese families have grown more affluent. In fiscal year (FY) 1990–91, the private sector's share of total educational expenditures was 17.7 percent, compared with 8.4 percent in FY1958–59. Most of five-year junior colleges in Taiwan are privately owned. Private sector participation is a cornerstone of vocational training in Taiwan (as in Korea and Singapore). Apart from alleviating the high costs of vocational and skill training for the public sector, it also ensures that training skills are relatively well matched to the needs of industry.

Human resources policies in Taiwan have been closely matched with economic policies. During the 1950s and 1960s, priority was placed on achieving universal primary education in order to educate Taiwan's growing population and prepare it for relatively unskilled work in labor-intensive industries. Since the 1980s, the government has emphasized high-level technical education to support Taiwan's move into high-tech industrialization and build up international competitiveness.

The government has taken a variety of measures to promote education in key areas of science and technology. It restructured key departments in colleges and universities, stressing the recruitment of teachers, revising curricula, and replacing old equipment. The new direction in educational policy is already reflected in a shift at the university level. Between 1967 and 1993, the percentage of students enrolled in engineering, mathematics, and computer and natural sciences combined increased from 25 percent of total students to nearly 40 percent. In the percentage of students enrolled in engineering alone, Taiwan leads not only fellow Asian Newly Industrialized Economies (NIEs) like Hong Kong and Singapore but also Japan, the United States, and Germany. Thus, at least in terms of the number of potential technical workers, Taiwan appears well equipped to meet the changing needs of industry.

In addition to developing the technical human capital base at home, the Taiwanese government has been actively seeking to expand technical manpower by recruiting directly from abroad. Over the past decade, both public and private enterprises have had considerable success in attracting overseas Chinese and Taiwanese students abroad by means of highly competitive salaries and other privileges.

Thanks to the rapid development of education, the quality of the work force has improved dramatically, and workers generally have little trouble adopting new methods of production or new technology. This constant upgrading of labor productivity has enabled Taiwan to change its comparative advantage from low-cost labor to a well-trained and highly skilled work force.

*Labor Markets.* Rapid industrialization in Taiwan has been made possible in large part because of a flexible labor market and strong government control of labor unions that was intended to keep wages low and maintain political stability. The economy absorbed as many as 400,000 people in the 1950s, during which time there was surplus labor from the agricultural sector and real wages rose very slowly. One of the most distinctive features of Taiwan's economic development was the achievement of full employment by 1971, after which time wages started to rise more rapidly. During the 1951–86 period, employment in Taiwan increased by 4.8 million persons, most of whom were absorbed by the manufacturing and retail trade sectors that grew out of the export promotion phase. In the 1980s, however, as labor-intensive exports became less competitive on the world market, increases in wages for unskilled labor began to lag behind those for skilled labor. Thus, flexible wage rates and mobile labor contributed to efficient labor utilization. Labor productivity has also increased rapidly due to the expansion of education and skill training.

The existence of a competitive labor market has been most beneficial for the efficient reallocation of factors of production, particularly in the course of rapid growth and industrialization.[56] The labor market in Taiwan has been guided by supply and demand: during the labor-intensive industrialization phase, for example, wages rose faster for unskilled than for skilled labor, reflecting the demand for workers in labor-intensive industries. This also contributed to achieving more equitable income distribution.[57]

The essential effects of growth and exports on income distribution worked as follows: a higher growth rate of income was generated for lower-income family groups by nonagricultural activities that were led by export expansion. Export expansion created markets, which in turn provided job opportunities.[58] Unskilled labor from the agricultural sector was thus absorbed into the export-oriented manufacturing sector. The rapid absorption of unskilled labor by the exporting sector at low opportunity costs contributed substantially to the rise in

---

56. Shirley W. Y. Kuo, "Economic Development in the Republic of China," in *Conference on Economic Development in the Republic of China, Taiwan,* July 22–27, 1987 (Taipei, Taiwan: Chung-Hua Institution for Economic Research, 1987), 50.

57. Ibid.

58. Ibid.

relative income of lower-income groups, leading to more equitable income distribution.

Until the mid-1970s, labor unions in Taiwan were tightly controlled by the government and operated under severe restrictions. Under martial law, strikes and collective bargaining were prohibited, and unions were under Kuomintang control, including party selection of union leaders and union activities. The government actively intervened in labor-management affairs, in part because it was concerned with providing a favorable investment climate for local and foreign businesses.

The situation changed drastically in 1987 with the lifting of martial law. At the end of 1989, there were 3,500 local unions in Taiwan with a membership of 2.53 million, corresponding to 30.5 percent of total labor. Strikes became legal for the first time in 1988. As the economy has matured, and with the growth of urban workers, the expansion of education, the internationalization of the Taiwanese economy, and the democratization of Taiwanese politics, labor has grown more active and more conscious of its rights and interests.

## Conclusions on the Role of Government

This section will attempt to draw some general lessons from Taiwan's development experience. As documented throughout this essay, the government has played a key role in Taiwan's economic development. It has intervened actively, frequently, and selectively in different aspects of industrial and trade policy, financial markets, and human capital and labor markets. Government intervention has been flexible and pragmatic, constantly taking account of changing domestic and international economic as well as political conditions.

However, it is important to emphasize two other aspects of the role of government in Taiwan's economic growth that appear to have been more important than selective intervention. *First, the government has played a key role in pursuing policies to restructure economic incentives, induce greater competition, facilitate the role of markets, and maintain macroeconomic and political stability.* Since the late 1950s, the government has sought to provide a competitive environment that stimulates and encourage firms to improve their performance and enhance their international competitiveness. When the economy outgrew the import substitution phase, the government introduced a series of major policy reforms during the 1960s that were intended to open up the local economy. To stimulate foreign trade, the new Taiwan dollar was devalued, a unified foreign exchange rate was established, the foreign exchange rate was converted to a floating rate system, and various trade controls were liberalized. Interest rates were kept at a positive real rate in order to encourage savings and capital formation.

In addition, the government has provided excellent macroeconomic management through strict fiscal discipline. By pursuing policies that discouraged social and economic inequity, such as land redistribution, and through the absence of policies encouraging the growth of large firms, the government also created a background of general social and political stability that enabled sustained growth.

*Second, the government has played a functional role in promoting economic development by establishing programs and institutions that support economic development through investments in physical and human infrastructure and in technological capability.* It has done so by building a solid physical infrastructure, making available efficient electricity, transportation, and communications systems. When bottlenecks in the infrastructure piled up in the early 1970s, the government revitalized the economy by upgrading the domestic infrastructure through the Ten Major Construction Projects, providing modernized and expanded electrification, transportation, and communications networks. These investments were complemented by an educational system that emphasized technical skills.

In the area of technology, the government put in place a comprehensive science and technology infrastructure designed to support and enhance the competitiveness of domestic firms. It created an environment conducive to technology transfer and development by offering an attractive climate for foreign investment, setting up research and industrial extension service institutions, and providing incentives for technology development. The government has also tried to compensate for structural weaknesses in the economy by developing institutions and programs that support the technological upgrading of small and medium enterprises through market and technological information, financial assistance, foreign linkages, enhanced productivity, and improved R&D.

The current restructuring of the Taiwanese economy toward high-technology industrialization appears to be shifting from a policy once heavily based on selective intervention in specific industries to one based on more functional intervention. This is possible largely because, having established the policy and institutional framework to support industrial development, government selective intervention is no longer necessary to develop key industrial sectors except in the high-technology area. With the Taiwanese economy now well integrated into the world economy and a solid institutional infrastructure in place to support outward-oriented growth, the government can focus on improving the functional areas of technology development and even on targeting a few high-technology industries. As Taiwan moves further into high-tech industrialization, government intervention will increasingly focus on four areas: (1) providing incentives to improve local R&D, (2) promoting the development of technical human capital, (3) providing incentives and regulations to address concerns about the environment, and (4) encouraging local exporters to move from simple subcontracting arrangements (where profit margins are low) to developing their own brand names (and higher-value-added products) and marketing and distribution channels. While this does not mean the abandonment of an industrial policy, it indicates a willingness on the part of the government to relax some of its previous economic controls now that the economy is mature and fully functional on its own.

On the whole, Taiwan's industrial policy influenced market incentives and market outcomes in a growth promoting direction. The measures taken were highly effective in promoting private sector growth because they provided economic incentives to the private sector and released its inherent dynamism. Industrial policy also integrated the Taiwanese economy in world markets, forcing domestic firms to compete in a global environment, while, at the same time, nurturing them at home through a system of incentives and strong support infrastructure.

## VII.   Recent Developments

### Introduction

Since the early 1990s, Taiwan has continued to redefine its role in the regional and global economy. Like the other original Asian "tigers," it has achieved a level of income that in many ways is comparable to that of an industrial country. However, along with the status of advanced NIE have also come many of the challenges confronting developing countries that are making the transition to developed status.

Over the past four decades, Taiwan has experienced rapid and dramatic economic expansion, but since 1991 real GDP growth has fallen below the target of 7 percent per year, reaching only 5.5 percent during the first quarter of 1994. Reflecting rising demand from the domestic market, imports are now increasing faster than exports, and the current account surplus reached its lowest level since 1981 in the first quarter of 1994. Although Taiwan's economic growth remains strong compared with most countries' and industrial output is expanding, the days of double-digit growth and massive trade and current account surpluses are over. The reasons behind this have as much to do with a changed domestic environment as with an increasingly competitive regional and international economy. The challenge now facing Taiwan is how to sustain growth by responding to new trends and conditions.

## New Developments

A number of regional and domestic developments are having and will continue
to have a profound impact on Taiwan's economic development and may slow
growth. Among the key regional trends are the following.

*Rising Domestic Costs.* High production costs, rising wages, and stringent
environmental restrictions since the mid-1980s have increasingly driven
Taiwanese and foreign manufacturers to relocate labor-intensive industries to other parts of Asia where labor and land are considerably
cheaper, and environmental protection standards are more relaxed. Over
the past two years, the majority of low-end manufacturing industries
such as textiles, footwear, and toys have moved production to less expensive sites in Asia, while higher-tech industries, especially computers, have remained in Taiwan. After Japan, Taiwan is the second-largest
foreign investor in many Southeast Asian countries, and it is the biggest foreign investor in Vietnam. In 1993, Taiwanese investment in
Thailand, Malaysia, Philippines, Indonesia, and Vietnam matched its investment in mainland China, where it is the second-largest investor after
Hong Kong.

*Labor Shortages.* There has been an increasing shortage of domestic labor
in recent years as a result of rising affluence, low birth rates, and an
increasing number of students staying on in higher education. With unemployment running below 1.5 percent percent, labor shortage is
becoming a growing problem for manufacturing, construction, and
other industries involving manual or semiskilled labor, and it has been
one of the main factors behind the relocation of light manufacturing
industries to lower-cost regions in Asia.

*Declining Inward Foreign Investment.* Despite government incentives,
direct foreign investment in Taiwan has been falling since 1991. From a
peak of U.S.$2.4 billion in 1989, inward investment flows have now ta-
pered off to the more moderate levels that are considered normal for
advanced industrial countries. In 1993, approved DFI in Taiwan was
U.S.$1.2 billion. Faced with competition from Southeast Asian NIEs,
the government is seeking to provide an environment that will encourage local manufacturers as well as multinational corporations to invest
in Taiwan as a high-end manufacturing base in Asia. As Taiwan is
already capital rich, the government is seeking to attract DFI primarily
as a means of bringing advanced technology from the United States,
Europe, and Japan. However, companies from these countries have been
somewhat reluctant to transfer their latest technologies. This reluctance
stems as much from the technological "nationalism" that is prevailing

in the increasingly competitive international economy as from foreign misgivings about Taiwan's commitment to intellectual property protection and its inadequate financial system (particularly when it is compared with Singapore and Hong Kong).

*Increasing Competition from the New Asian NIEs.* While first-generation NIEs such as Hong Kong, Korea, and Taiwan are striving to remain competitive by upgrading their industries and modernizing their infrastructure, the new crop of Asian NIEs like Thailand, Malaysia, Indonesia, and China offer the advantages of cheap and abundant labor, inexpensive land, and fewer environmental restrictions. The attractiveness of the new Asian NIEs as low-cost production bases has been facilitated by the liberalization of financial markets, which has allowed large-scale expansion of international capital flows in the 1990s, and it has further been enhanced by the increasing openness of some poorer Southeast Asian countries such as Vietnam.

In addition, a number of internal factors and developments are likely to hinder economic growth if not carefully managed.

*Over-regulated Banking Sector.* The state-dominated banking system is failing to meet the needs of small and medium enterprises that make up the backbone of Taiwanese industry and are currently forced to borrow from the curb lending market at high interest rates. An acceleration of bank privatization will be necessary to bring competition to the financial sector.[59]

*Inadequate Financial System.* In contrast to the significant upgrading in industry that has taken place, Taiwan's financial system remains underdeveloped. The formal financial regulatory framework is weak and, as seen as section VI, functions alongside a strong informal financial market that thrives on black market borrowings. Faced with an inadequate formal banking system, the Taiwanese continue to resort to a panoply of informal financing techniques ranging from "mutual savings societies" to underground lending by financial intermediaries.[60] Despite the recent liberalization of its financial system, Taiwan remains far behind Hong Kong and Singapore as a regional financial center.

*Fiscal Weakness.* Due to inefficient tax collection, government revenue levels fell below target in 1994, while public infrastructure costs have risen beyond projections. A rising budget deficit would further constrain public investment in infrastructure.

---

59. *The Economist,* June 24, 1994.
60. *Oxford Analytica,* March 14, 1994.

*Strained Infrastructure.* Sustained high growth has placed strains on existing infrastructure facilities. Although Taiwan's infrastructure is adequate compared to that of most of Southeast Asia, it is inferior to Singapore's, and this is one of the factors standing in the way of its goal of becoming a regional service center. Furthermore, as mentioned earlier, the current fiscal weakness and low levels of current account surpluses could slow down the government's ambitious U.S.$225 billion infrastructure program, which could in turn hinder growth.

*Rising "Quality of Life" Concerns.* Higher living standards, increased exposure to foreign ideas, and the rising political power of consumers have led to increased public demand for greater participation in the political process and a better quality of life. Overall, these are the concerns of a maturing and more affluent economy, and in that sense they are not impediments to economic development, as would be, for example, real structural shortcomings. Nevertheless, the growing democratization of Taiwanese politics means that the government may not be able to operate as unilaterally as it has in the past in formulating and implementing economic policies, and in that sense it may become a factor in slowing growth.

### The China Issue

While the Asian "tigers" share many of the same concerns and challenges, Taiwan faces a specific issue that has enormous relevance for its economic and political future: its expanding economic ties with China and the near- and long-term impact these are likely to have on Taiwan.

The Taiwanese economy has benefited tremendously from expanding ties with China over the past two years. Next to Hong Kong, Taiwan is the second-largest investor in China, with total investments estimated to range between U.S.$25 and $30 billion as of the end of 1993 (these include investments, remittances, and cash "gifts" by relatives).[61] Cheap wages, surplus labor, available land, and the cultural and linguistic advantages of dealing with ethnic Chinese have made China a very attractive investment location for many Taiwanese manufacturers. Furthermore, exports to China have helped sustain economic growth (in 1993, Taiwanese exports to China through Hong Kong were valued at more than U.S.$8.5 billion), and they have helped offset Taiwan's trade deficit with Japan.[62]

But Taiwan's rapidly expanding linkages with China are becoming a double-edged sword. On one hand, they have greatly benefited the Taiwanese

---

61. *New York Times,* July 5, 1994.
62. *Oxford Analytica,* August 15, 1994.

economy. On the other hand, they raise the risk of increasing Taiwan's economic dependence on the mainland, particularly when one considers that in 1994 exports to China represented 25 percent of total exports. A slowdown or contraction of the Chinese economy, or political instability arising from the death of China's aging leader, Deng Xiaoping, would have a profound impact on the Taiwanese economy. The extent of Taipei's economic dependence on China is evident in the recent dispute between China and the United States involving intellectual property protection. When the United States threatened trade sanctions against China, Taiwan ironically found itself on Beijing's side given the high volume of Chinese exports coming from Taiwanese-operated factories.

To offset the impact of possible economic or political instability on the mainland, Taipei has been strongly encouraging local manufacturers to diversify investments to Southeast Asia and other parts of the world over the past year. In fact, Taiwanese investments in China have declined recently as a result of a less welcoming tax environment for DFI in China as well as from growing concerns about the lack of a credible legal system there. This decline, it must be noted, is part of a general slowdown in DFI in China: for the first five months of 1994, foreign direct investment contracts in China fell 45 percent from those of a year earlier, from U.S.$58.76 billion to $32.7 billion.

Taipei's fear of dependence on the mainland extends to the political sphere as well. The estimated 20,000 to 25,000 Taiwanese enterprises that are now operating in China constitute a powerful interest group calling for reduced barriers to trade and investment. Furthermore, Taiwan's expanding economic and family linkages across the straits may well create demand for reunification with the mainland and hinder the government's goal of establishing Taiwan as a separate political and economic entity and possibly of seeking independence.

Nevertheless, both China and Taiwan recognize each other's economic importance, and trade linkages are likely to grow, regardless of what happens on the political side, where relations may become more acrimonious as Taiwan pushes harder to raise its international profile. This economic understanding was symbolized in recent developments: (1) Chinese president Jiang Zemin's conciliatory "Eight-Point Policy Statement" in February 1995, which laid the groundwork for further economic ties across the Taiwan Strait; (2) the March 1995 announcement by Taipei that it would allow transshipment of mainland goods through the port of Kaohsiung; and (3) Taiwanese president Lee Teng Hui's expected policy announcement in April 1995 about Taiwan's rapprochement with China.[63]

---

63. *Oxford Analytica,* March 22, 1995.

## Policy Trends and Developments

The clear trend in Taiwan's economic and political development over the past two years has been the shift toward liberalization and internationalization. Significant liberalizing trends in several areas underscore the government's desire to establish Taiwan as a model of economic and political development, in the hope that it will become further integrated into the world economy and gain legitimacy in world affairs. Financial and political liberalization are areas where liberalization and internationalization have been most significant.

*Financial Liberalization.* The recent reform of the banking sector is a positive step in facilitating Taiwan's integration into world financial markets and enhancing its ability to compete with Singapore and Hong Kong as a regional financial center (even though that latter prospect is not imminent). After many years of restrictive financial policies, the government announced the following measures in 1994 and 1995.

> Foreign banks will be allowed to set up branches in Taiwan. Foreign individuals and companies will henceforth be allowed to establish new, totally foreign-owned banks.
> Nonresident foreigners will be allowed to open bank accounts.
> The privatization of domestic state-owned banks will be accelerated. Although privatization of state banks has proceeded relatively slowly, competition in domestic banking has been enhanced by the entry of 16 new private banks, most of which were established in 1992. The fastest growing banks are private. The average growth rate of the 16 private banks in Taiwan's financial system was 64 percent, compared with 12 percent for the three largest banks, which are state-owned.[64]
> Foreigners are now allowed to own up to 12 percent of most Taiwanese stock.
> Foreign holders of convertible bonds will soon be able to convert to ordinary shares.
> Some form of individual foreign investment will be permitted by the end of 1995.
> A New Taiwan dollar bond will soon be issued, indicating that Taiwan is moving toward international use of its currency.[65]

*Political Liberalization.* In the last few years, the political process in Taiwan has been characterized by a move toward a more representative system. A key factor behind this shift is purely generational and demographic. As the

---

64. *The Economist,* September 25, 1994.
65. *Oxford Analytica,* March 10, 1995.

aging Kuomintang politburo passes away and the generation of Taiwanese born on the island after 1949 matures, there has been a growing demand for greater political participation, and this is reflected in changes in Taiwanese politics. Since 1992, all the members of the Legislative Yuan have been popularly elected. The opposition now holds 52 seats in the 161-seat legislature, and the ruling Kuomintang is moving toward a more moderate base, represented by President Lee Teng Hui, the first native Taiwanese to serve as president. An important milestone in Taiwan's political maturation process will be the first direct presidential election, which will be held in 1996.

While Taiwan's shift toward a more democratic political system is a reflection of popular demand rather than government engineering, the motivating factor behind reforms in the financial and trade sectors is based purely on the government's desire to achieve international legitimacy through further integration into the world economic system. The government's more aggressive forays into international diplomacy has not always been successful. In 1994, Taiwan applied for readmission to the United Nations, but the application was vetoed for the second year in a row. However, in recognition of its importance as the world's twelfth-largest trading nation, Taiwan was recently admitted as an observer to the World Trade Organization, and its accession to the General Agreement on Tariffs and Trade (GATT) is expected soon, pending negotiations on services.

This trend toward economic and political liberalization is likely to continue, particularly as a result of generational change and as Taiwan seeks to carve out a legitimate international role based on democratic values and free market principles.

## Conclusions

What is significant about these trends and developments—whether adverse or beneficial for the Taiwanese economy—is that they contribute to regional integration and lead to a virtuous cycle of growth for East Asia.

> The relocation of low-end manufacturing to Southeast Asia and China has contributed to the rapid industrialization of these countries—in very much the same manner as the relocation of "sunset" industries from the United States, Western Europe, and Japan 30 years ago accelerated Taiwan's industrialization—thereby starting a new cycle of economic growth.
>
> Competition from the Southeast Asian NIEs has played a catalytic role in pressuring Taiwan to open its market and upgrade its industry.
>
> Trade linkages with China have sustained exports in Taiwan, and further economic concessions between the two countries are likely to enhance Taiwan's ability to become a major regional service center.

## VIII.  Lessons for Other Developing Economies

A cursory glance at Taiwan's development experience may suggest that its successful economic growth was more the result of favorable initial conditions than of other factors and thus may imply that its success is not replicable. It is true that economic modernization in Taiwan was accelerated by a set of rather unique circumstances: the economic infrastructure laid out by the Japanese during the colonial period, the establishment of an ideologically mature and unified government from the mainland, the injection of administrative and entrepreneurial talent from mainland China, and timely and massive U.S. aid. And very probably, although its impact cannot be quantitatively measured, the Confucian cultural heritage emphasizing hard work, education, and discipline was conducive to rapid economic growth. Had these conditions not existed, Taiwan's economic development in the postwar period would probably have occurred at a much slower pace: without the Japanese-bequeathed physical and human infrastructure, and in the absence of U.S. aid, Taiwan would have had to build the infrastructure from scratch with its meager resources while shouldering its heavy defense burden on its own, and its policy of import substitution would probably have been less successful without U.S. aid to finance trade deficits and imports.

All countries start with a set of initial conditions, whether favorable or crippling, that define the environment in which their modern economic development takes place. Few of the historical, social, and cultural conditions that have facilitated Taiwan's postwar reconstruction can be replicated. Yet some elements are not unique. Scores of developing countries share a longer colonial history than does Taiwan, and many more have been the recipients of prolonged and massive foreign aid without achieving the same rates of economic growth. Likewise, the global experience of development assistance has shown that foreign aid, however massive, is often misallocated and inefficiently used.

However favorable and conducive to growth, a country's given physical or even sociocultural attributes are therefore not sufficient to sustain growth. They may facilitate growth initially, but without appropriate development strategies that build upon or modify initial conditions development is unlikely to progress very far. The success of the Taiwanese economy is largely the result of sound development policies that effectively built upon the foundations established and successfully exploited national social values. This section will attempt to distill lessons from Taiwan's experience for other developing countries.

### Political Stability and Development-Oriented Government

Political stability in Taiwan was the result of several factors: a consensus-based, outsider regime that was insulated from political pressure; the long presidencies of Chiang Kai-shek and Chiang Ching-kuo; and strong party dominance of the political system. This is not to recommend any particular form of political system but simply to observe that a stable and development-oriented government appears to be one of the elements of success. More useful for other countries, perhaps, is the lesson that economic policy making was efficiently managed by a core group of competent and highly pragmatic leaders who shared the conviction that government intervention should co-exist with private sector development. The top economic leadership was supported, in turn, by a highly qualified economic bureaucracy that was recruited through the competitive civil service examination and salaries that were competitive with those offered in the private sector.

## Macroeconomic Stability

Taiwan's experience suggests that macroeconomic stability is central to sustained growth. Macroeconomic stability provides the private sector with a stable environment in which entrepreneurs and consumers are able to plan and invest and focus on production and performance rather than the environment in which they operate. In Taiwan, macroeconomic stability was achieved thanks to generally prudent fiscal and monetary policies that were reflected in a strong commitment to combat inflation and promote capital formation. On the fiscal side, the persistent determination to curtail public expenditures and increase tax revenues have resulted in almost uninterrupted budget surpluses since 1964. Another important feature of efficient macroeconomic management in Taiwan has been the ability to respond quickly and flexibly to external shocks and changing domestic conditions.

## High Savings and Investment

Since growth depends in large part on investment, high rates of savings and investment are a critical factor in rapid growth. In Taiwan, gross savings have increased from 14 percent in 1953 to an average of more than 30 percent since the early 1970s. That increase was achieved in part as a result of low inflation, prudent economic management, government savings, income tax exemptions for savings, and several special features of the financial system, including positive real savings rates and a financial infrastructure (including an active curb market) that efficiently tapped savings from throughout the country and converted them into productive investments. High domestic investment, in turn, was stimulated by macroeconomic and political stability, a closed foreign capital account until 1987, slightly repressed interest rates through the formal banking system, and an economic policy that supported the development of the private sector and opened up many productive investment opportunities.

## Heavy Investment in Human Resources

Taiwan's rapid industrialization is based on huge investments in human resources. Quantitative increases and qualitative improvements in the educational and technical level of the labor force have played a key role in raising the work force's productivity and ability to produce more competitive products. Total national expenditures on education have grown at an average annual rate of 19 percent over the past 20 years. The close coordination of human resources and industrial policies has produced a close matching of labor skills to the evolving needs of industry. In the 1950s and 1960s, government policy focused on broad primary and secondary education to prepare Taiwan's growing population for the labor-intensive industries then being promoted. Since the mid-1970s, formal and vocational education in technical disciplines such as science, computers, engineering, and mathematics, was promoted to support the shift to high-tech industrialization. The emphasis on science and technology development is reflected in Taiwan's increasing technical human capital stock: between 1967 and 1990, the percentage of students enrolled in the fields of engineering, mathematics, computers, and the natural sciences combined increased from 25 to nearly 40 percent.

## Agriculture and Land Reform

In Taiwan, as well as in Korea and Japan, large early investments in agriculture and land reform not only dramatically increased productivity and efficient use of resources but raised political stability and income equalization. Unlike many developing countries, where agriculture is often neglected for the benefit of industry, the Taiwanese government—no doubt chastened by the consequences of its neglect of the peasantry on the mainland—promoted the balanced development of agriculture and industry, transferring the resources from one to nurture the growing needs of the other. Land reform was crucial both in providing the incentive to increase productivity and in allowing a more equal distribution of income, which, in turn, increased demand for the output of the industrial sector.

## Flexibility and Pragmatism in Industrial and Trade Policies

Taiwan's industrial and trade policies have shifted over time as domestic and international conditions have changed. The initial focus on land reform was followed by a period of import substitution. When that ran its course and began to falter, the government switched to an export promotion strategy, which carried over until the late 1980s. However, within that export strategy there was a period of secondary import substitution when the economy was hit by the double shock of expulsion from the United Nations and the first oil crisis. Since the 1980s, the government has pursued high-tech industrialization as a means of building Taiwan's international competitiveness in a world economy defined by ever more rapid technological change.

## Outward Orientation and Competition

The key feature of Taiwan's industrial and trade policies, however, has been its strong outward orientation since the late 1950s. This was achieved by a change in the incentive regime that made exports attractive. Key elements to this outward-oriented incentive regime were policy innovations that, while maintaining some protection of the domestic market, allowed exporters duty-free access to imported inputs necessary for exports and an undervalued exchange rate. An added bonus from this strong export orientation was that it forced local manufacturers to focus on the efficient use of technology to enhance their competitiveness. In addition, increased competition from exporting firms has compelled nonexporting firms to improve their productivity by upgrading their technology and management techniques. Export orientation also played a catalytic role in encouraging technological development through trade linkages and marketing channels. In addition, as the exporting sector and its associated duty-free regime grew as a share of the whole economy, it expanded competitive pressure on the rest of domestic production.

## Effective Government Institutions

The effectiveness of economic policies was to a large extent facilitated by core economic agencies that operated and functioned independently of the mainstream government structure. Almost all of the core government economic policy-making bodies in Taiwan today started out as independent agencies that had the resources and the broad authority to implement policies efficiently and rapidly without being hampered by mainline bureaucratic constraints. This design was particularly effective during the chaotic years of reconstruction, when reform programs and support infrastructure needed to be set up rapidly. Once economic development had stabilized, these special agencies were reorganized to take on more mainstream tasks. Thus, independent economic agencies can play an important role, at least during an initial period, in the successful implementation of policies. Much of their effectiveness, however, depends on the scope of their authority, the extent of their resources, and the quality of their leadership.

## Investment in Institutional Support Infrastructure for the Private Sector

Economic development is not just a matter of economic policies. The government complemented the general incentive and policy regimes during each phase of economic development with investment in institutional infrastructure that supported the increased efficiency of the private sector. In the early 1950s, the government provided agricultural extension services such as those developed and expanded by the Joint Commission on Rural Reconstruction. During the export promotion period, it invested in metrology, standards, and quality control systems to improve the quality of export products and created productivity improvement institutions such as the China Productivity Center. In addition, the government developed export marketing services such as the China External Trade Development Council. During the industrial consolidation phase, it expanded its investments in public research institutes such as the Industrial Technology Research Institute in order to be able to absorb the more complex foreign technology required for secondary import substitution. In the high-tech phase, the government increased its investments in the higher technology elements of the public R&D infrastructure such as the Electronics Research and Service Organization branch of ITRI and the Institute for Information Industries. It also developed the Science-Based Industrial Park to provide a convenient infrastructure to attract foreign high-technology investment to Taiwan.

## Technology Development Strategy

The experience of Taiwan suggests that the focus on high technology and heavy investments in public R&D infrastructure only make sense once the economy has reached a relatively advanced stage of economic development. The initial productivity growth was achieved by being very efficient at acquiring foreign technology, much of it informally through trade. The strong push for local R&D capacity came only after manufacturers had acquired technical skills through foreign alliances involving trade, direct foreign investment, technology transfers, subcontracting, working with foreign firms, and foreign studies. Only then did the government encourage industry to move upstream to heavy and petrochemical industries. Furthermore, the main function of the public R&D infrastructure has not been merely to push back the frontiers of knowledge, as in developed economies, but to adapt and disseminate foreign technologies to the needs of the local productive sector.

## Effective Use of Comparative Advantage

The ability to successfully exploit different factor endowments at different stages of development has enabled the Taiwanese economy to remain highly competitive, underscoring the modern economic principle that comparative advantage is not static but constantly created. In the 1950s and 1960s, the government promoted labor-intensive industries to take advantage of Taiwan's growing population, excess agricultural labor, and low wages. As wages rose and the unskilled labor supply grew short, the government made the shift to technology-intensive industries as a means of enhancing Taiwan's international competitiveness and gradually fostered the development of more technically skilled and highly educated manpower. Thus, over the years Taiwan has adjusted not only its economic policies to changing circumstances but its comparative advantage, which has shifted from low-wage and relatively unskilled labor to an increasingly technical work force with higher wages.

In short, the government's approach to development has been one of constant reevaluation, adjustment, and modification of economic policies to meet the demands of evolving national and international circumstances. This pragmatic and flexible approach to development has led to an economy that is constantly attuned to its changing environment.

APPENDIX

**TABLE A2.1.    Nominal and Real Exchange Rates in Relation to the U.S. Dollar**

| Year | Nominal XRs | Real XRs | Taiwan/U.S. CPI |
|------|-------------|----------|-----------------|
| 1950 | 10.30 | 45.78 | 22.50 |
| 1955 | 24.78 | 37.49 | 66.09 |
| 1960 | 39.85 | 38.65 | 103.11 |
| 1965 | 40.10 | 36.68 | 109.33 |
| 1970 | 40.05 | 37.59 | 106.54 |
| 1975 | 38.00 | 27.81 | 136.65 |
| 1980 | 36.06 | 29.10 | 123.90 |
| 1985 | 39.90 | 39.45 | 101.15 |
| 1990 | 27.11 | 29.22 | 92.77 |

Source: *Taiwan Statistical Data Book,* 1992.

*Note:* XR = exchange rate; CPI = consumer price index.

**TABLE A2.2. Ownership of Industrial Production in Manufacturing**

| Year | Total Industry | | Manufacturing | |
|------|--------|---------|---------|--------|
| | Public | Private | Private | Public |
| 1955 | 48.7 | 51.3 | 48.9 | 51.1 |
| 1960 | 43.8 | 56.2 | 52.1 | 47.9 |
| 1965 | 36.8 | 63.2 | 58.7 | 41.3 |
| 1970 | 20.6 | 79.4 | 72.3 | 27.7 |
| 1975 | 14.2 | 85.8 | 77.9 | 22.1 |
| 1980 | 14.5 | 85.5 | 79.1 | 20.9 |
| 1985 | 12.0 | 88.0 | 81.2 | 18.8 |
| 1990 | 11.1 | 88.9 | 81.0 | 19.0 |
| 1993 | 10.5 | 89.5 | — | — |

*Source: Taiwan Statistical Yearbook,* various years.

**TABLE A2.3. Hourly Compensation Costs for Production Workers in Manufacturing for Taiwan and Other Countries**

| Year | Taiwan | Korea | Hong Kong | Singapore | India | Sri Lanka | Pakistan | Brazil | Mexico | Japan | United States | Germany |
|------|--------|-------|-----------|-----------|-------|-----------|----------|--------|--------|-------|---------------|---------|
| 1975 | 0.39 | 0.33 | 0.76 | 0.84 | 0.19 | 0.28 | 0.21 | 0.87 | NA | 3.05 | 6.36 | 6.35 |
| 1976 | 0.46 | 0.43 | 0.87 | 0.86 | 0.28 | 0.24 | 0.23 | 1.01 | NA | 3.30 | 6.92 | 6.73 |
| 1977 | 0.53 | 0.57 | 1.03 | 0.91 | 0.32 | 0.32 | 0.29 | 1.12 | NA | 4.02 | 7.59 | 7.86 |
| 1978 | 0.62 | 0.77 | 1.18 | 1.05 | 0.37 | 0.26 | 0.36 | 1.33 | NA | 5.54 | 8.28 | 9.65 |
| 1979 | 0.79 | 1.02 | 1.31 | 1.26 | 0.37 | 0.23 | 0.38 | 1.43 | NA | 5.49 | 9.04 | 11.29 |
| 1980 | 1.00 | 0.97 | 1.51 | 1.49 | 0.44 | 0.22 | 0.35 | 1.38 | NA | 5.60 | 9.87 | 12.33 |
| 1981 | 1.21 | 1.03 | 1.55 | 1.79 | 0.42 | 0.21 | 0.37 | 1.65 | NA | 6.18 | 10.87 | 10.53 |
| 1982 | 1.24 | 1.10 | 1.66 | 1.96 | 0.39 | 0.24 | 0.35 | 1.76 | NA | 5.70 | 11.68 | 10.35 |
| 1983 | 1.29 | 1.17 | 1.51 | 2.21 | 0.41 | 0.25 | 0.34 | 1.24 | NA | 6.13 | 12.14 | 10.26 |
| 1984 | 1.42 | 1.22 | 1.58 | 2.46 | 0.42 | 0.25 | 0.30 | 1.07 | NA | 6.34 | 12.55 | 9.43 |
| 1985 | 1.50 | 1.25 | 1.73 | 5.43 | 0.35 | 0.28 | 0.32 | 1.12 | 1.60 | 6.43 | 13.01 | 9.57 |
| 1986 | 1.73 | 1.34 | 1.88 | 2.23 | 0.39 | 0.29 | 0.36 | 1.47 | 1.10 | 9.31 | 13.25 | 13.36 |
| 1987 | 2.26 | 1.65 | 2.09 | 2.31 | NA | 0.30 | 0.41 | 1.38 | 1.06 | 10.83 | 13.52 | 17.07 |
| 1988 | 2.82 | 2.30 | 2.40 | 2.67 | NA | 0.31 | NA | 1.46 | 1.32 | 12.80 | 13.91 | 18.28 |
| 1989 | 3.53 | 3.29 | 2.79 | 3.15 | NA | 0.31 | NA | 1.68 | 1.59 | 12.63 | 14.31 | 17.73 |
| 1990 | 3.95 | 3.82 | 3.20 | 3.78 | NA | NA | NA | 2.64 | 1.80 | 12.64 | 14.88 | 21.53 |
| 1991 | 4.42 | 4.32 | 3.58 | 4.38 | NA | NA | NA | 2.55 | 2.17 | 14.41 | 15.45 | 22.17 |

*Source:* U.S. Department of Labor, various years.

**TABLE A2.4.  Composition of Savings by Different Sectors as a Percentage of GNP**

| Sector | As Percentage of GNP | | | | | | |
|---|---|---|---|---|---|---|---|
| | 1960 | 1965 | 1970 | 1975 | 1980 | 1985 | 1988 |
| Household and private, nonprofit organizations | 4.79 | 8.20 | 11.05 | 11.04 | 11.48 | 15.00 | 15.63 |
| Private enterprises | 0.67 | 1.91 | 1.66 | −0.51 | 2.75 | 0.93 | 0.91 |
| Government enterprises | 1.85 | 1.72 | 2.55 | 2.12 | 2.80 | 2.48 | 1.86 |
| Government institutions | 3.45 | 2.14 | 3.08 | 6.34 | 7.16 | 4.83 | 7.49 |
| Reserves for depreciation | 7.00 | 6.75 | 7.25 | 7.73 | 8.08 | 9.37 | 8.82 |
| Gross national savings | 10.76 | 20.72 | 18.34 | 26.72 | 32.27 | 32.61 | 34.71 |

*Source:* Chiu, "Money and Financial Markets," 158.

TABLE A2.5.  Assets and Market Share of Financial Institutions (in NT$ billions at the end of 1988)

| | Number of Units[a] | As Percentage of Total | Assets | As Percentage of Total | 1961–88 Growth Rate | Share of Deposits Market | Share of Loans Market |
|---|---|---|---|---|---|---|---|
| Central Bank of China (CBC) | 1 | 0.02 | 2,249 | 25/11 | 20/3 | — | — |
| Domestic commercial banks (DCB) | 705 | 16.76 | 3,723 | 41.57 | 19.4 | 48.71 | 66.00 |
| Local branches of foreign banks | 38 | 0.90 | 193 | 2.16 | 27.7 | 1.01 | 4.12 |
| Medium business banks | 262 | 6.23 | 429 | 4.79 | 23.4 | 6.13 | 9.26 |
| Credit cooperative associations | 414 | 9.84 | 551 | 6.15 | 21.0 | 10.23 | 9.78 |
| Farmers' and fishery credit departments | 976 | 23.21 | 453 | 5.06 | 22.1 | 8.20 | 5.92 |
| Investment and trust companies | 49 | 1.17 | 181 | 2.02 | 26.6 | 3.26 | 2.92 |
| Postal savings system (PSS) | 1,577 | 37.49 | 933 | 10.42 | 33.4 | 17.80 | 0.18 |
| Life insurance companies | 70 | 1.67 | 217 | 2.42 | 30.6 | 4.35 | 1.76 |
| Property and casualty insurance companies | 92 | 2.19 | 26 | 0.29 | 18.8 | 0.31 | 0.03 |
| Offshore banks (U.S.$ billion)[b] | 22 | 0.52 | 13 | — | 74.8 | — | — |
| Total | 4,206 | 100.00 | 8,955 | 100.00 | 20.8 | 100.00 | 100.00 |

*Source:* Chang, "Financial Institutions and Deepening" based on Central Bank of China, *Financial Statistics Monthly* (October 1989); and Ministry of Finance, *Financial Statistics Abstract* (December 1988).

[a]The number of financial units is as of the October of 1989.
[b]Offshore banking commenced on July 1, 1984.

**TABLE A2.6.   Percentage Share of Government Enterprises in Total Output and Bank Loans, 1986–87**

|  | 1961–65 | 1966–70 | 1971–75 | 1976–80 | 1981–85 | 1986–88 |
|---|---|---|---|---|---|---|
| Percentage of total domestic output | 17.75 | 15.20 | 13.44 | 15.01 | 15.01 | 11.65 |
| Percentage of total loans outstanding | 23.48 | 14.40 | 14.27 | 16.52 | 16.95 | 8.63 |

*Source:* Chiu, "Money and Financial Markets," 163.

**TABLE A2.7.   Annual Interest Rates on Loans against Postdated Checks and Commercial Bank Rates on General Loans, Taiwan, 1963–86**

| Years | Loans against Postdated Checks[a] | General Loans and Commercial Loans |
|---|---|---|
| 1963–86 | 23.0 | 14.9 |
| 1970 | 22.6 | 12.5 |
| 1971 | 22.3 | 12.5 |
| 1972 | 23.2 | 11.7 |
| 1973 | 24.3 | 13.7 |
| 1974 | 32.8 | 15.5 |
| 1975 | 28.9 | 13.8 |
| 1976 | 29.3 | 12.5 |
| 1977 | 28.5 | 11.2 |
| 1978 | 28.2 | 11.2 |
| 1979 | 32.6 | 14.2 |
| 1980 | 34.6 | 14.2 |
| 1981 | 34.6 | 13.0 |
| 1982 | 31.1 | 9.0 |
| 1983 | 28.7 | 8.5 |
| 1984 | 27.4 | 8.0 |
| 1985 | 26.2 | 6.2 |
| 1986 | 23.0 | 5.0 |

*Source:* Biggs, "Heterogeneous Firms," 186.
[a] Based on a compounded monthly rate.

REFERENCES

Biggs, Tyler S. "Heterogeneous Firms and Efficient Financial Intermediation in Taiwan." In *Markets in Developing Countries: Parallel, Fragmented, and Black.* San Francisco: International Center for Economic Growth, 1992.

Central Bank of the Republic of China, various years. *Flow of Funds in the Taiwan District.* Taipei: Economic Research Department of the Central Bank of the ROC.

Chang, Kuo-hsing. "Financial Institutions and Deepening in Taiwan, ROC." In "The Central Bank of China and the Financial Market. Mimeo, 1990.

Chenery, Hollis B., and Moshe Syrquin. "Typical Patterns of Transformation." In *Industrialization and Growth: A Comparative Study,* edited by H. Chenery, S. Robinson, and M. Syrguin. New York: Oxford University Press, 1986.

Chiu, Paul C. H. 1992. "Money and Financial Markets: The Domestic Perspective." In *Taiwan: From Developing to Mature Economy,* edited by Gus Ranis. Boulder: Westview Press.

Dahlman, Carl J., and Ousa Sananikone. "Technology Strategy in the Economy of Taiwan: Exploiting Foreign Linkages and Investing in Local Capability," World Bank, mimeo, 1990.

Directorate-General of Budget, Accounting and Statistics. Various years. *Financial Statistics Monthly.* Taipei: Directorate-General.

Galenson, Walter, ed. *Economic Growth and Structural Change in Taiwan: The Postwar Experience of the Republic of China.* Ithaca: Cornell University Press, 1979.

Ho, Samuel P. *Economic Development of Taiwan, 1860–1970,* New Haven: Yale University Press, 1978.

Hou, Chi-ming. "Strategies for Industrial Development," *Industry of Free China* (October 1987): 1–18.

Hsieh, Alvin, and Tain-jy Chen. "The Role of Foreign Capital in the Economic Development of Taiwan." Conference Proceedings Series No. 7, July 22–27. Taipei: Chung-hua Institution for Economic Research, 1987.

Kuo, Shirley W. Y. "Economic Development in the Republic of China." In *Conference on Economic Development in the Republic of China, Taiwan, July 22–27, 1987.* Taipei, Taiwan: Chung-Hua Institution for Economic Research, 1987.

Kuo, Shirley W. Y. *The Taiwan Economy in Transition.* Boulder: Westview Press, 1983.

Li, K. T. *The Evolution of Policy behind Taiwan's Development Success.* New Haven: Yale University Press, 1988.

Mao, Yu-Kang, and Chi Schive. "Agricultural and Industrial Development of the Republic of China on Taiwan." In *Reference Papers on Economic Development and Prospect of the Republic of China,* compiled by the Board of Foreign Trade, Ministry of Economic Affairs (April 1991). Taipei: Ministry of Economic Affairs.

Pack, Howard. "Exports and Productivity Growth: The Case of Taiwan's Development." Mimeo, 1992.

Pack, Howard. "The Role of Industrial Policy in Taiwan's Development." Mimeo, April 1992.

Page, John, Jr., and Peter Petri. "Productivity Change and Strategic Growth Policy in the East Asian Miracle." World Bank, mimeo, 1993.

Pang, Chien-kuo. *The State and Economic Transformation: The Taiwan Case.* New York, Garland Publishing, 1992.

Rabushka, Alvin. *The New China: Comparative Economic Development—Mainland China, Taiwan, and Hong Kong.* San Francisco: Westview Press, 1987.

Schive, Chi. *Taiwan's Economic Role in East Asia.* Washington, D.C.: Center for Strategic and International Studies, 1995.

Small and Medium Business Administration, various years. "Trend Outstanding Loans Extended by Domestic Banks to Small and Medium Enterprises." Taipei: Small and Medium Business Administration.

*Statistical Yearbook of the Republic of China,* various years.Taipei: Directorate-General of the Budget. Accounting and Statistics.

*Taiwan Statistical Data Book,* various years. Taipei: Council for Economic Planning and Development.

Thorbecke, Erik. "Agricultural Development." In *Economic Growth and Structural Change in Taiwan: The Postwar Experience of the Republic of China,* edited by Walter Galenson. New York: Cornell University Press, 1979.

U.S. Department of Labor, various years. *Foreign Labor Statistics.* Washington: Bureau of Labor Statistics.

Wade, Robert. *Governing the Market: Economic Theory and the Role of Government in East Asian Industrialization.* Princeton: Princeton University Press, 1990.

World Bank. 1995. *World Development Report.* Oxford: Oxford University Press.

CHAPTER 3

# Korea: A Case of Government-Led Development

*Kim Kihwan and Danny M. Leipziger*

## I. Economic Performance

The Korean success story begins with a war-torn economy that had just lost two-thirds of its industrial capacity and 1.5 million lives in the Korean War. With a poor natural resource base and one of the world's highest population densities, Korea bore a strong resemblance to Japan. Armed with a literate and hard-working work force, a sense of common purpose, and the fierce nationalism that had kept the country independent and united for 12 centuries, Korea managed (in the terminology of Cho [1994]) to "condense" a century of growth into three decades. Unlike Japan, Korea did not have a large enough domestic market to contemplate anything other than export-driven development.

After a number of false starts in the 1950s, when Korea was almost totally dependent on U.S. foreign assistance, early attempts at "development" began, first in the form of reconstruction, indeed, led by the Ministry of Reconstruction.[1] The coming to power of President Park Chung Hee with his strategy of *suchul ipguk,* or "nation building through exports," heralded the beginning of Korea's modern development. In broad terms, Korea's real GNP has tripled every decade since 1962 (see fig. 3.1). Combined with a rapid slowdown in population growth,[2] this produced significant per capita income gains (see fig. 3.2). In 1962, per capita GNP in the United States, in real purchasing power terms, was 11 times greater than Korea's; by 1988, it was only 3.3 times greater. Korea also caught up significantly with Japan (see fig. 3.3) and outpaced its other East Asian neighbors (see fig. 3.4).

How was this achieved? According to Cho (1991), the Korean economic system in the 1960s and 1970s was a variant of authoritarian capitalism, in

---

1. For a description of these early years, see Chung 1986 and Song 1990.
2. According to Song (1990), the government systematically implemented population control plans at the national level very much like military campaigns. It also monitored the use of contraceptives and other family planning measures with almost the same attention it devoted to export promotion.

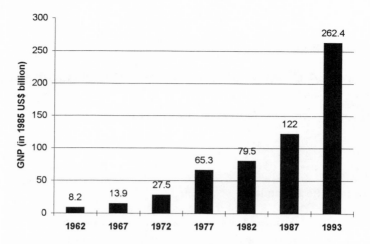

**Fig. 3.1.    Three decades of growth (GNP in 1985 U.S.$). (Data from Bank of Korea 1990, 1994.)**

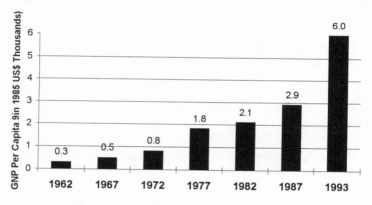

**Fig. 3.2.    Individual income growth (GNP per capita in 1985 U.S.$ thousands). (Data from Bank of Korea 1990, 1994.)**

which the enterprises were privately owned but the management was shared between the government and the owners. We concur with this assessment and see Korea's development history in its formative years as a government designed and managed effort, with the willing participation and execution of the private sector. What distinguishes Korean development from other efforts, however, was its devotion to exports and therefore its total acceptance of international prices as the yardstick of industrial performance. (For historical and other reasons, the same cannot be said for agriculture.) As a consequence of

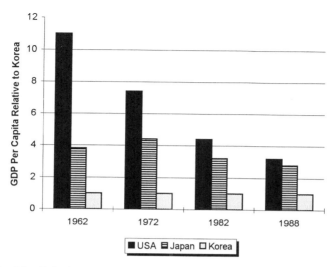

**Fig. 3.3. Relative income performance (GDP per capita relative to Korea in 1980 international prices). (Data from Summers and Heston 1988.)**

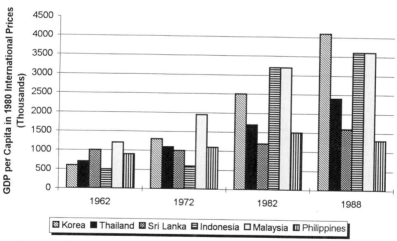

**Fig. 3.4. Comparative Asian performance (GDP per capita in 1980 international prices, thousands). (Data from Summers and Heston 1988; Noland 1990.)**

these efforts, Korea is one of the few nations that has transformed itself into a global trader (now ranked eleventh in world trade) much the same as Japan has done. Indeed, comparisons with Japan a decade or two earlier raise the question of the "Japanese model" and the role of government, issues we deal with in this essay.

## Export Dominance

The dominant feature of the Korean economy has been its export orientation. Exports, as a proportion of GNP, rose from 7.4 percent in 1967 to 27.2 percent in 1977 and 36.7 percent in 1987 (see fig. 3.5). The country's share of world trade rose from negligible proportions in 1962 to 2 percent in 1990. There is persuasive evidence from the work of Balassa, Krueger, and the *Word Development Report, 1991* (World Bank 1991) that outward-oriented countries have grown faster than those favoring production for domestic markets.[3] Indeed, the benefits of outward orientation are greater than what might be reasonably attributed to the achievement of allocative efficiency alone.[4] The Korean preoccupation with exporting is seen as the prime motivator of government policy.

The elements of the support system for exports have been described by Rhee et al. (1984) and others. They include the setting and monitoring of export targets, allocation of credit for export purposes, maintenance of an export-friendly tax and trade regime (see World Bank 1987), effective policies for technology acquisition (see Westphal et al. 1984), and strong international marketing efforts. One big influence has been the Korean Trade Promotion Corporation (KOTRA), which was established in 1962, as the export drive began. (It is a Korean characteristic to establish an institution to help implement major policy changes. Korea's technological drive, for example, began with the establishment of the Korean Institute for Science and Technology in 1961.) The interesting fact about KOTRA is that it was not government financed. It was supported by the exporters themselves, although it was clearly an instrument designed to achieve government objectives. Similarly, the Korean Traders Association (KTA) was influential in promoting contact between government and business. The KTA's Special Fund for Export Promotion (begun in 1969) was funded by mandatory contributions levied as 1 percent of most imports.

Firms and industrial associations clearly internalized government objectives. They were expected to perform in exchange for the benefits provided in the form of infrastructure, credit, and other policies described as the government's "modestly pro-export bias" by Westphal (1978). The yardstick of performance was exports not profitability. This helps to explain the high leveraging behavior of firms and their growth-at-all-costs strategies. Since the government

---

3. See Dollar 1992 for a recent confirmation that openness is clearly associated with superior economic performance.

4. Krueger et al. (1985) and others argue that open economies are more flexible than import-substituting economies because they have greater "cushions" of unessential imports to squeeze under adverse circumstances. According to Westphal et al. (1984) and others, openness can also facilitate the absorption and mastery of foreign technologies. Nishimizu and Robinson (1983) have shown that the rate of technical progress was faster in countries with outward-oriented policies than in those pursuing import-substituting strategies.

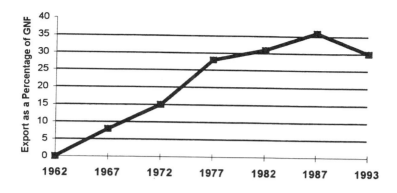

Fig 3.5.   **Export-led growth (exports as a percentage of GNP). (Data from Bank of Korea 1990, 1994.)**

favored economies of scale in production, marketing, and technology acquisition, it rewarded size with better access to credit.[5] It also used social pressures and practical penalties to ensure compliance. Since it controlled industrial entry and rationed credit, the task of enforcement was rather easy. As in Japan in earlier periods, a few general trading companies (GTCs) were sanctioned (licensed) and allowed preferential access to foreign exchange. These GTCs controlled the majority of exports, and through them the government had easy control over industry.

Korea's manufacturing is unusually dependent on imports (see Chenery, Robinson, and Syrquin 1986). This helps explain both the efficiency of production and the desire of Korean policymakers to change the structure of the economy. The model they followed was Japan.

## Changing Industrial Structure

The overriding characteristic of Korea's economy is not only its rapid shift from agriculture (37 percent of GDP in 1962 to 8 percent in 1991) to manufacturing (see fig. 3.6); just as striking were the dynamism and flexibility of manufacturing itself. This can be seen at the firm level in the story of the Handok Company (see sidebar), in the rapid transformation of Korea's leading exports (see table 3.1), and in changes in its output structure. The Handok story is mirrored in the pattern of exports, which shifted from the most basic raw materials (primarily minerals) in 1961 to labor-intensive exports in 1970, an increasing emergence of capital-intensive exports in the 1980s, and technology-intensive

---

5. See Leipziger 1988 on the size, leveraging, and profitability of Korean firms.

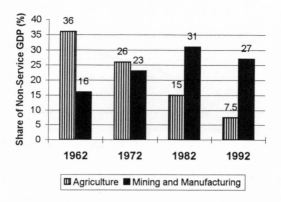

Fig. 3.6. Changing industrial structure (share of nonservice GDP, percentage). (Data from Bank of Korea 1990, 1994.)

exports by 1989. This pattern did not just happen; it was the result of careful planning and execution.

It is instructive to see the strong correlation between Korea's output structure in manufactures in 1983 vis-à-vis Japan's in 1965, and between Korea's "projected structure" for the year 2000 and Japan's composition in 1983 (see table 3.2). The strategy document for 2000 was prepared by the Korea Institute for Economics and Technology, the think tank affiliated with the Ministry of Trade and Industry. This industrial blueprint is only indicative, but performs a "signal" function for the now privatized but not independent banking system, serves as "guidance" for industry in that industrialists are expected to take general investment and marketing cues from these strategic objectives, and functions as a "coordinating" instrument for government through its educational, R&D, and technology policies.

**Korea's Industrial Flexibility at the Firm Level**
In 1971, the Handok Company was a wig manufacturer, with wigs accounting for 95 percent of sales. By 1976, Handok had diversified extensively, to the point where wigs were only 16 percent of sales. Paper products made up 51 percent of output, complemented by tuna (22 percent) and watches (9 percent). The industrial transformation was completed by 1981, when watches accounted for 85 percent of sales. By 1985, liquid crystal display manufacturing, including monitors and dashboard items, were beginning to emerge as new sales items (10 percent of sales) and the bulk of revenue came from computers and electronics (41 percent) and watches (45 percent). Handok is an example of industrial flexibility in a medium-sized firm employing about 3,500 people and generating sales of about 64 billion won in 1984.

**TABLE 3.1.  Industrial Flexibility: The Top Five Korean Exports for the Years 1961, 1970, 1980, 1985, and 1989**

| | 1961 | | 1970 | | 1980 | | 1985 | | 1989 | |
|---|---|---|---|---|---|---|---|---|---|---|
| | Export Item | Share (%) | Export Item | Share (%) | Export Item | Share (%) | Export Item | Share (%) | Export Item | Share (%) |
| | Iron ore | 13.0 | Textiles and garments | 40.8 | Textiles and garments | 28.6 | Textiles and garments | 23.1 | Electronic products | 29.4 |
| | Tungsten | 12.6 | Plywood | 11.0 | Electronic products | 11.4 | Ships | 16.6 | Textiles and garments | 24.3 |
| | Raw milk | 6.7 | Wigs | 10.8 | Steel products | 10.6 | Electronic products | 14.1 | Steel products | 6.9 |
| | Anthracite | 5.8 | Iron ore | 5.9 | Footwear | 5.2 | Steel products | 8.5 | Footwear | 5.8 |
| | Squid | 5.5 | Electronic products | 3.5 | Ships | 3.5 | Footwear | 5.2 | Automobiles | 3.8 |

*Source*: Korea Foreign Trade Association.

One example of the effectiveness of policy was the rapid development of heavy and chemical industries (HCI) in the 1970s (see fig. 3.7). The costs associated with this forced restructuring of industry are discussed later, but it is worth noting that the percentage of production exported by these infant HCI industries tripled between 1973 and 1983 to almost 23 percent. Herein lies the major distinction between Korean industrial policy interventions and similar efforts in other would-be industrializers, namely, that the ultimate goal from the start was international competitiveness (the classic infant industry case).

### Economic Welfare

Korea has not just had rapid economic growth; it has also shared the benefits of that growth. The basis for rural equity was laid with the postoccupation reform of confiscated land. This was followed by the 1954 land reform in which land was appropriated in exchange for five-year bonds (the value of which was largely eroded through inflation) and redistributed in small units. As important, however, is the lesser-known fact that, between 1962 and 1976, 25 percent of public investment was destined for agriculture, forestry, and fisheries (Sakong 1992). Some of these investments were part of the so-called *saemaul,* or "new village," movement to spur rural development. Song (1990) lists land reform, the asset destruction of the Korean War, and education as the major factors working for an equitable distribution of rural income. Leipziger and Petri (1994) add to this the clear system of agricultural price supports, which aimed to minimize urban-rural income differentials. Except for the early 1970s, the av-

**TABLE 3.2.    Comparison of Output Structures in Korea and Japan (percentage)**

| | Output | | | |
|---|---|---|---|---|
| | Korea | | Japan | |
| | 1983 | 2000 | 1965 | 1983 |
| Machinery | 10.4 | 12.1 | 12.2 | 14.3 |
| Electronics | 8.2 | 15.4 | 9.5 | 18.0 |
| Automobiles | 3.6 | 8.6 | 2.7 | 6.3 |
| Shipbuilding | 4.3 | 3.3 | 3.3 | 2.6 |
| Petrochemicals | 3.2 | 2.6 | | |
| Industrial chemicals | 3.4 | 4.6 | 4.6 | 3.1 |
| Petroleum refining | 9.9 | 3.8 | | |
| Iron and steel | 7.6 | 6.2 | 3.3 | 2.7 |
| Textiles (excluding garments) | 13.9 | 8.3 | 17.3 | 10.2 |
| Food | 10.9 | 7.0 | 6.7 | 4.3 |
| Other manufacturing | 24.6 | 28.1 | 40.4 | 38.5 |
| Total manufacturing | 100.0 | 100.0 | 100.0 | 100.0 |

*Source:* KIET 1985.

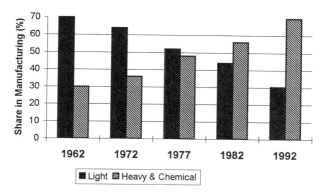

**Fig. 3.7. Heavy and chemical industry push (share in manufacturing, percentage). (Data from Bank of Korea 1990, 1994.)**

erage income differential between urban and rural households never exceeded 15 percent and usually was within a few percentage points.

Whether measured by the decile distribution ratio reported by Song (1990) or the Gini coefficients reported by Choo and Yoon (1984) and Kim and Ahn (1987), Korea's income distribution changed remarkably little during the high-growth years of 1965–85. Absolute poverty, as measured by Suh (1992), declined steeply, from 41 percent in 1965 to less than 10 percent in 1980. Figure 3.8 shows trends in absolute poverty, the share of the bottom four deciles of the income distribution, and the wage share in national income. Although Leipziger et al. (1992) argue that recent shifts in the value of assets have had an adverse impact on income distribution, especially because of underreporting of capital gains by the wealthiest decile, there is no doubt that Korea has contradicted the Kuznets hypothesis with broadly distributed income gains.

Welfare as measured by purchasing power relative to consumer goods increased by a factor of 3.2 between 1974 and 1989. Purchasing power relative to land and housing prices, however, has remained essentially unchanged. Even so, the average Korean is clearly better off with each passing decade. This trend is apparent from any number of social indicators. The one surprising statistic is the amount of leisure time reported (see Song 1990, 182): it was unchanged between 1970 and 1985, at 116 hours per week. A corollary is that Korea's average manufacturing workweek of 54.7 hours in 1984 was 10 percent higher than Taiwan, China's, 31 percent above Japan's or Germany's, and 34 percent above that of the United States. It is not apocryphal that Korean subordinates do not leave the workplace until their manager has departed.

However, Korea is no longer a society of repressed consumption. With car ownership growing exponentially, demographics favoring consumption, and capital controls being gradually lifted, savings may well have peaked, and the government's role as a savings mobilizer may be reduced over time. Although

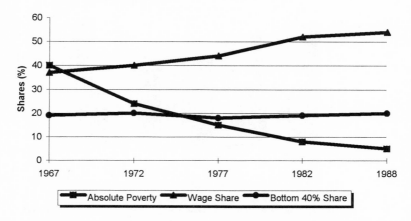

**Fig. 3.8. Measures of economic welfare. The absolute poverty line is defined as 121,000 won (1981 prices) per month for a five-person household. (Data from Suh 1992; Choo 1985; Bank of Korea 1990.)**

Koreans still lag behind in certain welfare indicators, particularly housing, three decades of rapid growth have produced unparalleled welfare gains.

## Characteristics of the Economy

*Chenery-Syrquin Norms*

One of the early attempts to analyze changes in economic structure for developing changes was the "norms" approach of Chenery and Syrquin (1975), later extended by Chenery (1989). The methodology is meant to explain the general evolution of structural variables as a function of income and population variables as well as net imports of goods and services. Deviations from the norm indicate unusual performance. Korea exceeded the norm for most key indicators as early as the mid-1960s (see table 3.3). It was not alone in beating the norms. Using the ratio of manufactured exports to GDP, for example, in which Korea reached the norm in 1966, Taiwan, China reached it in 1965, Malaysia and Thailand in 1978, and Indonesia in 1984, shows a clear pattern for first- and then second-generation industrializers.

Several recent studies have sought to explain East Asia's success (see World Bank 1991 for a general review), and most have singled out macro-management, in particular, exchange rate policy.[6] Though clearly crucial as a proximate policy variable, what enabled Korea to respond to a competitive exchange rate was its early infrastructure investments, its heavy spending on education, strong savings, and its energetic work force. Thus, when the sources of Korea's growth are examined in a Denison framework, as was done by Kim

---

6. See Krueger 1979, 1985.

and Park (1985), the major contributors were (in order of importance) labor, capital, economies of scale, and knowledge. During 1963–82, labor's contribution was relatively constant, but capital's contribution doubled in the second half of that period, when it added an average of 2.1 percentage points to growth annually. Advances in knowledge, measured as total factor productivity, averaged 1.1 percent during 1963–82 compared with almost 2 percent in Japan during 1953–71 (Denison 1979).[7] As for labor, it contributed greatly to Korea's growth, as sources of growth in employment levels and hours worked were twice as great as they were in Japan for the period cited by Denison. The contribution of education was equally relevant for Korea as it had been for Japan a decade earlier and in the United States during 1948–73.

## Human Capital

Even in 1960, Korea's level of educational attainment was high compared with most other developing countries (see Barro and Lee 1993). Between then and 1982, however, it showed exponential growth in secondary education. Enrollments rose from 27 to 82 percent of the relevant age cohort. As for tertiary education, the enrollment ratio rose from 11 percent in 1977 to 36 percent in 1987 (see tables 3.4 and 3.5).

According to Tan and Mingat (1992), who surveyed educational spending in Asia, Korea's mid-1980s average of 3.4 percent of GNP spent on public education was in line with the regional average, as it had been in previous decades.[8] What differentiated Korea from other Asian economies (except for the Philippines) was the amount of private spending on education: 2.5 times more than the Asian average, according to Tan and Mingat's index of private financing in higher education. According to data collected by the Korean Edu-

**TABLE 3.3.   Chenery-Syrquin Norms**

| Variables to GDP | Year C-S Norm was Reached | Average Annual Deviation[a] (%) |
|---|---|---|
| Gross Investment | 1966 | 23 |
| Manufactured Exports | 1966 | 58 |
| Manufactures | 1967 | 19 |
| Infrastructure | 1966 | 13 |
| Utility production | 1966 | — |
| Merchandise exports | 1971 | 74 |

*Source:* World Bank.

[a]Average annual deviation between C-S norms year and 1989.

---

7. Measured as output per unit of input, Korea (1963–82) added 3.24 in output per 1.0 unit of input, below Japan's (1953–71) performance but roughly equivalent to those of France, Germany, and Italy in the 1950–62 period (Denison 1979).

8. An interesting finding by Tan and Mingat (1992) is that among Asian countries the Gini coefficient for access to public education is lowest (most equal) in Korea.

cation Development Institute, when private spending on education is included, the country's total was 10 percent of GNP in 1990.

All anecdotal evidence confirms that Korean families place the highest premium on education. Korea is a country where government, in the name of equity, once tried to ban private tutoring, where research institutes regularly count the number of their doctoral-level staff, and where (merit-based) entrance to Seoul National University is a prized family accomplishment. Indeed, surveys by the Bank of Korea routinely report that education and housing are the two main motivations for saving.

### Infrastructure and the Role of Government

Most development observers are familiar with the disparaging international view of Korea in the late 1950s. Heavily dependent on U.S. foreign aid for food,

**TABLE 3.4.  Educational Achievement in Secondary Schools**

|  | Average Schooling Years[a] | | | |
|  | 1960 | 1970 | 1980 | 1988 |
|---|---|---|---|---|
| Korea | 0.81 | 1.67 | 2.75 | 2.86 |
| Philippines | 1.18 | 1.67 | 2.39 | 2.68 |
| Indonesia | 0.12 | 0.34 | 0.62 | 0.73 |
| Malaysia | 0.61 | 1.05 | 1.49 | 1.79 |
| Taiwan, China | 1.03 | 1.33 | 1.96 | — |
| All developing | 0.34 | 0.52 | 0.95 | 1.1 |
| OECD | 2.59 | 3.03 | 3.79 | 3.94 |

Source: Barro and Lee 1993.
[a] Defined as the average number of years of secondary schooling attained by the total  population.

**TABLE 3.5.  Educational Achievement in Higher Education**

|  | Average Schooling Years[a] | | | |
|  | 1960 | 1970 | 1980 | 1985 |
|---|---|---|---|---|
| Korea | 0.1 | 0.23 | 0.36 | 0.41 |
| Philippines | 0.25 | 0.38 | 0.61 | 0.71 |
| Indonesia |  |  |  |  |
| Malaysia | 0.06 | 0.06 | 0.06 | 0.08 |
| Taiwan, China | 0.17 | 0.21 | 0.37 |  |
| All developing | 0.04 | 0.07 | 0.13 | 0.18 |
| OECD | 0.28 | 0.41 | 0.60 | 0.70 |

Source: Barro and Lee 1992.
[a] Defined as the average number of years of higher educational achievement attained by the total population.

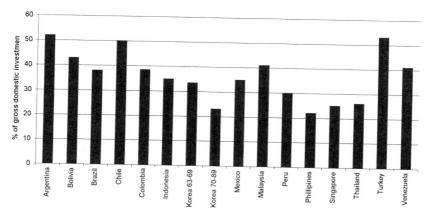

**Fig. 3.9.  Importance of public investment (percentage of gross domestic investment, 1970–89)**

fuel, and other raw materials, Korea was not seen as a promising place for major investments. According to Mr. Kim Chung Yum, the minister of finance in the early 1960s, the World Bank's president, Eugene Black, explained his rejection of Korea's investment priorities by noting that highways, steel plants, and national monuments produced the lowest return of any investments in developing countries (see J. Kim 1990). So Korea built the Seoul-Pusan Highway with domestic finance, after it had been rejected by both multilateral and bilateral donors.

Korea's infrastructure ranked well below those of Turkey, Colombia or Taiwan, China in 1960. Over the following ten years, one-third of gross domestic investment (GDI) consisted of infrastructure investment.[9] This trend continued in the 1970s when Korea's 33 percent infrastructure share in GDI was more than twice as high as Malaysia's and 50 percent higher than Thailand's. Its share was apparently less than those of other developing countries, however (see fig. 3.9), though this figure understates the true level of public infrastructure investments because government-invested enterprises (GIEs) did much of their own investing, especially in the 1970s. According to data reported by Sakong (1991), GIEs averaged 16 percent of GDI over the 1963–79 period. By 1980, Korea was well ahead of many developing countries (see table 3.6).

From the start, Korea put great reliance on self-financing. In its the First Five Year Plan (FFYP), the government stated that "investment resources for

---

9. The infrastructure category includes electricity, gas, water, transport and communications, and road and waterway investments.

the expansion of such government-run or controlled projects as the railroad, communications and electricity must be financed within the relevant corporations themselves by means of their management rationalization and the upward adjustment of public utility charges." The FFYP set Korean National Railway's (KNR) self-financing rate at 40 percent and that of the Korea Electric Power Corporation (KEPCO) at 45 percent.

A second feature of Korea's infrastructure is the scale of individual projects. The country's tendency to believe in its own projections has yielded ample rewards. Indeed, the economy's tendency to outperform its plan targets was not as awkward as it might have been had Korea merely invested in small bites. Much of the economic planning in the early days of Korean development was spearheaded by engineers, with economists entrusted merely with securing the requisite financing (D. Nam 1992).

It is hard to quantify the effect of infrastructure investments. However, strong evidence is presented by Kaufman (1991) that the economic rate of return on historical World Bank projects increases by 7 percentage points as the share of public investment in GDP increases from 5 to 10 percent.[10] The absolute rate of return rises from 13 to 20 percent in this "high infrastructure case," based on a large sample of 656 Bank projects. And K. S. Lee and A. Anas (1992) argue that in the few cases in which public infrastructure was lacking, Korean firms have had to undertake costly investments themselves, for example, to secure reliable utility supplies. Therefore, in addition to direct financial savings, Korean firms received greater certainty about public services. It can be argued that private firms were "crowded in" to make substantial investments because of the government's infrastructure program.

Of course, it is not merely capital expenditure per se that matters; it is also its quality, its maintenance, and its linkages with other complementary invest-

TABLE 3.6.  Building Infrastructure

| | Average Annual Growth Rate, 1960–80 (%) | | |
| --- | --- | --- | --- |
| | Electricity Generation (MKWH) | Length of Railway (KM) | Telephones Installed (per 1,000) |
| Korea | 17.0 | 4.7 | 20.9 |
| Taiwan, China | 12.9 | −0.5 | 21.9 |
| Turkey | 11.1 | 0.3 | 9.4 |
| Algeria | 20.5 | 0.4 | 13.3 |
| Argentina | 8.8 | — | 2.5 |

*Sources:* United Nations various years; World Bank's transport data; other sources.

10. I am indebted to K. S. Lee for bringing this evidence to my attention.

ments. Here Korea's technical capability and its planning apparatus played a large role in the success of its infrastructure program. Data collected by the World Bank's Operations Evaluation Department on 75 completed bank projects in Korea show that the proportion rated satisfactory was 95 percent, compared with 76 percent for the global sample of almost 500 projects. More telling are comparisons of ex-post rates of return: Korean projects averaged a 20 percent rate of return, compared with 18 percent for the East Asia region and 16 percent for all bank regions, or 3,000 total projects. Harberger (1978) reports that Korea's net productivity of capital in 1969–71 was more than twice as efficient as the average for the OECD countries and other Asian economies and second only to Taiwan, China (see Fry 1992 for recent estimates for Asian countries).

*The Importance of Savings*
Korea has become a nation of savers. Personal savings, which averaged 1 to 2 percent of GNP in the 1960s, advanced to a 7 percent average in the 1970s and exploded to 16 percent of GNP in the 1980s. When corporate savings, which have tended to outstrip personal savings except for the tail end of the heavy industry period (1976–78), and the modest but consistently positive government savings are added, the resulting national savings rises from 10 percent of GNP in the 1960s to 21 percent in the 1970s and peaks of 35 to 38 percent in the 1980s (see fig. 3.10). Savings behavior responds most directly to income gains and demographic factors and only secondarily to interest rates.[11] In the case of Korea, personal savings can be said to be largely autonomous rather than policy induced, in the sense of responding to sustained income growth and continuous declines in the population growth rates, which significantly lowered the dependency ratio.[12] Savers were also able to use a number of savings instruments, formal as well as informal.[13]

The primary objectives of Korean savings are education and housing. House prices (averaging multiples of six times income) and the shortage of mortgage lending, which forces self-financing of purchases, make housing the major motivation for savings.[14] Even the rental market's peculiarities (the advance deposit system or *chonsei*) make for a kind of forced savings.

11. See Fry (1984), who estimates the effects of Asian savings rates of income gains, population growth reductions, and improvements in real interest rates.
12. See Cho and Kim 1991 and Song 1990 on population dynamics and the importance of early and effective family planning efforts, which lowered the population growth rate from 3 percent per annum in 1960 to 2 percent in 1970.
13. "No-name accounts" were a popular instrument of financial savings. Savings societies are also prevalent and provide savers with credit on a revolving basis.
14. On the importance of the housing motivation on savings, see Renaud 1988, 1989.

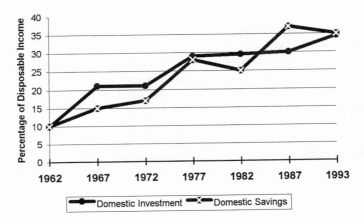

**Fig. 3.10.  Investment and savings. (Data from Bank of Korea 1990, 1994.)**

Despite its heavy savings, Korea's investment has been even larger at various critical periods. In 1962, foreign aid financed as much as 80 percent of investments, and throughout the 1960s foreign capital (either assistance or guaranteed foreign borrowings) was financing an average of 35 to 50 percent of domestic investment. In the post–oil shock periods of 1974–75 and 1980–81, Korea relied heavily on foreign borrowing; it was the world's fourth-largest debtor in the mid-1980s. The major role played by foreign capital in preceding and then complementing domestic savings is seen in figure 3.11.

Total official development assistance (ODA) per capita averaged more than U.S.$13 in the late 1950s (see Krueger 1979), which was considerable relative to Korea's then meager GNP. Only, perhaps, in the case of Taiwan, China did so much foreign aid flow into a poor developing country in such a short period of time. In the same fashion that foreign aid substituted for domestic savings in rapidly boosting investment levels, the question arises as to whether foreign direct investment (FDI) aids or deters domestic savings. In a provocative analysis, Fry (1992) argues that, for East Asia, FDI appears to reduce national savings. Of course, his sample of only five countries is dominated by Korea and Taiwan, China, both of which failed to encourage FDI in their early development years, although according to Korean policymakers in the early 1960s foreign investors were reluctant to invest in Korea.[15] Nevertheless, it took Korea until 1984 to become an active recipient of original FDI; like Japan, it seems to have opted for a domestically owned investment effort, which required mobilization and husbanding of national savings.

---

15. Interview with the Hon. Kim Chung Yum, former senior secretary to the late President Park.

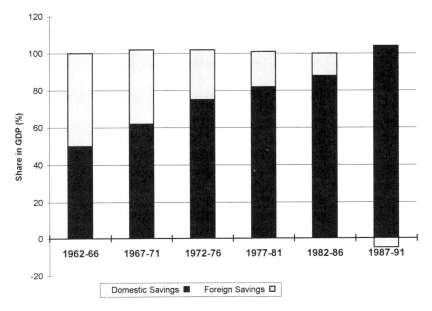

**Fig. 3.11.  Financing gross domestic investment (perecntage share in GDP). (Data from Bank of Korea 1990, 1994.)**

The Importance of Economic Management

Among many achievements of the Korean government's economic management, three stand out.[16] First, the real effective exchange rate was maintained within a narrow band of fluctuation. Second, the public sector deficit was kept under control. Third, despite occasional bouts of inflation, real wage increases were not allowed to outpace productivity growth.[17]

These achievements were the result of pragmatism and flexibility in economic management. This characteristic is exemplified by the government's comprehensive stabilization program in the early 1980s in response to the second oil shock and the sectoral imbalances of the HCI drive.[18] Unlike the previous "growth-first" era, the government gave top priority to price stability and implemented drastic policies such as freezing the budget. Even the exchange rate was kept overvalued to help reduce inflationary pressure, depressed exports

16. We are indebted to S. Y. Song for his collaboration in the preparation of this section.

17. The main exceptions occurred during the late 1970s, due to labor shortages resulting from the Middle East construction boom, and during the late 1980s, due to labor disputes in the wake of democratization and tightening labor markets.

18. See Corbo and Suh 1992.

notwithstanding. To quote an evaluation of the World Bank, "The remarkably successful measures of stabilization-with-structural adjustment undertaken by Korea in the first half of the 1980s are yielding handsome returns. . . . The substantial and swift adjustment Korea undertook in the early 1980s in response to the second oil shock and rigidities in the economy inherited from the 1970s was indeed impressive. . . . The adjustment was undertaken in two phases and is widely regarded as a model for other countries to emulate."[19] Other evidence of flexibility can be found in the relationship between the five year plans and annual management plans and budgets. The five year plans aimed to provide basic directions, principles, and plan targets, while policymakers were allowed enough room to maneuver to allow for policy responses to changing economic conditions (Jones and Sakong 1980).

Although the Korean government has consistently pursued an outward-oriented industrialization strategy, the conduct of economic policies has varied depending on the stage of development. It is useful to divide Korea's economic development into three periods. The first period (1962–71) can be characterized as encompassing a "growth at all costs" strategy emphasizing export promotion. The second period (1972–79) was dominated by HCI promotion and efforts to modernize farming. The third period (1980–88) was one of stabilization, liberalization, and increasing awareness of social welfare.

*Exchange Rate Management*
Both in terms of purchasing power parity and real effective exchange rates (REER), the won has shown very small changes over time. Its REER variability was reportedly the lowest among 95 Less-Developed Countries (LDCs) during 1976–85.[20] However, Korea has not always maintained a competitive exchange rate. The main exception occurred during 1975–79, when the exchange rate was fixed at a constant level for five years due to the burden of interest payments as external borrowing increased rapidly to finance the HCI drive. Another exception was during 1981–83, when the main concern was to help reduce inflationary pressure. Most recently, the won appreciated sharply during 1988–89 as a consequence of the undervalued won resulting from the Plaza Accord in 1985. This delay enabled Korea to establish a foothold in American markets.

It is noteworthy that the Korean government has consistently used devaluation in its economic reform packages. For instance, the won was devalued by 100 percent in 1964 to provide strong incentives for exports. Then it was devalued by 20 percent in December 1974 in response to the first oil shock and by 20 percent in January 1980 after the second oil shock. However, frequent use of devaluation puts further pressure on inflation. And the benefits of devaluation in terms of improvement in the trade balance have been less than anticipated due to Korea's heavy dependence on imports of raw materials and capital equipment. Nevertheless, despite the tradeoffs involved, a generation of Korean policymakers has used the exchange rate as the key variable to help achieve export targets.

*Inflation Control*
Throughout the 1960s and 1970s, controlling inflation was second only to the growth-oriented development strategy. Specifically, the Central Bank's financing of the National Investment Fund, used to promote the HCI drive, and the Grain Management Fund, used to support the prices of rice and barley in the 1970s, were mainly responsible for inflationary pressure. Accordingly, serious inflation emerged in the 1970s, running at times at a rate of around 20 percent. Since the early 1980s, however, the rate of inflation has decelerated substantially due to the government's comprehensive stabilization measures and then President Chun's personal aversion to inflation.

As aggregate demand policies were devoted to sustaining rapid economic growth, the government relied heavily on incomes policy, mostly in the form of price controls, to combat inflation. Ever since May 1961, when an across the board freeze on prices of goods and services was implemented, various forms of price control have been used as a means of slowing inflation. For example, the Price Stabilization Act of 1973 empowered the government to regulate prices of an extensive list of items and implicitly to control wages. Then, in 1976, the Price Stabilization and Fair Trade Act enabled the government to monitor price increases of items deemed to be under monopolistic control.

By the late 1970s, however, symptoms of administratively suppressed inflation in the form of supply shortages, black markets, and deteriorating product quality became serious. Furthermore, wages were increasing rapidly due to the labor shortages resulting from the Middle East construction boom, and inflation was galloping in the wake of the second oil shock and the huge liquidity inflow from the Middle East construction. In response, the government became strongly committed to price stabilization by implementing tight monetary and fiscal policies. It streamlined the operation of policy loans. It curbed expenditures, civil servant salaries, and rice purchase prices, culminating in a complete budget freeze in 1983. It kept the exchange rate overvalued to reduce inflationary pressure. It introduced the Monopoly Regulation and Fair Trade Act in 1981 to move away from direct interventions and toward promoting competition. In addition, it started a far-reaching import liberalization program to promote a more competitive environment. Government efforts paid off handsomely, with inflation averaging less than 3 percent a year during 1983–87, albeit aided by stable prices of raw materials, especially oil.

*Savings Promotion*

The main reason for Korea's relatively modest domestic savings until the mid-1980s was that the government had a low interest rate policy designed to reduce the cost of capital for export and strategic industries. Real interest rates were negative in the early 1960s and throughout the mid to late 1970s of the HCI drive period. As a result, potential financial savings were invested in either the curb market or property. One notable feature of Korea is the lack of capital flight, influenced no doubt by capital control but also by a strong sense of nationalism.

There was one notable exception to this policy of low interest rates, and it occurred during 1966–71. The government doubled the ceiling deposit rate in September 1965, from 15 to 30 percent, and kept high interest rates for five years. The amount of financial savings increased more than ten times in current prices within five years due mostly to shifts from the curb market. However, this policy stance was abruptly reversed in the wake of the Emergency Decree of August 3, 1972, which essentially froze curb market loans to debt-ridden firms in an effort to avoid a series of bankruptcies.

The surge in domestic savings since the mid-1980s can be explained by several factors. Personal savings increased substantially thanks to hefty increases in personal income and high real interest rates. Government savings also increased significantly, as budget deficits turned into surpluses. Business savings also increased substantially due to a lower tax burden and the booming economy. The development of nonbank financial intermediaries replaced the curb market and offered higher returns for savers. The government's policy of applying a low flat tax rate on most interest income, due in part to the lack of a "real name" system whereby asset holders are forced to use their own names in financial transactions, also helped to boost savings.

*Fiscal Management*

The government's fiscal stance was expansionist until the stabilization period in the early 1980s. The annual consolidated public sector deficit in 1971–82 averaged 3 percent of GNP. Initially, the main items of government expenditure were education, infrastructure, and defense. Government spending increased rapidly during the 1970s, largely because of policies designed to support grain prices and promote the HCI. Since 1969, the government has managed the Grain Management Fund, which was intended to pay a higher price to farmers and charge a lower price to urban wage earners. Deficits in the Grain Management and Fertilizer funds were financed through the Bank of Korea and were jointly responsible for as much as 37 percent of total growth of the money supply during 1976–78.

Since then, however, the public sector deficit has declined substantially, eventually turning to balance in the late 1980s. This turnaround was due to the fact that tax revenue increased from 10 percent of GNP in the early 1960s to the current level of 20 percent. This growth was helped by the tax reform of 1966–67: as the Office of National Tax Administration was created for effective tax enforcement, income tax rates were lowered, and a system of voluntary filing was adopted to promote compliance. The introduction of a value-added tax (VAT) in 1977 also boosted tax revenues significantly.

One notable feature of Korea's pattern of government expenditure is the low proportion spent on wages and salaries. At about 15 percent, it is considerably less than similar wages in the Philippines, Thailand, Malaysia, and Turkey (see table 3.7). Capital expenditure is not higher than in other, similar countries, and Korea's interest payments have been relatively small. In the 1964 budget, wages and salaries took a third of the budget, as did capital expenditures; by 1972, the former's share fell to 15 percent, and by the 1970s the latter's share averaged 21 percent. Korea thus was able to keep a tight grip on its government wage bill while passing a significant share of public investment over to GIEs and off the budget.

*Policy Flexibility*
Korea's flexible and pragmatic economic management was demonstrated by its successful responses to shocks. After the first oil shock in 1973, the government continued with its growth-oriented policies through export promotion (particularly overseas construction) and external borrowing. As a result, GNP grew at an average rate of more than 9 percent a year during 1974–78. One

**TABLE 3.7.   Consolidated Central Government Expenditures Composition (in percentage of total expenditures)**

| | Korea 1970–90 | Philippines 1972–90 | Thailand 1972–90 | Malaysia 1972–90 | India 1974–90 | Brazil 1970–89 | Turkey 1972–89 |
|---|---|---|---|---|---|---|---|
| Capital Expenditures | | | | | | | |
| Average of 1970–79 | 20.7 | 15.1 | 23.7 | 18.5 | 12.6 | 11.6 | 27.5 |
| Average of 1980–90 | 14.8 | 18.8 | 18.9 | 22.4 | 13.0 | 6.1 | 20.9 |
| Wages and salaries | | | | | | | |
| Average of 1970–79 | 15.8 | 28.6 | 23.3 | 30.6 | 17.3 | 15.5 | 34.0 |
| Average of 1980–90 | 14.5 | 28.9 | 30.0 | 29.7 | 12.5 | 9.6 | 25.9 |
| Other purchases of goods and services | | | | | | | |
| Average of 1970–79 | 26.0 | 26.0 | 30.7 | 16.7 | 15.8 | 8.7 | 14.6 |
| Average of 1980–90 | 26.4 | 23.2 | 29.5 | 15.0 | 14.9 | 7.2 | 14.6 |
| Interest payments | | | | | | | |
| Average of 1970–79 | 3.5 | 4.6 | 7.5 | 10.5 | 11.3 | 7.6 | 2.7 |
| Average of 1980–90 | 6.3 | 21.6 | 18.9 | 18.6 | 16.6 | 32.9 | 10.9 |
| Transfers | | | | | | | |
| Average of 1970–79 | 34.1 | 25.7 | 14.8 | 23.8 | 42.9 | 56.5 | 21.1 |
| Average of 1980–90 | 38.1 | 7.4 | 2.7 | 14.3 | 43.0 | 44.2 | 27.6 |

*Source:* IMF, government finance statistics.

inevitable consequence of this policy response was a rapid increase in external debt, from $4 billion in 1973 to $15 billion in 1978. (Such a rapid increase in external debt, which peaked at $47 billion in 1985, caused serious concerns for some time.)

Korea made a successful adjustment in the early 1980s in overcoming the second oil shock (of 1980) combined with sectoral imbalances in the aftermath of the HCI drive, bad harvests, and the political instability following the assassination of President Park. Shortages of daily necessities emerged, wages increased rapidly, and inflation accelerated, culminating in GNP recording negative growth for the first time and inflation galloping at 30 percent in 1980. In response, the government implemented comprehensive stabilization measures. First, restrictive fiscal and monetary policies were implemented: (1) government expenditure was restrained by reducing the grain price support program, deferring some public investment projects, and suppressing wages of civil servants; and (2) the money supply was restrained by reducing credit available to the government and reducing and rationalizing policy loans. Second, investment in the HCI was reduced and realigned: the government, in effect, forced each conglomerate to select one of the heavy industries for specialization. Third, the won was devalued, and interest rates were increased. Fourth, energy demand management policies were vigorously applied, and the full price of oil price increases was passed through. This structural adjustment program was highly praised by the World Bank for its speed and effectiveness.

An equally important observation is that when selective industrial intervention conflicted seriously with prudent macropolicy the former was abandoned. Thus, Korean policymakers had no fear of policy turnarounds and were able to shift gears quickly and efficiently. The policy flexibility of the Korean government is a model for other developing countries to emulate. A further example is the way in which trade liberalization was handled.

Trade liberalization began in earnest in 1981 when task force recommendations were adopted and plans announced to move from a 75 percent automatic approval list (based on number of items) to 95 percent by 1988. The public was convinced by official pronouncements that trade reform was needed to increase export competitiveness and appease trade partners. Precise annual targets were preannounced with the number of items to be added to the automatic approval list. This opening was a dramatic departure from the import licensing regime of the 1960s and the vigorous import restrictions that had attended the HCI drive. (At the height of HCI, 95 percent of all manufactures by value were restricted items.) Not only was trade liberalization a dramatic departure from past policy, but it was also implemented without backsliding and with a minimum of offsetting tariff increases. Once the political leadership was convinced that policy change was warranted, it was steadfastedly implemented in typical Korean fashion. By 1988, only 367 out of a total of 7,915 items remained on the restricted list.

## II.  Industrial Policy

Introduction

Although Korea's industrial policy began much earlier in the Park regime, many associate the Presidential Declaration on Heavy and Chemical Industrialization Policy of January 12, 1973, as the moment when Korea turned to modern industrialization. Korean documents in 1975, published by the HCI Promotion Council and kindly made available by Mr. O. Won Chul, its secretary, clearly state that:

> By combining educated cheap labor of good quality with foreign capital and technology which will be made available by the established credibility enlarged and absorption capacity of the Korean economy, the development of heavy and chemical industries will be made economically feasible.[21]

With these prophetic words, Korea launched its most controversial policy—the identification of and support for six strategic industries, including steel, petrochemicals, (nonferrous) metals, shipbuilding, electronics, and machinery. Each industry was supported by its own promotional law; according to government's 1975 manifesto, the first three were selected "with a view to enhancing self-sufficiency in industrial raw materials" and the other because "they are going to be developed into technology-intensive industries."[22]

What separates Korea from other developing countries is not only the fact that it was largely successful in its efforts but more importantly that it was conscious government policy from the outset to be internationally competitive. Again, quoting from the 1975 HCI manual:

> In the development of HCI, economy [*sic*] of scale, efficient operation, and competitive prices are prerequisite, since these are the industries which have vast inter-industry effects. The competitiveness of HCI is, therefore, fundamental to the whole economy. Economy of scale is especially required when we consider that domestic markets are so limited that HCI should be developed as export industries. In other words, economy of scale should be supported by an expansion of markets through export

21.  *Heavy and Chemical Industry* 1975, 8.
22.  Ibid., 11.

promotion. Most projects of the HCI, in this regard, are now under construction to have their unit production capacity running to an international level so that they may secure competitiveness on the world market, and enhance internal economy effect as well.[23]

The second feature that characterizes the HCI period was its detailed planning. The 1973 Industrial Site Development Promotion Law created the Industrial Site and Water Resource Development Corporation (1974), which was the key agent in building various industrial complexes, including Onsan and Changwon, and Yeocheon Chemical. Harbor, road, and water investments were coordinated and provided as part of social overhead capital investments.

The third distinctive aspect of Korea's industrialization planning was its forward-looking nature. Korean documents published in 1973 dutifully note Japan's export performance in 1955–71 and its composition of manufactures. Furthermore, Korean plans are explicit in saying that only up to date technology will be encouraged. This technological direction was undoubtedly aided by the return of U.S.-educated scientists and engineers, who were recruited with repatriation allowances, high salaries, and considerable power. Yoon (1992) reports that the "reverse brain drain" began with President Park's urging and the formation (with U.S. support) of the Korean Institute for Science and Technology (KIST) in 1966, an institution he strongly favored. This "technocratic aristocracy" did much to foster Korea's rapid technological advance.

The fourth and most controversial aspect of Korea's industrialization is its financing. Volumes have been written on the subject, including World Bank 1987, Amsden 1989, and Stern, et al. 1992. Not only were public resources directly mobilized for HCI financing via the National Investment Fund; even more significantly, banks were directed to lend to industry, often at preferential rates. In addition, the government provided a plethora of tax incentives as well as subsidized public services. The true cost of the HCI promotion will thus never really be known.

### Evolution of Industrial Policy[24]

Commentators have tended to divide Korea's industrial policy history into three distinct stages. The first was takeoff, generally thought of as 1961–73, when aggressive promotion of exports was combined with classic protection at home. Although interventions were manifold, the net effect was a regime favorable to exporters but generally neutral between one sector and another. By contrast, the HCI drive of 1973–79 represented a major shift in favor of specific industrial

---

23. Ibid., 12.
24. This section is based in part on previous work by Leipziger (1988), Leipziger and Petri (1989), and World Bank (1987).

targets and a wide-ranging commitment by government to use all levers at its disposal to steer resources to the HCI sectors and overtly direct its development. In the 1980s, following macroeconomic difficulties, this approach was replaced with a more neutral attitude, which was based largely on functional incentives but still had to cope with some of the costs of the HCI period.

*Industrial Takeoff*
This period featured a strongly dualistic trade regime of aggressive promotion of exports and protection of domestic markets. Korean policymakers maintained close control over trade, exchange, and financial policy, as well as over aspects of industrial decision making. In contrast to other countries, however, they used these instruments in an integrated fashion to pursue the primary objective of export growth. The net effect of these policies was a trade regime that was biased in favor of exports as a whole but essentially neutral with respect to the composition of exports.

The first instruments of export promotion were highly discretionary. Exporters were supported with multiple exchange rates, direct cash payments, permission to retain foreign exchange earnings for private use or resale, and the privilege to borrow in foreign currencies and import restricted commodities. Even as discretionary incentives were gradually replaced with more automatic instruments, exporters received significant concessions such as wastage allowances permitting them to import (on preferential terms) greater amounts of intermediate inputs than required in production, concessional interest rates on export loans, preferential access to working capital, and tariff exemptions to direct and indirect exporters. In part, these interventions allowed Korean exporters to avoid some of the distortions involved in the protection afforded to domestically oriented activities. Essentially, the policies amounted to off-budget subsidies for exporters.

Support for exports was channelled through the state controlled banking system. Government objectives were implemented through policy loans—bank loans explicitly earmarked for particular activities or industries and lent passively by banks at interest rates below those charged for general lending purposes. Following explicit government directives, banks used export performance as the criterion of creditworthiness.

By the late 1960s, therefore, the main features of industrial policy were: (1) moderate overall protection of domestic markets offset by special subsidies to exports; (2) approximately world market pricing of inputs and outputs across different export products; (3) high protection of the domestic market in industries with poor export prospects; and (4) high protection of final consumer goods relative to industrial raw materials and capital goods. Overall, protection did not significantly distort either the general level or the interindustry pattern of export incentives. Consequently, the emerging export structure reflected comparative advantage more closely than is generally the case in protected economies. Moreover, Korea's trade deficits reflected heavy imports of raw materials and intermediates, not of final consumption goods.

*The Heavy and Chemical Industry Drive*
Buttressed by the six promotional laws issued during the Second Five Year Plan (i.e., for industrial machinery in 1967, shipbuilding in 1967, electronics in 1979, steel in 1970, and petrochemicals in 1970), President Park's 1973 decree mobilized Korea's bureaucracy to achieve his goals. Targets set in the Third Five Year Plan included physical quantities of steel, ships, and autos to be produced by 1980. The most remarkable feature of these plans was that each industry designated for support was to go through four predetermined phases:[25]

1. *Minimum scale* during active government planning and support accompanies protection
2. *Optimum scale,* at which time government lending and support continues but the industry matures
3. *International scale,* by which time industries are expected to be self-sustaining and initiative is to come from business itself
4. *International first-class scale,* by which time the industry is expected to be internationally competitive

As can be seen in figure 3.12, it was expected to take 10 years from the time of heavy government support for HCI during the Third Five Year Plan until international competitiveness was reached in the Fifth Five Year Plan. By and large, Korean planners were correct: HCI exports reached world-class scale in the mid-1980s. By the late 1980s, indeed, trade liberalization had progressed very far in manufactures, and, helped by an appreciating yen, Korean exports in key sectors had successfully entered Western markets.[26]

Government support for industry was massive. It included import protection, fiscal preferences, and, most importantly, preferential access to credit. Evidence from Hong (1979, 1985) shows that restricted imports of machinery rose from 34 percent of the total in 1968 to 61 percent in 1978, while a similar measure for iron and steel rose from 28 to 75 percent. Tariff rates and domestic content laws were also used to protect infant industries. According to the World Bank (1987), only 41 percent of electrical appliances and electronics were subject to automatic approval in 1981, compared with an average of 75 percent for all import categories.

As for fiscal preferences, most tax obligations for promotional industries were exempted for five years and often cut in half for an additional three years.

25. HCI Promotion Council 1975.
26. The U.S. market was Korea's largest and most successful, although even these antidumping suits served to raise entry costs (see Leipziger and Shin 1991).

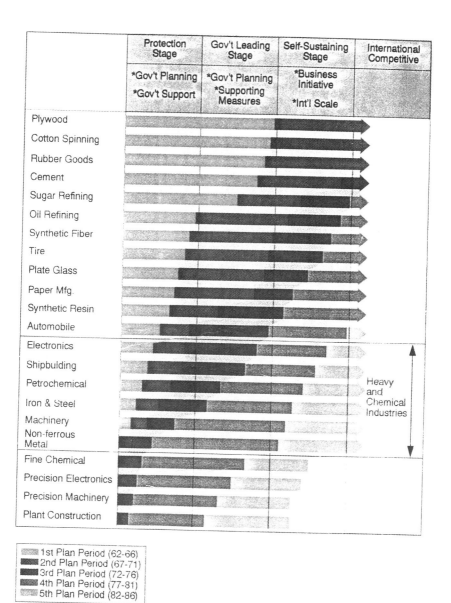

| | Protection Stage | Gov't Leading Stage | Self-Sustaining Stage | International Competitive |
|---|---|---|---|---|
| | *Gov't Planning *Gov't Support | *Gov't Planning *Supporting Measures | *Business Initiative *Int'l Scale | |

Plywood
Cotton Spinning
Rubber Goods
Cement
Sugar Refining
Oil Refining
Synthetic Fiber
Tire
Plate Glass
Paper Mfg.
Synthetic Resin
Automobile
Electronics
Shipbulding
Petrochemical
Iron & Steel
Machinery
Non-ferrous Metal
Fine Chemical
Precision Electronics
Precision Machinery
Plant Construction

Heavy and Chemical Industries

1st Plan Period (62-66)
2nd Plan Period (67-71)
3rd Plan Period (72-76)
4th Plan Period (77-81)
5th Plan Period (82-86)

**Fig. 3.12. Stages of HCl development. (Data from Heavy and Chemical Industry Promotion Council 1975.)**

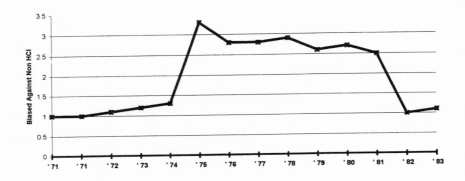

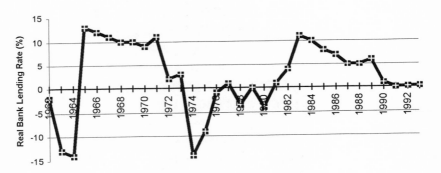

Fig. 3.14.   The real price of capital (real bank lending rate, percentage). GNP deflator is used for the inflation rate. (Data from Bank of Korea, *Economic Statistical Yearbook,* various issues.)

The bias toward the HCI sector produced a comparatively light tax burden compared with that of other industries (see fig. 3.13). The government relied heavily on its control of the credit system to provide "strategic" industries with access to substantially subsidized bank loans. The potential for subsidization was great due to the complicated system of interest rate ceilings that prevailed throughout the 1970s. Real bank interest rates were negative during most of that time (see fig. 3.14), and bank rates were anyway much lower than those in the informal credit markets.

The National Investment Fund (NIF) was specially created in 1974 to help finance the HCI drive. It was funded by the compulsory deposit of savings by all managers of pensions, savings, and postal savings accounts, and by life insurers or equivalent purchasers of NIF bonds. It lent as much as two-thirds of its portfolio to HCI projects; however, its real impact stemmed from its "announcement effect" on bank lending practices. Policy loans, the directed credit

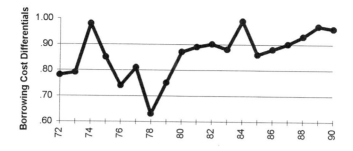

**Fig. 3.15. Financing the HCI expansion (borrowing cost differentials, average borrowing cost of HCI to average borrowing cost of light industry, 1.0 = neutrality). (Data from World Bank 1987.)**

instrument of government, rose from an already high 41 percent of total domestic credit in 1975 to 51 percent in 1978 with real interest rates being sharply negative at the height of the HCI drive (fig. 3.14).

It is this period of underpriced capital that has drawn the attention of Amsden (1989) and the criticism of Korea's neoclassical economists. At the same time that targeted capital-intensive industry received these preferences, light industries such as textiles faced fierce discrimination in access to credit. This pattern of increasing preferences for HCI industries is seen clearly in figure 3.15 (reproduced from World Bank 1987), wherein 1.0 represents neutrality in industrial finance. Even more importantly, the volume of credit destined for light industries fell from an average of 66 percent of the total in 1973–74 to 40 percent in 1975–79.[27]

*A Shift Toward Functional Incentives*
Unlimited support for strategic industries was abruptly reversed in 1980. Certainly, President Park's assassination was one reason for the change; but the second oil shock had derailed Korea's macroeconomic balances, and the excess capacity in HCI was no longer tolerable. Korea's rapidly rising incremental capital-output ratio (ICOR)—it reached almost 5.0 in 1975–80—showed that investment was yielding low returns. It became clear to economic policymakers that a shift in strategy was needed, as evidence of financial losses and structural distortions caused by the HCI drive mounted. Retrenchment was necessary.

The new government had simultaneously to stabilize the macroeconomy, solve mounting financial problems in major industries, and establish new directions for industrial policy. As far as industrial policy was concerned, the

27. See World Bank 1987, 156.

new approach was contained in the Fifth Five Year Plan, written in 1979. The plan's emphasis on indicative planning and a greater role for the market was eventually translated into a range of financial and import liberalization programs.

The government began to reverse its past preferences for heavy industry firms by reserving credit for small and medium firms. It reduced its role in specific decisions on credit allocation and abandoned policies that favored the HCI sector. In the area of industrial finance, the government: (1) sold the commercial banks to private shareholders, although it continued to exercise significant influence over banking decisions; (2) established new financial institutions and permitted some growth in the international activities of domestic banks and the domestic activities of foreign banks; (3) increased real interest rates, reducing the gap between the organized and unorganized sectors of the financial market; and (4) substantially reduced the scope of interest rate subsidies for particular borrowers.

Despite this general thrust toward neutrality, the government continued to play an active role in several areas of policy. Intervention since 1979 has focused on the restructuring of distressed industries, support for the development of technology, and the promotion of competition. Restructuring operations became frequent in the wake of sharp reversals in world markets and the over-ambitious investment programs of the 1970s. The firms and industries involved were large and highly leveraged, with their loans representing a significant share of commercial bank assets. These factors, coupled with the relative thinness of Korean capital markets, drew the government deeply into the restructuring process. The plans it helped orchestrate involved mergers, capacity reduction, and special financial rescheduling with commercial banks (issues discussed at greater length in Leipziger 1988). Although the government was no longer involved in picking winners, it did occasionally block industrial entry (such as when Samsung wanted to enter the automobile market), possibly for strategic economic reasons.

To many observers, the key to Korea's future industrial policy lies in its approach to financial reform. The residual difficulties of the financial sector include controlled interest rates; the still huge proportion of domestic credit going to "policy loans"; passive rediscounting at official behest, which manages to keep the questionable portfolios of some industries performing; and, above all, the implicitly socialized or shared risk between government and business on borrowed funds (on these see C. Nam 1990; S. Nam 1991; and Leipziger and Petri 1994.) Clearly, the remnants of past policies are part of the price Korea is paying for earlier intervention and its failure to establish an independent financial sector. The critical question is whether this is a price worth paying, the subject of the following section.

## An Assessment of HCI

The HCI episode in Korea is perhaps its most controversial period of economic history. Proponents like Amsden (1989) stress the virtues of having got the prices wrong in order to create dynamic comparative advantage. Opponents like Yoo (1990) stress the costliness of the distortions, the excesses and waste, and compare them unfavorably with Taiwan, China, which achieved at least as enviable a growth record without the forced transformation of its economy. The World Bank (1987) took a middle-ground position. It acknowledged that dynamic gains were made possible in record time, as evidenced by the high percentage of exports in a number of HCI sectors by 1983.[28] But it also recognized the low levels of capacity utilization in some industries, such as machinery and fabricated metals in the 1970s, which caused large economic losses. Moreover, light industries such as textiles suffered greatly as a result of the HCI drive[29] and, more importantly, lasting scars were left in the financial sector, the costs of which are still being borne (see C. Nam 1990).

Any verdict on HCI depends largely on the period during which the assessment is made and also on the approach adopted. Yoo (1990) attempts to measure the marginal products of capital applied to HCI and non-HCI activities and finds that the returns to invested capital were lower in the HCI sector. His findings are dependent on some critical assumptions, but the general proposition that capital's efficiency was not higher in HCI sectors, despite the subsidies showered on them, may well be true, measured in the late 1970s and early 1980s. An interesting test would be to extend the analysis to allow for some dynamic returns. Yoo, however, concludes that "the net effect of the HCI policy on the export competitiveness of the heavy and chemical industry group seems to have been nil or negative" when compared with Taiwan, China's performance.[30]

Kim (1990) reviews some of the outcomes of the HCI drive, including a deteriorating trade balance, sharply increased foreign debt (up from U.S.$4 billion in 1973 to $15 billion in 1978 before the second oil shock), an increase in inflation due to classical overheating, a weakening of financial discipline as firms denied credit borrowed heavily on the curb market, and rising unit labor costs as wages were pushed up by expanding labor demand. Kim also argues that income distribution worsened during the HCI drive.

Another interesting assessment of HCI is contained in Stern et al. 1992. In this treatment, the joint team from Harvard Institute for International Develop-

---

28. Ibid., 15.
29. Ibid., chap. 7.
30. Yoo 1990, 99.

ment (HIID) and Korea Development Institute (KDI) categorized investments in industries as follows: (1) those investments that were successful—defined as yielding rates of return higher than the cost of capital either ex ante (i.e., a normal industry) or ex post (i.e., an infant industry); and (2) those that were unsuccessful—yielding negative internal rates of return—despite ex ante expectations to the contrary (i.e., unsuccessful infants) or due to changes in relative prices (i.e., declining industries). The "market-conforming" industrial successes and failures are easy to discern. Among promoted industries, electrical equipment was a clear success based on existing comparative advantage of high-quality, low-cost labor and international markets pioneered by the Japanese. The example of a failed industry (which according to Stern exhibited initially positive rates of return) is fertilizers, for which the cost of raw materials caused losses. In the group of what Stern calls "non-market conforming industries," there are failures such as machinery and aluminum and successes such as steel and automobiles. Based on the sample of projects selected for analysis, Stern finds no evidence to suggest that Korean policymakers were more astute in picking winners than were policymakers elsewhere.

The World Bank (1987) concluded by saying that "the HCI drive was overambitious and resulted in serious misallocations of resources. Nevertheless . . . many of the goals of that policy were in fact achieved. Exports of HCI did not quite reach the target of 50 percent of total exports by 1980, but exceeded the target only a few years later and reached 56 percent in 1983. . . . In a comprehensive dynamic perspective, [they concluded,] it is difficult to demonstrate that an alternative policy would have worked better."[31] On an industry by industry basis, the World Bank's assessment does not differ much from that of Stern et al., but the overall judgment is quite different. Stern concludes: "In short, while there is no evidence to support the contention that Korean policymakers were able to pick winners, neither can we conclude that the shift to the HCI policy helped promote Korea's development."[32] Kim (1990), like the World Bank, highlights the weak capacity utilization in selected industries but concludes that "capital was transferred into physical assets, most of which were competitive when renewed growth in demand restored international prices to levels covering the replacement costs of efficient new producers."[33]

Since neither a full costing of the HCI drive nor a counterfactual exercise is possible, it is perhaps wise to accept the fact that short-term dislocations occurred, damaging both labor-intensive industries and the macroeconomy. Still, HCI's objectives were largely met once the effects of the second oil shock were

---

31. World Bank 1987, 45.
32. Stern, et al., 1992, V–22.
33. J. Kim, 34.

overcome. The structure of Korean manufacturing was radically altered, and HCI achieved, albeit with a delay, the goals set out in the Third Five Year Plan. Most of the distortions have proved reversible, except for the weaknesses of the financial sector, which remain today.

The interesting line of inquiry, from the point of view of replicability, is the assessment of infant industries. Why did some succeed while others failed? And how did Korea manage to get a sizable set of world-class industries? To answer the first question, we draw on the stories of Pohang Steel and the Changwon Complex (sidebars).

## Pohang Steel: Korea's Most Successful Infant Industry

In order to supply its emerging capital-intensive industries, Korea attempted in the early 1970s to build a state of the art, integrated steel plant. The Pohang Steel Company (POSCO) was a bold and successful gamble. According to Auty (1990), Pohang attained global competitiveness in 1981, when the third-stage expansion was completed, because it could quickly reach full capacity as each successive stage came online. What accounted for its success?

First, although Pohang was a state enterprise, it had powerful and independent leadership in the person of former general Park Tae Joon. Through his access to President Park, he was able to clear away bottlenecks and complete construction of Pohang in record time. Second, financing was secured largely through Japanese reparations funds (at subsidized interest rates); even more importantly, state of the art technology and technical assistance were provided by Nippon Steel. Third, the high potential productivity of a new steel plant was successfully captured by an efficient and cooperative work force and strong domestic demand. Low construction and operating costs, along with strong management, are reflected in Pohang's ability to produce steel as efficiently as Japan in the early 1980s, the true test of an infant industry. Put differently, Korean steel fits the Stern et al. (1992) typology of an industry whose economic rate of return ex ante fell short of the real price of capital but ultimately passed the efficiency of capital test ex post.

Pohang is also a case of government selecting an industry for promotion after, according to policymakers Kim Chung Yum and Choi Gak Kyu,[a] the private sector declined involvement and all aid donors rejected the project. It benefited from highly subsidized capital, a protected domestic market, discounted public services and utilities, and other preferences mandated by the Steel Industry Promotion Law of 1970. The verdict is unanimous that the industry is a technical success, while the verdict on financial success is mixed, with Auty (1991) doubtful and Amsden (1989) and Stern et al. (1992) convinced.

The strong conclusion that emerges, however, is that a risky major investment project such as Pohang could not have proceeded without direct government involvement. The project would not have succeeded without presidential support, independent corporate management, and world prices as the ultimate yardstick of technical efficiency. Korea's version of state capitalism yielded a dynamically efficient industry capable of supplying downstream users, financing its own second-generation expansion through retained earnings, and propelling Korea into a capital-intensive stage of industrialization perhaps a decade earlier than expected.

[a] Respectively chief secretary to the president and minister of commerce and industry at the time.

The differences between Korea's most successful and least successful infant industries are manifold. Pohang Steel was a clearly defined project with superior management, strong implementation, a captive domestic market, presidential backing, a proven technology, and, above all, a goal of exporting. Changwon suffered from divisive management, an overambitious and diffuse industrial mission, and a limited domestic market; above all, at heart it was an import-substitution activity. Pohang went on to become one of the world's most efficient steelmakers, while Changwon has undergone many ownership changes and industrial restructurings.

These contrasts need to be considered in light of the fact that more infants have succeeded in Korea than almost anywhere with the possible exception of Taiwan, China (see Wade 1990). This is despite the fact that Korea's industrialization drive involved much higher risks, as the chosen industries were highly capital intensive and large (e.g., shipbuilding, steel, and automobiles). These industries can be viewed in the following light.

First, Korean decision makers did select industries in which the achievement of dynamic comparative advantage was possible. It seems clear that their choices were influenced by the manufacturing structure of Japan.

Second, the scale of support was massive, and project execution was largely excellent. In cases where it was not, changes were made quickly and decisively.

Third, self-reliance and ultimately internationally competitive performance were expected, and the authorities were not patient with non-performers. Moreover, the government was basically indifferent about whether it used the private or the public sector to achieve its industrial goals. One need only look at the frequent ownership changes of the heavy machinery facilities at Changwon to see this point.

Fourth, the institutional environment in Korea favored success. Specifically, the scarcest resource, capital, was directed generously toward emerging growth industries, and tax incentives and protection were offered. Moreover, the five year plans signaled that the government stood behind these emerging industries, and a can-do (or cannot-fail) mentality was shared by industrialists and bureaucrats.

Fifth, tremendous efforts were made to absorb foreign state of the art technology, aided by the return home of Korean scientists and engineers.

Sixth, progress was continually monitored, and Koreans were not untouched by fear of political and economic reprisals.

Indeed, it is impossible to draw lessons from the HCI experiment or any other period of Korea's recent economic history without a clear discussion of the role of government in the industrialization process.

### The Changwon Industrial Complex: An HCI Fiasco

The Changwon Complex in the southern part of Korea mirrored to some extent the push into integrated steelmaking; however, the differences far exceeded the similarities. First and foremost, the heavy machinery complex was meant to supply the Korean Power Company with thermal power-generating equipment as well as machinery for other HCI subsectors. As such it resembled much more closely a traditional import-substitution industry. Second, it was entrusted to a subsidiary of Hyundai, a private company, and, since its scale was enormous (unparalleled, according to Stern et al. 1992, in the developing world and with a product diversification and degree of integration rarely found in the industrialized world), it was both risky and costly. Begun in 1976 and partially halted in 1979, it became a symbol of the unbridled engineering focus of the HCI drive, although, according to Stern and his associates, the ex ante rate of return was favorable. But it differed from steelmaking in that it had to rely on licensed technology in many areas and on uncertain markets. In fact, KEPCO's switch to a nuclear investment program undermined Changwon's viability. Changwon's coming online in the midst of Korea's worst economic crisis, in 1980–81, certainly hurt, but Changwon was beset by poor technical decisions and muddles as well. Restructuring continued in the early 1980s, but low capacity utilization continued to plague the complex, and by all accounts it was not a profitable investment.

*Source:* Stern et al. 1992; World Bank 1987.

## III.  The Role of Institutions

There can be no doubt that Korea's rapid economic development was government led. Various authors refer to market-conforming or market-guided policies, but it is instructive to see reality not only with hindsight and with the theoretical perspective of today but from the views of the policymakers then. According to D. W. Nam, Korea's finance minister (1969–74) and deputy prime minister (1974–78):

> In the 1960s, the Korean government had to take the initiative in almost all areas of development effort. It was busy introducing new institutions and reforming existing ones, building up social infrastructures, negotiating with foreign governments and international organizations for economic assistance, undertaking strategic investment projects, both public and private, and, above all, campaigning to mobilize and motivate people towards fulfilling the development objectives."[34]

The evidence is clear that the Korean government had: (1) a clear vision of its industrial, as well as agricultural, goals; (2) an ability to control the economy via economic instruments supplemented with jawboning and coercion when needed; (3) a willingness to share risks with industry or, put differently, to use business to achieve national goals; (4) an excellent track record of creating institutions such as development banks, trade promotion agencies, and general trading companies; and (5) a unique ability to make pragmatic policy decisions.

The evidence is also clear to Cho (1994) that "the system of resource use in Korea throughout the period of rapid growth, and particularly during the 1970s, deviated markedly from the competitive market system."[35] It may be that C. H. Lee (1992) is correct and that government and business formed a quasi-internal organization that could allocate capital efficiently. More likely it seems that government did not so much pick winners as create winners with widespread and lasting interventions. One should not let the 1973–79 period dominate Korean economic history unduly, however. Korea was highly successful in the 1960s and again in the 1980s. Much of this success revolves around: (1) Korea's bureaucracy and planning apparatus, led by the Economic Planning Board; (2) the unique relationship between business and government; and (3) the intangibles of policy making, which revolve uniquely around culture and country-specific circumstances but account in large measure for the pragmatism, consistency, and decisiveness of policy formulation and implementation.

## The Government and Bureaucracy

On taking power through a military coup in 1961, President Park Chung Hee made a commitment to achieving rapid economic development and national se-

---

34. D. Nam 1992, 7.
35. Cho 1994, 36.

curity. He believed that in order to attain these objectives a restructuring of the government would be necessary. He wanted to replace the existing cabinet style of government with a form in which power and authority are concentrated in the presidency. President Park also saw the need for an organization that would not only formulate consistent economic policies but coordinate their implementation. To fulfill this need, he approved a recommendation for establishing the Economic Planning Board (EPB).[36]

Set up in 1961, the EPB combined several policy functions previously entrusted to different ministries: (1) the planning function, originally located in the Ministry of Reconstruction, which had worked with the U.S. Agency for International Development (USAID) in the aftermath of the war; (2) the power of preparing the government budget, which was removed from the Ministry of Finance (MOF); and (3) the function of collecting and evaluating the national census and other statistics, which was taken from the Ministry of Internal Affairs. Responsibility and jurisdiction over the inflow of foreign capital and technology were vested in the EPB as well. The EPB had three main functions: (1) it planned and formulated economic policy programs, (2) it coordinated economic policies implemented by individual ministries, and (3) it evaluated policy programs implemented by individual ministries on a continuing basis.[37]

Since effective coordination of policies among ministries required both power and prestige, the EPB was made a "superministry." It was the only ministry in the government to be led by the deputy prime minister (DPM), who was also made chairman of the Economic Ministers' Council. Although the DPM and the Economic Ministers' Council were subordinate to the prime minister and the State Council on the organizational chart of the government, they were given considerable autonomy. Few economic policies and programs approved by the Economic Ministers' Council were overruled by the State Council.

Part of the reason for conducting economic policy in this way was that the DPM received his instructions directly from the president, that is, not through the prime minister. The DPM often reported first to the president when he needed to obtain informal approval on any new policy adopted in the Economic Ministers' Council. Thereafter, the policy proposal would be sent to the State Council for formal approval. In effect, the DPM was deputy to the president rather than the prime minister on economic policy matters.

Apart from establishing the EPB, a number of new government agencies were launched, and several existing agencies were revamped to advance

36. The idea of an EPB with a threefold function was originally suggested to President Park in a memorandum prepared by Chung Jae-Suk, who at the time was director of planning in the Ministry of Reconstruction. Mr. Chung later became minister of trade and industry (1972–80). This information was conveyed through the author's interview with Mr. Chung.

37. The evaluation and assessment of government policies and programs has also been carried out by the Office of the Prime Minister. But that office has concentrated more on noneconomic programs.

the goals of economic development. Three of them are noteworthy. The first concerns the National Tax Administration. Until this agency was completely restructured in 1966, the Korean government had only limited ability to collect the necessary revenues. Shortfalls had been made up largely from U.S. aid, and as that declined there was a critical need to increase tax revenues.

This need was met by reorganizing the internal tax office into the Office of National Tax Administration (ONTA). It was responsible for collecting a larger amount of taxes through vigorous enforcement of existing tax laws. To ensure effective tax collection, President Park not only specified tax collection targets but instructed ONTA to set up a tax collection situation room in the Office of the President, commonly called the Blue House.[38] The president himself would check progress on meeting tax collection targets on a daily basis. Without such concentrated efforts to increase tax revenue, the Korean government would not have come close to achieving an overall budgetary balance by 1968 in the face of rapidly dwindling U.S. aid.

The second notable change was the establishment of the Office of Labor Affairs. Historically, the labor movement in Korea began as part of the independence campaign, so it was very political. In the early years following World War II, it had been infiltrated by leftist groups. Furthermore, even in the early 1960s, there was a widely held fear that trade unions could be manipulated by North Korea to its advantage. In order to ensure peace on the labor front, it was necessary for the government to be attentive to the needs of ordinary workers. The office was therefore established not only to enforce new labor standards but to protect workers' rights in such areas as industrial disablement. Furthermore, it organized vocational training programs to help workers acquire the new skills needed for industrial development.

The third notable change was the establishment of the Ministry of Science and Technology (MOST). As the economy began to take off, there was an urgent need for Korea to increase the inflow of foreign technologies and develop its own technologies. To achieve these objectives, the Bureau of Technologies, established first in the EPB, was expanded and transformed into a full-fledged ministry in 1967.

### Bureaucracy: Staffing, Dedication, and Access

During the period from 1948 to 1960, the Korean bureaucracy was a kind of spoils system. Although civil service appointments were based on examinations, these were rather perfunctory. In April 1963, however, the National Civil Service Law was passed to serve as the legal base for professionalizing the entire national bureaucracy. It adopted three key principles: (1) with few exceptions, appointments to be based on the results of open competitive exami-

---

38. For an illuminating account of the significance and operational style of ONTA, see C. Kim 1991, 44–46, and Choi 1992, 33–34.

nations; (2) promotions to depend on the evaluation of the performance of each individual in a particular position; and (3) all civil servants to be guaranteed job security. This last point meant that regular civil servants could not be dismissed unless the grounds for dismissal were legitimate and due process was followed.

As far as recruitment is concerned, Korea's professional bureaucracy is a two-tier system, similar to that which exists in Japan.[39] This system allows exceptional people to begin at advanced levels and has attracted many well-qualified and ambitious individuals to government service. Those who pass the high civil service examination can start at a higher level (currently grade 5), which would take ordinary recruits several years to reach. Although many who have started at the bottom of the bureaucratic hierarchy are allowed to move on to higher grades based on on-the-job performance, the high civil service in Korea has always been dominated by those who have passed the high civil service examination. Competition for passing this examination has been intense. Between 1963 and 1985, some 157,000 persons took it, and only a little more than 2,600 (1.7 percent of the total) succeeded. Of these, nearly all had a college education, and more than three-quarters were under the age of 28.

Because of this rigorous selection process, senior civil servants have been highly regarded by the rest of society. This respect no doubt reflects the long Confucian tradition of honoring scholar-bureaucrats. Members of the advanced civil service have therefore tended to look upon themselves not only as the guardians of national interest but as an elite group of leaders. In this respect, the Korean bureaucracy today shares not only many characteristics of the Yi Dynasty bureaucracy but also those of the Japanese bureaucracy.

However, like its counterparts elsewhere, the Korean bureaucracy has some flaws. Often it has tended to be exclusive and not receptive to the views of outsiders. Fortunately, during the 1960s and 1970s these negative traits have been offset in various ways. For example, since the beginning of the Saemaul (New Village) Movement initiated by President Park in November 1970, many short-term educational forums and training sessions have been organized that civil servants are required to attend together with leaders from other sectors of society. Such occasions have helped Korean high civil servants to a greater understanding of the concerns and interests of the country as a whole. Members of the Korean bureaucracy have also maintained close links with outsiders with whom they were at school or university. And many high civil servants have been sent abroad to study, acquiring not just new technical competence and perspective but democratic values.

*Achieving Policy Consensus*
Besides the five year and annual economic management plans, under presidents Park and Chun, there were other mechanisms through which national consensus

39.  Choi 1992, 25–26.

for economic policy was obtained and its implementation monitored. Three in particular are worth noting. One of them was the monthly economic briefing held at the EPB. This meeting started out as an occasion for the EPB to report general economic trends to the president, but it soon acquired broader objectives. The president, all ministers, and other senior figures attended. In addition, the heads of big business and financial organizations were invited. The briefing covered not only macroeconomic trends but micropolicy issues.

Consensus building was also achieved at the quarterly Trade Promotion Conference. At this meeting, attended by the president, ministers, other high government officials as well as the heads of virtually all large trading firms in the country, the Ministry of Trade and Industry (MTI) would provide reports not only on the progress toward achieving annual export targets but the problems and difficulties facing industries in meeting their export goals. As in the case of the monthly economic briefing, the president made suggestions as to how problems might be handled. In addition, he used the meetings to recognize those individuals from the private sector who had made outstanding contributions toward achieving export targets.

The third important mechanism took the form of annual meetings between the president and senior officials of individual ministries. In January or early February, every ministry reported directly to the president on its plan of activities for the current year as well as its achievements over the previous one. After listening to the report, the president would comment on the past year's achievements and, if necessary, make changes to the plan for the current year. After attending such a meeting, a senior official was left in no doubt as to which direction the president wished him to lead his ministry for the year.

It is often assumed that a strong president can achieve his aims merely by issuing orders. In fact, people need to be persuaded to work with the government for the good of the country. Presidents Park and Chun made use of almost every occasion to expound on their economic policies and underlying philosophies. In the case of President Chun, he felt that such efforts did not go far enough. Therefore, he instructed the EPB to launch what he called the Public Economic Education Program, focusing on such issues as the merits of price stability and the need to work with Korea's trading partners.

In spite of the many mechanisms for ensuring consistency of policies and coordination among different ministries, it is worth emphasizing that the balance between microinvestment planning and macroeconomic management was not always achieved. This has been particularly true when a certain policy or a group of projects is backed by the Office of the President, which has a limited staff but the power to overrule other ministries, including the EPB. One example was the HCI drive in the 1970s. As President Park believed in the urgency of undertaking and completing the HCI projects for national security reasons,[40] a Special Task Force was put under the direction of one of the senior secretaries to the president for economic affairs.[41]

This senior secretary enjoyed virtually unlimited power to plan and execute HCI projects with little regard for the overall resource constraints of the economy. After he and his staff had designed various projects, the task of financing them was left to the MOF and the EPB.[42] Because the government had to complete many other projects, resources were greatly stretched, and inflation accelerated. During 1973–78, the average annual rate of consumer price inflation shot up to 18 percent, from 13 percent in 1968–72. Similar experiences were repeated in 1990–91, when President Roh allowed his senior secretary for economic affairs to bypass the DPM on policy matters involving housing construction and aid to the former Soviet Union.

*Rewards and Penalties*
Korean civil servants are by no means well rewarded financially, particularly in terms of salaries. Until recently, the average monthly salary of civil servants was only 50 to 60 percent of what someone with equivalent education, training, and experience received in nongovernment sectors. However, until the early 1980s, civil servants were the only professionals in Korea who enjoyed the benefit of pensions after retirement. Those pensions, together with lifetime job security, were significant incentives.

Nevertheless, the strongest incentive, particularly for high civil servants, has been social respect, which increases as they climb the ladder. This kind of nonpecuniary satisfaction reaches its peak when performance is recognized in the form of special citations, awards of honor, and personal appreciation by the heads of state. This was President Park's style.

Somebody who has served as a minister in the government is usually recognized for his achievements for the remainder of his life. For instance, he is still addressed as a minister, even years after leaving office. True to the Confucian tradition emphasizing the unity within a family, this kind of honor, which has been upheld for more than 500 years, is usually regarded as something to be shared by members of the entire family or clan. Partly for this reason, a family is often willing to give financial support to a promising young civil servant for many years.

40. In view of the growing tensions between North and South Korea, President Park strongly believed that through the development of HCI Korea would acquire the capacity to produce important weapons within two or three years instead of the four- to five-year minimum period that was thought required in the opinion of his advisers (C. Kim 1991, 323).

41. For a very informative discussion on why and how the Special Task Force came into being, see ibid., 320–24.

42. This information was conveyed through an interview with Mr. D. W. Nam, former minister of finance, deputy prime minister, and prime minister, conducted by the authors.

Procedures for awards and punishments are not symmetrical in Korea, at least not on the surface. Although achievement is openly recognized, failure seldom seems to be penalized. This may be the legacy of the Confucian tradition in which members of the *yangban* class were seldom punished openly. In any event, in the Korean context perhaps the most effective penalty has been the social disgrace of being dismissed from the government for wrongdoing. It is probably this stigma that ensures that, unless an individual civil servant has done something extremely serious, all that is required of him is a discreet submission of a resignation.

This asymmetrical system of awards and penalties has certain consequences. Because achievements are explicitly recognized, individuals are strongly motivated to work hard and do well. Since wrongdoing and shortcomings are not severely punished, individuals are less fearful of failure. On balance, this can result in more policy innovations, thus increasing dynamism for the whole organization. However, when a policy goes seriously wrong and few are held accountable, the cost tends to be shared by society as a whole.

*Policy Research Institutes*
For the most part, the Korean bureaucracy has been manned by generalists. This reflects the Confucian view that a person of superior intellect can handle almost any subject once he puts his mind to it. Partly because of this belief, Korean bureaucrats are seldom kept on one assignment for very long before being shifted to their next position. In addition, like their counterparts elsewhere, Korean bureaucrats have to devote their attention to immediate and short-term problems. To compensate for these weaknesses, several policy research institutes have been established to look at long-term issues based on special knowledge and expertise.

The first of them was the Korean Development Institute, established in 1971. The KDI's main function has been to help the EPB formulate medium- and long-term economic policies. It has been manned principally by Ph.D level economists and other social scientists trained abroad.

Stimulated by the success of KDI, other ministries have established institutes under their own umbrellas. Examples include the Korea Educational Development Institute (KEDI), founded by the Ministry of Education in 1972; the Korea Rural Economics Institution Institute (KREI), founded by the Ministry of Agriculture and Fishery in 1978; and the Korea Institute for Human Settlement (KIHS), established in 1978 by the Ministry of Construction. By 1992, there were at least 10 such institutes in Korea.

Over the years these institutes have greatly enhanced the quality of policy making in Korea. However, their contributions do not go unchallenged. In the opinion of some, the researchers have had too little experience of government, and as a result their policy recommendations have often been too theoretical and lacking in immediate applications. Such criticism is misplaced. After all, these institutes have been established precisely to offset the tendency of the government bureaucracy to focus only on immediate and short-term problems.[43]

## Business and Entrepreneurs

For many centuries, Korea was not a country in which entrepreneurship thrived. Due to the Confucian influence, merchants and businessmen were placed near the bottom of the social hierarchy. This tradition even survived through the period of Japanese occupation (1910–45).

During the three-year period of U.S. military occupation following the end of World War II, this tradition began to change somewhat, especially after an extensive land reform was carried out. As the maximum amount of land a family could own was limited to three hectares, many landowners (who traditionally had been greatly honored) were forced to seek new ways of life in such fields as business. Nevertheless, the emergence of a business class was by no means complete on the eve of Korea's economic takeoff in the 1960s.

To be sure, some Korean businessmen had managed to become rich during the period of reconstruction following the Korean War. But they were all suspected of having made their money through illegal means such as bribery. In response to continuing popular prejudice, President Park, shortly after coming power, arrested a large number of Korean businessmen, including the late founder of the Samsung Group, on charges of alleged accumulation of wealth through illegal means.

Ironically, President Park soon realized that he would need a large business class to perform entrepreneurial functions if he was to succeed in his development goals. So he set out to create just such a class, as will soon become clear.

President Park created a business class in various ways. First, as has already been described, he offered many financial incentives to those who were deemed capable of doing what the government wanted.[44] Second, he awarded successful industrialists with special prizes and medals. This kind of recognition also served to enhance the prestige of businessmen in the eyes of the Korean people. And, third, the government got closely involved with business itself.

It did so initially by sharing risks with private entrepreneurs. Because domestic savings were inadequate to finance investment, there was a need to attract foreign capital. Since few Korean businesses were strong enough to attract foreign loans on their own, the government provided the guarantees not

---

43. The most recent example of the long view is a project on "Korea in the Year 2000," completed by a consortium of government-funded research institutes under the coordination of KDI in 1988.

44. For a fuller discussion of these incentives in the 1960s, see Krueger 1979, 92–98.

only for the repayment of principal but for payments of interest. Over time, risk sharing between the government and businesses expanded into other areas.

One example is Korea's construction activities in the Middle East. After the first oil shock, the government encouraged Korean construction companies to win contracts in oil-producing countries in the Middle East. To help this happen, the government directed commercial banks to provide guarantees of performance. When some of the construction companies failed to fulfill contracts, the government had to ask other companies to take over the failing projects in return for a package of subsidized loans and special tax treatment.

The cooperative relationship between the government and private business has often taken an indirect form as well. When there was a need for the government to control the behavior of private firms in a given industry, it often did so through the industrial associations. What is remarkable about Korea's industrial associations is that so many of them have been created at the behest of the government rather than by the spontaneous desire of individual firms in the industry. Another remarkable aspect is that, regardless of how a given association was created, almost all its executive positions have been filled by former government officials—a Korean equivalent of Japanese "descent from heaven." Former officials are useful, of course, as lobbyists vis-à-vis the government and as convenient channels through which the government can exert its influence on the industries.

*Characteristics of the Korean Firm*

There are several features that distinguish Korean companies from their counterparts elsewhere. For the most part (and unsurprisingly), Korean firms have had a short history. Therefore, many are still owned and operated by their founders. They rely heavily on family members or close relatives to manage their businesses and are reluctant to seek the views of outsiders or salaried managers. This explains why they can often take decisions rather quickly.

Korean entrepreneurs are also hard working and aggressive—qualities that can be readily explained by the great hardships and social upheaval that the Korean people underwent during the Korean War. To foreign observers, Korean businessmen often care more about business expansion than profits. These traits can also be understood if one remembers that under the Confucian tradition Korean entrepreneurs have more freedom to hire than to fire their workers. In fact, they behave in a very patriarchal and authoritarian manner. They feel they are responsible for the welfare of their employees. In this, they are following the Confucian tendency to regard all forms of organization as nothing more than an extension of the family. In relation to the government, virtually all businessmen are highly cooperative, sometimes even subservient. This is not surprising if one bears in mind that many Korean businessmen owe their success to government support and encouragement; and, like the rest of society, they tend to regard policymakers and bureaucrats with great respect.

*The* Chaebul

Compared with other countries at similar stages of development, the average size of the Korean firm is quite large. Thirteen Korean firms were listed in the 1991 Fortune 500, compared with one each from Taiwan, Malaysia, and Thailand.[45] The large size of Korean firms is no accident. From the beginning, the Korean government felt that Korean firms could compete in the international market only if they were of a certain minimum size. This view was reinforced when the government encouraged the development of heavy and chemical industries (HCI) in the 1970s to upgrade its export structure. The very nature of the HCI drive was capital intensive and involved a scale economy. This policy also meant that it was more convenient for the government to deal with a smaller number of firms. The result was the emergence of a handful of large conglomerates, commonly known as the *chaebul.*

Other factors have also helped to produce the *chaebul.* Since Korea began its industrialization with a highly underdeveloped equity market, industrialists had to rely heavily on bank loans—and most banks were owned by the government. When interest rates on bank loans were set below market clearing levels, the demand for loans exceeded supply. It was necessary, therefore, for the government to ration loans by means of nonprice mechanisms, which led to a concentration of economic power in a limited number of firms. Over time, loans were readily available only to those "strategic" industries favored by the government.

The government also promoted the growth of the *chaebul* through its heavy involvement in certain investment decisions. When projects did badly, it had little choice but to get involved. It did so by either an outright bailout or by asking another group with a sound financial base to take over the unsuccessful venture. Bailouts began in the 1969–70, when some of the firms whose foreign borrowing had been guaranteed by the government were in financial difficulties. In order to induce another business group to get involved, the government usually offered incentives in the form of new loans to be used as "seed money" and special tax treatment.

What are the consequences of this concentration of commercial power? On the positive side, conglomerates enhanced the synergy effect—what is sometimes called the economy of scope. In addition, the *chaebul* not only acted as a marketing agent for small firms but provided short-term financing for them. This support was particularly helpful in the early stages of economic development, when small firms ran into difficulties while exploring market potential abroad.

These positive contributions of the *chaebul* need to be seen alongside some negative ones as well. When different firms or business units with different specialties are combined to form a *chaebul,* initially the synergy effects

---

45. *Asian Wall Street Journal,* September 24, 1992, S–18.

are multiplied and business risks are reduced. However, as the number of firms and units increases, profitable units have to be called on to subsidize inefficient and unprofitable ones (particularly through cross-holdings of equity). This tends to lock in resources to inefficient uses. In addition, the overall vulnerability of the group to business fluctuations increases. In the opinion of many, this is precisely the position that some Korean conglomerates have now reached.

Another consequence of the conglomerates is that, by preempting bank loans, they have prevented the healthy growth of small and medium industries. The absence of such a sector has been considered the weakest link in Korea's overall industrial structure, which is in sharp contrast to economies such as those of Japan and Taiwan, China.

Because of the preemptive effect of the *chaebul,* the general public in Korea has looked unfavorably not only on the *chaebul* but on the capitalist system as a whole. In the public's eyes, the emergence of the *chaebul* is an inevitable result of capitalist developments. In a country such as Korea, where capitalism has no deep cultural roots, a negative view of capitalism is extremely unfortunate for the *chaebul* as well as the long-term growth prospects of the country.

*State-Owned Enterprises*
Although the Korean government never intended to develop its economy along the socialist path, in the 1960s and 1970s the weight of state enterprises in the Korean economy was comparable to that in countries such as India.[46] Due to the pragmatism of the Korean government, it was more than willing to ignore ideological quibbles when it judged that establishing state enterprises was the only feasible way to meet certain critical needs of the economy. Such needs arose often when Korea began its economic development, since it had only limited capital and management expertise in the private sector.

More than 20 major state enterprises were set up by the government between 1961 and 1976. They included Korea National Airlines, Inc. (1962), Korea Electric Power Company (1962), Korea Petroleum Company (1962), Korea Petroleum Development Corporation (1977), Korea Mining Promotion, Inc. (1967), Inchon Heavy Industries, Inc. (1963), Korea Shipbuilding Corporation (1968), and Pohang Iron and Steel Company (1968). In addition, the government established some special banks and financial institutions, including Korea Small and Medium Industries Bank (1962), Korea National Citizens Bank (1963), Korea Reinsurance Corporation (1963), Korea Housing Bank (1967), Korea Exchange Bank (1967), Korea Development Bank (1969), and Korea Imports and Exports Bank (1976).

46. See Song 1990, 37–39.

Given the establishment of so many state enterprises, the average annual growth of their output during 1963–72 was 14.5 percent, well above the 9.5 percent growth of GDP. The share of the total value added accounted for by state enterprises also rose, from 6.5 percent in the 1960s to 9.1 percent in the 1970s.[47]

It should be noted that in the 1960s and 1970s most state enterprises were created in areas where initial capital requirements were large, the gestation period of investment long, and investment risks high—precisely the areas into which private enterprises were either unable or unwilling (or both) to move. In addition, new state enterprises had greater linkage effects on the economy than other enterprises did. Furthermore, state enterprises accounted for no less than 30 percent of the total fixed investment of the economy during 1963–81. In other words, state enterprises not only filled the gap left by private enterprises but played a critical role in propelling the overall development of the economy.

## The Intangibles of Policy

It has become clear that both the government and the private sector have made valuable contributions to the success of Korea's growth over the past 30 years. One should keep in mind that several cultural and historical factors unique to Korea have also influenced the economy's development. We examine five of those in this section: (1) the role of Confucianism, (2) the influence of Japan, (3) the effect of the Korean War, (4) the effect of the North-South division, and (5) the role and influence of the United States in Korea's development.

### *Confucian Background*

Confucianism was introduced into Korea by the Yi Dynasty, founded in 1392. Although it ceased to be an official state creed in 1894, it has continued to influence Korean society to this day.

Confucianism insists on a strict discipline based on a social hierarchy, with the king or ruler at the apex. All subjects owe unlimited loyalty to the king, and all rights and privileges the subjects enjoy are regarded as gifts from him. Below the king in status are teachers, who outrank parents. Children owe respect to teachers and obedience to parents. Other things being equal, men are considered to be superior to women, and elders superior to the young. All these traditions have been conducive to the emergence of an authoritarian government in Korea.

The Confucian approach to the betterment of the world is through good government and education. The ideal government in the Confucian view is headed by a wise king supported by scholar-bureaucrats who occupy the position in society directly below the king. Scholar-bureaucrats are to be recruited through rigorous and impartial examinations from among "superior men" who

---

47.  Ibid.

not only possess innate abilities but have successfully applied them to learning and the cultivation of character.

Below scholar-bureaucrats in the Confucian hierarchy are farmers. Artisans, who work with their hands to produce utensils and other artifacts needed in daily life, are placed below the farmers. Merchants and tradesmen are below the artisans and are considered to be only slightly higher than butchers and shamans. This view of social hierarchy, together with the notion of "superior men," goes far toward explaining why Korea's economic development has been led by government rather than the private sector.

This tradition has brought many benefits to Korea, but it has also done some harm. Because Confucianism has little respect for merchants or the business class, it maintains a strong antibusiness bias. In addition, the strong stress on family has tended to encourage nepotism in both government and business, while emphasis on personal loyalty has resulted in downplaying the need to govern society through law and order. Furthermore, the kind of education stressed in the Confucian tradition has had more to do with the development of a personal character fit for public service than with special knowledge and expertise in science and technology.

*The Japanese Influence*
For about 15 years after the end of World War II, anti-Japanese feeling was understandably very strong in Korea. Although most Koreans still have anti-Japanese sentiments, there is little question that Japan has had an enormous influence on Korea's economic development, particularly during the 1960s and 1970s. Many senior policymakers received much of their formal education under the Japanese system. Indeed, many spent their formative years in Japan, internalizing Japanese values such as respect for honesty and integrity.

The aspect these Korean policymakers admired most about contemporary Japan was its ability to industrialize through the adaptation of Western science and technology. As for Japanese history, they were most impressed with the Meiji Era, when a handful of oligarchs successfully led Japan to achieve the mercantilist goal of both "enriching the nation and strengthening arms." It is true that many Korean government leaders resented the Japanese oligarchs who colonized Korea, but these oligarchs also served as their role models.[48] The same was true of many Japanese institutions and approaches to economic development.[49]

---

48. It is very instructive to note that in naming Korea's new Constitution, adopted in 1972, President Park used the term *Yushin,* which happens to be the same terminology used by the Meiji Japanese oligarchs to characterize their reform policies.

49. It is also instructive to note in this connection that the organizational structure as well as the names of the bureaus in the Ministry of Trade and Industry in Korea are very similar to those of the Ministry of International Trade and Industry in Japan.

*The Legacy of the Korean War*

The Korean War brought untold suffering to the Korean people, to say nothing of the physical destruction it caused. Ironically, perhaps, this very destruction strengthened the determination of the Korean people to rebuild their nation.

The Korean War also caused people to free themselves of many culturally ingrained inhibitions, including the choice of profession. Under the Confucian influence, Koreans had held a low opinion of careers in fields other than government service and teaching. After the war, attitudes changed, and people became more willing to accept careers in business and military service. In addition, the Korean War made almost everyone equally poor. This tended to destroy social barriers and increase social mobility.

The war also raised the quality of manpower. Many soldiers freshly recruited from rural areas did not have the education and skills to use modern military equipment. They were trained to acquire skills in areas such as the operation of engineering equipment and were taught to appreciate the value of teamwork and discipline. After military service, they were able to apply these skills and disciplines to their work in civilian life. Many officers who had acquired managerial expertise during military service were able to make a smooth transition to management positions in civilian life. And all Koreans realized that, despite the extensive loss of physical assets, they still possessed human capital—their least vulnerable asset to wartime destruction. This, in turn, greatly increased the demand for education. The wartime policy of the government, which gave students enrolled in colleges and universities deferment from military service, encouraged people to opt for higher education. Thanks to this policy, the number of students enrolled in colleges and universities increased dramatically during the war years.[50]

For centuries the Korean people suffered innumerable invasions by foreigners. As a result of this history, Koreans had more than their fair share of xenophobia. They tended to believe that foreigners were synonymous with people who would harm Korea's interests. The Korean War proved that this was not necessarily the case. This time foreign soldiers came to Korea, under the U.N. flag, to help Koreans repel their enemies. This new experience had an enormous impact on the Korean psyche. For the first time in their history, Koreans began to appreciate the fact that they could work together with foreigners for mutual gains. Without this revelation, Koreans would have had great difficulty abandoning their centuries' old inward-looking orientation and adopting the outward-looking development strategy that they embraced so successfully in the early 1960s.

---

50. See Kim and McGinn 1980, 106–7.

*The North-South Division*
Few developments in Korea over the past 40 years or more can be understood without reference to the North-South division of the country. Because of this division, the security of the nation has been under constant threat. This fact alone goes far toward explaining the politics as well as the economics of the country. The ever-present threat from the North forced the country to pursue two goals simultaneously—increasing the wealth of the country and strengthening its arms. Put differently, Korea has forced Korea to produce both guns and butter for over 30 years.

Without the threat from the North, the military government under the leadership of General Park would probably not have come into being in 1961. Nor would so many Koreans have been willing to live under a series of authoritarian governments and sacrifice a great deal for rapid economic development. The urgency of sacrifice became all the greater in the 1960s when North Korea's GNP per capita was supposed to have exceeded that of the South. Because of this urgency, the time horizon of economic policymakers also became distorted. The value of any project yielding long-term benefits often was discounted in favor of short-term gains.

*The U.S. Influence*
Over the past 30 years or more, the United States has affected Korea's economic development in many ways. Given the geostrategic importance of Korea, the United States has maintained its military presence to ensure peace and stability on the peninsula. This has enabled Korea to devote a greater amount of resources to economic development than would otherwise have been possible. Even so, over the past three decades Korea has spent an average of 4 to 5 percent of its annual GNP on defense. It is worth recalling that whenever the U.S. resolve to defend Korea from an invasion from the North seems to waver, as happened during the early 1970s, Korea's economic policy has been immediately affected. The motivations behind the HCI drive in the 1970s can best be understood in this light.

Apart from providing basic security, the United States contributed greatly to Korea's early economic development through its generous aid. Without such aid, recovery from the destruction of the Korean War would have taken much longer. It should be noted, however, that this aid allowed the United States to influence Korean economic policy. After the completion of reconstruction in the late 1950s, U.S. aid donors began to pressure Korea to adopt an outward-looking development strategy. In the late 1950s and early 1960s, U.S. authorities made conscious use of their aid leverage to persuade Korean policymakers to adopt reforms on inflation, interest rates, the exchange rate, and tariffs as part of the efforts implementing the outward-looking strategy.

The United States facilitated this strategy not only by making its markets available to Korea but by helping Korea exploit market opportunities in other

Western nations. It sponsored Korea's membership in international organizations such as General Agreement on Tariffs and Trade (GATT), the International Monetary Fund (IMF), and the World Bank. Furthermore, many Koreans were given opportunities to study in the United States either through U.S.-funded scholarships or on their own initiative. Many promising young Korean policymakers were trained at various American universities and institutions under exchange programs financed by the U.S. government.

These educational exchanges have undoubtedly helped Korea's drive toward economic development, but their effects should not be exaggerated. Apart from a few individuals, the beneficiaries of exchange programs did not reach positions of influence until the late 1970s. As already noted, many of those who played key roles in policy making in the 1960s and 1970s were trained under the Japanese system.

## IV.  Recent Developments

### Economic Structure

Korea's economy has undergone several several structural changes during the 1990s that are reflected in the trade and investment regimes.

As recently as 1986, the United States was the destination for 40 percent of all Korean exports. By 1993, the percentage had fallen to around 20 percent, although the United States remains Korea's largest export market. The decline of the United States as a major trading partner relative to other countries reflects the rise in intraregional trade in Pacific Asia. Exports to Pacific Asia accounted for over 45 percent of Korea's total exports in 1993, up from 25 percent in 1986. Of this, the bulk goes to Japan (16 percent of total exports), members of the Association of Southeast Asian Nations (ASEAN; 10.5 percent), Hong Kong (8 percent), and China (5.5 percent).[51]

In terms of the commodity composition of Korean trade, the country remains primarily an exporter of manufactured goods. Machinery and manufactures continue to be the dominant export products, acounting for 45 and 42 percent of exports, respectively.

During the 1990s, Korean firms have ceded some export markets to other countries with a stronger comparative advantage in labor-intensive industries. Rising labor costs in Korea have been partially blamed for this development. In 1990, nominal wages in the manufacturing sector rose by 20 percent compared with an estimated productivity increase of only 12.5 percent. By 1993, this wage-rate growth had slowed to 10.9 percent.[52]

---

51.  Figures supplied by the International Monetary Fund.
52.  Korea Economic Institute of America 1995.

Partly in response to rising wages at home, Korean firms have expanded aggressively into offshore production.[53] Over the past decade Korea's direct investment abroad has surged. After a period of general discouragement of outward investment by the Korean government, FDI increased rapidly following liberalization measures initiated in the mid-1980s. Since 1987, Korea's FDI has increased at an average annual rate of nearly 77 percent. Since 1985, when Korea's FDI totaled only U.S.$116 million worldwide, Korean firms have increasingly acquired foreign productive facilities such that by 1992 FDI outflows totaled $1.2 billion.

Investments in manufacturing have led the way and have been concentrated in Asia and North America. North America currently receives nearly 43 percent of Korea's FDI, followed by Asia at 37 percent. However, since 1987, the share of Korean FDI in Asia has grown due to the rapid increase in Korean investments in China. In North America trade and basic metals products are the most heavily invested sectors, whereas in Asia mining and manufacturing receive the bulk of Korea's FDI.

Political tensions with North Korea continue to influence the pace and extent of economic relations on the peninsula. Following the conclusion of an agreement between the United States and North Korea in 1994 over North Korea's nuclear program, a new momentum has emerged for increasing peninsular economic exchanges. In 1994, the South Korean government lifted the ban on business contacts with the North, a move originally expected to revitalize inter-Korean economic activity. As yet significant economic relations have not materialized, primarily due to the North's reluctance to allow foreign investment outside the free trade zones in the Rajin-Sonbong area.

## Political Economy

Following the election of Kim Young Sam as president in 1993, the government unveiled its Five Year Plan for a New Economy, which articulated its conception of an internationally competitive Korea based on less government involvement and more private sector participation. The plan addressed four principal concerns: institutional reform, administrative deregulation, financial sector liberalization, and privatization.

*Institutional Reform.* In 1994, the Economic Planning Board, formerly the most prominent economic policy-making body in the country, was merged with the Ministry of Finance, a move that signified that the Korean government would set growth and development goals but would not adhere as stringently to

---

53. A recent survey by the Korea Institute for International Economic Policy (KIEP) indicated that the major motivation behind Korean firms' decisions to invest in developing countries is the lower wage cost relative to Korean labor. An appreciating won has also been cited as a motivating factor for increased Korean FDI (ibid.).

prospective targets as in the past. At the same time the Fair Trade Commission was separated from the MFE and given the power to investigate and take action against anticompetitive trade practices.

*Deregulation.* Foreign and domestic enterprises alike complained that government regulations were excessive and unnecessary and a burden to doing business. Deregulation has thus been a priority of the Kim regime. In 1993, the new government examined 1,079 business regulations that were recommended for relaxation or abolishment and selected 670 regulations for the deregulation list.[54] Rules on gaining government approval or licenses for market entry were relaxed in such businesses as overseas trade, harbor transportation, overseas construction, automobile repair, grain bargaining, pounding and pulverizing, and small restaurants. The streamlining of administrative procedures is expected to promote greater competition in overprotected and oversegmented business sectors that have been sheltered by excessive entry requirements.

*Financial Sector Liberalization.* Financial sector development in Korea has been lagging due to a variety of government regulations imposed in order to support government-led resource allocation. This sector has been considered one of the most significant bottlenecks for business. The most recent five year plan has set several goals, including: (1) elimination of underlying documentation requirements for financial transactions by 1997; (2) lifting the ceiling on foreign investments in the stock and bond markets; (3) allowing offshore borrowing for all firms, both domestic and foreign owned, by 1997; (4) easing government control on most lending and deposit rates; and (5) reducing "policy loans" such as compulsory lending requirements to small and medium-sized enterprises (SMEs). Finally the blueprint contains measures to introduce open market operations such as the use of treasury and public bonds as a major monetary policy tool and thus shift toward more indirect means of implementing monetary policy.[55]

The current five year plan will also open up 132 of 224 currently restricted businesses for FDI. In addition, the plan will lift joint venture requirements for 43 of 50 sectors currently subject to them by 1996. However, 92 sectors remained closed, most notably in financial services, media, real estate speculation, and fisheries. Intellectual property rights protection has also been strengthened in an attempt to make Korea more attractive to foreign investors.

Capital account liberalization has also allowed Korean firms to expand overseas investment, a move that is partly inspired by the need to remain internationally competitive in the face of rising labor and land costs at home. In 1994, Korean firms' outward investment rose by 88 percent. Most expansion

---

54. Korea Institute for International Economic Policy 1993, 20.
55. Kwon Okyn 1993.

has been in Asia, but Korean firms are also building auto plants in Canada and Uzbekistan and an electronics complex in Great Britain.

*Privatization.* The Kim government has revised the country's original privatization initiative, begun in 1987 as part of its overall plan of supplanting government decision making in the economy with private entrepreneurship. During the five year plan period, it has set a goal of privatizing (completely or partially) 58 of 136 public enterprises by 1998. An additional 10 state-owned firms are scheduled to be merged or restructured during the same period.[56]

## V.  Summary

Korea managed to turn its initial disadvantages into assets by pursuing total dedication to exporting in the post-1961 period. Relying first on foreign aid and later on rapidly increasing savings and external borrowing and a vigorous pursuit of technology (in lieu of DFI), it was able to capitalize itself. When combined with a talented labor force that worked record hours, it produced a highly productive and rapidly growing economy.

Public policy was at the center of development, as stable governments, aided by technocratic bureaucracies and research institutes, prodded the private sector to attain national export objectives. In addition to managing the macroeconomy, the government created state enterprises when needed, intervened in credit allocation to promote exports in the first instance, and selected industries in the HCI period. The trade regime was schizophrenic, with a proexport bias, as reflected in trade preferences and an aggressive real effective exchange rate policy, combined with import protection. Following the second oil shock, selective industrial policy was abandoned, trade reform began, and the banks were privatized. Much of the 1980s involved the dismantling of controls on trade and direct foreign investment and the gradual easing of equital flows. The 1990s has witnessed a reexamination of the role of government.

Korea is rightly held as perhaps the most successful newly industrializing country, and its experience is often examined for replicable lessons. This essay argues that Korea did very well on the economic fundamentals: the government pursued sound macroeconomic management, invested in infrastructure and human resources, and supported an outward-oriented private sector. When industrial intervention was tried in the 1973–79 period, it always had exporting as its final objective. Korea has a good record of developing infant industries. Nevertheless, the evidence is still mixed as to whether the HCI drive was necessary to maintain economic success. Costs and benefits are noted.

What Korea also had in abundance was excellent policy making and policy implementation, based on strong presidential leadership and political

---

56.  Nam Shun-Woo 1993.

stability. Social consensus and strong national identity, when combined with proequity policies (inland reform and rural investments), served to maintain social stability despite rapid economic change. Korea is a place where government clearly took the lead in development—strategy and implementation—and where it was highly successful.

REFERENCES

Amsden, Alice H. 1989. *Asia's Next Giant: South Korea and Late Industrialization.* New York: Oxford University Press.
Auty, Richard M. 1990. "Creating Competitive Advantage: South Korean Steel and Petrochemicals." *Tijdschrift voor Economischeen Sociale Geogiafie* 82: 15–29.
Auty, Richard M. 1991. "Multinational, State Enterprises and Heavy Industry: From Girvan to Blitzer." *IDS Bulletin* 22 (April): 53–58.
Bank of Korea. 1990. *National Accounts.* Seoul: Bank of Korea.
Bank of Korea. 1994. *Economic Statistical Yearbook.* Seoul: Bank of Korea.
Barro, Robert J., and Jong-Wha Lee. 1993. "International Comparisons of Educational Attainment." Paper presented at the World Bank conference How Do National Policies Affect Long Run Growth? Washington, D.C.
Chenery, Syrquin. 1989. *Patterns of Development, 1950–83.* Washington, D.C.: World Bank.
Chenery, Hollis, Sherman Robinson, and Moshe Syrquin. 1986. *Industrialization and Growth: A Comparative Study.* New York: World Bank.
Chenery, Hollis, and Moshe Syrquin. 1975. *Patterns of Development, 1950–70.* Oxford: Oxford University Press.
Cho, Lee-Jay, and Yoon Hyung-Kim, eds. 1991. *Economic Development in the Republic of Korea: A Policy Perspective.* Honolulu: East-West Center.
Cho, Soon. 1994. "The Dynamics of Korean Economic Development." Washington: Institute of International Economics. Mimeo.
Choi, Dong Kyu. 1991. *The Government in the Age of Rapid Growth.* Seoul: Korea Economic Daily Press. In Korean.
Choo, Hakchung. 1985. "Estimation of Distribution of Income and its Sources of Change in Korea, 1982." Korea Development Institute Working Paper 8515. Seoul: Korea Development Institute.
Choo, Hakchung, and J. Yoon. 1984. "Size Distribution of Income to Korea, 1982: Its Estimation and Sources of Change." *Korea Development Review* (March): 2–18.
Chung, Ju-Yung. 1986. *In Excitement This Morning As Well [Onul Achimedo Sulleimeul Ango].* Seoul: Samsung Publishing Co.
Corbo, Vitorio, and S. M. Suh, eds. 1992. *Structural Adjustment in a Newly Industrialized Country: The Korean Experience.* Washington, D.C.: World Bank.
Denison, Edward F. 1979. *Accounting for Slower Economic Growth: The United States in the 1970s.* Washington, D.C.: Brookings Institution.

Dollar, David. 1992. "Outward-Oriented Developing Economics Really Do Grow More Rapidly: Evidence from 95 LDCs, 1976–85." *Economic Development and Cultural Change* (April 1992): 540–42.

Fry, Maxwell. 1984. "Saving, Financial Intermediation, and Economic Growth in Asia." *Asian Development Review,* vol. 2 no. 1, 82–91.

Fry, Maxwell. 1992. "Foreign Direct Investment in a Macroeconomic Framework: Finance, Efficiency, Incentives, and Distortions." Mimeo.

Harberger, Arnold. 1978. "Perspectives on Capital and Technology in Less-Developed Countries." In *Contemporary Economic Analysis,* edited by M. J. Artis and A. R. Nobay. London: Longman.

HCI Promotion Council. 1975. *Heavy and Chemical Industry.* Seoul: HCI Promotion Council.

Hong, Wontak. 1979. *Trade, Distortions, and Employment Growth in Korea.* Seoul: Korea Development Institute Press.

Hong, Wontack. 1985. "Import Restriction and Import Liberalization in an Export-Oriented Developing Economy: In Light of Korean Experience." Seoul University. Mimeo.

Jones, L., and Il Sakong. 1980. *Government, Business, and Entrepreneurship in Economic Development: The Korean Case.* Cambridge: Harvard University Press.

Kaufman, Daniel. 1991. "Determinants of the Productivity of Projects in Developing Countries: Evidence from 1,200 Projects." Background paper for the 1991 *World Development Report.* Washington, D.C.: World Bank.

Kim, Chung-Yum. 1991. *Korea's Economic Development: President Park and the Miracle on the Han River.* Tokyo: Simul Press. In Japanese.

Kim, D., and K. S. Anh. 1987. *Korea's Income Distribution, Its Determinants, and People's Consciousness about Distribution Problems.* Seoul: Jung Ang University Press. In Korean.

Kim, Ji Hong. 1990. *Korean Industrial Policy in the 1970s: The Heavy and Chemical Industry Drive.* KDI Working Papers No. 9015. Seoul: Korea Development Institute.

Kim, Kwang-Suk, and Joon-Kyung Park. 1985. *Sources of Economic Growth in Korea: 1963–1982.* Seoul: Korea Development Institute.

Korea Economic Institute of America. 1995. *Korea's Economy, 1995.* Washington, D.C.: Korea Economic Institute of America.

Korea Institute for International Economic Policy. 1993. The Beginning of Korea's New Economy: *The Kim Administration's 100 Day Plan.* Seoul: Korea Institute for International Economic Policy.

Krueger, Anne O. 1979. *The Development Role of the Foreign Sector and Aid.* In the series *Studies in the Modernization of the Republic of Korea.* Cambridge: Harvard University Press.

Krueger, Anne O., Vittorio Lorbo, and Josi Fernando Ossa, eds. 1985. *Export-Oriented Development Strategies: The Success of Five Newly Industrializing Countries.* Boulder: Westview Press.

Lee, Chung H. 1992. "Government, Financial Systems, and Large Private Enterprises in the Economic Development of South Korea." World Development 20:187–97.

Lee, K. S., and A. Anas. 1992. *Impacts of Infrastructure Deficiencies on Nigerian Manufacturing: Private Alternatives and Policy Options.* World Bank Infrastructure and Urban Development Discussion Papers No. INU–98. Washington, D.C.: World Bank.

Leipziger, Danny M. 1988. "Industrial Restructuring in Korea." *World Development* 16, no. 1: 121–36.

Leipziger, Danny, David Dollar, Anthony Shorrocks, and Su-Yong Song. 1992. *The Distribution of Income and Wealth in Korea*. Washington, D.C.: World Bank, EDI Development Studies.

Leipziger, Danny M., and Peter Petri. 1989. "Korean Incentives Policy Towards Industry and Agriculture." In *The Balance Between Industry and Agriculture in Economic Development*, edited by Williamson and Panchamukhi. London: MacMillan.

Leipziger, Danny M., and Peter Petri. 1994. "Korean Industrial Policy: Legacies of the Past and Directions for the Future." In *Korea's Political Economy: An Institutional Perspective*, edited by Lee-Jay Cho and Yoon Hyung Kim. Boulder: Westview.

Leipziger, Danny M., and H. S. Shin. 1991. "A Look at Anti-Dumping Cases." *Open Economics Review* 2:1.

McGinn, Noel F. 1980. *Education and Development in Korea*. Harvard East Asian Monograph. Cambridge: Harvard University Press.

Nam, Chong-Hyun. 1990. "Export Promotion Strategy and Economic Development in Korea." In *Export Promotion Strategies*, edited by Chris Milner. New York: New York University Press.

Nam, Duck Woo. 1992. "Korea's Economic Take-off in Retrospect." Paper presented at the Second Washington Conference of the Korea-America Economic Association, Washington, D.C.

Nam, Sang-Woo. 1991. "The Comprehensive Stabilization Program." In *Economic Development in the Republic of Korea: A Policy Perspective*, edited by Lee-Jay Cho and Yoon Hyung Kim. Honolulu: University of Hawaii Press.

Nam, Shun-Woo, 1993. "Korea's Privatization Policy for the New Economy." *Economic Bulletin*. August.

Nishimizu, Mieko, and Sherman Robinson. 1983. "Trade Policies and Productivity Change in Semi-Industrialized Countries." *Journal of Development Economics* 16: 177–206.

Noland, Marcus. 1990. *Pacific Basin Developing Countries: Prospects for the Future*. Washington, D.C.: Institute for International Economics.

Okyn, Kwan. 1993. "Liberalization and Internationalization under the 'New Economy.'" *Economic Bulletin*. August.

Renaud, Bertrand. 1988. "Compounding Financial Repression with Rigid Urban Regulations: Lessons of the Korea Housing Market." World Bank Discussion Paper 21. Washington, D.C.: World Bank.

Renaud, Bertrand. 1989. "Understanding the Collateral Qualities of Housing for Financial Development: The Korean 'chonse' as Effective Response to Financial Sector Shortcomings." World Bank Discussion Paper 49. Washington, D.C.: World Bank.

Renaud, Bertrand. 1992. "Confronting a Distorted Housing Market: Can Korean Policies Break with the Past?" Paper presented at the Korea-U.S. Symposium on Korean Social Issues, Graduate School of International Relations and Pacific Studies, University of California at San Diego, June 26–27.

Rhee, Yung Whee, Bruce Ross-Larson, and Gary Pursell. 1984. *Korea's Competitive Edge: Managing the Entry into World Markets.* Baltimore and London: Johns Hopkins University Press.

Sakong, Il. 1993. *Korea in the World Economy.* Washington, D.C.: Institute for International Economics.

Song, B. N. 1990. *The Rise of the Korean Economy.* Oxford: Oxford University Press.

Stern, J, J. H. Kim, D. Perkins, and J. H. Yoo. 1992. "Industrialization and the State: The Korean Heavy and Chemical Industry Drive." Harvard Institute for International Development and KDF. Mimeo.

Suh, Sang-Mok. 1992. "The Economy in History Perspective." In *Structural Adjustment in a Newly Industrialized Country: The Korean Experience,* edited by Vitorio Corbo and S. M. Suh. Washington, D.C.: World Bank.

Summers, Robert, and Alan Heston. 1988. "A New Set of International Comparisons of Real Product and Price Levels: Estimates for 130 Countries, 1950–1985." *Review of Income and Wealth* 34 (March): 1–25.

Tan, Jee-Peng, and Alain Mingat. 1992. *Education in Asia: A Comparative Study of Cost and Financing.* Washington, D.C.: World Bank.

Wade, Robert. 1990. *Governing the Market: Economic Theory and the Role of Government in East Asian Industrialization.* Princeton: Princeton University Press.

Westphal, Larry E. 1978. "The Republic of Korea's Experience with Export-led Industrial Development." *World Development* 6, no. 3: 1–18.

Westphal, Larry E. 1981. *Empirical Justification for Infant Industry Protection.* World Bank Staff Working Papers No. 445. Washington, D.C.: World Bank.

Westphal, Larry E., Linsu Kim, and Carl Dahlman. 1984. "Reflections on Korea's Acquisition of Technological Capability." World Bank Discussion Paper 77. Washington, D.C.: World Bank.

Westphal, Larry E., Yung Whee Rhee, Linsu Kim, and Alice Amsden, 1984. *Exports of Capital Goods and Related Services from the Republic of Korea.* World Bank Staff Working Papers No. 629. Washington, D.C.: World Bank.

World Bank. 1987. *Korea: Managing the Industrial Transition.* Washington, D.C.: World Bank.

World Bank. 1988. *Review of Adjustment Lending.* Washington, D.C.: World Bank.

World Bank. 1991. *World Development Report 1991.* Washington, D.C.: World Bank.

World Bank. Various years. *World Tables.* Washington, D.C.: World Bank.

Yoo, Jung-ho. 1990. *The Industrial Policy of the 1970s and the Evolution of the Manufacturing Sector in Korea.* KDI Working Papers No. 9,017. Seoul: Korea Development Institute.

Yoon, B. S. 1992. "Reverse Brian Drain in South Korea: State-Led Model." *Studies in Comparative International Development* 27, no. 1: 2–26.

CHAPTER 4

# Singapore: Public Policy and Economic Development

*Teck-Wong Soon and C. Suan Tan*

## I. Defining Success

In November 1990, Lee Kuan Yew handed over the prime ministership of Singapore to Goh Chok Tong. In the three decades following self-rule in 1959, the first-generation leaders, as epitomized by Lee Kuan Yew, Goh Keng Swee, and S. Rajaratnam, had transformed the island-state from a "basket economy"[1] into one of Asia's four newly industrializing "minidragon" economies. In keeping with the central role played by a well-defined strategy between 1959 and 1990, the second prime minister set out his agenda in *The Next Lap* (Government of Singapore 1991) and *The Strategic Economic Plan* (MTI 1991). The first document places human resource development at the center of the continuing development effort and sought the people's support for the new leadership's efforts to raise living standards. The second document outlines the elements of a science-, technology-, and R&D-based strategy to transform Singapore into a developed nation on a par with Western Europe and the United States in 30 years' time.

Both the political transition and the economic platform reflected the two ingredients that have been crucial to Singapore's economic performance: social and political stability coupled with the moral authority enjoyed by the first-generation leadership. Our study will attempt to identify the nature of the interaction between economic growth and political conditions to see if there are policy lessons for other developing countries.

Section I reviews Singapore's 30-year developmental experience and structural change and brings into focus the underlying philosophy and rationale that influenced policy design and decision making throughout the period. Section II discusses the various developmental phases that Singapore has been

---

1. In a report in the *Far Eastern Economic Review,* David Bonavia concluded that an independent Singapore had no future and the "only sensible answer is a fresh accommodation with Malaysia to restore the natural economic relationship . . ." (1967, 38).

through during the last 30 years. By reference to the strategic framework, the rationale for the major economic policies adopted at the beginning of each developmental phase and the need for subsequent policy adjustments will become clear. Section III looks at the institutional framework for policy implementation and formulation. Singapore's public sector agencies comprise not only the government ministries and departments (that is, the civil service proper) but also a large number of statutory boards and state-owned enterprises (SOEs) that are generally referred to in Singapore as government-linked corporations (GLCs). Unlike SOEs in many other developing countries, which are usually inefficient and ineffective (Klitgaard 1991), these SOEs have been successful and profitable.

Section IV analyzes the design and implementation of vital policies, dealing particularly with how regulations were designed in a free market context to encourage savings and boost long-term growth. Section V reviews policy developments during the 1990s. Section VI concludes by placing public policy and the role of government in the wider domestic international context. The section analyzes the sources of growth and points to the importance of timing for interventions by the state. It offers some potentially useful lessons for other small, resource-poor, developing countries.

## Structural Change and Success

Over the 30-year period, there have been 5 phases of development.

Phase I     Labor-intensive, import-substitution industrialization
            (1959–65)
Phase II    Labor-intensive, export-orientated industrialization
            (1966–73)
Phase III   First attempt to upgrade the economy (1973–78)
Phase IV    Economic restructuring (1979–84)
Phase V     Retrenchment and further diversification (1985–90)

In constant Singapore dollar terms,[2] GDP increased 10-fold from $5 billion in 1960 to $53 billion in 1990. Given the high level of foreign participation in this growth, the indigenous GDP is much lower and has experienced a widening gap over time. In 1966 (when its data first became available), indigenous GDP was $6.7 billion, some 91 percent of the corresponding $7.4 billion for GDP. By 1990, the indigenous GDP of $36.5 billion amounted to only 64 percent of total GDP. Between 1960 and 1990, per capita indigenous GDP increased almost fourfold from $3,455 to $13,150. This is significantly lower

---

2. Unless otherwise specified, all dollar amounts refer to Singapore dollars.

than the sevenfold increase in per capita GDP, from $3,068 to $21,100, over the same period.

Table 4.1 highlights the main dimensions of structural change over the period and shows how economic openness has been a permanent feature. Trade has typically been around three times the GDP. Another striking feature is the tripling of gross domestic investment within the first decade, to 33 percent of GDP; by 1980, its share had reached 41 percent of GDP. The sectoral shares of GDP show the decline of primary activities from 3.3 percent in 1960 to a negligible .4 percent in 1990. Despite the countercyclical nature of construction activity, its contribution to GDP has remained at about 10 percent. The shifting importance of manufacturing and services is seen in the rapid growth in manufacturing's share, from 19 percent of GDP in 1960 to nearly 30 percent in 1980, followed by a slight decline to 26 percent for 1990. Trade and transport services have maintained their share at about 30 percent of GDP, while financial and other services have risen from 30 percent of GDP in 1970 to 38 percent in 1990.

TABLE 4.1.    Structural Change in Singapore, 1960–90 (all figures as percentage of GDP)

|  | 1960 | 1970 | 1980 | 1990 |
|---|---|---|---|---|
| Economic openness |  |  |  |  |
| Total trade | 356 | 210 | 370 | 327 |
| Exports | 164 | 82 | 165 | 155 |
| Imports | 192 | 130 | 205 | 172 |
| Gross domestic investment | 10 | 33 | 41 | 38 |
| Gross national savings |  |  |  |  |
| Private | — | 76.3[a] | 55.4 | 53.8[b] |
| CPF | — | 22.1 | 30.0 | n.a. |
| Non-CPF | — | 54.2 | 25.4 | n.a. |
| Public (government) | — | 23.7 | 44.6 | 46.2 |
| Sectoral shares |  |  |  |  |
| Agriculture, fishing, and quarrying | 3.3[c] | 2.5 | 1.3 | 0.4 |
| Construction | 11.5 | 11.7 | 8.9 | 6.7 |
| Manufacturing | 19.2 | 25.4 | 28.6 | 26.1 |
| Trade and transport services | 30.6 | 30.9 | 30.0 | 28.5 |
| Financial and other services | 35.4 | 29.5 | 31.2 | 38.3 |
| Payments balance and reserves (U.S.$m) |  |  |  |  |
| Overall balance of payments | — | 184 | 663 | 5,431 |
| Foreign exchange reserves | — | 1,012 | 6,567 | 27,748 |

*Sources*: Yearbook of Statistics, IMF International Finance Statistics, various years.
[a]For 1974.
[b]For 1988.
[c]For 1966.

Sound macroeconomic management and financial prudence account for the absence of external debt. The balance of payments has been solidly in surplus and foreign reserves have grown. Macroeconomic stability is manifest in relatively stable prices throughout the period. With the exception of the 1973–78 period of high oil prices, prices (as measured by the GDP Deflator, Consumer, and Wholesale Price Indices) increased on average by barely 4 percent a year.

One of Singapore's earliest successes was in family planning. The population rose from 1.6 million in 1965 to only 2.6 million in 1990. But with the postwar "baby boomers" growing into adults, from the 1960s onward the labor force expanded almost tenfold, from 162,000 to 1,524,000 in 1990. This growth slowed down, though, to only 1.5 percent a year during phase V, compared with the average annual 30 percent increase during phase II (all details are in the appendix.)

Other socioeconomic indicators include the impressive record of public housing. The number of people living in owner-occupied public flats rose from 9 percent of the population in 1970 to 92 percent in 1990. An additional 7 percent live in rented public flats. Literacy rates (among people above 10 years of age) rose from 72 percent in 1970 to 90 percent by 1990, and student enrollment ratios increased from 80 percent (for primary schools) and 43 percent (secondary) in 1970 to an average of 93 percent for both groups in 1990. Better quality education is also reflected in the significant declines in student/teacher ratios at both the primary and secondary levels.

Some of the main features of the developmental phases were as follows.

Growth in private consumption, from U.S.$4.1 billion in 1960 to U.S.$26.3 billion between 1960 and 1990.

Changes in the pattern of private consumption. Shares for food and clothing declined; those for rent and utilities, transport, and communications increased slightly; those for furniture and household equipment and medical services were broadly stable; and there were significant increases for recreation and education and other goods and services.

A sharp rise in domestic savings from 10 percent of GDP in 1965 to 40 percent in 1985, a year of recession.

A slowdown in the rate of foreign capital inflow in the 1980s, from 13.8 percent of GDP in 1973 to .1 percent in 1985.

A steep rise in gross fixed capital formation (GFCF), from 17 percent of GDP in 1965 to 42 percent in 1985.

Balanced growth in the secondary and tertiary sectors, with higher sectoral shares of employment in manufacturing in the earlier phases giving way to growth in services from phase IV.

Figure 4.1 illustrates the time paths for the sectoral shares of GDP. Over time, the share of construction and utilities (referred to as Overheads) has re-

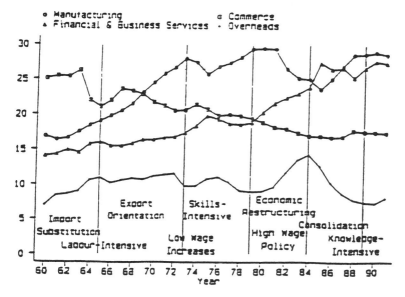

Fig. 4.1.   Changing sectoral composition and economic development

mained fairly stable except for the early 1980s. The rise in manufacturing continued through the early 1980s until the high wage policy and global recession
precipitated a decline. In contrast, the rise in the share of financial and business
services is more gradual. Significantly, the share of commerce and transport
services declined continuously, to about 17 percent in 1990.

### The Re-export Economy and World Trade

The openness of the economy and the role of international trade are reflected
in the high trade/GDP ratio of 200 to 350 percent. The impact of the 1970s oil
price hike is reflected in the highest annual average growth rates for trade values
during this period. Despite persistent current account deficits, continuous capital inflows have ensured growing balance of payment surpluses, from $1 billion
in 1973 to $9.9 billion in 1990. Official foreign reserves have increased at a
similar pace, from $5.8 billion in 1973 to $55.8 billion in 1990, equivalent to
about five to eight months' worth of imports.

Historically, re-exports have been an integral part of Singapore's entrepôt
trade. But export-oriented activities have evolved from those based on simple
processing and repackaging to the transforming of inputs into higher-value
outputs. Since Singapore has virtually no natural resources, all exports rely on
imported inputs and are therefore re-exports. Lloyd and Sandilands (1988) thus

consider Singapore to be a re-export economy, in which imported inputs are used in the production of some or all export-production activities. The result is a high trade/GDP ratio by international standards, with export-led economic growth hinging on how much value is added domestically.

A re-export economy has several implications for overall growth. The Dixit-Grossman model (1982) of a re-export economy shows that free trade and capital intensification will jointly raise the value-added content of tradables that use intermediate inputs. Because of the absence of a domestic resource base, export growth in any sector entails increased imports of intermediate goods as well as of final goods. Thus, export growth enhances production efficiency and export competitiveness. These gains are then fed back into the domestic sector via their impact on the prices of tradables (other exportables) and nontradables (such as labor and infrastructure).

Trade data show that Singapore's share of world trade has been rising continuously, from .7 percent in 1965 to 1.8 percent in 1990. Trade is concentrated in commodities such as beverages and tobacco (SITC 1), petroleum products, oil bunkers, chemical and medical products, and plastic materials (SITC 3 for mineral fuels, lubricants, and related materials), animal and vegetable oils and fats (SITC 4), and office machines, industrial machines, electric motors and resistors, television sets and radios, electronic components, ships, boats and oil rigs (SITC 7 for machinery and transport equipment). In these commodities, Singapore's share of world trade averaged about 2.5 percent in 1990.

## Economic Preconditions for Success

Of the four "minidragon" economies, Singapore is the smallest. In 1959–60, it covered 582 square kilometers and had a population of about 1.6 million. It also differed from the other "dragons" in the virtual absence of an agricultural sector, natural resources, and industrial tradition and entrepreneurship. Normally, these factors would have been considered a great handicap. But Singapore's policymakers turned them into an advantage by acting on the simple premise that "people are Singapore's only productive asset" (Goh Keng Swee 1977b, 81).

In retrospect, the government had little choice but to look to industrialization as a means of generating employment for its growing labor force. While the decision to use foreign investment, particularly that from the multinational corporation (MNC), was pragmatic, its outcome was by no means certain—especially in view of the tumultuous period preceding independence.[3] A hospitable, stable environment was thus recognized to be a necessary, but insuf-

---

3. For details of the political struggles during this period, see Bloodworth 1986, Chan 1971, and Rajaratnam 1966.

ficient, condition for attracting foreign investors. Developing an efficient infrastructure that would lower operational costs was essential for transforming Singapore into a competitive base for MNCs.

At the same time, the government recognized the need for a competent bureaucracy to help implement its policies. It also understood the vital importance of industrial peace. Having won its political mandate in 1968—partly because of the speed with which it solved the housing problem for the lower income group—the government was able to begin mobilizing labor's support for good industrial relations when it shifted to export-oriented industrialization.

From the start, it was clear that the government would have few qualms about intervening to supplement and/or reinforce market forces. Although such interventions do not always lead to the desired results, in Singapore's case they were designed so effectively that they created the preconditions for success. This emphasis on the design of economic policies and government intervention will be a recurring theme of this essay.

The strategic framework the government used has consisted of: (1) defining the constrained economic growth objective function, (2) identifying the two "engines of growth" to be used, and (3) setting the criteria for policy design.

To implement this framework, other strategic decisions were required:

The choice of MNCs as the vehicle for launching the industrialization process
Identifying government interventions to enhance industrialization
Minimizing domestic uncertainties and maximizing investor confidence in Singapore through macroeconomic stability
A free-market orientation and openness for competitive sourcing of inputs (including human resources), rapid transmission of external changes, and minimal scope for rent-seeking, unproductive activities
Facilitating the evolution of entrepôt trade via intensification of the international division of labor.

Figure 4.2 provides a schematic presentation of the guiding framework. More details on the rationale underlying this framework are in section V.

## II.  Industrial Policy

This section discusses the evolution of Singapore's industrial policy over the five developmental phases. It is worth noting that, apart from an initial five year plan (State of Singapore Development Plan 1960–64), the government did not produce any more five year plans. However, this does not mean that it

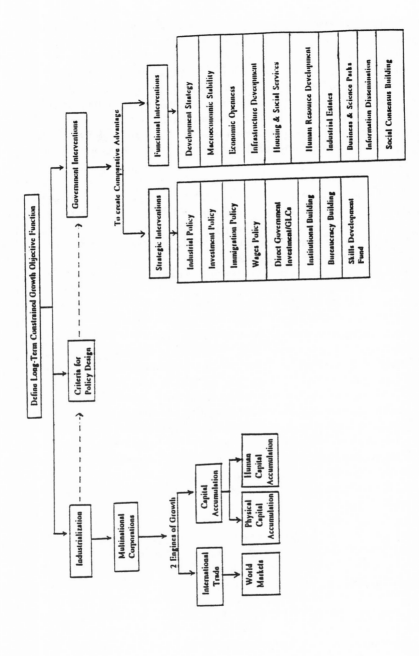

Fig. 4.2. Summary of the strategic framework for economic development

has not practiced planning. It took a flexible approach to planning, one that did not depend on a rigid time frame.

In view of its openness and vulnerability, Singapore has always emphasized the need for continuous monitoring of its external environment, with policy being refined as and when needed. However, the government usually ensured that any major modifications to its developmental strategy were thoroughly explained. Although the details of some policy changes might appear drastic (or draconian) to some observers and critics, these changes were, on closer examination, well coordinated and designed to work toward achieving the government's long-run objective for economic growth.

## Phase I: Labor-Intensive Import Substitution (1959–63)

*Initial Conditions.* When Singapore attained self-government in 1959, its social, economic, and political environment was not vastly different from those of other former colonial countries. It was an underdeveloped Third World country with widespread poverty, low levels of education, inadequate housing and health facilities, and high unemployment. These problems were compounded by rapid population increases and the complexities of its ethnic mix. But Singapore had two potential advantages: its hard-working people and its geographic location. Reflecting these endowments, the main economic activity at the time was entrepôt trade and the services supporting this trade (such as banking, regional shipping, warehousing, transportation, and some intermediate processing industries). Unfortunately, entrepôt trade was assessed as having "very limited possibilities for expansion" (Ministry of Finance 1961–64).

Under such dismal conditions, the People's Action Party (PAP) leadership, which assumed power in 1959, had little choice but to look toward industrialization as the basis for providing jobs. However, the small size of the domestic market was a handicap, so the new government considered it essential to expand this market through economic and political union with Malaya, thus creating the Federation of Malaysia. During this initial phase of development, the idea of Singapore as an independent nation was not even contemplated. Even so, its government made a firm and early commitment to provide the people with decent housing, basic medical care, and better education.

In becoming a member of the federation, Singapore was assured of a reasonably large hinterland, which could be protected by tariffs and quantitative import restrictions. Thus, like most developing countries, Singapore based its initial industrialization strategy on import substitution. Because of its severe unemployment at the time, the government sought to attract labor-intensive industries.

*Policy Responses.* To improve the dismal housing conditions of the people, the government established in February 1960 a new housing authority.

The Housing and Development Board (HDB) was given the objective of building and providing large-scale subsidized housing. The HDB was to embark on a mass housing program. The government also introduced in 1960 a five year plan in education whose main features were: (1) equal treatment for the four streams of education: Malay, Chinese, Tamil, and English; and (2) emphasis on the study of mathematics, science, and technical subjects.

These two features are instructive. The first reflected the reality of a multiracial society, and the second reflected the early realization of the types of education and training required for industrialization. As a first step toward achieving these aims, the government embarked on an accelerated school building program, aiming to provide a place for every school-age child in Singapore (Soon 1988).

In 1961, the government established a second statutory board, the Economic Development Board (EDB), to centralize all industrial promotional activities. To ensure success, the EDB had ample funds and strong powers (1) to grant loans or advances to, or subscribe to, stocks, shares, bonds, or debentures of, industrial enterprises; and (2) to acquire land for industrial sites. These powers enabled the EDB to provide capital to enterprises in need of assistance, to invest directly in industrial ventures, and to establish industrial estates furnished with all the required facilities—power, water, gas, roads, railways, and even a deep seaport. The EDB was also able to provide some discretionary incentives; the main one was the "pioneer status" award, introduced in 1959, which gave five-year tax holidays to labor-intensive companies.

*Economic Outcomes.* The anticipated benefits of the merger with Malaysia did not materialize. Instead, after Singapore joined Malaysia in 1963, severe internal political difficulties were encountered as well as an external challenge arising from a confrontation with Indonesia's President Sukarno.

In the initial phase, Singapore's achievements were modest. The manufacturing share of real GDP increased from 16.9 percent in 1960 to 19.1 percent in 1965, which was considered disappointing after the prodigious efforts of the government and the EDB. Real GDP grew at an annual compound rate of 5.7 percent during this period, a fair achievement given the economic slump of 1964. The total inflow of foreign investment during this period was S$157 million, not a large amount but still indicating some success in attracting foreign companies, particularly those aiming for the expanded Malaysian market.[4] However, even though 21,000 new jobs were created in manufacturing, unemployment was estimated to be well over 10 percent.[5]

4. Ryokichi (1969, 148) noted, for example, that "the anticipated formation of the Federation of Malaysia during 1962–63 . . . was a very important motivating factor, not only in bringing manufacturers to Singapore but also in increasing the size of plant and equipment."

5. No official unemployment figure was published. Yoshihara (1976) cites an unemployment figure of 12.3 percent from Blake 1967, 138.

Such modest achievements led economists and other commentators to suggest that this was a period in which Singapore's policies were ineffective and unsuccessful. Young (1992, 27), for example, noted "that the failure of Singaporean policies at this time is typified by the fate of the 17,000 acre Jurong Industrial Estate, created to attract foreign investment." Despite such assessments, it is important to realize the significance of this period in laying the foundations for Singapore's later success. Strong institutions were established, including the two strongest statutory boards, the HDB and the EDB.

Substantive social overheads were also developed during this period, as can be seen from the rise in the construction share of real GDP from 5.4 percent in 1960 to 9.4 percent in 1965. The government also boosted the capacity of educational and training institutions. Without all these initial efforts, it is doubtful whether Singapore could have survived the crisis it faced in the mid-1960s.

## Phase II: Labor-Intensive Export-Oriented Manufacturing (1966–73)

*Changes in Environment.* Singapore's difficulties with the Federation of Malaysia proved intractable and resulted in independence being thrust upon it in 1965. This reduced its access to the Malaysian market. A further blow came in 1967 when the British government announced its intention to withdraw its military base in Singapore by 1971. This threatened a further loss of investment confidence, an impending recession, and a worsening of the unemployment situation.

Although the situation seemed dire, the Singapore government's policy initiatives during the previous phase had already begun to bear fruit:

The government's success in tackling the housing problems led to its strong credibility with the people.

The heavy investment in education and vocational training was beginning to produce a substantial pool of semiskilled workers.

The EDB had developed several industrial estates, the largest on reclaimed swampland at Jurong. These estates offered industrial sites with excellent physical infrastructure at subsidized rates.

The EDB had developed its organizational capability and accumulated considerable experience in investment promotion. It was also entering into joint ventures with investors, the first of which was the Jurong Shipyard, a joint venture between the EDB and a Japanese firm.

Singapore's main economic problem remained high unemployment, so its main development priority had to be job creation. Without access to the

Malaysian market, the government had little choice but to abandon import substitution as its growth strategy. Industrialization behind tariff walls was clearly
not a feasible option for a small city-state with no raw materials. Instead,
the government switched its investment promotion efforts to labor-intensive,
export-oriented manufacturing.

*Policy Responses.* The Singapore government acted quickly to implement
its new approach. In 1967, the Economic Expansion Incentives Act provided
new tax incentives for investment:[6]

> Tax relief was allowed in certain circumstances for incremental income
> resulting from capital expansion.
> A 90 percent remission of tax profits was allowed to approved enterprises
> for periods of up to 15 years.
> Tax exemptions were allowed on interest on foreign loans, royalties,
> know-how, and technical assistance fees.

These incentives, though similar to those offered by many developing countries at the time, were more generous on average.

Though fiscal incentives and the efforts of the EDB did much to help the
new strategy, what was even more critical was the government's success in obtaining public support for its policies. In the 1968 general elections the PAP
won all 58 parliamentary seats. Seizing upon this success, the government introduced several policy initiatives that, in hindsight, translated the economic
preconditions created in the previous phase into economic success. With industrial stoppages widespread at the time, the government acted swiftly to promote
better industrial relations. The Employment Act of 1968 abolished some discriminatory practices, rationalized pay structures by doing away with abuses on
overtime, and reduced retrenchment benefits. In the same year, the Industrial
Relations (Amendment) Act removed a big source of friction between labor and
management by placing matters such as promotions, methods of recruitment,
transfers, task assignments, and retrenchment firmly within the prerogative of
management and not subject to negotiation. These legislative changes resulted
in a transformation of the role of trade unions, which had hitherto taken an adversarial and confrontational stance.

The PAP government had already strengthened its relationship with the
union movement by including six Central Committee members of the National
Trades Union Congress (NTUC) as parliamentary candidates in the 1968 general elections. Building on the changes in industrial relations, the NTUC held a
seminar on "Modernization of the Labor Movement" in November 1969, at
which the prime minister persuaded the union movement to shed its role as "a

---

6. Cited in Goh Keng Swee 1973.

combat organization . . . for class war" and accept the interests of the nation (NTUC 1970b). One of the key recommendations of the seminar, which was subsequently put into practice, related to the promotion of tripartism involving the government, employers, and labor for the purpose of achieving higher productivity, greater efficiency, and faster economic growth. These measures laid the foundation for a close relationship between the unions and the government, which came to be called the "PAP-NTUC symbiotic relationship." The promotion of tripartism and industrial peace must surely be regarded as an important component of industrial policy.

In the cause of investment promotion, the government reorganized the EDB in 1968, hiving off several of its functions to other agencies and statutory boards (see sec. III). The government also continued to stress the development of human resources and physical infrastructure. It intensified its efforts to improve telecommunications, port, and air services. And, to promote macroeconomic stability, it raised the contribution rate to the Central Provident Fund (CPF), a pension scheme established by the British colonial government in 1955, to 25 percent of workers' wages. This increased the amount of real savings available for noninflationary finance.

*Economic Outcomes.* These policy initiatives prompted a surge in direct foreign investment, particularly after 1967. In manufacturing, investment commitments during 1968–73 totaled more than S$2.3 billion. The bulk came from the United States, which replaced the United Kingdom as the largest source of foreign investment. Most of the early U.S. investments were in petroleum refineries and electronics. Singapore was also fortunate in that political uncertainties in Hong Kong resulted in some textile and garment plants moving from there to Singapore. These investments generated a large increase in industrial employment and exports. The number of workers in radios, televisions, semiconductors, and other electronic devices rose from 1,611 in 1966 to 44,483 in 1973. In textiles and clothing, the number of workers increased from 2,459 in 1966 to 35,012 in 1973. These two industries alone generated more than half the total growth of about 147,500 jobs in manufacturing employment during this period.

The government was able to seize fresh opportunities. Thus, when the Bank of America (BOA) proposed to set up a foreign currency unit in Singapore similar to its Eurocurrency unit in London, the government responded by exempting from tax the interest derived from nonresident deposits in these units, which came to be called Asian currency units (ACUs). BOA's entry was followed by a rapid succession of other banks, mainly foreign, and this resulted in the phenomenal growth of the so-called Asia Dollar Market (ADM). The subsequent expansion of financial services provided economic diversification and also facilitated the inflow of foreign investment by making financial resources more readily available. Indeed, it was the growth of the ADM that provided the impetus for Singapore's aspirations as a regional financial center.

Real GDP grew at an impressive 13 percent a year from 1966 to 1973, with the share of manufacturing rising sharply from 16 to 22.3 percent. Direct exports as a percentage of total sales in manufacturing rose from 43.3 percent in 1966 to 53.9 percent in 1973. Gross domestic capital formation as a percentage of GDP rose rapidly, from 21 to 40 percent in 1973.

### Phase III: First Attempts to Upgrade (1973–78)

With the attainment of full employment in the early 1970s, labor surplus was replaced with labor shortage. This created the need to import large numbers of workers from neighboring countries.[7] Singapore also experienced a sharp decline in the inflow of foreign investment from S$708 million in 1972 to $376 million in 1973.

Under such changed circumstances, the government maintained its long-term growth objective but modified its economic strategy. It moved its investment promotion efforts away from labor-intensive manufacturing industries and sought instead to upgrade and restructure the economy, putting greater emphasis on quality, skills, and technological content. A two-pronged approach to achieve this was announced by Hon Sui Sen (Hon 1973), then finance minister: to intensify efforts to attract manufacturing industry (such as petrochemicals, machine tools, precision engineering, sophisticated electronics, office equipment, and machinery) and to assist existing industries to upgrade their skill and technological levels.

Hon (1973) also announced a 10-point program designed to upgrade the skill and technological levels of the entire manufacturing sector, which included the following policy initiatives.

  A wage policy based on an orderly increase in cash wages under the guidance of the National Wages Council (which was established in 1972) to ensure the international competitiveness of wage costs in Singapore for medium- and high-technology industries

  Manpower development—intensified efforts to promote industrial training, including allowing training expenses by medium- and high-technology industries to be amortized for tax purposes

  An open door policy for admitting qualified foreign engineers, technicians, and other professionals and skilled workers needed for the

---

7. It was only natural that once the pool of domestic unemployed workers had been absorbed by the expansion of the manufacturing sector, inflow of foreign workers would follow. While detailed statistics are not published on a yearly basis, the 1970 Census of Population showed a total of 72,590 noncitizen and nonresident workers in 1970, about 11 percent of the work force.

implementation of various medium- and high-technology industrial projects

A special tax concession (five-year complete tax holiday) to industries with desired levels of technology

*Economic Outcomes.* This initial attempt to upgrade the economy was hindered by the first oil crisis in 1973 and the world recession that followed in 1974–76. Despite this, Singapore's real GDP grew by 7.4 percent a year in 1974–79, compared with the developing countries' average of about 4.8 percent. The government's efforts to attract investment achieved some success with the inflow of foreign investment recovering. However, economic growth was not achieved because of the upgrading of manufacturing, which actually showed a decline in 1975. Indeed, during the two low years of 1974 and 1975, growth came from construction (reflecting the investment in infrastructure) and financial services (as a consequence of the expansion of the ADM). As noted by Goh Chok Tong (1980), economic upgrading slowed down as "fear of recession and its resulting unemployment cause[d] the economy to cling on to labor-intensive industries" and kept wage increases down. Ironically, because of the low wages, manufacturing was able to grow toward the end of the 1970s, helped by the continuing inflow of foreign workers.

*Discussion.* That the government was able to recognize the need to upgrade and restructure the economy so soon after achieving full employment is a reflection of its perceptiveness with regard to fundamental changes in the economic environment. The policy initiatives announced in 1973 were noteworthy for being introduced at a time of prosperity—not out of desperation, as had happened at the beginning of the previous phase.

With the stylized strategic framework in mind, it is easy to see that Singapore's dependence on international trade made it determined to remain internationally competitive. This was reflected in the measures to ensure orderly wage increases through the National Wages Council (NWC). The establishment of the NWC might be regarded as a signal of the government's reluctance to permit market forces to determine wage increases. In the event, the NWC became a powerful instrument for promoting the tripartism considered essential for industrial peace.

Further, while acknowledging the role of direct foreign investment in economic development, the government also wanted to enhance the human resources and supporting infrastructure needed for a healthy business environment. In particular, it recognized the need to upgrade the skills of the entire work force. Thus, this phase saw the establishment of a strong foundation for industrial training. While the government continued to strengthen its educational institutions, it also initiated the establishment of joint industry training centers through the EDB. These EDB training centers, established in collaboration with MNCs, provided the framework for a highly successful Joint Industrial Training Scheme.

Although some analysts, as well as the government, consider this early attempt to upgrade industrially as having been aborted by the first oil shock and world recession, it was more a matter of imported labor moderating the upward pressure on wages as well as the move away from labor-intensive industries. Without foreign workers, many of the labor-intensive industries would have shifted prematurely out of Singapore during this phase. Without the skilled work force produced by the Joint Industrial Training Scheme, the MNCs would not have been able later to obtain the high-quality support services they required for the more capital-intensive industries sought by Singapore. The rapid growth of the ADM contributed to the growth of the financial and business sector, facilitated economic diversification, and resulted in Singapore becoming a financial center.

### Phase IV: Economic Restructuring (1979–84)

The environment prevailing in the late 1970s was essentially similar to that at the beginning of the previous phase. The labor market was tight, and the inflow of foreign workers continued unabated.[8] For its part, the government laid stress on upgrading and restructuring the economy. Success in attracting foreign investment had caused the economy to become highly dependent on foreign firms, especially in manufacturing (see table 4.2). Far from being disturbed by this, the government sought to increase the inflow of foreign investment. By this time, it had recognized that such efforts also required continual improvements in infrastructure and the skills of the work force.

With the slowdown in the industrialized economies, it was expected that they would turn more protectionist and provide less capital to the rest of the

**TABLE 4.2.   Share of Majority Foreign-Owned Firms in Manufacturing, 1980**

| Contribution To | Percentage |
| --- | --- |
| Gross output | 73.7 |
| Value added | 67.4 |
| Employment | 58.4 |
| Direct exports | 84.7 |

*Source: Report on the Census of Industrial Production 1980.*

8. The 1980 Census of Population showed that the number of foreign workers in Singapore had increased to nearly 120,000 in 1980, an increase of about 50,000 since 1970.

world. Moreover, unlike the mid-1960s and the 1970s, when there was little competition for foreign investment, the Singapore government expected other economies to offer inducements to MNCs.

Under these circumstances the government saw an increasing need for economic diversification. In its Economic Development Plan for the Eighties, released as an appendix to the 1980 budget speech (Goh Chok Tong 1980), it stressed that Singapore must diversify: (1) its economic activities into new, information-based services such as computer, medical, consultancy, and warehousing services; and (2) its markets, so as to reduce the threat of protectionism and expand its exports to developing countries.

The government's views on foreign investment were reiterated in no uncertain terms in this plan. It stressed that Singapore would not place unnecessary burdens or restrictions on foreign investors: "[W]e cannot reserve nor demarcate areas for local businesses, nor compel foreign companies to combine with local companies." The government reaffirmed its commitment to allow foreign companies 100 percent ownership of their investments in almost every field.

In its assessment of the previous efforts at industrial upgrading, the government concluded that low wages encouraged the inflow of labor-intensive, low-technology investments and, as such, were an obstacle to upgrading and restructuring. With this in mind, it decided to institute "corrective" or "high" wage increases over the three-year period 1980–83, to be followed by market-oriented wage increases. The EDB would also intensify its investment promotion efforts through an extensive network of 22 overseas offices in the United States, Japan, and Europe. In an apparent attempt at industrial targeting, 11 primary and supporting industries were designated for promotion: automotive components, machine tools and machinery, medical and surgical apparatus and instruments, specialty chemicals and pharmaceuticals, computers, computer peripheral equipment and software development, electronic instrumentation, optical instruments and equipment (including photocopying machines), advanced electronic components, precision engineering products, and hydraulic and pneumatic control systems.

Although these policy initiatives attracted much attention, the government's efforts in the area of education and industrial training received less publicity. In practice, both approaches were complementary: the EDB's success in attracting particular industries was predicated on the availability of suitably skilled workers. These promotional efforts by EDB substantiate the finding by an International Monetary Fund (IMF) study on foreign direct investments, which concluded that incentives per se were not directly significant for FDI. Rather, they were important in drawing attention to a relatively unknown place and providing the critical mass of investors needed to spur growth and development (IMF 1985).

*Economic Outcomes.* The economy responded positively to the various policy measures. The EDB's efforts helped to induce a large inflow of foreign investment in the desired industries. Net investment commitments in 1980–84 averaged S$1.7 billion per annum, led by strong expansion in new, higher-value-added industries such as computers, electronics, machinery, printing, and pharmaceuticals. While real GDP grew at 8.5 percent per annum during this period, growth in manufacturing output averaged only 5.1 percent. The construction sector, however, grew by a phenomenal 21.6 percent per annum and financial and business services sector by 11.3 percent.

*Discussion.* Given the heavy investment in manufacturing during this period, the growth in output was disappointing. Instead, the rapid development of financial and business services, with their productivity rising the fastest during this period, provided further impetus to Singapore's aspirations to become a financial center. A growing consensus was beginning to form on the need for Singapore to accelerate the diversification of its already well-diversified economy.

Although it is difficult to assess the full impact of the oil crisis, it did harm the oil- and marine-related industries. In contrast, the costs of the high-wage policy of 1979–84 are clearly seen in the lackluster performance of manufacturing. Its profits were squeezed by the higher relative unit labor costs coming at the same time as a prolonged global recession and hence reduced external demand. As table 4.3 and figure 4.3 reveal, productivity growth was maintained throughout 1979–84, but the return on equity investment fell from 1983, reaching its low in 1985.

## Phase V: Retrenchment and Further Diversification (1985–90)

Singapore had its first severe recession in 1985 when real GDP declined by 1.6 percent. Coming after a long period of growth, the recession took the government by surprise. The Economic Committee, established under then Minister of State for Trade and Industry Lee Hsien Loong, concentrated on the immedi-

TABLE 4.3.    Comparison of Average Wage Increases and Productivity Growth of Asian NICs, 1979–84 (percentage)

| Country | Wage Increases | | Productivity Growth |
|---------|---------|------|---------------------|
| | Nominal | Real | |
| Hong Kong | 12.9 | 1.1 | 3.9 |
| Taiwan, China | 15.2 | 6.6 | 4.8 |
| Singapore | 11.6 | 6.5 | 4.6 |
| South Korea | 17.7 | 4.1 | 3.9 |

*Source:* MTI 1985; table 2.2.

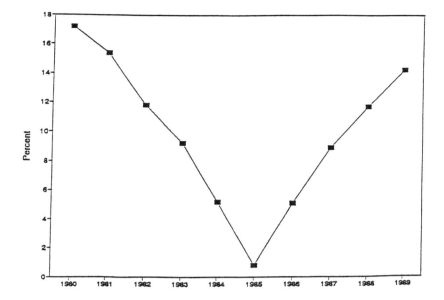

**Fig. 4.3.   Return on equity investment**

ate task of getting out of recession. The committee concluded that changed global demand had created structural problems for several key industries, in particular, the oil- and marine-related industries. It also noted a sharp rise in business operating costs, due to three main factors: (1) high labor costs result-ing from the increased rate of CPF contributions and from rapid wage increases continuing beyond the planned three years; (2) creeping rises in fees and charges levied by the Public Utilities Board, the Port of Singapore Authority, the Jurong Town Corporation, and other statutory boards; and (3) the strength of the Singapore dollar as a result of the success in attracting foreign capital.

Under such circumstances, the government maintained its long-term goal of economic growth. Recognizing that there was little it could do about external conditions, it considered that Singapore would have to deal with fundamental domestic problems. Thus, although it would have been politically expedient to improve international competitiveness through a weaker exchange rate for the Singapore dollar, the government chose instead to seek a reduction in labor costs and stuck to its strong exchange rate policy.

The employers' contribution rate to the Central Provident Fund was cut from 25 to 10 percent. Such a move meant a reduction in workers' earnings by 12 percent[9] and would have been difficult to implement without the support of

9. Since employers' contributions are part of workers' gross earnings, a 15 percent fall in employers' contributions results in a fall in gross earnings by 15 / 125 × 100 percent, or 12 percent.

the NTUC. Through the NTUC, the government also sought backing from the unions for two years of wage restraint. That the union movement supported the CPF cut and the wage restraint was a demonstration of both the symbiotic relationship between the government and the NTUC and the government's success in securing consensus on the measures needed to get Singapore out of recession. At the same time, the government lowered tax rates, reduced charges for utilities as well as for international telephone and telex services, and offered rebates on site rentals in the industrial estates, port fees, and so on.

As in the earlier phases, the EDB intensified its efforts to promote investment, particularly in high-value-added, technology-based manufacturing. It established a S$100 million Venture Fund to enable it to coinvest in new technology companies—even overseas when that would encourage the transfer of technology and investments to Singapore. The EDB was also charged with boosting investment in service industries, which (apart from the financial sector, which was promoted by the Monetary Authority of Singapore) had hitherto been left on their own. The EDB offered incentives for services similar to those for manufacturing, including pioneer status (tax holiday) and investment allowances. And the EDB stressed the notion of Singapore as a "total business center": the regional headquarters for the operations of MNCs in the Asia-Pacific region.

As in the earlier phases, the government's initiatives were successful, leading to a quick economic recovery. Real GDP grew by 1.8 percent in 1986, then by almost 10 percent in each of the following four years. Several MNCs set up their operational headquarters in Singapore.

Nonetheless, the severity and unexpectedness of the 1985 recession prompted several attempts to study its causes. The government's official response was the report of the Economic Committee. This was followed by Krause, Koh, and Lee 1987 and Lim and Associates 1988. These studies looked particularly closely at the high-wage policy. They questioned the overwhelming dependence of the economy on MNCs as well as the dominance of the government in economic management. The contribution rates to the CPF were considered to be excessive, and despite the government's efforts the studies also suggested that Singapore had underinvested in education. (These issues are considered in sec. IV and V.)

## What Constitutes Singapore's Industrial Policy?

The experience of the five developmental phases shows that the key elements of public policy were:

> Choice of industrialization as a developmental strategy, initially to create employment

Reliance on the private sector, particularly foreign MNCs, to establish and
run enterprises, though the government would step in should the private
sector fail to respond
Investment in human capital and infrastructure
Consensus building, maintenance of good industrial relations, and the
promotion of tripartism between government, industry, and labor
Maintenance of a stable macroeconomic environment through prudent
fiscal and monetary policies

The chief elements of industrial policy were the strategic interventions that
were manifested through:

Liberal fiscal incentives, initially to begin the industrialization process but
later to encourage specific kinds of investments and activities
Industrial targeting via investment incentives, which was modified over
time to reflect the shift from labor-intensive, low-technology industries
to skills- and capital-intensive industries

Indeed, Singapore has now begun to embark on its next phase: to encourage investment abroad. While growth has hitherto been largely dependent on
the inflow of foreign investment, future prospects depend also on the capacity
to build up large stocks of foreign assets.

The most recent account of the government's overall thinking comes in
the *Strategic Economic Plan* (1991), which was drawn up after work by eight
subcommittees comprising representatives from both government and business. The plan, which favors the positioning of Singapore as a global city, is a
reflection of the rational, incremental approach to policy formulation. It reiter-
ates the various elements of the strategic framework: emphasis on attracting
high-tech, knowledge-intensive industries; promotion of high-value innovative
and creative activities; investment to enhance human resources; and promoting
teamwork and cooperation between labor, business, and government. The one
new element of the plan is the call for the internationalization of local firms to
help them transcend the constraints of small size.

## III. Governance and Institutional Framework

However good the policies, they are unlikely to be effective without good governance and an appropriate institutional framework. This was recognized at
an early stage by the government in an analysis by Goh Keng Swee (1983). He
suggested that the fundamental problems with many developing countries stem
from inappropriate social and political institutions. He also noted that it is

essential to have as little corruption as possible but conceded that this was an issue that was unlikely to be raised in polite circles.

The purpose of this section is to examine how good governance has been achieved in Singapore, and the nature of its institutional framework. Apart from the civil service itself, much of the government's powers and activities are exercised by statutory boards. This section looks in detail at the Economic Development Board, and examines the major reorganization of the Monetary Authority of Singapore (MAS) in April 1981 as well as the review of the educational system in 1979–80.

## The Civil Service

The first generation of PAP leaders were quick to see the civil service as a vital instrument. Without its support and cooperation, their objectives could not be achieved. However, the civil service had identified itself with the British colonial government, so it was not particularly sympathetic to the goals of the PAP government (Vasil 1992, 136). To correct this bias, the PAP government set up a Political Study Center to raise the awareness of civil servants about the problems facing Singapore. In opening the Political Study Center in 1959, Prime Minister Lee Kuan Yew said:

> My theme to you today is simply this: You and I have vested interests in the survival of the democratic state. We the elected Ministers have to work through you and with you to translate our plans and policies into reality. You should give of your best in the service of our people.

In recognizing the value of a competent bureaucracy, the PAP government made it clear to the civil service that high standards of performance were expected; and it began to appoint increasing numbers of younger and highly qualified Singaporeans on merit, replacing the seniority system hitherto practiced by the British colonial government. The government placed particular emphasis on attracting people with technocratic-managerial skills and introduced a scholarship system to ensure a supply of qualified young graduates to the civil service. At the same time, it decided to substantially improve salaries and benefits in the civil service so as to bring them broadly into line with those of the private sector. The government sought also to ensure that these competent civil servants would not feel frustrated with the implementation of policies and programs devised by politicians. It involved them actively in the formulation of policies and accorded them high status. The best civil servants were later encouraged to go into politics. In the words of S. Rajaratnam, "[W]e involved them in something far more challenging and satisfying than just being civil servants—building houses, roads, keep the city clean. They were being stretched. It did not take long before we established a close link between us and the civil service. In fact, after the first two elections, the PAP became really an administration. It was no longer a party. And the civil service became a part of that" (quoted in Vasil 1992, 146).

## Statutory Boards

The public sector comprised not just the civil service, but a large number of statutory boards. Ow describes these boards as follows.

> Statutory boards are autonomous corporate bodies established by Acts of Parliament. As such, they are legal entities and fully liable in law and do not enjoy the legal privileges and immunities of government ministries and departments. Statutory boards enjoy a much greater degree of autonomy and flexibility in their day-to-day operations and financial matters than the civil-service proper. However, the statutory boards are under the supervision of their respective Ministers who lay down the major policy guidelines and are answerable to the Parliament. (1986, 241)

Although statutory boards are not unique to Singapore, they have been atypically effective there. In the initial phases, they were often given wide-ranging powers. The first statutory board established by the PAP government was the Housing and Development Board. Its success is in sharp contrast to that of its predecessor, the Singapore Improvement Trust (SIT), which was established in 1927 by the British colonial government. It built only 20,907 units[10] between 1947 and 1959, housing just 8.8 percent of the population. The HDB, on the other hand, quickly provided Singaporeans with housing standards much envied in other developing countries (Tan and Phang 1991). As table 4.4 shows,

TABLE 4.4.    **Home Ownership in Singapore, 1980 and 1990**

| Type of Dwelling | Home Ownership (%) | |
|---|---|---|
| | 1980 | 1990 |
| HDB flats | 60.8 | 91.7 |
| Private houses and flats | 72.0 | 87.2 |
| Others | 46.1 | 63.6 |
| Overall | 58.9 | 90.2 |

*Source:* Department of Statistics 1991, table 28.

10. Yeh 1975, table 2.

the proportion of households owning the homes they occupied rose from just under 60 percent in 1980 to 90 percent in 1990.

The success of the HDB and the Economic Development Board led to the establishment of other statutory boards. Indeed, as noted by Ow (1986), there is a statutory board in almost every important socioeconomic field.

| | |
|---|---|
| Industrialization and investment | EDB and the Jurong Town Corporation (JTC), established as an offshoot of the EDB in 1968 to take over from the EDB the development and management of industrial estates |
| Savings | The Central Provident Fund (CPF) Board and the Post Office Savings Bank |
| Infrastructure and essential services | The Public Utilities Board (PUB), the Telecommunications Authority of Singapore (TAS), the Port of Singapore Authority (PSA), and the Civil Aviation Authority of Singapore (CAAS) |
| Trade | The Trade Development Board (TDB), which replaced the Department of Trade in 1983 |
| Banking and finance | The Monetary Authority of Singapore and the Board of Commissioners of Currency, Singapore (BCCS) |
| Tourism | The Singapore Tourism Promotion Board (STPB) and the Sentosa Development Corporation (SDC) |
| Radio and television | The Singapore Broadcasting Corporation (SBC) |
| Housing | HDB and the Urban Redevelopment Authority (URA) |
| Education and training institutions | The National University of Singapore (NUS), the Nanyang Technological University (NTU), the Singapore Polytechnic (SP), the Ngee Ann Polytechnic (NP), and the Institute of Technical Education (ITE), which was established to take over the functions of the Vocational and Industrial Training Board (VITB) |
| Public transport | The Mass Rapid Transit Corporation (MRTC) |
| Promotion of information technology and science and technology | The National Computer Board (NCB) and the National Science and Technology Board (NSTB) |
| Taxation | The Internal Revenue Department was converted in 1992 to a statutory board, the Internal Revenue Authority of Singapore (IRAS) |

The flexibility of these statutory boards, particularly in the recruitment and promotion of their staff, has contributed significantly to their success.

Several of these statutory boards provided services similar to those that could be provided by commercial enterprises. Indeed, the success of these boards has resulted in their accumulating sizable surpluses. As they have traditionally not been required to pay income taxes or dividends, the government decided in the 1987–88 financial year to transfer S$1.5 billion to the government's consolidated funds from four statutory boards—PSA, TAS, CAAS, and URA. From that year also, statutory boards were required to give 33 percent of their operating surpluses to the government, which is the income tax rate of private enterprises. The statutory boards have remained profitable and continue to show large operating surpluses.[11]

## State-Owned Enterprises and Government-Linked Corporations

The government's participation in business activities was done largely through the statutory boards and a large number of state-owned enterprises. Since the initiative to privatize them (PSDC 1987), the SOEs have come to be referred to in Singapore as government-linked corporations. Including the statutory boards and the GLCs, the government's participation in the economy is fairly extensive, providing almost 18 percent of total employment in 1990 (see table 4.5).

The rationale for establishing SOEs and GLCs has been explained by Goh Keng Swee (1992). In at least one instance, that of Singapore Bus Services, Ltd. (SBS), the government was obliged to get involved because the private transport companies failed to provide satisfactory services to the commuting public. In other instances, SOEs were established to cope with, or take advan-

**TABLE 4.5.    Size of the Public Sector in Singapore, 1990**

|  | Sales (S$m) | Profits (S$m) | Number of Employees |
|---|---|---|---|
| SOEs and GLCs | 9,237 | 2,119 | 83,700 |
| Statutory boards | 9,615 | 2,592 | 59,500 |
| Government (including defense forces) | — | — | 123,000 |
| Total |  |  | 266,200 |
| Total work force |  |  | 1,516,000 |

*Source:* EDB, "Annual Reports of Statutory Boards," cited in Goh Keng Swee 1992.

---

11. The operating surpluses of 10 major statutory boards (CAAS, HDB, JTC, MRTC, PSA, PUB, SDC, SBC, Singapore Telecom [previously TAS], and URA) were reported in the annual *Economic Survey of Singapore* to have been about S$2.5 billion in 1991.

tage of, major events in Singapore's history. These included the establishment of Sembawang Shipyard to commercialize the British naval facility after Britain's military withdrawal. The attainment of independence provided Singapore with an opportunity in 1968 to set up its own shipping company, Neptune Orient Lines, to take advantage of the Far East Freight Conference, a cartel of British and European vessel owners. As this grouping virtually monopolized the freight business between Europe and the Far East, it ensured steady profits for its members. Also at independence, it was necessary for Singapore to establish its own defense forces. Although much military equipment could be imported, the government decided to establish an SOE to produce small-arms ammunition. Later, several other enterprises related to defense were established. The EDB has also established several joint venture companies, sometimes to demonstrate the government's commitment to a project.

The cumulative effect of government decisions to establish SOEs of one kind or another has been a large number of enterprises, which, as suggested by Goh Keng Swee (1992), can be analyzed in two tiers. First-tier companies are set up by the government (with the government usually as the sole shareholder) and funded from the development account. These are generally subsidiaries of one of three government holding companies, Temasek Holdings, Singapore Technology Holdings (for defense-related industries), and Health Corporation Holdings (for hospitals and medical services). Second- and lower-tier companies are subsidiaries of the first-tier companies. GLCs are funded by the Government Holding Companies but are closed down if they are unprofitable. Since 1983, GLCs have begun to be privatized to enhance the private sector in the country's future growth, not to raise revenue. In the main, GLCs have been established for strategic reasons (as in the assurance of the pork supply for the domestic market) or when the private sector's inexperience resulted in slow investments in industries that the government thought were integral to its long-term development goal. Table 4.6 shows the breakdown of these companies in Singapore.

The dominance and relative performance of the large GLCs have been analyzed by Low, Soon, and Toh (1989), using data from a credit information

**TABLE 4.6.  State-Owned Enterprises and GLCs in Singapore, 1990**

|  | Temasek Holdings | Technology Holdings | Corporation Holdings | Total |
|---|---|---|---|---|
| Number of companies | 39 | 5 | 6 | 50 |
| Number of subsidiaries | 469 | 97 | — | 566 |
| Capital (S$b) | 9.1 | 1.0 | 0.5 | 10.6 |
| Number of employees | 65,000 | 12,300 | 6,200 | 83,700 |

*Sources:* Goh Keng Swee 1992.

agency on the 500 largest Singapore companies. Despite incomplete data, the study revealed the extent of GLCs' involvement in the Singapore economy. Table 4.7 shows that only 4.4 percent of the 500 largest firms (or 22) were GLCs, but they accounted for 12.2 percent of sales, 19.5 percent of profits, and 22.9 percent of the assets of the 500 firms. It is also worth noting that about two-thirds of the GLCs were joint ventures.

Table 4.8 also shows that the GLCs are large and profitable. They have the highest average ratio of profits to sales (9.6 percent) compared with 4.9 percent for foreign firms and only 2.5 percent for non-GLC Singapore firms. However, in terms of the ratio of profits to assets, foreign firms had the best return (9 percent) compared with 5 percent for GLCs and only 2 percent for non-GLC Singapore firms.

While the success of the GLCs is generally acknowledged, the reasons for their success have been widely debated. In general, local businessmen argue that GLCs have an unfair advantage because of their close links with the government. However, Goh Keng Swee (1992) maintained that they are expected to operate on a competitive basis, just like private firms. Indeed, given the small size of the Singapore economy, the larger and more successful GLCs have to compete not only within Singapore but outside as well. Even in the defense-related industries, economies of scale dictate that they should not restrict their production to the domestic market. However, it is still possible that some GLCs have an inherent advantage in the domestic market because of their connections with the public sector. The government has shown itself willing to modify policies and regulations in response to justified complaints, and it has tried to ensure fair competition. For example, in 1983, traders complained about the monopoly of the Primary Industries Enterprise on the import of fresh pork from Malaysia; the government responded by allowing the free importation of pork, provided that it met veterinary and public health standards.

The government's insistence that the GLCs stand on their own must have contributed to their efficiency. Indeed, not all GLCs have survived (Goh Keng Swee 1992). The first closure was in 1981, of John White's Footwear, which

**TABLE 4.7. Percentage Distribution of Firms, Sales, Profits, and Assets of the Largest 500 Firms in Singapore, 1986**

|  | Firms | Sales | Profits | Assets |
|---|---|---|---|---|
| Foreign | 62.8 | 63.8 | 70.5 | 44.2 |
| Singapore | 37.2 | 36.2 | 29.5 | 55.8 |
| GLC | 4.4 | 12.2 | 19.5 | 22.9 |
| Non-GLC | 32.8 | 24.0 | 10.0 | 32.9 |
| Total | 100.0 | 100.0 | 100.0 | 100.0 |

*Source:* Low et al. 1989.

had difficulties in exporting to the Soviet Union. The second example was Singapore Textiles in 1985, which failed due to poor management. The defense-related industries also fared badly when they ventured into high-technology enterprises not related to the production of weapons. In general, it seems fair to argue that the GLCs, like the statutory boards, are successful largely because they have had to compete. Their competitiveness appears to stem from good management and their ability to recruit well-qualified and capable staff. More-over, they provide a useful countervailing force to the large MNCs (Low and Toh 1989).

It is worth noting one other source of concern. With the dominance of the MNCs in manufacturing and the success of the statutory boards and the GLCs, some have argued that the indigenous private sector may be "crowded out" (see, e.g., Krause, Koh, and Lee 1987). One response might be to allow smaller local enterprises to ride piggyback on the statutory boards and the GLCs in their current drive to invest overseas.

## The Economic Development Board

The EDB was the second statutory board established by the PAP government in 1961.[12] What is unique about it is that, unlike other statutory boards that were given one specific task, it has the all-embracing responsibility for promoting economic development.

The establishment of the EDB was recommended by the 1960–61 United Nations mission led by Albert Winsemius to help develop a blueprint for Singapore's industrialization. The approach and thinking of the mission were re-flected, inter alia, in its areas of expertise: industrial sites, electrical equipment and appliance industries, metal and engineering industries, chemical indus-tries, and shipbuilding, ship repairing, and ship breaking industries (Chow et al.

TABLE 4.8.  Comparative Performance of the 500 Largest Firms in Singapore, 1986

|  | Average Sales per Firm | Average Profits per Firm | Average Assets per Firm |
|---|---|---|---|
| Foreign | 110.8 | 7.3 | 81.6 |
| Singapore | 106.0 | 5.1 | 174.1 |
| GLC | 301.2 | 28.8 | 603.5 |
| Non-GLC | 798.5 | 2.0 | 63.8 |

*Source:* Low et al. 1989.

12. The first statutory board to be established was the Housing and Development Board (HDB).

1990). With the agreement of the Singapore government, the mission went beyond its original terms of reference and undertook a broad investigation to advise on economic policies and organization.

The Winsemius report provided the basis for Singapore's first development plan. It made two particularly notable observations. The first was that Singapore did not lack entrepreneurs but they were mainly in commerce and not in manufacturing. This suggested the need for the government to participate directly to operate certain basic industries if neither foreign nor local enterprises were prepared to do so. However, said the report, long-run government participation might harm the investment climate unless it was true to commercial and market principles.

The second point recommended the establishment of a nonpolitical EDB with divisions for financing, industrial facilities, projects, technical consulting, services, and promotion. The report recognized that the EDB's core function should be the promotion of investment and that it should eventually hand over its financing activities to an industrial development bank. The Winsemius report was accepted and its recommendations implemented almost immediately.

The EDB was established as a statutory board under the Ministry of Finance. Hon Sui Sen, who later became minister of finance, was its first chairman. Lim Kim San, who was then chairman of the Housing and Development Board and later assumed several ministerial positions, was the first deputy chairman.[13] Five other board members, representing banking, manufacturing, labor, the professions, and academia, were appointed. In its early years, the EDB had technical advisers from the United Nations and the International Labour Organization (ILO).

Even though investment promotion absorbed much of the EDB's energies, it put considerable effort into other activities. Initially, it concentrated on the four industries identified in the Winsemius report, namely, shipbuilding and repair, metal engineering, chemicals, and electrical equipment and appliances. As the EDB was established as a one-stop investment promotion agency, its various divisions provided their specialized services to potential investors.

Apart from the Finance Division and the Project Division, the EDB also had a Technical Consultancy Services Division (TCSD). The TCSD had three units. One was the Industrial Research Unit, established with assistance from the New Zealand government under the Colombo Plan. It was the forerunner of the Singapore Institute of Standards and Industrial Research (SISIR). The second unit was the Light Industries Services (LIS) Unit, established with seed money from the United Nations to provide extension services to small manu-

13. The pattern of civil servants going into politics has continued. The current prime minister, Goh Chok Tong, and some of the "younger," or second-generation, ministers in the Singapore government are former civil servants.

facturers to modernize and expand. Parts of it were later regrouped and centralized under the Engineering Industries Development Agency (EIDA), which became established as a company under the Companies Act. The third unit was the Manpower Development Unit, which organized management courses in conjunction with other bodies such as the Singapore Manufacturers' Association, the University of Singapore, and Singapore Polytechnic. These efforts were later handed over to the Singapore Institute of Management, which was set up in 1965. The Manpower Development Unit continued to provide industrial training and has been involved in several training centers and technical institutes in collaboration with both the MNCs and foreign governments.

Other activities of the TCSD include the establishment of the National Productivity Center (NPC) and the Product and Design Center, which was incorporated in 1967 as the Export Promotion Center. The Export Promotion Center was, in turn, absorbed into the International Trading Company, Ltd. (INTRACO) in 1968, which was established to boost trade with the centrally planned economies.

The most notable feature of the EDB's early work was its emphasis on developing its own abilities without becoming a sprawling bureaucracy. By 1968, when U.N. assistance ceased, the EDB had developed a core of competent local staff. As its functions have grown in scale and complexity, they have been hived off into separate, autonomous organizations. In 1968, with an economic crisis facing Singapore, the EDB reorganized itself and handed over several of its functions to new organizations:

1. The Industrial Facilities Division, including the Civil Engineering Branch, was absorbed into a separate statutory board, the Jurong Town Corporation, which took charge of all the industrial estates.
2. The Finance Division was transformed into the Development Bank of Singapore, to serve as an industrial bank.
3. The Export Promotion Center of the Technical Consultancy Services Division was absorbed into INTRACO, the government-owned trading company.[14]

When the EDB was charged with promoting service industries, it had to coordinate with even more government departments: the Ministry of Health (medical care), the Ministry of Education (education services), the Monetary

14. Despite the EDB no longer being a one-stop agency, it has been successful in providing a wide range of services to potential investors and industry through the coordination of the various government agencies, that is, a multiagency approach. With its constant contact with industry and its several overseas offices, the EDB has served as the "eyes and ears" of the government and provides useful feedback on changes in the business environment. In performing this role, it continues to maintain good relations with industry.

Authority of Singapore (financial services), and the National Computer Board (information services).

## Drastic Reorganization of Government Agencies

Not all reorganizations of government agencies were as gradual and orderly as that of the EDB. At least two important bodies have been drastically reorganized: the Monetary Authority of Singapore and the Ministry of Education. Both reorganizations were initiated after extensive reviews in 1979–80 by then Deputy Prime Minister Goh Keng Swee. While these reorganizations seemed draconian at the time, they nonetheless resulted in organizations with an improved sense of purpose.

*The Monetary Authority of Singapore.* The reorganization in April 1981 of the MAS, a statutory board with all the functions of a central bank other than currency issuance, was surprising. It occurred after a period of rapid growth in the Asia Dollar Market, and the MAS was widely regarded to have been extremely successful in promoting Singapore as a financial center. Indeed, it was expected to absorb the functions of the Singapore Board of Commissioners of Currency and become a full-fledged central bank. Instead, it ended up transferring one major function, managing Singapore's foreign reserves, to a new organization, the Government of Singapore Investment Corporation (GSIC). Although the internal review of the MAS was never released in full, it seems to have emphasized the need to manage Singapore's foreign reserves more actively.

The reorganization of the MAS involved almost all the senior management either resigning or losing their jobs. Lim Kim San, a former cabinet minister, became the new managing director. Senior bankers were seconded from the private sector, and other senior staff were recruited from abroad. The reorganization cut the MAS's staff from 503 to 369. Its responsibilities were clarified, and it was given sufficient funds to enable it to manage the Singapore dollar.

The reorganization of the MAS did not imply that Singapore had dropped its goal of becoming a financial center, even though the new management insisted that the Singapore dollar should not be internationalized. The MAS decided in 1984 to revamp the former Gold Exchange of Singapore, whose members were then engaged in questionable practices, and set up the Singapore International Monetary Exchange (SIMEX). With senior MAS managers serving in SIMEX initially, a mutual exchange arrangement was worked out with the Chicago Mercantile Exchange. SIMEX's subsequent growth reinforced Singapore's aim of becoming a financial center.

*The Ministry of Education.* Although this reorganization did not result in the sudden departure of senior managers, almost all the ministry's senior officials were replaced. The report of the review of the Ministry of Education (Goh and the Education Study Team 1979) was published as a public document and submitted to Parliament. It proposed the establishment of a Feedback and Monitoring Branch to ensure that officials took responsibility for decisions. It also recommended the strengthening of the professional staff in the ministry as well as the establishment of a Curriculum Development Institute of Singapore (CDIS). The new education minister, Goh Keng Swee, described the management system that he inherited in 1979 as dismal and identified two major weaknesses in its "management culture": the cult of obedience and the cult of secrecy. He therefore set up the Schools Council, consisting of school principals and senior ministry officials. It works by circulating a catalogue of Ministerial Committee Meeting (MCM) papers, which are kept in each school library or staff common room. All principals are free to submit comments on any paper.

## Integrating and Coordinating Mechanisms

Thynne (1989a) has observed that the governmental system in Singapore involves a concerted effort to ensure coordination and control by the prime minister and his cabinet. It places great emphasis on the development and maintenance of strong interorganizational connections and of centrally directed policy and administrative integration. It is in this sense that Singapore has been described as an administrative state. Coordination is also achieved because a relatively small group of senior civil servants and other government appointees each hold several different jobs (Thynne 1989a).

The coordination and control of statutory boards and GLCs has been described in detail by Thynne (1989b), from which the present discussion is drawn. In the case of statutory boards, the acts of Parliament that established them usually enable the ministers in charge not only to appoint the members of their governing boards and direct them on their policies but also to request and receive information on their projects and programs. In several cases, permanent secretaries and other senior officials are on the governing boards, so they participate directly in decision making and act as channels of communication between the boards and their ministers. In addition, ministers and board members often hold informal discussions before important questions of policy are considered at the board level.

The same mix of formal and informal processes are also features of the arrangements with SOEs and GLCs. Particularly noteworthy is the fact that the chairmen of the three government-owned holding companies have usually been senior permanent secretaries. They are well placed to enhance the capacity of the holding companies, not just by coordinating their main policies but by ensuring that company policies are consistent with broader national objectives. Given the power of senior civil servants, it is vital that they should not be tempted into corruption. The government's approach has been to reward these civil servants with high status and income, while at the same time instituting tough actions against anybody who is found to have abused his position.

## Tripartite Arrangements

The government's approach to tripartism is best seen through the National Wages Council (NWC), which was set up in 1972 to avoid the traditional and potentially damaging "free for all" wage negotiations between employers and unions. The NWC comprised representatives from the government, employers, and the labor movement. However, it is not a statutory body, and its recommendations do not have the force of law.

While the obvious rationale of the NWC was to guide wage increases, its real value is that it provides a forum for frank and open discussion. In this way, the recommendations of the NWC are arrived at by consensus rather than by majority vote. To achieve a consensus, the NWC requires fairly detailed information about the state of the economy, performance of companies, real wage increases, productivity increases, and various aspects of government policy. This enables it to have an objective discussion about wage increases without the confrontational element common in traditional wage negotiations. Despite the NWC being regarded as a wage formulating body, it has actually been involved in a wide range of subjects. According to the NWC:

> The NWC over the years has addressed itself on various issues, other than wage adjustments. These include the two-tier wage system, job-hopping, fringe benefits, CPF increases, exchange rate changes, income distribution, including intra-wage income distribution, the investment climate, productivity issues, the competitive position of the Singapore economy, wage policy in economic restructuring, flexible wage system, extension of retirement age, part-time workers, foreign workers and the training of workers. For example, it was the recommendation of the NWC that brought about the establishment of the Skills Development Fund, based on tripartite involvement and direction of the workers' training programs. (1992, 28)

The success of the NWC as a tripartite body has given the government a mechanism with which to obtain consensus and support for its economic policies. For example, it was through the NWC that the government implemented its high wage policy in 1979 to accelerate the pace of economic upgrading and restructuring. Following the 1985 recession, the NWC provided a ready forum for the support of the government's initiatives for wage restraint and reform.

The success of bodies such as the NWC has since been replicated in, for example, the Economic Committee (set up in 1985), the various subcommittees or working groups that provided inputs to the Strategic Economic Plan of 1991, and a wide range of sectoral master plans. Through arrangements such as these, the government draws upon the resources of the private sector and ensures widespread support for its policies.

## IV.  Design and Implementation of Vital Policies

### Influence of the Leadership's Characteristics

Throughout three decades of rapid economic growth, one fundamental factor has been political continuity. The same party has pursued the same development goals on the basis of the same philosophy.

This extraordinary continuity has been reinforced by the personal characteristics of the top leaders. They were of similar intellectual mold, with academic achievements (mainly in law and economics) from top British universities. Having experienced life under the colonial government and then the Japanese occupation forces during World War II, they were determined to work toward Singapore's independence. They took political power in the prime of their lives. They were intellectually curious, with an understanding of global trends, a hard-headed pragmatism, a capacity for hard work, and a belief in personal and professional integrity. Thus, the policies adopted in Singapore cannot be analyzed and understood apart from the people who were driving them.

### Vital Policies

Broadly speaking, five groups of policies were vital to Singapore's growth.

Industrial and trade policy
Infrastructure policy
Human development policy, including education and industrial training
Labor and wage policy, including industrial relations and immigration
Macroeconomic policy

Section II analyzed economic growth in terms of the five phases of development and highlighted the main elements of policy design and adjustments in each phase. This section will focus on the essential aspects of these and other policies and their interdependence.

*Industrial and Trade Policies.* To encourage industrialization, the government initially relied upon various incentives introduced in 1961: a five-year tax exemption for new industries qualifying for "pioneer" status, the protection of the domestic market via the introduction of import quotas and extension of import tariffs, public investment in establishing industrial infrastructure (sites and factories), and the supply of industrial utilities at subsidized rates. To spearhead industrialization, the EDB lent money at concessionary rates and, when appropriate, took direct equity investments. Given the high unemployment at the beginning of the period and the lack of domestic industrial entrepreneurs and experience, there were no restrictions or qualifications on industrial investments. In 1963, accelerated depreciation allowances for pioneer industries were introduced in an attempt to raise industrial performance.

At the same time, the government's concern with the longer term led to the 1961 Commission on Education Reform, which laid the foundation for diversifying education into the technical and vocational areas. The government also decided to send top students overseas for training on bursaries and scholarships.

The 1965 shift in industrial policy toward export promotion involved three features that were characteristic of all policy design and implementation. First, the government gave consideration to infant industries that were established during the short-lived import-substitution effort and needed time to adjust to the new policy environment. Second, it selected certain industries in electronics and marine-related activities for promotion and gave them preferential loans and/or EDB equity participation. Third, it identified science and technology as the means of creating dynamic comparative advantage.

The government also responded quickly to external shocks. When access to the Malaysian market was lost, it promptly raised protective tariffs to increase protection of domestic industries for a while. In the following year, it began phasing out protection, first by removing some quotas and gradually replacing others with import tariffs. Later it reduced the tariffs, believing that the industries had had enough infant protection and should by then have become competitive. Its switch to export promotion involved redesigning some policies, largely through the 1967 Economic Expansion Incentives Bill. In addition to the tax holidays granted to new industries under the 1961 Pioneer Industries Ordinance, the bill provided indefinite concessionary tax rates on export profits. This was meant to attract export-oriented industries and encourage foreign investments and entrepreneurship. From 1969 onward, trade was continuously liberalized, and by 1973 all quotas and almost all import tariffs were eliminated.

At the same time, the government boosted incentives for industrial investments by granting longer tax exemption periods and lower tax rates. To compensate the infant industries whose tariff protection had been withdrawn, it extended the original five-year tax exempt period by 10 years and gave 20-year tax exemption to all export industries. These long exemption periods reflected the policymakers' view that it might take a decade or more for the new industrialization strategy to take root. In the event, everything happened much sooner. By 1970, the tightening labor market prompted the Amendment Act of 1970, which reduced the generous tax incentives of the 1967 Economic Expansion Incentives Bill.

The government then switched to industrial upgrading and restructuring, favoring larger-scale industries so as to accelerate growth. The earlier incentives were now made conditional on (1) investments being at least S$1 billion (or S$150 million if 50 percent of the paid-up capital came from Singapore permanent residents); and (2) the discretion of the Ministry of Finance as to the kind of enterprise that would promote or enhance economic and technological development. The accelerated depreciation allowance also was restricted to larger investments. To accelerate industrial upgrading, the government revised the rules for tax relief (even for those industries still within the relief period), withdrawing it from those industries whose annual export sales were either below S$100,000 or less than 20 percent of total sales.

The onset of higher oil prices after 1973 led to further policy revisions. In 1975, the government brought in a Capital Assistance Scheme and extra EDB loans to encourage specialized projects of unique economic and technical benefit to Singapore and to assist SMEs in establishing high-technology industries. To strengthen export promotion, it withdrew pioneer status concessions from firms producing exclusively for the domestic market. It also restricted the type of industries qualifying for pioneer status to aircraft components and accessories, compressors, transformers, diesel and petroleum engines, electrical and portable tools, telephone exchange equipment, microwave equipment, magnets and magnetic materials, typewriters, cameras, watches and clocks, miniature lamps, and a large range of plastic raw materials.

A further round of policy reform took place in 1979. It was aimed at industrial upgrading as well as expanding into financial and other specialized services. To encourage existing industries to invest in improving productivity, tax incentives were broadened to include tax exemption of profits up to a predetermined level. This level was an approved percentage of fixed investment and was in excess of the normal capital allowances.

In the 1980s, the government sought to encourage incentives for manufacturing firms by introducing various fiscal schemes: (1) double deduction, on a case by case basis, of R&D expenditures (excluding building and equipment); (2) accelerated three-year depreciation for all plant and machinery used for R&D; (3) an investment allowance of up to 50 percent of all capital investments in R&D facilities (excluding building costs); (4) extension of existing industry building allowances of 25 percent and an annual allowance of 3 percent for new industrial building and other physical structures for R&D activities; and (5) capitalization and the writing off of lump sum payments for manufacturing licensing for five years.

The 1985 recession highlighted the poor performance and vulnerability of domestic small and medium enterprises. Many closed down, leading the government to introduce a series of policy initiatives after 1986 to try to bolster these SMEs.[15]

The initiatives included drawing in the MNCs to help develop the SMEs. This has paved the way for the next stage of development—joint product development by the MNCs and SMEs.

This approach began in 1986, with the Light Industries Upgrading Program (LIUP). The EDB was again the coordinating agency, with MNCs and their subcontractor SMEs taking part in the program. In 1989, the EDB launched the SME Master Plan to renew and redevelop SMEs. Like earlier government initiatives, it uses joint public-private sector collaboration to encourage and assist SMEs. As before, public assistance has been provided through information, training facilities, and concessionary loans. SMEs can seek professional and advisory services from university academics at concessionary fees. The design of programs under the master plan also benefited from contributions by the MNCs, larger firms, and local chambers of commerce. To reinforce these efforts, the government formed an Enterprise Development Council in 1990 to provide ideas and recommendations. The council comprises members of Parliament, CEOs of the major MNCs, prominent local entrepreneurs, and academics.

Unlike Hong Kong and Taiwan, China, where indigenous SMEs have been an integral part of the industrial landscape, SMEs in Singapore have emerged much later in the process. As a result, SMEs in Singapore have entered directly, instead of gradually, into relatively skill-intensive activities, thereby providing another contrast to its Asian counterparts.

*Infrastructure Policy.* Once basic housing for the lowest income group was provided in the mid-1960s, the public housing program was integrated into the industrialization program. Guidelines for the design and location of new housing estates, industrial estates, public amenities (such as schools, shopping, and recreational facilities), and the public transportation network were intended to facilitate (1) more jobs for women; (2) domestic transportation for the labor force as well as for goods (ranging from imported industrial inputs to

---

15. The unsatisfactory performance of the SMEs can be seen from statistics pertaining to the situation of SMEs in 1987: (1) while SMEs constitute about 90 percent of all small and medium establishments and 44 percent of employment, they contribute only 24 percent of value added and 16 percent of direct exports; (2) only a third of SMEs are in the manufacturing sector, the majority being in the commercial services trade; (3) the manufacturing SMEs contribute only 1.1 percent of total manufacturing value added and less than 1 percent of manufacturing output; (4) value added per worker in manufacturing SMEs averaged S$17,000, compared with $55,000 per worker in MNCs and larger enterprises; (5) among manufacturing SMEs, the share of output exported is only 4 percent, compared with 670 percent for the MNCs and larger manufacturing firms.

finished goods for export); (3) a reduction in pollution by noise and industrial effluence; and (4) improved quality of life. Industrial estates were spread around the island to minimize congestion (for further details, see Chia 1984).

Besides ensuring adequate domestic transport, the government has aimed to modernize and expand port capacity by the early development of container port facilities. Much has been done to expand ship repairing and oil rig construction facilities. Efficient airport facilities are now in place to boost trade and help Singapore develop into a regional communications and financial hub. Resources have also been allocated for a full-fledged, fiber-optic telecommunications system that would lower costs and allow for the future integration of new telecommunication services and facilities, whenever these come online.

Important though physical infrastructure is, it needs to be complemented with the development of a suitable "institutional infrastructure." Singapore's government has shown an awareness that, as the economy increases in complexity, there is a growing need for government bodies to be better at managing their affairs and implementing their policies. Change cannot happen suddenly, not least because experience is a vital part of any institution's effectiveness. But the process of change must be built into the way the public sector operates.

*Human Resources and Dynamic Comparative Advantage.* As in industrial and infrastructural developments, Singapore's approach to human resource development (HRD) has been gradual and systematic, with flexible timing of policy changes. The salient features of its HRD strategy were based on several considerations. First, although labor was the country's main asset, population growth had to be constrained because of limited land. Second, skills were necessary for effective technology transfer and industrial takeoff. Finally, dynamic comparative advantage in the longer term is relatively more dependent on accumulating human skills not physical capital.

The design of an HRD strategy was initially complicated by (1) the government's inheritance in 1959 of an educational system geared to lower-rung jobs in the colonial administration (2) the need to provide employment not only for the existing nontechnical labor force but for the postwar generation, which was about to enter the labor market in the 1960s, and (3) the multiracial population and the different language capabilities of school dropouts entering the labor force in the early 1960s.

Until 1959, the education system consisted predominantly of state schools where English was the medium of instruction (hereafter referred to as English schools) and Malay schools for the Malays. There were also some Chinese and Tamil schools, established privately to provide an education in the vernacular. It was against this background that language became an emotive issue that was exploited during the independence movement period and early years of independence. The immediate task for educational reform was therefore to resolve the issues of language and standardization. In recognition of political realities, Malay was designated the national language. At the same time, economic modernization via technical change dictated that English be designated the official language. Vernacular Chinese and Tamil became secondary languages.

To start a convergence process for the different language schools, the government brought in a national Primary School Leaving Examination in 1960 for all schools. Gradualism was both technically and politically expedient, since language was still being used as a political tool. In language, as in other social areas, the government was to accelerate change after its landslide election win in 1968.

After two commission reviews in 1961 and 1962, the commissioners recommended providing technical and vocational education at the secondary school level and creating technical colleges for Chinese secondary school dropouts.[16] The next major initiative in the HRD strategy did not occur until 1968, when the government extended the formal system to include technical and vocational education and established joint training schemes with MNCs and foreign governments.

Parallel to the industrial upgrading efforts of the early 1970s (phase III) and late 1970s (phase IV), these training schemes were also upgraded by first being "joint" with MNCs and then "joint" with the governments of industrial nations. The joint MNC-government schemes resulted in the Tata–Government Training Center (Tata-GTC, with India's Tata Iron and Steel) in 1972, the Rollei-GTC in 1973, and the Philips-GTC in 1975. Joint government-government training schemes began with the Japan-Singapore Training Center in 1979 to promote Japanese investment in Singapore. It was followed by the Japan-Singapore Institute of Software Technology (1979), the German-Singapore Institute (1980), and the French-Singapore Institute (1983). To coordinate technical training and guide future activities, a Council for Professional and Technical Education was established. Its members included the education minister, the permanent secretary of the Education Ministry, the heads of the two universities, the chairmen of the EDB and the Public Service Commission, and the deputy secretary-general of the NTUC.

At the same time, the decline in population growth enhanced the value of skilled labor. The government therefore set about reducing the dropout rates in primary and secondary schools. The education system was overhauled in 1979–80. By 1984, dropout rates had fallen to about 7 percent from about 30 percent in the 1970s. By 1986, almost every Singaporean child was receiving at least 10 years of schooling (Soon 1988). Despite all these efforts, a study of the 1985 recession suggested that Singapore was not investing enough in edu-

16. Chinese school students rarely qualified for admission at the time to the sole university where English was the medium of instruction.

cation. More reforms therefore followed. Entry requirements for preuniversity admission were raised and stricter standards applied to vocational and technical institutes, polytechnics (technical colleges), and universities.

Better schools and universities do a great deal to raise a country's skills, but they exclude adult workers. Hence, there was a complementary emphasis on continuing education and training through the NWC and the Skills Development Fund (SDF). The SDF was established to provide funds for training workers. Employers are required to pay a levy on the salaries of employees whose monthly earnings are below S$750. The levy was initially set at 2 percent of the employees' earnings, then raised to 4 percent in 1980. Over time, the SDF has become involved in assisting the development of domestic technological skills. For example, by 1984 it was introducing its fourth scheme, known as the "Initiatives in New Technologies," aimed at nurturing a nucleus of trained scientists and professionals for industries such as automation and robotics, microelectronics, information technology, biotechnology, optical and laser technology, engineering, and materials sciences.

*Wages and Industrial Labor Relations.* Another vital element in successful industrialization is harmonious industrial labor relations. Two factors underlie the design of Singapore's labor policy: the absence of an agricultural sector, and hence minimal property ownership for the bulk of people, and the politically instigated labor unrest of the 1950s and early 1960s. In the 1967 Employment Act and the 1968 Amendment of Industrial Relations Act,[17] it was clearly recognized that fiscal incentives per se were insufficient to attract investments. To create a hospitable investment environment, the politically diverse trade unions were consolidated into the National Trade Union Congress. The "carrot and stick" approach to shared growth was launched through a 1969 NTUC seminar on modernizing labor, which helped to win labor support for the government's long-term strategy. At the same time, several NTUC cooperatives in basic consumer goods and services were launched to help contain living costs and initiate the shared growth strategy.

The creation of the NWC provided another arm for consensus building and policy coordination. Although the NWC was formed when the labor market was tightening, and it started with guidelines to restrain wage increases, it was clear from its tripartite nature that it would also serve as a forum for a wider set of issues. This was vindicated by the major policy switch in 1979 from wage restraints to high wages in tandem with the revised goal of moving into higher-valued-added industrialization.

---

17. The 1967 Act standardized working terms and conditions by laying down a 44-hour work week, limiting the annual bonus to one month's wages, and provision of retirement and retrenchment benefits only after three and five years of service, respectively. The 1968 Act preempted potential labor unrest and redefined labor-management relations by conferring more managerial power on employers.

Because of Singapore's attractive working environment and incentives for skilled labor, immigrants came from many countries—not just those of the Association of Southeast Asian Nations (ASEAN) but from South Asia and the western industrialized nations. The number of immigrants grew sharply in the early 1970s when Singapore experienced severe shortages of skilled and unskilled labor. In 1973, migrants amounted to over 12 percent of the total labor force. Conversely, with the expected onset of the 1985 recession, target dates were set in 1984 to phase out all immigrant workers from nontraditional sources. (There were some exceptions, for the construction and ship repairing industries, where activities were countercyclical and export-oriented, respectively.) And the levy collected from employers of imported unskilled labor not only provided a source of government revenue but also ensured that immigrants did not detract from the government's long-term strategy to boost value added and wages.[18]

*Macroeconomic Stability and Financial Control.* Macroeconomic stability has been crucial to the apparent ease with which continuous policy adjustments have been accomplished. Since the government was also aiming to develop Singapore into a global financial center, this enhanced the need for currency stability and prudential regulations. Because of the small size of the economy, the balance between those regulations that impinge domestically and internationally becomes crucial.

Macroeconomic policy has been characterized throughout by low inflation, budget surpluses, and a strong currency. Current account deficits in the earlier years turned into current account surpluses and growing external reserves. Continuous budgetary surpluses (except for 1973–74 and 1987–88) were obtained through a buoyant tax structure, capital revenue from government land sales, a policy of restricting public expenditure by charging all government services (except public goods) at full cost, and by limiting growth of public sector employment.

Given the significant roles of public housing, infrastructure development, labor and wage policies, and the compulsory CPF savings scheme, all these activities fall within the purview of macroeconomic policy. Lee [Tsao] Yuan (1987a) identifies five areas of macroeconomic policy: (1) monetary and exchange rate policy, (2) CPF and public sector surpluses, (3) public sector construction, (4) other fiscal instruments (such as taxation), and (5) labor policy. To illustrate how these have been coordinated, the interaction between the CPF

---

18. The levy was originally introduced under the CPF scheme but evolved into a separate levy on imported unskilled labor working under work permits. Skilled and professional foreign workers on professional visit passes are not subject to this tax. This levy has increased over time with the rise of foreign unskilled workers. In 1992, the levy rate was S$250 per month for domestic helpers and S$300 per month for workers in other sectors. The levy is paid by employers and therefore is easy to collect.

funds, money supply, exchange rate stability, and the management of external reserves will be briefly reviewed.

The effect of CPF contributions on the money supply stems from the investment of CPF funds in government securities. This results in a sizable withdrawal of money from the system and a consequent rise in domestic interest rates. The higher rates are likely to result in more commercial banks borrowing from offshore banks or abroad, putting upward pressure on the Singapore dollar. Given the size of the monthly contributions (up to 40 percent of wages) to CPF and the regularity of CPF purchases of government securities, exchange rate stability has been maintained by the MAS selling Singapore dollars. The foreign exchange holdings from these dollar sales are then handed over to the Government of Singapore Investment Corporation for management.[19] CPF funds have therefore provided much of the government's capital for development. On average, about 40 percent of government expenditures went into development projects such as airport, harbors, highways, public housing, industrial estate development, water, sewerage, electricity and telephone systems, schools, and universities (Lee [Tsao] Yuan 1987a; Seah 1983).

In studying the record of price stability in Singapore, Grubel concluded that "at the most fundamental theoretical level, Singapore's record of price-level changes is explained by monetary policy. Inflation was high following periods of excess money creation and low when money supply more nearly equalled demand for it" (1989, 378). More recently, Teh and Shanmugaratnam (1992) provide the background to the evolution of monetary policy and the managed float of the exchange rate in the 1980s. In the main, the choice and effectiveness of monetary policy instruments were influenced by the high degree of openness to trade and capital flows. Since 1981, monetary policy has focused on an exchange rate policy aimed at controlling inflation. The consequent appreciation of the nominal exchange rate during most of the 1980s has helped offset increases in the foreign currency price of imports and dampened the effects of wage increases. The industrial relations and wage flexibility achieved through the NWC also benefited the exchange rate policy, since rigidity of nominal wages would have caused a stronger impact on export competitiveness. It should also be mentioned that the labor and wage legislation of the late 1960s engendered technical change, since technical change depends crucially on the legal and institutional framework and is therefore not exogenous. Thus Grubel's (1989) argument that the income policies of 1974–79 and 1979–84 were redundant, since market forces would have brought about the same wage adjustments, seems to discount the potential role of legislation and institutions in enhancing technical change.

In their 1992 study, Teh and Shanmugaratnam also conducted model simulations of exchange rate impacts. The simulations indicate that without the

---

19. To date, GSIC's policy has been to invest these funds abroad rather than locally.

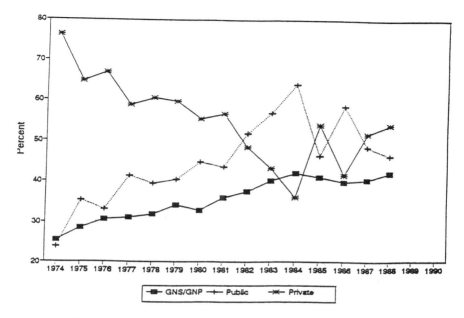

**Fig. 4.4.  National, public, and private sector savings, 1974–87**

Singapore Dollar's appreciation during 1988–91, inflation would have averaged 6 percent a year instead of the 3 percent it actually did. Furthermore, the lagged effects of a weak exchange rate in 1991 would cause the CPI in 1995 to be 25 percent higher than otherwise projected.

Much has been written about the high, "forced" savings rate in Singapore induced through the CPF scheme. In fact, the growth in domestic savings stems not from the CPF per se but from a rising rate of participation in the labor force, three decades of rapid economic growth, and the maintenance of budgetary surpluses. The CPF scheme differs from pay as you go social security systems in that CPF is fully funded and individually specific. Over time, the CPF scheme has also become more flexible by allowing members to use their funds for various approved purposes such as purchase of approved housing, medical and educational expenses, and investment in securities. As a result, the gross CPF contributions increasingly overstate the extent of CPF savings. In 1989, gross CPF savings amounted to 12.5 percent of GDP; but net CPF savings (gross CPF savings less withdrawals for various approved uses) was only 6 percent of GDP, which was less than the social security contribution rate in the European Community. Figures 4.4 and 4.5 show the changing shares of public and private sector savings and the decomposition of private savings into CPF and non-CPF savings.

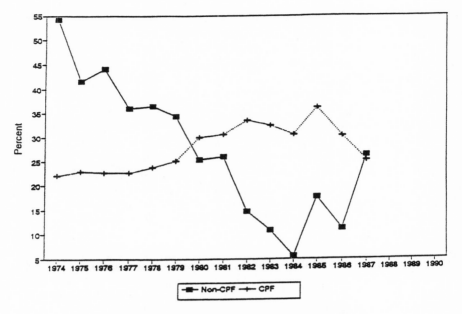

**Fig. 4.5.  Savings by private sector, 1974–87**

## Costs and Benefits of Policy Changes

Despite being a small and open economy vulnerable to external factors, Singapore has weathered the economic crises and uncertainties thrown upon it. As this paper has emphasized, much of this success is based on a long-term development strategy aimed at boosting growth. However, there have been occasions when policy was reversed or corrected, and these deserve attention as well.

One example was the switch from import substitution to export-oriented industrialization from 1965 onward, when policies were redesigned without prejudice toward industries that had been established during the import-substitution phase. Nonetheless, some firms were closed during this period—which was socially optimal since in the land-scarce (and eventually labor-scarce) economy prolonged protection would have been at the expense of overall growth. Another example involved the encouragement in the early 1980s of domestic self-sufficiency in pork. The government set stringent standards for controlling pig waste, which was to be partially subsidized by a levy per pig slaughtered at an abattoir. Despite effluence treatment by all farms, however, the level of pollution of the Straits of Johore by pig waste remained unacceptable. A review revealed that self-sufficiency was unwarranted because the domestic rearing of pigs depended on imported feed. Moreover, the production cost of pork was considerably lower in nearby China, Malaysia, and Thailand. The government therefore decided to phase out the pig farms in Singapore. Pig farmers were encouraged to take up alternative (and nonpolluting) farming such as hydroponic agriculture. Farmers who had invested substantially in effluent treatment were compensated by the government to the tune of about S$150 million.

Perhaps the biggest policy switch happened in 1985, when the government abandoned the high-wage policy it had adopted six years earlier. In a sense, the high-wage policy may be seen as a reward for the wage restraints accepted by labor during 1972–78. By the same token, labor's cooperative attitude during the renewed wage restraints of 1985–86 was in part due to the higher wages it had enjoyed in 1979–85. Labor also recognized that lower wages would mean fewer layoffs. In the event, retrenchment was minimal during the 1985 recession.

Because the 1985 recession followed on the heels of the unorthodox high-wage policy, various studies have tried to assess the policy's contribution to recession. Otani and Sassanpour (1988) showed that wage increases played a small role. If relative unit labor cost (unadjusted for exchange rate changes) had remained at 1980 levels during 1981–86, and all other exogenous variables were kept at actual values, GNP would have been unchanged in 1984–85 instead of declining. Lim and Associates (1988) showed that, had the 1986 cost-cutting measures been introduced in 1984, real GDP growth would have declined by only .5 percent instead of the actual 1.6 percent. In their recent study, Teh and Shanmugaratnam (1992) indicate that the 1985 recession stemmed from the coincidence of three factors: (1) a loss of international competitiveness as the high-wage policy from 1979, combined with the strong exchange rate policy from 1981, caused an increase in the real effective exchange rate; (2) a fall in cyclical domestic demand with the ending of the construction boom; and (3) a fall in cyclical external demand, especially in the electronics, ship repair, petroleum refining, regional tourism, and entrepôt trade industries that were important to Singapore.

Perhaps the biggest benefit of the recession was that it demonstrated Singapore's vulnerability to the global environment. The high-wage policy may also have been useful in helping to overcome some initial impediments to structural change. It ensured the deliberate creation of a critical mass of high-technology, knowledge-intensive, and skill-intensive industries and a basic level of manpower skills that made Singapore better poised for future growth.[20]

Lee [Tsao] Yuan has pointed out the inconsistency of having high wages and a strong Singapore dollar (Krause et al. 1987) simultaneously. Because of

---

20. We are grateful to Wanda Tseng of the IMF for this point.

the country's heavy dependence on exports, and hence on global competitiveness, wages are crucial to economic performance. By maintaining a strong and appreciating dollar, wages in purchasing-power parity terms increased by more than the increases provided by the NWC guidelines. A more circumspect and gradual approach might have been to forego the strong dollar target during the initial phase of the high-wage policy.

## V.  Recent Developments

### Overall Trends

During the 1990s, Singapore continued to maintain many of its hallmark macroeconomic policies of low inflation, fiscal discipline, and international orientation. Prudent fiscal policies have produced consistent and often substantial budget surpluses, which have been accompanied by low inflation of around 3 percent annually. Total trade has continued to increase (U.S.$193 billion in 1994), and the country has maintained its overall balance of payments surplus.

Economic growth during the early 1990s has been remarkable. Spurred by an annual average growth rate of over 8 percent, Singapore's per capita income grew from U.S.$12,462 in 1990 to U.S.$20,415 in 1994. Singapore labor costs continue to rise due to heavy labor demand linked to rapid growth but have been matched in general by commensurate increases in productivity, particularly in the manufacturing sector. Improved productivity continues to allow Singapore to attract foreign investment in higher-value-added and technology-based manufacturing industries as well as in high-quality services such as regional headquarters, financial services, research and development, design, packaging, and marketing. Net investment commitments rose steadily from U.S.$1.2 billion in 1990 to a record high of U.S.$2.8 billion in 1994, concentrated mainly in capital-intensive and high-value-added industries.

### Policy Developments

The government has continued to stress the need for restructuring and upgrading of the country's industrial base as well as the importance of education, training, and retraining for improving Singapore's human capital resources. At the same time the government has adopted regionalization as the basis for further expansion and encouraged Singapore companies to invest abroad. Major policy initiatives during the early 1990s have been aiméd at the labor, tax and investment regimes.

*Labor Market.* Even though they have been matched by productivity increases, rising labor costs remain a preoccupation, and the government has undertaken several measures to alleviate pressures on a tight labor market, increase the supply of workers, and increase the efficiency of labor resource use. The government has eased restrictions to allow firms to hire more foreign workers. At the same time, it has continued to stress the importance of education, skills training, and retraining. Government expenditure on education has nearly doubled from $1.2 billion in 1990 to $2.2 billion in 1994. Additional educational reforms include the intention to provide 10 years of general education in the school system, establishment of a third polytechnic, the expansion of the two universities, and the establishment of the Singapore Open University.

At the same time, the Skills Development Fund administered by the National Productivity Board (NPB) intensified its efforts to train and retrain Singapore's existing work force. In addition to providing training grants, the SDF has established training partnerships with trade associations, local corporations, and multinational enterprises. By 1994, these partnerships had enrolled some 118,552 trainees.

*Overseas Investment.* Faced with increasing domestic costs and continuing shortages of labor, labor-intensive industries are increasingly relocating to neighboring countries such as Malaysia and Indonesia. This move is supported by the Singapore government's announced strategy of supporting regionalization. By 1993, Singapore companies had invested almost $32 billion abroad, up significantly from $23 billion three years earlier.

*Tax Policies.* To ensure that the tax regime continues to be conducive to business, the government introduced the Goods and Services Tax (GST) in April 1994 as the basis for a major tax reform initiative that would reduce the burden of direct taxation. Tax deductions, subsidies, and rebates have also been approved to render the tax regime more progressive for lower-income groups.

*Savings and Investment Policies.* Given the Singapore government's historically prudent fiscal policies, which have resulted in consistent budget surpluses, policymakers have considered programs to return some of the surplus to the public. One measure to do so has involved encouraging widespread public ownership of government-linked corporations. For example, shortly before listing Singapore Telecom on the stock exchange in 1992, the Singapore government provided funds to allow citizens to purchase concessionary shares through the Central Provident Fund. This measure has introduced a high proportion of the population to the stock market. The government has also upgraded public housing and established an Edusave Program for all children enrolled in school.

As a result, Singapore now ranks fourteenth worldwide in terms of per capita income, ahead of Italy and the United Kingdom and just below Canada. This achievement was recognized by the recent OECD decision to graduate Singapore to developed country status.

## VI.  Policy Conclusions

### The Role of Government

Government has been integral to Singapore's rapid industrialization and growth. Government interventions, while extensive, have been purposeful. By constant reference to the broad but well-defined strategic framework, policy consistency was ensured without prejudice to flexibility. This is because the principles for when and how government should intervene were, in a sense, checked by the framework. It also allowed policy to be fine tuned rather than changed through "flip-flops." Underlying the policy design was the government's basic philosophy that Singapore "must excel in business and whatever it attempts." Public policy must therefore always be "directed to the support of this pursuit of business excellence" (Goh Keng Swee 1977a, 17). As figure 4.6 shows, this strategy has many complementary components. In Singapore's case, however, its essence has taken two main forms: MNC-led industrialization and a stable sociopolitical setting.

Through the MNC-based industrialization strategy, the government's role was focused on creating the conditions to attract foreign investment. At every stage, it sought to adopt policies that would boost productivity and make Singapore a place where MNCs could climb the value-added chain. This involved it in, above all, infrastructure and education. The constant upgrading and expansion of physical infrastructure may be viewed as an anticipatory and cautious approach to ensure that resources are ready for the future. The predominance of huge infrastructural investments, with initial slack because of their "lumpy" nature, partly accounts for the inadequacy of the total factor productivity (TFP) approach, as used by Young (1992), in assessing investment performance in Singapore.

The industrialization program also required considerable investment in human capital. Besides providing the requisite education and training infrastructure, the government chose a strategy of developing broad-based, basic skills that could be upgraded sequentially. By drawing lessons from the records of the various industrial approaches to science and technology in the United Kingdom, Germany, and Japan, the government decided to ensure economic realism in the development of industrial skills (Goh Keng Swee 1977a). Hence, industrialization was to be initiated through low-technology products. A set of core industries with an associated set of core skills would then lend themselves to faster progress to higher levels of technology.

With this emphasis on physical infrastructure and human skills, Singapore has been continually well placed to attract MNCs. Again, its approach was deliberate. Goh Keng Swee has stated that "it would take a very obtuse economist not to have recognized that the electronics industry was in a state of dynamic expansion in the mid-1960s" (1992, 1). The availability of low-cost but

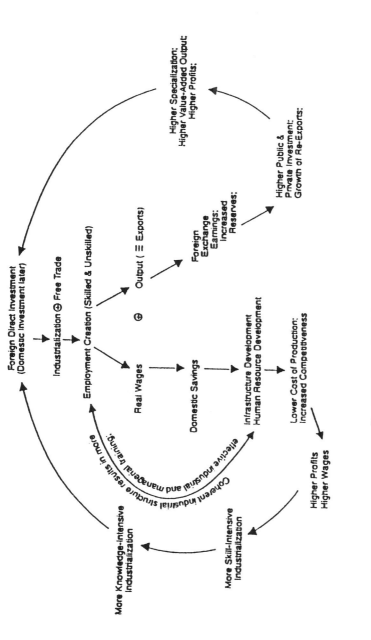

Fig. 4.6. Dynamics of development strategy

disciplined labor provided the basis for integrated circuits assembly, which became one of the first impetuses to Singapore's industrialization. As the electronics industry developed, so did Singapore's mastery of it, because of the government's increasing emphasis on science and engineering in the curriculum of secondary and tertiary education.

On its own, though, MNC-led industrialization would not have just happened. It occurred in the context of social and political stability, conditions that the government has worked hard to foster and secure. Singapore is situated between the Straits of Malacca and the South China Sea, right on the route of East-West trade. Because of the strategic and geopolitical importance of these waterways, politics has always been a major influence on Singapore's economic well-being. Since 1965, the country's foreign policy has been carefully crafted toward international cooperation to ensure economic and political survival. Concern with domestic sociopolitical stability is reflected in the firm disapproval of domestic and foreign detractors.[21]

Singapore has one other sociopolitical feature that is worth noting. The three-year national service that is compulsory for all male high school graduates before they are able to enroll for their tertiary education serves not only to provide defense training but an awareness of the geopolitical and security issues behind the country's political stance. Because of the significance of domestic and regional political stability to the country's developmental effort, and its reliance on imported potable water and imported labor, national service provided another channel for consensus building among the young.

The government has adopted a policy of nonalignment and internationalism so as to preserve territorial integrity and maintain even-handed relations with China, Russia, and the United States. However, until 1990, it did not have diplomatic relations with China, despite the long-standing strong commercial ties between the two countries. Reasons for this lacuna have varied over time. In the early 1970s, it stemmed from a fear that China's growing international prestige might encourage Chinese chauvinism in Singapore, which would have jeopardized the government's effort to establish a cohesive multiracial Singaporean society. At the same time, the government was concerned that Singapore should not be seen as a "third China" (after Taiwan, China) and that the Chinese-origin population not be considered a "fifth column" for China and that the Singaporeans not be considered Overseas-Chinese.

---

21. Examples of this stance include the 1971 termination of a foreign correspondent's stay because of his critical reporting and the 1976 PAP resignation from the London-based Socialist International (this is a loose federation of anticommunist, social democratic parties committed to the promotion of democracy and civil liberty with a charter that rejects any form of political cooperation with parties of political dictatorships) upon refusal by the Dutch Labor Party to withdraw its motion to expel the PAP for alleged violations of human rights and detention of political prisoners without trial (Vreeland et al. 1977, 105).

The political stability of the ASEAN countries after the mid-1960s was unambiguously positive for Singapore. This stability not only increased the confidence of firms based in Singapore, but it enabled rapid growth in the ASEAN countries themselves (apart from the Philippines). Political instability elsewhere in Asia benefited Singapore, especially the uncertainties surrounding Hong Kong. Singapore also gained from its proximity to the Vietnam War, becoming a major supplier to South Vietnam.

It was not just international politics that mattered; Singapore has also been affected by various changes in international economic relations. For example, Singapore's correction of the high-wage policy happened to coincide with the 1985 dollar-yen realignment, which resulted in increased exports to the United States, Singapore's largest trading partner. With growing protectionism against Japanese imports, Japan reacted by transplanting some manufacturing plants abroad. It altered its foreign investment philosophy to one aimed at reorienting the ASEAN countries toward Japan. With its higher technological base, Singapore became an original equipment manufacturing (OEM) base for Japanese industries as well.

## Lessons from Japan and Other Industrialized Countries

Singapore had to design a development approach compatible with its size, its lack of natural resources, and its sociopolitical objectives. Initially, small countries with resource constraints (such as Switzerland and Israel) were examined for lessons in development. Subsequently, as industrialization progressed and greater emphasis was placed on developing industrial training programs and worker skills, Singapore's policymakers looked to countries such as Germany and Japan for models that could be adopted and adapted to suit its conditions. They came up with two main conclusions: first, that science and technology must be used selectively in accordance with the given economic reality, and, second, that the attitude of workers in an industrialized society differs fundamentally from what exists in an entrepôt trading center.

The importance of economic relevance in the choice of science and technology was based on the leadership's comparison of postwar economic growth in Britain, versus that of (West) Germany and Japan (Goh Keng Swee 1977a). As a victor country, British scientists were able to build upon their advanced science foundation and focus their energies on basic research without paying heed to the relevance of their research to the country's industrial and economic needs. The practical approach toward science and technology adopted in Germany and Japan was in direct contrast. The defeat and losses suffered by these two countries and the need for postwar reconstruction possibly reinforced their pragmatic approach in directing the use, as well as the development, of science and technology toward economic ends. From the start, the building of a domestic technology base in Singapore was directed specifically at its industrialization goal.

Through this technology-minded industrialization strategy, Singapore's wages became explicitly linked to industrial countries' wages from 1972. Worker complacency would be put under pressure, since the industrial upgrading strategy translates into a "catch-up" process not only for the industries but for their workers. The Singaporean ideal was to have a combination of the best attributes of German and Japanese workers: German industriousness and skills, acquired through industrial training of a complex and demanding nature; and Japanese loyalty, capacity for hard work, and worker-management cooperation.

As shown earlier, industrial efficiency has been reinforced by an efficient and dedicated bureaucracy and the cooperation between it and the private sector. Although Singapore did not have a role model for its bureaucracy, the same qualities have been significant in the economic success of Japan, the Republic of Korea, and Taiwan, China. Grubel (1989) points out the similarity between the NWC in Singapore and tripartite, consultative processes in Sweden.

## The Relationship between Development Success and Social Attitudes

Two features influenced the social makeup of the population in 1959. One was entrepôt trading, which had provided Singapore's economic livelihood for more than a century; the other was the new immigrants who had come from southeastern China and southern India. Both features contributed to social attitudes that were receptive to the government's developmental efforts.

The long tradition of trade and services associated with an entrepôt society produced openness and outward orientation in the people's attitudes, as well as an emphasis on excellence so as to remain internationally competitive. Interaction with the industrialized countries that were importers of raw materials from, and exporters of manufactured goods to, Southeast Asia meant that Singapore had had constant exposure to new ideas from the West. Furthermore, the education system established by the colonial government produced an educated and urbane group in society well aware of the development and income gaps that existed between the developing and industrialized countries.

As described by Hasan (1976a), a "transition syndrome" among migrants lends itself to a positive approach to change and progress, since the initial departure from home was motivated by the search for better economic conditions. Sowell (1983) argues that this search, often coupled with persecution or political resentment by the indigenous populations, reinforces the strong motivation of immigrants to do well in their new countries.

In the early 1960s, many of the new immigrants from China and India still identified with their home countries and planned to return once they became financially secure. But gradually economic improvements coupled with home ownership led to the shifting of their allegiance to Singapore. By the early 1970s, these migrants had assumed full identity as Singaporeans.

The immigrants were also attracted by the changes taking place in Singapore's educational system. Before 1959, education was seen as the route to an administrative white-collar job, preferably in the offices of the colonial government or foreign trading firms. The educational reforms of the early 1960s, the establishment of schools for technical training, and growing employment opportunities from the 1960s onward in industries requiring technical skills caused the shift in the population's inclination toward scientific and technical training. Immigrants saw this as being more meritocratic than the old system was.

## Policy Lessons from Singapore's Experience

Singapore's success shows that even the most unpromising starting point need not stop a country from developing. What matters is a growth-oriented leadership with a realistic strategy and intelligent policies. In more detail, four basic elements are involved: (1) government with a vision of long-term development, (2) a stable and hospitable environment conducive to economic growth, (3) a public policy that emphasizes investment, and (4) the capacity for sustained accumulation of human and physical capital. Such an "integrative approach to development in which a single policy has been made to serve a plurality of purposes inevitably introduces an element of artificiality into strictly analytical studies of specific policies" (Sandhu and Wheatley 1991, viii).

Singapore's experience points to three crucial and general lessons: (1) the importance of sound economic policies, (2) the reinforcement of sound policies with policy implementation by a bureaucracy that is run on meritocratic lives, and (3) government's role in winning credibility within the state and with foreign investors. None of these is shrouded in mystery or workable only when applied in Singapore. The precise circumstance may differ from country to country, but the broad outlines are clear. There is much to admire about Singapore's economic development, and much to copy, too.

APPENDIX

*(see following page)*

**TABLE A4.1.  Key Economic Indicators, 1960–90**

| Indicators | 1960 | 1965 | 1970 | 1973 | 1978 | 1980 | 1983 | 1985 | 1990 |
|---|---|---|---|---|---|---|---|---|---|
| Population (millions) | 1.6 | 1.9 | 2.1 | 2.2 | 2.4 | 2.4 | 2.5 | 2.6 | 2.7 |
| GDP at 1985 factor cost (S$b) | 5.0 | 6.6 | 12.1 | 17.3 | 24.1 | 28.9 | 36.6 | 38.9 | 57.1 |
| Domestic exports (S$m) | 3.5 | 3.0 | 4.8 | 8.9 | 23.0 | 41.5 | 46.2 | 50.2 | 95.2 |
| Labor force (thousands) | 162 | 557 | 693 | 818 | 995 | 1,116 | 1,206 | 1,204 | 1,516 |
| Unemployment rate (%) | | 10.0[a] | 6.1 | 4.6 | 3.6 | 3.8 | 3.2 | 4.1 | 2.0 |
| GDP Deflator (1985 = 100) | 42.9 | 44.6 | 47.8 | 59.1 | 74.1 | 87.0 | 100.5 | 100.0 | 110.0 |
| CPI (1985 = 100) | 40.9 | 40.7 | 43.2 | 56.7 | 75.6 | 85.3 | 97.0 | 100.0 | 106.3 |
| GDFCF (S$b) | | 1.0 | | 5.6 | 8.1 | | 17.5 | 16.4 | 22.0 |
| (GDFCF/GDP) ratio (%) | 9.7 | 16.7 | 32.5 | 34.9 | 35.7 | 40.7 | 47.5 | 42.2 | 37.9 |
| GNS (S$m) | | | | | | | | | |
| (GNS/GDP) ratio (%) | | | | 29.1 | 34.0 | | 46.1 | 40.1 | 40.5 |
| Overall balance of payments (S$m) | | | | 1,005.2 | 1,511.5 | | 2,237.3 | 2,942.0 | 9,892.5 |
| Official foreign reserves (S$m) | | | | 5,800.1 | 11,400.0 | | 19,755.3 | 27,080.0 | 55,795.2 |
| Number of months of imports | | | | 5.6 | 4.6 | | 4.0 | 5.6 | 6.1 |

*Source:* World Bank, various years.
*Note:* All dollar values are for constant 1985 dollars.
[a]Estimate.

**TABLE A4.2. Growth Rates of Key Economic Indicators, 1959–90 (percentage per annum)**

| Indicators | 1959–60 to 1965 | 1965–72 | 1973–78 | 1979–84 | 1985–90 |
|---|---|---|---|---|---|
| Population | 2.68 | 2.09 | 1.54 | 0.65 | 1.71 |
| Labor force | na | 36.73 | 4.59 | 3.30 | 1.50 |
| Employment | na | 21.62 | 4.05 | 3.08 | 3.79 |
| GDP (1985$) | 5.89 | 14.08 | 7.63 | 8.66 | 6.38 |
| GNP (1985$) | | | | | |
| GNP, Indigenous (1985$) | na | 11.16 | 5.99 | 9.17 | 3.37 |
| GNP, Indigenous (1985$) | na | 10.35 | 6.53 | 9.52 | 1.95 |
| Per capita GDP | na | 9.93 | 6.00 | 8.02 | 4.59 |
| Per capita indigenous GDP | na | na | 4.38 | 8.55 | 1.63 |
| Per capita GNP | | | | | |
| Per capita indigenous GNP | na | na | 4.91 | 8.88 | 0.24 |
| Inflation rates | | | | | |
|   GDP deflator | 0.78 | 2.29 | 5.99 | 5.38 | 1.45 |
|   WPI | na | na | na | 4.89 | −1.23 |
|   CPI | na | 1.29 | 9.55 | 4.72 | 1.16 |
| GDP Sectoral growth | | | | | |
|   Agriculture/Fishing/Quarrying | na | na | −5.64 | −5.93 | −15.42 |
|   Construction and Utilities | na | na | −3.30 | 6.38 | −10.96 |
|   Manufacturing | na | na | 0.43 | −2.60 | 1.74 |
|   Trade and Transportation | na | na | 1.16 | −1.89 | 0.08 |
|   Financial and Other Services | na | na | 0.19 | 2.33 | 2.54 |
| Employment sectoral growth | | | | | |
|   Agriculture/Fishing/Quarrying | na | na | 43.70 | −11.32 | −11.09 |
|   Construction and Utilities | na | na | −3.74 | 6.94 | 5.44 |
|   Manufacturing | na | na | −2.91 | −0.42 | 1.09 |
|   Commerce and Transportation | na | na | 1.99 | −0.86 | −0.24 |
| Private Consumption | | | | | |
| Government Consumption | | | | | |
| Domestic Savings | 11.50 | 32.61 | 21.17 | 20.40 | 7.40 |
| Domestic Savings 1985$ | 10.81 | 29.62 | 14.32 | 14.20 | 6.29 |
| DS/GDP | 9.07 | 15.43 | 6.13 | 5.11 | −0.36 |
| Foreign Savings | 4.49 | 33.69 | 3.05 | 9.48 | 2152.60 |
| Foreign Savings 1985$ | 3.68 | 30.74 | −4.12 | 2.65 | −2046.10 |
| FS/GDP | −1.91 | 16.32 | −10.89 | −5.76 | −112.85 |
| Gross Fixed Capital Formation | 19.74 | 28.54 | 13.71 | 20.42 | 4.58 |
| GFCF/GDP | 13.01 | 11.83 | −0.45 | 5.05 | −4.99 |
| Public GFCF/GFCF | −8.07 | −3.63 | 10.28 | 0.40 | 4.07 |
| Private GFCF/GFCF | −6.66 | −1.06 | 6.77 | −0.99 | 2.67 |
| Exports | −1.96 | 10.65 | 26.55 | 15.14 | 11.51 |
| Imports | −0.84 | 13.57 | 22.48 | 13.64 | 10.99 |
| Exports and Imports | −1.53 | 12.28 | 24.09 | 14.28 | 11.22 |
| Exports/GDP | −8.07 | −3.63 | 10.28 | 0.40 | 4.07 |
| Imports/GDP | −6.66 | −3.63 | 6.77 | −0.99 | 2.67 |
| Exports and Imports/GDP | na | −2.19 | 8.16 | −0.40 | 2.75 |

*Source:* World Bank, IMF, various years.

**TABLE A4.3.  Indicators of Living Standards in Selected Years, 1960–90**

| Item | 1960 | 1965 | 1970 | 1973 | 1975 | 1978 | 1980 | 1985 | 1990 |
|---|---|---|---|---|---|---|---|---|---|
| **Housing** | | | | | | | | | |
| Share of total population in public flats (%) | | | 35 | 43 | 54 | 68 | 73 | 84 | 87 |
| Share of above population in owner-occupied flats (%) | | | 9 | 16 | 22 | 37 | 42 | 64 | 80 |
| **Education** | | | | | | | | | |
| Literacy rate (%)[a] | | | 72 | 73 | 78 | 83 | 84 | 86 | 90 |
| Student enrollment ratio—primary | | | 81 | 85 | | | | | |
| —secondary | | | 43 | 50 | 78 | 79 | 79 | 92 | 93 |
| Student-teacher ratio—primary | 33 | 30 | 30 | 29 | 30 | 29 | 30 | 26 | 26 |
| —secondary | 28 | 24 | 22 | 23 | 26 | 25 | 22 | 22 | 21 |
| **Health** | | | | | | | | | |
| Per capita government expenditures on health (S$) | | | 40 | 47 | 63 | 76 | 96 | 195 | 187 |
| Number of persons/doctor | | | 1,522 | 1,401 | 1,395 | 1,265 | 1,222 | 972 | 753 |
| Number of persons/dentist | | | 5,212 | 5,362 | 8,979 | 7,287 | 6,977 | 5,157 | 400 |
| Number of persons/hospital bed | | | 301 | 273 | 249 | 244 | 252 | 256 | 274 |
| **Utilities** | | | | | | | | | |
| Per capita electricity consumption (kilowatt hours) | | | | | | 2,195 | 2,530 | 3,448 | 5,270 |
| Per capita water consumption (cubic meters) | | | | | | 81 | 90 | 104 | 120 |
| **Transport and Communications** | | | | | | | | | |
| Number of persons/public bus | | | 705 | 459 | 458 | 401 | 371 | 293 | 285 |
| Number of persons/private car | | | 15 | 12 | 16 | 17 | 16 | 12 | 10 |
| Number of persons/taxi | | | | | 420 | 305 | 255 | 234 | 220 |
| Telephones/1,000 persons | | | 78 | 114 | 141 | 229 | 291 | 420 | 480[b] |

Culture and recreation

| | | | | | | | |
|---|---|---|---|---|---|---|---|
| Daily newspaper circulation/1,000 persons | 200 | 202 | 198 | 227 | 255 | 279 | 302 |
| National Library members | | | | | | | |
| —Under 12 years old (%) | 15 | 9 | 22 | 26 | 29 | 49 | 35 |
| —Over 12 years old (%) | 5 | 7 | 9 | 9 | 11 | 29 | 25 |
| Entertainment | | | | | | | |
| Radio and TV/1,000 persons | 76 | 105 | 124 | 150 | 165 | 188 | 217 |
| Cinema attendance/person | | | 18 | 19 | 17 | 9 | 8 |

*Source:* World Bank *Social Indicators*, UN *Human Indicators*, various issues.

*Note:* Data prior to 1970 are not available.

[a] For population above 10 years of age.

[b] Estimate.

**TABLE A4.4. Initial Conditions for Each Phase, 1959–90**

| Indicator | 1959 | 1960 | 1965 | 1973 | 1978 | 1985 | 1990 |
|---|---|---|---|---|---|---|---|
| Population (millions) | na | 1.63 | 1.86 | 2.19 | 2.35 | 2.56 | 2.71 |
| Labor force (millions) | na | na | 0.56 | 0.82 | 1.00 | 1.20 | 1.49 |
| Unemployment rate (%) | na | na | 10.0 | 4.56 | 3.60 | 4.10 | 2.00 |
| GDP (S$b, 1985$) | na | 5.44 | 6.12 | 16.23 | 22.59 | 41.65 | 57.07 |
| GNP (S$b, 1985$) | na | na | na | na | na | na | na |
| Indigenous GDP (S$b, 1985$) | na | na | 6.0 | 13.73 | 17.93 | 30.12 | 46.39 |
| Indigenous GNP (S$b, 1985$) | na | na | na | 14.23 | 19.06 | 33.41 | na |
| Per capita GDP (S$, 1985$) | na | 3,068 | 3,560 | 7,913 | 10,227 | 15,217 | 21,481 |
| Per capita indigenous GDP (S$, 1985$) | na | na | 3,225 | 6,284 | 7,577 | 11,774 | 15,725 |
| Per capita indigenous GNP (S$, 1985$) | na | na | na | 6,512 | 8,100 | 13,063 | na |
| GDP deflator (1985 = 100) | na | 42.9 | 44.6 | 59.1 | 74.1 | 100.0 | 110.0 |
| WPI (1985 = 100) | na | na | na | na | 78.5 | 100.0 | 93.5 |
| CPI (1985 = 100) | na | 40.9 | 40.7 | 56.7 | 75.6 | 100.0 | 106.6 |
| Sectoral shares of GDP (%) | | | | | | | |
| Agriculture | na | na | 3.3 | 2.0 | 1.6 | 1.0 | 0.4 |
| Construction and utilities | na | na | 11.5 | 10.2 | 9.6 | 11.9 | 6.7 |
| Manufacturing | na | na | 19.2 | 28.6 | 27.9 | 22.1 | 26.1 |
| Trade and transportation | na | na | 30.6 | 30.6 | 31.9 | 28.5 | 28.5 |
| Financial and other services | na | na | 35.4 | 28.7 | 28.9 | 36.6 | 38.3 |
| Sectoral shares of employment (%) | | | | | | | |
| Agriculture | na | na | na | 0.7 | 2.0 | 0.9 | na |
| Construction and utilities | na | na | na | 8.7 | 6.4 | 9.6 | na |
| Manufacturing | na | na | na | 36.3 | 28.2 | 25.5 | na |
| Commerce, transportation, and communication | na | na | na | 30.3 | 34.9 | 33.6 | na |
| Private sector consumption (S$b, 1985$) | na | 4.1 | na | 11.0 | 14.4 | 17.2 | 26.3 |
| Consumption shares of (%) | | | | | | | |
| Food and beverages | na | 45.1 | na | na | na | 30.1 | 23.1 |
| Clothing | na | 8.0 | na | na | na | 9.1 | 9.5 |
| Rent and utilities | na | 9.3 | na | na | na | 12.5 | 11.7 |

| | | | | | | | |
|---|---|---|---|---|---|---|---|
| Furniture and household equipment | na | 10.7 | na | na | na | 11.4 | 10.6 |
| Medical services | na | 3.1 | na | na | na | 4.0 | 5.1 |
| Transportation and communications | na | 12.7 | na | na | na | 15.7 | 16.4 |
| Recreation and education | na | 6.1 | na | na | na | 13.6 | 19.1 |
| Other goods and services | na | 17.1 | na | na | na | 20.7 | 25.7 |
| (+) Residents' expenditures abroad | na | 1.6 | na | na | na | 6.4 | 9.4 |
| (−) Nonresidents' expenditures locally | na | 9.9 | na | na | na | 23.5 | 30.4 |
| Government consumption (S$b, 1985$) | na | na | na | na | na | 5.4 | 6.2 |
| Gross fixed capital formation (S$b, 1985$) | na | na | na | na | na | 20.2 | 14.7 |
| Savings and investment | | | | | | | |
| Domestic savings (S$b, 1985$) | na | -.1 | .7 | 5.0 | 8.2 | 15.6 | 25.4 |
| Foreign savings (S$b, 1985$) or net foreign borrowing | na | .7 | .7 | 2.4 | 1.4 | .007 | -3.9 |
| Foreign direct investment (S$b) | na | na | .5 | .8 | .4 | 1.8 | 6.1 |
| (Domestic savings/GDP) | na | -2.7 | 10.2 | 29.1 | 34.0 | 40.1 | 44.6 |
| (Foreign savings/GDP) | na | 14.0 | 6.8 | 13.8 | 5.8 | 0.1 | -6.8 |
| (GFCF/GDP) | na | 9.7 | 16.7 | 34.9 | 35.7 | 42.2 | 37.9 |
| Sectoral distribution of GFCF (%) | | | | | | | |
| Construction and public works | na | 53.4 | 54.2 | 41.5 | 39.1 | 60.9 | 38.8 |
| Transport equipment | na | 14.0 | 6.8 | 13.8 | 5.8 | 0.1 | -6.8 |
| Machinery and equipment | na | 32.7 | 39.1 | 39.3 | 36.8 | 27.5 | 49.9 |
| Ownership distribution of GFCF (%) | | | | | | | |
| Public sector | na | 70.9 | 45.4 | na | na | 35.5 | 18.4 |
| Private sector | na | 29.1 | 54.6 | na | na | 64.5 | 81.6 |
| Exports (S$b) | na | 3.5 | 3.0 | 8.9 | 23.0 | 50.2 | 95.2 |
| Imports (S$b) | na | 4.1 | 3.8 | 12.5 | 29.6 | 57.8 | 109.8 |
| Total trade (S$b) | na | 7.6 | 6.8 | 21.4 | 52.6 | 108.0 | 205.0 |
| (Exports/GDP) (%) | na | 164 | 106 | 87 | 129 | 129 | 152 |
| (Imports/GDP) (%) | na | 192 | 134 | 123 | 166 | 149 | 175 |
| (Total trade/GDP) (%) | na | 356 | 240 | 210 | 295 | 277 | 327 |
| Exchange rates (S$/US$) | na | 3.06 | 3.06 | 2.46 | 2.27 | 2.2 | 1.81 |

Source: World Bank *World Tables*, IMF, various issues.

REFERENCES

Aw, Bee Yan. 1991. "Singapore." In Papageorgiou, Michaely, and Choksi 1991.

Blake, D. J. 1967. "Employment and Unemployment in Singapore." In Chalmers 1967.

Bloodworth, Dennis. 1986. *The Tiger and the Trojan Horse.* Singapore: Times Books International.

Bryant, Ralph. 1991. "The Evolution of Singapore as a Financial Centre." In Sandhu and Wheatley 1989.

Chalmers, W. E. 1967. *Critical Issues in Industrial Relations in Singapore.* Singapore: Donald Moore Press.

Chan, Heng Chee. 1971. *The Politics of Survival, 1965–1967.* Kuala Lumpur: Oxford University Press.

Chenery, H., and M. Syrquin. 1986. "Typical Patterns of Transformation." In Chenery and Robinson (1986).

Chia, Siow Yue. 1984. "Export Process and Industrialization: The Case of Singapore." In E. Lee 1984.

Chia, Siow Yue. 1986. "Direct Investment and the Industrialization Process in Singapore." In Lim and Lloyd 1988.

Chia, Siow Yue. 1991. "The Character and Progress of Industrialization." In Sandhu and Wheatley 1989.

Chow, Kit Boey, Chew Moh Leen, and Elizabeth Su. 1990. *One Partnership in Development: UNDP and Singapore.* Singapore: United Nations Association of Singapore.

Department of Statistics. 1991. *Home Ownership Survey.* Singapore: Department of Statistics.

Department of Statistics. Various years. *Monthly Digest of Statistics.* Singapore: Department of Statistics.

Dixit, Avinash K., and G. M. Grossman. 1982. "Trade and Protection with Multistage Production." *Review of Economic Studies* 49 (October): 583–94.

Dutta, M., ed. 1992. *Asian Economic Regimes: An Adaptive Innovation Paradigm.* Greenwich: JAI Press.

Findlay, Ronald. 1991. "Theoretical Notes on Singapore as Development Model." In Sandhu and Wheatley 1989.

Goh Chok Tong. 1980. "We Must Dare to Achieve." Budget speech. Transcript.

Goh Keng Swee. 1973. "Investment for Development: Lessons and Experiences of Singapore, 1959 to 1971." Paper presented at the Third Economic Development Seminar, Saigon, January 17, 1973.

Goh Keng Swee. 1977a. *The Practice of Economic Growth.* Singapore: Federal Publications.

Goh Keng Swee. 1977b. "A Socialist Economy That Works." In *Socialism that Works*, edited by C. V. D. Nair. Singapore: Federal Publications.

Goh Keng Swee. 1983. "Public Administration and Economic Development in Less Developed Countries." Harry G. Johnson Memorial Lecture No. 4. London: Trade Policy Research Centre.

Goh Keng Swee. 1992. "MNCs Brought Jobs, Sparked Change." *Sunday Times*, August 23, 1992.

Government of Singapore. 1991. *The Next Lap.* Singapore: Times Editions.

Grubel, Herbert G. 1989. "Singapore's Record of Price Stability, 1966–84." In Sandhu and Wheatley 1989.

Hasan, Riaz. 1976a. "Symptoms and Syndrome of the Development Process." In Hasan 1976b.

Hasan, Riaz, ed. 1976b. *Singapore: Society in Transition.* Kuala Lumpur: Oxford University Press.

Hirono, Ryokichu. 1976. "Japanese Investment." In Hughes and You 1969.

Hon, Sui-Sen. 1973. "The New Phase of Industrial Development in Singapore." Address to the Singapore Press Club, March 23, 1973. Transcript.

Hughes, Helen, and You Poh Seng, eds. 1969. *Foreign Investment and Industrialization in Singapore.* Canberra: Australian National University Press.

IMF. 1985. *Foreign Private Investment in Developing Countries.* IMF Occasional Papers No. 33, Washington, D.C.: International Monetary Fund.

IMF. Various years. *International Financial Statistics.* Washington, D.C.: International Monetary Fund.

Klitgaard, R. 1991. *Adjusting to Reality.* San Francisco: International Center for Economic Growth.

Koh, Ai Tee. 1991. "Diversification of Trade." In Sandhu and Wheatley 1989.

Krause, Lawrence. 1991. "Government as Entrepreneur." In Sandhu and Wheatley 1989.

Krause, Lawrence B., Koh Ai Tee, and Lee [Tsao] Yuan. 1987. *The Singapore Economy Reconsidered.* Singapore: Institute of Southeast Asian Studies.

Lee, Eddy, ed. 1984. *Export Processing Zones and Industrial Employment in Asia: Papers and Proceedings of a Technical Workshop.* International Labor Organization. Geneva.

Lee Kuan Yew. 1970. "The Harsh Realities of Today." Opening Address to the 1969 NTUC Seminar on the Modernization of the Labor Movement, Singapore. Transcript.

Lee Kuan Yew. 1978. Speech delivered to the Twenty-sixth World Congress of the International Chamber of Commerce, Florida, October 1978. Transcript.

Lee [Tsao] Yuan. 1987a. "The Government in Macroeconomic Management." In Krause et al. 1987.

Lee [Tsao] Yuan. 1987b. "Economic Stabilization Policies in Singapore." In Rana and Alburo 1987.

Lim Chong Yah and Associates. 1988. *Policy Options for the Singapore Economy.* Singapore: McGraw Hill.

Lim Chong Yah and Peter J. Lloyd, eds. 1988. *Singapore: Resources and Growth.* Singapore: Oxford University Press.

Lim Chong Yah and Ow Chwee Huay. 1971. "The Singapore Economy and the Vietnam War." In You Poh Seng and Lim Chong Yah. (Eds.) *The Singapore Economy.* Singapore: Eastern Universities Press.

Lloyd, P. J., and Roger Sandilands. 1988. "The Trade Sector in a Very Open Re-export Economy." In Lim and Lloyd 1988.

Low, Linda, and Mun-Hong Toh. 1988. "Economic Planning and Policymaking in Singapore." *Economic Bulletin for Asia and the Pacific* 39: 22–32.

Ministry of Finance. 1961. *State of Singapore Development plan 1961–1964*. Singapore: Ministry of Finance.

Mirza, Hafiz. 1986. *Multinationals and the Growth of the Singapore Economy*. New York: St. Martins Press.

MTI. 1980. *Report on the Census of Industrial Policy*. Singapore: Ministry of Trade and Industry.

MTI. 1985. *Report of the Economic Committee*. Singapore: Ministry of Trade and Industry.

MTI. 1986. *The Singapore Economy: New Directions*. Singapore: Report of the Economic Committee, Ministry of Trade and Industry.

MTI. 1991. *The Strategic Economic Plan*. Singapore: Economic Planning Committee, Ministry of Trade and Industry.

NTUC. 1970a. *Modernization of the Labor Movement*. Singapore: National Trades Union Congress.

NTUC. 1970b. *Why Labor Must Go Modern*. Proceedings of the 1969 NTUC Seminar on the Modernization of the Singapore Labor Movement. Singapore: National Trades Union Congress.

NTUC. 1980. *Progress into the 1980s*. Singapore: National Trades Union Congress.

NWC. 1992. *Twenty-one Years of the National Wages Council*. Singapore: Singapore National Printers.

Ong, Yen Har. 1970. "Future Directions of the Singapore Labor Movement." In NTUC 1970a.

Otani, Ichiro, and Cyrus Sassanpour. 1988. "Financial, Exchange Rate, and Wage Policies." *IMF Staff Papers* 35 (3): 474–95.

Ow, Chin Hock. 1992. "Development Strategies, Economic Performance, and Relations with the United States: Singapore's Experience." In Dutta 1992.

Papageorgiou, Demetris, Michael Michaely, and Armeane M. Choksi, eds. 1990. *Liberalizing Foreign Trade*. Oxford: Oxford University Press.

Phang, Sock Yong. 1989. "Welfare Implications of the HDB Policy on the Public Housing Price Gradient." *Singapore Economic Review* 34: 16–32.

Rajaratnam, S. 1966. "Democratic Socialism." Speech delivered to the Democratic Socialist Club of the University of Singapore, September 17. Transcript.

Rana, Praduma B., and Florian A. Alburo, eds. 1987. *Economic Stabilization Policies in ASEAN Countries*. Singapore: Institute of Southeast Asian Studies.

Ryokichi, H. 1969. "Japanese Investment." In Hughes and You 1969.

Sandhu, Kernial, and Paul Wheatley, eds. 1989. *Management of Success: The Moulding of Modern Singapore*. Singapore: Institute of Southeast Asian Studies.

Seah, Linda. 1983. "Sources of Finance for Economic Growth in Singapore, 1965–75, with Special Reference to the Public Sector." Ph.D. diss., Department of Economics and Statistics, National University of Singapore.

Soon, Teck Wong. 1988. *Singapore's New Education System: Education Reform for National Development*. Singapore: Institute of Southeast Asian Studies.

Soon, Teck Wong. 1991. "Private Sector Led Development through Direct Foreign Investment." National University of Singapore. Mimeo.

Sowell, Thomas. 1983. *The Economics and Politics of Race: An International Perspective*. New York: Quill.

Stoever, William A. 1982. "Endowments, Priorities, and Policies: An Analytical Scheme for the Formulation of Developing Country Policy toward Foreign Investment." *Columbia Journal of World Business* 17 (fall): 3–15.

Syrquin, Moshe, and Hollis B. Chenery. 1989. *Patterns of Development: 1950 to 1983.* World Bank Discussion Papers No. 41. Washington, D.C.: The World Bank.

Teh, Kok Peng, and Tharman Shanmugaratnam. 1992. "Exchange Rate Policy: Philosophy and Conduct over the Past Decade." In *Public Policies in Singapore,* edited by Linda Low and Toh Mun Heng. Singapore: Times Academic Press.

Thynne, Ian. 1989a. "The Administrative State." In Woon 1989.

Thynne, Ian. 1989b. "The Administrative State in Transition." In Thynne and Ariff 1989.

Thynne, Ian, and Mohammed Ariff, eds. 1989. *Privatization: Singapore's Experience in Perspective.* Singapore: Longman Press.

United Nations. Various years. *Human Indicators of Development.*

Vasil, Raj. 1992. *Governing Singapore.* Singapore: Reed International.

Vreeland, Nena, B. G. Dana, G. B. Hurwitz, P. Just, and R. S. Shinn. 1977. *Area Handbook for Singapore.* Washington, D.C.: American University, Foreign Area Studies.

Winsemius, Albert. 1984. Speech delivered at the General Electric International Personnel Council Meeting, Singapore, June 19. Transcript.

Woon, Walter, ed. 1989. *The Singapore Legal System.* Singapore: Longman Press.

World Bank. Various years. *Social Indicators of Development.* Washington, D.C.: World Bank.

World Bank. Various years. *World Tables.* Washington, D.C.: World Bank.

Yeh, Stephen H. K. 1975. *Public Housing in Singapore: A Multidisciplinary Study.* Singapore: Singapore University Press.

Yoshihara, K. 1976. *Foreign Investment and Domestic Response.* Singapore: Eastern Universities Press.

Young, Alwyn. 1992. "A Tale of Two Cities: Factor Accumulation and Technical Change in Hong Kong and Singapore." Sloan School of Management, MIT. Mimeo.

# Part 2
# The Cubs of East Asia

CHAPTER 5

# Malaysia: Growth, Equity, and Structural Transformation

*Ismail Muhd Salleh and Saha Dhevan Meyananthan*


## I. Introduction

Over the past three decades, Malaysia has achieved growth, equity, and structural transformation in an ethnically diverse society. What was the role of the government versus markets in this process? What were the forms of government intervention? What were the costs and benefits? Could the Malaysian government have acted in other and better ways? In evaluating government actions, the right emphasis is not on a simple state versus market approach but on the closeness of fit between strategy, circumstances, and institutional capability, on one hand, and development goals on the other (Klitgaard 1991). This essay will use this approach to illuminate the nature, causes, and results of state intervention. It is divided into five sections. First, there is a definition of development success and then an examination of the conditions Malaysia faced at the time of independence and its major development since then. Section III analyzes the state's role in development, paying particular attention to trade and investment, human resources, agriculture, infrastructure, state-owned enterprises, and the financial system. Section IV takes a brief look at Malaysia's institutional capacity for implementing reforms, and section V assesses the role of government intervention in Malaysia's development and draws some lessons from its experience.

### Development Success

Although national development includes economic, social, cultural, and political elements, this study treats economic development as the core concern. Except for the severe 1985–86 recession, Malaysia has had relatively uninterrupted and rapid growth since 1957. Between 1960 and 1990, real GDP increased sevenfold at an annual growth rate of 6.8 percent.[1] Per capita real

---

1. The recession of 1985–86, when Malaysia experienced negative growth, naturally lowers the overall figure. During the period 1967–74, the growth rate averaged 7.7 percent per year, and

GDP multiplied threefold, rising (in 1980 ringgit) from M$1,634 (U.S.$534) to M$5,301 (U.S.$1,960) at an average 4 percent per year (IMF 1991).[2]

Aggregate growth is not the only measure of economic welfare; equity is another important consideration. Figures show that inequality in income distribution has been reduced, particularly between ethnic groups. The incidence of poverty fell among all ethnic groups, with those in the rural sector (where the Bumiputera population predominates) showing large gains. There was also some success in changing the ownership of wealth. In 1970, the Bumiputeras owned an estimated 2.4 percent of corporate equity; by 1990, their share had increased to 20.3 percent (Government of Malaysia 1991b).

The government adopted the goal of universal education in the 1960s, and by 1990 about 96 percent of all students managed to complete at least six years of primary schooling. Health services, too, have expanded considerably. The ratio of population per doctor declined from 4,302 in 1970 to 2,594 in 1990, and the number of hospitals and government clinics expanded from 1,838 to 2,784 (Government of Malaysia 1991b). The results have been striking. Life expectancy among men has increased from 62 to 70 years since 1970 and for women from 66 to 74 years. During the same period, infant mortality rates have declined from 41 to 13 per 1,000 births (Government of Malaysia 1991b).

A third criterion for economic development is resilience—the ability of the economy to withstand internal and external shocks. In the case of an open economy like that of Malaysia, resilience means diversification away from the production and trade of a few commodities. This structural transformation from a lower-value-added, farm-based economy to a higher-value-added, modern industrial economy (Kuznets 1966; Chenery et al. 1985) is characterized by a decline in the share of agriculture and a corresponding rise in industry. This Malaysia has done: in 1957, manufacturing contributed less than 10 percent of the GDP while agriculture made up more than 40 percent; by 1990, manufacturing accounted for 27 percent of the GDP, compared with agriculture's 19 percent, and 60 percent of total exports compared with 10 percent for agricultural commodities. Structural transformation has not lessened the economy's involvement in trade. Exports increased from 56 percent of GDP in 1960 to 65 percent in 1990; the corresponding figures for imports are 44 and 65 percent.

*Structural Transformation.* How do Malaysia's rates of structural transformation compare with the pattern of modern economic growth first defined by

from 1975–81 it averaged 8.3 percent per year (Bruton et al. 1992). Since the recession, the annual growth rate has resumed a steady 7 percent.

2. These are computed point to point in 1980 prices. Since income levels over a long period are not strictly comparable, these figures should be treated only as indicative of the magnitude of change. In deriving the 1957 figure, the deflator for 1960 was used, based on the assumption that there was zero inflation in the intervening period.

Kuznets (1966) and expanded by Chenery and Syrquin (1975)? Using the results from the updated study by Syrquin and Chenery (1989) for 108 economies in 1950–83, Malaysia's GDP shares of agriculture, manufacturing, and services were compared with the predicted pattern. The results, presented in table 5.1 and figures 5.1 through 5.5, show that Malaysia, by virtue of its abundant natural resources, has a GDP share of agriculture that is five to 10 percentage points higher than other countries at the same income level. The gap narrows as income rises. More importantly, the pattern of agriculture's share of GDP decline mirrors the path of successful transformation undergone by other countries (fig. 5.1). Of course, the agriculture share would have fallen anyway, as a consequence of growth, with or without state intervention. Growth, however, can be achieved without structural transformation. The fact that growth in Malaysia was achieved with structural transformation, and that the period of transformation was fairly short, suggests that policies have played a major role.

A more dramatic achievement was made in manufacturing (fig. 5.2). In 1960, its GDP share was 11 percentage points below the predicted value. It leveled by about 1980, and by 1990 it exceeded the predicted value by three percentage points. This rapid "catch-up" in manufacturing strongly reflects the success of the industrialization policies pursued by the government.

Similarly, agriculture's share of the labor force (fig. 5.3) follows the predicted general decline but at a faster rate. By 1990, the agricultural labor share was 10 percentage points lower than the predicted share. This implies that there has been a successful transfer of labor from farming to industry and services. In both industry and services (figs. 5.4 and 5.5), the labor shares generally follow the predicted upward trend; however, they had higher actual shares of total employment compared with their predicted values at later stages of development (much higher in the case of services).

The improvements in the structure of the economy, compared with the average patterns, indicate the effectiveness of the policies being pursued. This achievement is reinforced by what happened in industry. The increase in its share of GDP was accomplished alongside a strong performance from agriculture. As shown by the growth performance of other resource-rich, primarily exporting, developing countries, transforming into an industrial-based economy amid resource abundance is difficult without prudent management. Moreover, the "Dutch disease" syndrome, caused by large capital inflows (arising, for example, from resource booms), results in real exchange rate appreciation. This discriminates against the traditional exporters—a fate that Malaysia has successfully managed to avoid through vigorous promotion of private sector investments.

One area in which structural development has not been successful, however, is in overcoming regional disparities. There is still a wide margin of difference in the incidence of poverty between states, one that essentially follows

**TABLE 5.1. Comparison with Economic Structure Predicted by Chenery-Syrquin's Average Patterns, 1960–90**

| Variable | 1960 C-S (a) | 1960 Act. (b) | 1960 Diff. (b)–(a) | 1970 C-S (a) | 1970 Act. (b) | 1970 Diff. (b)–(a) | 1980 C-S (a) | 1980 Act. (b) | 1980 Diff. (b)–(a) | 1990 C-S (a) | 1990 Act. (b) | 1990 Diff. (b)–(a) |
|---|---|---|---|---|---|---|---|---|---|---|---|---|
| **Demand (share of GDP)** | | | | | | | | | | | | |
| Private consumption | 0.69 | 0.62 | -0.07 | 0.67 | 0.62 | -0.05 | 0.64 | 0.51 | -0.13 | 0.62 | 0.45 | -0.17 |
| Government consumption | 0.13 | 0.13 | 0.00 | 0.13 | 0.16 | 0.03 | 0.13 | 0.17 | 0.04 | 0.13 | 0.11 | -0.02 |
| Investment | 0.23 | 0.13 | -0.10 | 0.24 | 0.20 | -0.04 | 0.25 | 0.30 | 0.05 | 0.26 | 0.27 | 0.01 |
| Exports | 0.26 | 0.56 | 0.30 | 0.26 | 0.46 | 0.20 | 0.26 | 0.58 | 0.32 | 0.25 | 0.65 | 0.40 |
| Imports | 0.26 | 0.44 | 0.15 | 0.27 | 0.44 | 0.17 | 0.26 | 0.55 | 0.29 | 0.24 | 0.65 | 0.41 |
| **Production (share of GDP)** | | | | | | | | | | | | |
| Agriculture | 0.27 | 0.34 | 0.07 | 0.22 | 0.32 | 0.10 | 0.17 | 0.23 | 0.06 | 0.14 | 0.19 | 0.05 |
| Mining | 0.09 | 0.07 | -0.02 | 0.10 | 0.06 | -0.04 | 0.11 | 0.10 | -0.01 | 0.11 | 0.10 | -0.01 |
| Manufacturing | 0.16 | 0.05 | -0.11 | 0.18 | 0.12 | -0.06 | 0.21 | 0.20 | -0.01 | 0.23 | 0.26 | 0.03 |
| Construction | 0.06 | 0.03 | -0.03 | 0.07 | 0.04 | -0.03 | 0.07 | 0.04 | -0.03 | 0.07 | 0.03 | -0.04 |
| Services and utilities | 0.48 | 0.45 | -0.03 | 0.38 | 0.46 | 0.08 | 0.49 | 0.43 | -0.06 | 0.43 | 0.42 | -0.01 |
| **Employment (share of total)** | | | | | | | | | | | | |
| Agriculture | 0.60 | 0.57 | -0.03 | 0.52 | 0.51 | -0.01 | 0.44 | 0.37 | -0.07 | 0.38 | 0.28 | -0.10 |
| Industry | 0.14 | 0.17 | 0.03 | 0.18 | 0.18 | 0.00 | 0.22 | 0.22 | 0.00 | 0.25 | 0.27 | 0.02 |
| Services | 0.26 | 0.26 | 0.00 | 0.31 | 0.32 | 0.01 | 0.35 | 0.40 | 0.05 | 0.39 | 0.46 | 0.07 |

*Sources:* (1) Predicted shares based on actual population sizes of 8.10, 10.39, 13.70, and 17.86 million and per capita GNP in 1980 U.S. dollars of 712, 1,085, 1,653, and 2,247 for the four selected years using Chenery-Syrquin's average regressions for 1950–83, as given in Syrquin and Chenery 1989. (2) Actual demand aggregate shares based on IMF 1991. (3) Production and employment shares based on relevant Malaysia Plans.

*Note:* C-S = Chenery-Syrquin's regressions; Act. = Actual; Diff. = Difference.

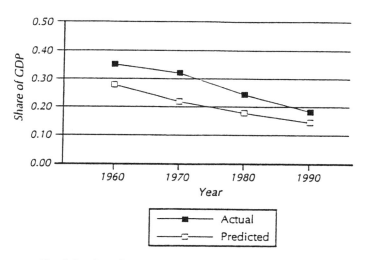

**Fig. 5.1.   Actual vs. predicted GDP shares (agriculture)**

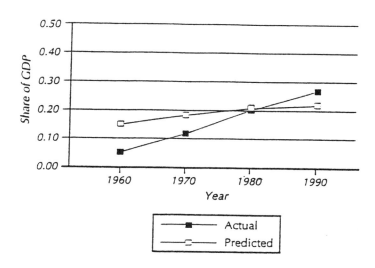

**Fig. 5.2.   Actual vs. predicted GDP shares (manufacturing)**

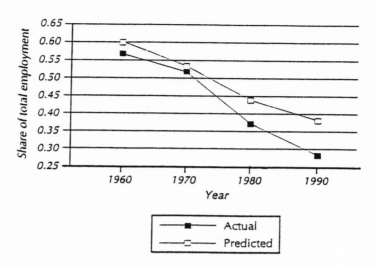

**Fig. 5.3.   Actual vs. predicted labor shares (agriculture)**

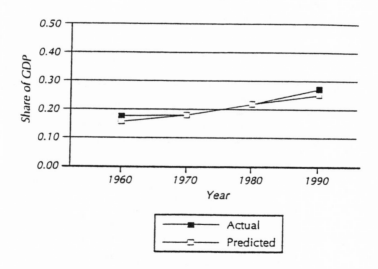

**Fig. 5.4.   Actual vs. predicted labor shares (industry)**

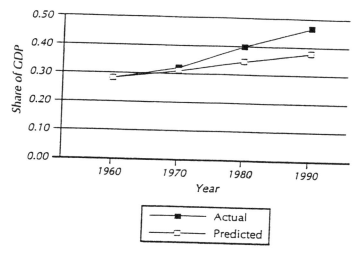

Fig. 5.5.   Actual vs. predicted labor shares (services)

rural-urban lines. A similarly stark difference exists in the distribution of GDP between states. While Selangor accounts for 18.4 percent of GDP, Perlis accounts for slightly less than 1 percent and Kelantan and Melaka less than 3 percent. This disparity is mirrored in the Federal Government Development Allocation by state, where urban or industrial regions like Selangor (7.8 percent) and Wilayah Persekutuan (8.4 percent) get the lion's share of development allocation, while smaller rural states like Perlis (.9 percent) and Melaka (1.7 percent) are left wanting (Sulaiman 1992). One cause of this imbalance is a lack of coordination and cooperation between the policies of the federal government and those of the states (some of which are controlled by opposition parties). It is at this federal-state intersection that Malaysia's spirit of political compromise seems most often to break down.

*Growth.* Though Malaysia has seen steady growth since independence (apart from the recession of the mid-1980s) it does not compare with the success stories of Taiwan, China and Korea. According to the *World Development Report* (World Bank 1992a), Malaysia's GNP per capita growth rate from 1965–90 was 4 percent a year, compared with an average of 6 percent for Asian NIEs (newly industrialized economy). To a large degree this difference can be explained by the inefficiencies that were allowed to proliferate in many parts of Malaysia's economy.

The inefficiencies in its education system were exacerbated by its political structure. From the time of independence on, Malaysia's government consisted of a basically unopposed bureaucracy, which, in the 1970s and 1980s, was willing to employ large numbers of college graduates who were not technically trained. The combination of these circumstances led to a weak managerial class in Malaysia and poor standards of accountability. As Malaysia's public sector grew to massive proportions in the late 1970s and early 1980s, this weakness was a major factor in the failure of many public enterprises and threatened to become a serious problem for Malaysia's privatization efforts as well. Only when the economy collapsed in the mid-1980s did the government face the problem of managerial accountability.

## Initial Conditions

For more than 80 years Malaysia (then Malaya) was under British colonial rule. Achieving independence in 1957 under a parliamentary democratic system, the country was bequeathed an economy with growth potential as well as weaknesses.

*Economic Conditions.* With a land area of 330,000 square kilometers, and a population of 6.2 million, Malaya already enjoyed a fairly high standard of living relative to its neighbors. It produced rubber, coffee, other forest products, and tin. About 35 to 40 percent of GDP came from agriculture in 1960, twice the average for all developing countries (Bruton et al. 1992). Agriculture itself was strongly dualistic, with large, foreign-owned plantations on the one hand and smallholder rubber and rice farming on the other. Almost 60 percent of the work force was in agriculture and fishing. Industrial activity was largely devoted to the processing of raw materials. In 1960, industry and construction together accounted for only 11 percent of GDP, with another 23 percent coming from trade and finance.

The external orientation of the economy meant that exports and imports constituted a high percentage of income. In 1960, exports were equivalent to 55 percent of GDP and imports 42 percent. The country was therefore susceptible in terms of trade shocks, and it has been ever since.

As described by Bruton et al. (1992), maintenance of order was the primary British concern, which also led to a strong sense of macroeconomic stability. Order would attract foreign capital, and it was best served by a balanced budget, a strong balance of payments, low taxes, and zero inflation. The increased investments would boost government revenues, which would allow for additional social services, which would also contribute to the improvement of the estate economy. Infrastructure, particularly transport, was relatively well developed but concentrated around the plantations and mines. Thus, concern for macroeconomic stability was established at the time of independence.

*Political and Social Conditions.* There was significant immigration from China in the nineteenth and twentieth centuries. These immigrants contributed to the trading sector and the opening and development of tin mining.[3] Their control was later diluted by British colonialists with access to superior technologies and greater capital.

Under the British, a large number of workers were imported from India as well, laying the foundations for a multiethnic society. In 1957, 49 percent of the population was Malay, 37 percent was Chinese, and 12 percent was Indian, with others making up the remaining 2 percent. Some 81 percent of the Malays lived in rural areas compared with 27 percent of the Chinese and 59 percent of the Indians. Malays were by far the poorest of the three groups. Snodgrass (1980) estimated that 56 percent of the Malay households had a monthly income of less than M$120, compared with 13 percent for the Chinese and 20 percent for the Indians. The colonial legacy was also characterized by the concentration of wealth in foreign hands. Most fledgling industries were owned by foreigners and ethnic Chinese.[4] In 1963, the Borneon states of Sabah and Sarawak joined the federation. Although rich in timber, oil, and other resources, they added yet more ethnic and political diversity to the country.

Malaysia also inherited the British colonial institutions: a strong central government, a small and efficient administration, and a parliamentary system. The firmly entrenched legal code would give the government a strong base for implementing and administering its policies over the coming decades. However, these institutions also served to codify certain social disparities that have affected Malaysia ever since, particularly in the areas of education and health.

As colonial powers withdrew from the region after World War II, a campaign for independence began in Malaya. A political group called the Alliance took power. It was a coalition of the leading Malay (United Malay National Organization [UMNO]), Chinese (Malayan Chinese Association [MCA]) and Indian (Malayan Indian Congress [MIC]) political parties, and it has remained in government ever since. In essence, each of Malaysia's economic plans has been a social contract promising equitable growth to all three groups.

To sum up, the newly independent Malaysia found itself left with a valuable institutional tradition and a coalition government willing to seek compromise. But this coalition faced a highly complex society that was troubled by an unbalanced economic structure, ethnic inequality, and large inter- and intra

---

3. The Chinese population in Peninsular Malaysia was estimated at 856,000 in 1921. It rose to 1.29 million in 1931 and 1.89 million in 1947. By 1957, it had reached 2.33 million (Bruton et al. 1992).

4. Another structural issue of importance in the rural context was the heavy concentration of village-level enterprises in Chinese hands. A particular instance of this was the rice market, which was monopsonistic at the purchasing and distribution levels. Small-scale Malay rice farmers generally sold their produce to the local Chinese rice miller, who was in a dominant situation in the local market. These setups aggravated ethnic tensions and resulted in the government devoting substantial resources to rural development in the 1960s.

regional disparities. Providing economic growth for the entire society would prove to be the government's greatest challenge, and the question was what role it should play in the economy. One standard justification for state intervention is some type of "market failure," resulting in a suboptimal allocation of resources. In the case of Malaysia, inequality in general, and interethnic inequality in particular, was precisely one such market failure. Racial equity was necessary for political stability, itself a vital precondition for rapid growth. In many senses, this was something that the market, composed of individual units, could not fully value.

## Development Phases

Given the initial complexities, it is not surprising that public policy has continually evolved over the past 30 years in response to changing social, political, and economic conditions. To provide a context for policy, we distinguish three development phases, more or less according to the degree of state intervention.

*Market-Led Development, 1957–70.* In the first decade after independence, the government essentially continued the colonial laissez-faire policies for industry but intervened extensively to promote rural development and provide a social and physical infrastructure. Its aim was to reduce the economy's dependence on rubber and tin, so it sought to boost the infrastructure and amenities that would encourage other forms of private sector production.

However, the government biased its interventions toward the rural areas. Agricultural and infrastructural projects, which accounted for 52 percent of spending in the first Malayan plan, were aimed largely at the eastern part of the country. This was comparatively underdeveloped and also contained a large proportion of ethnic Malays. Over the course of the first three five-year plans (1956–70), agriculture and rural development accounted for 22.3 percent of spending, while industrial development received only 2.4 percent (Bowie 1991). The government's hands-off industrial policy was the implicit social contract arising from the political compromise reached after independence. That compromise gave the Malay party (UMNO) the leading role, while the Chinese political party (MCA) kept control over the industry and commerce portfolios.

Although the government promoted import substitution during this phase, it did not pursue a strong protectionist policy that would have boosted manufacturing at the expense of agriculture. Bruton et al. (1992) attribute this policy stance partly to the continuing political influence of the large plantations. Apart from broadening the industrial base, the import-substitution policies were also aimed at reducing dependence on imported consumer goods, promoting the use of domestic natural resources, and creating employment opportunities.

Instead of direct industrial intervention, the government chose to operate through the creation of a favorable investment climate. It offered general financial inducements in the form of tax holidays, industrial estates, and the provision of supporting services and infrastructure, which were institutionalized in measures such as the Pioneer Industries Ordinance (PIO) of 1958. In the late 1960s, government industrial intervention was increased following the formation of the Federal Industrial Development Authority (FIDA), a government body responsible for promoting and regulating industrial development.[5]

*Macroeconomic Developments.* Starting around 1960, the Malaysian economy was on its way to stable growth. During the 1960s, the average GDP growth rate was 6 percent per year. During this and later periods, overall performance was largely determined by the achievements of exporters. Taxes on rubber, palm oil, and tin exports provided the bulk of government revenue. The export sector also had an influence on the money supply, but the Central Bank (established in 1958) has always closely controlled inflation and the period was marked by an unusual level of price stability.

Investment averaged 14 percent of GDP, but the savings rate was twice as high. Savings, strongly affected by commodity prices, outstripped investment until about 1971. One explanation for the low investment rate was the inherent caution of the entrepreneurial class (World Bank 1985). Fiscal prudence was another cause. The country had a balanced budget and a balance in the external current account, and its foreign currency debt was around 10 percent of annual exports (Bruton et al. 1992). The labor market could not keep up with the growing number of new entrants, and unemployment by the end of the 1960s was reaching 7 percent.

Although economic growth during this period was impressive by developing countries' standards, there was relatively little reduction in the level of absolute poverty for many people, particularly the Bumiputeras.[6] Widespread poverty coupled with relatively high unemployment and underemployment among the Bumiputeras contributed to discontent, which, together with communal politics, resulted in the 1969 ethnic conflict. This event was a watershed in Malaysia's social and economic policy.

*State-Led Development, 1971–85.* The 1969 ethnic conflict prompted a major rethinking of the Malaysian government's approach to development. The result was the New Economic Policy (NEP) of 1971. In retrospect, the NEP can be seen as a response to the failure of the "trickle-down" effects of market-

---

5. Formed in 1965, it was renamed the Malaysian Industrial Development Authority in 1968.

6. The term *Bumiputera* was coined to refer collectively to the Malays and other indigenous groups after the formation of Malaysia in 1963 when Sabah, Sarawak, Singapore, and Peninsular Malaysia combined as a federation.

led development to achieve a socially acceptable pace of income, employment, and wealth between the economically disadvantaged Bumiputeras and the other ethnic groups. In essence, this second phase of Malaysia's development policies was the product of a second social contract.[7]

The NEP's aim—growth with equity—was embodied in the twin objectives of eradicating poverty and restructuring society to redress economic imbalances between the ethnic groups. The NEP thus gave impetus to a more active and direct state role in resource allocation, production, and trade, primarily through public enterprises. The aims of the government were to establish new industrial activities in selected areas and create a Bumiputera involvement in commercial and industrial life. "The efforts to attain these objectives will, in turn, be undertaken in the context of rapid structural change and expansion of the economy so as to ensure that *no particular group* experiences any loss or feels any sense of deprivation in the process" (Government of Malaysia 1973, emphasis added).

The government set two targets: the Bumiputera group would, within 20 years, manage and own at least 30 percent (as opposed to 2.4 percent at the time) of total commercial and industrial enterprises, and employment at all levels and in all sectors, particularly the *modern* and *urban sectors,* must reflect the ethnic composition of the population (Government of Malaysia 1970). To achieve its ownership target, the government began a policy of velvet nationalization, basically buying and restructuring the equity of foreign-held companies through trustee companies, notably the Permodalan Nasional Berhad (National Equity Corporation).

In the pursuit of growth, the government stressed the diversification of agriculture and more intensive use of natural resources. It established regional development authorities to integrate agricultural, commercial, and rural development in selected regions. The decline in rubber and other commodities accelerated government programs supporting cocoa and palm oil cultivation as well as extensive forestry. Significant reserves of petroleum and natural gas were also discovered in the eastern part of Peninsular Malaysia and offshore Sabah and Sarawak, and the extraction and refining were taken over by the government. Malaysia became a net exporter of oil, with a surplus that grew from M$607 million in 1976 to M$3.4 billion in 1980.

This period also saw a shift from import-substitution to export-oriented policies. The latter aimed to encourage the production of light manufactures such as textiles, footwear, and garments. Export incentives, tax breaks, and other indirect subsidies were given to "pioneer" industries, particularly through the setting up of export processing zones (EPZs) or free trade zones (FTZs).

---

7. The eventual structure of the 1957 Constitution was the product of the first social contract.

These incentives, coupled with the availability of low-cost, semiskilled, female workers led to the rise of the semiconductor industry in Malaysia.

During this period, both state and market forces were operating on the economy at the same time, though not necessarily always in contention. On the one hand, state interventions via licensing and quotas (principally through the Industrial Coordination Act [ICA]) and regulated prices (e.g., controlled prices for state procurement through state-owned enterprises) acted to restrain the market. On the other hand, the government was encouraging private sector development through the promotion of investments in exported-oriented industries. The net effect was a mixed economy that was increasingly state dominated.

*Macroeconomic Developments.* During the 1970s, external demand accelerated and the prices and production of major commodities increased. However, import prices rose rapidly as well. This prompted some tightening of monetary policy, so that inflation was held at about 4.5 percent a year. In 1980, after the second oil shock, the inflation rate rose to 9 percent. The commodities boom led to the familiar appreciation of the exchange rate ("Dutch Disease").[8] In late 1984, speculation against the ringgit was heavy and was met with intervention by the Central Bank. The adjustment of the OECD countries to the second oil shock and the consequent recession led to a softening of the markets for Malaysia's exports. This resulted in a deterioration in the terms of trade and in growth and in weakened domestic savings. The growth rate dropped from around 8 percent in 1979 to 6 percent in 1982. The precipitous drop in commodity prices created difficulties for the conduct of fiscal and monetary policies, together with a buildup of external debt. As the government acted on a broad front to address the immediate financial problems (through reductions in expenditures), the severity of external conditions persisted. By this time the increasingly restrictive features of the ICA were also being felt, and investment fell. The economy lunged to a negative 1 percent growth rate in 1985.

The financing of investment in the country, which had relied largely on domestic savings prior to 1980, shifted to external borrowing after 1980. As in other resource-rich countries, the weight of primary commodities in GNP made income, the major determinant of savings, sensitive to variations in primary commodity prices. The commodity price boom of the late 1970s and the oil exports after 1977 encouraged policymakers to lift their sights and spurred a vast expansion of the development effort. Gross national savings (as a percentage of GNP), which was 20.6 percent between 1971 and 1975, rose to 30 percent during the second half of the decade (fig. 5.6). But by the first half of the 1980s the fall in commodity prices and income had squeezed savings to 27 percent of

8. It has been estimated that the exchange rate overvaluation was 12 to 20 percent (Ariff 1991; World Bank 1985).

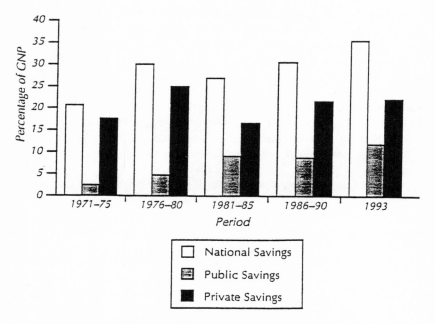

**Fig. 5.6.    Gross national savings. (Data from Herbert 1993; Government of Malaysia 1993.)**

GNP, and the ambitious targets of government expansion had to be financed largely by foreign borrowing. External borrowing swelled from M$4.86 billion (9.46 percent of GNP) in 1980 to reach a peak of M$50.5 billion in 1986 (76 percent of GNP).[9]

During 1971–80, substantial structural changes took place. The share of agriculture in GDP declined from 30 percent in 1970 to 20 percent in 1980, and that of manufacturing increased from 13 to 20 percent. Employment in manufacturing rose at 7.6 percent per year, in construction at 6.8 percent, and in utilities at 6.5 percent. The unemployment rate as a percentage of the labor force fell from 7.5 percent in 1970 to 5.3 percent in 1980.

---

9. Prior to 1980, financing of investment was largely done from domestic savings, the bulk of which was contributed by private savings (18 to 25 percent) of GNP. A large part of this is accounted for by "contractual" or forced savings (5 to 7 percent of GNP) of the Employees Provident Fund (EPF), a compulsory provident scheme introduced in 1952. The rate of contribution increased progressively from 10 percent in 1952 to 13 percent in 1975, to 20 percent of wages by 1980. EPF is the biggest holder of government debt (60 percent). Public savings (current surplus of the public sector), on the other hand, ranged from 2.4 to 9.4 percent and has been contributed to by a few large and commercially viable nonfinancial public enterprises (NFPEs) in utilities, commodities, and petroleum.

*Adjustment and Liberalization, 1986–90.* The 1985–86 recession triggered a second round of market liberalization and a more active promotion of private sector growth. The shift was given new impetus by the Promotion of Investments Act (1986), which provided incentives for manufacturing, agriculture, and tourism. Many of the old methods were again used as instruments of change (e.g., pioneer status and investment tax allowances), but they were made even more generous (Government of Malaysia 1991a). The Industrial Coordination Act (1975) was amended to exempt companies with less than $2.5 million shareholders' capital from the licensing and reporting requirements. The government also kept public spending under control, focusing on providing the infrastructure and conducive environment needed for private enterprise to thrive.

During this period, the nation's outstanding external debt was reduced by about M$9 billion to M$41.5 billion in 1990 through prepayments by both the public and private sectors. In addition, recourse to external borrowing was reduced in favor of foreign equity funding and domestic borrowing. The period also saw the depreciation of the ringgit, which provided a boost to manufactured exports.

*Macroeconomic Developments.* The pattern of growth shifted during this period. Previously led by the external sector, domestic demand became more important, in part due to the rise in consumer spending after the 1985–86 recession. The surge in private investment, however, can be largely attributed to the Promotion of Investment Act of 1986. The four years of sustained growth resulted in some problems associated with a successful economy. Toward the end of the 1980s, there were signs of overheating arising from labor shortages and rising inflationary pressures. Imports, concentrated largely in intermediates and capital goods, outstripped exports, and the balance of payments deteriorated.

## II. Sector Analysis

### Investment and Trade

In the decade or so following independence in 1957, the government's import-substitution policy was motivated by a wish to encourage the development of local industry and promote employment.[10] In some senses, it may have been an intellectual fashion of the times as well. Relative to many other developing nations, however, Malaysia has had a fairly liberal trade regime. Compared with the six countries in the Balassa study (Power 1971), the average effective rate of protection for manufacturing in Malaysia was 7 percent in the 1960s, whereas

---

10. Another important fact is the contribution of import duty revenues for total government revenues, though this has declined over time. Import duties accounted for a total of 43 percent of inland revenues in 1960, falling to 23.3 percent in 1970 and 16 percent in 1980 (Lee 1986, 105).

for the others it was between 21 and 92 percent. Still, the number of items on the tariff schedule increased from 25 in 1962 to 200 in 1963 (Lee 1986).

The effects of the import-substitution policies are revealed in two studies on the sources of manufacturing growth. Hoffman (1973) found that import substitution accounted for 51 percent of the growth in manufacturing output during 1959–68. Applying the same methodology, Vijayakumari (1992) compared two periods, 1973–81 and 1982–85, and found that domestic demand expansion and, to a lesser extent, import substitution were the main contributors to manufacturing growth during the earlier period. The results of the two studies, summarized in table 5.2, show that import substitution was a much bigger source of demand than export expansion was during the 1960s and 1970s, even though export promotion policies took effect in 1968.

Under the 1968 Pioneer Industries Ordinance, the minister of commerce and industry was empowered to grant pioneer status to any firm that could establish an economic rationale for assistance and demonstrate that this was in the public interest. By acquiring this status, a firm received a tax holiday. This was an effective inducement only when firms made a profit, and it appears that only a handful of firms actually did so. Given the 2 percent payroll tax levied until 1971 and the obvious capital bias of the incentive scheme, it is not surprising that employment did not grow rapidly in pioneer firms (Bruton et al. 1992). Seventy percent of the value added of pioneer firms during this period came from foreign-owned firms.

The Tariff Advisory Council (TAC) was set up in 1959 as an investigative and advisory body on matters of tariff protection and exemptions, with its members drawn from the private sector. Following the departure of Singapore from the federation in 1965 and the resulting loss of a significant part of the industrial base, the Action Committee on Tariffs and Industrial Development (ACTID) was set up in 1966. Its managers came from the senior ranks of the bureaucracy. ACTID was responsible not only for regulation and application of the tariff scheme; it also considered applications for pioneer status and therefore had control over many matters of industrial development. Over the next three decades, overall nominal and effective rates of protection declined in absolute

TABLE 5.2.    Sources of Demand for Manufacturing Output Growth

| Source of Growth | 1959–68 | 1973–81 | 1982–85 |
|---|---|---|---|
| Domestic demand | 39.6 | 143.5 | −5.5 |
| Export expansion | 9.5 | −79.7 | 137.5 |
| Import substitution | 50.9 | 36.2 | −32.0 |

*Source:* Hoffman 1973; Vijayakumari 1992.

terms across most sectors. Malaysia continued to remain a comparatively open economy.[11] But, although tariffs were relatively low, they varied widely across sectors. During the 1960s, the highest rates were for nondurable consumer goods, whereas some export activities had negative rates (Power 1971).

By 1970, the domestic market was showing signs of saturation. Import substitution was not providing enough employment opportunities, as it tended to encourage capital-intensive industries using more skilled labor (Linnerman 1987).

In 1968, the Investment Incentives Act (IIA) shifted the basic structure away from import substitution. The incentives, administered by ACTID, extended measures such as accelerated depreciation, reinvestment allowances, and investment credits for nonpioneer industries. Manufactured exports also received an ad valorem incentive. The major export incentives given to domestic firms have been amended over the years, but their main content can be summarized in four points: (1) an export allowance that provided a deduction of taxable income, the amount of the subsidy depending upon export performance and domestic input content; (2) tax deductions for promotional expenses for exports; (3) an accelerated depreciation allowance for companies that exported at least 20 percent of their output; and (4) export financing and insurance facilities from the government at preferential rates.

By the mid-1970s, however, these modifications appeared to be insufficient to meet the objectives of the NEP. Despite government efforts, industrialization was not moving fast enough.[12] Foreign investment, chiefly from the United States and Japan, was not providing satisfactory linkages to the domestic economy. The NEP's goal of 30 percent wealth ownership for the Bumiputeras by 1990 was clearly not going to be reached.

To push the economy toward these equity objectives, the government brought in the Investment Coordination Act in 1975. It was aimed at controlling industrialization and enforcing the NEP's goals. Policy changed from attempting to increase the size of the pie (theoretically providing more for all) to determining the size of the slices. The ICA initially required all manufacturing enterprises with 25 or more employees (or with paid-up capital greater than

---

11. Relative to many other developing nations, the Malaysian government has had a fairly liberal trade policy. Tariff and other trade barriers were erected in the past, but effective protection rates have remained fairly low. The average effective protection rate was only 4 percent in 1965, rising to 39 percent in 1978 (Ariff 1991). This compares, for example, with an average effective protection rate in the Indonesian manufacturing sector in 1984 of 141 percent. When the various policies implemented by the government are examined, these relative magnitudes should be borne in mind.

12. The NEP was, after all, a result of the perception that (following the disturbance of 1969) the process of redistribution was not proceeding fast enough.

M$250,000) to obtain a license to manufacture.[13] It made the granting of licenses conditional upon compliance with NEP guidelines. It was hotly contested by Chinese business groups, which feared it was a mandate for the minister to discriminate in favor of the Bumiputeras. The Associated Chinese Chambers of Commerce and Industry (AACIM) called the ICA "a sword hanging over the private sector. . . . [T]he ICA, if it remains, will constitute a continuing threat to the private sector" (Bowie 1991). Private domestic investment fell, and the strong local reaction no doubt affected foreign investors. Foreign direct investment (FDI) dropped from 6.3 percent of GNP in 1974 to 3.9 percent in 1975 and continued to slide to 2.9 percent by 1979.

The timing could hardly have been worse. The 1971 Free Trade Zone Act had been designed to attract multinational companies (MNCs) to produce for world markets (see sidebar). FTZs and licensed manufacturing warehouses (LMWs) had played an integral role in Malaysia's shift from import substitution to export-oriented manufacturing. FDI had grown from .9 percent of GNP in 1968 to 6.3 percent (and 19 percent of GDP) in 1974, the year before the ICA was enacted.[14] Downturns in both foreign and domestic investment would exacerbate external economic difficulties in the coming years.

After the severe recession of the mid-1980s, pragmatism dictated another policy shift. The government introduced general liberalization to promote the private sector and amended the scope of the ICA. Only manufacturing companies with shareholder funds of M$2.5 million and above or engaging 75 or more full-time employees needed to apply for a license (as opposed to the original M$250,000 and 25), and, increasingly, exemptions were granted. The Promotion of Investment Act replaced the IIA in 1986. It provided a wider range of incentives for investments in manufacturing, agriculture, and tourism and included small- and medium-scale enterprises (SMEs).

### Export Processing Zones or Free Trade Zones

Under the FTZ Act of 1971, certain industrial estates were designated as FTZs. The official incentive package has four main components.

*Duty-free imports of Raw Materials and Capital Equipment.* The FTZ Zone Act of 1971 defines the zones as outside the Federation of Malaysia for purposes of customs duties and taxes. All imported raw materials, components, and capital equipment that are directly related to production may therefore enter the zones without payment of customs duties or other taxes. The exemption does not cover imported capital equipment not di-

---

13. Exemptions from the licensing requirements were given to rice and rubber milling, crude palm oil processing, and so on (Government of Malaysia 1984).

14. A census in 1978 of firms located in FTZs found that 94 percent of them were foreign controlled (Linnerman 1987, 366).

rectly related to production, for example, office equipment, building materials, and vehicles. For these items, duty is, in principle, payable. Similarly,
all goods manufactured in and exported from an FTZ are exempt from
sales and excise taxes. Goods may be moved from one FTZ to another
without payment of duty or other taxes. Goods entering Malaysia and destined for one of the FTZs must travel from the port of entry to the zone by
means of a bonded container truck. This vehicle is sealed by Customs Department officials at the point of entry, and its seal must be intact when it
arrives at the FTZ customs checkpoint. Goods exported from the FTZ must
be transported in the same manner. Goods purchased by FTZ firms from
within Malaysia are treated as exports from Malaysia. The domestic seller
is responsible for the payment of any export duty.

   *Streamlined Customs Formalities.* Imports into the FTZs and exports
from them can be made with less customs documentation than normally
applies to such imports and exports, provided that bonded vehicles are
used for transport to or from the port of entry or exit. Sales within FTZs or
between one FTZ and another can also be effected with minimum documentation. The streamlining of administrative formalities applies only to
the Customs Department, however. The fact that Malaysia's FTZs were established and are still controlled at the state rather than the federal level
means that there is no federal body with overall responsibility for them.
For FTZ firms, this means that they have to deal with the various federal
departments individually. Elsewhere in Asia, a single body has typically
been created with authority to intercede between FTZ firms and the various government agencies at the federal, state, and local levels. The absence of such an authority in Malaysia means that delays do occur and
policy has tended to be uncoordinated.

   *Infrastructure Facilities.* Except for the customs policing of the zone
perimeter, the infrastructure facilities available to FTZ firms are similar to
those provided in other types of industrial estates within Peninsular
Malaysia. Most FTZ firms have constructed their own factory buildings, and the others have not been encouraged to occupy government-
provided buildings on a long-term basis. Government-owned buildings
are rented at or slightly below commercial rates, but the land within the
FTZs is leased to zone firms at well below market rates. This is the most
significant subsidy in the provision of infrastructure to FTZ firms.

   *Company Income Tax Incentives.* A complex system of tax incentives
has been established to grant relief from the normal rate of company
income tax in Malaysia. These tax incentives are not unique to the FTZ
firms, but they are an important component of the overall incentive package. Their stated aim is to encourage investment in export-oriented
manufacturing. There are three major systems of tax relief, known as

pioneer status, labor utilization relief, and investment tax credit. These three systems are mutually exclusive. The first two entail complete exemption from company income tax for the specified period, and the third involves an exemption that may be only partial. Only one other tax incentive may apply in addition to these three, the export promotion deduction. A fifth major category of tax exemption, the locational incentive, applies instead of pioneer status or labor utilization relief if the firm locates in a designated locational incentive area. These areas do not include any of the regions currently possessing FTZs, but suitably located licensed manufacturing warehouses[a] may be eligible for locational incentive status.

*Source:* Warr 1987.

[a] In 1975, the 1967 Customs Act was amended to allow firms to be designated as licensed manufacturing warehouses, which in effect allows them to operate as firms located in FTZs.

These reforms were rewarded with an upturn in FDI and economic growth. The growth of FDI in the late 1980s was markedly different from that of the 1970s, however. Whereas FDI in the 1970s was dominated by Japan and the United States, important contributions are now being made by the "new wave" of Asian NIEs, particularly Taiwan, China. It moved from a meager .3 percent of approved FDI in 1982 to 36 percent in 1990 (passing even Japan in the process).

As for trade policy, two recent studies have revealed a decline in the effective rates of protection (ERP) in the late 1970s and 1980s. The Malaysian Industrial Policy Study of 1984 found an average weighted ERP value of 31 percent in 1979–80. The average ERP estimated by Edwards (1990) for 1987 is 17 percent. In an earlier study, he found an average ERP value of 45 percent in 1969. The general consensus is that the ERP in manufacturing has been declining but dispersed since the early 1970s. This is consistent with the shift from import substitution to export promotion in the 1970s and with the trade liberalization in the 1980s. One exception was an increase in the ERP for heavy industries (discussed later).

The new wave of foreign investors has had a dramatic impact on the Malaysian economy. SMEs being the hallmark of Taiwan's industrial structure, it is not surprising that many Taiwanese investors are setting up SMEs in Malaysia, and the same is broadly true of the other NIEs. This trend has begun to include Japanese investors as well. Partly due to Malaysia's investment incentives and partly to industrial restructuring at home, the newcomers are geared primarily toward exports. Eighty-two percent of foreign projects in 1988–89 exported more than half their output (as opposed to 24 percent of such projects in 1984–85), and 74 percent export more than 80 percent. Since many of these new SMEs are involved in the component industries, they increased interindustry and interregional linkages.

This is true within Malaysia as well. Whereas most FTZs were initially on the west coast, new FDI projects have been more willing to move inland and to the outlying areas. This is partly due to their smaller scale of operation and partly to recent infrastructural development. Some investment zones now cater to a particular line of manufacturing. For example, the 80-hectare Olak Lempit furniture park in Banting (Selangor) contains 59 firms, both foreign and local.

For the future to remain bright, foreign and domestic firms must play complementary roles. Though Malaysia continues to encourage FDI, it still holds to equity objectives through which "identification of race with economic function" will be eliminated. These goals help to create the political stability and infrastructure that make Malaysia a desirable place for foreign investment.

Another looming problem is the lack of product diversification. FDI in Malaysia is still concentrated on electronics and textiles (see sidebar). This weakness is coupled with a growing labor shortage, especially of skilled workers. Every move to establish new industries and modernize the old ones must be linked with programs to develop the skills of the work force.

### The Electronics Industry in Malaysia

The electronics industry accounts for the largest share of manufacturing output, value added, exports, and employment. During 1981–88, its output expanded rapidly from M\$3.58 billion to \$9.42 billion, an average increase of almost 15 percent per year. Exports also increased rapidly; by 1987, electronics exports were Malaysia's top revenue earner, contributing M\$6.9 billion to the national accounts. Most of this was due to the well-established MNC semiconductor firms. Malaysia now has one of the largest installed semiconductor assembly capacities in the world and is a major testing location for semiconductor devices. According to the *Electronics Data Yearbook, 1987,* published by Benn Electronics, the total electronics production of Malaysia in 1987 was U.S.\$2,772 million, some 9 percent of the world's total.

What were the factors that led to this development? The industry took a foothold in 1967 when a Japanese multinational set up a consumer electronics plant in Malaysia to take advantage of the domestic market. In 1971, the semiconductor business began when an American multinational invested in Malaysia. Many other multinationals did the same following active government promotion of foreign investment to develop labor-intensive industries. This was part of export-oriented strategies adopted in the early 1970s. Initially feared to be a "footloose" industry associated with assembly-type operations in free trade or export processing zones, electronics has developed into a major area of high-technology investment and development. It has become the main catalyst in the country's manufacturing and export-led growth. In the process, Malaysia has achieved the status of being the world's leading exporter of semiconductors and the third-largest producer after Japan and the United States.

The Investment Incentives Act of 1968 and the establishment of free trade zones in 1972 encouraged the influx of foreign companies into the electronics industry. Beyond the general incentives to foreign investment, however, the electronics industry was singled out. In the early 1970s, as U.S. semiconductor makers were relocating their labor-intensive assembly operations to the developing countries, the Malaysian Industrial Development Authority (MIDA) coordinated specific investment missions to attract their attention. Later, during the recession of the mid-1980s, as U.S. investment declined in Malaysia, MIDA aimed its efforts at the surrounding Asian NIEs. These countries, especially Taiwan, began to move their plants to Southeast Asian countries due to rising labor cost and currency appreciation at home. Their reliance on SMEs and component industries fits well into Malaysia's entrenched electronics industry and has had a significant impact on the boom.

The electronics industry is characterized by a high growth rate; rapid technological change, which necessitates continual investment in facilities and equipment, technology, and skills transfer; and development of ancillary industries. In terms of growth, the industry value added expanded by 28 percent in real terms between 1973 and 1981 and 10 percent between 1981 and 1988. Its contribution to GDP increased steadily from 2.12 percent in 1981 to 2.98 percent in 1988. Correspondingly, its share of manufactured exports rose from 48 to 56 percent. During the same period, industry employment increased from 16 to 22 percent of total manufacturing sector employment. One of the key reasons behind the success of the industry was, in fact, the wealth of available labor and the efficient use that was made of it.

Malaysia has benefited from the industry's rapid technological changes and competitive nature. Over the last two decades, continuing investments by the MNCs have transformed the industry from a labor-intensive operation in the early 1970s to a highly capital- and technology-intensive operation today. The investments have gone into upgrading equipment, expanding production facilities, developing backward and forward integration, establishing local research and development capabilities, and improving quality. These investments have resulted in a gradual progression of the industry into areas of higher technology, for example, automated assembly equipment, computer-aided manufacturing, device testing, robotics, and computer-aided design. Consequently, there has been some success in the transfer of skills and technology. Many MNCs have established formalized apprenticeship programs for precision tool engineering, local and overseas scholarships, and skills development courses. The equipment, materials, and infrastructural support required by the electronics sector have resulted in the creation of ancillary industries. These linkages are gradually being developed as the country's industrial base deepens.

The Penang Skills Development Center (PSDC) is a good example of the forward thinking that has propelled the industry. PSDC is a public-private sector joint venture. It was given tax exempt status while much of its equipment is donated by the industry. It provides training courses not just to its members but to the entire manufacturing sector. As a nonprofit organization, it has emerged as one of the leading training institutes in the country, becoming a model for other states to follow.

*Sources:* Salleh 1992; Meyanathan and Salleh 1993.

*Heavy Industry.*[15] In 1980, the new prime minister, Dr. Mahathir bin Mohamad, launched a state-sponsored heavy industry project. The Heavy Industries Corporation of Malaysia (HICOM) was incorporated in November 1980 with an authorized capital of M$500 million to "plan, identify, initiate, invest [in], implement and manage projects in the field of heavy industries" (HICOM 1984). Joint ventures would be established between HICOM and foreign investors, relying heavily on Japanese capital and know-how.

Mahathir had long been an advocate of the Look East policy for the industrialization of Malaysia. As the minister of trade and industry in 1978–81, he had campaigned strongly for heavy industry investment. The HICOM projects were intended to push Malaysia into diversification, create modern manufacturing activity outside the FTZ enclaves, and foster linkages between industries. State involvement was necessary to overcome private investors' caution about high-cost, high-risk ventures with long gestation periods.

Initially, HICOM was provided with M$125 million under the Fourth Malaysia Plan (1981–85). It was one of 20 public enterprises in which the Ministry of Finance was a major shareholder. As such, the ministry appointed the Board of Directors of HICOM and had a direct say in the appointment of the

---

15. The conventional definition of heavy industries covers products that are bulky and heavy and require enormous capital, a high level of technology, and skilled manpower. These industries include paper and paper products, chemical products, basic metals, fabricated metal products, shipbuilding, petroleum refineries, machinery, and equipment. The Heavy Industries Corporation of Malaysia defines heavy industries as those possessing all or some of the following characteristics: (1) large-scale in nature, (2) large investment outlays, (3) long gestation periods, and (4) rates of return generally not attractive if measured purely by normal commercial standards and thus not attractive to domestic private investors (Chee 1992).

chief executive.[16] It also provided HICOM with subsidized loans—generally 2 to 4 percent lower than market rates (Chee 1992)—or stood as the guarantor of foreign loans. The Implementation and Coordination Unit (ICU) in the Prime Minister's Department is also responsible for monitoring and controlling HICOM. ICU is charged with reviewing HICOM's annual report, approving financing of new projects, and conducting ex post evaluations of projects.

By 1988, HICOM had set up nine companies employing a total of 4,350 workers and involving investments of about M$2 billion. Most were involved in manufacturing and were set up in different states to try to correct regional imbalances in industrial development.

The best known of the HICOM ventures was the national car project, or PROTON, a joint venture with Mitsubishi. It ran into immediate problems, which revealed many of the weaknesses of the HICOM experiment. Financial arrangements were particularly favorable to the Japanese partners. HICOM was required to provide 70 percent of the capital, which it financed mainly by means of foreign borrowing. The PROTON venture's losses were largely due to forces beyond HICOM's control: world recession and the revaluation of the yen. Even so, for a project that was supposed to lessen Malaysia's dependence on world markets, this was certainly ironic.

The limited size of the domestic market was also a factor. PROTON had an initial plant capacity of 80,000 units, with a plan to expand to 120,000 by 1988. Some economists questioned the viability of producing 80,000 units when the minimum efficient scale of production for a single plant was considered to be 200,000 (Bowie 1991). In fact, production measured 100,000 in 1983, the year PROTON was established, and dropped to 70,000 in 1985 and 33,500 in 1987 before reaching 104,000 in 1992. To recoup losses, HICOM shifted its policy and tried exporting the automobiles to foreign markets (e.g., to the United Kingdom).

With the deepening world recession, Malaysia was faced with twin deficits in its fiscal and external accounts. Ultimately, government policy changed sharply, as the equity imperative seemed to slip in importance compared with the growth imperative. In a stern rebuke to the project's management, Finance Minister Daim Zainuddin said in 1988: "The recession is only part of the problem. If a company fails something must have gone wrong. I am prepared to listen [to problems] up to a point. Beyond that I don't want to hear anymore. . . . Either you perform or say goodbye" (*Far Eastern Economic Review* 1988). HICOM officials said goodbye and were replaced with managers from one of PROTON's foreign partner institutions. Again, the irony of the move was not lost on HICOM's critics.

---

16. The first chief executive was a former civil servant.

Though HICOM turned out to be a loss maker until recently, the Malaysian government did what it could salvage the situation. Saga, an automobile produced by PROTON, has reached the 60 percent local content required to enter Western markets, and exports (notably in the United Kingdom) have gone forward (Machado 1989–90).[17] PROTON has turned around and has been making a profit since 1990.

### The Public Sector

In contrast to the policy before independence, the public sector since independence has been geared to the country's social and economic development.

*Government Expenditure.* During the 1950s and 1960s, the development strategy aimed to reduce the dependence of the economy on rubber and tin. The government launched a program to diversify and modernize agriculture and promote industrial development. It also spent more on the infrastructure and amenities needed to facilitate private sector production.

Public spending changed in the 1970s in response to the 1969 riots. As a proportion of GDP, it rose from 29.2 percent in 1970 to 39.9 percent in 1979 and peaked two years later at 58.4 percent. The public sector deficit and public debt also increased during the same period (see table 5.3). The growth of public enterprises was only one aspect of the widening scope of the public sector. Three types of enterprises were classified as public:

> Departmental enterprises that were required by law to maintain their financial accounts in accordance with commercial standards, for example, the National Electricity Board, Telecommunications Department, and Waterworks Department.
>
> Public corporations and bodies established by state and federal statutes. These were 100 percent government owned and included the Federal Land Development Authority (FELDA) and the Malaysian Rubber Development Corporation (MARDEC).
>
> State-owned companies established under the 1965 Companies Act. Although wholly or partly owned by the government and accountable to Parliament, they were involved in commercial activities and competed with domestic or foreign enterprises. Included in this category are the Heavy Industry Corporation of Malaysia (HICOM), Petroleum Nasional Berhad (Petronas), Malaysian International Shipping Corporation (MISC), Malaysian Airlines System (MAS), and several other enterprises created by the federal government and the State

---

17. Local content in 1993 had reached about 80 percent (*Business Times,* July 9, 1993).

**TABLE 5.3.   Consolidated Public Sector Finance as a Percentage of GNP**

| | 1970 | 1979 | 1981 | 1983 | 1985 | 1987 | 1989 | 1990 | 1991 | 1993 |
|---|---|---|---|---|---|---|---|---|---|---|
| Revenue | 24.6 | 30.7 | 32.9 | 33.2 | 36.5 | 32.61 | 31.49 | 30.40 | 34.75 | 34.83 |
| Operating expenditures | 20.9 | 26.8 | 31.1 | 30.6 | 30.8 | 31.15 | 28.05 | 27.72 | 26.71 | 24.89 |
| Current surplus or deficit | 3.7 | 3.9 | 1.9 | 2.6 | 5.6 | 1.45 | 3.45 | 2.68 | 8.05 | 8.65 |
| Nonfinancial public enterprise surplus | 0.8 | 1.2 | 5.1 | 6.6 | 7.8 | 4.78 | 3.91 | 3.86 | 5.53 | 4.63 |
| Total public sector current surplus or deficit | 4.5 | 5.0 | 6.9 | 9.2 | 13.5 | 6.23 | 7.36 | 6.54 | 13.57 | 13.27 |
| Development expenditures | 8.3 | 13.1 | 27.3 | 26.2 | 18.3 | 11.29 | 13.36 | 14.84 | 13.13 | 13.84 |
| General government | 7.6 | 11.0 | 22.6 | 16.8 | 9.6 | 7.43 | 8.67 | 10.05 | 8.92 | 8.17 |
| Nonfinancial public enterprises | 0.7 | 2.1 | 4.7 | 9.4 | 8.6 | 3.86 | 4.69 | 4.79 | 4.21 | 5.67 |
| Total expenditures | 29.2 | 39.2 | 58.4 | 56.8 | 52.4 | 42.44 | 41.40 | 42.56 | 39.84 | 38.74 |
| Overall surplus or deficit | -3.7 | -8.1 | -20.4 | -17.0 | -4.7 | -5.05 | -6.00 | -8.29 | 0.44 | -0.57 |
| (GNP growth) | 5.8 | 22.6 | 8.2 | 9.2 | -3.2 | 5.4 | 7.7 | 6.5 | 10.8 | 10.7 |
| (GDP growth) | 6.2 | 9.3 | 6.9 | 6.3 | -1.0 | 5.3 | 7.6 | 6.5 | 11.9 | 10.3 |

*Sources:* Government of Malaysia, Ministry of Finance, *Economic Report,* various years; Bank Negara Malaysia, "Annual Report," various issues.

Economic Development Corporation (SEDC), the investment arm of the states.

The amount owed to the federal government by statutory bodies, government-owned companies, and state governments stood at M$1.2 billion in 1970, the equivalent of 24 percent of the federal government's outstanding debt. By 1982, the figure was approximately M$17 billion, 37 percent of outstanding debt. Public enterprises were specifically defined in the Second Malaysia Plan (1971–75) as one of the instruments for redistributing wealth and creating a Bumiputera commercial and industrial community. The result was more regulation, affirmative action, and an increased share of government in production through a proliferation of public enterprises. This proliferation continued strongly through 1975–85. At least 453 public enterprises (more than 50 percent of all that exist today) were created during this period.

This expansion of public expenditures coincided with a severe world recession. By the end of 1982, it was clear that it could not continue. The government started to curb its operating expenditures and sharply reduced its development expenditures. It also checked the growth of public enterprises and announced a master plan for privatization. "Malaysia Incorporated," as Mahathir called it, gave strong emphasis to an increased role for the private sector. Public spending as a proportion of GDP peaked in 1982 at 38 percent, and then began a gradual but steady decline.

*Nonfinancial Public Enterprises (NFPEs).* The government saw the expansion of NFPEs as being central to the tasks of stimulating growth in areas where private sector participation is lacking, promoting regional development and social restructuring, ensuring political control, reducing bureaucratic constraints, and "nationalizing" foreign-controlled companies through the purchase of equity. More importantly, NFPEs have been used as a policy weapon to improve the welfare of the poor and raise the relative economic position of the Bumiputeras.

For the government, there were a number of advantages in using the NFPEs as development agents. First, they were free from normal government controls. Second, they were not subject to the same parliamentary scrutiny as was a government ministry or department. Third, they were empowered to establish subsidiary companies. Finally, their ownership structure could be easily varied to meet the requirements of the NEP. Thus, once a state-owned or state-controlled enterprise was financially viable, some or all of its shares could be transferred to private Bumiputera individuals.

The expansion of NFPEs has been financed continuously by an increase in public development expenditures. During the First Malaysia Plan (1966–70) period, the allocation to NFPEs totaled M$1.4 billion, or 32 percent of all public development expenditures. With the implementation of the NEP in 1971, this

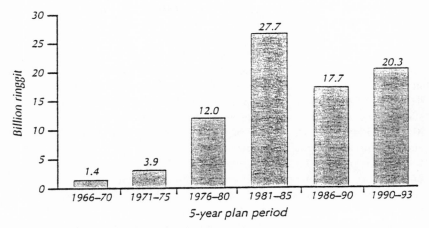

Fig. 5.7. Public development expenditures on NFPEs by 5-year plan periods. (Data from government of Malaysia, Ministry of Finance, *Economic Report,* various years.)

figure increased to M$3.9 billion (40 percent) during the Second Malaysia Plan (1971–75) period, M$12 billion in the Third Malaysia Plan (1976–80), and M$27.7 billion (56.6 percent) in the Fourth Malaysia Plan (1981–85) before declining to M$17.7 billion in the Fifth Malaysia Plan (1986–90) (see fig. 5.7 and table 5.4).

The NFPEs also relied heavily on loans from both the domestic and international markets under federal government guarantee. Outstanding loans due to the federal government by the various statutory bodies and NFPEs totaled M$40.7 billion in 1986, up from M$18 billion in 1982 and M$1.2 billion in 1970. The largest numbers of NFPEs were created in manufacturing and services, but they were pervasive throughout the economy (see table 5.5).

Under the Fifth Malaysia Plan (1986–90), many public enterprises were reclassified as NFPEs. Those with government equity ownership exceeding 50 percent, and an annual revenue exceeding M$5 million was included in the operational definition of the public sector. In view of the large impact that public enterprises have on domestic investment and the balance of payments, an Inter-Agency Committee was formed in 1984 to define the coverage of NFPEs for monitoring and reporting purposes. The following year, a Central Information Collection Unit (CICU) was formed and jointly operated by the Treasury and the National Equity Corporation (see sidebar) to monitor and analyze the nearly 900 enterprises with government equity participation.[18]

---

18. A total of 141 agencies with at least 51 percent government equity and an annual revenue turnover of more than M$5 million were initially identified for monitoring purposes. Of

## The National Equity Corporation

One of the major objectives of the New Economic Policy of 1971 was to redistribute wealth. The government set a target goal of 30 percent ownership for Bumiputeras by 1990. Since 1978, the Malaysian government has set out to distribute the capital stock purchased from British, Chinese, and other companies among the Bumiputera masses. First, it wanted to prevent that stock from being concentrated in the hands of high-ranking officials and rich Malays. Second, it wanted to create an organizational device to prevent the shares distributed to Bumiputeras from being resold to non-Malays (this had taken place earlier despite the efforts of the National Investment Company [NIC]). To meet these two objectives, the government came up with a unit trust scheme known as the Amanah Saham Nasional (ASN). This scheme had three implementing arms: (1) the Yayasan Peraburan Bumiputera (YPB) or Bumiputera Investment Fund; (2) the Amanah Saham Nasional Berhad (ASNB), the National Investment Trust Corporation; and (3) the Permodalan Nasional Berhad (PNB) or National Equity Corporation. These institutions worked with the Perbadanan Nasional Berhad (PERNAS), the National Corporation set up in 1969 to carry out the Bumiputera policy by buying stock and forming joint ventures.

PNB was set up to accumulate and manage capital on behalf of the Malays. YPB worked as PNB's investment planning and decision-making body (with Prime Minister Mahathir serving as its head), while ASNB

TABLE 5.4. **Actual Malaysia Plan Development Expenditures (percentage of total)**

| Sector | Second Malaya Plan (1961–65) | First Malaysia Plan (1966–70) | Second Malaysia Plan (1971–75) | Third Malaysia Plan (1976–80) | Fourth Malaysia Plan (1981–85) | Fifth Malaysia Plan (1986–90) | Sixth Malaysia Plan (1991–95)[a] |
|---|---|---|---|---|---|---|---|
| Agriculture | 18 | 26 | 24 | 22 | 16 | 21 | 16 |
| Industry | 2 | 6 | 19 | 15 | 14 | 11 | 11 |
| Infrastructure (including communications) | 26 | 17 | 19 | 18 | 20 | 22 | 20 |
| Human resources | 19 | 16 | 17 | 17 | 22 | 25 | 25 |
| Services | 13 | 15 | 5 | 9 | 10 | 10 | 9 |
| Security and administration | 22 | 20 | 16 | 19 | 18 | 11 | 19 |

*Source:* Government of Malaysia, respective *Malaysia Plans.*
[a]Projected figures.

these, 56 were selected for initial scrutiny because they formed the bulk of the NFPE expenditures and borrowings (Salleh and Osman-Rani, 1991).

works as a wholly owned subsidiary of PNB. Following YPB planning, and using YPB interest-free loans, PNB acquired at face value the stock of profitable companies from among the shareholdings acquired by the Ministry of Trade and Industry and from those held by public subsidiaries and affiliated companies. Beginning in April 1981, PNB began moving into the investment trust business, working through the ASNB and aiming its efforts at Malays as individuals.

By 1981, the government had invested over M$2 billion in 674 companies. The plan was to sell the purchased equity shares to Bumiputera within 20 years. The government selected 21 companies from among the firms in which it had invested and decided to sell M$660 million worth of their stock shares to Bumiputeras. In all, M$252 million worth of these shares were transferred to PNB to establish the National Trust Fund, and the remaining M$108 million were to be transferred to Bumiputera companies, their employees, and Bumiputera organizations. Ten of the companies chosen as equity share recipients were subsidiaries of PERNAS, including the Malaysia Mining Corporation Bhd., Bank Bumiputera Malaysia Bhd., Kontena Nasional Sdn. Bhd., Malayan Banking Bhd., Komplek Kewangan Malaysia Bhd. (the financing arm of the Council of Trust for Indigenous People [MARA]), and three subsidiaries of the Bank Pembangunan Malaysia Bhd. (Development Bank of Malaysia).

PNB has been able to borrow interest free and noncollateral loans from the government. Under such favorable conditions, PNB has been rapidly increasing its stockholdings. Apart from the stocks acquired from the government and public enterprises, PNB itself has used its borrowed government capital to make investments. These investments are concentrated in the mining, plantation, financial, and industrial sectors. The investment into plantations has been aimed primarily at buying up British enterprises; most of that going into the financial sector has been used to buy up mainly Chinese banks and enterprises.[a] Both of these sectors have

**TABLE 5.5.   Growth of Public Enterprises in Malaysia (number of enterprises)**

| Sector | Before 1960 | 1960–70 | 1971–80 | 1981 Onward |
| --- | --- | --- | --- | --- |
| Agriculture | 4 | 6 | 73 | 59 |
| Building and construction | 2 | 7 | 56 | 65 |
| Extraction industry | 0 | 3 | 22 | 6 |
| Finance | 3 | 14 | 61 | 44 |
| Manufacturing | 5 | 35 | 172 | 102 |
| Other industrial | 0 | 0 | 0 | 10 |
| Services | 5 | 10 | 135 | 143 |
| Transportation | 5 | 13 | 28 | 23 |

*Source:* Central Information Collection Unit, Permodalan Nasional Berhad.

been very profitable, so they are the most effective places to invest to raise the proportion of capital owned by the Malays.

Forty-four percent of the qualified Bumiputera population, as of 1990, had their money invested under the trust system, their total investment amounting to M$6.7 billion. In 1985, Bumiputeras held 17.8 percent of total Malaysian stock. It is fair to say that ASN has contributed greatly toward the goal of raising Bumiputera equity ownership to 30 percent.

*Sources:* Horii 1991; Saruwatari 1991.

[a]In the 1960s and 1970s, all of Malaysia's local banks (with two or three exceptions) were synonymous with Chinese business. Chinese-controlled banks have now diminished in importance, and the banking business has become dominated by government-sponsored or privately held Bumiputera capital. Chinese capital has not been a force in Malaysia's manufacturing sector but rather tends to be concentrated in real estate, hotels, finance, and commerce.

Public holding corporations were another instrument of state intervention. For example, PERNAS was set up in 1969. As its capitalization under the NEP increased, PERNAS became the most successful of the public holding companies. In late 1975, it employed about 4,000 people and operated eight subsidiaries in a wide range of activities, from trade and mining to property development and securities trading. The Urban Development Authority (UDA) had the principal responsibility for supplying Malays in business with office space and other premises in urban areas. SEDC activities, like those of PERNAS, were wide ranging, encompassing agriculture, manufacturing, the provision of business and office premises, and wholesale and retail trading (Gale 1981).

These and other institutions provided direct assistance to Bumiputeras to enable them to compete with non-Bumiputera capital. For example, to prepare more Bumiputeras for skilled jobs in manufacturing and commerce, many agencies offered training facilities. MARA, Bank Bumiputera, and to a lesser extent Malaysian Industrial Development Finance (MIDF) extended credit to Malay businessman at concessionary rates.

We shall assess the financial performance of NFPE's, bearing in mind the shortcomings of the profitability criterion because of the special treatment usually given to NFPEs in the allocation of licenses, government contracts, and other assistance. Table 5.6 shows the percentage of profitable companies in the

**TABLE 5.6.   Profitable Companies in the NFPE Sector**

|                     | 1981 | 1982 | 1983 | 1984 | 1985 | 1986 |
|---------------------|------|------|------|------|------|------|
| Number of companies | 498  | 576  | 631  | 676  | 702  | 574  |
| Percentage          | 61.6 | 55.5 | 56.7 | 58.0 | 54.8 | 55.2 |

*Source:* Ministry of Public Enterprises, cited in Salleh and Osman-Rani 1991.

NFPE sector. It varied between 55 and 60 percent during 1981–86. A large proportion of the profitable companies were in finance, transportation, and extraction. Those in services and manufacturing fared very badly. Those in agriculture were rather erratic, again due to a combination of international conditions and management troubles.

The heavy losses continued up to 1988, the year of the latest available data. They show that, of the total of 770 companies monitored, 378 reported accumulated profits of M$4.6 billion, while 383 companies had accumulated losses of M$5.6 billion (Salleh and Osman-Rani, 1991). Most of the large losses came from the large NFPEs involved in heavy industry.

The poor financial performance of the NFPEs has been attributed to various factors. One is the lack of accountability due to the absence of performance guidelines, overemphasis on social and political considerations, and lack of managerial skills and experience. This failure to develop strict guidelines, performance criteria, and management training programs suggests that the Look East philosophy of Dr. Mahathir was never developed from theory into a detailed program.

Another factor was the easy access to funds, which meant that NFPEs were inclined to do little in-depth preinvestment study and did not prepare themselves to cope with the expansion. They also had a strong tendency to operate on high gearing ratios.[19] Puthucheary (1984) estimated that of the M$33 billion invested in federal-owned companies in 1984, only M$2.5 billion was in equity capital. The rest took the form of outstanding loans that were easily borrowed from the commercial banks.

*Privatization.* The poor performance of the NFPEs led to the privatization policy announced in 1981. By 1992, 40 NFPEs had been taken over by the private sector, and 14 projects involving infrastructure and utility construction had been privatized. At the state level, 120 smaller enterprises belonging to the various SEDCs were sold. Other divestitures involved transferring various entities to the PNB, the Bumiputera Trust Corporation (see sidebar). The aim of the whole process was "to increase private sector involvement [in the economy] and, at the same time, reduce the financial and administrative burden of the Government."[20] The Privatization Plan was, in fact, an admission that mistakes had been made during the second phase of Malaysia's development in trying to fulfill the goals of the NEP. Malaysian Airlines was the first to be sold, followed by several other prominent enterprises. An Interdepartmental Committee at the Prime Minister's Office (supported by technical committees) is responsible for the implementation of privatization. Public sector reforms de-

---

19. Ratio of debt capital to equity capital.
20. Wahab 1987.

signed to reduce and rationalize the size of the civil service have been in force since 1985.

Privatization poses special problems for Malaysian policymakers because of the inherent tension between the dual objectives of unleashing the energies and resources of the private sector, on the one hand, and the desire to protect and promote Bumiputera interests on the other. It is still far from certain that the privatization effort has achieved its stated objectives. Most of the enterprises selected for privatization were natural monopolies (such as the airlines, the municipal water supply, the toll road, electricity, and the telecommunications company); selling them did not change their monopolistic status.

The broader social tensions can be seen clearly in the policies toward the employees of privatized enterprises, who were protected by government regulations. They have been given the option of joining the new enterprise, retiring, or remaining in the public sector. While the benefits of stability are undeniable, this policy has raised concerns that the efficiency that privatization is intended to promote is being stymied by excessive staff.

## Human Resource Development

Malays had long insisted that the limited opportunities they had experienced under colonial rule were largely due to the inequities of the British education system. It came as no surprise, then, that the first phase of Malaysia's development saw a focus on education as a means of achieving economic and social improvement. Through the Education Ordinance of 1957, a national system of education was established. Malay was designated the national language, but the role of other languages continued. Malay and English were made compulsory in all primary and secondary schools. In 1962, primary school fees were abolished, and three years later the school leaving age was raised to 15 to provide a minimum of 9 years of education for every child. This was in line with the National Educational Policy, which was promulgated after the passing of the Education Act of 1961.

Education was a primary concern of the early Malaysia plans. In the 1960s, it was the third-largest item in the development budget, after land development and transport. Recurrent expenditures on education were also high, amounting to 20 percent of total expenditures in those early years (Bruton et al. 1992). Development expenditures on education rose from 9.4 percent of the total in the Second Malaysia Plan to 16.1 percent in the Fifth Malaysian Plan, before dropping to 15.1 percent in the sixth Malaysia Plan.

Between 1956 and 1968, total primary enrollment increased by 60 percent. Enrollment in Malay-language schools increased by more than 50 percent and in Chinese-language schools by almost 30 percent. English-language instruction more than doubled. The statistics were even more dramatic in the secondary schools. Total enrollment between 1956 and 1968 jumped by a factor of more than five, and in Malay-language schools by a factor of 45. All evidence suggests that the poorest people believed in the potential of education and wanted more educational opportunities for themselves and their children.

Not only did enrollment show a rapid increase, but the adult literacy rate grew from 53 to 60 percent between 1960 and 1975. This increase, though admirable, has been slower than those of many of Malaysia's foreign competitors (see table 5.7). The facts are disturbing; nearly all of the other second-tier Asian countries boast a greater success rate in tackling illiteracy. Korea and Hong Kong not only began with much higher adult literacy rates but have shown a 20 percent increase over the same period. To some degree, Malaysia's relative lack of success must be the result of the problems inherent in a multi-ethnic society. Compared with homogeneous societies like those of Korea and Taiwan, China, it faces problems of language and culture that invariably lead to inefficiencies in the educational system.

In the universities, by the late 1960s, 35 to 40 percent of total students enrolled were Malays, a promising sign of social equity and a major objective of the government. However, a new problem was starting to arise: "credentialism." Many investigators (e.g., Meerman 1979) began to argue that the strong bias toward liberal arts by university students was a major handicap for an economy that needed to diversify technologically. The fear was that many students, and Malays in particular, merely wanted a degree (of any kind) because that was the principal requirement for a government job. By 1983, a survey by the Institut Pengajian Tinggi (IPT), or Institute of Advanced Studies, found that 67 percent of all university scholarship students went to work for the government and another 14.5 percent took jobs with statutory bodies. For Malays, the

**TABLE 5.7. Literacy among Asian Nations (percentage)**

| Country | 1960 | 1975 | 1985 | 1990 |
|---|---|---|---|---|
| Malaysia | 53[a] | 60 | 73 | 78 |
| Republic of Korea | 71 | 93 | — | 96 |
| Hong Kong | 70 | 90 | 88 | — |
| Singapore | 75[a] | 86 | — | — |
| Indonesia | 39[a] | 62 | 74 | 77 |
| Philippines | 72 | 87[a] | 86 | 90 |
| Thailand | 68 | 84 | 94 | 93 |
| India | 28[a] | 36 | 57 | 48 |
| Japan | 98 | 99 | — | — |

*Source:* Tan 1992.

[a]Figures are for years other than those specified—generally not more than two years distant from those specified.

numbers were 70 and 16 percent (Mehmet and Yip 1986). As the government succeeded in increasing Bumiputera participation in higher education, it felt compelled to guarantee those students a job in public service.

Throughout the 1960s and into the 1970s, the population was growing rapidly.[21] This put a growing stress on the educational system; many schools adopted morning and afternoon sessions to cope with the increasing number of students, but this made school administration difficult and exacerbated the problem of finding adequately trained instructors. As the Malaysian educational system tried to absorb more and more students, it suffered a drop in standards. By 1990, Malaysia had 13,855 untrained teachers, 11.5 percent of all instructors in the country (Tan 1992). As table 5.8 shows, Malaysia was falling behind its competitors on the secondary level as well.

If worrying trends were beginning to appear in the late 1960s, the government's interventionist policies of the 1970s did nothing to help. In attempting to further the goals of the NEP, the government promoted Bumiputera participation in higher education. The Third Malaysia Plan was based on the assumption that there was a critical underinvestment in Malay human capital. It provided detailed occupational and educational requirements through 1990 and recommended "a sizeable expansion in the production of scientific and technical personnel" and a "vast expansion of personnel and facilities for education at the secondary and tertiary levels of education in the sciences and technologies."

As a result of these forecasts and expectations, there was a rapid expansion in the Malaysian university system, with five new universities opening during 1969–80 and a fourfold increase in enrollment. At the same time, there was a

**TABLE 5.8.  Educational Achievement in Secondary School**

| Country | Average Schooling Years[a] | | | |
|---|---|---|---|---|
| | 1960 | 1970 | 1980 | 1988 |
| Korea | 0.81 | 1.67 | 2.75 | 2.86 |
| Philippines | 1.18 | 1.67 | 2.39 | 2.68 |
| Indonesia | 0.12 | 0.34 | 0.62 | 0.73 |
| Malaysia | 0.61 | 1.05 | 1.49 | 1.79 |
| Taiwan, China | 1.03 | 1.33 | 1.96 | — |
| All developing | 0.34 | 0.52 | 0.95 | 1.1 |
| OECD | 2.59 | 3.03 | 3.79 | 3.94 |

*Source:* Barro and Lee 1993.

[a] Defined as the average number of years of secondary schooling attained by the total population.

21. Urban population increased from 26 percent in 1965, to 29 percent in 1980, to 42 percent in 1989.

vast expansion in government scholarships. The IPT survey showed that two out of every three students in Malaysian universities in 1982 were on a government scholarship. Scholarships were granted on need, as opposed to merit, with informal quotas set to enhance Bumiputera participation. The survey concluded that the Malaysian government was a virtual monopsonist of higher-level manpower (HLM); almost none of the HLM coming out of the universities had an impact on the private sector. Fully 90 percent of the 1982–83 graduates on scholarship were under bond to the government, and two-thirds of these were committed to seven years' service.

Overseas education increased dramatically during this phase, particularly among non-Bumiputera students, who felt pushed out of the Malaysian universities. During the mid-1970s, overseas enrollment nearly equalled the enrollment in Malaysia's universities. By 1987, there were some 65,000 students at the tertiary level within Malaysia, compared with 40,000 students studying overseas, mostly non-Bumiputeras (Klitgaard 1991). These statistics naturally raised the question of a "brain drain."

The 1980s have seen a changing approach to this complex situation. In 1983, scholarships were changed from a need to merit basis. Furthermore, if students fail to perform well, their scholarships are treated as loans that must be repaid. This change has provided hope that market forces will ease the problem of a skills mismatch and that the government scholarships will begin to produce more trained technical and professional manpower and fewer "generalists." In addition, the government decided to shift the cost burden of overseas education (which had led to a large outflow of foreign exchange). As a result, overseas enrollment dropped from 39 percent in 1980 to 29 percent in 1990.

Another encouraging sign in the 1980s was the increasing role of the private sector in education. The enclave nature of some MNCs located in FTZs has caused training to be limited to in-plant experience. In general, however, the human capital in advanced integrated circuit (IC) design and masking has been far superior in Malaysia to that of any other country in Southeast Asia. A growing number of private sector institutions have begun to offer tertiary education to make up for what they perceive to have been a "government failure" during the 1970s and early 1980s. Also, the rapid pace of industrialization and growing diversification have led to a growing demand for middle-level technicians with higher wages. As a result, more children and young adults seem willing to get vocational training for these "blue collar" positions that traditionally Malaysians have shunned.

These changes are welcome and badly needed. Tan and Mingat's (1992) recent study of 15 Asian countries showed that Malaysia had lower than expected postbasic enrollment ratios given its GNP per capita of about M$2,300 and a high share of GNP spent on education (6 percent). This study showed that as a percentage of GNP per capita, recurrent unit costs were 25 percent above the average for Asian countries (at all levels of education) and 39, 12, and 24 percent above, respectively, for primary, secondary, and tertiary education. At the same time, Kharas and Bhalla (1988) show that the quality of the labor force has increased at the rate of 1 percent per year since 1973. At all levels, the trend is clear: Malaysia is spending more on education than are countries such as Korea and Taiwan, China, and it is getting relatively less out of it.

The same could be said of the government's efforts to create a Bumiputera entrepreneurial class. After more than 20 years of credit provision, training, advisory services, quotas, and price allowances in supplies and works contracts, the issuance of licenses in local authority areas, allocation of shares in new companies, and the provision of buildings, the government still laments the lack of a vibrant Bumiputera entrepreneurial class—a class that can venture out without political crutches. Many Bumiputera entrepreneurs fell into financial difficulties during the recession in the mid-1980s; the government later set up a fund to help some of them. Many of the successful small Bumiputera entrepreneurs have been the ones who have skills in their own trades, know the market, and have a good sense of management and thrift. Recent efforts include establishing joint ventures between Bumiputeras and non-Bumiputeras and between successful and aspiring Bumiputera entrepreneurs (Meyanathan and Salleh 1993).

At the same time, there have certainly been gains in other types of Bumiputera employment. In 1990, Bumiputeras made up 30 percent or more of all doctors, veterinary surgeons, surveyors, and engineers, with respectable contingents of lawyers, dentists, and architects as well.

## Infrastructure

One of the reasons for Malaysia's success in the past three decades is its steady support of infrastructure. Every Malaysian plan has devoted about 20 percent of its expenditures to building the country's infrastructure. This farsighted approach has paid many dividends.

In the first decade after independence most of the government's concern with infrastructure focused on the agricultural areas. It invested in drainage and irrigation facilities to promote rice cultivation among the predominantly Bumiputera rice farmers and to maintain the price of rice. These projects went hand in hand with other land development projects. The 1956–60 plan devoted M\$38.3 million to drainage and irrigation alone, about 4 percent of total expenditures. The 1961–65 plan spent M\$108 million on these projects, also about 4 percent of total expenditures. Building the rural infrastructure was also vital to the goals of poverty reduction and the development of a Bumiputera ownership class. The Bumiputeras made up the bulk of poor land workers, and the land development scheme was a concentrated effort to set up Bumiputeras as smallholders, particularly in the rubber and oil palm industries.[22]

In the 1970s, this concern began to change. When, with the 1968 Investment Incentives Act, the government began to court foreign investment, an efficient infrastructure became one of the most powerful incentives in the package. The government built roads for the transportation of equipment, materials, and goods, and it created the FTZs. Although the government did not encourage any firms to occupy a government-provided factory building on a long-term basis, government-owned factories and buildings were rented to firms at or slightly below commercial rental rates, and the FTZ land was leased to firms at well below market lease rates.

The infrastructure shift toward industry has continued ever since, even during the recession of the mid-1980s. It is a tribute to the planners that they kept the long-range benefits of building and maintaining infrastructure firmly in mind during this period rather than giving in to any temptation to save on immediate expenditures by reducing infrastructure development. Malaysian planners have been astute in anticipating the future need for infrastructure and have avoided the creation of severe supply bottlenecks. Consequently, as the new FDI began to take shape in the late 1980s, there was no time lag needed to prepare the way.

## Agriculture

At the time of independence, agriculture accounted for about 70 percent of total exports and almost 60 percent of the labor force. Despite this, Malaysia had a trade deficit in food and could not reach self-sufficiency in its main food crop—rice. By 1980, agriculture's share in GDP had fallen to 22.2 percent (while manufacturing had risen from 13.4 percent in 1970 to 20.5 percent in 1980), and agricultural employment was down to 40.6 percent of the total (Meyanathan and Sivalingam 1986).[23]

The need for economic diversification was recognized even before independence. In the Draft Development Plan of the Federation of Malaya, covering 1950–55, the dependence of the economy on a limited range of products (rubber and tin) was highlighted. Similarly, in the First Malaya Plan, covering 1956–60, economic diversification was listed among the priority objectives.[24] It called for diversification in agriculture ". . . by providing more land, by diversifying and intensifying production, by supplying better planting material,

---

22. Another major thrust of this early phase was the building of schools.

23. As discussed in the HRD section, this was, in part, due to large-scale demographic changes in Malaysia's population.

24. The First Malaya Plan was based on a 1955 World Bank report entitled *The Economic Development of Malaya* (World Bank 1955).

encouraging the use of fertilizers and off-season cropping, by improving cultivation techniques, extending cooperation and fisheries and the practice of
poultry rearing and animal husbandry" (60).

Using public sector surpluses, the government began to implement a
range of policies designed to widen the agricultural base after independence.
These policies included measures to influence prices, subsidies on agricultural
inputs, the provision of extension services, and technological and research support. These policies influenced the flow of factors to the production of different
commodities by modifying the private rates of return. The provision of protection against imports, together with fiscal incentives or taxes, also influenced the
differential rates of return between commodities. This effect was particularly
strong on rice production, which was officially supported in the 1960s and
1970s. Import subsidies were also introduced for agricultural machinery and
fertilizer to encourage double cropping. As a result, the number of wet rice
fields rose, from 2 percent in 1960 to 57 percent of total cultivated area in 1975
(Young et al. 1980). The contribution of off-season crops also rose from 2 to 40
percent of total annual rice production. Increases in rice yields were also
achieved as a result of improved inputs and the provision of extension and
credit services.

The earliest institution set up by the government to implement land-
use development programs was the Rural Industrial Development Authority
(RIDA). Along with the Malaysian Agricultural Research and Development
Institute, RIDA worked to extend the amount of land that could be put to
use (mainly through drainage programs) and to help smallholders and non-
landowners buy this land. Due to the rapid increase in the rural population,
the Federal Land Development Authority was established in 1956. Its main objective was to resettle farmers with uneconomical farm sizes into new land
schemes, thereby increasing their incomes and alleviating overcrowding on traditional farms. In fact, FELDA was using policies to favor smallholders in an
attempt to increase Bumiputera landownership.

To avoid confiscating land from large private estates, the government
chose to develop unused fringe land. Through the efforts of these land schemes,
private estates gradually decreased both in absolute and relative terms from
1960 to 1980; smallholders, both traditional and organized, increased dramatically (by 34 times) over the same period. The development of new land
schemes was considered to be more socially and politically acceptable as a
redistributive scheme than were land reforms (Tamin 1990). The NEP then
provided new impetus for pursuing land development schemes on large tracts
of undeveloped forest land. To develop the targeted regions, various regional statutory bodies were established: Johor Tenggara Regional Authority
(KEJORA) in 1972, Trengganu Tengah Development Authority (KETENGAH)
in 1973, and Kelantan Selatan Development Authority (KESEDAR) in 1978.

Following the NEP, state intervention extended deeper into agriculture. The Agricultural Bank (Bank Pertanian) was founded in 1969 to provide greater access to credits for agricultural development. The activities of the Federal Agricultural Marketing Authority (FAMA), which was established in 1965, were expanded. The National Paddy and Rice Authority (LPN) was created in 1971 to manage the price support system for rice farmers. The Rubber Industry Replanting Board was established in 1952 to rejuvenate the industry by providing money for replanting with new, high-yielding clones. As the agricultural diversification drive intensified in the 1960s and 1970s, the rubber replanting fund was approved for smallholders to plant approved crops, particularly oil palm (see sidebar).

### The Oil Palm Industry

Malaysia's oil palm industry has grown phenomenally over the past three decades. Since 1965, Malaysia has been the world's largest exporter of palm oil products and, since 1972, the largest producer of palm oil. In 1984, it produced over 60 percent of the world's palm oil and accounted for more than 80 percent of the global exports of palm oil. Over the past three decades, total planted hectarage grew 36 times, expanding from 55,000 hectares in 1960 to about 2 million in 1990. During the same period, crude palm oil production rose from about 100,000 tons to about 6 million. It is now the leading crop in the country, contributing 5.4 percent of total export earnings in 1990 compared with 4 percent for rubber.

Until the establishment of processing facilities in 1975, only crude palm oil was exported. By 1984, more than 98 percent of the crude palm oil was processed locally into various products. The output of processed palm oil and other products grew at an average rate of 30.5 percent per year in that period. This impressive growth sums up the success of the crop diversification efforts and the trade and investment incentives given by the government to stimulate the growth of the processing industry in the 1970s.

*Industry Profile.* The composition of private-public ownership of oil palm plantations has changed tremendously since 1960. Then private sector estates accounted for all oil palm plantings. By 1990, federal and state government agencies controlled 46 percent of the total planted area, compared with 45 percent in private sector estates and the rest in smallholdings. There has also been an increase in ownership by Malaysians. Of the total of 1,668 oil palm estates in 1990, 93 percent were owned by Malaysians, compared with 81 percent out of a total of 975 estates in 1980.

*Intervention and Effects.* An account of the state's role in the development of the oil palm industry can be drawn from the various Malaysian five-year development plans. These plans contained numerous policies and programs that directly or indirectly supported the development of the industry. The major policy motivating the industry's growth was encapsulated in the diversification effort to reduce the economy's dependence on two commodities, rubber and tin. In tandem with the diversification effort was the rural development program to resettle and absorb the expanding rural labor force and reduce rural-urban migration. Among the major implementation agencies set up to spearhead the program were the Federal Land and Development Authority, the Federal Land Consolidation and Rehabilitation Authority (FELCRA), and the Rubber Industry Smallholders Development Authority. In 1990, FELDA managed about 588,000 hectares, or 67 percent, of public sector holdings, FELCRA about 12 percent, RISDA about 4 percent, with the various state land schemes comprising the rest. FELDA also worked toward reorganizing the smallholders into efficient production units. RISDA, on the other hand, provided smallholders with replanting grants to convert their rubber holdings into oil palm.

While the economic diversification policy stimulated rural land development, the industrialization policy provided the impetus for the development of palm oil downstream activities. Incentives were already provided under the 1958 Pioneer Industries Ordinance to set up processing activities. These incentives were boosted by the Investment Incentives Act of 1968, which geared the industries toward exports. The incentives enjoyed by the palm oil refining industry include pioneer status, investment tax credits (ITC), and export incentives. As of 1984, 70 percent of the total of 54 refineries were given ITC, 17 percent were operating under pioneer status, and the rest were without incentives. Of the total of 51 palm kernel mills, 18 percent were given pioneer status, 20 percent were accorded ITC, and the rest were without incentives.

Since 1980, the government has been reforming the commodity export tax structure to alleviate the incidence of producer taxes on smallholders. An export duty scheme, featuring different rates of duties on crude and processed palm oil, was introduced in 1976 to encourage further value-added processing. An export duty exemption is also granted to processed palm oil according to the level of processing.

Currently, Malaysia is the world's largest producer of palm oil, with half of the acreage under the control of public sector authorities. The government set up the Palm Oil Research Institute of Malaysia (PORIM), which suggested utilization of Cameroon weevils as a pollinating agent for increasing yield productivity (standard agricultural technological externality). The Malaysian Industrial Development Authority promoted local refineries through tax and other incentives such as exemptions from the licensing requirements of the Industrial Coordination Act.

*Source:* Meyanathan 1989; Government of Malaysia 1991a.

The achievements of the land development agencies, particularly those of FELDA, highlight the success of state intervention in agricultural and rural development. As shown in table 5.9, both FELDA and Rubber Industry Smallholders Development Authority (RISDA) have contributed significantly to the expansion of oil palm cultivation. FELDA and the agricultural research institutes have been quite successful in bridging the productivity gap between the private plantations and the smallholdings that it manages. FELDA's average plantation yield by 1988 was almost equal to that of the private estates.

However, there have been notable failures of government intervention as well. FELCRA's objective in taking over the Fringe Alienation Scheme in 1962 was to give landless peasants 10 acres each and boost all smallholders up to 10 acres. This was converted into the Land Rehabilitation Scheme in 1966, under which FELCRA assumed the responsibility for management of the land by controlling the sales of products and taking over the farmers' debts to the government. By 1970, when FELCRA began a renamed Fringe Alienation Scheme, some farmers were denied ownership because they had merely held and not developed their uncultivated land. This scheme was called the "sharing system," since participating farmers were given part shares in the land, with FELCRA acting as a trustee. They were guaranteed equitable wages from FELCRA until they could pay off their debts.

The National Agricultural Policy (NAP) of 1984 clearly states that estate-type management is preferable in the future for rubber, oil palm, and rice farming. However, present policy clearly limits capital expenditures on land development and promotes the conversion of FELDA estates into industrial land. This has brought instant wealth to some farmers.

### Finance

The financial system in Malaysia is fairly sophisticated compared with those of other countries at a similar stage of economic development. Financial deepen-

**TABLE 5.9.  Oil Palm Hectarage in Peninsular Malaysia**

| Year | FELDA | RISDA | Estates | Others | Total |
|---|---|---|---|---|---|
| 1970 | 7,219 | 438 | 68,289 | 0 | 75,947 |
| 1980 | 307,530 | 16,185 | 495,412 | 87,465 | 916,590 |
| 1988 | 477,502 | 98,661 | 782,877 | 168,503 | 1,527,543 |
| 1990 | 602,590 | — | 894,742[a] | 379,920 | 1,877,252 |
| 1993 | 570,580 | 40,687 | 787,338 | 424,368 | 1,822,973 |

Source: Government of Malaysia, Department of Statistics 1988; Government of Malaysia, Ministry of Primary Industries 1994.
[a]Includes RISDA figure.

ing and innovations have proceeded rapidly, especially since the second half of the 1970s (Ahmad 1990). The financial system covers a broad spectrum of institutions and markets, including the Central Bank, the commercial banks, the finance companies, and the merchant banks. By 1990, the number of bank branches had risen to 1,000, making an average population to bank office ratio of roughly 18,000 to 1.

Other than the state's role in maintaining a stable monetary system, it was involved in three main types of intervention: (1) ownership structure of banks, (2) directed credit, and (3) the export credit refinancing scheme.

*Ownership.* In colonial times, foreign banks accounted for the bulk of deposits and loans advanced. By March 1980, however, domestic banks took about 66 percent of the total deposits and advanced about 55 percent of the total loans. By 1990, out of a total of 38 commercial banks, 22 were domestic incorporated banks.

Three banks with large government shareholdings (Malayan Banking, United Malayan Banking Corporation, and Bank Bumiputera) have become very active in collecting deposits and advancing loans. Although Bank Bumiputera was established in 1965, it has expanded rapidly, with strong government support, and is now the second-largest domestic bank (after Malayan Banking). It is wholly owned by the government, with the objective of promoting Bumiputeras in the banking industry. From 1970 onward, Bumiputera equity stakes in the country's commercial banks began to increase. By the beginning of 1982, they had increased to 77 percent of the entire banking industry.[25]

One reason for the increased ownership by Bumiputeras (and the government) in the banks has been profitability. Another has been the desire to shift the pattern of lending. The government has a strong influence on the financial system through its stakes in the major banks and development finance institutions that were established in the 1970s. Guidelines on lending and the regulation of interest rates set by Bank Negara, the state development bank, shaped the direction and cost of credit throughout the country.

*Directed Credit.* Following the NEP in 1971, the Central Bank changed its approach toward banking in order to fulfill the social and restructuring objectives of the government (Yusof et al. 1992). It required banks to provide designated priority sectors with ready access to credit at a reasonable cost. It first issued guidelines for bank lending in 1975, directing commercial banks and finance companies to provide at least half of their increase in net credit during the year to the priority sectors. It also imposed ceilings on the interest rates that could be charged to certain types of priority borrowers. The list of priority sectors, which was modified yearly according to development needs, originally included the Bumiputera community, small businesses, food produc-

---

25. In 1992, there were nine banks under Chinese management (Hara 1991).

322     Lessons from East Asia

tion, housing loans (including loans for low-cost houses of M$25,000 or less), manufacturing, and other sectors such as agriculture, fishing, forestry, building, construction, and property development (Yusof et al. 1992).

Although the Central Bank administered these guidelines flexibly, it ensured compliance by penalizing those who failed to meet them. The delinquent institutions were required to deposit with the Central Bank an amount equal to the shortfall for one year at an interest rate to be determined by the bank. These deposits would then be lent to institutions that had the capacity to lend to the private sector. In 1976, the directive was made more specific: 25 percent of the loan increase had to be channelled to manufacturing industries, 20 percent to Bumiputera borrowers, and 10 percent to food production. The stringency of the guidelines has been reduced progressively in the third phase of development as more targets have been met. Although it is not possible to separate the effects of organic change from the government's scheme, the direction of bank lending, as shown in table 5.10, does reveal a balanced distribution of loans to the various sectors.

The guidelines also covered the implementation of schemes like the General Guarantee Scheme (GGS) and the Special Loan Scheme (SLS) administered by the Credit Guarantee Corporation (CGC). CGC was set up in 1972 to guarantee cover for loans by the commercial banks to small businesses. Between 1973 and 1990, the cumulative loans by CGC to Bumiputeras numbered 81,270, with a total value of M$1,007 billion. Non-Bumiputeras received a total of 75,572 loans amounting to $2,217 billion. According to Yusof et al. (1992), the priority lending guidelines did not seriously distort the capital market be-

TABLE 5.10.   Direction of Commercial Bank Lending (millions of ringgit and percentage of total)

| Sector | 1970 | | 1980 | | 1990 | | 1993 | |
|---|---|---|---|---|---|---|---|---|
| Agriculture | 240 | (10.2) | 1,648 | (7.8) | 4,238 | (5.2) | 4,125 | (3.5) |
| Mining and quarrying | 51 | (2.2) | 211 | (1.0) | 833 | (1.0) | 631 | (0.5) |
| Manufacturing | 466 | (19.7) | 4,694 | (22.3) | 18,742 | (23.2) | 26,931 | (23.0) |
| Electricity | na | na | 279 | (1.3) | 202 | (0.2) | na | na |
| General commerce | 756 | (32.0) | 4,644 | (22.1) | 11,642 | (14.4) | 13,662 | (11.7) |
| Real estate, building, and construction | 207 | (8.8) | 3,117 | (14.8) | 14,599 | (18.1) | 20,692 | (17.6) |
| Housing | na | na | 2,323 | (10.6) | 9,587 | (11.9) | 14,508 | (12.4) |
| Transport and storage | 17 | (0.7) | 400 | (1.9) | 1,342 | (1.7) | 2,001 | (1.7) |
| Financing, insurance, and business services | 80 | (3.4) | 1,297 | (6.2) | 9,105 | (11.3) | 16,983 | (14.5) |
| Other | 543 | (23.0) | 2,509 | (11.9) | 10,473 | (13.0) | 17,702 | (15.1) |
| Total | 2,360 | (100.0) | 21,031 | (100.0) | 80,763 | (100.0) | 117,235 | (100.0) |

Source: Malaysia, Bank Negara Malaysia, Quarterly Economic Bulletin and Annual Report, various issues.
Note: Na = not available. Totals may not add up to 100 percent due to rounding.

cause the Central Bank ensured that the fixed interest reflected the actual cost of funds to the banking institutions.[26]

The other form of priority lending is directed government credit. This involves the provision of loans by the federal government to various government agencies, statutory bodies, and corporations in which the government owned equity. The interest rates charged depended on the purpose of the loan. For instance, no interest was charged for loans to antipoverty projects. Restructuring, infrastructural, strategic, and similar projects carried an interest rate of 2 to 5 percent, while commercial projects were charged the full cost of the funds to the government (Yusof et al. 1992). Thus far in the 1990s, the government has charged an interest rate of half the cost for antipoverty program loans, while loans for other social restructuring programs may be charged up to the full cost of the funds to the government. The funding of commercial projects at subsidized rates has been stopped. This more market minded approach shows up in the figures: in 1975, total government loans amounted to 22 percent of total banking system loans, but the proportion declined to 16 percent in 1980 and 9.8 percent in 1989.

After the NEP, four major institutions were created specifically for development banking: Bank Pembangunan Malaysia Berhad (BPMB), Malaysian Industrial Development Finance (MIDF), Bank Industri Malaysia (BIM), and Bank Pertanian Malaysia (BPM). These institutions have concentrated on furthering NEP equity goals in various parts of Malaysia's economy. BPMB has been involved in implementing a World Bank–assisted program for the development of small-sized enterprises (SSEs). MIDF concentrates on the development and modernization of manufacturing. Bank Industri Malaysia works on stimulating export-oriented, high-technology industries. BPM deals mainly with agriculture.

With the exception of Bank Industri Malaysia (see sidebar), these institutions have been hampered by the poor performance of many of their debtors. BPMB, for instance, has had a failure rate of about 30 percent, with an additional 20 percent of the SSEs experiencing severe financial troubles. To some degree this has been the result of a shortage of viable projects, and even viable projects have not properly prepared their business proposals. Recently, the development institutions have widened their sectoral targets, accepting more applications from non-Bumiputeras (Asian Development Bank 1990).

### Bank Industri Malaysia

The success of the Bank Industri Malaysia can be attributed to its strict attention to detail. Even though it is willing to finance high-risk pro-

---

26. After 1987, it was linked to the base lending rate of the banking institutions, subject to market levels (Yusof et al. 1992).

jects that commercial banks will reject, it still has had a good success ratio with its loan projects.

Bank Industri has a thorough research team on which it relies heavily. It has adopted a target market approach, and the research staff plays the key role in identifying and evaluating new areas of the economy for the bank to penetrate. The researchers undertake very detailed industry studies, looking at all aspects of a potential project in order to gain familiarity with its strengths and weaknesses and gain market intelligence on the opportunities and threats awaiting it.

Once it has approved a project, Bank Industri insists on being an active partner. It stays jointly involved in the financial management with its partner, often operating joint bank accounts with the clients, which requires the bank to countersign all checks for payment of expenses. Bank Industri is vigilant in monitoring the progress of its clients, frequently visiting business sites, and is quick to provide financial management advice.

*Source:* Asian Development Bank 1990.

The debt problems caused by the promotion of heavy industries and NFPEs in the early 1980s had a major impact on the financial sector and forced some changes in policy. Bank Negara has tried to strengthen the financial system by imposing capital adequacy ratios, single customer limits, and provisions for nonperforming loans. Rescue operations were conducted to assist ailing financial institutions. As the economy began to recover from the recession of 1985–86, structural changes took place in the financial sector. A number of institutions have been consolidated through mergers and acquisitions, forming more resilient units. New legislation has strengthened insurance companies and cooperatives and improved their supervision. Finally, Bank Negara has encouraged increased competition within the banking system by removing entry barriers between the various financial markets.

*Export Credit Refinancing.* The ECR program has promoted Malaysian exports since 1977 by providing exporters with easy access to credit at preferential rates for both pre- and postshipment costs. The ECR's objective is to promote the export of manufactured goods and agricultural products that have high value-added and local content, and the government approves the selection of goods according to these criteria. The minimum amount of ECR financing is M$10,000, and the minimum drawdown is $2,000.

ECR is very popular among exporters, and its utilization has risen from M$140 million in 1977 to $9.6 billion in 1989. The sharpest rise came after 1986, when the scheme was restructured so as to simplify its administration and clarify the procedure for bankers and exporters. In 1977, when the scheme was initiated, only 3 percent of gross manufactured exports used ECR. By 1989, the proportion had risen to 22.5 percent, well up from 1988's figure of 16.3 percent.

Another important feature of the recent restructuring of the scheme was a shift toward preshipment financing. This benefits Malaysia more directly by providing the exporter and his suppliers with financing for "bridging" (Meyanathan and Salleh 1993).

## III. Institutional Capacity

As the previous sections have shown, the Malaysian government increased its intervention in the economy during the second phase of the country's modern development, then shifted back again during the third period. Its ability to make these changes is partly a function of political will and partly of institutional strength and pragmatism.

*Political Will.* Malaysia inherited, at independence, a parliamentary democratic system along with the administrative, legal, and legislative systems of the British. The Constitution provides for a king, who is himself elected by rotation from among the nine sultans for a term of five years. It has a bicameral Parliament, consisting of the upper house (Senate) and the lower house (House of Representatives). Members of the lower house are elected for five years. The federal government is headed by the prime minister, whose cabinet consists of ministers who are members of either house. The cabinet comprises leaders of the governing coalition of ethnic-based parties. The distribution of cabinet posts by political parties is based on the number of seats secured by each party in the coalition during the elections and also on the need for equitable representation for the coalition parties.

Parliament is not the sole repository of legislative power. The Constitution (in 1957 and 1963) provided for the legislative assemblies of each of the 13 states to make laws for their respective states. Federal-state relations are therefore an important factor in the role of the government in fostering development. The federation was intended to have a strong central government, with some autonomy for the states based on their control over local government and land matters. However, the federal government is constitutionally empowered to enact legislation through Parliament to provide for uniformity of law and policy. In particular, it has the power to acquire states' land for national development and national interest projects. More importantly, the federal government has been able to influence the activities of the states through its spending and its control over their borrowing.

Since the beginning of modern politics in Malaya and Malaysia, the concept of a coalition of ethnic-based political parties has always been a successful one. This coalition, the Alliance part—representing Malays (UMNO), Chinese (MCA), and Indians (MIC)—has been in power since 1955. After 1969, the Alliance was broadened to include several other parties and became the National Front. The Alliance and the National Front have been replicated in the political life of the various states. UMNO is recognized as the dominant party in the coalition, but tensions among the partners are not unknown. Even so, the notion of unity at the highest level of government has been used to fend off internal and external challenges from opposition parties (Z. Ahmad 1982).

The strength of the coalition lies in its ability to achieve national goals based on continuing development and modernization for all, while still favoring the economically disadvantaged but politically dominant Malay group. Although Malaysia is a secular state, with Islam as the major and official religion, the country still harbors the potentially explosive forces of religious extremism and narrow communalism. In the light of these forces, the importance of the government's prodevelopment stance cannot be overemphasized.

Except for 1969, the coalition has won a two-thirds majority at each of the eight elections (from 1955 to 1989). This majority has allowed it to pass legislation as well enjoy the credibility needed for policy reform. The pragmatism displayed by the government in implementing the NEP policies has been a major contribution to political stability. In a virtuous cycle, political stability facilitates economic growth, which in turn contributes to political stability. Specifically, the growing Bumiputera middle class is seen as a stabilizing force that has helped to create the more stable political climate and racial relations of the 1980s.

Have political leadership and vision been factors in explaining the turning points in Malaysian policy? Clearly, the answer is yes. The ruling party's political dominance has allowed for strong political leadership, particularly by the prime minister. The first prime minister, Tungku Abdul Rahman (1957–70), who led the country to independence, is usually identified with the forging of national unity and a preference for the functioning of markets. The second prime minister, Tun Abdul Razak (1970–76), is associated with rural development and modernization and the third, Tun Hussein Onn (1976–81), with stability and clean government. The present prime minister, Dato Seri Mahathir Mohammed, is identified with strategic vision, heavy industrialization, the work ethic, public sector reforms, and the move toward attaining "developed nation" status by the year 2020.[27]

*Institutional Strengths.* Since Malaysia's experience with colonialism was a relatively fortunate one and independence was gained without violence, it began its development with an outward-looking rather than inward-looking view of the world. It had no inhibitions about trading with and accepting aid from the West and made good use of capital and technical assistance from both

---

27. This personal influence extends beyond the prime minister. One of the strongest and most controversial personalities in the government was former Finance Minister Daim Zainuddin. A product of the private sector, he was willing to face head-on the growing problems of government expenditures and debt. While some say he is antagonistic to the Bumiputera cause, there is no doubt that the liberalized policies of the late 1980s are partly Daim's doing (*Far Eastern Economic Review* 1988).

unilateral and multilateral donors (Higgins 1982). The Office of the Prime Minister, particularly its Economic Planning Unit (EPU), has been the key institution for development planning. The EPU, which was established in 1961 and took over the planning function from the Treasury, is staffed by capable technocrats who produce the long-term (10–20 years) and medium-term plans (five-year plans), as well as the midterm reviews.[28] It has a wide range of other responsibilities: advising the government on economic matters, drawing up detailed development plans, economic analysis, the review and evaluation of projects, and programming and coordinating technical assistance.

The annual budget is prepared by the Treasury in cooperation with the EPU. The Treasury allocates operating and development budgets, and the EPU appropriates development allocations across sectors and states. Also working out of the Prime Minister's Department, the ICU ensures the coordination and implementation of government policies, programs, and projects at the national, intergovernmental, and federal and state levels. The prime minister is also assisted by a special committee of ministers for socioeconomic development. He advises the cabinet before any planning document is approved for tabling in Parliament. The National Development Planning Committee, which consists of senior civil servants appointed by the government, also has a big say in the formulation of development plans; it undertakes periodic reviews and suggests adjustments in accordance with changing circumstances. While the EPU's focus is on macroeconomic planning, the National Development Planning Committee's main concern is the effective implementation of projects and programs (Ariff 1991). From the mid-1980s onward, there has been a tendency for think tanks, academies, and other private sector organizations to have greater input into the policy formulation process.

Implementing development plans and monitoring their progress has proved to be far more difficult than the actual planning itself due to coordination problems inherent in the multiple levels of government (federal, state, and local) and the multitude of ministries, departments, agencies, and so on (Ariff 1991). The highest form of coordination occurs at the political level. Below this, fairly good coordination has been established by interagency planning groups and technical working groups established by the EPU for preparing plans and formulating policies. At the state level, the need for coordination is more extensive, as the government must deal with many organizations and the state planning committees.

Malaysia inherited the legacy of a closely administered political structure and a highly effective bureaucracy. This has made the implementation of policies easier (including the National Front's modernization policies), but,

28. The Prime Minister's Department consists of the EPU, the Implementation Coordination Unit, the Public Services Department, the Manpower Planning Unit (Mampu), the Microelectronics Institute of Malaysia (Mimos), the Islamic Center, and the National Security Council.

paradoxically, it could also destroy the regime's credibility through inefficiency and incapacity (Z. Ahmad 1982). However, the evidence indicates that the bureaucracy, though nonpartisan, is strong and highly committed to achieving the government's goals. The bureaucracy occupies a central position in the policy process in terms of formulation, evaluation, analysis, periodic reviews, and adjustments. Members of the Malaysian civil service have always worked closely with the political leadership and have been well paid, especially compared with their counterparts in the faster growing NIEs.

Despite this institutional strength, policy miscalculations were made in the second period. Implementation capacity, in particular, suffered. One example was the difference between allocations and expenditures in the Third and Fourth Malaysia Plans (see table 5.11). Although a small lag was noticeable in implementing the allocation of the Third Malaysia Plan, this increased tremendously during the next term. In short, the government's reach exceeded its grasp.

Another instructive comparison is between Malaysia and Korea. While Malaysia's public capital expenditures increased from 18.5 percent of total government spending in the 1970s to 22.4 percent in the 1980s, Korea's dropped from 20.7 to 14.8 percent. While Malaysia spent about 30 percent of its total government expenditures on wages and salaries in the 1970s and 1980s, Korea kept its personnel expenditures down to about 15 percent (dropping, in fact, from 15.8 percent in the 1970s to 14.5 percent in the 1980s) (IMF, Government Finance Statistics). As the next section will show, Korea's relative efficiency was accompanied by strong economic growth.

## IV.  Evaluation and Lessons

Evaluating the results of policies is fraught with difficulties. Even when a defined set of criteria exists, it is difficult to arrive at a definitive conclusion when effects are not measurable or, as is the case with Malaysia's tension between growth and equity, when there are policy tradeoffs. Another complicated problem is the issue of attribution—to what extent can the observed changes be attributed to a particular policy? And, finally, the issue of "what might have been" can only be guessed at, never known. Our approach is to use a macroeconomic framework and compare the actual conditions with average patterns, or with the patterns of neighboring countries, and sometimes to compare the results with the position before a policy went into effect.

Before evaluating the role of government in Malaysia, it is important to distinguish intervention from distortion. Intervention concerns a government's attempt to influence economic performance through strategic expenditures. Distortion has to do with a government arbitrarily masking the signals that its economic performance sends (for example, through price or currency

**TABLE 5.11.** Allocations and Actual Expenditures, Malaysia Plans (in M$ millions)

| Section | (A) Allocations 1971–75 | (B) Expenditures 1971–75 | (C) Difference A–B (%) | (D) Allocations 1976–80 | (E) Expenditures 1976–80 | (F) Difference D–E (%) |
|---|---|---|---|---|---|---|
| **Economic** | | | | | | |
| A. Agriculture and rural development | 2,278.82 | 1,793.53 | 21 | 6,464.31 | 4,672.41 | 28 |
| B. Mineral resources development | 0.69 | 0.56 | 19 | 21.29 | 15.70 | 26 |
| C. Commerce and industry | 1,658.62 | 1,433.20 | 14 | 4,255.98 | 3,246.21 | 24 |
| D. Transport | 1,562.06 | 1,233.92 | 21 | 4,462.98 | 3,246.21 | 24 |
| E. Communications | 155.42 | 174.93 | (13) | 1,252.71 | 1,152.08 | 8 |
| F. Energy and public utilities | 378.07 | 285.86 | 24 | 1,931.69 | 1,582.52 | 18 |
| G. Feasibility studies | 43.69 | 34.42 | 21 | 91.58 | 59.12 | 35 |
| **Social** | | | | | | |
| A. Education and training | 881.43 | 695.92 | 21 | 2,152.79 | 1,548.18 | 28 |
| B. Health and population | 218.82 | 183.25 | 16 | 529.42 | 307.40 | 42 |
| C. Information and broadcasting | 102.20 | 85.23 | 17 | 110.20 | 69.10 | 37 |
| D. Housing | 173.06 | 166.01 | 4 | 1,705.53 | 1,291.04 | 24 |
| E. Sewerage | 12.60 | 8.60 | 32 | 170.95 | 69.10 | 60 |
| F. Culture, youth, and sports | 18.98 | 12.90 | 32 | 93.66 | 54.64 | 42 |
| G. Local councils, welfare, and community services | 30.04 | 21.36 | 29 | 225.87 | 115.88 | 49 |
| H. Kampong and community development | 30.34 | 29.45 | 3 | 172.00 | 113.75 | 34 |
| I. Purchase of land | 84.02 | 84.02 | 0 | 334.21 | 66.90 | 80 |
| **Security** | | | | | | |
| A. Defense | 810.00 | 705.85 | 13 | 4,969.43 | 2,672.36 | 46 |
| B. Internal security | 321.33 | 316.13 | 2 | 1,339.98 | 857.44 | 36 |
| **Administration** | | | | | | |
| A. General services | 173.94 | 135.07 | 22 | 808.28 | 437.15 | 46 |
| B. Ministry of Foreign Affairs | 16.31 | 14.88 | 9 | 54.15 | 28.17 | 48 |

*Source:* Government of Malaysia (1970, 1973, 1976, 1984).

controls). In Malaysia, there has been a great deal of government intervention, particularly in the 1970s when the NEP boosted public expenditures and programs. But there has been relatively little distortion. Malaysia's ERP has always been low relative to that of other Asian countries. Also, the exchange rate has not been used as an explicit policy instrument. Malaysia's experience is, therefore, quite different from Korea's. Data compiled by Thomas and Wang (1992) show that, whereas Korea's price distortion index is higher than Malaysia's and its total expenditures much lower, as a proportion of GDP, its growth and total factor productivity growth (TFPG) have been higher. Japan also used distortion of the real value of the yen as an explicit economic policy. Clearly, no blueprint for development success exists. The issue comes down to efficiency. How well does government strategy fit the existing circumstances of the country and how efficient is government spending in implementing that strategy? These questions ultimately matter far more than the actual amount of spending.

*Equity.* When it comes to evaluating government intervention, the issue of equity is fairly straightforward. Given the events of 1969 (particularly with the memory of Indonesia's troubles in 1966 fresh in the mind), the Malaysian government had every reason to make equity a primary strategic goal. Despite the economic strains that the NEP caused, it also brought benefits. Poverty has been reduced. Although there is still an unacceptable regional disparity in income, all states have shown a marked decline in the incidence of poverty over the past 15 years (see table 5.12).[29] Of particular note has been the drastic reduction in hard-core poverty, down to 2 percent in Malaysia and Sarawak and 1.7 percent in Peninsular Malaysia. The incidence of poverty itself has been cut significantly in most regions; between 1976 and 1990, the incidence of poverty fell in Malaysia from 46.4 to 17.1 percent, and then even further to 13.5 percent by 1993 (Government of Malaysia 1991a, 1991b, 1993). In terms of annual income growth, the Bumiputera recorded the highest rate, at 6 percent, compared with 3.5 percent for the Chinese and 1.4 percent for the Indians during 1970–87. At the start of the NEP in 1970, the average Bumiputera household had substantially lower income per capita than did either Chinese or Indian households; both gaps had narrowed by 1987. Still, by 1987, the average Bumiputera (M$2,246) and the average Indian ($2,640) had below-average incomes ($2,761). The goal of 30 percent Bumiputera ownership was not reached, but Bumiputera wealth ownership did increase from 2 percent in 1970 to 20.3 percent in the early 1990s. This allowed the government to compromise, using PERNAS and PNB gradually to buy more wealth for the

---

29. This was due to both the redistributive policies of the government and the labor-intensive industrialization effort.

Bumiputeras through the rest of the century. The Gini coefficient, which was calculated at .42 in the late 1950s, rose to .50 by 1970 and continued to rise until 1976 (to .53). Since then it has shown a steady decline. In the late 1980s, it was nearly the same as it had been 30 years earlier.

Critics of NEP equity strategies can make a good case for themselves, however, in terms of the direct costs on growth and indirect costs on the incentive structures for both Bumiputeras and non-Bumiputeras. Although Bumiputeras have benefited most from Malaysia's successful growth, the average Bumiputera household has not caught up with the other ethnic groups, especially the Chinese. Also, despite heavy spending on education, Malaysia still lags behind other Asian countries when it comes to literacy.

The final judgment is inevitably a compromise. On equity, success *was* achieved. More importantly, the government created the *perception* that this issue was of prime importance, thereby fostering policies of the past six years to be implemented without undue social disturbance and cries of foul play. Still, in tackling the issue of equity, a government may choose between equality of opportunity and equality of outcome. Malaysia chose to focus on equality of outcome in the 1970s and 1980s, and this had many negative ramifications. It now seems that the government is ready to focus on equality of opportunity, while building up human skills so that all Malaysians will be able to take advantage of opportunity when it comes.

A look at Malaysia's total factor productivity growth for the entire period since independence shows Malaysia (2.2) operating at acceptable standards, albeit somewhat behind Hong Kong (4.7), Taiwan, China (3.9), and Korea

TABLE 5.12.    Incidence of Poverty by State, 1976 and 1990

| State | 1976 (%) | 1990 (%) |
|---|---|---|
| Johor | 29.0 | 10.1 |
| Kedah | 61.0 | 30.0 |
| Kelantan | 67.1 | 29.9 |
| Melaka | 32.4 | 12.4 |
| Negeri Sembilan | 33.0 | 9.5 |
| Pahang | 38.9 | 10.3 |
| Pulau Pinang | 32.4 | 8.9 |
| Perak | 43.0 | 19.3 |
| Perlis | 59.8 | 17.2 |
| Sabah | 58.3 | 34.3 |
| Sarawak | 56.5 | 21.0 |
| Selangor | 22.9 | 7.8 |
| Terengganu | 60.3 | 31.2 |
| Wilayah Persekutuan | 9.0 | 3.8 |

*Source:* Sulaiman 1992.

(2.4).[30] When we break this down further, however, the 1980s show themselves
to have been a most inefficient period. Table 5.13 gives some indication of the
economywide effects of public policies between the 1970s and the 1980s.

The problem seems to have been the inefficient use of capital. Based on
data computed by the Malaysian Institute of Economic Research, Malaysia's
incremental capital output ratio (ICOR), which measures the efficiency in the
utilization of capital, rose from 3.65 in 1971–80 to 7.21 in 1981–85 before
dropping to 4.7 in 1986–90. The ICOR computed for the public sector increased from an average of 6.75 in 1971–80 to 15.51 in 1981–85, while the
corresponding figures for private sector investment were 2.27 and 3.87.
Malaysia invested heavily but did not have the human capital to use it properly.

**TABLE 5.13.   Sources of Malaysia's Growth**

|  | 1971–75 | 1976–80 | 1981–85 | 1986–89 |
|---|---|---|---|---|
| GDP at factor cost | | | | |
| Output growth | 6.50 | 7.72 | 5.71 | 5.93 |
| Contribution by | | | | |
| Capital | 0.81 | 2.62 | 3.49 | 1.36 |
| Labor | 2.52 | 2.44 | 2.47 | 2.57 |
| (Labor quality) | 0.40 | 0.43 | 0.65 | 0.96 |
| Structural change | 0.09 | 0.10 | 0.11 | −0.07 |
| Residual (TFPG) | 3.03 | 2.56 | −0.35 | 1.76 |
| GDP (excluding government and housing) | | | | |
| Output growth | 5.94 | 7.84 | 5.22 | 5.86 |
| Contribution by | | | | |
| Capital | 0.94 | 3.49 | 4.04 | 1.41 |
| Labor | 1.98 | 2.15 | 2.49 | 2.76 |
| (Labor quality) | 0.44 | 0.41 | 0.65 | 0.89 |
| Structural change | 0.03 | 0.04 | 0.05 | 0.00 |
| Residual (TFPG) | 2.99 | 2.15 | −1.37 | 1.68 |
| GDP (excluding government, housing, and resource rents) | | | | |
| Output growth | 5.96 | 7.43 | 4.96 | 5.21 |
| Contribution by | | | | |
| Capital | 0.75 | 2.31 | 3.01 | 1.02 |
| Labor | 2.29 | 2.51 | 2.97 | 3.34 |
| (Labor quality) | 0.51 | 0.48 | 0.78 | 1.20 |
| Structural change | 0.03 | 0.05 | 0.06 | −0.01 |
| Residual (TFPG) | 2.88 | 2.06 | −1.08 | 0.86 |

*Source:* World Bank 1991.

30. Thomas and Wang 1992.

Monitoring and implementation capacity within the government failed to keep pace with the rapid growth of the public sector programs. Financial control and economic appraisal of projects suffered. The government spent heavily on "social infrastructure" and "commerce and industry," areas that make extensive demands on design and appraisal skills and on administrative capacity.

The drastic deterioration of efficiency in the 1980s was in direct contrast to what happened elsewhere. Hong Kong and Korea were both able to raise their TFPGs substantially from 1960 to 1970 (Hong Kong's grew from 2.4 in the 1950s to 4.3 in the 1960s, while Korea's rose from 2.0 to 4.1 during the same periods) and have managed to maintain fairly stable levels ever since. Taiwan, China has maintained a TFPG consistently above 3 since the 1950s. They also differed from Malaysia in their decisions to promote small industries and enterprises. Industrial parks and districts, for example, were set up in Taiwan for small capitalists and entrepreneurs. Consequently, between 1966 and 1976, the number of manufacturing firms in Taiwan increased by 150 percent, while the average size of individual enterprises increased by only 29 percent. Taiwan's success in this endeavor stands in stark contrast to Malaysia's experiment in heavy industry.

Lessons

We have emphasized that, although Malaysia's statistical results can be compared with those of other NIEs (for example, Taiwan, China and Korea), it is difficult to compare their developmental success because Malaysia's socioeconomic environment and objectives were so different. Malaysia's circumstances demanded a complex strategy and efficient implementation. It did not always succeed in this. However, it has provided some clear lessons from which others can learn.

The flexibility of Malaysia's government has been a crucial factor. Despite having a monolithic structure, the government has repeatedly shown itself to be willing to adapt to changing conditions. It has had to walk a tightrope of compromise between growth and equity concerns, and, while shifting conditions have caused it to shift its emphasis from time to time, it has resisted the temptation to drop either objective. It has even been willing to pronounce certain policies and their implementation outright failures. What success Malaysia is now enjoying is primarily due to this characteristic.

Beyond this virtue, Malaysia did have some initial advantages. Unlike Taiwan, China and Korea, it began with a wealth of natural resources. This enhanced its ability to draw in foreign investment and continued to provide a sense of economic stability. This gave it some freedom to experiment with other policies. If some of these experiments were unsuccessful (e.g., HICOM), others were tremendously successful (e.g., the oil palm and electronics industries).

Malaysia also benefited from institutional strength. Having a legal and political structure in place has paid dividends in terms of the speed with which strategy is converted to policy. Built-in checks, the openness of the economy, and low levels of distortion all helped to create strong institutions that have been able to achieve stability quickly. The successful structural transformation and the benefits Malaysia has reaped from developing its infrastructure are, in no small part, due to this institutional strength. The same can be said of the recent growth that has resulted from the liberalizing policies of the late 1980s. This strength does have a drawback, however, for it suggests that the policies of the NEP, however extravagant, should have been implemented with a greater degree of efficiency than we have seen. This points to the insufficient development of human resources in the 1960s and 1970s as a crucial reason for the economy's poor performance in the 1980s.

Finally, and most importantly, the Malaysian story highlights the importance of political sustainability. The country is engaged in a long-range plan, which it is pursuing with flexible short-term objectives. The benefits of this kind of thinking can be seen most clearly in the way the government has always insisted that economic performance be considered a means to social enrichment rather than an end in itself. Malaysia's development policies were, for a long time, considered sui generis. Today, with the end of the cold war, the Balkanization of nations, and the ensuing ethnic conflicts, the Malaysian experience seems highly relevant to the rest of the world.

## Recent Development

Since 1990, Malaysia has continued sustaining respectable growth rates (about 8 percent) while maintaining macroeconomic stability. The concern by 1995 was to keep growth in check to prevent overheating of the economy. By 1993, poverty had declined to 13.5 percent. The country is now being guided by the more growth-oriented National Development Policy, which replaced the New Economic Policy in 1991, with distribution policies focused more on eradicating the "hard-core" poor.

In tandem with Malaysia's growth, a number of internal and external developments have captured the minds of policymakers. These include:

(1) Sustaining foreign direct investment flows that were more that U.S.$4 billion in 1992, the highest for the developing world on a per capita basis, with much of it flowing into the export sector

(2) Encouraging Malaysian investments in other developing countries,

including regional "growth triangles," and integrating further within Southeast and East Asia in trade and investments

(3) Upgrading education, skills, labor productivity, and technological effort at all levels to overcome the effects of a labor shortage economy

(4) Investing in strategic alliances through government-linked companies to acquire strategic technological know-how

(5) Investing in environmental technologies and resources to overcome the negative environmental consequences of rapid growth and the urban onslaught

(6) Aligning short- and medium-term plans to reflect the objectives of Vision 2020, the desire to attain developed country status by the year 2020.


APPENDIX

**TABLE A5.1.  Mechanisms and Instruments of Shared Growth in Malaysia, Phase I: 1957–68**

| Sector | Objectives | Instruments | Institutions | Sources of Funds |
|---|---|---|---|---|
| Agriculture | Increase land ownership<br>Increase incomes | New land development<br>In situ development | RIDA<br>MARA | Federal government |
| Education (entrepreneurial training) | Create BCIC | Loans<br>Scholarships<br>Training<br>Consultancy | RIDA<br>MARA | Grants and loans from federal government |
| Finance | Create BCIC | Establishment of Bank Bumiputera (loans) | Central Bank | Federal government |
| Industry | Increase corporate ownership | Share reservation and acquisition | NIC<br>MITI | Federal government |
| | Promote small Bumiputera enterprises | Public support services | MARA | Grants and loans from federal government |

*Note:* BCIC = Bumiputera Commercial and Industrial Community
MARA = Council of Trust for the Development of Indigenous People
MITI = Ministry of International Trade and Industry
NIC = National Investment Company
RIDA = Rural Industrial Development Authority

**TABLE A5.2. Additional Mechanisms and Instruments of Shared Growth in Malaysia, Phase II: 1969–90**

| Sector | Objectives | Instruments | Institutions | Sources of Funds |
|---|---|---|---|---|
| Industry | Increase corporate ownership | Share acquisition investments<br>Joint ventures<br>Licensing (ICA) | PERNAS<br>PNB<br>HICOM<br>SEDCs<br>MITI/FIC | Grants and loans from the federal government |
|  | Create BCIC | Priority sector lending<br>support services for SMEs | Central Bank<br>MPE/MRD |  |
| Finance | Create BCIC | Loans<br>Equity investments | ABM<br>DBM | Federal government |
| Housing and urban development | Create BCIC<br>Ownership of urban properties | Investments<br>Investments | UDA<br>SEDCs | Federal government<br>Federal government |
| Agriculture and land development | Increase land ownership | New land development | SADCs<br>RISDA | Federal government |
|  | Increase incomes | In situ development | MARDI<br>LPN | Grants and loans from federal government |

(continued)

**TABLE A5.2.**—*(Continued)*

| Sector | Objectives | Instruments | Institutions | Sources of Funds |
|---|---|---|---|---|
| Transport | Create BCIC | Loans<br>Licensing | MARA<br>MPE | Grants and loans from federal government |
| Construction | Create BCIC | Loans<br>Licensing | MARA<br>Ministry of Works/MPE | Grants and loans from federal government |
| Government procurement | Create BCIC | Administrative guidelines | MOF | |

*Note:* ABM = Agricultural Bank of Malaysia
BCIC = Bumiputera Commercial and Industrial Community
DBM = Development Bank of Malaysia
FIC = Foreign Investment Committee
HICOM = Heavy Industries Corporation of Malaysia
LPN = National Paddy and Rice Authority
MARA = Council of Trust for the Development of Indigenous People
MARDI = Malaysian Agricultural Research and Development Institute
MITI = Ministry of International Trade and Industry
MOF = Ministry of Finance
MPE = Ministry of Public Expense
MRD = Ministry of Rural Development
PERNAS = Perbadanan Nasional Berhad (National Corporation)
PNB = Permodalan Nasional Berhad (National Equity Corporation)
RIDA = Rural Industrial Development Authority
RISDA = Rural Industrial Development Authority
SADS = State Agricultural Development Corporation
SEDC = State Economic Development Corporation
SME = Small and Medium Enterprises
UDA = Urban Development Authority

REFERENCES

Ahmad, Jaafar. 1990. "Review of Financial Infrastructure and Institutional Development." In *The Malaysian Economy: Policy and Structural Change*. Tokyo: Institute of Developing Economies.

Ahmad, Zakaria Haji. 1982. "The Political Structure." In *The Political Economy of Malaysia*, edited by E. K. Fisk and Osman Rani. Kuala Lumpur: Oxford University Press.

Ariff, Mohamed. 1991. "Managing Trade and Industry Reforms in Malaysia." In *Authority and Academic Scribblers*, edited by Sylvia Ostry. San Francisco: International Center for Economic Growth.

Asian Development Bank. 1990. "Malaysia: Study on Small and Medium Enterprises with Special Reference to Technology Development." Staff working papers, Manila. April.

Barro, Robert J., and Jong-Wha Lee. 1993. "International Comparisons of Educational Attainment." Paper presented at the World Bank Conference How Do National Policies Affect Long Run Growth? Washington, D.C.

Bowie, Alisdair. 1991. *Crossing the Industrial Divide: State, Society, and the Politics of Economic Transformation in Malaysia*. New York: Columbia University Press.

Bruton, Henry J., G. Abeysekera, N. Sanderatne, and Z. A. Yusof. 1992. *The Political Economy of Poverty, Equity, and Growth: Sri Lanka and Malaysia*. New York: World Bank and Oxford University Press.

Chee, Peng Lim. 1992. "Heavy Industrialization: The Malaysian Experience." Paper presented at the ISIS-HIID Conference on the Malaysian Economy, Kuala Lumpur, June.

Chenery, Hollis, Sherman Robinson, and Moshe Syrquin. 1985. *Industrialization and Growth*. Washington D.C.: World Bank and Oxford University Press.

Chenery, Hollis, and Moises Syrquin. 1975. *Patterns of Development 1950–70*. London: Oxford University Press.

Demery, D., and L. Demery. 1992. *Adjustment and Equity in Malaysia*. Paris: OECD Development Center.

Edwards, Chris. 1990. "Protection and Policy in the Malaysian Manufacturing Sector." In *Policy Assessment of the Malaysian Industrial Policy Study and the Industrial Master Plan*, vol. 3. Vienna: UNIDO.

*Far Eastern Economic Review.* 1988. "Malaysia's Controversial Finance Minister Proves an Able Economic Manager: The Diam Stewardship." September, 52–56.

Gale, Bruce. 1981. *Politics and Public Enterprise in Malaysia*. Kuala Lumpur: Eastern Universities Press.

Government of Malaysia. *Bank Negara. Annual Report*. Various Issues. Kuala Lumpur: Government Press.

———. *Quarterly Economic Bulletin*. Various issues. Kuala Lumpur: Government Press.

———. 1970. *The Second Malaysia Plan, 1970–1975*. Kuala Lumpur: Government Press.

———. 1973. *Mid-Term Review of the Second Malaysia Plan*. Kuala Lumpur: Government Press.

————. 1976. *The Third Malaysia Plan, 1976–1980*. Kuala Lumpur: Government Press.

————. 1984. *Malaysian Industrial Policies Studies Project: Final Report*. Kuala Lumpur: Government Press.

————. 1990. *Government of Malaysia Annual Report*. Kuala Lumpur: Government Press.

————. 1991a. *The Sixth Malaysia Plan, 1991–1995*. Kuala Lumpur: Government Press.

————. 1991b. *The Second Outline Perspective Plan, 1991–2000*. Kuala Lumpur: Government Press.

————. 1993. *Mid-Term Review of the Sixth Malaysia Plan, 1991–1995*. Kuala Lumpur: Government Press.

Government of Malaysia, Department of Statistics. 1988. *Handbook of Oil Palm, Cocoa, Coconut, and Tea Statistics*. Kuala Lumpur: Government Press.

Government of Malaysia, Economic Planning Unit. 1965. *The First Malaysia Plan*. Kuala Lumpur: Government Press.

Government of Malaysia, Ministry of Finance. Various years. *Economic Report*. Kuala Lumpur: Government Press.

Government of Malaysia, Ministry of Primary Industries. 1994. *Statistics on Commodities*. Kuala Lumpur: Government Press.

Hara, Fujio. 1991. "Malaysia's New Economic Policy and the Chinese Business Community." *The Developing Economies* 29 (4): 350–70.

HICOM [Heavy Industries Corporation of Malaysia]. 1984. *Annual Report*. Kuala Lumpur: HICOM.

Herbert, Clifford. 1993. "Role of Government in Mobilising National and Public Sector Savings." Paper presented at the First Malaysian National Conference on Savings, Kuala Lumpur, July.

Higgins, B. 1982. "Development Planning." In *The Political Economy of Malaysia,* edited by E. K. Fisk and Osman Rani. Kuala Lumpur: Oxford University Press.

Hoffman, Lutz. 1973. "Import Substitution–Export Expansion and Growth in an Open Developing Economy: The Case of West Malaysia." *Weltwirtschaftliches Archiv* 109 (3): 452–75.

Horii, Kenzo. 1991. "Disintegration of the Colonial Economic Legacies and Social Restructuring in Malaysia." *The Developing Economies* 29 (4): 281–313.

IMF [International Monetary Fund]. Various issues. *International Financial Statistics*. Washington, D.C.: IMF.

IMF [International Monetary Fund]. Various issues. *Government Finance Statistics*. Washington, D.C.: IMF.

Kharas, Homi, and Surjit Bhalla. "Growth and Equity in Malaysia: Policies and Consequences." Paper presented at the Eleventh Economic Convention on the Sixth Malaysia Plan: The Way Forward, Kuala Lumpur, September.

Klitgaard, Robert. 1991. *Adjusting to Reality: Beyond the State versus Market in Economic Development*. San Francisco: ICS Press.

Kuznets, Simon. 1966 *Modern Economic Growth: Rate Structure and Spread*. New Haven: Yale University Press.

————. 1971. *Economic Growth of Nations: Total Output and Production Structure*. Cambridge: Harvard University Press.

Lee, Kiong Hock. 1986. "The Structure and Causes of Malaysian Manufacturing Protection." In *The Political Economy of Manufacturing Protection: Experiences of ASEAN and Australia*, edited by C. Findlay and R. Garnaut. Sydney: Allen and Unwin.

Leipziger, Danny. 1992. "Korea: The Case of Effective Government-Led Development." Paper presented at the World Bank Workshop on the Role of Government and East Asian Success, Honolulu, November.

Linnerman, H., ed. 1987. *Export Oriented Industrialization in Developing Countries.* Singapore: Singapore University Press.

Machado, Kit. 1989–90. "Japanese Transnational Corporations in Malaysia's State Sponsored Heavy Industrialization Drive: HICOM Automobile and Steel Projects." *Pacific Affairs* 62 (4): 504–31.

Maisom Addullah. 1992. "Patterns of Total Factor Productivity Growth in Malaysian Manufacturing Industries, 1973–89." Paper presented at the ISIS-HIID Workshop on the Malaysian Economy, Kuala Lumpur.

Meerman, Jacob. 1979. *Public Expenditure in Malaysia: Who Benefits and Why.* Oxford: Oxford University Press.

Mehmet, Ozay, and Yip Yat Hoong. 1986. *Human Capital Formation in Malaysian Universities: A Socio-Economic Profile of 1983 Graduates.* Kuala Lumpur: University of Malaya Press.

Meyanathan, Saha Dhevan. 1989. "Adjustments in the Palm Oil Industry in Malaysia." In *Trade, Protectionism, and Industrial Adjustment in Vegetable Oils*, edited by Joseph Tan, Loong Hoe, and Shankar Sharma. Singapore: Institute of Southeast Asian Studies.

Meyanathan, Saha Dhevan, and Ismail Haron. 1987. "ASEAN Trade Co-operation: A Survey of the Issues," In *ASEAN at the Crossroads,* edited by Noordin Sopiee, Chew Lay See, and Lim Siang Jin. Kuala Lumpur: Institute of Strategic and International Studies.

Meyanathan, Saha Dhevan, and Ismail Muhd Salleh. 1993. "Industrial Structure and Small and Medium Enterprise Development in Malaysia." EDI working paper, Washington, D.C.

Meyanathan, Saha Dhevan, and G. Sivalingam. 1986. "Malaysia." In *Food Trade and Food Security in ASEAN and Australia,* edited by Anne Booth and Cristina C. David. Canberra: Australian National University Press.

Osman-Rani, H., J. K. Sundaram, and Ishak Shari. 1981. *Development in the Eighties with Emphasis on Malaysia.* Kuala Lumpur: University Kebangsaan Malaysia.

Power, J. H. 1971. "The Structure of Protection in West Malaysia." In *The Structure of Protection in Developing Countries*, edited by Bela Belassa. Baltimore: Johns Hopkins University Press.

Puthucheary, M. 1984. "The Political Economy of Malaysian Public Enterprises." In *Malaysian Economy at the Crossroads,* edited by Lim Lin Lean and Chee Peng Lim. Kuala Lumpur: Malaysian Economic Association.

Salleh, Ismail. 1992. *Dynamic Input-Output Analysis and Sectoral Projections of the Manufacturing Sector.* Vol. 12: *Electronics and Electrical Industry.* Geneva: United Nations Industrial Development Organization for the Government of Malaysia.

Salleh, Ismail, and H. Osman-Rani. 1991. *The Growth of the Public Sector in Malaysia.* Kuala Lumpur: Institute of Southeast Asian Studies.

Saruwatari, Keiko. 1991. "Malaysia's Localization Policy and Its Impact on British-Owned Enterprises." *The Developing Economies* 29 (4): 371–86.

Sieh-Lee, Mei Ling, and Chew Kwee Lyn. 1985. "Redistribution of Malaysia's Corporate Ownership." In *South East Asian Affairs, 1985.* Singapore: Institute of Southeast Asian Studies.

Snodgrass, D. R. 1980. *Inequality and Economic Development in Malaysia.* Kuala Lumpur: Oxford University Press.

Spinanger, Dean. *Regional Industrialization Policies in a Small Developing Country: A Case Study of West Malaysia.* Kiel: Institute for World Economics.

Sulaiman, Dato' Ali Abul Hassan bin. 1992. *Inter-Ministerial Coordination and the Role of the Prime Minister's Department in Malaysia.* Kuala Lumpur: Economic Planning Unit, Prime Minister's Department.

Syrquin, M., and H. B. Chenery. 1975. *Patterns of Development, 1950–1970.* London: Oxford University Press.

———. 1989. *Patterns of Development, 1950–1983.* World Bank Discussion Papers No. 41. Washington, D.C.: World Bank.

Tamin, Mokhtar. 1990. "Agriculture and Structural Transformation." In *The Malaysian Economy: Policy and Structural Change,* edited by H. Yokoyama. Tokyo: Institute of Developing Economies.

Tan, Jee Peng, and A. Mingat. 1992. *Education in Asia: A Comparative Study of Cost and Financing.* Washington, D.C.: World Bank.

Tan, Poo Chang. 1992. *Consequences of Population Change on Education.* Kuala Lumpur: Faculty of Economics and Administration, University of Malaya.

Thomas, Vinod, and Yan Wang. 1992. "Government Policies and Productivity Growth: Is East Asia an Exception?" Paper prepared for the World Bank Workshop on the Role of Government and East Asian Success, Honolulu, November.

Vijayakumari, K. 1992. "Industrial Restructuring and Its Implications for Employment, Wages, and Human Resource Development." Institute of Strategic and International Studies. Mimeo.

Wahab, Haji Yahya Abdul. 1987. "Investment Opportunities in Government Privatization Projects." Speech delivered at the Malaysian-Arab Trade and Investment Conference, Kuala Lumpur, November. Transcript.

Warr, Peter G. 1987. "Malaysia's Industrial Enclaves: Benefits and Costs." *The Developing Economies* 25 (1): 30–55.

———. 1989. "Export Processing Zones: The Economics of Enclave Manufacturing." *World Bank Research Observer* 4 (1): 65–88.

World Bank. 1955. *The Economic Development of Malaya.* Washington, D.C.: World Bank.

World Bank. 1985. *Malaysia: Development Strategies and Their Financing.* Washington, D.C.: World Bank.

———. 1990. *Malaysia: Matching Risks and Rewards in a Mixed Economy.* Washington, D.C.: World Bank.

———. 1991. *Growth, Poverty Alleviation, and Improved Income Distribution in Malaysia: Changing Focus of Government Policy Intervention.* Washington, D.C.: World Bank.

————. 1992a. *World Development Report: Development and the Environment.* Washington, D.C.: World Bank.

————. 1992b. *Malaysia: Fiscal Reforms for Stable Growth.* Washington, D.C.: World Bank.

Young, Kevin, Willem Bussink, and Parvez Hassan. 1980. *Malaysia: Growth and Equity in a Multiracial Society.* Baltimore: Johns Hopkins University Press.

Yusof, Zainal Aznam, et al. 1992. "The Impact of Financial Reform in Malaysia." Paper presented at the World Bank Conference on the Impact of Financial Reform, Washington, D.C., April 2–3.

CHAPTER 6

# Thailand: The Institutional and Political Underpinnings of Growth

*Scott R. Christensen, David Dollar, Ammar Siamwalla, and Pakorn Vichyanond*

## I.  Introduction

Rapid economic growth in East Asia has sparked a great debate. The role of the state is the central issue in that debate. Proponents of a minimalist state argue that East Asian governments have succeeded because they have confined themselves to the maintenance of macroeconomic equilibrium, the provision of basic physical and social infrastructure, and boosting education. In this view the state has an important role but one confined largely to establishing the conditions for the efficient operation of markets (Krueger 1979; Kuznets 1977).

Proponents of the activist state, on the other hand, argue that some East Asian countries have succeeded because their governments have intervened extensively in the economy.[1] These interventions, particularly in the credit and foreign exchange markets, have got prices deliberately wrong in order to favor specific industries and firms. The policies are effective because they are supplemented by disciplinary mechanisms. Macroeconomic equilibrium has been maintained in these countries, but growth has always taken precedence. The authorities have sometimes gone against the canons of macroeconomic propriety, and it was growth that eventually rescued them from their problems.

The experience of Thailand may be of some help in this debate. Here is another East Asian economy that has achieved excellent economic growth. Although not as spectacular as that of Japan, Korea, and Taiwan (China), Thai growth has been remarkably steady. Even in the worst years, in the mid-1980s, per capita incomes continued to grow. But the Thai case is different: neither the minimalist nor the activist analysis accurately describes Thailand's economic policy and state interventions. This essay deals with the role of the

---

1. In this paragraph we have followed the most articulate presentation of the activist view, that in Amsden 1989. The book maintains that the same story applies not only to Korea but to Japan and Taiwan (China) as well. See also Johnson 1982 and Wade 1990.

state in fostering growth and considers the issues of the effectiveness of state intervention and how far the model has been copied (from, say, South Korea or Japan).

The paper advances two main arguments. First, Thai economic policy has been most effective in maintaining a macroeconomic environment conducive to trade, investment, and the growth of private firms. It has been least effective in identifying and implementing sectoral objectives. Thai sectoral policies have not been guided by a strategy of picking winners and have often been marked by patronage and rent seeking. And, second, we argue that an activist state may require certain institutional skills that on many measures have eluded Thai economic policy making, at least on the sectoral side. Macroeconomic stability, combined with the dynamism of private firms (and particularly of bankers), has helped overcome certain weaknesses on that side. But these mitigating factors may not be enough if the government wants to guide the economy into industrial deepening or technological upgrading.

The paper is organized as follows. Section II reviews Thailand's macroeconomic policy and performance. Section III examines sectoral policies and their results. Section IV looks at the institutions of economic policy making in Thailand, and section V analyzes the political economy of macroeconomic decision making. The final section provides some conclusions about the Thai government's success in promoting growth and industrialization.

## II.  Overview of Thailand's Development

Thailand has had one of the fastest growing economies in the world in recent years. However, its growth has been striking for much longer. During 1955–88, only four developing economies achieved a higher growth rate of per capita GDP than Thailand's at 3.9 percent a year: these were Brazil and Malaysia (slightly faster) and Taiwan (China) and Korea (much faster).[2] Thailand's success is more likely to be relevant to the typical developing economy because Korea and Taiwan (China) had some distinctive features that are not likely to be replicated.[3]

The most notable feature of Thailand's record is macroeconomic stability. Sound macroeconomic policies, combined with a relatively open regime for foreign trade and investment, have resulted in sustained and rapid growth. Investment in primary education has been helpful, but investment in secondary

---

2. This comparison ignores small economies and city-states such as Hong Kong and Singapore. Growth rates were calculated from real per capita GDP figures derived from the International Comparison of Prices (ICP) Project, release 5.

3. A long period of Japanese colonialism, extraordinary amounts of U.S. aid, and a Confucian culture that emphasizes education are three examples of characteristics that distinguish Korea and Taiwan (China) from other developing economies.

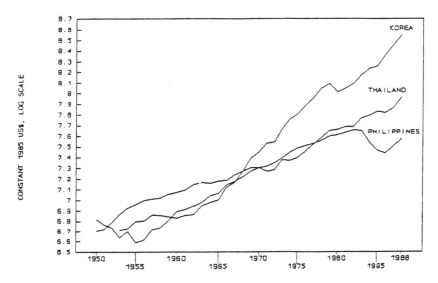

**Fig. 6.1.   Real per capita GDP in Thailand, Korea, and the Philippines,
1950–88**

education has been weak, especially compared with that of the successful
newly industrialized economies (NIEs). This weakness has been the main
factor holding the economy back from even faster growth.

Thailand's growth has brought a rapid decline in absolute poverty. It
has also been associated with an increase in inequality. Development has been
concentrated sectorally (in industry rather than in agriculture) and geogra-
phically (in Bangkok and its environs). Thus, the story of Thailand's postwar development is largely one of success, though the imbalances show that
the benefits of development have not been spread as widely as they might
have been.

## Sources of Growth

The Thai economy did not do well in the years immediately following World
War II, as the country retained a policy of heavy state involvement that dated
from the 1930s. Real per capita GDP declined between 1950 and 1955 (fig.
6.1). However, beginning in the mid-1950s, Thailand switched to an emphasis
on private sector development and an outward orientation. Since that shift in
strategy, the economy has grown steadily and rapidly. Since 1955, the middling
but steady performance of the Thai economy has enabled it now
to have an income level higher than that of the Philippines, considered a likely

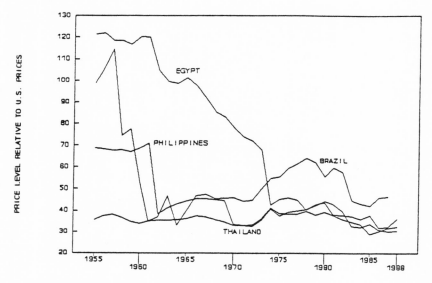

**Fig. 6.2. Price levels in Thailand and other developing countries, 1955–88**

star in the 1950s. On the other hand, it is now at a much lower level of development than is Korea, surely the least promising economy in Asia in the 1950s but since then a stellar performer.

In terms of conventional growth theory, Thailand's rapid development is something of an anomaly. Investment averaged only 14 percent of GDP during 1955–88, well below the investment rate in Korea or the Philippines.[4] The new empirical growth literature, on the other hand, sheds considerable light on Thailand's success. It has identified three variables that are highly correlated with per capita growth in developing economies: school enrollment rates, measures of outward orientation, and macroeconomic stability.[5]

Macroeconomic stability is one of Thailand's strongest features. A good summary measure is the price level in Thailand, measured in U.S. dollars (see fig. 6.2), in essence, the real exchange rate. Certainly some variation in the real exchange rate is necessary and desirable as the external environment changes and development proceeds. But no country needs a roller-coaster, which is what most developing economies have experienced. Thailand stands out as an economy whose real exchange rate has been low and stable continuously since 1955.

---

4. This investment figure is from the unpublished ICP release 5 (see note 2). Comparable figures for the Philippines and Korea are 18.7 and 22.6 percent, respectively.

5. See, for example, Barro 1991 or Dollar 1992a.

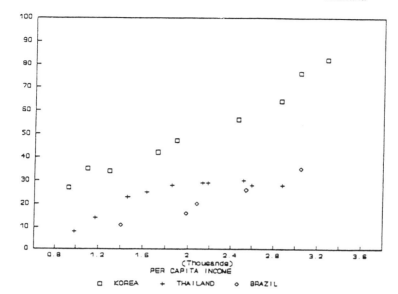

**Fig. 6.3. Secondary school enrollment in Thailand, Korea, and Brazil**

That stability is also a sign that Thailand is a relatively outward-oriented economy.[6] Other potential measures of openness have been proposed in the literature, and most of them show that Thailand is indeed relatively open[7]— only "relatively," however, since Thailand has heavily protected a few capital-intensive industries. The pattern of selective protection is not untypical, even among developing countries that are measured empirically to be relatively open. In the case of Korea, for example, agriculture has been largely protected.

Education is an area where Thailand's performance is more complex. In cross-country studies, the primary school enrollment rate in 1960 is a variable that has been found to be highly correlated with economic growth in subsequent years. Thailand's 1960 rate of 83 percent was high relative to that of other countries in its income group. On the other hand, Thailand does not have a particularly high enrollment rate in secondary schools, a variable that also has a significant impact on growth. Thailand's rate in 1960 was 13 percent, well behind those of Korea (27 percent) and the Philippines (26 percent) and at about the same level as that of Brazil (11 percent). More importantly, Thailand's secondary school enrollment rate has not increased much over time (see fig. 6.3).

6. On the basis of its low price level, Dollar (1992b) categorizes Thailand as "very outward oriented."

7. See the discussion in Bhattacharya and Linn 1988 or the *World Development Report, 1987,* (World Bank 1987).

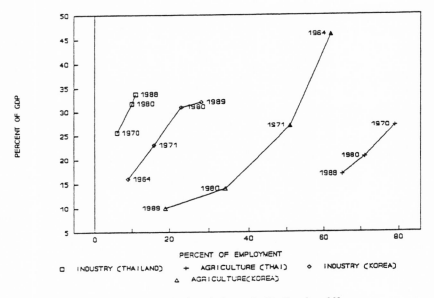

**Fig. 6.4.   Industry and agricultural shares in Thailand and Korea**

## Effects of Growth

Rapid economic growth has transformed Thailand over the past few decades. But even as absolute poverty has declined, some income gaps have widened. Today, the Bangkok region, with 16 percent of the population, produces about one-half of GDP and nearly two-thirds of industrial output. This contrast is linked to another one: between industry and services, on the one hand, and agriculture on the other. Industry's share of GDP increased steadily from about one-quarter in 1970 to more than one-third in 1988. But one of the startling characteristics of Thailand, in contrast to, say, Korea, is that this transformation of production has *not* been associated with a comparable shift in employment (see fig. 6.4). The employment share of industry grew by only a few percentage points during this period. In 1988, nearly 70 percent of the labor force was still in agriculture, producing only 17 percent of GDP, although it must be pointed out that the size of the labor force in agriculture is overestimated, probably, as many who claim to be in the agricultural labor force obtain a significant proportion of their incomes from working outside their farms in nonagricultural activities. Nonetheless, Thailand has always had a more favorable land-labor ratio than other Asian countries, creating a weaker incentive to leave agriculture. Indeed, the area of cultivated land actually increased by nearly 50 percent between 1970 and 1980, so that the land-labor ratio was rising, contrary to the experiences in most developing countries.[8] One would therefore expect to find a larger share of the labor force in agriculture in Thailand than in the NIEs.

The uneven development of different regions and sectors in Thailand has resulted in a deterioration in the household distribution of income (table 6.1). The share of income going to the richest 20 percent of the households rose from 49 percent in the mid-1970s to 56 percent in the mid-1980s. The Gini co-efficient of inequality has shown a similar trend.

Despite the increase in inequality, the number of households living below the poverty line fell from nearly 60 percent of the total in the early 1960s to 30 percent in the mid-1970s and 24 percent in the mid-1980s. Urban poverty de-clined particularly sharply, so that poverty in Thailand today is largely a rural phenomenon, concentrated in the north and northeast.[9]

## III.   Sectoral Interventions

The government has pursued a fairly activist policy of intervening to pro-mote particular industries and even firms. The main instruments of industrial policy have been the trade regime and the Board of Investment (BOI), which have combined to favor large industry. In the 1960s and 1970s, they supported capital-intensive, import-substituting activities. In the 1980s, they shifted in

TABLE 6.1.   Thailand: Income Shares by Quintile, Selected Years (percentage of total income)

| Quintile | 1975–76 | 1980–81 | 1985–86 | 1988–89 |
|---|---|---|---|---|
| First | 49.26 | 51.47 | 55.63 | 54.98 |
| Highest top 10% | 33.40 | 35.44 | 39.15 | 37.58 |
| Second top 10% | 15.86 | 16.04 | 16.48 | 17.12 |
| Second | 20.96 | 20.64 | 19.86 | 20.3 |
| Third | 14.00 | 13.38 | 12.09 | 12.20 |
| Fourth | 9.73 | 9.10 | 7.87 | 7.98 |
| Fifth | 6.05 | 5.41 | 4.55 | 4.51 |
| Second bottom 10% | 3.62 | 3.28 | 2.75 | 2.74 |
| Lowest bottom 10% | 2.43 | 2.13 | 1.80 | 1.76 |
| Total share | 100.00 | 100.00 | 100.00 | 100.00 |
| Gini coefficient | .0426 | .453 | .500 | .478 |
| Variance of logarithm of income | .530 | .602 | .737 | .689 |

*Source:* Hutaserani (1990) and Jitsuchon (1991).

8. Siamwalla (1991) analyzes the impact of this land expansion on Thailand's develop-ment path.
9. Hutaserani 1990.

favor of exporters but were still biased toward large-scale producers. But there is little reason to believe that these interventions have not been important in explaining Thailand's economic success, as we shall demonstrate.

## Trade

The trade regime has been one of the main tools of Thai industrial policy. Before the mid-1950s, it was extremely restrictive. Rice exports were controlled by a state monopoly, exporting was discouraged by significant export taxes, and there was a system of multiple exchange rates. As part of the policy shift in the mid-1950s, the government liberalized the trade regime by unifying the exchange rate in 1955 and removing the government rice export monopoly.[10]

Even after these reforms, Thailand still had substantial import protection for certain industries. As of the mid-1960s, the country had moderate levels of effective protection for finished consumer goods. Their nominal tariffs were 25 to 30 percent ad valorem, whereas tariffs on machinery and materials tended to be 15 to 20 percent. In the 1970s, Thailand increased effective protection for finished consumer goods, raising their nominal tariffs to the 30 to 55 percent range while maintaining machinery tariffs at low levels. The main protected industries were textiles, automobiles, and pharmaceuticals.[11]

The protection for automobile assembly was particularly strong. At times, vehicle imports were banned or subject to domestic content rules. In the late 1980s, even after some easing of protection, the effective protection rate for motor vehicles was still around 70 percent. Textiles also continued to receive high protection.[12]

In general, the most heavily protected industries were capital-intensive manufactures. This policy discriminated against agriculture and labor-intensive manufactures, the sectors in which the country had static comparative advantage in the 1960s and 1970s. There was also discrimination against agriculture in the form of export taxes, notably for rice. It seems very likely that this regime had a significant effect on the *pattern of industrialization* in Thailand. On the basis of comparative advantage, one would have expected the leading sectors in Thailand to be agriculture, related processing industries, and labor-intensive manufactures.

The effect of these incentives can be seen in the distribution of value added among manufacturing industries (table 6.2). In 1970, manufacturing value added was concentrated in food processing and traditional labor-intensive activities, though even at that point Thailand had a surprisingly large share of its

10. See Jitsuchon 1991 for a discussion of trade policy in this period.
11. Sibunruang 1986.
12. Bhattacharya and Linn (1988).

value added in heavy industries. The import-substituting strategy was especially strong during the 1970s, and manufacturing value added shifted toward heavy industries (with the share rising from 31.9 percent in 1970 to 42.6 percent in 1979). This policy no doubt helps to explain why industry's share of GDP rose substantially in the 1970s while industry's share of the labor force showed little increase.

In 1981, Thailand's trade policy began to promote exports more explicitly. The second oil shock exposed underlying weaknesses in the country's balance of payments, resulting from the import-substituting policies of the 1970s. Remaining export taxes were reduced, and the exchange rate was devalued by 8.7 percent. The government also made an effort to rationalize tariffs. In 1982, it cut the top rate from 100 to 60 percent and also reduced the average rate. However, budgetary problems soon led to the imposition of an import surcharge, undermining the effort to reduce average protection. By the mid-1980s, effec-

**TABLE 6.2.   Thailand: Gross Domestic Product Originating from Manufacturing at Current Market Prices (millions of baht)**

|  | 1970 | % | 1979 | % | 1986 | % |
|---|---|---|---|---|---|---|
| Heavy Industries |  | 31.9 |  | 42.6 |  | 36.7 |
| Chemical and chemical products | 845 | 3.6 | 3,881 | 3.3 | 8,787 | 3.4 |
| Petroleum refineries and petroleum products | 1,331 | 5.7 | 9,021 | 7.7 | 25,677 | 10.0 |
| Rubber and plastic products | 679 | 2.9 | 3,843 | 3.3 | 6,172 | 2.4 |
| Nonmetallic mineral products | 1,007 | 4.3 | 4,473 | 3.8 | 10,289 | 4.0 |
| Basic metal industries | 6,317 | 2.7 | 3,528 | 3.0 | 3,202 | 1.3 |
| Transport equipment | 1,221 | 5.2 | 9,884 | 8.4 | 12,470 | 4.9 |
| Textiles | 1,759 | 7.5 | 15,390 | 13.1 | 27,326 | 10.7 |
| High-Skill Labor-Intensive Industries |  | 9.7 |  | 11.1 |  | 13.8 |
| Fabricated metal products | 756 | 3.2 | 3,509 | 3.0 | 6,552 | 2.6 |
| Machinery | 733 | 3.1 | 2,978 | 2.5 | 6,095 | 2.4 |
| Electrical machinery and supplies | 442 | 1.9 | 2,869 | 2.4 | 7,656 | 3.0 |
| Other manufacturing industries | 554 | 1.5 | 3,815 | 3.2 | 14,862 | 5.8 |
| Traditional Light Industries |  | 19.2 |  | 20.1 |  | 23.3 |
| Wearing apparel except footwear | 2,126 | 9.0 | 10,524 | 8.9 | 35,513 | 13.9 |
| Leather, leather products, and footwear | 538 | 2.3 | 2,077 | 1.8 | 7,288 | 2.9 |
| Wood and wood products | 654 | 2.8 | 5,671 | 4.8 | 5,432 | 2.1 |
| Furniture and fixtures | 484 | 2.1 | 2,184 | 1.9 | 3,744 | 1.5 |
| Paper and paper products | 367 | 1.6 | 1,686 | 1.4 | 3,921 | 1.5 |
| Printing, publishing, and allied industries | 336 | 1.4 | 1,508 | 1.3 | 3,668 | 1.4 |
| Food and Related Industries |  | 39.3 |  | 26.2 |  | 26.0 |
| Food | 4,681 | 19.9 | 14,294 | 12.2 | 33,258 | 13.0 |
| Beverages | 2,820 | 12.0 | 10,123 | 8.6 | 20,981 | 8.2 |
| Tobacco | 1,733 | 7.4 | 6,353 | 5.4 | 12,136 | 4.8 |
| Total value added | 23,503 |  | 117,611 |  | 255,029 |  |

*Source:*  Bank of Thailand and National Statistical office, various years.

tive protection for manufacturing in Thailand (52 percent) was still substantially higher than in other East Asian economies such as Korea (28 percent), Malaysia (23 percent), and the Philippines (23 percent).[13]

Some of the bias toward heavy industries was corrected in the 1980s, partly because of these modest changes in tariffs and more importantly because of the Board of Investment (discussed in the next section). The value-added shares of heavily protected industries such as transport equipment and textiles declined between 1979 and 1986. Overall, the weight of heavy industries in manufacturing value added decreased from 42.6 to 36.7 percent. The industries whose shares expanded were labor intensive: traditional products such as garments as well as new, higher-skill areas such as electronics and jewelry. Still, as of 1988, this policy shift had done little to raise the low employment share of industry.

Only in the past few years has Thailand done much to liberalize manufactured imports. In 1990, the government cut tariffs on capital goods used in manufacturing from 20 to 5 percent. It followed this in 1991 with large reductions in tariffs on automobiles and computers. In 1992, the government reduced duties on chemicals, textiles, iron, aluminum, and glass.

## The Board of Investment

The other powerful instrument of industrial policy in Thailand has been the Board of Investment. It was established in 1960 to implement a new investment promotion act. Its activities were initially carefully circumscribed; laws dictated which industrial activities it should promote, and each promotion certificate was subject to cabinet approval.[14] BOI incentives included a holiday on income tax (initially for two years). However, the BOI's most significant power was over imports. It could exempt particular firms or industries from import duties on machinery, components, and raw materials as well as imposing bans and surcharges on competing imports.

In 1962, the Promotion of Industrial Investment Act gave BOI more flexibility and independence. It allowed BOI itself to issue promotion certificates and to add to the list of eligible activities. The 1962 act also created three basic groups of promoted activities, with different incentives based on their perceived importance to the economy. Full exemption was granted to a range of mostly heavy industries, including basic metals, machinery, and chemicals. A second group, mostly involved in assembly (i.e., of motor vehicles, agricultural machinery, or electrical appliances), received half-exemption, and another (including agricultural processing industries, textiles, and pharmaceuticals) got one-third exemption.

---

13. Ibid., 1988.
14. This description of the evolution of BOI policy is based on Sibunruang 1986.

There were various adjustments to the investment promotion laws in the 1970s, but the basic thrust remained: to promote capital-intensive industrialization. This was capital intensive in two senses of the phrase: first, the industries promoted tended to be ones that employed a lot of capital per worker, and, second, the strong incentive to import machinery favored capital-intensive techniques within each industry.

Almost all promotional certificates awarded in the 1960s went to firms producing for the home market. Apart from that general principle, however, "[n]o really clear and explicit criteria were developed to form the basis for a decision" to promote individual firms (Ingram 1971, 289). The BOI never provided a coherent import-substitution philosophy, and its practices were often inconsistent. For instance, it never developed performance criteria to judge whether the firms fulfilled any stated policy objective and rarely evaluated the firms it promoted. There is evidence that the import-substituting policies did not succeed in "picking winners." Wiboonchutikula's study of total factor productivity (TFP) growth in Thai manufacturing found that TFP growth has been low in import-competing sectors and relatively higher in export industries.

When Thailand started to favor export promotion in the early 1980s, the BOI was called upon to play a different role. A major study of its work was carried out under a UNDP/IBRD technical assistance project, and it recommended substantial reforms. In January 1983, the BOI announced its criteria in approving investment promotion and providing tax privileges. This was the first time that clear criteria for the approval of projects were published. In addition, some of the specific characteristics favored—generation of foreign exchange through exporting, employment creation, utilization of local raw materials, and industrial decentralization—represented a shift in the thrust of Thai industrial policy.

## Export Promotion Policies

Even as it switched to export promotion, the Thai government stressed that its efforts were not intended to distort markets but to reinforce market competition.

The most important change in incentives came through the real exchange rate. Throughout the 1960s and 1970s, the Thai baht had been tied to the U.S. dollar, with only minor adjustments from time to time. This passive policy served Thailand well while the Bretton Woods system of fixed exchange rates was in effect. However, problems arose once the major currencies began to float. Linking the baht to the dollar led to a rise in the real effective exchange rate in the early 1980s, despite the 8.7 percent devaluation against the dollar in 1981. The big change in Thailand's real exchange rate came in 1984 when the Bank of Thailand started tying the currency to a basket of major currencies, not just the U.S. dollar, preceded by an immediate 14.8 percent devaluation of the nominal exchange rate against the dollar. Furthermore, the new policy gave the government more flexibility, as the basket to which the baht was tied was not precisely defined. As the U.S. dollar fell against major East Asian currencies in the second half of the 1980s, the Thai government allowed the dollar weight in the basket to increase, so that the baht was devalued significantly against the Japanese yen and the new Taiwan dollar.[15] The real effective exchange rate depreciated by nearly 30 percent between 1983 and 1991.[16]

These developments resulted in a large increase in the incentive to export from Thailand, spurring Thai firms to export and also attracting direct foreign investment from the economies whose currencies had appreciated. Other Thai policies supported the export drive:

Tax privileges and refunds
Zoning
Electricity cost reduction
Refinancing facilities
Marketing assistance
International trading firms
Quality control

The BOI gave priority to export projects in addition to ones using local input, projects employing a large labor force, and those located outside the Bangkok area. It granted numerous tax exemptions to export-oriented projects, including duties and business taxes on imported raw materials or components or re-exported items, business taxes on domestic input, export duties, and certain deductions from taxable corporate income. Roughly half of the projects that the BOI promoted in the 1980s were export oriented.

Even firms that were not promoted by BOI could claim similar tax refunds on their export activities, and their claims were dealt with by the Customs Department in conjunction with Fiscal Policy Office. Under these schemes, exporters were entitled to receive rebates on customs duties, business taxes, municipal taxes, excise taxes, and other taxes previously collected on particular inputs.

The government also streamlined customs procedures and abolished unnecessary regulations so that exporters were able to expedite their processing and shipments. It established export processing zones (EPZs) and bonded warehouses. Firms in EPZs enjoyed privileges such as exemption from import duties, export duties, and business taxes. Foreign investors were permitted to own land, to bring in necessary technicians or experts, and to remit much of

---

15. Jitsuchon 1991.
16. This is calculated from the International Monetary Fund's (IMF) index of real effective exchange rates.

their foreign exchange. EPZ factories also benefited from good transportation and telecommunications, and they could get a 20 percent reduction in their electricity bills as long as they were qualified for the Fiscal Policy Office's tax rebate scheme. Each EPZ had bonded warehouses for storing duty-free imported inputs destined for export production. These warehouses helped exporters to limit the burden of customs duties and storage expenses. Once again, however, the deregulation within EPZs tended to assist large firms while leaving the incentive regime for small firms quite distorted.

In addition to tax privileges, exporters received concessionary credits. The central bank has been extending refinancing facilities (RFs) to certain economic sectors (exports, industry, and agriculture) since 1956. Typically, an eligible entrepreneur wishing to obtain a cheap loan can issue a promissory note to be discounted by his bank and rediscounted by the central bank, both at below-market rates. Some 95 percent of RFs were absorbed by exporters.

The Thai government also provided exporters with marketing assistance, by organizing international trade exhibitions, setting up trade missions, establishing commercial and trade offices abroad, and lobbying. Thailand sought to emulate the role that international trading firms have played in the Japanese export drive. Such firms were given special privileges from the BOI on condition that their performance was satisfactory. This policy, however, did not succeed in creating strong trading firms.

The export drive raised several noteworthy points. First, quite a few of the measures—and particularly the most critical one, the refund of taxes on inputs—corrected an existing distortion. Second, these measures, even though technically they were sectoral in nature, were spearheaded by the macroeconomic technocrats, and many of them involved the Ministry of Finance. With the exception of the Ministry of Commerce, the sectoral ministries were bypassed entirely.

As a result of these new policies, Thailand's exports of labor-intensive manufactures increased rapidly. Between 1970 and 1979, light manufactures increased from 1.4 percent of Thailand's exports to 12.8 percent. By 1986, their share had soared to 30.8 percent of total exports. The main industries involved were clothing, footwear, artificial flowers, jewelry, and integrated circuits (see table 6.3).

Although the BOI's new emphasis on export promotion supported the export drive, its importance should not be exaggerated. In general, BOI has been a follower not a leader. For example, the BOI started to favor electronics in the early 1980s, yet the industry did not make much progress. It was not until the mid-1980s, with the large devaluation in the real exchange rate, that electronics really took off. In 1987, the BOI approved more electronics promotions, with increased investments, than in all its 27 years of existence.[17] There are other sectors that the BOI did little to promote until they were already very successful: canned tuna, canned fruit, and jewelry are good examples. In recent years the importance of the BOI in sectoral policies has diminished as the tariffs and taxes upon which its incentives were based have been reduced. Its role since 1992 has shifted to spreading Thai industry out of Bangkok into the provinces. Generous privileges (e.g., an eight-year income tax holiday) are now given to firms that locate their factories in the outlying provinces, while the list of industries to be located in Bangkok that can receive BOI privileges is now sharply curtailed.

While the trend in the 1980s was toward general export promotion, that decade also witnessed the Eastern Seaboard Program. This program was primarily a regional development scheme, but the original conception involved a targeted sectoral policy to develop heavy industry as well. The program was organized around the newly discovered natural gas supply in the Gulf of Thailand. The initial plan was to develop a national fertilizer complex, steel mills, gas and oil processing, and petrochemicals (all import substituting) as well as export-oriented light manufactures. At the end of the day, many of the heavy projects were abandoned because the technocrats resolved that the projects would overextend the financial resources of the government. In particular,

TABLE 6.3.  Distribution of Thailand's Exports, 1970, 1979, and 1986 (percentage)

|  | 1970 | 1979 | 1986 |
|---|---|---|---|
| Heavy Manufactures | 13.6 | 17.6 | 10.4 |
| Iron and steel | 0.3 | 0.4 | 0.9 |
| Nonferrous metals | 11.8 | 9.6 | 1.6 |
| Chemicals and plastics | 0.2 | 0.7 | 1.6 |
| Transportation equipment | 0.0 | 0.2 | 0.4 |
| Textiles | 1.3 | 6.7 | 5.9 |
| High-skill, light manufactures | 0.8 | 6.4 | 17.1 |
| Machinery | 0.1 | 0.3 | 2.1 |
| Electrical machinery | 0.1 | 3.3 | 8.3 |
| Metal products | 0.2 | 0.6 | 0.7 |
| Other industries | 0.4 | 2.2 | 6.0 |
| Traditional light manufactures | 0.6 | 6.4 | 13.7 |
| Wood products, paper | 0.3 | 1.4 | 1.4 |
| Rubber products | 0.1 | 0.3 | 0.7 |
| Leather and leather products | 0.1 | 0.4 | 0.8 |
| Clothing, footwear | 0.1 | 4.3 | 10.8 |
| Primary products | 83.3 | 66.8 | 54.4 |

*Source:* United Nations, various years.

17.  Chitayarangsan 1990, 73.

the steel mills and fertilizer complex never materialized. The export-oriented factories built on the industrial estates have done well, so that the Eastern Seaboard Program has been successful as a regional development scheme and has contributed to the 1980s export boom. The abortive attempt to target the development of heavy industrial complexes, on the other hand, was a failure. The facilities that were built, notably in petrochemicals, survive today because of continuing import protection but have not been major contributors to the country's industrial development.

In general, while the government provided generous incentives for industry in the 1980s, particularly for exports, the economy probably would have developed even more successfully with a regime geared toward broad-based liberalization of manufactured imports rather than for the government to continue with restrictions combined with other countervailing policies to neutralize them. The flaw in the Thai system was that it kept so many small and medium firms out of exporting or supplying exporters. For a large firm that could get BOI promotional benefits, there was a strong incentive to export in the 1980s. For smaller firms, on the other hand, the incentive largely remained to produce for the domestic market. This combination resulted in Thailand becoming a significant exporter of manufactures. However, labor-intensive manufacturing has not had the same effect on production and employment that it has had in the NIEs.

Given Thailand's natural comparative advantage in agriculture arising out of the favorable land-labor ratio, the government, by altering relative prices from those prevailing in international markets, discriminated against agriculture and labor-intensive manufacturing in favor of heavy industry. A neutral policy could have boosted agricultural productivity by raising agricultural prices. Stronger development of secondary education in rural areas also would have helped by increasing the ability of farmers to absorb new information and technologies and equipping other rural dwellers to move off the land and into industry and services. To complement this, the government could have invested more in physical infrastructure in rural areas.

Financial Policies

Thailand has a relatively well-developed financial system. Broad money (M2) is about two-thirds of GDP in Thailand, a ratio typical of a developed country and far higher than the norm for a country at Thailand's level of income. By and large, the government has not relied much on credit control and directions. The exception is some credit directed toward agriculture and small-scale industry—ironically, the same sectors discriminated against by the combined effect of the trade regime and the BOI's activities. However, the real thrust of financial policies has come via interest rates and the regulation of the financial system. By these methods, the government has helped the development of strong commercial banking.[18]

Commercial banks are the dominant financial institutions, accounting for 59 percent of all financial assets in 1988. Five large private banks are particularly prominent; together they made 65 percent of all commercial bank loans in 1988. Their growth has been nurtured by the government's policy of setting ceilings on both deposit and lending rates. These ceilings have almost always been well above the rate of inflation, thus avoiding the severe distortions common in many developing countries. On the deposit side, for example, ceilings in the 1980s were in the 10 to 13 percent range, while inflation was very low. As a result, actual deposit rates bumped up against the ceiling only very rarely.

The ceilings have probably had more effect on the lending side. The prime lending rate of commercial banks was normally well below the lending ceiling. But commercial banks typically make loans to less creditworthy customers at rates well above the prime. Thus, it is likely that some of these customers have been denied a loan by the interest rate ceilings. Even so, the commercial banks increased their dominance of the Thai financial system during the 1970s and 1980s, which suggests that regulation did not hamper their ability to compete. Early in the 1990s, the government further liberalized the financial system by fully deregulating interest rates.

Other aspects of regulation worked in favor of the banks. There were, for example, no markets for commercial paper or corporate bonds. One reason for this lacuna was restrictions on the issuance of debt by companies whose shares are not traded on the stock market. Many Thai industrial firms are closely held and so were unable to issue their own paper. These regulations contributed to the development of industrial groups of closely held firms clustered around the major commercial banks.

The Thai government therefore decided it was right to introduce some distance between commercial banks and industrial firms and to diversify the ownership of banks. It introduced complex requirements for bank ownership, bank holdings of equities, and bank lending to related firms. For example: (1) no one person can own more than 5 percent of a bank's outstanding shares; (2) a commercial bank must not have fewer than 250 shareholders, each of whom holds not more than .5 percent of outstanding shares, but who together hold more than 50 percent; and (3) three-quarters of shareholders must be Thai nationals.

It is generally agreed that these regulatory efforts have failed. The big banks are typically family controlled and closely linked to industrial firms

---

18. Data in this section are from the World Bank's *Financial Sector Study* (World Bank 1990).

owned by the same families. The unfortunate result of this regulation is that it becomes difficult to sort out who owns what, which complicates the efforts of the Bank of Thailand to assess the quality and riskiness of bank portfolios.

The Bank of Thailand has also supported the banks by providing soft loans in times of trouble. There is no explicit deposit insurance in Thailand, nor is there a formal mechanism for taking over insolvent institutions. But the government has provided implicit guarantees by not allowing big banks to fail. This policy was tested in the early 1980s, during a time of slow growth following the second oil shock. Several nonbank financial institutions were closed. Some commercial banks had serious financial difficulties. The Bank of Thailand's options were limited by features of Thai law that made it hard to transfer claims once legal action commenced. Therefore, troubled financial institutions had to remain in existence in order to foreclose on debtors or collect overdue debts. In addition, the Bank of Thailand's legal authority to intervene was weak, so its only realistic option for preventing the failure of major banks was to provide low-interest loans. Many such loans are still on the bank's books.

In practice, therefore, the Thai banking system has been loosely regulated. Restrictions on banks tend to be minor, concerning interest rates and lending to related parties. At the same time, regulation has protected the banks by limiting the activities of foreign competitors and hampering the growth of markets for corporate debt that would compete with bank lending. By bailing out troubled banks with soft loans, the Bank of Thailand has limited the downside risk, not just for depositors but for bank shareholders as well.

Since 1992, the government has tried another tack. It introduced a comprehensive law to supervise and regulate the financial markets. In particular, the issuance of commercial paper is now liberalized, reducing the monopoly over lending that the banks previously enjoyed. The Stock Exchange of Thailand is now maturing as a financial resource mobilizer.

*Direction of Lending.* Beginning in 1975, the government stipulated that a certain share of credit must go to agriculture. It claimed that the commercial banks, based in Bangkok, were ignoring the farmers. The original target was for commercial banks to allocate 5 percent of their previous year's deposit base to agricultural lending. By 1987, the target had reached 14 percent for direct lending to the rural sector plus 6 percent for agribusiness. Shortfalls had to be deposited in the Bank for Agriculture and Agricultural Cooperatives (BAAC), a development bank for agriculture. (After 1992, this requirement was liberalized so that 20 percent of the deposit is to be lent within the province in which the bank branch is located.)

In practice, commercial banks have exceeded the 6 percent target for lending to agribusiness. But their lending to agriculture has usually fallen short of the 14 percent target, so they have had to make deposits into the BAAC. They are comfortable lending to large farmers with clear title to their land, but only about one-half of agricultural land is covered by land titles they regard as acceptable. As a result, many small farmers do not benefit from the government's policy of directed credit. They have to rely on informal moneylenders who charge interest at 5 percent a month.

The BAAC has done something to fill the gap. It generally lends to medium-scale farmers at interest rates far below informal market rates but above deposit rates. It accounts for about 25 percent of agricultural lending, compared with 55 percent for commercial banks and an estimated 20 percent for the moneylenders. The BAAC has some privileged access to funds, notably low-interest loans from the Bank of Thailand and the deposits from commercial banks. These subsidies, however, are not large. More important, the BAAC is quite efficient, particularly as far as short-term working capital loans are concerned. Overdue loans at the end of the year were only 82 percent of the total in the late 1980s, and most of these were eventually recovered.

The government's effort to build up a similar development bank for industry has been less successful. The Industrial Finance Corporation of Thailand (IFCT) was established in 1960 to provide long-term project financing for private industry. As a development bank it was unusual in that initially it was fully private. Later the government became a minority shareholder. Thai commercial banks have been the main shareholders, with foreign banks holding significant shares as well. The IFCT is successful in the sense that it is financially sound. However, it has never played much of a role in financing investment in Thailand. Its loans outstanding amount to about 1 percent of the total in the financial system, and even in manufacturing its share of lending is only 3 percent. The reason for its relative failure is that there was no real niche for the IFCT to fill.

It should also be noted that equity rather than debt has been the main source of long-term financing for most manufacturers. The ratio of long-term debt to equity in 1988 was .09 in textiles, .12 in electronics, and .06 in the motor industry. These figures are a bit misleading, as firms in these industries have large amounts of short-term debt to commercial banks that is routinely rolled over and has some of the character of medium- and long-term debt. Their overall debt to equity ratio is therefore around 1.0. Thailand has an active and growing stock market, but many large industrial firms remain closely held. Retained earnings are the main source of the growth in equity in Thai industry.

## Direct Foreign Investment

The Thai government has traditionally had a liberal attitude toward foreign direct investment (FDI). Beginning with the first one in the early 1960s, every plan has had a clear policy of promoting FDI. Thai law makes no major distinctions between domestic and foreign investment. This is true for tax laws and most regulations. An important exception is that foreigners are generally not allowed to own land in Thailand, so they rely on long-term leases. The Alien Business Law also identifies some industries that are closed to foreigners, particularly various types of farming. There are some restrictions on the number of foreign technicians and managers who can work in Thailand.[19]

These regulations are minor and can be circumvented if a foreign firm receives BOI promotion. A promoted foreign firm is allowed to own land, produce in the prohibited sectors, and normally bring in the expatriate staff it requires. As with domestic firms, BOI promotion also enables a company to get access to imported machinery, parts, and materials without paying significant tariffs. Thus, BOI policy strongly affects the choice of industries in which foreign firms will invest.

Changes in BOI policy on FDI have mirrored the board's general policy shifts. We have indicated already the shift from import-substituting industries to export industries in the early 1980s. In ownership, in the 1960s and 1970s, it preferred joint ventures with Thai nationals over 100 percent foreign ownership, but in 1983 the "criteria in approving investment promotions" indicated that companies aiming at the domestic market should be at least 50 percent Thai-owned (and 60 percent in agriculture and services). Where more than 50 percent of the output is exported, foreigners can hold a majority share in promoted investments. And plants that export all their output can be owned 100 percent by foreigners.

In combination with the large real devaluation of the exchange rate, particularly vis-à-vis the yen in the mid-1980s, this policy led to a surge of manufacturing FDI into Thailand. The inflow averaged U.S.$270 million per year during 1980–85, but by 1990 it had reached U.S.$2.4 billion. Firms from neighboring economies whose currencies have appreciated, notably Japan and Taiwan (China), have moved some production to Thailand. Investment has been particularly strong in electronics and footwear. FDI has made a large contribution both to the overall growth of industry and to diversifying and expanding Thailand's exports.

## Provision of Infrastructure

Where and how a government spends money on infrastructure has a large impact on industrial development. The Thai government has a good record in the provision of basic infrastructure, notably railroads, electricity, irrigation, highways, and (extending the concept of infrastructure somewhat) primary education. Its weaknesses have been in urban water supply, urban roads, and the telephone network, but even here it has been under pressure to perform.

19. Sibunruang and Tambunlertchai 1986.

In the cases of railroads at the turn of the century and roads in the 1960s and 1970s, the Thai government did not merely respond to demand; it anticipated it. However, its decisions were often driven by military rather than economic considerations. Investments in the transport network made it possible for the Thai state to increase its presence in the countryside. It is no accident that the decision to spend heavily on roads was made in the 1960s when the military dominated the government and the state was increasingly challenged by a communist insurgency. The road network eventually had a major economic impact in promoting agricultural growth, but this was regarded by the policymakers as quite incidental.

Some of the same factors were also at work in the development of universal primary education. In the aftermath of the coup d'état against the absolute monarchy in 1932, the government undertook immediately to expand education as a means of promoting nationalism and support for the new regime. The government also wanted to equip ethnic Thais to compete with the Chinese, anti-Chinese sentiments then being quite strong. Within a few decades, primary education became universally available. In the 1960s, the period of compulsory primary education was raised from four years to six. The consequent rise in the quality of the labor force played a big role in boosting agricultural productivity.

As economic growth and industrialization accelerated in the 1980s, the supply of infrastructure became a severe bottleneck. The problem was largely caused by the slowdown in infrastructural investments during the austerity program of the early 1980s. Government investment, mostly for infrastructure, declined from 5.4 percent of GDP in 1970 to 4.0 percent in 1980 and 2.7 percent in 1990 (National Statistical Office, various years).

With the need to speed up investments in transport and communications, conflicts between the economic technocrats and the elected politicians came to a head. The technocrats wanted to privatize some of the projects. But in many areas state enterprises had monopoly powers under the law, so the only way private firms could enter the fray was by obtaining concessions from them. The awarding of these concessions then became the battleground; the technocrats lost, particularly during the government of General Chatichai Choonhavan. The country also lost. Not only was corruption rife in the negotiation of many of these contracts, but the negotiation, and, with the departure of the granting government, the renegotiation, also took a damagingly long time.

## IV.  Institutions of Economic Policy Making

So far, this paper has argued that Thailand's development has been a strange mix of strong macroeconomic management and poorly coordinated sectoral interventions. The second half of this essay examines the institutional and political bases for this combination.

The institutional origins of economic policy in Thailand lie in the politics of national state formation in the nineteenth century. Three political features have molded state institutions and economic policy instruments: the bureaucracy, the system of administrative law, and patronage.

## Bureaucratic Autonomy, Administrative Law, and Patronage

Under challenges from the British and the French, the monarchy established a functional bureaucracy in 1892. It thereby warded off the threat of colonial intervention while centralizing political power and bringing outlying regions under its legal domain. A code of civil law was imported from France, empowering the functionally organized ministries of government with administrative autonomy. To this day, the bureaucracy retains a considerable part of its legal discretion.

In 1932, a coup d'état did away with the absolutist powers of the monarch and introduced a parliamentary form of government. Since then, although there have been many constitutions, all governments have been at least nominally accountable to the legislature. But the autonomy of the civil service has endured.

Thailand's code of administrative law has three main features. First, it gives great authority to subordinate laws, which are controlled by permanent officials and ministers. Acts of Parliament typically have very little policy content. Rather, they give discretion to the relevant agencies and affect the relative bargaining power among them. Armed with this authority, officials then introduce whatever regulations and notifications they see fit. This leads to the second feature of the Thai system: that Parliament has little power to scrutinize the activities of the bureaucracy. Rather, the politicians' source of power lies in ministerial appointments. The third feature of the legal code is that, as a matter of principle, *the rights of the individual are not protected uniformly from the state.* This gives officials considerable autonomy in deciding who wins and loses in the regulation and allocation of resources.

These legal points should be seen against the political background of Thailand's tradition. Laws in Thailand are very long-lived, but not because of any foresight on the part of the legislators. The real explanation is that the legislature is not very productive in making laws, especially when members of Parliament are elected—as they have been for most of the past two decades. Although a coalition government is normally appointed with the consent of the Parliament and is nominally accountable to it, as soon as the government is in office it directs its majority to vote for as brief a session of Parliament as possible to prevent members from becoming too obstreperous. Parliament, then, is usually in session for three months, but it convenes for only about 12 days. Its main tasks are to pass the annual budget and, for opposition MPs, to debate no-confidence motions against the coalition. These ensure that there is little time left for legislative business. Again, this is symptomatic of a Parliament that is used primarily as a device for winning seats in the Cabinet.[20]

The low productivity of the legislature has various consequences. First and most obviously, Thai laws are sometimes badly out of date. For example, the current legislation guiding the allocation of the electromagnetic spectrum was passed in 1934. And other key pieces of legislation—like the Import and Export Commodity Act of 1979 and the National Forestry Act of 1964—are almost identical versions of documents enacted much earlier. Second, it reinforces the bureaucracy's penchant for proposing laws that give it all-encompassing powers to cover as many future contingencies as possible. Third, since the laws give the bureaucracy such broad powers, it is difficult to liberalize particular sectors of the economy. Even if the bureaucrats and the ministers agree on a liberalization program, it cannot be fully credible because the next change of government may lead to a policy reversal.

In this context, coups d'état perform a useful function. In the first flush of a coup, the junta usually assumes broad legislative powers, and its decrees remain on the books on a par with acts of Parliament. It also appoints members to sit in the legislature, and this body will then break the legislative logjam developed in previous elected Parliaments. Thais are now living under laws the vast majority of which were passed by unelected legislatures.

Despite their wide-ranging legal powers, however, officials are not impervious to extrabureaucratic demands. They are vulnerable to intervention both from above (the military and political elites) and below (lobbying and other forms of influence from interest groups and firms) (Crouch 1984). A Cabinet position enables a minister to influence how state agencies use their discretionary powers. Moreover, Thai officials, like most regulators, are vulnerable to "capture" by industry interests that seek benefits from regulation or protection (Stigler 1971). These opportunities for patronage make the bureaucracy a key mediator and participant in rent seeking. But officials remain independent and powerful because of the mandates of the legal code.

As for Cabinet ministers, they exert patronage depending on which portfolios they hold. Table 6.4 shows the distribution of Cabinet portfolios among the main coalition parties for all *elected* coalition governments between 1975 and 1991. Prior to the coup of February 1991, agriculture was evenly rotated among the top parties; industry was dominated by the Chart Thai Party; com-

---

20. It bears consideration that elected parliaments are often under pressure from the military, both the appointed Senate, which also votes on bills, and individual officers who have been known to threaten coups to keep the elected lower house in line. This, however, does not in itself account for the aspirations of elected MPs to the Cabinet. For more discussion, see Christensen 1991.

**TABLE 6.4. Allocation of Economic Portfolios among Leading Coalition Partners, 1975–91 (total posts in elected coalitions)**

| Ministry/Portfolio | N | Chart Thai | Social Action Party | Democrat | Technocrat | Military/Police |
|---|---|---|---|---|---|---|
| Finance |  |  |  |  |  |  |
| Minister | 9 | 1 | 1 | 1 | 5 | 1 |
| Deputy | 13 | 4 | 2 | 1 | 4 | 0 |
| Industry |  |  |  |  |  |  |
| Minister | 9 | 7 | 1 | 0 | 0 | 0 |
| Deputy | 15 | 3 | 3 | 3 | 2 | 1 |
| Commerce |  |  |  |  |  |  |
| Minister | 9 | 1 | 6 | 2 | 0 | 0 |
| Deputy | 13 | 2 | 8 | 1 | 1 | 0 |
| Communication/Transport |  |  |  |  |  |  |
| Minister | 9 | 2 | 1 | 0 | 0 | 4 |
| Deputy | 21 | 4 | 3 | 4 | 0 | 4 |
| Agriculture/Cooperatives |  |  |  |  |  |  |
| Minister | 9 | 3 | 1 | 3 | 0 | 0 |
| Deputy | 25 | 4 | 7 | 4 | 0 | 1 |

*Source:* Christiansen 1992, Fongsamut 1989.

merce was controlled by the Social Action Party; technocrats were usually assigned to the Finance Ministry; and the military, in addition to the defense portfolio, often laid claim to the transport and communications posts. After 1975, the agriculture, commerce, and industry posts were favored by the leading parties. In the late 1980s, the communications post became lucrative with the privatization of numerous mass transit and telecommunications projects. Many were allegedly used as sources of graft by ministers in the governments of Generals Prem Tinsulanond and Chatichai Choonhavan.

The typical style of the parties is to manage sectoral policy in an activist fashion geared to satisfying particular groups of supporters. With rice prices, for example, politicians have favored government procurement at above-market prices for some farmers, but they have not introduced programs that would raise prices for all farmers (Siamwalla and Setboonsarng 1989). Trade quotas and factory permits also create opportunities for political parties and individual politicians. In the case of textiles, efforts to liberalize these regulations were often obstructed by elected ministers, who preferred to use controls on factory capacity for allocating largesse to client firms (Doner and Laothamatas 1992, app. on textiles and apparel).

These general features of state intervention—autonomy, discretion, and patronage—do not in themselves produce "good" or "bad" policy management. Rather they are formal and informal rules of the game that act as incentives and shape competition among political and bureaucratic elites.

### The Division of Management: Macro- and Micropolicies

Between 1932 and 1957, the state was very activist. Its interventions were not guided by an industrial development philosophy as such but were made in the name of economic nationalism or "rescuing capital from the aliens," the overseas Chinese. In practice, military elites started to collaborate with immigrant Chinese traders, bankers, and nascent industrialists, who exchanged payoffs or shares in their firms for assurance against harassment. Ruling military officials also created franchises for themselves, usually to support their factional struggles for control of the government. Nearly 100 state enterprises were created before 1957, and most of them were poorly managed. The results were generally negative because officials used the offices and legal discretion of the state to create and diversify their revenue bases (Riggs 1966; Skinner 1957; Golay et al. 1969). Initially they and the military intervened in the country's thriving rice industry. Later, military elites used the ministries to create state enterprises in manufacturing.

After a coup in 1958, policy reforms curbed state intervention and altered the economy's course. The management of macroeconomic policies was reorganized, producing an organizational and political split between macro- and microeconomic policies (Christensen 1993, chap. 3; Christensen 1992; Doner and Laothamatas 1992).

In consultation with the World Bank, the new government created agencies and put them in the Office of the Prime Minister. The most critical ones were the National Economic and Social Development Board (NESDB) and the Bureau of the Budget (BOB). These, along with the Ministry of Finance and the Bank of Thailand, formed the core macroeconomic agencies. Officials from these four agencies are referred to frequently as "the technocrats." In addition, the BOI was created. The government cut back on subsidies for state enterprises, reformed the accounting systems in the line ministries, and empowered the budget bureau to scrutinize their spending. The provision of infrastructure was inscribed in the five-year development plans launched in 1961. The reforms cut losses, stabilized fiscal management, and ensured more centralized planning and monitoring of public investments.

Credit policies were revised as well, again in an effort to curb patronage. After several quasi-state enterprises went bankrupt and foreign loans were squandered, the government stopped guaranteeing private sector debts. The Bank of Thailand provided selective credit only on a very limited basis, almost entirely in the form of rediscounted promissory notes or "packing credits" for exporters.

The reforms were successful in part because they had a political constituency that made them feasible and legitimate. The new government had the support of entrepreneurs and military officers hostile to the group that had promoted the nationalist policy. Leading Chinese firms favored a more stable macroeconomic environment and had lobbied, before the coup, for less state intervention (Hewison 1985, 266–67). As for the armed forces, they were discovering that technocratic management formed the basis for a lucrative defense budget. Military initiatives began to intrude on debt management only in the late 1970s.[21]

The fact that many Thai technocrats had the same views and training was also important for the success of the reforms. Although the reforms were supported by the World Bank, they were formulated and carried out by a group of Thai economists. These people shared an esprit de corps inspired by a long tradition of financial conservatism, a tradition inherited from British advisers and from the monarchy's fear that debt would lead to loss of sovereignty.

This "Gladstonian orthodoxy" had a deflationary bias and emphasized financial conservatism (Silcock 1967). Transmitted primarily through the

---

21. It was not until 1984 that an officer, the army's commander in chief, took a position on a macroeconomic issue, in this case the 14 percent devaluation of the baht because it thwarted the planned purchase of F–16s from the United States (Phongpaichit 1991). Six months later that officer was dismissed from his post.

Ministry of Finance and the Bank of Thailand, the orthodoxy shaped the outlook of the first generation of postwar technocrats and influenced officials in the other macroeconomic agencies. Moreover, it had a political bias that despised patronage and the corruption that went with it. Evers and Silcock wrote that the liberal exchange and trade regime was "partly the result of opposition [by technocrats] to the opportunities for private gain which a protective system would bring . . ." (Evers and Silcock 1967, 97). The technocrat who did most to institutionalize this philosophy was Dr. Puey Ungphakorn, the former governor of the Bank of Thailand. We stress that this specific philosophy—which has favored a relatively open trade regime, only minimal central bank discretion over credit and foreign exchange allocations, and fiscal conservatism—was initially made possible and then was sustained for two decades by a growing surplus of exportable agricultural produce.

In contrast, sectoral policies were changed only slightly. The five-year development plans launched in 1960 helped to ensure the development of infrastructure such as irrigation, roads, and electric power. But in the area of industrial policies, there was virtually no coherent or coordinated strategy, in part because the institutional framework was not conducive to it. Moreover, patronage still influenced some of the important decisions by the line ministries.

Beginning in the late 1950s, the civil service gradually changed. It had been an office-holding class, which once owed its allegiance to the king. It became a more meritocratic institution that was involved in policy-based discussions with the private sector. This change owed much to foreign scholarships and training, which had previously been confined to nobles and top officials. For example, in 1987, 61 percent of the top-ranked (C9 through C11) officials had achieved a master's or higher degree, mostly from abroad. And over one-quarter of serving permanent secretaries at the ministries held doctoral degrees in their fields of service (Xuto 1987). Education and skill have made officials more inclined to involve the private sector in policy issues and to recognize the value of what private firms bring to bear. In addition, technical training expanded the pool of "engineering technocrats," especially infrastructure specialists. Many of these officials, writes Muscat (forthcoming), were "socialized in a work ethic of professionalism and national interest," a departure from previous practice. Yet the organization of sectoral policies and public services remained fragmented. Agencies whose officials received professional training often became dominated by "organizational cultures" that operated without reference to the work of other agencies.

The segmentation and ad hoc nature of sectoral policies continued into the "democratic" period when the main economic ministries—agriculture, commerce, communications, and industry—became the main sources of largesse for elected politicians. The advent of democracy in Thailand did not encourage a popular coalition to take power and reform the established structures of power (Chantornvong 1988). Rather it saw the rise of political elites whose ambition was to seize control of the state apparatus, in particular the sectoral ministries (Christensen 1991). In every elected coalition government since 1975, Cabinet jobs at these ministries have nearly always been held by the top coalition parties. An added dimension to this is that, in an elected government, many Cabinet ministers represent provincial constituencies and are thus keen to transfer resources to the countryside.[22]

Unlike the situation in much of Latin America, however, the rigidity and insulation of the budget process make it virtually impossible for politicians "to use macro-economic policies to raise the incomes of lower-income groups" (Sachs 1990, 10). Moreover, as Parliament has only a minimal say on public spending, appropriations are free of "electoral cycling" (Doner and Laothamatas 1992). As a result, elected Cabinet ministers rely on sectoral policies to satisfy the demands of party supporters and voters (Christensen 1992).

The division of macro- and micropolicies has given technocrats the autonomy to pursue their conservative macroagenda, one that has assisted rapid growth. But it has also meant there has been very little connection between macro- and sectoral policies. The macroeconomic technocrats tend to distrust the line ministries, believing they are dominated by narrow bureaucratic interests. In their view, any promotion of private firms generates rent seeking rather than socially optimal objectives. The relationship between the two policies, in other words, is marked by tension and constraint rather than coordination and complementarity.[23]

In planning, for example, until the mid-1980s the NESDB had no real involvement with the line ministries. In trade policy, there has been a sharp distinction between tariffs as a source of revenue and as an instrument of trade strategy. The Finance Ministry has applied tariffs, still a valuable source of government revenue. But its officials usually have "few institutional linkages to and little real knowledge about particular industries" (Doner and Laothamatas 1992, 49), and tariffs are seldom coordinated with the implementation of nontariff barriers by the Ministry of Commerce and the Board of Investment.

As for fiscal policy, the Budget Bureau tends to perceive itself as the "policeman" of the ministries (Dhiravegin 1987). Although the budget process entails close collaboration between it and the various departments, they concentrate on the allocation of funds rather than project-based evaluation.

22. We note, however, that distributive pressures come primarily from political elites and the provincial elites that form the parties' support networks rather than from the rural public at large.

23. An important exception to the generalization that macroeconomic technocrats tend to ignore microeconomic problems is their entry into energy sector planning in the early 1980s. But that followed a period when patchwork policies and corruption in this very large sector in the aftermath of the second oil crisis threatened to upset macroeconomic equilibrium.

Program budgeting has been tried, but it never took hold: it was too big a departure from the Budget Bureau's standard operating procedures.

These adversarial arrangements, and the lack of formal links between macro- and sectoral officials, often hamper the effectiveness of overall development strategy. Structural adjustment efforts in the mid-1980s are a good example. They produced successful macroeconomic stabilization, but did little to restructure key industries, including automobiles and textiles (Doner and Laothamatas 1992). Similarly, not enough has been done in areas where sectoral regulation is sometimes necessary, such as implementation of rural property rights, agricultural research and dissemination, and technological research (Doner and Siroros 1992; Doner and Laothamatas 1992).

### The Private Sector and the State

Government-business relations have changed a lot since 1960. They are now less a matter of ministries and their clients and more a matter of equal partners involved in policy-based consultation. Much of this change has occurred because of the way the private sector has organized itself. It has formed business associations—initially the Board of Trade, the Thai Bankers Association, and the Federation of Thai Industries—which, by the late 1960s, were consulted regularly by ministry officials and macroeconomic technocrats. This had been almost unthinkable only a decade earlier, when the Sino-Thai business elite were deemed (or officially scorned as) the pariahs of society. Sectoral trade associations have also proliferated, from 48 in 1967 to 233 in 1987 (Thanapornpun 1990, app. 5–3). In the context of favorable macroeconomic policies and inconsistent sectoral policies, Doner notes that firms "found associations to be increasingly useful in their responses to changing market conditions" (Doner 1991). All these consultative exercises reach their peak in the Joint Public-Private Consultative Committee, or JPPCC, created by the NESDB in 1980. The JPPCC gathers heads of the leading business associations to talk to leading technocrats and economic ministers. It deals mainly with issues involving overall development strategy.

Another private sector change was the formation of large, vertically integrated, business groups.[24] Initially they came from the largest Sino-Thai firms, and were supported by the top commercial banks. The banks were also instrumental in increasing private sector flexibility by financing exports and attracting

---

24. We follow Leff's definition of a business group as "a large-scale firm that invests and produces in several production lines that involve vertical integration or other economic and technological complementarities. . . . The groups mobilize capital from wealthy people linked by family or other personal ties; in addition they often possess their own banks and other financial intermediaries" (1979, 52).

savings.[25] They helped ensure that the private sector was not entrenched in import substitution industries (Christensen 1993, chap. 3; Doner and Laothamatas 1992).

A third influence on the private sector, and its links with the public sector, has been Japanese foreign direct investment, which is concentrated in the textile, metals, electrical machinery, and automobile industries. By the late 1980s, Thailand was one of the chief recipients of Japanese FDI; indeed, in 1988 it attracted more than did the four Asian newly industrialized countries (NICs) combined (Doner 1992, 8–9).

In general, the effects of Japanese investments and joint ventures on growth and the transfer of technology have been specific to individual industries. For example, in textiles, bureaucratic fragmentation has frustrated the efforts of Japanese and Thai firms to negotiate the development of a textile technology institute with the Ministry of Industry. In other industries, Japanese organizations have been more successful at promoting coordination in industrial upgrading. For example, as Doner has shown, the Japanese International Cooperation Agency (JICA) has been the major supporter of the Metalworking and Machinery Industries Development Institute, which provides technical support for small and medium-sized firms (Doner 1992, 35).

Despite these differences among individual industries, the cumulative sectoral effects of Japanese FDI have been to facilitate institutional development in the private sector and to expand cooperation between Thai business associations and the government (Doner 1991, 1992; Unger 1990). Market linkages between Thai and Japanese firms have encouraged the emergence of interfirm cooperation and subcontracting networks. Japanese FDI has also promoted "cooperation clubs" in the automobile industry, which facilitate sharing of information among Japanese and Thai makers of components (Donor 1992, 40). Finally, Japanese FDI and related institutions have helped lend strategic direction to the Thai private sector, a change that has been valued by officials (Laothamatas 1992).

A comparison with other countries in Southeast Asia suggests that, on its own, Japanese FDI does not explain the emergence of these forms of public-private cooperation. But it is clear that the impact of Japanese investment in Thailand has been to strengthen the resources and capabilities of Thai firms and to boost their bargaining power with the bureaucracy. More research is required to determine precisely why that leverage has encouraged less rent seeking than elsewhere in the region (e.g., in the Philippines). But private

---

25. It is true that overtly the banks' traditional role has been to finance short-term trade credits, but it would be simplistic to conclude that this is all, or even primarily, what they do. The commercial banks have backed many entrepreneurs through good times and bad, and even rolled over their debts, until some of them became heads of large conglomerates.

sector efficiency and public-private consultations have not always been enough to correct critical market failures with regard to FDI. Sectoral policies have not ensured the right levels of education and training among the work force now required by foreign firms, Japanese or otherwise. And the sectoral machinery has been sluggish in providing the institutional framework needed to ensure more transfers of technology and spillovers of knowledge, the textile institute being a prime example.[26]

## V.  Macroeconomic Policy Making

The symbol of the success of Thai macroeconomic management is the nominal exchange rate. But its relative stability has come about because of firm fiscal and monetary restraint, the subjects considered in this section of the essay.

### Fiscal Management

In each fiscal year, four agencies cooperate with one another in planning government spending, taxing, and borrowing. By the time these agencies first meet, the Budget Bureau has already negotiated the outlines of the following year's departmental budgets. Strictly speaking, the relevant line ministers are responsible for the expenditure requests to the Budget Bureau, but in practice they leave it to their officials. The normal way for the bureau to fend off ministerial requests is to say that there is no money.

Meanwhile, the National Economic and Social Development Board proposes the public investment projects envisioned in the ongoing five-year development program. The Ministry of Finance is mainly in charge of estimating revenues from different sources, and the Bank of Thailand decides on the right approach to public borrowing.

The Budget Bureau then submits the following year's budget for the Cabinet to approve and submit to the Parliament. The Cabinet seldom tampers with the budget. Within the Parliament, most of the work of considering the budget is done by the Budget Scrutiny Committee. In this committee, Cabinet members can propose amendments to increase or reduce spending, whereas ordinary members of Parliament can propose only expenditure cuts. Thus, both the overall budget and its composition are largely immune to political considerations.

The Budget Bureau is legally in charge only of the expenditure side of the budget, yet it dominates the whole fiscal process. Its practice is essentially that of a housekeeper, indeed, a Victorian housekeeper. It estimates the revenues, accepts the Bank of Thailand's opinion on how much deficit financing the economy can tolerate, and then decides how much spending to allow. Most

---

26. The authors are grateful to Richard Doner for insights regarding this point.

Thai governments, particularly those involving elected politicians, have sought to avoid raising tax rates (with the exception of customs tariff rates).[27] In most parliamentary systems, the budget is a centerpiece of policy making, with opportunities for politicians to control both taxes and spending. Not so in Thailand. The rigidity of the budget process effectively prevents elected representatives from developing programs or responding to voter demands through public spending. Again, we believe this is a main reason why ministers rely on sectoral interventions to boost their popularity.

It is interesting to speculate why Thai politicians, particularly elected ones, avoid changing tax rates. Of course, most politicians would like to avoid discussing, let alone raising, taxes. For a society riven by the income gap between rural and urban areas, however, the wealth of Bangkok might have made it a convenient milch cow. The fact that this has not happened is as much a testimony to the political clout of the private sector in Bangkok (plus its undoubted ability to evade taxes) as to the guile of the macroeconomic technocrats.

As if these various devices were not enough, the technocrats' instincts have been reinforced by the 1959 budgetary law. It limits deficits to no more than 20 percent of government expenditures. In 1974 the law was amended to exclude refinancing payments from the calculation: in each fiscal year the government can borrow up to 20 percent of that year's total appropriations plus 80 percent of the part allocated to principal repayments.

Roughly 80 percent of government spending consists of current expenditures and within that the bulk consists of salaries and other inflexible items. This means that, when revenues are squeezed, the cuts fall on capital items. Also, government has had little leeway to introduce programs involving recurrent expenditures such as subsidies or the introduction of new tasks like environmental regulations. Only when there is a spurt of economic growth, as in the late 1980s, could new tasks be undertaken. From a politician's point of view, the budget constraint implies that very little patronage can be financed by the central government. The pressure (indeed the requirement) to provide patronage has to be met by other means: hence the use of tax expenditures by the Board of Investment or extrabudgetary funds to shore up commodity prices (selectively) or keep down petroleum prices.[28] Another major leakage has been the deficits of the state enterprises, particularly in the late 1970s and the early

---

27. Listed tariffs have been on an upward surge throughout most of the post-1958 period, so that, if listed tariffs were actually collected, Thailand's would be one of the most protected economies in the world. But the listed tariffs are what Parliament allowed the government to collect. The standard practice of the Customs Department is to adjust the rates that are to be actually collected well below listed tariff ceilings.

28. *Tax expenditures* is a term used in public finance literature to indicate special reductions from the levels specified in the relevant tax codes. They have some of the characteristics of the expenditure side of the government budget, hence the term.

1980s. In the late 1980s, some politicians discovered privatization as a means of financing their patronage.

In addition to aggregate control over debts, the budget process pays special attention to foreign debts. In 1976, after a military coup and amid growing concern about the communist threat, the armed forces proposed a major arms purchase totaling 20 billion baht (U.S.$1 billion at the prevailing exchange rate). To put some controls on the raising of public debt, an act authorizing the Ministry of Finance to raise loans from abroad was issued in November 1976. This act limited the government's annual foreign borrowing to no more than 10 percent of budgetary appropriations with the same ceiling being applied to government guarantees for borrowing by public agencies and state enterprises. These measures were reinforced by an emphasis on monitoring and curbing the growth of foreign debt. For example, in December 1961, the Council of Ministers stipulated 5 percent as the ceiling for the ratio of external public debt service to the country's export earnings. In July 1964, this was increased to 7 percent, and was applied throughout the 1970s.[29] In addition, the debt service drawn out of the fiscal budget each year was not allowed to exceed 13 percent of the government revenues in that year.

Whatever the regulations say, however, the principle of budgetary restraint will not survive a determined onslaught by a government trying to spend its way out of its problems. Unlike many other countries, Thailand has generally avoided this fate. Perhaps it is because macroeconomic imprudence almost immediately leads to external complications and assigns responsibility to the decision makers involved. Because of the fear of being thus "caught," Thai politicians (whether they are elected or from the military) have not tampered as much with macroeconomic policy as with sectoral policies. Of the four agencies chiefly involved in formulating Thailand's macroeconomic policies, three are controlled directly by the prime minister, who tends to take a less sectional position on any given issue (even if he is an elected member of Parliament). The fourth agency is the Ministry of Finance, which has normally been headed by a technocrat. Even General Chatichai Choonhavan, an elected politician, at one point found it prudent to appoint a technocrat as minister of finance.

## Macroeconomic Policies at Work

Even a conservative macroeconomic policy, managed by technocrats who are immune to distributional pressures, cannot insulate the economy against external shocks. The proper test of policy and institutions is how much damage is inflicted, the speed and nature of the response, and how well the stresses are

---

29. When debt service payments on loans for national defense were included, the public debt service ratio was not to exceed 9 percent each year.

managed. This section looks at the events of the late 1970s and the early 1980s, following the second oil shock. Unlike the first oil shock in 1973, when commodity prices rose and thus lessened the impact on Thailand's external position, the second shock reduced Thailand's terms of trade considerably. The effect of these adverse developments was magnified by the decision to keep the baht tied to the dollar. Further, between 1979 and 1981, economic policy came under the control of a banker turned populist politician, Boonchu Rojanasathien. He is unique among Thai politicians in having a macroeconomic program that he was allowed by the prime minister to implement. He obtained this freedom partly because he could claim to have some expertise—he was president of the Bangkok Bank—and, more importantly, because he was respected by foreign bankers. Boonchu set about pursuing a strongly expansionist policy. Adjustments to the second oil shock were not made, and state enterprises were allowed to run large losses financed by short-term loans from the government.

Between 1980 and 1985, Thailand found itself under severe financial strains, particularly on its external account. To try to contain inflation, the government prevented state enterprises from increasing their prices. This led to an increase in the public sector deficit which contributed to the rise in the trade deficit from roughly 6 percent of GDP in the 1970s to a record 9.8 percent in 1983. The external current account deficit also rose as a proportion of GDP.

Thailand's increased reliance on foreign capital coincided with two peaks of interest rates in the global money markets, one in 1981 and another in 1984. The country's external debt service ratio rose beyond the critical benchmark of 20 percent. The baht came under pressure, partly because of the external deficits and also because the U.S. dollar, to which the baht was pegged, rose significantly between 1981 and 1984. Thailand's overall balance of payments position plunged into deficit in 1983, and an uncomfortably large portion of its relatively small foreign reserves (about three months' worth of imports) was earmarked for obligations such as IMF commitments.

To cope with these problems, the Bank of Thailand devalued the baht twice, in 1981 and 1984. It then opted for a managed float, specifying daily exchange rates in accordance with the fluctuations of prominent currencies. The purpose of this exercise was to maintain the baht-dollar parity within a somewhat wider band. The commercial banks' credit expansion was capped in order to curb import demand. Specific sectors—such as exports and low-income housing—were exempted from austerity measures or were given special assistance, a rare instance of the use of selective credit controls. Public foreign borrowing in each year was restricted to an exact ceiling—U.S.$1.6 billion in fiscal year (FY) 1985 and U.S.$1 billion in FY1986–88, which was far more restrictive than the level allowed by the debt service ratio rule. Moreover, the Bank of Thailand began financial deregulation in an attempt to strengthen the competitiveness of exporters.

These restructuring efforts produced excellent results. Economic growth accelerated from 3.5 percent in 1985 to 4.9 percent (1986), 9.5 percent (1987), 13.2 percent (1988), and 12.0 percent (1989). Some of this success was due to external good luck—oil price decreases, the revaluation of the yen and other Asian NIEs' currencies, low overseas inflation and interest rates—but the reforms contributed to the upswing. More than that, they helped the economy to diversify. New types of exports and a significant rise in the export share of GDP contributed to a fall in the current account deficit, from 5.5 percent of GDP in 1980–85 to only 1.6 percent in 1986–89. Gross domestic investment also grew strongly, mostly due to the revaluation of the yen and other Asian currencies.

The Boonchu episode of 1979–81 demonstrates that Thailand is not immune to populist pressures. Once the rules of financial conservatism were broken, however, it did not take long for the technocrats to reestablish control. In our view, the discipline of a de facto fixed exchange rate has been the chief anchor in macroeconomic management. An additional benefit is that the exchange rate regime has stabilized expectations in the private sector. The last domestically generated inflation in Thailand was as far back as 1942–46. Otherwise, Thai inflation has been broadly similar to that of the United States.

## VI.  Developments since 1991

In February 1991, the military once more made its entry into Thai politics, removing from his prime ministership General Chatichai Choonhavan, who despite his title was an elected member of Parliament. The military leaders then appointed as prime minister Anand Panyarachun who was at that time a businessman but who had been until 1977 a diplomat with a distinguished record in public service. His two turns at the helm of the government, lasting altogether one and a half years, saw one of the most extensive reforms undertaken by the Thai government since the late 1950s.

The government completely liberalized the petroleum sector. It substantially liberalized the financial sector, but at the same time it introduced somewhat more discipline into the financial markets by creating the Securities and Exchange Commission. The purpose of this new regulator was clearly to make the markets function better. On the fiscal front, it grasped a particularly thorny political nettle by introducing a value-added tax, replacing what has become an archaic indirect tax system. It also initiated discussions with the private sector with a view to substantially reducing import tariffs, although it did not stay long enough to implement the reforms. What it did do was push Thailand and other ASEAN countries into creating an ASEAN Free Trade Area (AFTA) with a 15-year timetable (since then shortened to 10 years) for implementation of almost completely free trade among the six member countries.

No doubt these achievements were possible because the Anand government did not have to share power with an elected Parliament. Not that it had an easy time with the military that appointed it, for soon afterward it clearly showed its disappointment with Anand and his policies, particularly with his attempts to block some of the privatization concessions with which part of the military was involved. That Anand was able to push through these reforms in the face of military opposition and yet remain enormously popular, and, more importantly, that his reforms remain substantially on the books to this day, almost three years later, testify to the sea change in attitudes that has taken place in Thai society at large. Since 1985, it has become widely recognized that Thailand is part of the global economy, and that to survive within that economy it has to be competitive. Further, to remain competitive, Thailand cannot afford to have the state coddle particular firms or sectors indefinitely. These firms and markets have to meet the market test. This change in attitude has now tempered the patronage system built around the sectoral policies discussed previously. The system has not died out, but now these sectoral policies have to meet the more stringent test.

With the return of an elected Parliament and full-fledged democratic government in September 1992, there was no wholesale reversal of the radical (by Thai standards) reforms of the Anand government. With sectoral interventions somewhat thwarted by this attitude, the new government turned to a regional policy. It began to push for more decentralization of both economic and political power away from Bangkok. Policies were put in place to promote that aim included the granting of BOI privileges mostly to firms located outside Bangkok and surrounding provinces and the intensification of public expenditure on provincial and rural infrastructure. These policies were pursued while at the same time ensuring that the heavy infrastructural investment needed for Bangkok itself was financed through the private sector rather than drawing exclusively on general tax revenues.

One area where the sectorally oriented patronage system has not quite disappeared is in infrastrucuture investment. The emphasis on granting private concessions as a means of financing these investments, particularly in Bangkok, has ensured lengthy delays in providing much-needed relief for traffic and communications congestion in Bangkok.

It is easy to deride these policies as patronage under another guise, with regional rather than sectoral policies as the objects of contention. There is no doubt that the old patronage system is still very much alive in Thai politics. But even if this form of patronage was the guiding principle of the current government, there is at least some efficiency arguments to be made in favor of such regional policies. The principal one is the increasing congestion within Bangkok and the need to lower the social costs (in terms of the disruption of family life) of migration that would be incurred if growth is concentrated in Bangkok. One can also add the equity argument that the current disparity in income between Bangkok and the provinces demands such corrective measures.

If proof is needed that many of the reforms of 1991–92 are politically sustainable in a more democratic era, we can point to the case of tariff reforms, which, it will be recalled, were initiated by the Anand government. Despite the potential political minefields, the new elected government has proceeded with the implementation of these reforms, which will bring the various tariffs down to six levels with a maximum rate of 30 percent by 1997.

Section II pointed to Thailand's low rate of secondary school enrollment as a weakness. Even here, the elected government was seriously tackling this issue, having raised the reenrollment rate at the end of the primary level from less than half to 85 percent. Furthermore, just prior to its resignation in May 1995, it was on the verge of bringing in loan programs aimed at students, schools, and colleges. These programs would have sped up the expansion of investment in schooling considerably. The effort was as much guided by the need to remain globally competitive as it was to provide expanding opportunities for Thais.

Although the elected government that continued Anand's reforms and brought in some of its own has fallen, it is not expected that the reforms will be substantially reversed since these reforms now command a solid constituency.

## VII.  Conclusion

A simple description of Thai economic policy making in the postwar period would give the impression that the Thai state has been highly active in promoting growth. On closer examination, much of the action was full of sound and fury that in fact signified very little. This is particularly true of sectoral policies, for which any attempt to establish a well-conceived and systematic policy has been defeated either by corruption or by frequent shifts in personnel and direction. The government never tried to discipline firms and industries to "deliver"; it would not or could not control the allocation of credit and foreign exchange, as some other East Asian governments did.

The Thai government has done well in the one area, which, in our view, has been essential for the growth of the economy: macroeconomic management. The stable monetary environment has made it possible for the private sector to grow and concentrate on productive rather than speculative investments. The growth of the private sector has, in turn, been fed by strong banks, which in Thailand perform some of the functions of investment coordination that are undertaken by the state in other countries. Certainly one vital lesson from Thailand is that a developing country can do very well by sticking to the fundamentals: macroeconomic stability, outward orientation, and sustained investment in physical infrastructure and primary education.

It is also clear that the key to an even better performance for Thailand is not a more activist state in the sense of one that intervenes more at the industry and firm levels. As this essay has shown, the Thai state has intervened a lot at these levels, but its actions have not been very effective, well coordinated, or carried out with a clear developmental purpose in mind. No doubt some will argue that *better* sectoral interventions could have helped the economy grow more rapidly. However, that is to wish for Thailand a state apparatus that it—and most other developing countries—simply do not possess.

In drawing lessons from Thailand's development, we choose to find a middle ground between the two extreme models laid out in the introduction: the minimalist state and the interventionist state. We do not think that Thailand would have done better with more promotion of specific industries and firms. There was enough of such promotion, and it brought very few benefits. What Thailand could have used—and could have achieved—is a more sectoral vision when making decisions about infrastructure. "Infrastructure" tends to get lumped together with general or functional incentives. The specific choices about infrastructure, however, almost inevitably affect sectoral development. For example, spending on primary education and roads in the 1960s paved the way for agricultural expansion. Spending on power and ports also helped in the earlier stages of industrialization. One shortcoming, even in this successful period, was the inadequate regional spread of infrastructural investments, so that most industrial plants ended up concentrated in and around Bangkok. However, as was pointed out in section VI, this imbalance is being sharply reversed.

Even though Thailand may have been successful so far, it is less well prepared for the next stage of industrialization. In particular, its investments in secondary education and its output of technicians and engineers fall seriously short of what is necessary to sustain the pace of industrialization.

The relevance of Thailand's experience to other countries is not clear. Countries that still depend substantially on agricultural exports and have a weak state apparatus may benefit by adopting Thailand's strong emphasis on macroeconomic stability. For them, good macroeconomic performance can partially compensate for poor sectoral policies by allowing the buildup of a strong private sector, including a financial system capable of coordinating investments.

The sectoral policies that worked well in Thailand were those that involved the choice of infrastructure investments. Good choices speed up development, whereas bad choices result in serious enough bottlenecks to throttle growth. To make such choices intelligently involves some vision of the changing industrial structure during various phases of economic growth and also some investment coordination between the private and public sectors. Thailand's experience in this respect has been at best variable.

As for the government intervening to fix prices, Thailand's experience does not support the view that deliberate distortions can play a positive role in development. The Thai government has deliberately distorted prices, but that has not contributed to growth. The question of whether a different method of intervention would have done better remains unanswered.

REFERENCES

Amsden, Alice H. 1989. *Asia's Next Giant: South Korea and Late Industrialization.* New York: Oxford University Press.

Bank of Thailand. Various years. *Annual Report.* Bangkok: Bank of Thailand.

Barro, Robert J. 1991. "Economic Growth in a Cross Section of Countries." *Quarterly Journal of Economics* 105 (May): 407–43.

Bhattacharya, Amarendra, and Johannes Linn. 1988. *Trade and Industrial Policies in the Developing Countries of East Asia.* World Bank Discussion Papers No. 27. Washington, D.C.: World Bank.

Chantornvong, Sombat. 1988. "Tocqueville's *Democracy in America* and the Third World." In *Rethinking Institutional Analysis and Development,* edited by Vincent Ostrom, David Feeny, and Hartmut Picht. San Francisco: International Center for Economic Growth.

Chitayarangsan, Rachain. 1990. "Industrial Structure: Electronics Industry in Thailand." In *Thai Economy in the Changing Decade and Industrial Promotion Policy,* edited by Samart Chiasakul and Mikimasa Yoshida. Tokyo: Institute of Developing Economies.

Christensen, Scott R. 1991. "Thailand after the Coup." *Journal of Democracy* 2 (3) 94–106.

Christensen, Scott R. 1992. "Capitalism and Democracy in Thailand." Paper presented at the annual conference of the Association for Asian Studies, Washington, D.C., April 2–5.

Christensen, Scott R. 1993. "Coalitions and Collective Choice: The Politics of Institutional Change in Thai Agriculture." Ph.D diss., University of Wisconsin-Madison.

Crouch, Harold. 1984. *Domestic Political Structures and Regional Cooperation in Southeast Asia.* Singapore: Institute of Southeast Asian Studies.

Dhiravegin, Likhit. 1987. *Allocation for Development: The Role of the Bureau of the Budget.* Bangkok: Thailand Development Research Institute.

Dollar, David. 1992a. "Exploiting the Advantages of Backwardness: The Importance of Education and Outward Orientation." World Bank. Mimeo.

Dollar, David. 1992b. "Outward-Oriented Developing Economies Really Do Grow More Rapidly: Evidence from 95 LDCs, 1976–1985." *Economic Development and Cultural Change* 40 (April): 523–44.

Doner, Richard F. 1991. *Driving a Bargain: Japanese Firms and Automobile Industrialization in Southeast Asia.* Berkeley: University of California Press.

Doner, Richard F. 1992. "Japanese Foreign Investment and the Creation of a Pacific-Asia Region." Paper presented at the NBER Conference on Japan and the United States in Pacific Asia, December.

Doner, Richard F., and Anek Laothamatas. 1992. "The Political Economy of Structural Adjustment in Thailand." Paper prepared for the World Bank Project on the Political Economy of Structural Adjustment in New Democracies. Mimeo.

Doner, Richard F., and Patcharee Siroros. 1992. "Technology Development and Collective Action in Southeast Asia: Notes from the Thai Case." Paper presented at the Annual Meeting of the Association for Asian Studies, Washington, D.C., April 2–5.

Doner, Richard F., and Daniel H. Unger. 1991. "The Politics of Finance in Thai Economic Development." Paper prepared for the Project on Government, Financial Systems, and Economic Development: A Comparative Study of Selected Asian and Latin American Countries, East-West Center, University of Hawaii, November 31–December 1.

Evers, H. D., and T. H. Silcock. 1967. "Elites and Selection." In *Thailand: Social and Economic Studies in Development,* edited by T. H. Silcock. Singapore: Donald Moore.

Fongsamut, Ark. 1989. "The Thai Cabinet System." M.A. thesis, Faculty of Political Science, Chulalongkorn University. In Thai.

Golay, Frank H., Ralph Anspach, M. Ruth Pfanner, and Eliezer B. Ayal. 1969. *Underdevelopment and Economic Nationalism in Southeast Asia.* Ithaca: Cornell University Press.

Haggard, Stephan. 1990. *Pathways from the Periphery: The Politics of Growth in the Newly Industrializing Countries.* Ithaca: Cornell University Press.

Hewison, Kevin J. 1985. "The State and Capitalist Development in Thailand." In *Southeast Asia: Essays in the Political Economy of Structural Change,* edited by R. Higgott and R. Robison. London: Routledge and Kegan Paul.

Hutaserani, Sugarya. 1990. "The Trends of Income Inequality and Poverty and a Profile of the Urban Poor in Thailand." TDRI *Quarterly Review* 5 (December): 1.

Ingram, James C. 1971. *Economic Change in Thailand,* 1850–1970. Stanford: Stanford University Press.

International Bank for Reconstruction and Development. 1959. *A Public Development Program in Thailand.* Baltimore: Johns Hopkins University Press.

International Monetary Fund [IMF]. Various years. *International Financial Statistics.* Washington, D.C.: IMF.

Jitsuchon, Somchai. 1991. "Retrospects and Prospects of Thailand's Economic Development." Working Papers No. 2, Economic Planning Agency, Tokyo. Mimeo.

Johnson, Chalmers. 1982. *MITI and the Japanese Miracle: The Growth of Industrial Policy, 1925–1975.* Stanford: Stanford University Press.

Krueger, Anne. 1979. *The Development of the Foreign Sector and Aid.* Cambridge: Harvard University Press.

Kuznets, Paul. 1977. *Economic Growth and Structure in the Republic of Korea.* New Haven: Yale University Press.

Laothamatas, Anek. 1992. *Business Associations and the New Political Economy of Thailand: From Bureaucratic Polity to Liberal Corporatism.* Boulder: Westview Press.

Leff, Nathaniel H. 1979. "Entrepreneurship and Economic Development: The Problem Revisited." *Journal of Economic Literature* 17 (March): 46–64.

Manarangsun, Sompop. 1977. "The History of Fertilizer Policies in Thailand." M.Econ. thesis, Thammasat University.

Muscat, Robert J. Forthcoming. "Political Instability and Development Disarray."

National Statistical Office. Various years. *Quarterly Bulletin of Statistics*. Bangkok: National Statistical Office.

Phongpaichit, Pasuk. 1991. "The Politics of Economic Policy Reform in Thailand." Paper presented at the seminar on the Politics of Economic Policy Reform in Southeast Asia, Asian Institute of Management, Manila, October 14–15.

Riggs, Fred G. 1966. *Thailand: The Modernization of a Bureaucratic Polity*. Honolulu: East-West Center Press.

Sachs, Jeffrey D. 1990. *Social Conflict and Populist Policies in Latin America*. Occasional Papers No. 9. San Francisco: International Center for Economic Growth.

Sathirathai, Surakiart. 1987. *Laws and Regulations concerning Natural Resources, Financial Institutions, and Export: Their Effects on Economic and Social Development*. Bangkok: Thailand Development Research Institute.

Siamwalla, Ammar. 1991. "Land Abundant Agricultural Growth and Some of Its Consequences." Bangkok, Thailand Development Research Institute. Mimeo.

Siamwalla, Ammar, and Suthad Setboonsarng. 1989. *Trade, Exchange Rate, and Agricultural Pricing Policies in Thailand*. Washington, D.C.: World Bank.

Sibunruang, Atchaka. 1986. "Industrial Development Policies in Thailand." World Bank. Mimeo.

Sibunruang, Atchaka, and Somsak Tambunlertchai. 1986. "Foreign Direct Investment in Thailand." Thailand Development Research Institute, August.

Silcock, T. H. 1967. "Money and Banking." In *Thailand: Social and Economic Studies in Development,* edited by T. H. Silcock. Singapore: Donald Moore.

Skinner, G. William. 1957. *Chinese Society in Thailand: An Analytical History*. Ithaca: Cornell University Press.

Stigler, George. 1971. "The Theory of Economic Regulation." *Bell Journal of Economics and Management Science* 2:3–21.

Summers, Robert, and Alan Heston. 1988. "A New Set of International Comparisons of Real Product and Price Level Estimates for 130 Countries, 1950–1985." *Review of Income and Wealth* 34:1–25.

Thanamai, Patcharee. 1985. "Patterns of Industrial Policymaking in Thailand: Japanese Multinationals and Domestic Actors in the Automobile and Electrical Appliance Industries." Ph.D. diss., University of Wisconsin-Madison.

Thanapornpun, Rangsun. 1990. *The Process of Economic Policy Making in Thailand: Historical Analysis of Political Economy, 1932–1987*. Bangkok: Social Science Association. In Thai.

Unger, Daniel. 1990. "Big Little Japan." Paper presented at the Eighth Annual Conference of the Defense Academic Research Support Program.

United Nations Economic and Social Commission for Asia and the Pacific. Various years. *Foreign Trade Statistics*. New York: United Nations.

Wade, Robert. 1990. *Governing the Market: Economic Theory and the Role of Government in East Asian Industrialization*. Princeton: Princeton University Press.

Wiboonchutikula, Paitoon. 1987. "Total Factor Productivity Growth of Manufacturing Industries in Thailand." In *Productivity Changes and International Competitiveness of Thai Industries,* Bangkok: Thailand Development Research Institute.

World Bank. 1987. *World Development Report.* Washington, D.C.: World Bank.

World Bank. 1990. "Thailand Financial Sector Study," Report No. 8403–TH.

World Bank. Various years. *World Tables.* Washington, D.C.: World Bank.

Xuto, Somsakdi. 1987. *Civil Servants at the Administrative Level.* Bangkok: Public Policy Studies Project, Social Science Association of Thailand. In Thai.

CHAPTER 7

# Indonesia: Development Transformation and the Role of Public Policy

*Amar Bhattacharya and Mari Pangestu*

## I. Introduction

Indonesia straddles the equator spread across an archipelago of more than 13,000 islands with an area of more than 2 million square kilometers. With a population of 184 million in 1992, it is the world's fifth most populous nation. The five big islands—Java, Sumatra, Sulawesi, Kalimantan, and Irian Jaya— account for 92 percent of the area and 94 percent of the population. Two-thirds of the population lives on Java, which has one of the highest population densities in the world. Some 95 percent of the population are Malay and 90 percent are followers of Islam, but there are more than 300 ethnic and linguistic groups. Like other Southeast Asian nations, Indonesia has an ethnic Chinese minority. It comprises 2.5 percent of the population but plays a disproportionate role in trade, services, and industry.

Like Malaysia, but unlike the East Asian countries of the north, Indonesia has a rich and diverse base of natural resources. Java has extremely fertile soil, and the outer islands are well suited for tree crops. Farming is well developed, comprised of rice, tree crops, spices, and fisheries. Indonesia is also rich in mineral resources, including oil.

Indonesia's history and development after Independence has two parts: the years under the helm of President Soekarno (1948–65), often referred to as the Old Order; and the period under President Soeharto, or the New Order period, which has spanned the last 30 years. Economic activity picked up after Independence but gradually lost momentum and then declined in the final years of the Soekarno era. Since then, Indonesia has had rapid and sustained growth, aided in part by the oil boom of the 1970s.

This essay analyzes Indonesia's transformation over the past 25 years and the role that public policy has played in bringing this about. The next section reviews the trends underlying this transformation. Section III reviews the key elements of the policy and institutional framework. Section IV analyzes the

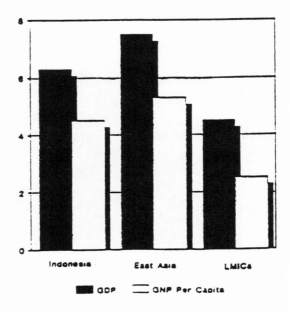

Fig. 7.1.   Growth performance, 1965–90

reform process, section V looks at recent developments in the regulatory environment, and section VI summarizes the main conclusions.

## II.   Development Transformation since 1965

### Long-Term Development Trends

Twenty-nine years ago, Indonesia was one of the poorest countries in the world. Its per capita income in 1967 was only U.S.$50, about half that of Bangladesh, Nepal, and Nigeria. Poverty was widespread; estimates suggest that, in 1970, 60 percent of the population (or 70 million people) were living in absolute poverty. Infant mortality was among the highest in the world, and life expectancy was lower than in other low-income countries in Asia. Indonesia was also lagging behind in education, with a substantially higher adult illiteracy rate and considerably lower primary and secondary enrollment rates than those of its neighbors.

Since then, Indonesia has made substantial progress. It achieved GDP growth of almost 7 percent per annum in 1965–90, far above the average for low- and middle-income developing countries and comparable to other East Asian economies (see fig. 7.1). Even during the 1980s—when Indonesia was

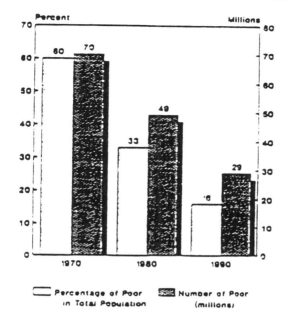

**Fig. 7.2.** Incidence of poverty

hit by a series of external shocks—it managed growth in excess of 5 percent a year. Over the past three decades, per capita income has increased at an average annual rate of 4.5 percent. The percentage of poor, the absolute number of poor, and the severity of poverty have all fallen sharply, which results in Indonesia having the sharpest annual reduction in the incidence of poverty among the countries analyzed in the 1991 *World Development Report* (World Bank 1991). At the same time, infant mortality has fallen sharply, and life expectancy has increased by 20 years. Universal primary education was achieved, secondary and tertiary enrollment has risen sharply, and the adult illiteracy rate has fallen by almost two-thirds (see fig. 7.2 and table 7.1).

The economy has also undergone substantial structural change (table 7.2). First, it has become much more open, with total trade flows now accounting for more than 50 percent of GDP. The growing openness of the economy was spurred by the oil and commodity boom of the 1970s and, more recently, by the acceleration of nonoil exports. Second, investment and savings rates rose steadily from the low levels of the early and mid-1960s to a peak in 1981 but then declined a little in the aftermath of external shocks. Third, there has been a rapid change in the composition of output. The share of agriculture has been more than halved. Oil and mining was the dominant sector during the 1970s, but manufacturing has since emerged as a major sector, making the largest

**TABLE 7.1.  Human Resource Development, 1960–90**

| | Life Expectancy at Birth (years) | | Infant Mortality Rate[a] | | Adult Illiteracy Rate[b] | | Primary Enrollment Ratio[c] | | Secondary Enrollment Ratio[d] | | Population per Physician | |
|---|---|---|---|---|---|---|---|---|---|---|---|---|
| | 1960 | 1990 | 1960 | 1989 | 1960 | 1990 | 1960 | 1989 | 1960 | 1989 | 1960 | 1984 |
| Indonesia | 41 | 61 | 225 | 64 | 61 | 23 | 71 | 118 | 6 | 47 | 46,780 | 9,410 |
| East Asia and Pacific | | | | | | | | | | | | |
| Philippines | 53 | 64 | 134 | 42 | 28 | 10 | 95 | 111 | 26 | 73 | na | 6,570 |
| Malaysia | 54 | 70 | 105 | 22 | 42 | 22 | 96 | 96 | 19 | 59 | 7,020 | 1,930 |
| Thailand | 52 | 66 | 149 | 28 | 32 | 7 | 83 | 86 | 13 | 28 | 7,950 | 6,290 |
| South Korea | 54 | 71 | 120 | 23 | 29 | 4 | 94 | 108 | 27 | 86 | 3,540 | 1,160 |
| South Asia | | | | | | | | | | | | |
| India | 43 | 59 | 165 | 95 | 72 | 52 | 61 | 98 | 20 | 43 | 4,850 | 2,520 |
| Sri Lanka | 62 | 71 | 71 | 20 | 25 | 12 | 95 | 107 | 27 | 74 | 4,490 | 5,520 |
| All developing countries | 46 | 63 | 233 | 65 | na | 40 | na | 105 | na | 43 | na | 4,980 |

[a]Number of infants per thousand live births, in a given year, who die before reaching one year of age.
[b]Proportion of the population over the age of 15 who cannot, with understanding, read or write a short, simple statement about their everyday lives. Illiteracy rate is for 1960 except for the following: Indonesia and India (1961); Malaysia (1970) and Sri Lanka (1963).
[c]Gross enrollment of all ages at primary level as a percentage of primary school-age children.
[d]Computed in the same manner as the primary enrollment ratio.

*Source:* World Bank *Social Indicators of Development*, various years.

contribution to overall growth in the second half of the 1980s. Fourth, with the stagnation in oil output and the sharp decline in oil prices in the 1980s, the reliance on oil revenues has diminished in terms of both foreign exchange earnings and budgetary contribution. Fifth, there has been a significant shift toward the private sector following the reforms of the 1980s. Its share of total investment has increased, and the private sector is estimated to have contributed 73 percent of overall growth since 1983. Finally, the level of external debt, which was reduced during the 1970s, rose sharply during the 1980s, so that Indonesia is among the five largest developing country borrowers in the world.

These longer-term trends have been influenced by: (1) big shifts in Indonesia's external environment and (2) the evolution of policy. Indonesia benefited from the oil and commodity boom of the 1970s, with a terms of trade effect that amounted to 12 percent of GDP by 1981. In contrast, Indonesia was adversely affected by sharp declines in oil and commodity prices as well as exchange rate movements during the 1980s. Together these led to negative external shocks of 15 percent of GDP by 1988.

Government policy has also changed over time, partly in response to changes in the external environment (table 7.3). The Soekarno era following Independence in 1948, and, in particular, the period of guided economic devel-

**TABLE 7.2.    Structural Change**

|  | 1965 | 1970 | 1980 | 1990 |
|---|---|---|---|---|
| As percentage of GDP | | | | |
| Openness | | | | |
| Total trade | 14.0 | 22.2 | 46.8 | 54.7 |
| Nonoil exports | 4.0 | 7.0 | 11.5 | 15.7 |
| Imports | 7.5 | 10.6 | 15.5 | 26.3 |
| Gross domestic investment | 8.0 | 10.8 | 18.7 | 24.6 |
| Gross national savings | 7.9 | 9.5 | 32.8 | 26.3 |
| Sectoral shares | | | | |
| Agriculture | 55.0 | 47.5 | 24.3 | 35.9 |
| Manufacturing | 8.5 | 10.9 | 13.4 | 18.8 |
| Other industry | 6.5 | 8.9 | 29.7 | 19.1 |
| Services, etc. | 30.0 | 32.7 | 32.1 | 39.1 |
| External debt | 50.0 | 32.5 | 30.0 | 66.6 |
| As percentage of exports | | | | |
| Oil LNG exports[a] | 40.0 | 40.5 | 78.5 | 44.8 |
| Debt service | 11.0 | 6.0 | 13.9 | 27.3 |
| Private investment | | | | |
| as percentage of total | — | — | 51.0 | 64.7 |

*Source:* Central Bureau of Statistics and World Bank staff estimates.
[a]LNG = liquified natural gas.

opment (1958–65), were characterized by a growing inward orientation and government control. Next came the initial years of the New Order government of President Soeharto (1967–73), during which macroeconomic stability was restored, the government liberalized the trade and payments regime, and there was a more favorable stance toward domestic and foreign private investment. The third phase was the oil and commodity boom period of 1973–81. While the government maintained generally sound macroeconomic policies and continued to pursue its longer-term development objectives, the trade and investment regime became increasingly inward looking and subject to government control. Then came the decline in oil prices and associated shocks in 1982. Between then and 1985, the government restored macroeconomic stability and initiated key fiscal and financial reforms, but it continued to pursue strongly inward and state policies. In 1986, Indonesia suffered a second and even sharper decline in oil prices as well as a rise in debt service payments due to the depreciation of the U.S. dollar. In response, the government adopted a second round of stabilization measures (1986–88). It also embarked upon some structural reforms designed to create a more outward-oriented and competitive economy. Since 1988, growth has been led by nonoil exports. External imbalances persist, but they are due to the resurgence of private investment and consumer demand. The government has extended and deepened the reform process but at a slower pace.

The remainder of this section describes the main developments in each of these periods. A detailed analysis of the policy framework is provided in section III.

**TABLE 7.3. Trends in Key Economic Aggregates (real growth, percentage per annum)**

|                        | 1960–67 | 1967–73 | 1973–81 | 1982–88 | 1988–91 |
|------------------------|---------|---------|---------|---------|---------|
| GDP                    | 1.7     | 7.9     | 7.5     | 3.3     | 7.1     |
| Nonoil GDP             | 1.7     | 7.3     | 8.0     | 4.3     | 7.7     |
| Agriculture            | 1.6     | 4.1     | 3.4     | 2.9     | 3.0     |
| Manufacturing          | 1.0     | 9.5     | 14.1    | 5.2     | 11.0    |
| Services               | 2.0     | 9.0     | 10.0    | 5.0     | 7.8     |
| Fixed investment       | 1.1     | 23.5    | 11.7    | –0.5    | 13.5    |
| Public                 | —       | —       | 11.0    | –2.0    | 8.2     |
| Private                | —       | —       | 12.3    | 0.7     | 16.9    |
| Nonoil exports         | 2.1     | 25.6    | 0.0     | 7.6     | 16.5    |
| Per capita GDP         | –0.5    | 5.5     | 5.2     | 1.3     | 5.3     |
| Per capita income      | –0.4    | 5.6     | 9.1     | –0.2    | 5.1     |
| Per capita consumption | –0.6    | 3.0     | 5.5     | 1.4     | 5.0     |

*Source:* Central Bureau of Statistics and World Bank staff estimates.

*The Soekarno Era, 1949–65.* In the period after Independence, economic policy was characterized by a strong sense of nationalism rooted in anticolonial, anti-Chinese sentiment. Despite several early attempts at liberalization, the policy regime became increasingly inward oriented and interventionist (Pitt 1991; Glassburner 1971). A pervasive regime of import and investment licenses was established, which promoted a new group of Indonesian importers and traders who earned substantial rents and became a powerful lobby for trade restrictions.

Following the centralization of power in 1958 after the regions' unsuccessful attempts to secede, Soekarno expounded a populist platform of "Guided Democracy and Guided Economy" based on direct state control of production and trade. Dutch interests were nationalized, and state enterprises took over all aspects of the economy, including the import monopolies established in the earlier period.

The result was chaotic. Inflation accelerated to 1,000 percent by 1965, foreign exchange reserves dwindled, and debt service exceeded foreign exchange earnings. The increased external borrowing and expansion of the money supply were the direct outcome of military adventures, including a confrontation with Malaysia, and showcase projects. Under these conditions, economic growth stagnated. Per capita income fell by 15 percent between 1958 and 1965, so poverty (which was already widespread) increased further.

*New Order Government: The Initial Years, 1967–73.* A coup attempt in September 1965 led to the demise of the Old Order of guided democracy. Following a turbulent period, when thousands of people died, a New Order government emerged under the leadership of Soeharto, although Soekarno remained formally as president until 1967.

Despite its tenuous position, the New Order government moved early and decisively to restore macroeconomic stability and introduce market-minded reforms (Pitt 1991). It eliminated the fiscal deficit through drastic expenditure cuts and passed a "balanced-budget" law in 1967 prohibiting domestic financing of the budget in the form of either debt or money creation. It also adopted a stringent monetary program to bring down inflationary pressures. The exchange rate was adjusted to realistic levels through large devaluations, and the administered system of foreign exchange allocation was gradually replaced by a market mechanism. Following the unification of the exchange rate in 1970 and a further devaluation in 1971, the capital account was fully liberalized.

In parallel, the government made sweeping changes in the trade and incentive regime, taking a more favorable line on private investment, including foreign investment. It abolished the import licensing system, and, while there was some increase in tariffs in 1968, it considerably reduced import protection. It also removed most domestic price controls and returned some nationalized enterprises to previous owners. A new Foreign Investment Law, giving a 30-year guarantee of nonnationalization and compensation, was enacted in 1967. Indonesia rejoined the International Monetary Fund (IMF) and the World Bank, which enabled it to receive substantial foreign assistance for its adjustment program and work out arrangements to reschedule its debt.

The stabilization and adjustment program was successful in restoring macroeconomic stability and spurring recovery. By 1969, inflation had been reduced to less than 20 percent, and the external accounts were brought into balance.

With this success, the government's policy focus shifted to long-term development. The first five year plan (REPELITA I) was formulated in 1969, with emphasis on agriculture, social sectors, infrastructure, and industry to support agricultural production. In many ways, this plan established the long-term development objectives of the New Order government for the next 20 years.

*The Oil and Commodity Boom, 1973–81.* Indonesia benefited from the first and second oil booms of the 1970s as well as from the boom in other commodity prices. Net oil and liquified natural gas (LNG) earnings rose from U.S.$.6 billion in 1973–74 to a peak of U.S.$10.6 billion in 1980–81. In that year, oil and LNG accounted for 75 percent of export earnings and 70 percent of budget revenues. The surge in oil earnings provided the government with the opportunity to intensify its development efforts; it also posed the familiar "Dutch disease" problem—how to protect the competitiveness of the nonoil economy from the adverse consequences of oil windfalls.

Compared with many oil exporters, Indonesia used its extra resources well (Gelb 1988). It achieved economic growth averaging close to 8 percent per year based on a strong expansion of public and private investment (see table 7.4). The nonoil economy remained buoyant, especially agriculture and manufacturing. Indonesia also had sound macroeconomic management and, following the Pertamina crisis of the mid-1970s (when the state-owned oil company defaulted on foreign loans), a conservative strategy for borrowing. By the end of the decade, the current account of the balance of payments was in surplus and debt service payments were below 13 percent of exports.

Major progress was also made in reducing poverty, improving living standards, and expanding infrastructure. The government's commitment to rural development was clear in its heavy spending on agriculture (especially rice) and rural infrastructure. The government also did much to improve the availability of education, health, and family planning services. As a result of these physical and social investments, Indonesia was able to make extremely rapid progress during the 1970s on reducing poverty and improving social indicators.

Despite these impressive achievements, there were various policies that marked a reversal of the liberalization of the late 1960s and accentuated the adjustment challenges that emerged in the 1980s. First, the incentive regime became progressively inward oriented and complex, creating a substantial bias against exports in favor of rent seeking. Second, the distortions in the trade regime were reinforced by investment licensing and by credit allocation at subsidized interest rates. Third, the public sector expanded substantially. Public enterprises assumed a dominant role in many sectors and public investment moved into heavy industries, petrochemicals, and mining. The civil service expanded rapidly, as did the scope of bureaucratic interventions. Fourth, the economy became heavily dependent on oil revenues, and competitiveness of the nonoil economy was eroded through a rise in the real exchange rate.

*External Shocks of the 1980s.* Indonesia experienced major external shocks during 1982–88 from two main sources: (1) a sharp decline in the external terms of trade, largely due to the fall in oil prices and to a lesser extent in commodity prices; and (2) the depreciation of the U.S. dollar vis-à-vis major currencies during 1985–88, which added substantially to Indonesia's external debt burden.

The magnitude and trends of external shocks are shown in table 7.5. They prompted two periods of adjustment: first from 1982 to 1985 and then from 1986 to 1988. During the first period, the negative external shocks averaged 3 percent of GDP (Ahmed 1989). During the second, the external shocks were much larger, averaging 15 percent of GDP.

**TABLE 7.4.  Economic Performance during the Oil Boom, 1973–82 (real growth rates, percent per annum)**

|  | 1973 | 1974–78 | 1979 | 1980 | 1981 | Average (1973–81) |
|---|---|---|---|---|---|---|
| Economic Activity |  |  |  |  |  |  |
|   GDP | 11.7 | 6.9 | 7.8 | 7.9 | 7.4 | 7.5 |
|   Nonoil GDP | — | 7.3 | 9.5 | 9.2 | 8.7 | 8.0 |
| Gross National Income | 11.4 | 9.2 | 12.4 | 19.2 | 14.0 | 11.4 |
| Fixed Investment | 12.0 | 11.1 | 8.7 | 15.4 | 12.0 | 11.7 |
|   Public | — | 10.6 | −10.0 | 46.0 | 8.5 | 11.0 |
|   Private | — | 12.5 | 13.0 | −2.0 | 16.4 | 12.3 |
| External Trade |  |  |  |  |  |  |
|   Nonoil exports | — | 4.5 | 8.6 | −9.0 | 19.0 | 0.0 |
|   Nonoil imports | — | 8.4 | 6.5 | 14.4 | 21.3 | 10.5 |
| Other Indicators[a] |  |  |  |  |  |  |
|   Domestic inflation | 30.6 | 19.2 | 20.4 | 17.0 | 10.2 | 17.9 |
|   Overall public sector |  |  |  |  |  |  |
|     balance/GDP | −2.6 | 0.0 | 2.2 | 1.8 | −1.3 |  |
|   Current account/GNP (%) | −4.0 | −2.0 | 3.9 | 2.7 | −2.9 |  |
|   Debt service ratio (%) | 11.3 | 21.5 | 14.5 | 10.1 | 10.4 |  |

*Source:* Central Bureau of Statistics and World Bank staff estimates.
[a]For the last year of multiyear periods.

*The First Adjustment Period, 1982–85.* The first period of stabilization followed the weakening of oil prices in 1982, the onset of a worldwide recession, and the decline in the prices of several important primary exports (e.g., rubber, palm oil, and tin). By 1982–83, Indonesia's current account deficit had widened to U.S.$7.2 billion (7.8 percent of GNP). In response, the government began a broad-based adjustment program, designed to achieve external balance and fiscal stability while reducing the economy's dependence on oil revenues. To restrain imports and improve the competitiveness of Indonesia's nonoil exports, the rupiah was devalued by 28 percent in March 1983 and thereafter was managed flexibly. Public expenditure was sharply reduced through the rephasing of many large projects and cuts in subsidies. At the same time, the government encouraged savings through comprehensive financial and tax reforms and made major efficiency improvements in customs, ports, and shipping. However, trade and industrial policies became even more inward oriented and subject to government intervention.

By 1985–86, the macroeconomic measures had restored financial stability (table 7.6). The current account deficit declined to U.S.$1.9 billion (2.4 percent GNP) in 1985–86, and inflation came to less than 5 percent. These adjustments, however, led to short-term costs in the form of slower growth of output and incomes, reduced private and public investment, low rates of capacity utilization, and financial difficulties for industrial enterprises.

*The Second Adjustment Period, 1985–88.* In 1986, the economy again suffered a series of setbacks. This led to a 34 percent deterioration in the terms of trade and a jump in the debt service ratio from 26 percent in 1985 to 37 percent in 1986. Once again, the government took timely actions to restore macroeconomic stability. These included: (1) the introduction of an austere budget for fiscal year (FY) 86–87, with investment cut by one-quarter in real terms; and (2) a 31 percent devaluation of the rupiah in September.

**TABLE 7.5.    Impact of External Shocks, 1983–84 through 1988–89 (percentage of GNP)**

| | Actual | | | | | | Average |
|---|---|---|---|---|---|---|---|
| | 1983–84 | 1984–85 | 1985–86 | 1986–87 | 1987–88 | 1988–89 | 1983–88 |
| Loss of income | | | | | | | |
| Terms of trade effect | | | | | | | |
| (1981 prices) | 2.5 | 2.0 | 5.7 | 15.6 | 13.3 | 14.1 | 8.9 |
| Exchange rate effect | | | | | | | |
| (1981 exchange rate) | –0.2 | –0.3 | –0.4 | 0.3 | 0.9 | 1.5 | 0.3 |
| Interest rate effect | 0.6 | 0.4 | 0.1 | 0.0 | –0.5 | 0.0 | 0.1 |
| Total effect | 2.9 | 2.1 | 5.4 | 15.9 | 13.7 | 15.6 | 9.3 |

*Source:* IMF and World Bank staff estimates.

The government also embarked upon a program of trade and other regulatory reforms that marked a break from the policies of the previous 15 years. It aimed to stimulate nonoil exports and investment by reducing trade restrictions and other regulations that had led to a "high cost" economy. Its first package, announced in October 1986, eliminated import licensing for 197 items accounting for 19 percent of import value. Later reforms included: (1) a reduction in nontariff barriers as well as in tariffs; (2) investment delicensing and the relaxation of controls on foreign investment; (3) financial deregulation that built on the 1983 reforms by lowering entry barriers, increasing competitive pressures, and reducing the role of subsidized credits; and (4) deregulation in other bottleneck areas such as shipping. These measures are discussed in further detail in section IV.

As a result of these programs, good progress was made in restoring financial stability. The current account deficit fell from 5.8 percent of GNP in 1986 to 2 percent by 1990 and the fiscal deficit from 4.1 percent of GDP to 1.3 percent. Inflation declined to less than 7 percent in 1989. The debt service ratio, which had risen sharply in 1986, began to decline briskly due to the strong

**TABLE 7.6.  Economic Performance during the Adjustment Period (real growth rates, percentage per annum)**

| | Actual | | | | | | Estimates | |
|---|---|---|---|---|---|---|---|---|
| | 1982 | 1984–85 | 1986 | 1987 | 1988 | 1989 | 1990 | 1991 |
| Economic activity | | | | | | | | |
| GDP | −0.3 | 4.6 | 5.9 | 5.0 | 5.6 | 7.4 | 7.1 | 6.5 |
| Nonoil | 4.2 | 5.2 | 6.2 | 5.8 | 7.3 | 8.2 | 7.8 | 7.1 |
| Gross national income | −0.9 | 4.0 | −0.5 | 5.9 | 6.2 | 7.7 | 8.2 | 7.2 |
| Fixed investment | 8.7 | −5.8 | −5.5 | 2.6 | 10.3 | 13.0 | 16.2 | 11.5 |
| Public | 18.2 | −2.9 | −19.1 | −4.5 | 10.3 | 6.8 | 9.6 | 5.6 |
| Private | −0.1 | −8.6 | 8.7 | 8.1 | 11.4 | 16.8 | 19.9 | 13.7 |
| External trade | | | | | | | | |
| Nonoil exports | −0.5 | 10.4 | 4.1 | 25.3 | 14.2 | 21.5 | 6.7 | 12.2 |
| Nonoil imports | 14.2 | −11.8 | −13.6 | 5.0 | 8.0 | 18.9 | 25.4 | 6.7 |
| Other indicators[a] | | | | | | | | |
| Domestic inflation[b] | 7.6 | 8.1 | 5.8 | 9.6 | 9.3 | 6.3 | 7.9 | 8.5 |
| Overall public sector | −4.3 | −3.0 | −4.1 | −2.8 | −3.1 | −1.3 | 1.8 | −1.0 |
| Balance/GDP | −7.8 | −2.6 | −5.8 | −2.3 | −2.3 | −2.0 | −3.8 | −4.1 |
| Current account/GNP (%) | 16.8 | 24.6 | 39.7 | 34.8 | 34.4 | 31.6 | 27.3 | 31.2 |
| Debt service ratio (%)[c] | | | | | | | | |

*Source:* Central Bureau of Statistics and World Bank staff estimates.

[a]For last year of multiyear periods.
[b]As measured by the 17 cities consumer price index (adjusted).
[c]Debt service excludes prepayments.

performance of nonoil exports. Overall growth was exceptionally strong (more than 6 percent per annum for nonoil GDP) given the magnitude of external shocks.

*Nonoil, Export-Led Recovery.* The pace of economic growth quickened in 1989, led by nonoil exports and private investment. However, this has led to substantial excess demand, exacerbated by an easing of monetary policies in late 1989 and early 1990. Consequently, imports surged and exports decelerated, leading to a widening of the current account deficit, a surge in external borrowing, and an acceleration of inflation. The government has responded by tightening monetary policy and curbing external borrowing for public and quasi-public-sector projects. These measures gradually began to take effect. Investment and output growth decelerated slightly in 1992 but still remained in excess of 5 percent per annum.

### Impact on Economic Outcomes

Table 7.7 summarizes the trends in key economic aggregates since 1960. After the stagnation of the early 1960s, growth accelerated following the reforms of 1966. The growth momentum was sustained by the oil boom of the 1970s. Growth decelerated sharply in the 1980s in the face of adverse external shocks, but this never turned into decline. Policy adjustment led to a recovery of growth in the closing years of the decade.

*Investment and Savings.* Figure 7.3 shows the trends in investment and savings rates since 1965. Starting from very low levels, both increased rapidly

**TABLE 7.7. Trends in Key Economic Aggregates (real growth rates, percentage per annum)**

|  | 1960–67 | 1967–73 | 1973–81 | 1982–88 | 1988–91 |
|---|---|---|---|---|---|
| GDP | 1.7 | 7.9 | 7.5 | 3.3 | 7.1 |
| Nonoil GDP | 1.7 | 7.3 | 8.0 | 4.3 | 7.7 |
| Agriculture | 1.6 | 4.1 | 3.4 | 2.9 | 3.0 |
| Manufacturing | 1.0 | 9.5 | 14.1 | 5.2 | 11.0 |
| Services | 2.0 | 9.0 | 10.0 | 5.0 | 7.8 |
| Fixed investment | 1.1 | 23.5 | 11.7 | –0.5 | 13.5 |
| Public | — | — | 11.0 | –2.0 | 8.2 |
| Private | — | — | 12.3 | 0.7 | 16.9 |
| Nonoil exports | 2.1 | 25.6 | 0.0 | 7.6 | 16.5 |
| Per capita GDP | –0.5 | 5.5 | 5.2 | 1.3 | 5.3 |
| Per capita income | –0.4 | 5.6 | 9.1 | –0.2 | 5.1 |
| Per capita consumption | –0.6 | 3.0 | 5.5 | 1.4 | 5.0 |

*Source:* Central Bureau of Statistics and World Bank staff estimates.

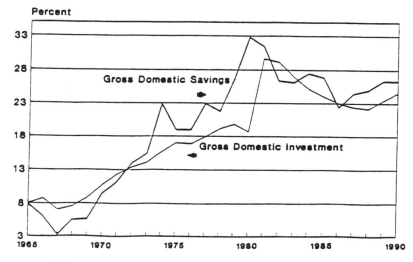

**Fig. 7.3. Investment and savings trends (percentage of GDP)**

following the policy reforms of 1966. The sharp increase in savings during the 1970s reflected the growth in oil earnings. Investment rose as well but with a lag and not to the same extent. The high savings and investment rates during this period reflect the fact that Indonesia was relatively prudent in its use of oil revenues, saving a larger proportion as well as directing more resources toward investment. The end of the oil boom inevitably led to a decline in national savings. Since 1987, however, positive real interest rates and economic recovery have reversed the decline in national savings, despite a much larger burden of debt service payments.

The investment rate also declined sharply between 1982 and 1987. This was due to a fall in public investment and was the direct outcome of the government's fiscal adjustment in response to falling oil revenues. Private investment declined as a share of GDP but did not fall in real terms. Gross domestic investment has recovered since 1987, spurred by the sharp increase in private investment after deregulation and other reforms. Consequently, the share of private investment in total investment rose from 52 percent in 1981 to 63 percent in 1990.

*Export Performance.* The stabilization and liberalization measures of the late 1960s stimulated a recovery in nonoil exports. At the time, nonoil exports were largely primary commodities; together with oil, they accounted for 97 percent of total exports. Even more than Thailand and Malaysia, Indonesia had a resource-based economy until the 1980s, and this was reflected in the structure of its exports.

During the 1970s, the surge in oil revenues dominated earnings from other exports. But primary commodity exports also grew rapidly, despite the appreciation of the exchange rate, because of the boom in world prices. When world commodity prices began to decline in 1980, commodity exports fell. This decline was reinforced by a ban on log exports introduced in 1981. However, the ban on exports was successful in stimulating the development of the plywood industry. It became Indonesia's first major manufactured export and is still today its largest. In addition to plywood, textiles became a significant export item during the first half of the 1980s.

But the major boost to manufactured exports, and to nonoil exports in general, came after the exchange rate adjustment and the reforms of 1986. The major improvement in competitiveness that followed boosted all nonoil exports, including primary commodities, but manufactured exports grew especially rapidly. Within manufactured exports, plywood and textiles remained the largest items, but other labor-intensive manufactures grew even faster. Manufactured exports rose from only 12 percent of total exports in 1985 to 45 percent in 1991, surpassing both oil and primary commodities.

*Efficiency and Productivity Growth.* Indonesia's investment and growth have been strongly influenced by external conditions and shifts in the policy stance. To disentangle the effects of external influences from underlying performance, table 7.8 analyzes the pattern of various aggregate efficiency indicators.

The table shows that rapid growth during 1967–73 was spurred by its investment—its growth, as well as its efficiency, induced by the policy reforms of

**TABLE 7.8.   Aggregate Efficiency Indicators, 1973–88**

|  | 1967–73 | 1973–81 | 1982–85 | 1985–87 | 1988–91 |
|---|---|---|---|---|---|
| Rate of return on investment (percent per annum)[a] | 53.4 | 31.4 | 13.1 | 26.0 | 17.0 |
| Incremental capital output ratio (ICOR) | 1.8 | 2.8 | 7.8 | 5.3 | 3.7 |
| Total factor productivity (TFP) change Growth rate of | | | | | |
| Value added[b] | 7.8 | 8.0 | 4.0 | 5.9 | 7.5 |
| Factor inputs | | | | | |
| Labor | 2.8 | 3.0 | 2.8 | 7.3 | 2.1 |
| Capital[c] | 7.6 | 10.7 | 9.8 | 6.8 | 8.4 |
| Total factor productivity[d] | 2.1 | 0.9 | –2.5 | –1.1 | 2.2 |

*Source:* World Bank staff estimates.
[a]Rate of growth of nonoil GDP as a percentage of average investment rate during the period.
[b]Using nonoil GDP.
[c]Capital stock derived by using the "perpetual inventory method."
[d]TFP change is calculated as the difference between rates of growth of value added and factor inputs (labor and capital). The inputs are weighted by their income shares.

1966. This can be seen from the high return on investment, the low incremental capital-output ratio (ICOR), and the magnitude of the change in total factor productivity (TFP).

The substantial increase in investment, financed through the oil boom, also fueled the growth of the nonoil economy during 1973–81. Given the low initial capital base, these investments continued to yield a fairly high average return. But, as investment went into more capital-intensive areas, the ICOR rose. Economywide efficiency also declined as policy became more inward oriented.

The legacy of promoting investment behind protective barriers became more apparent in the early 1980s after the collapse of oil prices. The government's initial response was to protect industry even more through a proliferation of non-tariff barriers (NTBs). Capital productivity fell sharply during 1982–85, as did the rate of return on investment and TFP.

Following the reforms of the mid-1980s, there has been a turnaround in productivity and efficiency indicators. ICOR levels have fallen steadily as more labor-intensive export industries have emerged as the engine of growth. The decline in TFP was reversed, and its growth in 1988–91 was matched only by its performance during 1967–73.

## III.   Continuity and Change in the Policy Framework

Overview of Policy Directions

Over the past 30 years, Indonesian policy has been marked by continuity. Not surprisingly, the areas of continuity are those where there was an early and clear consensus among the country's leadership. These areas are: (1) macroeconomic stability, (2) agricultural and rural development, (3) improvement in social conditions and human resource development, and (4) infrastructure. The emphasis on agriculture, improvements in social welfare, and upgrading the nation's extremely weak infrastructure base was shared by a broad group of leaders. Their views on agriculture were reinforced by the food crisis of 1974–75, when Indonesia was unable to buy enough rice in the international market. As for the emphasis on macroeconomic stability, it came from the chaotic experience of the mid-1960s: the hyperinflation of the 1965–66, from which emerged the Balanced Budget Law of 1967; the capital flight, and the complete erosion of investor confidence, from which stemmed the decision to open the capital account; and the debt difficulties and rescheduling in the early years of the New Order government (1968–69) and the Pertamina debt crisis of 1975, which led to caution about external borrowing.

There were, in contrast, two areas where government policy was more ambivalent. The first was a willingness to rely on the market economy. Although the New Order government took some steps during the late 1960s to liberalize the economy, they did not last; they were overtaken by concerns about the concentration of ownership in the Chinese minority, distrust of foreign investment, and a desire to regulate private activity toward desired social ends. The rapid expansion of the government machinery during the 1970s was itself a powerful force for boosting the role of the state in ownership and control.

The second area of policy volatility involved the tradeoff between growth and equity. Social and regional equity have been a shared concern of both the Old Order and New Order governments. During the oil boom, it was easier for the government to manage the tradeoff because it could afford to expand rural and social infrastructure. During the reforms of the 1980s, however, the social cost of adjustment has been a continuing theme. The government managed the tradeoff between growth and equity by protecting social expenditures and creating an early supply response. Even so, and despite strong economic growth, many people are concerned about the equity and regional impact of the new prosperity. They fear that the new liberalization has created vested interest groups. In response, the government has continued to use suasion and regulation in an attempt to meet social and equity objectives.

## Macroeconomic Policies

The combination of a balanced budget, an open capital account, and generally cautious external borrowing has created a prudent and responsive macroeconomic framework. The open capital account has kept a check on monetary expansion through its influence on external reserves. At the same time, although external borrowing and the drawdown-buildup of government deposits have allowed fiscal policy to deviate from a strict balanced budget rule, the absence of domestic borrowing and money creation has ensured that Indonesia avoided the fiscal excesses common in many other developing countries. The fiscal rule also provided an impetus to undertake longer-term fiscal reforms during the 1980s on both revenue and expenditures. An added feature of macroeconomic policy was active exchange rate management as an instrument to maintain the competitiveness of the nonoil economy.

*Fiscal Policy.* During the 1970s, government spending grew very rapidly. However, oil revenues were so large that the government was able to build up a substantial stock of assets. During the 1980s, fiscal policy had to change, to achieve macroeconomic stabilization and less reliance on oil revenues. The government was largely successful in achieving both of these objectives. Initially, it did so by cutting investment. Many large capital-intensive projects were rephased in 1983, and public investment continued to decline in real terms until 1987. In addition, the government undertook a sweeping tax reform in 1984–86 to boost nonoil tax revenues and improve the efficiency of the tax system (Ahmed 1989; Asher 1991). As a result, nonoil taxes as percent of nonoil GDP rose from 8.3 percent in 1982–83 to 13.2 percent in 1991–92. The government also reduced current outlays through a three-year freeze on civil salaries (1986–88) and much slower growth in the civil service. These steps turned a public sector deficit of 4.9 percent of GDP in 1982–83 into a surplus after 1990. The unexpected surge in private investment since 1988 has created extra demand pressures requiring an even more cautious fiscal stance.

*Monetary Policy.* Fiscal policy was complemented by monetary and financial policies designed to contain inflationary pressures, prevent capital flight, boost savings, and improve the allocation of financial resources. When monetary policy was lax, as in late 1989, the open capital account provided an immediate signal of inconsistent policies, and the government was prompt to respond. Reserve money growth as well as growth of monetary aggregates have been substantially reduced over the adjustment period. The ability to bring down inflation and preserve depreciation in the real exchange rate is testimony to the soundness of fiscal and monetary management albeit at the cost of high interest rates in periods such as 1990–92.

*Exchange Rate Management.* Indonesia has pursued a more active exchange rate policy than other Southeast Asian countries have, particularly during the 1980s. After several devaluations in the late 1960s, the nominal exchange rate remained unchanged for a long period after 1971. With the surge in oil revenues, the result was a real appreciation of currency. This prompted growing concerns about the competitiveness of the nonoil economy. The government responded with a 34 percent devaluation of the exchange rate, even though there were no balance of payments pressures. The devaluation was eroded over the next 18 months because of the second oil price increase of 1979–80 (Pitt 1991). Without the devaluation, however, the real exchange rate would have appreciated even more.

Indonesia had two maxi-devaluations during the 1980s—one in March 1983, at the start of the first stabilization period, and the second in September 1986. Whereas the first devaluation was primarily aimed at closing the large current account deficit, the second was specifically intended to improve the competitiveness of the nonoil economy. Indonesia changed to a managed float system after the 1978 devaluation, but the float was applied actively only after 1988.

As a result of these policies, Indonesia has been able to sustain a real depreciation of 55 percent since 1983. This has contributed to successful adjustment in four ways: by (1) stimulating a strong export response that reduced the transitional costs of adjustment, (2) restraining imports, (3) facilitating trade liberalization, and (4) improving competitiveness and thereby supporting a strong recovery of private investment.

*External Borrowing.* Indonesia has gone through several cycles of external borrowing. It borrowed excessively in the early 1960s, which led to the debt reschedulings of the late 1960s. In 1975 there was a second surge in borrowing, partly driven by the state oil company (Pertamina). Following the resolution of the Pertamina crisis, the government brought in strict controls on public enterprise borrowing and used the windfalls to reduce external indebtedness. By 1980, the debt service ratio was down to 13 percent.

However, in the early 1980s, the government turned to commercial borrowing to finance several large public sector investments. When oil prices declined in 1982, it borrowed even more to meet the financing gap. Much of this increased borrowing was yen-denominated, so when the yen appreciated in 1986–87 the level of debt and debt service rose considerably.[1]

When oil prices declined again in 1986, external borrowing was more prudently managed than in the first adjustment period. The government relied on concessional official financing rather than commercial financing to support the balance of payments. Although borrowing rose after 1986, the debt service ratio declined from 40 percent in 1986–87 to 30 percent in 1991–92, thanks to the recovery of nonoil exports. A third surge in external borrowing occurred in 1990, this time largely due to private sector investment. A growing number of large public and quasi-public projects also added to borrowing pressures. In response, the government moved to restrain aggregate demand and set up a ministerial team to establish borrowing ceilings for public and quasi-public entities.

In general, Indonesia's external borrowing over the past 30 years has been prudent. It has been used to finance development expenditures and facilitate smooth adjustment. Nonetheless, the scale of external borrowing in the 1980s has left Indonesia with a debt burden that is significantly larger than that of other East Asian economies and has largely offset the "oil advantage" that Indonesia had previously enjoyed. In 1991, public debt service totaled $8.5 billion, more than the revenues received from oil (excluding LNG).

## Trade and Regulatory Policies

*Initial Liberalization, 1966–71.* Despite three liberalization attempts in 1951, 1955, and 1957, the Indonesian economy became progressively inward oriented and regulated during the Soekarno period. The first major liberalization occurred during 1966–71, when the New Order government dismantled the import licensing system, removed most price controls, eliminated direct allocations of foreign exchange, and opened the economy to foreign investment (Pitt 1991). These changes were introduced with extraordinary speed, unlike the reforms of the 1980s, and against a backdrop of chaotic macroeconomic and social conditions. However, although the import licensing system was

---

1. Depreciation of the U.S. dollar added $12.1 billion (31 percent) to Indonesia's public debt between 1985 and 1988.

eliminated, not much change was made to the protective structure of tariffs. And it was notable that improvement in incentives to exporters came before the liberalization of the payments system for imports.

*Inward Orientation and Regulation, 1973–85.* The appreciation of the real exchange rate after 1971 led to increased pressures to protect industry. By 1980, Indonesia's import regime was characterized by disparate tariff rates and a range of nontariff barriers (NTBs). The NTBs included an importer licensing system, import bans and quotas, and various informal quantitative restrictions (e.g., the complex port and customs clearance procedures). During the early 1980s, the government expanded the role of import licensing controls with the intention of boosting import substitution in such basic goods as cement, chemicals, fertilizers, synthetic fibers, and iron and steel. The Ministry of Trade issued several decrees in late 1982 and early 1983 increasing the number of products requiring an "approved-importer" license.[2] It also cut the number of approved traders, often to as few as two or three (usually state owned) companies. Besides nominating who may import, some decrees also established the Department of Trade's authority to fix formal quotas. For manufactured goods, these decisions were based on consultation with the Department of Industry and were often linked to local content programs. These programs, designed to increase the local content of various domestic assembly activities, initially covered motor vehicles, tractors, diesel engines, and motorcycles but were then extended to construction equipment, diesel engines, home appliances, and electronic goods.

By 1985, a plethora of decrees had brought a wide range of products under different forms of import control. This made it extremely difficult for potential investors or policymakers to get a clear picture of the impact of the existing trade regime on the economy. It is estimated that in 1985 some 1,484 items (28 percent of the total) were restricted to holders of an approved-importer license. These items accounted for about 26 percent of total import value and 32 percent of domestic value added (excluding construction and services).[3] However, the level of protection for domestic producers varied significantly. In the most restrictive cases (e.g., some iron and steel, plastics, and agricultural products), imports were channeled through a sole importer, often accompanied by a binding quota. In other cases, where licenses were restricted to a few approved traders, imports may have been informally controlled through approval of the

---

2. This restricted the right to import such goods to designated traders or producers. The actual degree of restriction depended on such factors as the number of license holders and whether a quota was in effect.

3. These calculations include oil and petroleum products, for which there are very few license restrictions. Excluding these items would increase the coverage of license restrictions to 30 percent of import value and 53 percent of domestic value added (excluding construction and services).

annual import plan by the Department of Trade. At the other end of the spectrum, there were the approved-importer quotas. Of the 1,484 items under approved-importer license, less than one-quarter were subject to formal quotas. In addition, there were 24 products for which imports were banned. These included automobiles, motorcycles, TVs, and radios.

The combination of NTBs and high tariffs produced high rates of protection in many manufacturing activities. Overall, the regime favored import substitution over exports. It also favored "basic," or "upstream," industries over "final product," or "downstream," industries. As a result, resources were drawn into relatively inefficient capital-intensive activities supplying the domestic market. The more labor intensive or efficient downstream producers were penalized, and export growth was reduced.

*Domestic Regulations and Foreign Investment Policies.* The private sector in the 1970s and the early 1980s was not just hindered by trade-related regulations but also by a multitude of domestic controls and procedures. The combination stifled competition, inhibited flexibility, encouraged rent seeking and held back productivity improvements. The main elements of the regulatory framework were: a restrictive investment and capacity licensing system, extensive controls on foreign investment, a proliferation of provincial and local regulations, cumbersome land and labor laws, and an increasingly outmoded framework of corporate law.

The main instrument of investment licensing was the investment priority (DSP) list, which regulated entry into specific industries for both foreign and domestic investors. The DSP list specified four categories of investment: those open to foreign investment, those open to domestic firms seeking incentives,[4] those open to small- and medium-scale industry and domestic investors without incentives, and those closed to further investment. The DSP list often indicated the number of projects for which licenses would be given as well as the permitted capacity.

Apart from the investment license, a firm had to obtain several other licenses and permits, including many at the provincial or local level, before it could commence operations. These included: the import and export licenses described earlier, a domestic trading license, a storage permit, land rights, a location permit, a nuisance license (including pollution control approval), a building permit, a safety permit, tax registration, and a permanent operating license. Although many of these licenses served legitimate regulatory concerns, the procedures for obtaining them were complex. They represented a significant barrier to entry in terms of time, money, and uncertainty. The entire

---

4. The incentives provided to domestic investors in this category (and to all foreign investors) are exemptions from import duties on capital equipment and the equivalent of two year's supply of raw materials.

process of getting approval often took more than two years from the investment proposal stage.

Foreign firms wishing to invest in Indonesia were subject to even tougher
rules than were domestic firms. These included: (1) generally more restrictive
investment licensing criteria; (2) minimum initial requirements for local ownership plus specified phasing for the transfer of the company from foreign to
local ownership; (3) a ban on domestic trading of outputs and the marketing of
Indonesian exports as well as restrictions on what domestic inputs could be purchased; (4) limitations on land lease; and (5) limited access to domestic capital,
including export financing.

*Public Enterprises.* Investment by public enterprises (PEs) rose sharply in
the 1970s and early 1980s supported by burgeoning oil revenues. By the mid-
1980s, there were 214 centrally owned PEs plus many others at the provincial
and local public levels. The central enterprises range widely in agriculture,
manufacturing, trading, banking, other services, and public utilities, and they
are supervised by 14 ministries. The stated objectives of PEs are: (1) to earn
profits and contribute to government revenues, (2) to contribute to national economic development, (3) to provide public utility services, (4) to undertake
pioneering activities that the private sector would not, and (5) to provide guidance to the private sector and cooperatives and to complement their overall
activities. PEs are required to prepare corporate plans on a rolling basis, though
less than half have complied with this condition. The annual budgets of PEs
are examined by their supervising (technical) ministries and the Ministry of
Finance, which provides finance for them in the government budget. PEs are required to submit monthly financial reports to their supervising ministries and
the MOF. The audit of PE accounts is undertaken by an independent audit
agency (BPKP).

The PEs in Indonesia have suffered from two systemic weaknesses. First,
their financial performance has been poor because of overstaffing, multiplicity
of objectives, insufficient autonomy, and management weaknesses. Second,
they have been concentrated in sectors that faced limited domestic or import
competition. Consequently, their outputs were often priced well above world
prices, putting a burden on other segments of the economy.

*Deregulation and Outward Orientation, 1985–91.* Beginning in 1985, the
government started to reduce and simplify regulations in order to encourage
the private sector. Deregulation has gathered momentum over the past six
years, culminating in major reforms of trade policy, investment licensing, and
transport.

In March 1985, the government announced an across the board reduction
in the range and level of import tariffs. The tariff ceiling was reduced from 225
to 60 percent, with tariff rates for most products ranging from 5 to 35 percent.
The number of tariff levels was also reduced from 25 to 11, although the full

benefit of this rationalization was mitigated by the proliferation of licensing restrictions. Second, the government overhauled customs, parts, and shipping operations and placed the sensitive job of certifying imports in the hands of private surveyors (SGS). As a result, the time and cost of customs clearance were reduced considerably.

During 1986, the government moved to the next stage of trade policy reform. It insulated exporters from the adverse effects of the import regime, and it began to dismantle the import licensing system. In May, it announced measures that gave major exporters access to unrestricted and duty-free imports. In October, following the 31 percent devaluation of the exchange rate, it took the first steps to dismantle the complex import licensing system. The intention was to phase out nontariff barriers and move toward an import regime based solely on tariffs. Since then, the government has announced five further trade packages to reduce NTBs, reform the tariff structure, and reduce some export restrictions.

*Reform of NTBs.* As is shown in table 7.9, the share of imports subject to NTBs fell from 43 percent in 1986 to 13 percent in June 1991, and the proportion of domestic production protected by NTBs has declined from 41 to 22 percent. The NTB coverage of domestic production of tradables is lower, covering only 8 percent of total production value. Nevertheless, some important subsectors in manufacturing, such as engineering goods, paper products and food processing, and a significant proportion of agricultural goods, remain subject to NTBs.

TABLE 7.9.  **Impact of Reform Packages on Import Licensing Coverage since 1986**

|  | Mid-1986 | End of 1988 | June 1991 |
|---|---|---|---|
| NTB coverage as |  |  |  |
| % of CCCN items | 32 | 16 | — |
| % of HS items | — | — | 10 |
| % of import value | 43 | 21 | 13 |
| % of total production value | 41 | 29 | 22 |
| Memo items |  |  |  |
| % of domestic production coverage of NTBs |  |  |  |
| Manufacturing | 68 | 45 | 32 |
| Agriculture | 54 | 41 | 30 |
| Mining and minerals[a] | 0.2 | 0.2 | 0.2 |

*Source:* World Bank staff estimates.

*Note:* There is a discontinuity in the series from the end of 1988 due to two causes: the shift from CCCN to the HS system of tariffs and the update from 1985 to 1987 production weights for calculating production coverage ratios of NTBs. However, this discontinuity does not change the trends since 1986. It should be noted that the food, beverage, and tobacco industries are included in the manufacturing sector.

[a]Including oil and gas.

*Tariff Reforms.* The average level and dispersion of tariffs have also fallen considerably (table 7.10). The (unweighted) average tariff is now 20 percent, compared with 37 percent before 1985. The latest reforms have concentrated on cutting tariff rates above 35 percent as part of the general move toward a tariff structure with a ceiling of 30 to 35 percent. At present, around 83 percent of all items have tariff rates at or below this range. In line with the government's efforts to promote an open economy, the reforms in the tariff structure have ensured that over half of the domestic output from import-competing sectors have tariffs of 10 percent or less.

*Reform of the Export Regime.* One big change in export incentives was the creation of a duty exemption and drawback facility in May 1986. This facility partially protects exporters from the antiexport bias that still exists in the economy by allowing them to import their inputs free of duty and bypass the import licensing restriction (for those products under NTBs).[5] In addition, the provision of preshipment export finance guarantees (PEFGs) and export credit insurance/guarantees (ECIs) have been valuable moves for exporters. Even so, less has been done to improve export incentives than to liberalize imports. Over one-quarter of domestic tradables are still subject to some form of export control.

*Other Regulatory Reforms.* Beginning in 1985, the government began to liberalize the investment licensing system, initially through the streamlining of licensing and approval procedures. In 1989, it went much further, replacing a partial and complex positive list with a short negative list of activities closed to private investment. Virtually all areas of manufacturing that were open to domestic investors were also opened to foreign investment. Since 1989, the government has continued to reduce the scope of the negative list.

**TABLE 7.10.   Changes in the Tariff Schedule (including surcharges)**

|  | Pre-1985 | 1989 | 1991 |
|---|---|---|---|
| Average tariff rates (%) |  |  |  |
| Unweighted | 37 | 27 | 20 |
| Weighted |  |  |  |
| By import value | 22 | 12 | 10 |
| By domestic production | 29 | 19 | 15 |
| Index of dispersion[a] | 62 | 93 | 83 |

*Source:* World Bank staff estimates.
[a]Measured by the coefficient of variation.

5. Import duty and value-added tax exemptions can be given for either a firm's total imported inputs—if the firm exports 65 percent or more of total production—or on a consignment basis (where a particular import order is directly linked to an export order).

As a result of these reforms, investment licensing is no longer a significant barrier to entry of firms in the tradable goods sectors. Investors are largely
free to respond to the more competitive environment. The deregulation has also
led a much greater degree of competition from foreign firms. This trend has
been assisted by other measures to reduce impediments to foreign investment.
In particular, divestiture requirements have been relaxed, and virtually eliminated for export-oriented investment, and the differential treatment between
domestic and foreign firms in trade and access to finance has been considerably
reduced.

A third area where major regulatory reforms were introduced in 1989 was
shipping, which plays a particularly important role in Indonesia. The 1989 reforms transformed the industry from one that was highly regulated to one of
the most liberal in the world.

*Effects on Effective Rates of Protection and Competition.* The scale of the
trade reforms can be gauged from the effective rates of protection (ERPs). Although the estimates for 1975 in table 7.11 are not strictly comparable with

**TABLE 7.11.  Effective Rates of Protection in Manufacturing**

| Industry | Effective Rate of Protection (%) | | |
|---|---|---|---|
| | 1975 | 1987 | 1990 |
| Basic industries | 38.7 | 8.0 | 5.0 |
| Nonoil | — | –1.0 | 1.0 |
| Oil refining | — | –1.0 | –1.0 |
| Iron and steel basic industries | 18.2 | 13.0 | 10.0 |
| Chemicals | 28.4 | 14.0 | 13.0 |
| Cement | 63.6 | 60.2 | 53.6 |
| Capital goods industries | 15.3 | 150.0 | 97.0 |
| Engineering goods | — | 152.0 | 139.0 |
| Intermediate goods industries | 49.0 | 42.0 | 40.0 |
| Wood and cork products | –1.2 | 25.0 | 33.0 |
| Rubber and plastic products | 426.0 | 57.0 | 48.0 |
| Consumer goods industries | 116.2 | 87.0 | 64.6 |
| Food, beverages, and tobacco | 336.2 | 122.0 | 124.0 |
| Paper and paper products | 87.3 | 31.0 | 20.0 |
| Textiles, cloth, and footwear | 231.8 | 102.0 | 35.0 |
| Manufacturing total (excluding oil refining) | 74.1 | 68.0 | 59.0 |
| All tradables (excluding oil sector) | 29.7 | 26.0 | 24.0 |
| Import-competing sector | 61.0 | 39.0 | 35.0 |
| Export-competing sector | –6.0 | –2.0 | –1.0 |

*Source:* World Bank staff estimates.

those for 1987 and 1990 because of differences in methodology, they suggest that the level and dispersion of effective protection, as well as the antiexport bias, have been substantially reduced since the 1970s and the 1980s. ERPs remain high for engineering and food industries, which are also the ones with NTBs. Despite the reforms, the level and dispersion of ERPs are still high compared with countries that have completed comprehensive trade liberalization, and there is a continuing bias against exports.

The trade and regulatory reforms also appear to have led to an increase in competitive pressures. Table 7.12 presents three types of evidence on the degree of competition. First, the four-firm concentration ratio is an indication of the degree of competition between domestic firms in the domestic market. Second, the import penetration ratio (imports as a percentage of output available in the total domestic market) indicates the degree of competition posed by imports. Third, the export share measures how much firms are subject to competition in foreign markets.

Overall, competition appears to have been promoted most in textiles, wood products, and other manufactures. The areas where competition is still limited tend to be dominated by the public sector and conglomerate interests. This is also an important reason why there has been less progress on import deregulation and domestic competition in these sectors.

## Financial Markets and Policies

In the New Order period, the role of government in financial markets and policies has changed from extreme intervention to a more market-oriented approach. As with deregulation elsewhere in the economy, the turning points in policy are related to the fall in oil prices.

*Initial Conditions.* During the Old Order period, more and more of the financial sector came under government control. As Woo et al. (1994) point out, this was mainly due to an ideology that was averse to financial capitalism. By 1965, government control was extensive. After a series of nationalizations, the financial system was dominated by state banks acting as commercial, savings, and development banks. There were the five units of Bank Negara Indonesia (unit I of BNI functioned as the central bank), Bank Dagang Negara (state commercial bank), 23 development banks (1 state-owned Bappindo and 22 regional development banks), two private savings banks, and 87 private commercial banks.

As pointed out by Nasution (1983), the central bank also served to implement government spending since the government borrowed from it in excess of the stipulated 30 percent of treasury reserves.

*Pre-Oil-Boom Period: Rehabilitation and Consolidation.* At the beginning of the New Order period, the immediate concern was to reestablish the

**TABLE 7.12. The Effects of the Reforms on Competition in the Industrial Sector (in percentage)**

| Sector | 1985[a] | | | | | 1989[b] | | | | |
|---|---|---|---|---|---|---|---|---|---|---|
| | Government[c] Share | Conclusion Ratio | Import Penetration | ERP | Export Share | Government[c] Share | Conclusion Ratio | Import Penetration | ERP | Export Share |
| Food, beverage and tobacco | 22.1 | 60.2 | 4.4 | 122.0 | 8.4 | 16.8 | 39.7 | 6.2 | 149.5 | 6.3 |
| Textiles | 30.2 | 40.6 | 5.8 | 0 | 11.5 | 4.7 | 13.8 | 8.7 | 79.1 | 16.7 |
| Wood and wood products | 22.6 | 18.8 | 0.6 | 102.0 | 28.0 | 3.2 | 11.9 | 0.7 | -2.9 | 34.6 |
| Paper and paper products | 33.1 | 45.3 | 25.2 | 0 | 1.9 | 16.9 | 33.1 | 21.6 | 16.8 | 5.7 |
| Chemicals and plastics | 51.2 | 49.7 | 33.2 | 25.0 | 3.0 | 30.4 | 18.3 | 33.0 | 39.6 | 4.7 |
| Nonmetallic minerals | 65.5 | 60.2 | 12.0 | 31.0 | 2.2 | 36.5 | 34.2 | 12.6 | 63.3 | 8.9 |
| Basic metals | 84.6 | 87.1 | 42.0 | 14.0 | 19.0 | 82.7 | 88.1 | 37.8 | 8.3 | 25.0 |
| Machinery and equipment | 37.7 | 49.7 | 54.0 | 57.0 | 1.8 | 18.7 | 30.0 | 48.4 | 148.0 | 2.8 |
| Other manufacturing | 39.1 | 75.5 | 35.6 | 13.0 / 152.0 | 19.9 | 0.09 | 32.6 | 33.9 | 86.1 | 32.0 |
| Average (unweighted) | 42.9 | 54.1 | 23.6 | 0 / 124.0 / 0 / 71.1 | 10.6 | 23.3 | 32.5 | 22.5 | 65.3 | 15.2 |
| Two sectors with highest public presence | 75.0 | 73.6 | 27.0 | 35.0 | 10.6 | 60.0 | 61.1 | 25.2 | 35.8 | 16.9 |
| Two sectors with lowest public presence | 22.4 | 39.5 | 2.5 | 73.5 | 18.2 | 4.0 | 12.8 | 4.7 | 38.1 | 25.6 |

*Source:* Central Bureau of Statistics, Census of Manufacturing Industry, and World Bank staff estimates.

[a] Import penetration and export shares have been calculated for 1986.

[b] Government share and concentration ratios as percentage of value added by sector.

[c] Includes joint ventures.

financial institutions as part of the rehabilitation program. In 1967, the government permitted foreign banks to operate in Indonesia through subsidiary branches, though they could not offer savings deposits, were limited to two branches, and could not lend outside Jakarta. Foreign banks were allowed in on a full-branch basis until 1969; then entry was closed.

Second, the government restructured the state-owned financial institutions through a series of laws in 1967–69. BNI I became Bank Indonesia, the central bank, and the other units became four independent state-owned banks: Bank Rakyat Indonesia, BNI 1946, Bank Ekspor-Impor Indonesia, and Bank Bumi Daya. Together with Bank Dagang Negara there were five state commercial banks, each with its own area of specialization, arranged so that at least two of the state banks covered each major economic sector.

Bank Negara Indonesia 1946: industry-transportation, agriculture-livestock, and export producing sectors

Bank Rakyat Indonesia: cooperatives, agriculture-livestock, fisheries, and rural development

Bank Dagang Negara: mining and export production

Bank Bumi Daya: mining, export production, and plantations

Bank Ekspor-Impor Indonesia: export production and marketing, plantations

The state-owned development bank, Bappindo, was given the task of providing long-term development funds, and Bank Tabungan Nasional remained the main savings bank. Altogether, there were 11 types of banks differentiated by ownership and function.

State banks were also given certain privileges that strengthened their positions vis-à-vis private banks: access to BNI, implicit government guarantees and extensive networks of branches, and the fact that state-owned enterprises were required to deposit government funds in state banks. This favoritism had several reasons behind it. First, state banks were the dominant players and had the bigger branch networks. Second, the government wanted a strong presence in the economy, based on Article 33 of the Constitution. The usual interpretation of the article is that economic activities that affect the daily lives of the people should be controlled by the government through state enterprises.

The central bank also played an influential role in the country's financial development by extending credits to nonfinancial institutions that were mainly government related. Nasution (1983) notes that the official reason for its actions goes beyond the lender of last resort function; the Central Bank has a broader mandate "to finance the implementation of government programs." As such, direct credit was used to support large projects that could not be financed by commercial banks and also to "hide" subsidies paid by the government to stabilize food item prices.

In 1968, the dominance of the state in the financial system was quite plain. State banks held 74 percent of the total assets of deposit-taking banks, and Bank Indonesia and the state banks between them accounted for 93 percent of total commercial bank credit. The large number of private domestic banks (10 foreign exchange and 112 non–foreign exchange banks) accounted only for 25 percent of assets and 6.3 percent of credit.

The development of the financial sector and the improving investment climate led to the inflow of the capital needed to rehabilitate the economy. However, the banking sector remained underdeveloped: in 1970, the M1/GDP and M2/GDP ratios remained low, at 7.1 percent and 9.37 percent.[6]

*Oil Boom Years.* The states's dominance of the financial sector continued right through the beginning of the oil boom. During the boom years, government oil revenues were abundant and were channelled into the domestic economy through a system of liquidity credits and credit allocations. In April 1974, with the start of the Second Five Year Development Plan, Bank Indonesia introduced a program of direct credit control and allocation. Its main features were:

1. Credit ceilings for individual banks, with subceilings for various categories of loans.
2. A complex rediscount mechanism, designed to reallocate credit and provide subsidies. The proportion of the loan for any particular credit program and the rediscount rate were regulated. The interest rate on the loan was also regulated.
3. Controls on interest rates of deposits (greater than three months) of state banks. Private banks were free to set their own rates.

The initial rationale for credit control was to sterilize the increase in the money supply resulting from the oil boom. The government set ceilings for types of credit for each bank and specified the interest rates on lending. However, increasingly the system was used to allocate credit by state banks in their function as the agents of development. This function, "which meant that they [the banks] were expected to be more pioneering than a normal bank would be and that they had to take more risks than a normal bank would be willing to take," [7] was seen as an implicit market failure argument.

---

6. M1 is cash in circulation and checking accounts; M2 is equal to the amount of M1 plus savings and money market accounts.
7. Rachmat Saleh, governor of the central bank in 1978, quoted in Woo 1994, 22.

Liquidity credits were a major source of funding, accounting for 48 percent of total credit by 1982. Although the bulk of their liquidity credits went to the state banks (93 to 98 percent during the 1976–82), they also helped the private domestic banks to grow. The role of the state banks increased; together with Bank Indonesia credits, they accounted for around 85–90 percent of all bank credits in 1974–82.

There were several criteria for subsidizing credit: economic (e.g., industrial development), food security (i.e., food stocks), distribution to the "weak" (indigenous) economic sector (e.g., small-scale credit), and support for rice production (e.g., agricultural credit programs). In 1976, the main sectors receiving subsidized credit were: food stocks (31.2 percent), medium-term investment credit (11.1 percent), agricultural credits (27.2 percent), Krakatau Steel (11 percent), Perumtel (3.5 percent), and small-scale credit (7.9 percent). By 1982, the targets had become more diverse; food stocks (4.8 percent), agricultural production (3.8 percent), and state-owned enterprises (3.8 percent) had lost share, while small-scale credit accounted for a large percentage (23 percent). The other sectors that began to get a share of subsidized credit were industrial production, construction, and exports.

The financial sector also grew rapidly during 1974–82, and the share of state and private banks in total lending expanded from 86 to 92 percent. The gains of these banks came at the expense of joint ventures and foreign banks, whose share fell from 13 to 8 percent.

The number of foreign banks remained the same, since new entry was prohibited, and the number of private banks fell from 97 in 1978 to only 60 by 1982. This was due to a ban on new entry and a Bank Indonesia policy to encourage the merger of private banks. The number of bank offices did not increase much due to the stringent conditions imposed on private banks and the fact that state banks had liquidity credit funds and captive deposits from state-owned enterprises and the government. Both Woo and Nasution (1989) and Suwidjana (1984) suggest that the system of credit allocation determined the structure of the banking system because Bank Indonesia could set the shares assigned to any bank. The ceilings also acted to minimize entry into the banking system.

As for the securities market, up to 1982 its was not very active and provided only a small proportion of total credit. A large number of the companies that went public were foreign and did so to comply with the divestment requirements and to take advantage of generous tax concessions.

What have been the effects of this financial system? First, investments financed by credits contributed to overall economic growth, but their productivity was poor. Allocation of credit ensured the growing state participation in the economy, notably in the industry. State-owned enterprises received 52 percent of total credit in 1978 and 37 percent in 1982.

Second, as pointed out by Woo et al. (1994) nonmarket credit allocation allowed subsidized credit to increase its coverage, and on even more generous terms. This occurred because of pressure from various interest groups such as estates, sugar plantations, and construction firms.

Third, an efficient banking system did not develop. State banks did not mobilize savings, then lend and perform their intermediation function. Instead, their main function was to channel money: they were provided with low-cost and captive funds and told which sectors to lend to and at what interest rates. As Woo et al. (1994) point out, the state banks (unlike the private banks) usually did not use all of their credit allocations. This could have been due to bureaucratic difficulties in obtaining a loan from state banks, inability of bank officers to select acceptable projects, and/or that officers of state banks may have demanded side payments from prospective borrowers. In fact, state banks did have problems of mismanagement and high default rates during this period. In 1977, the government had to bail out one of the state banks, Bank Bumi Daya. As for private banks, their ability to intermediate between lender and borrowers was limited by the their credit ceilings.

Fourth, real interest rates on state bank deposits were negative throughout the period of regulated interest rates. The ratio of money supply to GDP remained low and did not increase very much. For M1, it rose from 7.1 percent in 1974 to 11.36 percent in 1982 and for M2 from 9.37 to 17.68 percent.

Fifth, the credit ceilings were not successful in sterilizing the inflow of money from oil revenues. This was because of leakages from foreign borrowing, themselves due to the open capital account. There were practical problems associated with adjusting ceilings quickly and by the right amount.

*Initial Oil Price Decline: First Phase Financial Reforms.* The response to the initial oil price decline in the early 1980s was to deregulate the financial sector, recognizing the need for greater domestic savings to finance further development. In part, the move was also aimed at increasing the efficiency and competitiveness of the financial sector. The main reforms were:

1. The removal of all credit ceilings
2. A reduction in the number of credit categories financed by liquidity credit
3. The removal of controls on deposit and lending rates (outside of those still being refinanced by Bank Indonesia) of state banks
4. The removal of remaining subsidies on deposit rates paid by state banks

The consequences of the deregulation were as expected. The removal of interest rate controls led to an immediate rise in interest rates and deposits. Real interest rates turned positive, especially for state banks. Total time deposits increased substantially, but demand deposits barely changed. Thus, the M1/GDP ratio declined after the 1983 reform, while the M2/GDP ratio increased dramatically, from 17.7 percent in 1982 to 29.6 percent in 1988.

At the same time, the assets of the banking system and the value of credit given continued to increase rapidly, particularly for private domestic banks. Their share of total assets rose from 12.3 percent in 1982 to 26.4 percent in 1988 and of total credit of commercial banks from 12.1 to 25 percent. And banking became more competitive: the interest rate spread of state banks fell from 3.3 to 2.3 percent, and of private banks from 7.6 to 6.6 percent.[8]

In a more competitive environment, the sluggishness of the state banks was due to their size and the fact that they still functioned as state-owned enterprises. They did try to adjust: for instance, BNI 1946 retrenched some 600 people, many state banks offered early retirement, and all went in for substantial training and upgrading. However, they were still subject to the regulations and structure of any other state-owned enterprise, so their ability to change has been limited.

*Second External Shock: Liberalization of the Financial Sector.* The second external shock, in 1986, prompted an extensive reform of the financial sector between 1988 and 1992. The October 1988 deregulation removed most of the entry barriers. New banks, whether joint ventures or domestic, can be set up with capital requirements of Rp.50 and Rp.10 billion, respectively, and sound domestic private banks are eligible for a foreign exchange license. Regulations on opening new branches were substantially relaxed, and foreign banks were allowed to open one subbranch in six other major cities. State-owned enterprises were also allowed to deposit 50 percent of their funds in private banks. Reserve requirements, which were thought to be high by international standards and were thus increasing the cost of bank services, were drastically reduced. They fell from 15 percent for demand deposits and 10 percent for savings and time deposits to 2 percent of deposit liabilities. Other measures included the establishment of legal lending limits for loans to a single borrower and to groups of borrowers. Banks were allowed to issue shares, and the tax exemption on interest on time deposits was also removed to equalize the treatment of interest payments and dividends.

Later, several other policy changes were made in the financial sector. In December 1988, some capital markets deregulation eased the requirements for companies to go public, eliminated the limits on price fluctuations, and gave priority to the state-owned corporation Danareksa. Foreign joint ventures and local companies were allowed to become securities companies. In mid-1989, the percentage of foreign participation was set at 49 percent (except for the purchase of bank shares), a change that promoted a surge of overseas interest. The

---

8. See Chant and Pangestu 1994.

equalizing of the treatment of dividends and interest payments also boosted the attractiveness of shares.

Other measures followed, intended primarily to clarify the meaning of various rules. In March 1989, the authorities set out the definition of bank capital, stipulated that banks could not invest in stocks, and replaced foreign borrowing ceilings by a net open position of 25 percent of equity. This was followed in February 1991 by detailed criteria for bank soundness, higher professional standards for bank directors and commissioners, and a ruling that banks had to meet the Bank for International Settlements (BIS) capital adequacy requirements of 8 percent by the end of 1993.

Finally, the new banking law was passed in July 1992 and ratified in October. It stipulated that there would be no more specialized banks and only two types of banks: general and people's banks. People's banks are not allowed to provide demand deposits or participate in the clearing process and foreign exchange services. Foreigners can now purchase bank shares. The legal status of state banks was changed to that of a limited liability company to allow them more autonomy and to be managed as private corporations. In October 1992, the capital requirements to set up domestic and joint venture banks were raised by five times for the former and doubled for the latter. This move appears to have been motivated by the wish to limit the number of new banks. Liquidity credits were also reduced as of April 1990, a change related to the deadline given by GATT to Indonesia to remove the subsidized export credit scheme by April 1991.

What have been the effects of such extensive liberalization? Since 1988, the growth of the financial sector has been dramatic. The number of new banks increased from 61 to 119 in 1991, and the number of foreign banks increased from 11 to 29. The relaxation of branching requirements led to a big increase in the number of bank offices, especially of private domestic banks whose branches expanded from just 559 in 1988 to 2,639 by end of 1991.

The range of new products and services has also increased. Various types of savings schemes tied to lottery prizes and gifts were introduced, so savings deposits outside of the government programs increased from Rp.605 billion in 1988 to Rp.9064 billion by June 1992. There was also stiff competition for qualified staff.

The shares of the state banks in assets and credit fell to 50 and 54 percent, respectively, by 1991; state banks are still dominant but no longer predominant. They faced strong competition for deposits as well as credit to prime customers, and this pressure initially led to an increase in the deposit rate but very little increase in the lending rate. Later, as deposits increased and banks became very liquid, deposit rates also started to come down. This combination led to an unprecedented increase in credits. They were given not just for production but also for consumer loans, real estate, and reportedly for the stock market. The share of total credit going to "other" sectors outside of agriculture, industry, service, and trade increased from 6 percent in 1988 to 12 percent in 1990. Monetary growth was very high during this period: 40 percent in 1989 for M1 and M2, and 18 percent for M1 and 44 percent for M2 in 1990. As a result, GDP growth was also rapid, reaching an average of 7.4 percent per annum in 1989–90. Inflation also rose, reaching almost 10 percent in 1990, and the current account deficit increased.

In response, the central bank began to reduce liquidity credits in 1990 and tightened its monetary stance. This led to some banks experiencing liquidity problems. As a result, deposit rates began to rise dramatically as banks competed for deposits to offset their tight liquidity. Banks and nonbanks also began to borrow abroad.

In 1990, some banks had a run on their deposits after rumors spread that they were in difficulty. The mood was aggravated when in August 1990 it was revealed that Bank Duta, one of the 10 biggest domestic foreign exchange banks had incurred losses of U.S.$400 million in foreign exchange dealings. It became clear that at the time Bank Duta went public earlier in the year the losses had already been incurred. The fact that the bank's financial statements did not reveal this to the public was considered to be fraudulent and added to the growing lack of confidence in the stock market.

By the beginning of 1991, money supply growth was high and inflationary concerns were increasing. This led to the second Sumarlin shock, in February 1991, when Rp.8 trillion (U.S.$4.2 billion) of deposits of state enterprises were withdrawn from the banks and shifted into SBI (Bank Indonesia Certificates).[9] As a result, deposit rates were increased by 4 to 5 percent, which did at least stave off further speculation. At the same time the government brought in tougher regulations on bank soundness, such as capital adequacy requirements and loan to deposit ratios, with strict deadlines for meeting the requirements.

By June 1991, interest rates offered by state banks on time deposits ranged from 22 to 25 percent, and the highest interest rate offered by private banks was 28 percent. In July 1991, the minister of finance attempted to "talk down" interest rates by calling a meeting of 68 state and private banks to urge them to lower interest rates. This resulted in some reduction in official interest rates, prompting the banks to turn to noninterest competition. They offered time, savings, and demand deposits with lottery features and gifts and some informally agreed-upon negotiable rates with large deposit holders. The effective interest rate is thought to have remained high, and there was the undesirable result that announced interest rates did not provide the correct information to the public. Furthermore, the lending rate did not fall in line with the deposit rate.

---

9. The Sumarlin Shock is named for the former Finance Minister Sumarlin who implemented strongly contractionary monetary policies.

In September 1991, the banking system was hit by another set of regulations aimed at correcting the balance of payments deficit and curbing the inflow of capital so as to control monetary growth and inflation. The government imposed ceilings on borrowing for public sector projects and borrowing by banks amounting to $5 to 6 billion over five years.

These "three shocks"—tight money, prudential regulations, and off-shore borrowing ceilings—have caused considerable problems for the banking system. The tight liquidity position has been relaxed, and interest rates on SBI and deposits have fallen. However, the interest rate on lending has not come down in tandem, partly because of the usual lag but also because of increased provisions for problem loans.

Furthermore, despite some monetary easing, banks are still slow to increase their lending. They have been constrained by the need to satisfy their capital adequacy ratios (CAR) by the rule that 20 percent of credit must go to small business and by the slowdown in the economy. Banks are placing the money they raised in deposits into Bank Indonesia certificates and SBI, and their value outstanding has increased dramatically, from Rp.9 trillion at the end of the first quarter of 1991, to Rp.15.5 trillion by mid 1992, and almost Rp.18 trillion as of October 1992. Banks are willing to place their funds in SBI at a loss because it is classified as a nonrisky asset and thus does not affect their CAR. The central bank governor also recently announced that part of the increase in SBI sales was purchases by foreigners in search of high interest rates. It should also be noted that some of the increase in credit reflects the increase in banks lending to customers with problem loans in order to service their debt.

At present there are signs of some financial instability in the banking sector, although it is difficult to say on what scale. Some banks with problems have already been "rescued" by arranging for a merger or takeover by another bank. The problem loans appear to have arisen in the period of rapid expansion after the deregulation. Strengthening of supervision is crucial in dealing with the new competitive environment. It remains to be seen whether there will be any further fallout of new banks and whether the central bank can avoid a financial crisis.

On the other hand, there are some signs of financial strength. Fixed investment has grown more rapidly than has the credit extended by banks, which suggests that the nonfinancial sector is able to obtain the finance it needs.[10] This is partly due to the explosive growth in the capital markets. Since the 1988 deregulation, the market capitalization expanded from just Rp.482 billion to Rp.15.8 trillion by April 1991. The number of companies listed jumped from 24 to 128 by the end of April 1991. Share prices increased rapidly in 1989–90, then plummeted in 1991. They have since recovered but not back to their earlier peaks.

---

10. See Chant and Pangestu 1994.

## Agricultural Development

Indonesia's long-term agricultural growth of 4 percent per annum over the 1965–90 period compares favorably with most other developing countries and helped to underpin its overall growth. At the heart of Indonesia's agricultural transformation was the drive for self-sufficiency in rice. Based on a strategy of massive investments in agricultural infrastructure and services, a favorable incentive regime (including large and growing subsidies for fertilizers), and strong central direction, rice output grew by 4 percent a year between 1965 and 1990, compared with 2.2 percent for Thailand, .6 percent for Malaysia, and 2.6 percent for the Philippines.

For the rest, nonfarm food crops, tree crops (in the outer islands), and livestock have been the main contributors to agricultural growth. The government played a major role in the development of tree crops, starting with the nationalization of colonial enterprises and followed by a major expansion of smallholder plots. These were linked to nuclear or large estates and financed by highly subsidized credit. These measures were not as successful as the ones for rice, being more expensive and often not achieving planned yields. Nevertheless, the area planted in and production of palm oil, copra and coconut oil, tea, and coffee expanded during the 1970s and 1980s. Like Malaysia and Thailand, and unlike most other developing country producers, Indonesia was thus able to maintain its income terms of trade for primary exports in the face of declining prices. Since tree crops are produced mainly in the outer islands, the strategy has fostered more balanced regional development.

In addition to its interventions in rice and tree crops, the government has sought to promote a diversification of farm crops through area controls and special programs (e.g., sugarcane and soybeans). These policies have not been successful (Tabor 1992), suggesting that the "rice model" is not readily applicable to other crops.

Agricultural growth slowed during the 1980s as a result of the limits on irrigation expansion, near-complete adoption of high-yielding varieties, and depressed commodity prices. Rice output decelerated further in the late 1980s, but estate crops, livestock, and fisheries continue to expand at over 4 percent per annum and are now bigger contributors to agricultural growth.

## Manufacturing

Indonesia's manufacturing output grew by more than 12 percent a year in 1965–90, a record exceeded only by the four "East Asian NIEs." Although this growth took place from an exceptionally low base, Indonesia's industry has nevertheless been transformed. The share of manufacturing in GDP increased from 8.5 percent in 1965 to 19 percent in 1990 and surpassed agriculture as the largest sector of the economy in 1995.

The stabilization and liberalization program of the late 1960s provided the first stimulus to manufacturing growth. Companies benefited from the resurgence of consumer demand, the dismantling of controls on foreign exchange, and improved access to inputs (Hill 1992).

During the next phase, which lasted from 1973 to 1985, the government sought to accelerate the pace of industrialization through a combination of import-substitution policies, regulation of investment, and state ownership. Indonesia was more successful than other oil exporters were in moderating the rise of its real exchange rate. Nevertheless, in the face of a gradual erosion of competitiveness and pressures from domestic interests, the trade regime became increasingly protectionist. The government began to rely more on investment licensing to regulate domestic and foreign private investment. It also invested in capital- and resource-intensive industries such as oil refining, LNG, chemicals, pulp and paper, fertilizer, cement, and steel. The result was that, although industrial growth accelerated in the 1970s, it became increasingly inefficient. An added policy intervention that had a significant impact was the ban on log exports in 1981 aimed at boosting the development of wood-based industries.

The high cost structure of industry and the end of the oil boom prompted a reassessment of industrial strategy in the early 1980s. Although REPELITA IV proposed a further push to heavy industry, economic circumstances strengthened the hands of policymakers who favored a different approach. As part of the fiscal adjustment of 1983, several large public projects were cut back or shelved. But the big shift in strategy came after the second oil shock of 1986. An export incentive package was introduced in May 1986 with the aim of boosting nonoil exports. Then it became clear that more comprehensive reforms were needed to achieve that objective, so the government announced a large devaluation in September 1986 and the first of a series of trade reforms in October 1986. Just as had happened in the late 1960s, the stabilization and adjustment program of the mid-1980s boosted manufacturing output, exports, and investment. What was particularly striking was the speed with which manufacturers responded to the reforms.

The rapid growth of manufacturing production has brought about large structural changes but in ways that are different from those of other East Asian economies. Unlike these economies, Indonesia's manufacturing industry has been primarily based on the exploitation of natural resources. As shown in Table 7.13, 60 percent of output and 90 percent of exports in 1977 were resource based.[11] By 1988, the proportion of output was still more than 50 percent, but there had been a noteworthy shift in exports to labor-intensive goods. In contrast to exports, imports are relatively skill and technology inten-

---

11. If agriculture and oil are included, the resource-based structure of production is even more striking.

sive, reflecting Indonesia's liberal policy on technology imports and foreign investment.

These trends suggest that Indonesia has moved to a labor-intensive path of export-led growth at a much later stage than other East Asian countries have. The devaluation of 1986 and the sharp appreciation of the yen boosted Indonesia's comparative advantage in labor-intensive production,[12] making it the cheapest source of unskilled labor in the region apart from China.

Both foreign and domestic firms have responded to these attractions, helped by the deregulation of imports and investment licensing. Foreign investment approvals increased 10-fold between 1986 and 1991 to over $8 billion, and domestic investment rose by a similar proportion to $30 billion. The approval data also show that 70 percent of foreign investment approved was export oriented, compared with 38 percent in 1986. Although the share of labor-intensive sectors in these investment plans is higher than in the past, capital-intensive, resource-based investments still account for a significant share of total investment. The share of engineering goods, although rising, is much smaller than in other East Asian economies.

## Infrastructure

In addition to stimulating agricultural growth and developing human resources, expanding and upgrading infrastructure was one of the early priorities

TABLE 7.13.  Industrial Output, Exports, and Imports by Factor Intensity: Selected Periods (medium- and small-scale industries, percentage of period total)

| Factor Intensity | Output | | Exports | | Imports | |
|---|---|---|---|---|---|---|
| | 1977 | 1988 | 1977 | 1988 | 1977 | 1988 |
| Resource based | 59.2 | 54.0 | 89.5 | 63.1 | 27.2 | 14.2 |
| Agriculture | 46.2 | 30.1 | 67.3 | 15.6 | 20.5 | 6.4 |
| Timber products | 4.6 | 16.0 | 4.8 | 32.5 | 2.2 | 3.7 |
| Minerals | 8.4 | 7.9 | 17.4 | 15.0 | 4.5 | 4.1 |
| Unskilled labor | 22.9 | 26.2 | 1.8 | 22.9 | 9.6 | 10.7 |
| Technology | 6.9 | 10.7 | 4.3 | 6.8 | 28.6 | 40.5 |
| Skilled labor | 11.0 | 9.0 | 4.5 | 7.2 | 34.5 | 34.6 |
| Total | 100.0 | 100.0 | 100.0 | 100.0 | 100.0 | 100.0 |

*Source:* World Bank staff estimates.

12. The rupiah was devalued by 31 percent against the dollar in September, but when combined with the depreciation of the dollar against the yen the rupiah's competitiveness vis-à-vis the yen improved by a massive 65 percent.

of the New Order government. This was reflected in the guidelines of state policy and successive five-year development plans. The expansion and improvement of infrastructure had two objectives: to provide the conditions for sustaining economic growth and to integrate and foster equitable development of the regions and rural areas.

This emphasis on infrastructure is reflected in the large share that it received in the budget. On average, 40 percent of government development expenditures have been allocated to economic infrastructure. Even during the 1980s, when the government had to cut real spending on everything, it boosted infrastructure's share. With the recovery of growth and the surge in private investment, the government is placing renewed emphasis on infrastructure, but it is now opening up many areas of infrastructure investment to the private sector (e.g., power, telecommunications, ports, and roads).

The stress on infrastructure has paid rich dividends (see table 7.14). For example, the installed capacity of the state electricity company (PLN) has increased 18-fold since 1970; the number of telephone lines rose sevenfold; and the length of paved roads increased almost sixfold, nearly 80 percent of which was at the district level. In telecommunications, Indonesia became the first developing country to install a domestic satellite system.

Human Resource Development

Section I highlighted Indonesia's impressive progress in human resource development. This was the direct result of a government commitment at the highest levels, which ensured the establishment of successful institutions for the delivery of basic services and the allocation of substantial resources (financed in part by the oil boom of the 1970s) through special programs. The

TABLE 7.14.    Expansion of Selected Infrastructure, 1970–90 (percentage per annum)

|  | 1970–75 | 1975–80 | 1980–85 | 1985–90 |
|---|---|---|---|---|
| Power |  |  |  |  |
| PLN sales | 11.5 | 18.1 | 14.2 | 16.0 |
| Telecommunications |  |  |  |  |
| Telephone lines | 4.6 | 15.4 | 7.5 | 13.2 |
| Transport |  |  |  |  |
| Paved roads | 10.2 | 11.3 | 8.0 | — |
| Water |  |  |  |  |
| Land under irrigation | 2.9 | 1.8 | 5.0 | 1.0 |

*Source:* Various Government of Indonesia publications and World Bank Staff estimates.

measures underlying the progress in each of the main areas are described in the following sections.

*Family Planning.* Indonesia's success in family planning is largely due to BKKBN, a centrally directed but community-oriented coordinating ministry created to promote family planning and community welfare. BKKBN was successful in making safe and affordable contraceptive methods available in villages and involving the community in adopting these methods. As a result, contraceptive use rose from 10 percent in the 1960s to 50 percent in 1991, matching countries with much higher per capita levels of income; this was reflected in a near halving of the fertility rate, from 5.6 to 3.1.

*Nutrition and Infant Mortality.* Indonesia has done much to reduce the incidence of malnutrition among children. The growth of food production and rural incomes has been a leading cause, but government programs (including nutrition education and distribution of Vitamin A capsules) have played their part. These gains, along with fertility declines, have contributed to a sharp reduction in infant mortality, as have government programs of immunization against childhood diseases. Access to health services expanded during the 1980s with the establishment of a network of nearly 6,000 health centers, each serving several subcenters and 40 village-level health stations.

*Basic Education.* A massive program of school building, teacher training, and subsidies (abolition of official fees) during the 1970s and 1980s enabled Indonesia to achieve universal primary education for boys and girls. There are currently 26.5 million students being served by 146,000 schools and 1.1 million primary school teachers. This effort helped boost adult literacy from 56 percent in 1970 to almost 80 percent by 1990. Government programs also brought about large increases in secondary-level enrollment during the 1970s and 1980s, so that primary and secondary enrollment rates compare favorably with those of countries with higher per capita incomes.

*Tertiary Education.* Indonesia has also done so much to expand tertiary education. Enrollments rose from 2 percent in 1970 to 9 percent by 1990, with most of this increase coming from private institutions. Private universities and colleges now account for two-thirds of postsecondary enrollment.

## IV.   The Institutional Framework and Implementation of Reforms

A country's institutional setup covers the rules that affect the behavior of people or groups—rules that can be in the form of formal institutions or can work more informally (Campos 1992). In addition, it is crucial to understand the dynamic between groups. The aim of this section is to explain the main elements of the institutional setup underlying policy making in Indonesia and

then to analyze how this ties in with other factors to explain the policy outcomes discussed in earlier sections.

## The Political System and State Autonomy[13]

The dominance of a single political party in East Asia is often thought to be a
reason for the state's ability to adopt and implement long-term public policies,
because potential conflicts can be internalized. In most cases there is a mechanism through which society's wishes can be made known, but the dominant
party has control (Campos 1992). The essential characteristics of Indonesia's
system are as follows.

First, the election of the Indonesian political elite is largely unaffected by
financial contributions from certain groups in society. Most decision makers
are not elected politicians but bureaucrats. For most of the New Order period,
abundant oil revenues ensured that the government was not beholden to individual business groups.

Second, the adoption of a corporatist strategy has ensured that policy
making occurs without direct societal pressure. The approach to the restructuring of the political system in the New Order period was greatly influenced by
the experience of the mass political mobilization of the Soekarno years. The
result was a network of functionally based, representative organizations, which
would serve as the conduits for channeling societal aspirations upward to state
leaders and would be imbued with a collectivist spirit. "It was seen as both an
indigenous and, more broadly, an Asian alternative to what was regarded as the
divisive Western capitalist and liberal democratic thinking associated with a
pluralism and competitive party system" (MacIntyre 1991, 24).

Such a strategy entailed centralizing power, which was justified on
grounds of national security. Part of the strategy involved the establishment of
a single body to represent various groups in society, especially the five mass
organizations of labor, youth, women, peasants, and fishermen. The leadership
of these strategic groups was overseen by the state. In the same spirit, the nine
opposition political parties were merged into two: the Development Unity
Party (PPP), which combined the former Muslim parties; and the Indonesian
Democratic Party (PDI), which combined the other nationalist and Christian
parties. Another part of the strategy was to prevent the establishment of party
offices in the villages and small towns in order to limit the reach of the opposition parties. This rule was removed at the election in May 1992.

Third, control within the state itself was achieved in several ways. Civil
servants were put under the Civil Servants Corporation (KORPRI), and since
they were integrated into the state political party GOLKAR they have com-

---

13.  This section draws from MacIntyre 1991.

prised a reliable part of the voting population. Civil servants, such as village heads, could "campaign" in the villages. The army was also reorganized to reduce the power of regional commanders.

MacIntyre (1991) characterizes the structure that developed as one that was managed "by a military and bureaucratic elite" in which GOLKAR, KORPRI, and the armed forces were instruments. The development of this structure culminated in a 1985 law requiring all social and political organizations to adopt the state ideology of Pancasila. This is based on five social and humanitarian principles, but it is used by the government to head off factional interests. As such, in the largest Muslim country in the world, there is no political party carrying a religious banner. Conflict within the state was effectively defused, and a national political consensus achieved, through a consultative process between the state and corporatist representatives.

## The Process of Economic Policy Making

Indonesia's economic stabilization and rehabilitation in the mid-1960s did much to influence the policy-making process. The structure of the process, the existence of capable technocrats, and the pragmatic leadership of the president were all important in ensuring that economic policy remained largely insulated from outside pressures.

The official decision-making process has several layers (see fig. 7.4). One, the Economic Stabilization Council, which is chaired by the president, was formed in 1968 to oversee the economic rehabilitation program. The members are the governor of the central bank, the coordinating minister of state for economic, financial, and industrial affairs; the chairman of the National Planning Agency (Bappenas); the ministers of agriculture, finance, trade, industry and cooperatives, transport and communications, and mining and energy; the junior minister of cooperatives; and the chairman of Bulog, the State Logistics Board responsible for food procurement. The council gradually came to involve all ministries that fall under the Economic Coordinating Ministry (EKUIN).

The second is the Cabinet on Economic Affairs, which meets the first Wednesday of the month and more often if there are special issues to be tackled. Policy proposals come from the relevant ministries and are discussed at these meetings. Policies requiring presidential decrees and recommendations to the president must be channeled through the cabinet secretary.

The third layer, the Monetary Board, is chaired by the minister of finance. The governor of Bank Indonesia is vice chairman, with other board members being the ministers of trade and the National Planning Agency as well as some nongovernment advisers. The Monetary Board discusses monetary and financial policies. In addition, an intraministerial team (COLT) for the monitoring and management of external debt was set up in 1991.

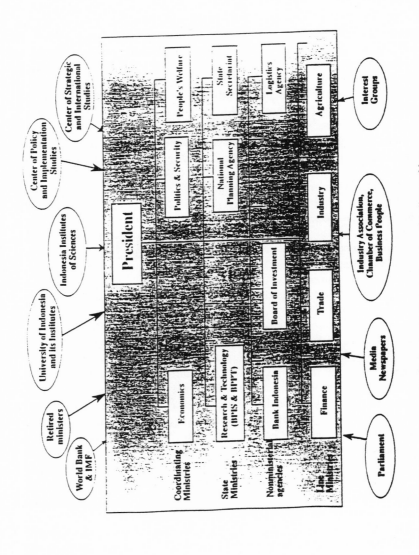

Fig. 7.4. Institutional structure of policy making

Coordinating Ministries

Economics

People's Welfare

Politics & Security

State Ministries

Research & Technology (BPIS & BPPT)

National Planning Agency

State Secretariat

Nonministerial agencies

Bank Indonesia

Board of Investment

Logistics Agency

Line Ministries

Finance

Trade

Industry

Agriculture

President

World Bank & IMF

Retired ministers

University of Indonesia and its Institutes

Indonesia Institutes of Sciences

Center of Policy and Implementation Studies

Center of Strategic and International Studies

Parliament

Media Newspapers

Industry Association, Chamber of Commerce, Business People

Interest Groups

In practice, however, policies are approved away from these meetings. The minister or ministers will coordinate discussion and pursue the issue with the president in a bilateral meeting. Only when a policy has the "green light" is it formally presented rather than discussed at these meetings. Thus, a crucial component in policy making is the informal meetings that take place outside the cabinet meetings. The cohesiveness of the economic ministries is essential for smooth coordination and cooperation on economic issues. Indeed, the main economic ministers meet on the Monday before the Wednesday cabinet coordination meeting, and also through the Monetary Board, to discuss macroeconomic issues. These meetings are used to sort out differences so that a consensus can be presented to the president.

## The Dynamics of the Cabinet

Economist members of the cabinet have played an important role since the beginning of the New Order period. Many of them came from the Faculty of Economics, of the University of Indonesia (FEUI). The role of the economists in the cabinet can be traced through several developments that began toward the end of the Old Order period.

First was the return of a group of Western trained economists in the early 1960s. Until then the prevailing ideology was not market minded; it stressed planning and the strong role of government in directing the economy, and it was based on the Indian model of planning. No doubt this kind of thinking influenced the five year plans that characterize Indonesian economic planning from the beginning of the New Order period.[14]

Second was the beginning of the close relationship between the commander of the Staff and Command School of the Army (SESKOAD) in Bandung and the FEUI economists. The economists were invited to teach at the school. At SESKOAD, 50 percent of the courses consisted of nonmilitary subjects, and the FEUI economists taught the economics courses.[15] These nonmilitary courses were deemed necessary to prepare the armed forces for their dual function (Dwifungsi): their military role, and their sociopolitical role. President Soeharto was one of the senior army officers in the school at the time. The relationship between the army and the FEUI academics was gradually institutionalized and extended to the navy and air force. It became an influential ingredient in the removal of the Old Order government.

The basis of economic policy of the New Order government was discussed at the Second Army Seminar in August 1966. The economists presented

---

14. See Thee, forthcoming.
15. Law Faculty members of Padjadjaran University, Bandung, were asked to teach law, and Political Science Faculty members of Gadjahmada University, Yogyakarta, were asked to teach political science.

the army leadership with "a 'cookbook' to rehabilitate the country. General Soeharto as the Army top commander did not only accept the cookbook but also wanted the 'cooks' to become his economic advisers" (Sadli, quoted in Thee, forthcoming).

The influence of economists in policy making can be explained as follows. First, their ability to work as a team came from their institutional link with FEUI, long-standing relations with one another, and their similarity in outlook. Second, they had early success in renegotiating Indonesia's debt, obtaining foreign aid from the West as well as Japan, and creating the Intergovernmental Group on Indonesia (IGGI). The group, and particularly the Economic Expert Team of the President of the Republic of Indonesia (Tim Ahli Ekonomi Presiden Republik Indonesia), did much to restore Indonesia's international creditworthiness at the beginning of the New Order period. In all their work, the president gave them full support, shielding them from political and military pressures.

Other than the inner group,[16] the technocrats would come together in times of crisis. The Pertamina affair was one example. In the mid-1970s, Pertamina, the state oil company, borrowed heavily abroad for its projects, which were not controlled by the government. In early 1975, it announced it was unable to repay some of its short-term debts. Despite the fact that Pertamina had been controlled by the army, President Soeharto did not protect the company for that reason. In fact, he supported the technocrats, as he saw the need to protect state revenues for the long-run interests of the country. After the resolution of the crisis, the technocrats prepared a new law to manage Pertamina. It involves monitoring by the government through a Board of Supervisors and requires Pertamina to hand over oil revenues directly to the government.

Even after leaving the cabinet, some technocrats remained influential in their official roles as external advisers. Their successors in the cabinet were initially from FEUI. But, since the early 1980s, economists from other institutions (such as the Faculty of Economics at Gadjahmada University) have become part of the team.

Other groups in the cabinet have also affected the direction of economic policy. The first group comprises the engineers and nationalists who basically believe that the costs of protection are justified to acquire technological capability and develop domestic industries. Beginning in the mid 1970s, the Ministry of Industry was heavily protectionist, following import substitution and the development of strategic industries by the state. Its approval led to the usual phasing of import substitution, from final to intermediate and capital

16. The members of the inner group were the minister of finance, the central bank governor, and the head of the National Planning Agency.

goods, and to the development of state-owned enterprises in steel, fertilizer, and cement. From the late 1970s until the mid-1980s, the ministry wanted to "deepen" (through backward and forward linkages) the industrial structure and local content policies. During the oil boom years the economists were willing to follow this basic import-substitution strategy, but when oil prices fell they were strongly proderegulation. However, they lost the argument: the first response to the fall in oil prices was to increase protection. A new junior ministry was created in 1983, the Ministry for the Utilization of Domestic Components.

A second influence on economic policy has been the Ministry of Research and Technology, which wants Indonesia to enter high-tech industries. Theoretically it covered nine industries. In the mid-1970s, the minister embarked on several "high-tech" projects to develop an aircraft and shipping industry. The justification was both technological development ("leapfrogging") and strategic interest. During the oil boom, when state oil revenues were buoyant, the technocrats had little ability to prevent these projects. Indeed, as recently as 1989, the ministry's mandate was expanded with the creation of the Agency for the Development of Strategic Industries. Ten state-owned enterprises were moved from the control and management of the Ministry of Industry and placed under the Ministry of Technology.

In general, however, the deterioration in Indonesia's environment has provided more support for reforms and a market-based approach. For instance, the minister of industry has become one of the most active proponents of deregulation, and the Ministry for the Utilization of Domestic Components was no longer thought to be necessary in the 1988 cabinet.

## External Influence over Policy

Although policy making is centrally directed by the president through the cabinet, there are other channels of influence over policy.

*Formal Policy Inputs.* The strength of the research departments in individual ministries varies, depending on the availability of researchers and the coordination within and between ministries and agencies. The government has also used external consultants, although the core group of economic ministers and their advisers have produced most of the policy ideas and provided the push for reforms. The external agencies involved in advisory work include the Harvard Advisory Group (which later became the Harvard Institute for International Development), the World Bank, and the IMF.

Academics, independent research agencies (e.g., the Center for Strategic and International Studies [CSIS], CPIS, and LIPI), and domestic consultants have not had much influence on policy. However, given the close links between the universities and the government, many academics are seconded to the government as senior officials.

*External Influence over Policy.*[17] The main sources of pressure for policy change are Parliament, the press, business associations (especially the umbrella organization of the Chamber of Commerce and Industry), and labor unions. Their influence has varied over time but has grown in the postreform era of the mid-1980s.

*Parliament.* It consists of two bodies: the People's Consultative Assembly (MPR) and the House of Representatives (DPR). The MPR is the highest authority in the country: it selects the president and sets the Broad Guidelines for State Policy (GBHN) which outlines the government's policy goals. However, in practice, it is government controlled, since more than half of its members are government appointed and meet only once every five years.

The DPR, the main legislative body, has had some impact on policy. MacIntyre (1991) points out that its role is often underestimated. It is dominated by the government and centers around the president and his ministers, none of whom is a member of Parliament. The list of potential and incumbent members of DPR is controlled by the government at every election. Even so, it has had some influence because its various committees can delay or force changes in government legislation. Policy debates in committee hearings are also important. Although committees cannot compel government officials to provide information, their hearings receive wide press coverage, so officials have to take them seriously.

*The Press.* The press operates under self-censorship as well as formal censorship. Self-censorship means the tacit understanding that certain sensitive issues (security, religion, and ethnicity) will not be reported irresponsibly. However, MacIntyre (1991) points out that press commentary and letters to the editor play a useful role in public debate. Furthermore, despite constraints, the press has maintained a critical and lively debate on political as well as economic issues. There are many recent examples of the media acting as a forum for public debate, for example, throughout the clove monopoly controversy and the automotive deregulation. Different groups within the state also use the media to influence the shaping of public policy.

*Business-Government Relations.* The main "official" representative of business interests is the Indonesian Chamber of Commerce and Industry (KADIN). Its leaders have close ties with the government. They are often seen as a tool of government rather than as representing government interests directly.

Substantive business-government dealings are conducted through individual industry associations. Roughly 350 of them are registered in Indonesia, and two-thirds are members of KADIN. By and large, they are not active in representing their sectoral interests, although some have influenced policy. Two

---

17. See MacIntyre 1991 for more details.

examples are the Association of Plywood and Wood Manufacturers and the textile associations.

The associations of the processed wood industries have been influential in the introduction of export bans, restrictions, and taxes on downstream products. The growth of the sector can also be attributed to the priority credits it received. The association has run a cartel-like operation to control the amount and price of plywood exports (it has the right to veto an exporter who does not comply), bring forward regulations on the banning of raw and semiprocessed rattan, impose prohibitive taxes, and control the distribution and production of rattan goods.

The textile associations have also successfully lobbied for policy changes. For instance, the Spinning Industry Joint Secretariat managed to have the import monopoly on cotton removed. Apart from direct lobbying, the association has used the press effectively. Other than associations, big business groups rely on their own close relationships with the decision makers.[18]

*Labor Groups.* The term *perburuhan* ("labor") has acquired negative connotations for the New Order government because it was long associated with communist-motivated labor organizations. The New Order government wanted to depoliticize the labor unions by favoring industrywide unions that would not be affiliated with political parties. It adopted the German model of collective labor agreements. Thus, in 1973, the All Indonesia Labor Federation (Serikat Perkerja Seluruh Indonesia, or SPSI) was formed, closely following the German model. Although the law allows the freedom to form unions, in practice the state controls worker organizations and strictly supervises the establishment of unions. Furthermore, strikes were illegal until 1990. Since then there has been an increase in strikes, with 61 in 1990 and 130 in 1991. Legally, a strike is allowed only if the Ministry of Manpower team in charge of the settlement of labor disputes fails to resolve the case and permission is granted to strike. The government also sets minimum wages, which are differentiated by area and reviewed periodically.

## Other Important Institutional Factors

*The Bureaucracy.* In general, policy making has been highly centralized. The autonomy of the state and individual ministers in carrying out economic policy is clear. Although state intervention was pervasive in the prereform period of the 1980s, the government lacked the capacity to monitor and implement the complex system of regulations. It is commonly observed that Indonesia's top decision makers are of the highest quality, but the bureaucracy as a whole is weak.

18. Ibid., 44.

The bureaucracy has not been able to attract the best people because of low pay and an emphasis on seniority rather than performance. The government has periodically tried to correct these systemic weaknesses. In general, an important consideration in the design of policy reforms was simpler rules and reduced scope for the discretionary power of bureaucrats.

*The Legal System.* There are major deficiencies in Indonesia's framework of law and its accounting system. These deficiencies are felt most by banking and large- and medium-scale businesses (especially foreign investors). The country also has a poor record in its legal system due to delays in court, contradictory judgments, corruption, and difficulties in enforcing decisions. There is also a shortage of information on laws and regulations, which creates great uncertainty. For instance, there is no reliable information on land records and transactions, property or security, or public credit. Although the absence of an efficient legal system does not prevent commercial activity, it creates entry barriers and adds to the cost of doing business in Indonesia.

## Continuity and Changes in Government Policy

Indonesia has had mixed success with government intervention, especially where the issues concerned have produced no clear consensus. However, the general institutional factors that led to the adoption of the "right policies" have been, first, the strong leadership provided by President Soeharto. It was development oriented, pragmatic, and had a central vision. Second, strong central authority has allowed the state to undertake painful economic reforms, especially since 1986.

Third is the astute use of external agencies and consultants. They have provided valuable policy advice and technical support, which have helped to fill an analytical gap though they have hardly influenced the actual decisions to undertake reforms. However, the government has created a deliberate impression of "external pressure" to adopt reforms, especially after the second external shock in 1986. For example, in past few years major deregulation packages were announced just before the annual meeting of donors to discuss Indonesia's foreign aid. This approach causes less domestic political fallout and creates a sense of irreversibility.

To understand how these factors and the institutional framework have interacted in the implementation of policy, it is helpful to look at each area in turn.

*Macroeconomic Policy.* Macrostabilization has long been the top priority in Indonesia, a principle that emerged from the Old Order period. The New Order government inherited hyperinflation, large budget deficits, and external debt. Macrostabilization is enshrined in various written and unwritten rules such as the balanced budget law, an open capital account, inflation in single digits, reserves at a minimum of five months' imports, and limits on government-related debt.

The influence of economists has been particularly powerful in the conduct of macroeconomic policy, and it has not been challenged by other groups in the cabinet. Their analytical capacity has been used to explain the continuous stress on macrostabilization and the appropriate responses in the form of devaluation, austerity measures, and management of the external debt. Although macroeconomic measures are easier to implement than are structural adjustment measures affecting certain groups, the fact that there was broad agreement on macropolicy (including the firm support of the president) explains the government's ability to conduct successful macroeconomic policy.

*Industrial Policy.* Indonesia has had mixed success with industrial policy—the phrase being used to describe attempts to promote or favor a certain sector.

Rice is an example of successful targeting. Broad-based support came not from the decision makers but from the society as a whole. But in the case of industry there are no comparable achievements to record. Based on various rationales such as strategic industries, increase in value added, and increased local content, industries such as cement, fertilizers, steel, aircraft, plywood, and automobiles have received government support and protection. As already discussed, the efficiency and productivity of these investments are still in question.

## V. Recent Developments in the Regulatory Environment

The government has demonstrated continuity in undertaking reforms in the regimes affecting investment, trade, and the financial sector. Underlying the strong push for deregulation in investment and trade appears to be competition, and a convergence of external pressures to undertake liberalization due to commitments under the ASEAN Free Trade Area (AFTA) Agreement. However, ambivalence remains as how to best increase Indonesia's technological capability, reduce economic concentration, and address distribution problems.

There has been a significant relaxation of the restrictions on foreign investment operating in Indonesia. Beginning in 1988 and into the early 1990s, Indonesia enjoyed an increase in foreign investment due to improvements in the investment climate as well as relocation by Japan and the East Asian NIEs. However, dramatic liberalization of restrictions on ownership, divestment minimum capital requirements were undertaken in June 1994. These moves need to be evaluated in light of the previous nationalistic stance toward foreign investment which has seen waves of liberalization and restrictions on foreign investment since the 1970s. The June 1994 package allowed for 100 percent foreign ownership with little restrictions, virtual elimination of the need to divest foreign ownership to Indonesian hands, the opening up of nine sectors previously closed in the infrastructure area, and the elimination of the need for minimum capital requirements.

The liberalization moves were perceived as being a response to increased competition for FDI in the region and diversion to China as indicated above. The effect has been positive, with approved investments going up to U.S.$23 billion in 1994 and to U.S.$30 billion at the end of October 1995, compared with U.S.$8 billion in 1993. These high numbers need to be interpreted cautiously since the realization rate is likely to be low given that a large number of these projects are large infrastructure and energy-related projects, which have not been realized or have long gestation periods. Nevertheless, the upward trend in investment approvals can still be taken in part as a positive response to the deregulation measures. The only sector which remains closed to foreign investment, and which is deemed to be important, is the domestic distribution sector. Streamlining of investment approvals and reducing bureaucratic hurdles and facilitation costs are also deemed to be important factors on Indonesia's investment climate.

After a period of little progress in trade liberalization in the 1991–94 period, May 1995 brought a trade liberalization package announcement which contained tariff reductions that brought down the average unweighted tariff from 20 percent to 15 percent. The approach to liberalization has also become more progressive and transparent with the announcement for the first time of a tariff reduction schedule for around two-thirds of tariff lines which will bring average unweighted tariffs to 7 percent by the year 2003. There is also a separate and longer time schedule for the reduction of high tariff sectors (that is, automotive, chemical, and metal industries).

However, there has been little progress on removal of nontariff barriers, especially for certain agriculture products and processed foods. Furthermore, export restrictions and domestic trade restrictions remain. The latter restrictions include industry cartels, prices controls, entry and exit controls, nontransparent and nonmarket interventions. The restrictions are imposed by a combination of central and provincial governments, as well as government backed private sector associations. These need to be deregulated to reduce the high costs of doing business and increase efficiency.

The lackluster performance of nonoil exports in the 1993–95 period has also prompted some changes in policies related to facilitating exports such as the creation of the stand alone export processing zones (EPZs), and improvements in customs clearance and the duty exemption scheme which at one stage had become a bottleneck due to overload and onerous documentation requirements. However, the main challenge faced by nonoil experts is increased competition from other low-cost economies in the region, especially given the rise in nominal wages and low labor productivity in Indonesia, improving productivity, human resource development, enhancing technological capability, building up a strong and internationally competitive supporting industries (that is, components, parts, machinery, and tools), and maximizing the benefits of foreign linkages.

In the financial sector, steps have been taken to continuously improve the legal and institutional setup governing banking, financial institutions, and the capital markets. During the 1993–95 period the banking, customs, capital markets, and company laws were passed. However, the challenge to strengthen the financial sector remains, which will include: (1) restructuring of the state banks and overcoming its bad debts and insolvency, partly due to the lack of prudential credit approvals which included owner-related projects; (2) implementing the soundness regulations by the central bank; (3) revitalizing the domestic capital and money markets, especially enhancing the lack of a secondary market; and (4) improve disclosure as well as implementing strengthened regulations.

Finally, abuses of market power and lack of transparency in certain areas highlights the urgency to speed up legal, regulatory, and institutional reforms that will ensure fair domestic competition and a level playing field. Other than continued deregulation and improving the incentive system, legal reforms and their implementation will play an important role.

## VI.  Conclusions

Indonesia's transformation since 1965 highlights not only its development success but also the differences in its structure, initial conditions, and strategy compared with those of other East Asian economies. The main differences are: (1) size (with a population of 182 million, Indonesia is larger than Thailand, Malaysia, and the Philippines combined); (2) low-income status (Indonesia started from a much lower base than did other East Asian countries); (3) natural resources (Indonesia has a much richer resource base than other East Asian economies do, including oil); and (4) as a result, unlike the other East Asian economies, Indonesia has until recently pursued a resource-intensive and home-market-oriented industrialization strategy rather than one based on labor-intensive, export-led production.

Public policy and institutions have played a central role in Indonesia's success. However, the record on state intervention is varied. Policies have been successful in promoting desired outcomes, macroeconomic management, agriculture, human resources, and infrastructure development. But intervention in the financial and industrial sectors did not yield the hoped-for results and required later measures to undo its legacy.

*Macroeconomic Management.* Indonesia's record on macroeconomic management has been one of its strongest assets. Although its sequencing of reforms does not match conventional wisdom, the open capital account has exerted financial discipline and enabled Indonesia to avoid many of the problems faced by other developing countries, particularly oil exporters. However, the open capital account combined with the potential volatility of export earnings and incipient weaknesses in the financial system have led to long periods of high real interest rates.

*Agricultural Strategy.* The attainment of self-sufficiency in rice was perhaps the most valuable achievement. It was based on a judicious combination of incentives and central direction. Public investments in supporting infrastructure and agricultural services were crucial to Indonesia's success. The substantial expansion of tree crops in the 1980s was also based on state intervention but with less impressive results. Public programs in other areas of agriculture have generally not been successful, creating distortions that must now be removed without offsetting dynamic gains.

*Human Resource Development.* Indonesia has closed the gap in social indicators with other countries in the region, largely thanks to aggressive programs in family planning, health, and education. Combined with the success in rice, they have achieved one of the fastest reductions in poverty and improvements in key social indicators among all developing countries.

*Infrastructure Development.* Government intervention was successful in accelerating and upgrading the country's infrastructure. The development of public institutions in key subsectors was an important ingredient underlying this success. The expansion of infrastructure, in turn, has supported sustained and broad-based economic growth.

*Financial Sector.* Selective government interventions—such as credit allocation, credit ceilings, and interest rate ceilings—have been largely ineffective and inefficient tools for promoting development. The failure was due to the multiplicity of objectives, weak management of credit allocation, and the damage done to efficient financial intermediation. In fact, the government has done much more to boost the financial sector through deregulation and an emphasis on competition and efficiency. There is, however, a clear need for a government role in bank supervision, setting and improving prudential regulations, and improving the legal framework.

*Industrialization Strategy.* The record of the past three decades in Indonesia suggests that inward orientation and selective interventions have generally not been successful in promoting industry. In the 1970s, the results were disappointing. Although a lot of industrial investment was made behind protective barriers and under public ownership, the productivity of these investments was low and the investments were a burden on the rest of the economy. In contrast, as shown in figure 7.5, manufacturing grew most rapidly during the two major liberalizations of the 1960s and the 1980s, when exports recovered and private investment surged. In the reforms of the 1980s, when the industrial structure was more developed, much of the extra investment went to

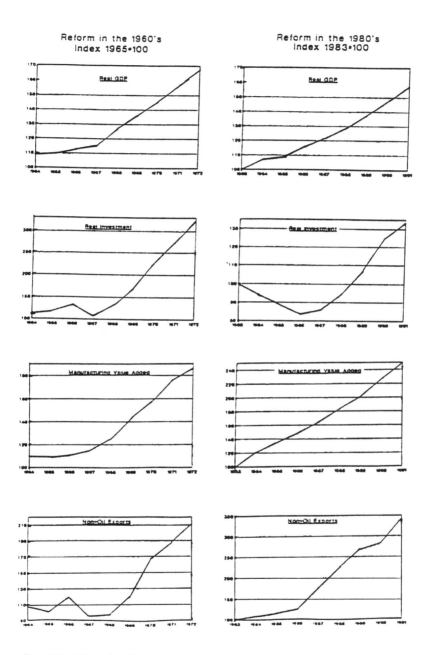

Fig. 7.5. Liberalization and supply response: the experience of two episodes

*new* labor-intensive export industries. This suggests that functional rather than selective interventions are likely to be the most effective in developing industry.

*Institutional Setup.* One lesson from Indonesia is that strong leadership and a cohesive team can work well in a crisis and ensure continuity of policy. A second lesson is that the limitations of the bureaucracy necessarily limit the scope for government interventions. Scarce managerial and administrative resources in the public sector need to be used to strengthen capacity in core functions such as macroeconomic management, legal and regulatory reforms, and the delivery of basic services. A final lesson is that, although direct public intervention has been crucial in some sectors, the state's role will become increasingly an indirect one as the private sector assumes more and more power and responsibility.

REFERENCES

Ahmed Sadiq. 1989. "Indonesia: External Shocks, Policy Response, and Adjustment Performance." World Bank internal discussion paper, Asia Regional Series Report No. IDO 39, June.

Asher Mukul G., and Anne Booth. 1992. "Fiscal Policy." In Booth 1992b.

Binhadi, and Paul Meek. 1992. "Implementing Monetary Policy." In Booth 1992b.

Booth, Anne. 1992a. "Growth and Structural Transformation in the New Order Aspects of Economic Liberalization: Problems for the Future." In Booth 1992b.

Booth, Anne, ed. 1992b. *The Oil Boom and After: Indonesian Economic Policy and Performance in the Soeharto Era.* Singapore: Oxford University Press.

Campos E. 1992. "Institutions and Public Policy." Issues paper for the East Asia Miracles Project, World Bank.

Chant, John, and Mari Pangestu. 1994. "An Assessment of Financial Reform in Indonesia: 1983–90." In *Financial Reform: Theory and Experience,* edited by Gerard Caprio, Jr., Izak Aityas, James Hanson, and others.

Cole, David C., and Betty F. Slade. 1992. "Financial Development in Indonesia." In Booth 1992b.

Gelb, Alan. 1988. *Oil Windfalls: Blessing or Curse.* Washington, D.C.: World Bank.

Glassburner, Bruce. 1971. "Economic Policy Making in Indonesia." In *The Economy of Indonesia: Selected Readings,* edited by Bruce Glassburner. Ithaca: Cornell University Press.

Hanna Don. 1992. "Indonesian Experience with Financial Sector Reform." Paper presented at the ECLAC/UNU-WIDER/UNCTAD seminar Savings and Financing Policy in Developing Countries, Santiago, Chile, October 5–6.

Hill, Hal. 1992. "Manufacturing Industry." In Booth 1992b.

Krueger, Anne. 1974. "The Political Economy of the Rent Seeking Society." *American Economic Review.* 64, no. 3: 291–303.

Krueger, Anne. 1978. *Liberalization Attempts and Consequences.* Cambridge, Mass: Ballinger Press.

MacIntyre, Andrew. 1991. *Business and Politics in Indonesia.* Sydney: Allen and Unwin.

McKinnon, Ronald I. 1991. *The Order of Economic Liberalization: Financial Control in the Transition to a Market Economy.* Baltimore: Johns Hopkins University Press.

Meier, Gerald M. 1991. *Politics and Policy Making in Developing Countries.* San Francisco: International Center for Economic Growth, ICS Press.

Michaely, Michael, Demetris Papageorgiou, and Armeane M. Choksi. 1991. *Lessons of Experience in the Developing World: Liberalizing Foreign Trade.* Vol. 7. Oxford: Basil Blackwell.

Nasution, Anwar. 1983. *Financial Institutions and Policies in Indonesia.* Singapore: Institute of Southeast Asian Studies.

Nelson, Joan M., ed. 1990. *Economic Crisis and Policy Choice: The Politics of Adjustment in the Third World.* Princeton: Princeton University Press.

Pangestu, Mari. 1991. "Managing Economic Policy Reforms in Indonesia." In *Authority and Academic Scribblers,* edited by Sylvia Ostry. San Francisco: International Center for Economic Growth, ICS Press.

Pangestu, Mari. 1992. "The Indonesian Economy: Booms and Macro-economic Pressures." In *Southeast Asian Affairs.* Singapore: Institute of Southeast Asian Studies.

Pangestu, Mari, and Achmad Habir. 1989. "Privatization and Deregulation in Indonesia." *ASEAN Economic Bulletin* (March): 224–41.

Pitt, Mark. 1991. "Indonesia." In *Liberalizing Foreign Trade: Indonesia, Pakistan, and Sri Lanka,* edited by Demetris Papageorgiou, Michael Michaely, and Armeane M. Choksi. Cambridge: Basil Blackwell.

Rodrick, Dani. 1990. "Trade Policies and Development: Some New Issues." John F. Kennedy School of Government, Harvard University, Discussion Paper No. 181 D, March.

Sjahrir and Mari Pangestu, 1992. "Adjustment Policies of Small Open Economies: The Experience of Indonesia." In *Economic Reforms and Internationalization: China and the Pacific Region,* edited by Ross Garnaut. Sydney: Allen and Unwin.

Soesastro, M. Hadi. 1989. "The Political Economy of Deregulation." *Asian Survey* 29, no. 9 (September): 853–69.

Stiglitz, J., and Marylou Uy. 1992. "An Issues Paper on Financial Markets and Policies in East Asian Economies." World Bank, draft paper.

Sundararajan V., and Lazaros Molho. 1987. "Financial Reform and Monetary Control in Indonesia." Paper presented at the conference Challenges to Monetary Policy in Pacific Basin Countries, Federal Reserve Bank of San Francisco, San Francisco, September 23–25.

Suwidjana, N. 1984. *The Jakarta Dollar Market.* Singapore: Institute of Southeast Asian Studies.

Tabor, Steve. 1992. "Agriculture in Transition." In Booth 1992b.

Thee Kian Wie. Forthcoming. "Recollections of My Career: Professor Sadli." *Bulletin of Indonesian Economic Studies.*

Warr, Peter G. 1992. "Exchange Rate Policy, Petroleum Prices, and the Balance of Payments." In Booth 1992b.

Woo, Wing Thye, Bruce Glassburner, and Anwar Nasution. 1994. *Macroeconomic Policies, Crises, and Long-Run Growth: The Case of Indonesia, 1965–90.* Washington, D.C.: World Bank.

Woo, Wing Thye, and Anwar Nasution. 1989. "Indonesian Economic Polices and Their Relations to External Debt Management." In *Developing Country Debt and Economic Performance,* edited by J. D. Sachs and S. M. Collins. Vol. 3. Chicago: University of Chicago Press.

World Bank. 1991. *World Development Report.* Washington, D.C.: World Bank.

World Bank. Various years. *Social Indicators of Development.* Washington, D.C.: World Bank.

World Bank. Various years. *World Tables.* Washington, D.C.: World Bank.

CHAPTER 8

# The Philippines: Three Decades of Lost Opportunities

*Homi J. Kharas*

## I. Introduction

The Philippines is the major outlier in the economic performance of East Asian countries. For over a generation, it has been the slowest growing market economy in the region. During the 1980s, this performance gap widened significantly—per capita growth in the Philippines turned negative while that in neighboring countries accelerated. The economy became progressively deindustrialized and decapitalized over this period, which was marked by political as well as economic instability. More recently, there are signs that the Philippines may be turning a corner. Following an extensive period of structural adjustment, GDP growth, exports, foreign investment and capital inflows, international reserves, and the stock market have surged. Government officials have used these indicators to suggest that the Philippines is "back in business."

This essay examines whether the Philippines is finally ready to join the ranks of the East Asian miracle economies. Skeptics recall that the whole postindependence record has been marked by brief growth spurts, interrupted by serious balance of payments crises that required prolonged periods of consolidation and adjustment. In 1962, 1970, 1983, and more recently in 1990, a shortage of foreign exchange necessitated a major currency depreciation, which cut back import growth, ignited domestic inflation, and retarded overall economic progress. These past setbacks have disrupted the momentum of growth and frustrated cumulative gains achieved in previous years.

This analysis seeks to unravel the policies and institutional forces that have shaped economic developments. Section II highlights the stop-and-go nature of past macroeconomic management and recent changes in the instruments of control. Section III reviews changes in industrial policy. Section IV describes social policy and outcomes. Section V examines the political and institutional setting under which "crony capitalism" flourished. Last, Section VI assesses recent developments in the 1990s and returns to the initial question of whether the Philippines can now legitimately aspire to join the ranks of East Asian high performers.

## Summary Performance Indicators

*Growth.* The Philippine economy experienced unsteady but fairly robust growth in the 1950s and 1960s. As long as primary commodity exports produced enough foreign exchange, the economy prospered. But, whenever international commodity markets slumped, so did growth. An import-substitution strategy in manufacturing was thought to provide a solution to break out of this cycle, but, in common with other countries, the Philippines found that, after a briefly successful initial phase, this increased its dependence on foreign exchange, as higher demand for imported intermediates and capital goods more than offset lower demand for consumer products.

Starting in the mid-1960s, the government undertook heavy investments in public infrastructure to spur private investments and prop up domestic demand. A heavy dependence on imports at a time of modest export growth and rapid fiscal and monetary expansion necessitated a major devaluation in 1970.

Growth averaged between 5 and 6 percent yearly through the 1970s, as the government was able to finance heavy public infrastructure spending through external debt accumulation. Despite the increase in international interest rates during the early 1980s, the government continued to incur short-term debt in order to service its foreign obligations. This strategy also allowed the authorities to accommodate the severe terms of trade deterioration that followed each of the two oil shocks.

The economy experienced a major recession in 1984–85 following the declaration of a moratorium on foreign debt service payments in 1983 and a crisis precipitated by domestic political upheaval and massive capital flight. The peso was devalued thrice and eventually allowed to float in October 1984. A series of adjustment programs were put in place to restore key macroeconomic balances. A fragile consumption-led recovery from 1986 to 1989 was interrupted by another foreign exchange shortage following the Gulf War. A coup attempt staged in the heart of the country's financial district also affected confidence. Yet the broad process of liberalization was continued by economic officials, despite tactical retreat on a number of fronts.

The boom and bust cycles experienced by the Philippine economy have led to a widening gap between the Philippines and its high-performing Asian neighbors. These countries grew on average by 8.2 percent from 1965 to 1980 and by 6.9 percent in the 1980s, while the Philippines grew by only 5.7 and, .9 percent, respectively. The Philippines lost out to Korea and Taiwan (China) in the 1970s and to Malaysia, Indonesia, and Thailand in the 1980s (fig. 8.1). Strikingly, the figure shows that the Philippines has lost about 25 years' worth of development since 1960.

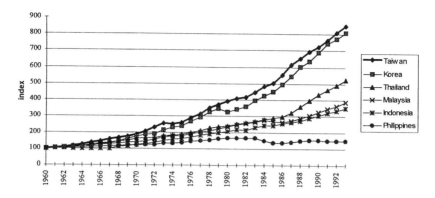

**Fig. 8.1. GDP per capita Index (constant price data, 1960 = 100). (Data from World Bank.)**

*Total Factor Productivity.* One reason for the poor growth record in the Philippines was disappointing total factor productivity (TFP) growth. TFP growth in manufacturing averaged .6 percent in manufacturing between 1956 and 1970 and then turned negative in the 1970s (−1.2 percent). Hooley argues that this negative rate was caused primarily by a shift to less efficient industries.[1] This continued through the early 1980s but finally reversed itself after the economy started its recovery in 1986.

*Export Shares.* Low productivity growth cannot be easily explained by an inward orientation of policies. By many measures, the Philippines has been quite outward oriented. It was one of the first countries in the region to explicitly adopt export-promotion policies, in the 1960s, and through the mid-1970s the Philippines had a higher share of world export markets than did Malaysia, Thailand, or Indonesia. It was only after this, and particularly during the 1980s, that Thai and Malaysian manufactured export performance far outstripped that of the Philippines (fig. 8.2).

*Sectoral Performance.* In the immediate aftermath of World War II, Philippine industrialization took off—the share of manufacturing doubled from 11.9 percent of GDP in 1946–49 to 21.3 percent in the 1950s. But this transformation mostly reflected the end of the reconstruction boom that took place immediately after the war. A longer lasting structural transformation of resources from agriculture to industry did not materialize. From 1960 to 1990, the share of industry and manufacturing in total GDP stagnated.

Agriculture has remained a mainstay of the economy: even in 1990, agriculture accounted for 22 percent of GDP, agricultural-based industry a further 13 percent, and services associated with trade in agriculture another 14 percent.

---

1. Hooley 1985.

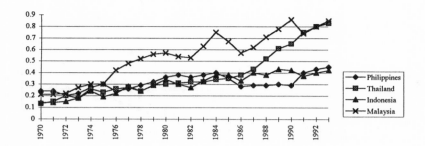

**Fig. 8.2. Share of World Markets in Manufactures (manufactured exports as a percentage of world manufactured exports). (Data from International Monetary Fund.)**

Thus, the fortunes of the Philippine economy continue to depend on agriculture.

Dependence on agriculture has been a major constraint on economic performance. Both trade and exchange rate policy have been biased against agriculture, limiting sectoral investment and growth. At the same time, during the 1980s, the terms of trade moved sharply against agriculture, largely as a result of international price developments. For example, the ratio of average prices of rice to urea, at 2.5, was 50 percent higher in the 1970s than in the 1980s. Finally, long periods of natural resource exploitation, which kept growth high through the 1970s, came to a halt during the 1980s. Depletion of forests, fisheries, and soil resources increasingly dimmed growth after 1980.[2]

*Labor Force Transformation.* Without major structural change in output, the labor force also stayed put. This is important because labor productivity in agriculture is only one-half that in services, and one-fifth that in industry, because almost 80 percent of the agricultural labor force consists of self-employed or unpaid family workers, whereas industrial sectors use wage employees and achieve a much finer division of labor.

In the Philippines, the share of labor in low-productivity agricultural occupations has declined slightly between 1970 and 1990, by about 10 percentage points, but there was only a 1 percentage point increase in industrial wage labor. The rest moved into the informal service sector. By contrast, in Korea and Malaysia, both the decline in self-employed agricultural workers and the increase in industrial wage labor were substantially higher over a comparable period (table 8.1).

*External Debt Accumulation.* Prior to 1970, the response to balance of payments crises in the Philippines was devaluation and a contraction in domestic demand and growth. But, with the development of international capital

---

2. See Cruz 1992.

**TABLE 8.1.  The Transformation of Philippine Employment**

| | Philippines | | | Korea | | | Malaysia | | |
|---|---|---|---|---|---|---|---|---|---|
| | 1970 | 1990 | (1970–90) | 1970 | 1990 | (1970–90) | 1973 | 1989 | (1973–89) |
| Total employment | 100.0 | 100.0 | 0.0 | 100.0 | 100.0 | 0.0 | 100.0 | 100.0 | 0.0 |
| Industry[a] | 16.5 | 15.2 | -1.3 | 14.3 | 27.3 | 13.0 | 18.86 | 25.89 | 7.03 |
| Wage | 10.7 | 11.8 | 1.1 | 10.2[b] | 23.7[b] | 13.5[b] | 14.62[c] | 22.79[c] | 8.17[c] |
| Nonwage | 5.8 | 3.4 | -2.4 | 4.1 | 3.6 | .5 | 4.24 | 3.10 | -1.14 |
| Services[d] | 29.7 | 39.5 | 9.8 | 35.2 | 54.5 | 19.3 | 36.60 | 48.47 | 11.87 |
| Wage | 22.5 | 24.8 | 2.3 | 21.0[b] | 35.1[b] | 14.1 | 24.7[c] | 36.66[c] | 11.95[c] |
| Nonwage[e] | 7.2 | 14.7 | 7.5 | 14.2 | 19.4 | 5.2 | 11.89 | 12.08 | -.7 |
| Agriculture | 53.8 | 45.3 | -8.5 | 50.5 | 18.2 | -32.3 | 44.55 | 25.64 | -18.91 |
| Wage | 8.5 | 9.5 | 1.0 | 7.6 | 1.4 | -6.2 | 15.50 | 8.81 | -6.69 |
| Nonwage[c] | 45.3 | 35.8 | -9.5 | 42.9 | 16.8 | 26.1 | 29.06 | 16.83 | -12.23 |

*Source:* Philippines 1970: Philippine Census of Population and Housing National Summary, vol. 2, Table 11.9; 1990: NCSO Special Tabulation. Korea 1970: Republic of Korea 1982, table 9; 1990: Republic of Korea 1990. Malaysia 1973, 1989: Household Income Surveys.

[a]Industry refers to mining and manufacturing only.

[b]Includes both private and public wage earners.

[c]Peninsular Malaysia only.

[d]Service refers to construction, utilities, transport, commerce, finance, community, and personal services.

[e]Nonwage includes self-employed employer and unpaid family workers.

markets, debt offered an attractive alternative to policymakers. Total foreign debt rose from U.S.$2.3 billion in 1970 to $17.3 billion in 1980 and $30 billion by 1991. The debt to GDP ratio climbed sharply from 10 percent in 1965 to a peak of over 90 percent in 1986, and the Philippines became one of the most heavily indebted developing countries.

*Poverty.* Without significant change in occupations, it has been hard for the Philippines to make progress on poverty reduction in the same way that other East Asian countries have. The general perception is that poverty incidence in the Philippines has at best remained constant and that even the little growth that did occur did not trickle down to the poor.[3] But this perception is not quite accurate. The measurement of Philippine poverty has been complicated by the use of official poverty lines that are high relative to other countries and have increased more rapidly than the consumer price index over time. When adjustments are made for these factors, the elasticity of Philippine poverty reduction with respect to GDP growth is quite comparable with that achieved in other East Asian countries (table 8.2).

*Overall Assessment.* These summary statistics point to an economy that has stagnated along many dimensions—growth, exports, sectoral shares, productivity, and the structure of jobs—while displaying symptoms of failed development strategies—high external debt and high levels of poverty. This is all the more disappointing because after World War II the Philippines seemed to have the best potential of any Asian economy, second only to Japan.

## Dashed Expectations

The basis for high expectations for Philippine development around 1960 was broad.

First, the country was endowed with a good natural resource base, consisting of arable land, rich mineral deposits, diverse marine resources, and ample forest cover.

**TABLE 8.2.   Elasticities of Poverty**

| Country | Elasticity of Poverty |
| --- | --- |
| Philippines | .17 |
| Thailand | .18 |
| Korea | .25 |
| Malaysia | .20 |

*Source:* World Bank estimates.

3. See, for example, Romulo 1989.

Second, it enjoyed special relations with the United States, which, until recently, dominated foreign aid, trade, and investments. Various agreements gave the Philippines open access to U.S. markets, preferential quotas and prices for sugar and textiles, and a political comfort that made the Philippines a favorite destination for U.S. foreign investment.

Third, in 1970, 83 percent of the population above 10 years of age were literate, with minimal differences between males and females.[4] The Philippines had a head start in providing universal primary education through public schools supplemented by a network of private educational institutions, particularly at the secondary and tertiary levels.[5]

Fourth, there was an early start in developing labor-intensive manufacturing for export. Between 1970 and 1984, the Philippines increased its market share in world manufactured exports from .24 to .4 percent, significantly higher than that of Thailand or Indonesia.

Fifth, the Philippines had already achieved a domestic savings rate of about 20 percent by 1970, a level comparable with that of the other "miracle" countries in midmiracle stage.

It is commonly supposed that a major disadvantage of the Philippines relative to neighboring countries was its skewed distribution of income (a Gini coefficient of .5 in 1961) and wealth. However, too much emphasis should not be placed on this. While it is true that the Philippines had a substantially less egalitarian income distribution than did Taiwan (China) or Korea, countries that had benefited from land reform and high primary school enrollment drives, it did not differ in any significant fashion from Indonesia, Thailand, or Malaysia.[6]

The indicators of poor performance, despite favorable initial conditions internally and externally, suggests that the tortuous path of development in the Philippines can be attributed to policy mistakes. In the following sections, we discuss these policy choices and their implementation. One conclusion that emerges from this analysis is that the roots of policy-induced distortions go deep and were negatively impacting economic performance for a considerable period of time. Initially, however, this was disguised by the presence of natural

---

4. These educational attainment rates, especially for females, are considerably better than those in Malaysia, Thailand, and Indonesia in 1970.

5. The number of people educated in technology and of those working in R&D, two measures used by UNESCO (United Nations Economic and Social Committee) to compare labor force skills across countries, was also much higher in the Philippines than in Korea, Malaysia, Thailand, or Indonesia (around 1982).

6. The *World Development Report,* 1991 (World Bank 1991c) shows the share of income going to the lowest 20 percent to be higher in the Philippines than in Thailand or Malaysia. Booth (1992) also concludes that land distribution in the Philippines is not less egalitarian than in Indonesia or Thailand.

resource wealth, which was systematically depleted. Later, external debt accumulation, which further reduced national wealth, disguised the inherent economic weaknesses of the system. Against this backdrop, the period of structural adjustment in the 1980s receives a much better scorecard than is suggested by growth, which, at .5 percent, was by far the lowest in the region. But we argue below that the macroeconomic and structural changes that took place over this period have set the stage for robust, sustained growth in the 1990s.

## II.  Macroeconomic Performance and Management

It is important to have some perspective on Philippine economic performance to differentiate two hypotheses: (1) that the Philippines had reasonable growth until it lost its way in the 1980s and (2) that sustainable performance has been poor for some time but was disguised for over 20 years by mortgaging the future. This second hypothesis seems to fit the facts best.

By some standards, the 1960s and 1970s were periods of modest progress, with annual growth rates between 5 and 6 percent. But these growth rates are biased upward by faulty accounting due to natural resource depletion and the debt buildup and so do not represent sustainable development. Over time, natural resource degradation has limited further expansion of resource-based subsectors, while the burden of debt service has served as a drag on continued growth. Making the appropriate adjustments shows the historical performance of the Philippines to have been much worse. The low growth of the 1980s, then, is not a further deterioration in performance as much as a period of consolidation and restructuring to reposition the economy on a sustainable growth path.

### Natural Resource Degradation

In the 1970s, growth was largely stimulated by agricultural expansion and the exploitation of extractive subsectors in forestry, fisheries, and upland agriculture. In agriculture, growth was boosted by higher and more stable rice yields made possible by the use of a combination of modern varieties and chemical inputs on irrigated lands. Coastal fisheries and logged-over upland areas were also able to absorb excess labor from lowland areas temporarily, thereby increasing measured GDP.

A number of disaggregated case studies point to the temporary nature of some of the recorded growth.[7] In the late 1960s, deforestation due to logging, shifting cultivation, pests, and diseases was estimated to have proceeded at a rate of around 300,000 hectares a year. This declined to around 180,000 in the 1980s and dropped below 100,000 hectares annually in the 1980s. As of 1992,

---

7. See Cruz 1992.

the Philippines had 6.2 million remaining hectares of forested area, of which only about a sixth is primary growth forest. The government has pursued reforestation efforts more vigorously, restoring over 100,000 hectares a year since 1989, compared with around 40,000 hectares a year during the 1970s and 1980s. With the forest resource destroyed and fresh administrative attention focused on sustainable development in the 1980s, it is not surprising that value added in forestry fell by 51 percent between 1980 and 1985 and by a further 14 percent by 1990.

A recent study has found that half a hectare of irrigated area has been lost for every hectare of forest cleared and converted to nonforest uses.[8] The Bureau of Soils and Water Management estimated that 9 out of the 11 million hectares of actively utilized land in the country, and the 3 million hectares available for expansion, are susceptible to natural soil erosion due mainly to their having slopes ranging from 8 to 15 percent. As many as 18 million upland farmers have cleared residual forests and practiced shifting cultivation on these slopes, making soil erosion a major environmental issue. In addition, polluted water systems and the adverse effects of prolonged use of chemical fertilizers and pesticides have led to a decline in the productivity of cropland in the plains.

Populations of a million or more coastal fishermen have likewise depleted the near-shore fisheries resources. Commercial vessels have encroached into shallow waters reserved for municipal fishing, while mangrove areas have been converted to aquaculture, with detrimental effects to ecological balance and future productivity of the fisheries sector. By the early 1990s, it was estimated that a fifth of the country's major fishing grounds had been overfished.

## External Debt Accumulation

A second major adjustment to growth must be made to reflect the buildup of external debt over the 1970s. Total external debt grew 10-fold from $2.3 billion in 1970 to $24.3 billion in 1983. But there was no equivalent expansion in the asset side of the country's ledger. Some of the debt (especially general purpose debt from commercial banks) went to finance an expansion in current public expenditures. Another portion helped create new public enterprises performing traditional private sector activities. Unfortunately, a large number of these investments were ill conceived, overpriced, or eventually proved unprofitable, leaving few real assets behind. A third portion financed loans from government financial institutions, guaranteed by the national government, to the private sector. These investments, too, were of low quality.[9] Finally, some

8. World Bank 1992.
9. The Asset Privatization Trust later took over these assets and sold them for an average discount of about 50 percent relative to face value.

of the external borrowing simply financed private sector capital flight, which totaled almost $10 billion between 1970 and 1982. In each of these instances, the future debt service burden is not being met by higher incomes generated by borrowing but out of future savings that otherwise could have been used for investment.

For all intents and purposes, then, Philippine debt accumulation in the 1970s represented an accommodation of an unsustainable growth strategy and a mortgaging of future growth. The legacy was a decade-long boom followed by a prolonged period of economic stagnation.

This contrasts with the rapid increase in foreign investment flows into Singapore and Hong Kong during the same period, which represented a balanced buildup of assets and liabilities. Taiwan (China), meanwhile, did not have to worry about a large current account deficit, as government spending and imports were restrained whenever export revenues slowed. Consequently, it is crucial to adjust relative GDP growth performance for the distinct patterns of debt accumulation in comparing Philippine growth performance with that of its neighbors and over different periods of time.

## Illusory Growth of the 1960s and 1970s

The impact on decadal growth of adjusting GDP growth for the effects of foreign debt accumulation and natural resource degradation is shown in table 8.3. The methodology used is to estimate the growth in net worth rather than the growth in GDP. The concept is that growth in net worth reflects sustainable development. Net worth is derived as domestic capital stock less the value of external debt. Domestic capital stock, in turn, is estimated as a constant multiple of GDP less the estimated depletion of natural resource wealth. The overall effect is to reduce growth substantially. The interpretation is that the Philippines cannot be considered a country that was growing relatively well but lost its way in the 1980s; rather, it should be considered a country where distortions and mismanagement consistently provided a drag on sustainable growth. It is for this reason that structural reforms during the 1980s did not yield immediate

**TABLE 8.3.   GDP Growth Revised for Resource Depletion and Foreign Debt**

| Average Annual GDP Growth Rate (%) | 1970s | 1980s |
|---|---|---|
| Measured | 5.6 | 0.45 |
| Adjusted for natural resource degradation | 4.6 | −0.90 |
| Adjusted for natural resource degradation and foreign debt | 3.6 | −2.30 |

*Note:* The heading 1980s refers to 1980–87 only.
*Source:* World Bank estimates.

benefits. Much was required to propel the economy onto a new growth path with which it had little prior experience.[10]

## Fiscal Imprudence

The Philippines' record in macroeconomic stability, while at times inconsistent, has never been poor. There have only been two years (1974 and 1985) with inflation greater than 20 percent during the last three decades, and most years saw single-digit inflation rates. Public sector and current account deficits have rarely exceeded 5 percent of GDP. From a cross-country perspective, even when only neighboring regional comparators are taken, these indicators of macroeconomic policy look quite favorable. But the reality in terms of macroeconomic outcomes was much worse. Looking at the deviations of GDP per capita from its trend growth, the Philippines stands out with a coefficient of variation of 2.7 (see table 8.4). In the end, this instability translated into lower savings and investment and, in turn, into a lower level of growth.

Another indicator of poor macroeconomic outcomes is the rapid growth in public debt, both external and domestic. Total public debt grew from 28 percent of GDP in 1976 to 112 percent in 1986. This expansion in public debt would seem to be at odds with relatively low annual deficits of the public sector, but there is an easy explanation. The deficits do not include the effects of implicit public guarantees and bailouts such as programs that allowed the private sector to service its external debt obligations at favorable, precrisis, exchange rates. This is just one of many examples of public sector bailouts of the private sector—other examples include bailouts of rural credit institutions, pro-

**TABLE 8.4.   Variance Analysis of Growth in East Asia**

| Country | Average Annual Growth Rate of GDP per Capita, 1960–93 (%) | Sample Variance | Coefficient of Variation (standard error/mean) |
|---|---|---|---|
| Philippines | 1.2 | .11 | 2.71 |
| Korea | 6.6 | .16 | .61 |
| Taiwan | 6.7 | .09 | .45 |
| Malaysia | 4.2 | .07 | .65 |
| Indonesia | 3.9 | .10 | .82 |
| Thailand | 5.2 | .07 | .51 |

*Source:* World Bank calculations.

10. Obviously, a similar methodology should be used to correct the GDP growth figures for other countries. For Malaysia, this does not appear to have much impact (see World Bank 1991b), and for nonagriculturally based economies such as Korea, Hong Kong, and Singapore it is a nonissue. But some studies suggest that it may be important for Indonesia (Cruz and Repetto 1992).

tection for selected industries in trouble, and bailouts of social security and pension schemes.

Another example of an unrecorded deficit comes from the bad loans of major public sector financial entities. Specialized government banks were established in the 1950s but experienced strong expansion in the 1970s, extending subsidized credit to state enterprises and private clients favored by the executive. These banks depended on credit from the Central Bank, which rediscounted and subsidized loans for priority activities. In addition, their foreign borrowings were obtained with a guarantee from the national government. In 1982, the assets of the four government financial institutions (GFIs)—the Philippine National Bank (PNB), the Development Bank of the Philippines (DBP), the Land Bank of the Philippines (LBP), and the Philippine Veterans Bank (PVB)—exceeded the combined assets of the 28 private commercial banks. PNB catalyzed investments in industry and rural programs, DBP focused on long-term finance, and LBP catered to clients in agriculture. When major clients' undertakings failed, these banks extended further credit or, in some cases, took over direct management control of the company but with little operating improvement. This led to unsustainable losses that eventually required additional emergency financing from the Central Bank, fresh government equity infusions or deposits of the working cash balances of the national treasury.

Much of the credit extended by public banks, ex post, turned out to be unrecoverable, and so it should count as public transfers to the private sector. But, while these debts were being rolled over, they were not accounted for as nonperforming loans and therefore do not show up in public deficit calculations.

A simple accounting framework can be used to derive the average implicit public sector deficit over the period. We define the average implicit deficit as the deficit that would have generated the same growth in public debt over the period as that which is actually observed. Algebraically, this is given by

$$\dot{D}/\text{GDP} = (D/\text{GDP}) + (D/\text{GDP}) * (\dot{\text{GDP}})/\text{GDP},$$

where • is the derivative with respect to time. The left-hand side of the above identity is the average implicit deficit expressed as a percentage of GDP.

The only parameters that are required to derive the average implied deficit are the growth rate of the public debt to GDP ratio, the initial public debt to GDP ratio, and the growth rate of GDP. Given that the debt to GDP ratio increased from 33 percent in 1970 to 91 percent in 1990, we can compute the average implied deficit as 8.4 percent of GDP, considerably larger than the 5 percent conventionally measured average deficit. This shows the true extent of fiscal imprudence in the Philippines over the 1970s and 1980s (see app., table A8.1).

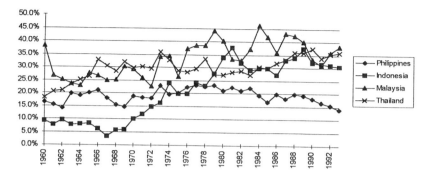

**Fig. 8.3. Domestic savings as a percentage of GDP. (Data from World Bank.)**

By itself, the deficit number for the Philippines does not tell the whole story of the lack of fiscal control. Even quite large deficits may be tolerated if domestic savings are buoyant and the tax system is sufficiently elastic so that higher interest payments associated with growing debt can easily be met. Neither of these conditions held in the Philippines. Domestic savings, which had been at a reasonable level of 21 percent of GDP in 1950, fell sharply after the mid-1970s to a low of just 16 percent by 1990 (fig. 8.3).

The pattern, then, is one of fiscal opacity rather than fiscal prudence. The buildup of public debt in the Philippines is indicative of a system of transfers and unrecorded expenditures by public entities financed not through the budget but through the financial system, which was underpinned by the government. Periodic financial crises led to a succession of events requiring public debt accumulation.

### Inefficient Public Investments

During the first half of the 1970s, public spending on infrastructure quadrupled, constituting half of total public capital outlays by 1976. Later, large, complex projects were launched, such as the Manila Bay reclamation project and the Cultural Center Complex, a new building for the legislature, numerous government offices and official residences, and showcase medical centers, most of which were overpriced and overdesigned for local conditions. While these projects boosted aggregate demand during the construction phase, they produced little new output. On the contrary, they may even have reduced output, as they required expanded bureaucracies to manage them, taking recurrent financing away from higher priority areas.

Part of the problem with "white elephant" projects was the politicized nature of investment screening. Economic profitability is only one of 31 criteria, with a weight of 4.4 percent, used to rank projects according to the official project selection guidelines of the National Economic Development Authority. Other criteria, such as location and labor absorption, are more important and easier to manipulate for political purposes.

Nonbudget public spending also grew rapidly in the 1970s. The government took over private companies and established new enterprises that competed directly with the private sector in such diverse areas as iron and steel, petrochemicals, transport, water supply, and energy. The number of government corporations almost trebled from 75 to 207 in a span of 10 years from 1970 to 1980. There was no pressure on these enterprises to improve cost efficiency or increase cost recovery through market-based pricing, as various tax exemptions, subsidies, and other preferences protected them from private competitors. In addition, the Philippines did not have adequate risk-sharing arrangements for such large, foreign-financed projects as the Bataan Nuclear Power Plant,[11] nor did it close loss-making ventures fast enough. Because of perennial losses, corporate equity became the single largest component of the capital outlays of the national government between 1981 and 1983.

### III.  Swings in Industrial Performance and Policy

It is in the area of industrial performance that the Philippines stands out furthest from its neighbors. Until 1960, Philippine industry grew strongly, based on war reconstruction and then an import-substitution policy. But once easy import-substitution opportunities in consumer goods were exhausted in the early 1960s, the industrial sector stopped playing a leading role in development. This underperformance of industrial growth raises two issues: first, what were the characteristics of industrial policy that held back growth, and, second, why has the response of the industrial sector to policy change been so slow?

Before describing the details of industrial policy, it is useful to examine the seeming paradox of the Philippines. From 1960 to the early 1990s, industrial performance was poor, with negative total factor productivity growth.[12] The paradox is that this occurred in spite of the initial advantages favorable to general economic growth and additional advantages favoring the industrial

---

11.  The Bataan Nuclear Power Plant never did become operational, and it saddled the economy with U.S.$2 billion in foreign debt. This can be contrasted with the case of Malaysia's Perwaja Steel Plant. Built as a joint venture with Nippon Steel, this billion dollar project was to use a new direct reduction technology, which never worked. But, thanks to risk-sharing clauses in the contract, the Malaysian government received U.S.$500 million in compensation from its Japanese partner.

12.  Page 1990.

sector. The latter included: (1) special access to U.S. markets and heavy investments by U.S. multinationals and the domestic private sector, (2) an early appreciation of the importance of exports,[13] (3) a reasonably diversified export structure, (4) early entry into the most dynamic manufactured export sectors of the past 25 years (electronics and garments), and (5) relative capital equipment prices about the same as world prices.[14]

## Import Substitution and Commodity Exports, 1950 to 1967

The Philippines adopted extensive import and foreign exchange controls in 1950 when reduced war payments and an overvalued exchange rate triggered a balance of payments crisis. Free access to U.S. markets, embedded in the 1946 Philippine Trade Act, was also approaching its end.[15] Import controls on consumer goods formed the bedrock of an import-substitution industrialization policy, assisted by the grant of nationality status to Americans for investment purposes. A comprehensive tariff law was enacted in 1957 to serve as the main instrument of protection in the 1960s, and quantitative controls were phased out. The resulting cascading tariff structure simply mirrored the protection previously offered by import licenses to import-substituting industries.[16] Tax relief was provided for capital equipment imports of firms in basic industries, and preferential access to subsidized long-term finance was given to favored industries. The growth rate of manufacturing value added hit its all-time peak at 12 percent per annum in the second half of the 1950s, led by a small number of large firms in consumer goods industries.

By the early 1960s, opportunities for further import substitution had been virtually exhausted and capital outflows triggered a balance of payments crisis. The response was orthodox—import controls were dismantled and the peso was devalued from P2 to P3.90 to the dollar. This had a favorable initial effect on the country's reserves but rapid increases in import volumes and declines in terms of trade caused large balance of payments deficits to resurface toward the second half of the 1960s. The overall decline in protection affected manufacturing adversely, with the average rate of growth of manufacturing falling from 7.7 percent during 1957–59 to 3.7 percent in 1960–65. Tariffs were adjusted

---

13. In 1970, the Philippines had about the same share of world manufactured exports as Korea and a higher share than Thailand, Indonesia, or Malaysia.

14. Aitken (1992) uses this statistic as a key indicator of the incentive for firms to access international technology.

15. The Laurel-Langley Agreement of 1956 spelled out the details of the transition away from special privileges for Philippine goods.

16. The average effective rate of protection for import-competing industries during this period was 59 percent according to Bautista and Power 1979.

upward in 1965 to compensate for the elimination of import controls, and moderate controls on foreign exchange for consumer goods imports were restored from 1967 to 1970. A floating exchange rate system was finally adopted in 1970 in view of severe pressures on the balance of payments position and the level of international reserves.

One important legacy of the 1960s was that neither the devaluation of 1962 nor the liberalization (tariffication of quotas and reduction in effective protection) of industrial policy seemed to have any success in accelerating industrial growth or raising manufactured exports. This experience was the foundation of a subsequent period of much more activist industrial policy, focusing on specific incentives for exports, priority investments, and aid for distressed industries.

### Industrial Activism and Debt Accumulation, 1967–82

Two pieces of legislation ushered in the 15-year activist period of Philippine industrial policy: the Investment Incentives Act (Republic Act 5186) in 1967 and the Export Incentives Act (RA 6135) in 1970. These opened priority areas of the economy to foreign investments and conferred special benefits for the establishment of pioneer and export-oriented enterprises under the administration of the newly created Board of Investments. They encouraged the formation of joint ventures and allowed full foreign ownership in priority areas, provided Filipino equity participation was admitted to the extent of 60 percent within a span of 30 years. Export processing zones were set up in various parts of the country. Special manufacturing programs were established in an effort to push the growth of nontraditional, light manufactured exports such as automotive, garments, and semiconductor assembly. Special privileges granted through bonded manufacturing warehouses meant that export operations had to be kept separate from domestic production. Export duties were imposed on primary commodity exports to encourage further domestic processing of indigenous raw materials for export. The Development Bank of the Philippines, meanwhile, opened a low-interest refinancing window to assist distressed domestic-oriented industries with excess capacity such as textiles, cement, and pulp and paper.

The impact of these measures was seen in a sharp increase in manufacturing investment, but they were not efficient. Much of the investment (especially in chemicals and basic metals) was through state enterprises or publicly sponsored, and it relied heavily on external debt accumulation for its financing. The subsectoral distribution of manufacturing value added changed little—food, beverages, and tobacco continued to account for half of all manufacturing, suggesting that much of the investment in new or priority sectors was wasted. Indeed, at an aggregate level, total factor productivity growth, which had been a modest .6 percent between 1956 and 1970, fell to a negative 1.2 percent per year in the 1970s.

## Structural Adjustment and Paying the Piper, 1982–93

The Philippines was one of the first countries to attempt a structural adjustment program when it initiated trade liberalization and financial reform in 1980 in response to the second oil price shock and weakening primary commodity prices. Interest rates, which had been regulated by the Central Bank, were gradually liberalized, and banks were permitted greater scope, becoming "universal" following the German model. Trade liberalization focused on substantially reducing tariff rates, in particular at the high end of the spectrum where the maximum tariff was brought down from 100 to 50 percent. The program also envisaged a reduction in administrative restrictions on imports (on 960 of 1,304 regulated items), but this moved slowly and was soon reversed when balance of payments problems began to mount in 1982–83. Fiscal incentives, meanwhile, were rationalized in the early 1980s, but various exemptions were restored through a series of presidential decrees because of political pressure from well-entrenched lobbies.

The early structural measures introduced between 1980 and 1982 were designed to reverse the perceived problem of inefficient resource allocation and low productivity. But they were implemented in the face of a rapidly deteriorating macroeconomic situation (fiscal deficits and losses in reserves). The private sector response was predictable: capital flight (estimated to have totaled more than $2.5 billion in 1980–81), lower domestic savings, and falling private investment. By 1983, an internal recession and a desperate balance of payments situation emerged. As the Philippines failed to come to an agreement with the IMF for the first time in over a decade, access to international capital dried up still more, and a full-fledged crisis erupted.

In 1984, the economy plunged into a deep crisis, and industrial policy was subsumed into crisis management. Across the board levies on imports and an economic stabilization tax on all exports were imposed. The peso was devalued thrice within one year. A major recession ensued: manufacturing output fell by 11 percent in 1984 and by 8 percent in 1985. Many of the capital-intensive sectors established in the 1960s and 1970s as "preferred" sectors for industrial development, such as transport equipment, cement, and chemicals, collapsed and virtually disappeared.

The structural adjustment effort was resumed in 1987 and intensified further in the early 1990s when the government embarked on a broad spectrum of initiatives designed to create a more neutral and stable incentive system and a more outward-oriented policy regime. These efforts consisted of removal of quantitative restrictions (QRs), reduction in the average level and dispersion of tariffs, reduction and rationalization of fiscal incentives, liberalization and encouragement (through debt-equity swaps) of foreign investment, and privatization of state-owned enterprises.

Once account is taken of the backtracking associated with macroeconomic crisis, the Philippine reforms appear to be comprehensive and relatively fast. Table 8.5 shows some comparative indicators in a range of policy areas. Average tariff rates have been more than halved since 1980, and the import-weighted level of 15 percent is comparable with that in other reforming countries. The effective rate of protection has also been reduced to an estimated 22 percent. Quantitative restrictions were almost completely phased out, barring a few items retained for health and safety purposes. Privatization has progressed with commendable speed, both for small assets and for large companies. What is more, the Philippines took the lead in initiating Build-Operate-Transfer programs for power generation in 1992. And the liberalization in foreign investment can be gauged from the doubling of foreign direct investment (FDI) in the important manufacturing sector between 1980 and 1991.

## Competition Counts: Better Late Than Never

It took a decade for the Philippines to establish a sound macroeconomic base where market-determined wage, interest, and exchange rates could complement microreforms. Since then, the focus of industrial policy has shifted from promotion of intermediate targets—private sector, foreign investment, exports—to promotion of competition from within and without. It is the implementation and acceptance of this change that has brought about a resurgence of industrial sector growth and offers hope for sustained strong performance in the future.

The idea that it is competition that really counts is based on two indicators that show the effects of past Philippine industrial policy. They are the high concentration of industry and the absence of quality enhancement. Both indicators provide evidence that industry had ossified over the 15 year period of heavy industrial policy interventions. It is only when the national vision shifted away from protection to embrace the concept of a dynamic, competitive, private sector that prospects for industrial growth truly improved.

*Industry Was Highly Concentrated and Inefficient.* A substantial amount of economic activity is accounted for by a relatively small number of firms operating across a range of sectors. Less than 10 percent of the firms employ more than 200 workers, yet they account for 64 percent of total manufacturing employment and 77 percent of value added. In 1983, 58 out of 130 manufacturing subsectors in the Philippines had four-firm concentration ratios higher than 80 percent, and there were no subsectors where the concentration ratio was

**TABLE 8.5. Indicators of Policy Reform**

| Policy Area | Philippines | | | | Indonesia | | | Mexico | | | Chile | | |
|---|---|---|---|---|---|---|---|---|---|---|---|---|---|
| | 1980 | 1985 | 1991 | 1995 | 1982 | 1985 | 1991 | 1982 | 1985 | 1991 | 1973 | 1980 | 1989 |
| Average tariff rate (%) | | | | | | | | | | | | | |
|   Unweighted | 43 | 28 | 27 | 21 | 37 | 27 | 20 | 27 | 23 | 13 | 105 | 10 | 10 |
|   Import weighted | n.a. | 18 | 19 | 15 | 22 | 13 | 10 | n.a. | 12 | n.a. | 94 | 10 | 10 |
| Import licensing (% coverage) | | | | | | | | | | | | | |
|   Unweighted | 52 | 35 | 5 | 1 | n.a. | 32[a] | 10 | 100 | 12 | n.a. | 50[b] | 0[b] | 0[b] |
|   Import weighted | 33[c] | 33 | 13[d] | 1 | n.a. | 43[a] | 13 | 100 | 35 | 14 | n.a | n.a. | n.a. |
| Public enterprises (number) | n.a. | 700[e] | 304 | 79 | 208 | 214 | 211 | 1,155 | 920 | 285 | 498 | 43 | 27 |
| FDI[f] from United States and Japan (U.S.$m) | | | | | | | | | | | | | |
|   Total | 283 | 188 | 355 | — | 2,586 | 1,306 | 1,752 | 834 | 778 | 769 | n.a. | 118 | 265 |
|   In manufacturing | 127 | 117 | 215 | — | 203 | 195 | 208 | 647 | 627 | 632 | n.a. | 29 | 147 |

*Source:* Philippine Tariff Commission; NEDA; Department of Finance; World Bank staff reports; Luders 1990.

*Note:* Fiscal expenditures is current government expenditures as a percentage of GDP. External debt is external medium- and long-term public debt as a percentage of GDP. FDI for 1980 is average 1981–84; 1985 is average 1985–88; 1991 is actual 1989.

[a]For 1986.
[b]Approximate.
[c]For 1981.
[d]For 1990.
[e]For 1987.
[f]Foreign direct investment.

**Employment**          **Value Added**

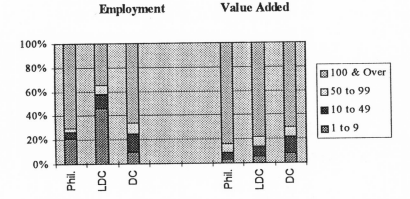

Fig. 8.4.    Manufacturing size structure of the Philippines, less-developed countries, and developed countries. Less-developed countries (LDCs) are the Philippines, Indonesia, India, Singapore, Korea, and Taiwan (China). Developed countries (DCs) include Japan, the United States, (former West) Germany, and the United Kingdom. Data for the Philippines are for 1988. For other countries they are the most recent available. (Data from Philippine Census of Establishments, 1988, NSO; Hooley and Ahmad 1990, table 1.)

less than 20 percent. The average concentration ratio was the highest among a sample of 10 developing countries studied by Frischtak.[17]

It must be pointed out that this structure did not emerge from a mere lack of attention to small and medium-sized firms. There is a long history of credit and livelihood programs for small enterprises in the Philippines. However, much of the attention has been devoted to micro- and cottage-based industries rather than the middle-tier or medium-sized firms that have the potential to increase the contestability and competitiveness of industries. In fact, the package of fiscal incentives, credit subsidies, and technical assistance for small firms may even have discouraged them from expanding and challenging the position of large enterprises. These benefited from preferential access to cheap capital, administrative controls on imported inputs, and fiscal breaks. Under this structure of easy profits, the incentive to innovate and export was low. As a consequence, the share of value added by enterprises with 50 to 99 employees in the Philippines was about half that in other developing countries (fig. 8.4).

*Low Quality.* To examine the issue of quality, we decomposed exports into goods where quality competition (requiring sustained technological and marketing efforts) has been important (such as microelectronics and shoes) and those where product quality has not undergone significant improvement inter-

17. Frischtak, Bita, and Ulrich 1989.

nationally (certain types of garments). In the case of the former, the Philippines had great difficulty in maintaining market share, while in the latter case it has had more success. But this success has been strictly a consequence of a higher volume of sales—unit values, and, indeed, local content, did not increase, suggesting that the type of product has remained unchanged. The problem was that the numerous industrial incentives offered by the government were geared toward production, not competition, so there was insufficient emphasis on the establishment of the supporting institutions that would promote broader industrial development, particularly in the areas of quality control, marketing support, and technological upgrading. While its competitors in labor-intensive manufactured exports managed to diversify into more complex, high-technology, product lines, the Philippines got stuck in the first phase of assembly industries, mainly using imported inputs and cheap domestic labor. In contrast, other Asian countries have seen sharp increases in both unit values and local content, showing that their export success was achieved by moving up the value-added ladder both within product categories and by diversifying into new, higher-value-added exports.

## IV.  The Social Compact

One legacy of years of underperforming growth is a level of poverty in the Philippines that far exceeds its neighbors—61.8 percent of the population, or 34.5 million people by official estimates in 1988. Along with the concentration of industrial power documented previously, these poverty estimates paint a picture of an unequal society that may have jeopardized its growth because of an inefficient and fragile social compact.

### Wasted Human Capital

The dominant explanation of poverty is the inefficiency with which assets are used. Human capital in particular has yielded low returns, not because Filipinos have lacked access to schooling but because low growth and the pattern of capital-intensive growth reduced the demand for labor.

Consider the case of schooling. Figure 8.5 shows that as early as 1965 expected years of schooling for both males and females in the Philippines far exceeded the level that would have been predicted given its level of per capita income and the experiences of other countries.[18] Even though most of the East Asian countries appear as outliers, the Philippines stands out as an exception even by these standards. Enrollment rates have been very high at all levels of

---

18. The expected years of schooling are calculated for a synthetic cohort based on primary, secondary, and tertiary enrollment ratios. The regressions include higher-order income terms. See World Bank (1993).

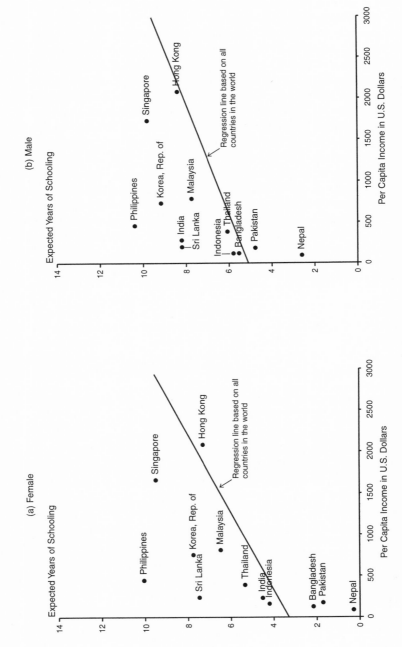

**Fig. 8.5. Cross-country regressions for (a) female and (b) male expected schooling in 1965 with selected Asian countries indicated**

education (54 percent secondary school enrollment in 1975 was more than double that of Thailand [26 percent] or Indonesia [20 percent]). High literacy rates also indicate that a broad segment of the population is well educated.

The real problem has been absorption into the labor force. Table 8.6 shows a steadily increasing rate of unemployment and underemployment over successive five-year periods (eliminating medium-term cyclical effects). Open unemployment is not an indicator of poverty, however, but a signal of high returns in searching for the right job. This can be inferred from the profile of unemployment, which shows that most (70 percent in 1988) of the unemployed have at least a high school education, more than half were less than 24 years of age, and only 10 percent were household heads.

The doubling in the rate of underemployment is a better indication of deteriorating job creation. The weak labor market resulted in two decades of falling real wages,[19] to a nadir in 1980, before recovery set in (fig. 8.6 and table 8.7). Several forces contributed to this pattern. On the supply side, the labor force grew by more than 4 percent a year in the 1970s and 1980s. While im-

**TABLE 8.6.   Rate of Unemployment and Underemployment (five-year averages)**

| Years | Unemployed (%) | Underemployed (%) |
|---|---|---|
| 1970–75 | 5.35 | 11.76[a] |
| 1975–80 | 5.40[b] | 12.68[b] |
| 1980–85 | 9.93 | 24.88 |
| 1985–90 | 10.46 | 21.88 |
| (1991–94) | (14.4) | (23.6) |

*Source:* 1970–89: NSO, *Yearbook of Labor Statistics,* 1990, 1991–94: NSO (1991) 1991, 4.
*Note: Unemployed* is defined as persons in the labor force who did not work or had no job/business during the reference week but were reported available and actively looking for work. Also considered as unemployed are persons without jobs or businesses who were reported as available for work but were not looking for work because of their belief that no work was available or because of temporary illness/disability, bad weather, pending job application, or waiting for job interview.
*Underemployed* is defined as employed persons who expressed the desire to have additional hours of work in their present jobs or in additional jobs or to have a new job with longer working hours. Data for 1956–76 and 1987 onward use the "past week" reference, while those for 1977–86 use the "past quarter" reference period. No labor force survey was conducted in 1979. Prior to August 1976, the labor force covers household population 10 years old and older. Since then the definition of *labor force* covers household population 15 years old and older. Prior to 1987, the concept of underemployed defines the number of employed persons wanting additional work; from 1987 onward, the concept was changed to number of employed persons wanting more hours of work.
[a]1971–75.
[b]1975–78 and 1980.

19. Wages refer to the average basic daily wage of common laborers in industrial establishments in Metro Manila.

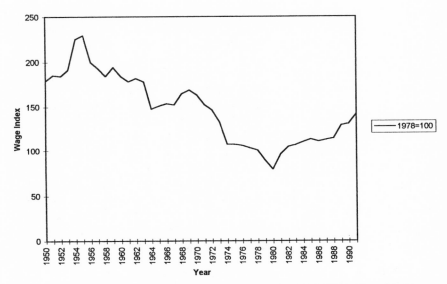

**Fig. 8.6.   Philippine real wage movements, 1950–91. (Data from World Bank.)**

portant, this does not explain the correlation of the timing of major wage declines with the oil shocks of 1973–74 and 1979–80, nor does it explain the reversal in the pattern of wage movements after 1980. And supply of labor explanations should impact equally on agricultural wages, which, in contrast to industrial wages, have been steady throughout the period.

Other explanations link wage movements to the pattern of industrial and trade policy. If policy-induced distortions and the real exchange rate act to favor capital-intensive, import-substituting industries, then the returns to capital will rise and the returns to unskilled labor, which is intensively used in the nontraded sector (construction), will fall. Lal (1986) uses this argument to explain why wages fell during discrete periods when protectionist industrial policies were being applied.

The insight provided by Lal's analysis, that real wages were unsustainably high during the 1970s and reflected the high degree of industrial protection, is a key to understanding later wage movements in the Philippines. But the model does not capture the recovery of wages after 1980. An additional part of the story must lie in the political links between business, industrial labor, and government. Worker "insiders" in Philippine manufacturing were able to gain a share of total profits (including protectionist rents) in return for the political support of the government and industrial peace. The fluctuations in wages reflect the difficulties in maintaining profits in the face of a stagnant domestic

**TABLE 8.7. Comparison of Industrial Wage Trends: Unskilled Industrial Labor versus Manufacturing Average**

| Year | Real Earnings (1978 pesos/month) | | Earnings Ratio Manufacturing Average | | Rate of Growth in Real Earnings (%)[a] | |
|---|---|---|---|---|---|---|
| | Unskilled | Manufacturing Average | Unskilled | | Unskilled | Manufacturing Average |
| 1972 | 548.6 | 768.8[b] | 1.40[b] | | — | — |
| 1975 | 400.9 | 631.4 | 1.57 | | -9.9 | -8.1[b] |
| 1978 | 374.6 | 591.2 | 1.58 | | -2.2 | -2.2 |
| 1983 | 397.6 | 688.1 | 1.73 | | +1.2 | +3.1 |
| 1988 | 426.4 | 771.4 | 1.81 | | +1.4 | +2.3 |

*Source:* National Statistical Office, Philippine Census of Manufacturing, Large Establishments, various years.
*Note:* The manufacturing average refers total compensation unless otherwise indicated.
[a]Rates of growth refer to compound growth rate from last year for which data are reported.
[b]The manufacturing average in 1972 refers to wages only. The estimated growth rate, 1972–75, refers to the growth in wages only.

economy and price increases of important intermediate inputs such as oil.[20] The turnaround in wages after 1980 can then be explained first by the launch of a new wave of public incentives to industry (through directed credit and the construction of large public enterprises), later by the decline in international oil prices, and still later by economic recovery. This view of manufactured labor as a protected sector is buttressed by looking at the empirical evidence of the ratio between average wages in manufacturing and GDP per capita (table 8.8). At 2.7, this ratio is far higher than those of comparable East Asian economies, suggesting that Philippine manufacturing evolved either in a much more human-capital-intensive direction than the other countries did or that wages in manufacturing were substantially protected relative to wages in other segments of the economy.

By organizing to protect their own wages, even at the cost of fewer manufactured jobs, labor and business in the Philippines blocked one of the principal channels through which human capital accumulation could be profitably used. Instead of fueling the transformation of labor from low-productivity rural jobs to higher-productivity urban wage jobs, human capital accumulation in the Philippines simply encouraged greater migration to the unskilled, low-productivity, urban service sector where migrants could hope to someday gain employment in a protected, formal sector job.[21]

TABLE 8.8.   The Competitiveness of Philippine Labor

| Country | Year | Firm Size | Ratio of Manufacturing Wage to GDP per Capita |
|---|---|---|---|
| Philippines | 1988 | 10+ | 2.7 |
| Turkey | 1988 | 25+ | 3.2 |
| Thailand | 1986 | 10+ | 2.2 |
| Colombia | 1988 | 10– | 1.9 |
| Indonesia | 1986 | 20+ | 1.8 |
| Mexico | 1988 | n.a. | 1.7 |
| Chile | 1986 | 10+ | 1.6 |
| Malaysia | 1987 | 5+ | 1.6 |
| Sri Lanka | 1987 | 5+ | 1.4 |
| Korea | 1987 | 5+ | 1.4 |
| Japan | 1988 | 4+ | 1.2 |
| Singapore | 1988 | 5+ | 0.8 |

Source: Annualized Manufacturing Wage: United Nations, various years. GDP per capita: IMF

20. Later in the 1980s, the price of petroleum, fixed by the government through subsidies given to the Oil Price Stabilization Fund, became one of the most politicized prices in the economy.

21. One other avenue that was actively used was migration (or labor contracts) abroad. In 1991, there were an estimated 433,889 registered contract workers abroad and a far greater number of legal and illegal immigrants to other countries, with over 1 million estimated to be in the United States alone.

### Exceptional Assistance for the Poor

Aside from market-based mechanisms for redistributing national income, the Philippines has had important private and public nonmarket mechanisms. These have been important components in maintaining limited progress in betterment of the living standards of the poorest in the economy.

*Private Transfers.* Private transfer networks are very extensive in the Philippines. In 1988, 88 percent of urban households and 93 percent of rural households were involved on a monthly basis as transfer recipients, donors, or both. Twenty percent of urban households received transfers from abroad.[22] On average, transfers accounted for 12 percent of total income for households that were net recipients. Transfers tend to be very progressive, accruing largely to households that, lacking transfers, would have been at the bottom of the income distribution. This is not surprising, as a significant portion of transfers appears to be from a working spouse supporting families back home. Perhaps because of these extensive transfers, income distribution in the Philippines may have improved slightly over a 30-year period. And the level of income distribution (as given by the Gini coefficient or the share of the bottom 20 percent) is comparable with that in other Asian countries (table 8.9).

*Public Distributional Policies.* Through its tax and expenditure policy, the public sector can have a major role in promoting a more equitable social outcome than the market solution. In the Philippines, however, tax policy is implemented in at best a distributionally neutral fashion. Expenditures, while seemingly progressive, may not yield equal benefits to recipients of different social classes, particularly expenditures on education, as has been noted.

*Taxes.* The Philippine tax system is known for its low collection rates and its reliance on indirect taxes. Perhaps only 50 percent of taxes due are actually collected. Income taxes, on businesses and individuals, have hovered around 3 percent of GNP. As in most countries, tax avoidance and evasion in the Philippines appears to be largely the province of the rich. One study suggests that the richest decile pays only about one-quarter of what is due and actually pays

**TABLE 8.9.  Income Distribution, 1961–88 (percentages)**

|  | 1961 | 1971 | 1985 | 1988 |
|---|---|---|---|---|
| Total |  |  |  |  |
| Top 20 percent | 56.4 | 53.9 | 53.1 | 52.6 |
| Bottom 30 percent | 8.0 | 7.4 | 9.4 | 9.2 |
| Gini coefficient | 0.50 | 0.49 | 0.447 | 0.460 |

*Source:* For 1985 and 1988, World Bank staff calculations for 1961 and 1971, International Labour Organization 1974.

22.   Cox and Jimenez 1995.

only about 2 percent of its income in taxes.[23] This sharply reduces the potential for progressivity built into the income tax schedule and contributes to a general sense that taxes are unfair.

Because of low yields on income taxes, there has been considerable reliance on indirect taxes for revenue raising purposes. The most important indirect taxes have been excises on petroleum products, alcohol, and tobacco, as well as import tariffs. Household budgets reveal that the poor spend a disproportionate share of their income on these items, and hence several analysts have concluded that indirect taxes are regressive.[24] But it is important to also consider general equilibrium effects of indirect taxes, especially for items such as petroleum, which are important inputs into production. When these are factored in, the distribution of taxes in the Philippines is approximately neutral.[25] The intuitive reasoning is that, while the poor may consume more of a taxed product directly, the rich consume these products indirectly through their consumption of products that use these taxed inputs intensively in production.

*Expenditures.* Education is the largest component of the government budget outside of general obligations such as administration, defense and interest payments. Unlike the situation in many other countries, the incidence of public spending on education in the Philippines is quite progressive. The bulk of spending is allocated to primary and secondary schooling. Because of an extensive network of private schools (secondary and university in particular) to which children from richer families go, public education spending does reach the poorest groups. The same can be said of public health spending. As a result, public expenditure acts as a significant redistribution mechanism in the Philippines. For example, the lowest quintile may receive benefits from public expenditures amounting to more than one-third of its income, while the richest quintile would only receive benefits worth 5 percent.[26]

This mechanism, however, is made less effective because of the problems in the labor market previously documented. Giving the poor an asset, such as education, is of little value in the end if the returns of that asset are reduced by distortionary labor market policies.

## V.  Politics and Governance

The absence of an explicit social contract to share wealth and growth equitably is rooted in a long tradition of political control by elite groups in the Philippines. On the surface, the Philippines was one of the first Asian republics, a country with a long democratic tradition; a clear separation of powers between executive, legislative, and judiciary branches; and a vibrant, free press. But it

---

23. Manasan 1990.
24. See for example, Yoingco 1989.
25. Devarajan and Hossain 1995.
26. World Bank 1993, 468.

also experimented with a "benign dictatorship" model, during the martial law years under President Marcos in the 1970s, when ostensibly technocrats were granted control over economic management. Both of these models have shown weaknesses: graft and corruption, inefficient bureaucracies, and an inability to forge a national consensus on development strategy.

## Utang Na Loob (Debt Inside Oneself)

The extended family is the most important social and economic unit in the Philippines, and kinship ties are the basis on which many interactions take place. These are broadened through ritual kinship to create a network of strong interfamily groups. The strength of the groups is reinforced by a binding system of reciprocal obligations (*utang na loob*), which demands that all favors be returned in like or greater value. These favors sometimes extend across several generations. They have led to a web of complex linkages that encourage patronage between superiors and subordinates and perpetuate the domination of elite groups deriving their power from the extensiveness of their networks.

Because membership in an "in" family group means so much to economic prospects, Philippine society has been broadly perceived as highly unequal. This reflects significant horizontal rather than vertical inequality; that is, people with otherwise similar characteristics may face quite different opportunities and incomes depending on their connections, and this can be a source of tension. The vertical inequality of Western economies, rooted in class distinctions, is less of an issue.

*Concentrated Political Power.* Part of the reason why family groups have been able to retain so much power is that the design of the political system has rewarded incumbents handsomely. This derives from two features of the system. First, power has been concentrated in the hands of the executive branch, through a series of legal provisions. The president can rule by decree and can veto congressional legislation, subject only to an overrule by a two-thirds majority in Congress. The president also has the power to make a large number of executive appointments within the national government structure, in a number of municipalities, and for judges and regulatory bodies. Finally, the president largely controls the budget process, although Congress sets ceilings on specific expenditure items. Control of the presidency can thus yield enormous returns to "inside" groups.

A second feature of the political system that rewards incumbents is the use of pluralistic, "winner takes all," voting rules. Small, well-organized groups can take advantage of such a system, and, indeed, Philippine politics has been dominated by two parties—Nacionalistas and Liberals—with very similar policy platforms. To the victor went the spoils. Hence, it became common to see the major political families also associated with major business interests, an unfortunate side effect of a fledgling democracy.

*Corruption.* Superimposed on the family groups, this political structure naturally gave rise to a system in which patronage politics flourished. Periodically, campaigns against corruption would be launched.[27] Indeed, President Marcos justified martial law in 1972 partly on the basis of removing pervasive graft and corruption. But Marcos instead acted to reinforce the powers of the presidency and created new sources of power—public enterprises, regulatory bodies, and public financial bodies—embedded in the military establishment, thereby introducing the term *cronyism* into the economic vocabulary of the country. This persisted until the arrival of people's democracy in 1986, under Mrs. Aquino, and the establishment of the Philippine Commission on Good Government. These marked a watershed in Philippine politics, toward a reformulation of the role of the state away from rent distribution, a trend that has been reinforced in the democratic transition of power to President Ramos and by the extensive decentralization of authority to local municipalities that has taken place in the past decade.

The series of coup attempts against President Aquino testifies to the strength of the pressures to revert to the old system. Many actions of the Aquino presidency, from pricing policies of electricity and oil to land reform and utility licensing, fit the model of traditional Filipino politics, but the larger trend was toward a distinct reduction in the power of the executive as a necessary ingredient in reducing corruption, accompanied by serious efforts at liberalization to reduce the scope of rent seeking.

### Constrained Technocrats

A common feature of the high-performing Asian economies has been the ability of its technocrats to formulate and implement policies consistent with national goals independent of day to day pressures from interest groups. In the Philippines by contrast, macroeconomic policy has been constrained by political factors at key points in time. Government technocrats have started out in control of the overall strategy but have not enjoyed political support at key moments. An early example of this is the payments crisis of 1961. A lame-duck administration spent millions in defense of a fixed overvalued exchange rate, leaving the politically unpleasant task of floating the rate to the incoming administration.[28]

Former President Marcos, who ostensibly declared martial law in 1972 to free the executive branch from excessive intervention by Congress at a time

---

27. Even recent surveys show graft and corruption as the number one economic problem cited by respondents to Social Weather Stations.

28. In fact, a two-tiered rate was established. The official rate, applied to 20 percent of exports, remained fixed at P2 per dollar, while the unofficial rate floated at about double this level.

when the economy needed his utmost attention, most obviously subordinated economic policy making to special interests. The formation of sugar and coconut marketing monopolies is one example. Another relates to the economic response to the second oil price shock in 1980. While technocratic advisers encouraged an orthodox downward adjustment of public spending and exchange rate depreciation, the government chose the opposite course. Public investment, financed by external borrowing, was used as a "countercyclical maneuver." The real effect was to accumulate an incremental $3.6 billion in external debt to shore up failing projects and run down international reserves by $.8 billion (in 1981 alone) to finance private sector capital flight at a favorable (to them) exchange rate.

Even under President Aquino—two decades later and following a major political upheaval—political constraints on technocratic economic policy making remained. The president held office during a particularly turbulent time politically. Right-wing military rebels (who launched six coup attempts against her), left-wing communist insurgents, a fragmented legislature, and significant union activity necessitated compromise politics. But the economic costs of this were high. Electricity and water prices were kept low, bleeding the utilities, which could not afford to embark on new expansion. And, when international oil prices rose during the Gulf crisis in 1989, domestic oil prices were kept unchanged. The cumulative subsidy to oil and energy consumers (off-budget initially) reached P9 billion in 1989 or about 1 percent of GDP.

Without technocratic underpinnings, macroeconomic management suffered from a lack of vision, transparency, and consistency. Private sector anticipation of policy reversals further accentuated business cycles. Even within the government, there was no confidence that stated policies would be implemented. Budgets were formulated on the basis of optimistic economic and tax revenue forecasts, but line departments of the government correctly based their own capital expenditure programs not on promised budgets but on actual monthly allocations. The inefficiencies of this system in terms of stop-and-go programs and resource misallocations were high.

### Weak Institutions Hinder Implementation

The politicized nature of economic policy making has also been reflected in weak public institutions. Often, even when good policies were articulated, institutional weaknesses—poor human and financial resources and organizational inadequacies—hindered actual implementation. The inefficiencies of Philippine tax collections have already been mentioned. Customs administration was so poor that a Swiss firm, the Societe Generale de Surveillance, was brought in to improve performance. Even important bodies such as the Central Bank and the National Power Corporation were debilitated.

The story of the Central Bank is an example of how economic crises could cripple an institution. By the mid-1980s, the Central Bank had accumulated a large negative net worth position, continued net income losses, and a significant negative net foreign asset position. In response to its negative net foreign assets, the Central Bank adopted a strong exchange rate policy, even when a weaker currency may have been in the national interest. To reduce its income losses, it resorted to heavy taxation of financial intermediaries (zero-interest reserve requirements), perhaps beyond what monetary policy considerations alone would require. And it further relied on the treasury to hold deposits (some at zero interest) of such magnitude that short-term changes in the money supply depended as much on the budget as on the monetary authorities. In brief, the Central Bank had become weakened in its monetary control and supervisory functions and needed major reserves and restructuring in 1993, receiving more than U.S.$8 billion in fresh capitalization.

The story of the National Power Corporation (NPC) shows how weak the institutional basis for setting even basic economic prices had become. By the late 1980s, even though full cost recovery was an official government policy, the NPC was running substantial losses and was unable to finance much needed investments in new power generation. Each effort at raising prices to levels sufficient to cover costs was met with public demonstrations, court challenges, and judicial rulings against tariff increases. Unable to mobilize resources and simultaneously faced with cumbersome environmental regulations, NPC did not add a single megawatt of new capacity during the six-year tenure of President Aquino. Major power shortages of up to 12 hours crippled the economy in 1993. The solution to the institutional crisis was to encourage private sector participation in power generation, and the Philippines became an early pioneer in this with the Hopewell contract in 1992.

## VI.   Recent Developments and Growth Prospects

The Philippines is in the middle of a boom. Growth started to recover in 1993 but was stalled by major power shortages. As capacity increased, growth jumped from 2.3 percent in 1993 to 5.1 percent in 1994 and 6 percent for 1995. Business and government officials are confident that a further acceleration to 7 percent per year is achievable. This would place the Philippines firmly in the ranks of other countries in the region.

Other macroeconomic indicators are also giving positive signals. Exports had risen by over 30 percent in dollar terms by the first half of 1995, and, importantly, they will have a faster growth rate than imports for the first time in many years. So the current account balance, which had swelled to 3 percent of GDP in 1993 when domestic demand started recovering, is on a downswing. This is significant because the current account had always been the Achilles' heel of previous expansions, including the most recent one in 1986–89.

The fact that the current account is falling during an expansionary phase when investment rates are rising is a good sign. Investment has risen to 25 percent of GDP, still short of the level it will have to reach to sustain 7 percent growth, but a considerable increase over the 20 percent level of a few years ago. Just as significant is the rise in domestic savings rates, from 18 percent in 1993 to 22 percent in 1995. Both the investment and saving figures suggest a return of confidence in economic opportunities. And high levels of foreign investment—now totaling $1.4 billion per year—suggest that this confidence is shared by foreigners as well as domestic residents.

Inflation has also been contained, despite a variety of supply shocks that have affected the agricultural sector. The inflation rate held to single-digit levels in 1995 for the fourth consecutive year, although the absolute level (8 percent in 1995) is still well above the 5 percent average for ASEAN countries. Inflation should continue to be manageable, as there are no pressures on money creation from the public sector deficit. The budget has been kept almost in balance through continued privatization revenues and tight control over expenditures.

## Lessons Learned and Playing Catchup

Despite these solid macroeconomic outcomes, there is still a sense of fragility about the Philippine recovery. After the Mexico crisis, the Philippines was one of the worst affected Asian economies, but the impact was of short duration— the Central Bank was only forced into dollar sales for a period of one month before capital inflows started to return.

Rather, the sense of fragility reflects the considerable gap in policy performance between the Philippines and its neighbors, a gap that now appears wider than the gap in economic outcomes. On the policy front, the government has suffered some reversals. There have been problems in raising tax collections relative to GDP, and the authorities continue to rely on distortionary measures such as documentary stamp taxes and other fees and charges that raise the cost of financial operations. The Oil Price Stabilization Fund, which in the past had been responsible for a substantial accumulation of public sector debt, is once more running a deficit. The National Power Corporation still depends on transfers from the treasury to finance its program and has been slow to put in place a more permanent solution of restructuring and privatization. There are pressures to raise social spending and teachers' salaries to improve the quality of public services. And there is a sense that the strategy that has been used to keep deficits at bay, namely, aggressive privatization of public assets, cannot be maintained for much longer.

In short, the most pressing policy problem in the Philippines remains today what it has been for several years—putting public finances on a transparent, sustainable footing. As we have argued, this means more than getting the budget balanced. It also means taking care of contingent public liabilities. And, while the restructuring of public financial institutions has addressed the biggest of these problems, there remain others that could potentially surface—the social security system; the Land Bank of the Philippines, which finances land purchases for redistribution to small farmers; and the array of take-or-pay contracts with the private sector that provided the sweetener for getting private infrastructure investment.

The government has plans for dealing with these issues. Reform proposals cover corporate income taxes, the value-added tax, and excise taxes; mechanisms for automatic setting of oil prices; budgetary rules and the measurement of public liabilities; and civil service reform. But an abiding lesson of Philippine economic history is that implementation rather than policy design is critical. And the complex interplay between the executive, Congress, and the judiciary, which determines what can and cannot be implemented, continues.

The other side of the implementation coin is the strength of public sector institutions. Some progress has been made with respect to public financial institutions especially, but creating a strong bureaucracy is a long process. In the Philippines, this will be further complicated by the need to decentralize expenditures to local bodies to match the decentralization of revenues that has already been mandated by law. The lessons may have been learned, but they still must be applied.

The Philippines is well on its way to overcoming its unenviable position as the sick man of East Asia. Like the rest of the region it has embraced the ideas of export-led growth, private sector development, and a reduced role for the state, and it has painstakingly implemented many of the changes required to take these ideas from concept to practice. But in other areas it still has some distance to go. Institutions weakened by decades of political patronage and fiscal mismanagement can only be restored to good health over a period of years. And the mortgaging of the future, reflected in debt and other contingent liabilities, is still an overhang that constrains achievement of the country's full economic potential.

APPENDIX

**TABLE A8.1.  Average Implicit Public Sector Deficit**

| | GDP ($U.S. million, current) | Total External Debt ($U.S. million) | Total Domestic Debt ($U.S. million) | Total Debt | Total Debt/GDP (%) | Growth Rate of Debt/GDP (%) | GDP Growth Rate (%) | Implicit Deficit to GDP (%) |
|---|---|---|---|---|---|---|---|---|
| 1970 | | | | | | | | |
| 1971 | 7,408.58 | 1,777.5 | 666.49 | 2,443.99 | 33.0 | | | |
| 1972 | 8,021.88 | 1,962.1 | 840.14 | 2,802.24 | 34.9 | 5.9 | 8.3 | 4.8 |
| 1973 | 10,083.6 | 2,028.3 | 1,079.62 | 3,107.92 | 30.8 | −11.8 | 25.7 | 3.8 |
| 1974 | 13,780.9 | 2,428.2 | 1,455.10 | 3,883.30 | 28.2 | −8.6 | 36.7 | 7.7 |
| 1975 | 14,894.2 | 3,063.8 | 1,516.45 | 4,580.25 | 30.8 | 9.1 | 8.1 | 6.1 |
| 1976 | 17,098 | 4,436.5 | 1,770.84 | 6,207.34 | 36.3 | 18.1 | 14.8 | 10.9 |
| 1977 | 19,648.6 | 8,183.4 | 2,061.67 | 10,245.07 | 52.1 | 43.6 | 14.9 | 23.6 |
| 1978 | 22,706.4 | 10,772.1 | 2,421.85 | 13,193.95 | 58.1 | 11.4 | 15.6 | 15.0 |
| 1979 | 27,501.8 | 13,281.5 | 2,587.12 | 15,868.62 | 57.7 | −0.7 | 21.1 | 11.8 |
| 1980 | 32,450.5 | 17,417.2 | 2,912.29 | 20,329.49 | 62.6 | 8.6 | 18.0 | 16.2 |
| 1981 | 35,646.4 | 20,883.2 | 3,627.63 | 24,510.83 | 68.8 | 9.8 | 9.8 | 12.9 |
| 1982 | 37,140.2 | 24,550.8 | 4,138.59 | 28,689.39 | 77.2 | 12.3 | 4.2 | 11.7 |
| 1983 | 33,211.3 | 24,394.4 | 3,765.18 | 28,159.58 | 84.8 | 9.8 | −10.6 | −1.4 |
| 1984 | 31,407.9 | 24,355.2 | 3,457.46 | 27,812.66 | 88.6 | 4.4 | −5.4 | −1.0 |
| 1985 | 30,734.8 | 26,621.5 | 4,082.92 | 30,704.42 | 99.9 | 12.8 | −2.1 | 9.2 |
| 1986 | 29,867.9 | 28,208.1 | 5,302.01 | 33,510.11 | 112.2 | 12.3 | −2.8 | 9.1 |
| 1987 | 33,195.5 | 29,762.2 | 7,329.51 | 37,091.71 | 111.7 | −0.4 | 11.1 | 12.0 |
| 1988 | 37,884.9 | 28,965.6 | 9,267.45 | 38,233.05 | 100.9 | −9.7 | 14.1 | 3.4 |
| 1989 | 42,574.6 | 28,376.2 | 10,360.90 | 38,736.90 | 91.0 | −9.8 | 12.4 | 1.3 |
| 1990 | 44,310.7 | 30,232.3 | 10,007.60 | 40,239.90 | 90.8 | −0.2 | 4.1 | 3.5 |

*Source:* World Bank.

REFERENCES

Aitken, Maxwell. 1992. "Measuring Trade Policy Intervention: A Cross-Country Index of Relative Price Dispersion." World Bank PRD Papers No. 838.

Balisacan, A. N. 1993. "Agricultural Growth, Landlessness, Farm Employment, and Rural Poverty in the Philippines." *Economic Development and Cultural Change* 41: 533–62.

Bautista, Romeo, and John Power. 1979. *Industrial Promotion Policies in the Philippines*. Manila: Philippine Institute for Development Studies.

Booth, A. 1992. "Poverty in Southeast Asia." London: University of London. Mimeo.

Cox, Donald, and Emmanuel Jimenez. 1995. "Private Transfers and the Effectiveness of Public Income Redistribution in the Philippines." In *Public Spending and the Poor: Theory and Guidance,* edited by D. Van der Walle and K. Neal. Baltimore: Johns Hopkins University Press.

Cruz, Willy, and Robert Repetto. 1992. *The Environmental Effects of Stabilization and Structural Adjustment Programs: The Philippine Case.* Washington, D.C.: World Resources Institute.

Devarajan, S., and S. I. Hossain. 1995. "The Combined Incidence of Taxes and Public Expenditures in the Philippines." World Bank. July. Mimeo.

Esfahani, Hadi Salehi. 1993. "Regulations, Institutions, and Economic Performance: The Political Economy of the Philippines' Telecommunications Sector." University of Illinois, Urbana-Champaign. March. Mimeo.

Frischtak, Claudio, Bita Hadjimichael, and Ulrich Zachau. *Competition Policies for Industrializing Countries.* Policy and Research Series No. 7. Washington, D.C.: World Bank.

Hooley, Richard. 1985. *Productivity Growth in Philippine Manufacturing: Retrospect and Future Prospects.* Monograph Series No. 9. Manila: Philippine Institute for Development Studies. December.

Hooley, Richard, and Ahmed Muzaffer. 1990. *The Role of Small and Medium-scale Manufacturing Industries on Industrial Development: The Experience of Selected Asian Countries.* Manila: Asian Development Bank.

International Labor Organization. 1974. *Sharing in Development.* Geneva: International Labour Organization.

International Monetary Fund [IMF]. Various years. *International Financial Statistics.* Washington, D.C.: IMF.

Lal, D. 1986. "Stolper-Samuelson-Rybczyuski in the Pacific." *Journal of Development Economics* 21: 181–204.

Luders, Rolf. 1990. "Chile's Massive SOE Divestiture Program: 1975–1990, Failures and Successes." Paper presented to Conference on Privatization and Ownership Changes in East and Central Europe. World Bank, Washington, D.C., June 13–14.

Manasan, R. 1990. "An Assessment of Fiscal Policy in the Philippines." Philippine Institute of Development Studies, Working Papers No. 9006. Mimeo.

National Statistical Office [NSO]. 1988. *Philippine Census of Establishments.* Manila: NSO.

National Statistical Office [NSO]. Various years. *Philippine Census of Manufacturing, Large Establishments.* Manila: NSO.

National Statistical Office [NSO]. Various years. *Yearbook of Labor Statistics.* Manila: NSO.

National Statistical Office [NSO]. 1991.*Current Labor Statistics.* September. Manila: NSO.

Oshima, H., E. de Borja, and W. Paz. 1986. "Rising National Income per Worker and Falling Real Wages in the Philippines in the 1970s." *Philippine Review of Economics and Business* 23:151–90.

Power, John H., and Gerardo Sicat. *The Philippines: Industrialization and Trade Policies.* London: Oxford University Press.

Presidential Management Staff. 1992. *The Aquino Management of the Presidency.* Vols. 1–10. Manila.

Republic of Korea. 1982. *Annual Report on the Economically Active Population.* Seoul: National Bureau of Statistics.

Republic of Korea. 1990. *Annual Report on the Economically Active Population.* Seoul: National Bureau of Statistics.

Romulo, Alberto. 1989. "Growth, Poverty, and Employment." In *Economic Growth and Income Distribution,* edited by H. Kurth. Quezon City: MOED Press.

United Nations. Various years. *Yearbook of Industrial Statistics.* New York: United Nations.

Van der Walle, D., and K. Neal. "Private Transfers and the Effectiveness of Public Income Redistribution in the Philippines."

World Bank. 1989. "Philippines: Environment and Natural Resource Management Study." Washington, D.C.: World Bank. Mimeo.

World Bank. 1991a. "The Challenge of Development." In *World Development Report, 1991.* Oxford: Oxford University Press.

World Bank. 1991b. "Growth, Poverty Alleviation, and Improved Income Distribution in Malaysia: Changing Focus of Government Policy Intervention." Report No. 8667–MA. Mimeo.

World Bank. 1991c. World Development Report. Washington, D.C.: World Bank.

World Bank. 1992. "Irrigated Agriculture Sector Review." Washington, D.C.: World Bank. Mimeo.

World Bank. 1993. *The Philippines: An Opening for Sustained Growth.* 3 vols. Report No. 11061–PH. Washington, D.C.: World Bank.

World Bank. 1994. "Philippines: Recent Macroeconomic Developments and Reform Efforts." Report No. 13109–PH. Mimeo.

Yoingco, A. Q. 1989. *A Study of the Burden of Philippine Taxes.* Manila: Philippine National Science Society.

# Part 3
# Cross-Country Studies

CHAPTER 9

# Government Policies and Productivity Growth: Is East Asia an Exception?

*Vinod Thomas and Yan Wang*

## I. Introduction

Developing countries have diverged sharply over the past quarter of a century in rates of output and productivity growth. Some have experienced stunning success, others disappointing failure. As a group, the East Asian economies consistently outperformed other developing regions, and their achievement has attracted the attention of policymakers everywhere. Although there are considerable differences among the East Asian economies, their generally superior performance justifies an East Asian focus in the analysis of government policies and growth.

Governments the world over have tried to speed up economic growth by intervening in the marketplace. The failures have far outnumbered the successes. But some of the successes have been spectacular. East Asian economies such as Japan, Korea, and Taiwan (China) have made remarkable progress under moderately interventionist policies. And now China, with only gradual market reforms, is achieving the most rapid and sustained growth of any large country in the world. The region's success raises three crucial questions. Was the nature of government interventions very different in East Asia than in other regions? Were the effects of government interventions very different in East Asia? What might account for these differences?

In considering these questions, this essay distinguishes government interventions from market distortions. Intervention does not necessarily lead to growth-reducing distortions. Whether they do depends on their scope, quality, and scale. The essay shows that the main reason for East Asia's superior performance is not that governments there intervened less—in fact, on average, they intervened as much as anywhere else in areas such as public expenditures. Rather, the East Asian governments intervened efficiently and in ways that contained and minimized overall price, trade, and macroeconomic distortions. The key to the region's better results is not so much unique cultural factors as it is the development of effective policies, institutions, and practices. That key is available for other countries to copy.

## II.  East Asia's Outstanding Perfomance

Between 1965 and 1993, average incomes in East Asia and the Pacific (as the developing region is defined in World Bank 1994) rose at 5.5 percent a year (table 9.1), which was nearly double the rate for all low- and middle-income countries (LMICs). Over the period as a whole, economies such as Korea and Taiwan (China) saw average incomes rise more than fivefold. In the shorter period of the 1980s, China experienced a dramatic 8 percent annual growth in average income in the 1980s. The slowest growing country in the East Asian group was the Philippines, whose per capita income rose at about 1.1 percent a year in 1965–93.

East Asia's high rates of investment in physical and human capital are often (and rightly) cited as major contributors to its spectacular performance. Its economies have consistently invested a larger share of output than other developing countries—nearly 40 percent higher in 1992. As for human capital, in 1992 their primary enrollment rate was 16 percent higher and their infant mortality rate 40 percent lower than the average for all developing countries.

Total factor productivity is known to be a powerful contributor to economic growth. East Asia's above-average increase in total factor productivity is

**TABLE 9.1.  Growth, Investment, and Social Development: East Asia and All Low- and Middle-Income Countries (LMICs)**

|  | East Asia | | All LMICs | |
|---|---|---|---|---|
|  | 1965 | 1992 | 1965 | 1992 |
| Growth rates (%) | | | | |
| GNP per capita, 1965–93 | 5.5 | — | 3.1 | — |
| Exports, 1965–92 | 10.0 | — | 4.2 | — |
| Structure of demand (% of GDP) | | | | |
| Gross domestic investment | 22 | 34 | 20 | 25 |
| Gross domestic savings | 22 | 33 | 20 | 24 |
| Education[a] | | | | |
| Primary enrollment ratio | 88 | 119 | 78 | 102 |
| Secondary enrollment ratio | na | 50 | 22 | 45 |
| Health[b] | | | | |
| Infant mortality per 1,000 | 95 | 39 | 117 | 65 |
| Adult life expectancy at birth | — | 68 | — | 64 |

*Source:* World Bank 1994.

[a]The most recent year is 1991 not 1992.

[b]Based on incomplete country coverage and presented purely for illustration.

a key to its high growth rates. Although it had higher investment rates than others did, it had even higher productivity growth: several times higher, as this essay will show. Previous work has suggested a strong link between productivity growth and government policies in all developing countries (World Bank 1991), a link confirmed by studies of individual countries in East Asia. An example is the acceleration of growth in Korea after 1959 and again after 1982, in China after 1979, and in Indonesia after 1985: all those changes can be attributed to policy improvements.

This essay highlights the link between policies and productivity growth within a cross-country framework. It first presents a formal framework for assessing this link and then uses that to derive cross-country averages. It examines country differences within East Asia to give a sense of how representative the cross-country averages are. It also reviews some of the tangible and intangible ingredients of East Asian policies.

## III.  The Analytical Approach

To assess the link between policies and productivity growth, we use two alternative models. One follows the tradition of neoclassical growth theory, using a quasi-Solow model. The other comes out of the recent literature on endogenous growth. We apply these models to explore, on the one side, the link between economic and productivity growth, and, on the other, the extent of distortions and government intervention. To explain the effects that are specific to East Asia, we examine the region's 10 economies closely and compare them with other countries in the sample, differentiating them according to policy "deepening" (extent of trade and price reforms, shares of expenditures) and policy "productivity" (a bigger coefficient of the policy variable).

The first approach applies a Cobb-Douglas production function (CD model), which emphasizes certain familiar production inputs. The unexplained residual of an economy's growth rate is considered to be the growth rate of total factor productivity, which is assumed to be a function of government policies, a regional dummy for East Asia, and some interaction terms between East Asia and these policies. That is,

$$\Delta \ln Y_{it} = a_{i0} + \sum_j \gamma_j P_{ijt} D + \sum_j \delta_j P_{ijt} D + \Theta D + \sum_{X=k,l,h,e} \beta_x \Delta \ln X_{it}, \quad (1)$$

where $Y_{it}$ is the output of $i$ country in year $t$ and $X_{it}$ represents such inputs as physical capital ($k$), labor ($l$), land ($h$), and educational capital ($e$), all measured by log differences. The term $P_{ijt}$ is policy indicator $j$ for country $i$ in year $t$; the indicator could be an individual policy variable or a composite index. The term $D$ is a regional dummy variable for East Asia, and the terms $P_{ijt}D$ are interaction terms between East Asia and policies and distortions.

Empirically, the model can be estimated in two ways: by estimating (a) equation 3 with all input variables and government policies or (b) the production function first and then taking the unexplained residual as total factor productivity growth (TFPG) and estimating:

$$\mathrm{TFPG}_{it} = \alpha_0 + \sum_j \gamma_j P_{ijt} + \sum_j \delta_j P_{ijt} + \Theta D. \qquad (2)$$

This essay highlights the results of the second approach, since its focus is on the effects of government policies and regional factors rather than on productive inputs. Because TFPG is measured after the effects of traditional and nontraditional (education) inputs are accounted for, TFPG can be related to policy and to some factors specific to the region.

In the second approach, which is closely related to recent models of endogenous growth, we begin with a simple linear output-capital model. Output ($Y$) is proportional to a broadly defined capital ($K$) that incorporates both physical and human capital, and labor enters the model through $K$.[1] Assuming that the economy is closed to capital flows (saving = investment), the growth rate of output per capita ($g$) is a function of the rate of accumulation of new physical and human capital ($i$), the capital-output ratio (parameter $\alpha$) and the depreciation rate ($\delta$). Government policies affect growth through their influence on the real rate of return to capital, which in turn affects the rate of investment and economic growth. We can express this function as

$$g_{it} = \alpha_0 + \sum_j \gamma_j P_{ijt} + \sum_j \delta_j P_{ijt} D + \Theta D, \qquad (3)$$

where $g_{it}$ is the growth rate of GDP per capita for country $i$ in year $t$, and $P_{ijt}$, $D$, and $P_{ijt} D$ are defined as above.

The data set is derived from pooled cross-country time-series statistics compiled for the *World Development Report, 1991* (World Bank 1991) and GDP data from the national accounts, as reported in the World Bank data base; figures on government expenditures are from the International Monetary Fund (IMF) government finance statistics data base. The data set contains information on GDP growth rates (1960–90), capital, labor, land, education, and other inputs for 68 developing countries for 1960–87. It also contains variables reflecting a wide range of public policies—outward orientation, price distortions, foreign exchange premiums in the parallel market, and fixed capital formation. And it quantifies public sector investment as well as government expenditures in education, health, and economic services. (Data on these policy variables are not available for all countries and all years, however; see app., table A9.1, for sources and descriptions.)

---

1. The analysis here has benefited from the work of Rebelo (1991), King and Rebelo (1990), Barro (1990), and Easterly et al. (1991).

Table 9.2 provides some descriptive statistics on growth and government policies for 10 East Asian economies and 58 other developing countries.[2] In growth of income per capita, the East Asian group has outpaced the others during the past three decades. Total factor productivity growth (TFPG1 and TFPG2),[3] calculated as the unexplained residuals in two estimated CD production functions, shows a similar trend. East Asia averages more than 2 percent

**TABLE 9.2.   Economic Growth and Government Policies: East Asia and Other Low- and Middle-Income Countries (LMICs)**

| Growth or Policy Indicator | East Asia (10 economies) | Other LMICs (58 economies) |
|---|---|---|
| Performance Indicator (1987 dollars) | | |
| Average annual growth in GDP per capita (%, 1960–90) | 4.68 (4.9) | 1.26 (5.4) |
| Total factor productivity growth (%, 1960–87) | | |
| TFPG1 | 2.58 (1.15) | 0.92 (1.14) |
| TFPG2 | 2.22 (1.11) | 0.40 (1.27) |
| Incentives and Stability | | |
| Trade policy index ([TPI] 1977–88) | 2.08 (1.0) | 1.69 (0.9) |
| Parallel market premium (%, 1960–90) | 14.16 (48.2) | 52.70 (155.9) |
| Inflation rate (%, 1961–89) | 8.92 (15.0) | 17.98 (35.2) |
| Real interest rate (%, 1970–88) | 3.71 (7.9) | −3.01 (19.6) |
| Government Expenditures (% of GDP, 1960–89) | | |
| Public sector investment | 8.53 (4.3) | 8.97 (5.8) |
| Consumption | 7.01 (3.4) | 8.88 (5.1) |
| Total expenditures | 19.50 (5.6) | 24.90 (11.5) |
| Fixed capital formation | 2.86 (2.0) | 3.40 (3.0) |
| Social expenditures | 8.62 (2.7) | 10.18 (5.4) |
| Education | 3.12 (1.4) | 3.13 (1.8) |
| Health | 0.79 (0.5) | 1.51 (1.3) |

*Source:* Authors' estimates.

*Note:* Simple group means are presented. Standard deviations are in parentheses. Government expenditures are for consolidated government. See appendix for a description of variables and time periods covered. The 10 East Asian economies are China, Hong Kong, Taiwan (China), Indonesia, Japan, Korea, Malaysia, the Philippines, Singapore, and Thailand.

2. The 10 East Asian economies are China, Hong Kong, Taiwan, Indonesia, Japan, Korea, Malaysia, the Philippines, Singapore, and Thailand. We include Japan because it made the transition to high-income status in the past 30 years. The total factor productivity growth rates of these 10 economies are listed individually in the appendix (table A9.1). See table A9.2 for a list of the 68 countries.

3. TFPG11 was calculated based on a CD production function with traditional inputs only (eq. 3) in table A9.1, while TFPG2 is based on a CD production function with both traditional and nontraditional inputs—education (eq. 4 in table A9.1).

productivity growth a year, compared with less than 1 percent for the other developing countries.

Indicators of government interventions are categorized in two ways: measures of distortion and measures of government action. Among the distortion indicators, we look at trade outward orientation and macroeconomic and price stability. Again, East Asia does better than the others: it was more outward orientated, had a stronger record of positive real interest rates, and achieved lower inflation rates and exchange rate premiums in parallel markets. These results indicate that the East Asian group has had a superior policy framework. But the question remains whether the policies were also more productive.

We next consider the category of government interventions measured by the shares of GDP going to public sector investment, government consumption, total and decomposed expenditures, and government fixed capital formation. The share of public investment is similar for East Asian and other developing economies, but the share of government consumption in GDP is smaller in East Asia. The differences in these categories are not particularly marked. But again the key question, investigated later, is whether public expenditures in East Asia were more productive.

## IV.  Distortions, Interventions, and Growth

Distortions and interventions are multidimensional concepts, just like the concepts of economic well-being and quality of life. It is now fully recognized that measuring the quality of life using individual variables such as GDP per capita is not sufficient. That is why many attempts have been made to construct composite measures of the quality of life. Similarly, there is no completely objective way to measure "policy" due to its complexity and multidimensionality. We cannot draw any firm conclusions from an examination of individual government actions. One way around the problem is to look at as many individual policy measures as possible. But not all measures are available for all countries for the same time periods—a genuine weakness, which could result in selectivity bias. In this essay, therefore, we construct composite policy indexes drawing on all data available on complementary policy indicators. This approach allows for international comparisons and, we believe, is more objective than relying on individual policy measures.

We constructed two composite indexes, one for incentives and macroeconomic stability (INDEX1) and one for government expenditures (INDEX2). INDEX1 includes seven variables: four that have already been mentioned—the trade policy index, inflation, real interest rates, and the parallel market premium—plus an index for outward orientation (Dollar 1992), an index for trade liberalization (Papageorgiou, Michaely, and Choksi 1990), and an index for agricultural disprotection (Krueger, Schiff, and Valdes 1991). (These three are not included in table A9.1 because their coverage is incomplete.) INDEX2 includes public sector investment, total government expenditures, fixed capital formation, and productive expenditures (including education, health, and economic services), all as shares in GDP.

To construct the composite index, we used the Borda ranking technique. It is based on public choice theory and has been used in evaluating welfare across countries.[4] The Borda rule provides a method of rank-order scoring that allows policy indicators to be aggregated even though they were originally measured in different units and for different countries and periods. Each country receives a point equal to its rank for each criterion of ranking for policy variables. The points are then added for each country to obtain its aggregate score, and then the countries are reranked on the basis of their total scores.[5] The Borda rule gives an equal weight of one to every nonmissing policy variable. This method allows us to aggregate and construct a composite indicator that reflects different dimensions of public policies. The missing value problem is partially alleviated. Even if a policy variable is missing for a country throughout the period, we still have an observation: the rank score of the country would depend on the average rank score of the nonmissing policy variables.

Figure 9.1 shows the positive association between incentives and stability (INDEX1) on the one side and GDP growth on the other. Figure 9.2 does the same for productivity growth. A few countries appear as outliers. For instance, in East Asia incentives (or less distortion) seem to be associated with lower growth in the Philippines; the same is true of Cote d'Ivoire, Gabon, and Togo in Africa. All the East Asian high-performing economies for which data are available appear in the top right of the graphs, indicating better incentives and more stability with higher growth in GDP per capita and in TFPG. In both figures these countries appear in a cluster slightly above and separated from the others, again suggesting that the policies reflected by INDEX1 appear to be more effective in these economies than in others.

Figures 9.3 and 9.4 show a possible nonlinear relationship between government expenditures and growth. Most of the East Asian economies appear in the upper-middle range of the graph—the top portion of an inverted U curve. Five of the six East Asian economies with data have moderate expenditures and high growth of output. However, moderate intervention alone is not

---

4. Dasgupta (1989) used the Borda rule in constructing a composite index of well-being. The strengths and limitations of the Borda rule have been investigated by Goodman and Markowitz (1952), Smith (1973), and Fine and Fine (1974). The Borda rule has also been used in evaluating country performance for IDA allocations by the World Bank.

5. We first rank the countries by individual policies. Then we take each country's rank score, say, $i, j, k,$ and $l$ for the selected policies, and calculate the mean to get the country's Borda score: $(i + j + k + l) / 4$. Finally, we rank each country's average Borda score, which results in a single rank—the composite policy index.

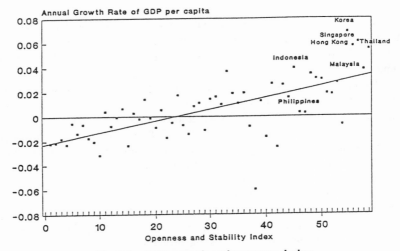

Fig. 9.1.   GDP growth and openness index

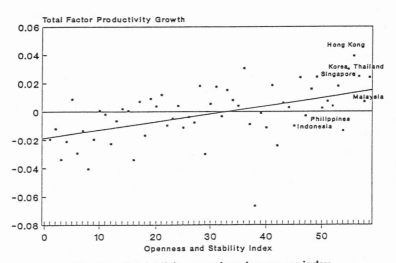

Fig. 9.2.   Productivity growth and openness index

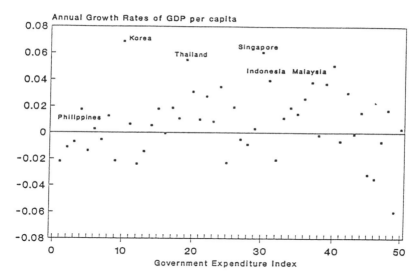

**Fig. 9.3.   GDP growth and government expenditures**

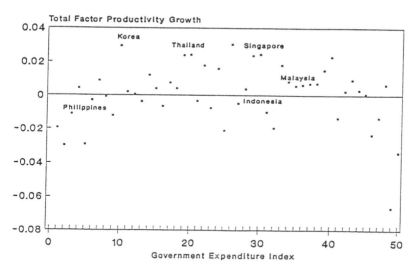

**Fig. 9.4.   Productivity growth and government expenditures**

necessarily associated with high performance: only seven of the 31 countries with moderate rates of government expenditures have performed well. Performance probably depends on the quality of implementation, the quality of human capital, the instrument applied (price subsidies, say, or favorable credit and tax treatment), and the sectors chosen, as well as some intangible factors.

We then estimate three equations (GDP per capita growth, TFPG1, and TFPG2) for the two composite indexes based on country-average data using different specifications and with and without the regional dummy for East Asia and the interaction terms. Tables 9.3 and 9.4 summarize the results of these regressions. INDEX1 is positive and significant in all equations using both specifications, indicating a link between incentives (or lack of price distortion) and stability and growth (table 9.3). It is also able to explain as much as 43 percent of the variation in growth in income per capita and 23 percent of that in total factor productivity growth. Up to 52 percent of the variation in GDP growth rate can be explained by this index, a regional dummy, and the

**TABLE 9.3.   Growth and a Composite Index on Incentives (using average data for 1977–90)**

| Dependent Variable | (1) zgdpcap | (2) TFPG1 | (3) TFPG2 |
|---|---|---|---|
| Specification 1 without regional dummy | | | |
| INDEX1 | .0010 | .0005 | .0006 |
| | (6.71) | (4.32) | (4.38) |
| constant | −.0225 | −.0135 | −.0185 |
| | (−4.60) | (−3.21) | (−4.14) |
| $N$ | 59 | 59 | 59 |
| Adjusted $R^2$ | .4316 | .2330 | .2384 |
| $F$ value | 45.04 | 18.62 | 19.15 |
| Specification 2 with a dummy and an interaction term | | | |
| INDEX1 | .0007 | .0005 | .0005 |
| | (4.39) | (3.18) | (3.19) |
| EA.INDEX1 | .0018 | .0021 | .0020 |
| | (1.50) | (1.76) | (1.60) |
| East Asia | −.0719 | −.1049 | −.1007 |
| | (−1.06) | (−1.67) | (−1.50) |
| Constant | −.0172 | −.0119 | −.0167 |
| | (−3.65) | (−2.70) | (−3.59) |
| $N$ | 59 | 59 | 59 |
| Adjusted $R^2$ | .5230 | .2528 | .2529 |
| $F$ value | 22.20 | 7.54 | 7.54 |

*Source:* Authors' estimates.

*Note:* Equation 1 concerns averages for 1977–90, while equations 2 and 3 are for 1977–87. The dependent variable, TFPG1, is calculated based on equation 3, and TFPG2, is based on equation 4 in the appendix, table A9.1. See appendix, table A9.1, for a description on the construction of INDEX1 and other variables.

**TABLE 9.4. Growth and a Composite Index on Government Expenditures (using average data for 1977–90)**

| Dependent Variable | (1) zgdpcap | (2) TFPG1 | (3) TFPG2 |
|---|---|---|---|
| **Nonlinear specification** | | | |
| INDEX2 | .0028 | .0025 | .0027 |
| | (3.02) | (4.09) | (4.35) |
| INDEX2sq | −.0001 | −.0001 | −.0001 |
| | (−3.12) | (−4.38) | (−4.62) |
| Constant | −.0171 | −.017 | −.0217 |
| | (−1.6) | (−2.50) | (−3.17) |
| Adjusted $R^2$ | .1359 | .2637 | .2862 |
| $F$ value | 4.85 | 9.78 | 10.822 |
| **Kinked specification** | | | |
| INDEX2k1 | .0009 | .0009 | .0009 |
| | (1.70) | (2.57) | (2.73) |
| INDEX2k2 | −.0023 | −.0016 | −.0017 |
| | (−2.4) | (−2.5) | (−2.6) |
| Dummy for INDEX2k2 | .1035 | .0711 | .0759 |
| | (2.62) | (2.71) | (2.85) |
| Constant | −.0051 | −.0077 | −.0118 |
| | (−.56) | (−1.3) | (−1.9) |
| Adjusted $R^2$ | .1048 | .1947 | .2113 |
| $F$ value | 2.912 | 4.949 | 5.376 |
| **Kinked specification with regional dummy and interaction terms** | | | |
| INDEX2k1 | .0007 | .0008 | .0009 |
| | (1.42) | (2.33) | (2.52) |
| INDEX2k2 | −.0018 | −.0017 | −.0018 |
| | (−2.05) | (−2.6) | (−2.7) |
| Dummy for INDEX2k2 | .0856 | .0805 | .0856 |
| | (2.28) | (2.86) | (3.01) |
| EA.INDEX2k1 | .0010 | .0001 | .0001 |
| | (.76) | (.06) | (.03) |
| EA.INDEX2k2 | −.0001 | −.0007 | −.0008 |
| | (−.18) | (−1.2) | (−1.3) |
| East Asia | .0279 | .0148 | .0174 |
| | (1.21) | (.86) | (.99) |
| Constant | −.0080 | −.0095 | −.0139 |
| | (−.94) | (−1.5) | (−2.2) |
| Adjusted $R^2$ | .3112 | .2122 | .2354 |
| $F$ value | 4.689 | 3.200 | 3.514 |

*Source:* Authors' estimates.

*Note:* Number of observations = 50. Equation 1 concerns averages for 1977–90, while equations 2 and 3 are for 1977–87. See appendix, table A9.1, for a description of the construction of INDEX2 and other variables.

interaction terms. A quadratic function form was attempted but is not shown since the coefficients are not significant in all three equations.

East Asia appears to be more efficient in trade policies and in maintaining macroeconomic stability. In all three equations, the interaction term between East Asia and INDEX1 is positive and significant (at 90 percent confidence), indicating a bigger slope coefficient. And this relationship holds when the specifications are changed. An $F$-test was also conducted to compare a restricted model—without the dummy and the interaction term—with a full model. The results suggest that the full model is significantly "better" in its specification than is the restricted model; in other words, East Asia has a slope coefficient that is different from that of other LMICs.

Three specifications are estimated for INDEX2: a linear form, a quadratic form, and a "kinked" specification. None of the three equations using linear specification shows a statistically significant association between INDEX2 and growth, and its explanatory power is negligible. That specification is not shown in table 9.4. The nonlinear quadratic specification fits the data better: in all three equations, INDEX2 is consistently positive, with a negative coefficient for the quadratic term and $t$-ratios ranging from 3.0 to 4.9. These results suggest that government interventions, as measured by expenditures, have a positive and significant association with growth, but that the effect gradually weakens as countries get richer. This finding is consistent with those we found using panel data and those of previous studies by Barro (1990) and Easterly et al (1992).

The merit of the "kinked" specification is that it is easier to interpret the coefficients and interact with the regional dummy variables. The cut-off point is where INDEX2 equals 30. We also tried other cut-off points, and the results were not sensitive for those between 20 and 30. In all six equations, with or without interaction and dummy variables, the first segments of the fitted lines (INDEX2k1) have positive and significant coefficient and negative intercepts. The second segments (INDEX2k2) have negative and significant slope coefficients and positive intercepts (as shown by the dummy for INDEX2k2). This suggests that government intervention as measured by expenditures is positively associated with GDP and productivity growth up to a point, but it then becomes harmful.

Is government spending more efficient in East Asia? The answer is ambiguous. To investigate this question, we included interaction terms between East Asia and INDEX2 in the kinked specification. The $t$-ratios show that interaction terms, individually, are insignificant in all three equations. All the East Asian countries are clustered around the top portion of the "kinked" line. The results of $F$-tests conducted to compare the restricted model—the one without the East Asia dummy and the interaction term—and the full model reject the restricted model only in the equation for GDP growth. This suggests that East Asia dummy and interaction terms, as a group, should not be ignored.

When both INDEX1 and INDEX2 are included in the regressions (not shown), the coefficients of the two indexes are robust. In both quadratic and kinked specification for INDEX2, the coefficients of INDEX1 are positive and significant, with *t*-ratios ranging from 6.1 to 2.2. INDEX2 still has the kinked relationship with growth. The signs remain the same, and the *t*-ratios improve. Interaction terms for East Asia and INDEX1 remain positive and significant. Interactions for East Asia and INDEX2 are mostly insignificant, except for two cases. The magnitude of the coefficients does not change much. The two indexes have a correlation coefficient of 0.16 and are insignificant (probability $> |R| = 0.26$). This confirms the notion that government intervention does not necessarily lead to market distortion.

To test the robustness of our results, we also built two composite indexes based on annual data. INDEX1a was constructed using only four variables, the trade policy index, real interest rates, parallel market premium, and inflation rates. The other three policy indexes included in the INDEX1 based on average data were excluded because of incomplete coverage. INDEX2a was built on the same set of policy variables as the INDEX2 based on average data. There were 222 observations for INDEX1a and 488 for INDEX2a.

INDEX1a is positively and significantly associated with GDP and productivity growth, with *t*-ratios ranging from 6.1 to 2.0. Interaction terms for East Asia and INDEX1 are always positive and significant, with *t*-ratios ranging from 2.1 to 2.5. INDEX2a, again, shows some features of nonlinearity: in the quadratic specification, the index itself has a positive coefficient with a negative coefficient for its quadratic term; both are significant. In the kinked specification with the cut-off point at INDEX2a = 250, the first segment (INDEX2ak1) of the line is positive and significant; the second segment is negative and significant in the equation for GDP per capita. These results are consistent with those found using indexes based on country-average data and hence are not shown.

Our hypotheses are supported by both the quasi-Solow model and the endogenous growth model. The regression results for the policy indexes based on average data and those based on annual data are highly consistent. Overall, the results are not sensitive to different approaches and specifications.

## V. Country Differences

So far this essay has presented only a group portrait of East Asian performance and policies. When the group is disaggregated, it turns out that every one of the 10 has done better than the average for 58 other developing economies, whether in 1960–90 or in 1975–90 (table 9.5). The variations in performance are also smaller for the 10 East Asian countries than for the other 58. Nevertheless, within East Asia, country differences are substantial, as indicated by the standard deviation.

The story is similar for country policies. Table 9.6 shows that East Asia as a whole had a policy framework that was superior to those of the other countries. However, by some measures country differences are as large within the region are as they are elsewhere. An exception is macroeconomic stability. Not only was it more pronounced in East Asia, but variations within the region were also less than in the other 58 countries. For a measure of sectoral distortions through agricultural protection, East Asia even has a higher variation than other regions do. Korea's direct protection of agriculture stands in contrast to the practice of the other countries. These differences reflect the fact that there was no single, regionwide approach adopted by all the successful East Asian economies.

The same is true of government interventions (table 9.7). In several East Asian economies (China, Taiwan [China], Malaysia, and Singapore), the public sector's share in investment was significantly higher than the average for the region and for the 58 countries elsewhere. Within East Asia there was also wide variation in the public sector's share in value added (although data were available for only four countries). For the region, the share of public investment in GDP was about the same as that elsewhere; for government consumption, however, the East Asian share was significantly smaller.

Political and civil incentives (measured by Gastil's index of liberty [Gastil

**TABLE 9.5.  Growth Performance: East Asia and Other LMICs, 1960–90 and 1975–90**

| Country | GDP per Capita Growth | | TFPG1 | | TFPG2 | |
|---|---|---|---|---|---|---|
| | 1960–90 | 1975–90 | 1960–90 | 1975–90 | 1960–90 | 1975–90 |
| China | 4.13 | 6.00 | 2.71 | 3.06 | 1.88 | 2.84 |
| Hong Kong | 5.97 | 5.72 | 4.66 | 4.28 | 3.96 | 4.03 |
| Taiwan (China) | 5.21 | 4.67 | 3.88 | 4.08 | 3.63 | 3.85 |
| Indonesia | 3.20 | 3.88 | 0.82 | −0.71 | 0.33 | −0.91 |
| Japan | 5.28 | 3.29 | 2.46 | 1.56 | 2.33 | 1.47 |
| Korea, Rep. | 6.61 | 7.03 | 2.38 | 3.26 | 2.13 | 3.05 |
| Malaysia | 3.95 | 3.78 | 2.21 | 1.08 | 1.95 | 0.80 |
| Philippines | 1.40 | 0.76 | 1.02 | 0.20 | 0.81 | 0.01 |
| Singapore | 6.25 | 5.79 | 3.10 | 2.21 | 2.84 | 1.98 |
| Thailand | 4.81 | 5.31 | 2.56 | 2.63 | 2.34 | 2.42 |
| East Asia | 4.68 | 4.63 | 2.58 | 2.16 | 2.22 | 1.95 |
| | (4.9) | (3.8) | (4.2) | (3.2) | (4.2) | (3.2) |
| Other LMICs | 1.26 | 0.26 | 0.91 | 0.09 | 0.39 | −0.32 |
| (58 Economies) | (5.4) | (5.3) | (4.9) | (4.8) | (4.9) | (4.8) |

*Source:* World Bank data and author's estimates.

*Note:* Simple country means and group means are presented. Standard deviations are in parentheses.

**TABLE 9.6. Distortion: Trade Incentives and Stability in East Asia and Other LMICs**

| Country | Incentive Regime | | | Macro Stability | | | Sectoral Incentives: Agricultural Disprotection[a] | |
|---|---|---|---|---|---|---|---|---|
| | TPI | Cmpindex | Dollar | PMP | Inflation Rate | Real Interest | Direct | Indirect |
| China | — | — | — | — | — | — | — | — |
| Hong Kong | — | — | 101.90 | -0.53 | 6.10 | — | — | — |
| Taiwan (China) | — | 10.61 | — | — | — | — | — | — |
| Indonesia | 1.25 | — | 101.43 | 6.13 | 28.51 | 1.18 | — | — |
| Japan | — | — | — | 2.34 | 5.49 | — | — | — |
| Korea, Rep. | 3.38 | 13.36 | 101.27 | 18.15 | 10.88 | 2.93 | 0.52 | -0.26 |
| Malaysia | — | — | 101.33 | 1.17 | 3.29 | 4.11 | -0.10 | -0.08 |
| Philippines | 1.28 | 10.56 | 101.47 | 10.85 | 10.60 | 1.95 | -0.05 | -0.23 |
| Singapore | — | 14.08 | 101.15 | 0.85 | 3.19 | — | — | — |
| Thailand | 2.67 | — | 101.95 | 0.25 | 5.26 | 8.37 | -0.29 | -0.15 |
| East Asia | 2.08 | 11.89 | 101.30 | 12.26 | 8.93 | 3.71 | 0.3 | -0.18 |
| | (1.02) | (3.51) | (0.47) | (37.32) | (15.0) | (7.94) | (0.39) | (0.09) |
| Other LMICs 58 economies | 1.69 | 9.18 | 99.83 | 42.30 | 17.98 | -3.01 | -0.13 | -0.25 |
| | (0.93) | (3.81) | (1.29) | (74.40) | (35.15) | (19.60) | (0.24) | (0.17) |

*Source:* Authors' estimates.

[a] This is based on Krueger, Schiff, and Valdes 1992. See description for "total" in appendix.

*Note:* Simple country and group means. Standard deviations are in parentheses. See appendix for a description of variables and time periods.

**TABLE 9.7. Interventions: Public Enterprises, Government Expenditures, Freedom, and Liberty in East Asia and Other LMICs**

| Country | Public Sector as Percentage of GDP | | Consolidated Government Expenditures as Percentage of GDP | | | | | | Freedom and Liberty[a] | |
|---|---|---|---|---|---|---|---|---|---|---|
| | Investment | Value Added | General government consumption | Total | Fixed Capital Formation | Education | Health | Transportation and Comunications | Civil Liberty | Political Liberty |
| China | 14.28 | — | — | — | — | — | — | — | 6.23 | 6.31 |
| Hong Kong | 3.86 | — | 6.91 | — | — | — | — | — | — | — |
| Taiwan (China) | 11.48 | — | 16.48 | — | — | — | — | — | 4.92 | 5.23 |
| Indonesia | 8.76 | 19 | 9.88 | 19.51 | 6.18 | 1.76 | 0.43 | 2.46 | 5.23 | 5.00 |
| Japan | 5.41 | — | 8.82 | — | — | — | — | — | 1.00 | 1.54 |
| Korea, Rep. | 6.73 | 3–10 | 10.60 | 16.18 | 1.31 | 2.84 | 0.24 | 0.68 | 5.46 | 4.77 |
| Malaysia | 11.56 | — | 15.30 | 28.51 | 2.52 | 4.47 | 1.16 | 2.23 | 4.08 | 2.92 |
| Philippines | 5.16 | 2.4 | 8.56 | 14.02 | 1.16 | 2.24 | 0.65 | 2.50 | 4.62 | 4.69 |
| Singapore | 10.97 | — | 10.78 | 21.06 | 3.03 | 3.74 | 1.37 | — | 5.00 | 4.62 |
| Thailand | 7.11 | 5–6 | 10.89 | 17.77 | 3.14 | 3.57 | 0.88 | 1.50 | 4.08 | 4.15 |
| East Asia | 8.53 | 9.5 | 10.92 | 19.46 | 2.87 | 3.12 | 0.79 | 1.84 | 4.51 | 4.36 |
| | (4.27) | | (3.4) | (5.6) | (2.04) | (1.43) | (0.52) | (0.41) | (1.52) | (1.46) |
| Other LMICs (58 countries) | 8.97 | 10.9[b] | 13.52 | 24.90 | 3.04 | 3.07 | 1.50 | 1.85 | 4.60 | 4.74 |
| | (5.75) | | (5.14) | (11.6) | (2.96) | (1.78) | (1.30) | (1.57) | (1.55) | (1.96) |

*Note:* Simple country and group means. Standard deviations are in parentheses. See appendix for a description of variables and time periods.

[a]Based on Gastil 1989.

[b]From Nair and Filippides 1988. This estimate for 1984 is for 28 developing countries.

1989] was no greater in East Asia than in other developing countries. The pattern varied from country to country, with some in East Asia showing significantly less openness than the average for other developing countries.

Finally, East Asian countries have been investing heavily in infrastructure. Although the shares of government expenditures in transportation and communication are similar, the averages for road densities (unpaved and paved) are much higher for East Asia than in other LMICs (290.4 and 251.9 km/area, respectively, using available data), and so is its rail density. Cross-country variations are substantial. The road and rail densities in Korea, for example, are at similar levels as in Spain, whereas the rail density in China (5.5 km/area) is much lower than that of India (18.8 km/area).[6]

## VI.  East Asian Policies and Effects

These differences among countries in the region suggest that it would be a mistake to think that they all adopted a single, uniform model of development. There are, nonetheless, certain broad policy features shared by the successful East Asian economies that have contributed to their rapid economic growth. Chief among these have been outward orientation, low price distortions, macroeconomic stability, and heavy investment.

With *trade and price policy,* the better policy framework in East Asia (as measured by various indexes) was associated with better performance. Governments did not intervene much less than elsewhere, but their interventions were "market friendly" and involved few distortions. In trade, for example, government intervention was subjected to the tests of international competition. Interventions that failed such tests were changed or abandoned.

This work highlights the importance of *macroeconomic stability,* as reflected in inflation, interest rates, and the parallel market premium for the exchange rate. The region's macroeconomic stability accounts for its particularly low overall distortion index. Its current account deficit for the past quarter of a century has remained below 1 percent of GDP, a remarkable achievement. China's influence on this statistic is strong, but even without China the current account deficit would be small.

Discipline in public borrowing was also a beneficial factor in East Asia. Until 1987, outstanding government bonds in Taiwan (China) were legally restricted to 40 percent or less of the central government's annual budget. Thailand limits its budget deficits to 20 percent of total expenditures. In Indonesia, a balanced budget law and a paucity of exchange controls serve as checks on irresponsible fiscal behavior that could precipitate currency speculation and crisis.

---

6. These calculations are based on data from *World Road Statistics* and *International Railway Statistics* (available from author on request).

Malaysia has run large deficits at times (as high as of 19 percent of GNP in 1982) but has cut them sharply (to 5 percent in 1990) when they threatened to damage economic growth.

These constraints on public borrowing did not always apply to public spending. In Taiwan (China), government spending was 26 percent of GNP in 1980 and 35 percent in 1989, well above the level in many developing countries. But the public sector has been a net saver since 1964, never crowding out the private sector. State enterprises contributed 49 percent of value added in industry in 1955; their share is now down to 11 percent but not because of privatization. These state enterprises grew in real value, but the private sector grew much faster. This pattern may help explain why public investment is not significantly related to growth (in our earlier analysis) whereas private investment played a major role. Meanwhile, government consumption has hampered growth less in East Asia than elsewhere, probably because it did little to crowd out private investment.

Though our essay did not consider the effects of *investment in education,* this has long been recognized as vital to competitiveness and growth. Total factor productivity is larger in East Asia partly because of the larger contribution of education. It also seems likely, from the evidence presented here and elsewhere, that East Asia's investment in education was a key element in its better policy framework. There was a strong positive interaction between incentives and low price distortions on one side and education on the other.

It is now widely accepted that East Asian governments have intervened in the economy (particularly in the 1960s and 1970s) but that they did so more efficiently than other governments did. Less well known is the region's even greater success with market reforms in the 1980s compared with other developing countries, including those that were also reforming. The gap in average income growth between East Asia and other developing regions (except South Asia) roughly tripled after 1982 compared with the period before. So the familiar question—why were East Asia's interventions more successful?—needs to be matched by another: why were its reforms more successful as well?

Various country studies provide some answers. First, policy changes in East Asia were deeper than those of other developing countries. A simple average of nine measures of exchange rate and trade restrictiveness (e.g., advance import deposits or surrender requirements for export proceeds) fell by half in East Asia from 1979 to 1990, far more than the average for other developing countries. Nor were its reforms offset by new impediments: for instance, many developing countries imposed reference prices on imports while tariffs were being reduced.

Second, the reforms were carried out vigorously. Indonesia, Korea, Malaysia, and Thailand took nearly 30 percent of direct foreign investment in developing countries in 1990, primarily, it seems, because they took measures to change the business climate as well as policies. Indonesia and Korea introduced "one-stop" offices for ministerial clearances, Malaysia removed numerous impediments to industrial licensing, and Thailand emphasized the warmth of its welcome. Such intangibles may explain why changes in policies alone cannot explain differences in results.

Third, the supply response to reforms depends critically on complementary conditions—manpower skills and flexibility, infrastructure, and institutional factors. Where incentives, investments, and institutions are missing or inadequate, output responds weakly to reform. Much depends on the building of consensus, public-private partnership, and the bureaucracy's capacity for policy planning and implementation. While certain policies and reforms in East Asia brought larger benefits than elsewhere, the reforms themselves are insufficient to explain the payoffs. Again, unquantifiable factors played a part.

Yet these intangible influences were not there from the start; they had to be developed and nurtured. It is striking that Singapore's savings rate (including mandatory savings) rose from 1 percent of GNP in 1965 to about 40 percent today, perhaps the highest in the world. Cultural and institutional changes triggered Korea's success; an example is the way Confucianism elevated the status of the bureaucracy while at the same time inspiring it to nurture business values.

## VII.   Conclusion

The broad findings of our essay are quite clear. Growth is damaged by trade and price distortions and by macroeconomic instability. However, it is not obviously affected, one way or the other, by government expenditures. In East Asia, price distortions and macroeconomic instability were relatively lower than those in other developing countries, so did less to hamper growth. By contrast, government expenditures in East Asia were broadly in line with those in the rest of the developing world, as a share of GDP.

When it comes to reforms aimed at reducing price distortions, these were more productive in East Asia than in developing countries overall. Some of East Asia's success is attributable to a superior policy framework and some to the greater returns achieved by a given policy framework or set of reforms. A positive and significant interaction between East Asia and its policy framework suggests that the region has been more efficient in getting payoffs from a superior policy framework. Government expenditures have a less clear and nonlinear relation with economic growth, with most East Asian economies belonging to the middle range of an inverted U curve.

These findings have a powerful relevance for developing countries everywhere. There was not something uniquely or inherently East Asian about the region's economic success. The essential ingredients—avoiding serious price and trade distortions and establishing macroeconomic stability—are key for generating growth anywhere. Numerous countries have recognized this fact and have been reforming their policy regimes over the past decade: the East Asian experience is a basis for this approach, not an exception.

But the region does seem to be an exception in getting the most from its reforms and making public expenditures work to promote growth rather than hinder it. East Asian countries have been effective in blending the roles of market and state. The combination of modest distortions, macroeconomic stability, and effective government spending, together with various intangibles such as consensus building and efficient bureaucracies, has made possible the rapid productivity and economic growth of the region. The intangible factors may not be linked to immutable cultural traits, and the bulk of the East Asian experience is one that can be copied elsewhere.

APPENDIX

**TABLE A9.1.  Description of Variables Used in the Analysis**

| Variables | Descriptions |
|---|---|
| Dependent variables | |
| zgdpkd | Growth rates of GDP at constant 1980 prices, U.S. dollars, 1960–89. Source: World Bank central data base (WBDB). |
| zgdpcap | Growth rates of per capita GDP at constant 1987 prices, U.S. dollars, 1960–90. Calculated based on GDP_MP and population figure in WBDB. |
| TFPG1 | Total factor productivity growth, residual from a Cobb-Douglas production function with capital, labor, and land as inputs for 1960–87 (eq. 3 in table A9.1). |
| TFPG2 | Residual from a Cobb Douglas production function with physical capital, labor, land, and education as inputs (eq. 4 in table A9.1). |
| Indicators of incentives and stability (or distortions) | |
| Trade policy index (TPI) | Index of trade restrictiveness from most restrictive (1) to least restrictive (5), for 38 countries in 1977–88. Source: Thomas, Halevi, and Stanton 1991. |
| PMP | Parallel market foreign exchange premiums based on the differences between official exchange rates and black market rates: PMP = [(BMER-OER)/OER]*100, where BMER is the parallel market exchange rate and OER is the official end of period exchange rate. Source: BMER—International Currency Analysis, Inc., *World Currency Yearbook*. OER is from WBDB. |
| Inflation | Inflation rates calculated as log differences of consumer price index when it exists, else log differences of wholesale price index (1961–89 for 84 countries). Source: WBDB. |

**TABLE A9.1.** —*Continued*

| | |
|---|---|
| Real | Real interest rates for 34 countries in 1970–88. Inflation was subtracted from the nominal interest rate. Source: Gelb 1989. |
| Cmpindex | Index of trade liberalization from one (least liberalized) to 20 (most liberalized) for 19 countries in 1960–85. Source: Papageorgiou, Michaely, and Choksi 1990. |
| Dollar | Purchasing power parity-based outward-orientation index for 92 countries, calculated as the weighted average of mean price distortion in the period of 1973–85 and of its standard deviation. Source: Dollar 1992. |
| Total | Total disprotection of agriculture for 18 countries in 1960–86. It has two components: direct and indirect disprotection. The first one measures the direct taxes/ subsidies on agriculture. The second measures the impact of economywide policies on agricultural incentives. Source: Krueger, Schiff, and Valdes 1992. |

Government expenditures

| | |
|---|---|
| invpub | Ratio of public sector investment to GDP. The public sector investment is defined as capital expenditures of the consolidated general government plus those of public corporate entities. Source: DEC analytical Data Base (IEC, World Bank). |
| gconx | Share of general government consumption in GDP for 1960–89. Source: WBDB. |
| gexptot | Share of consolidated government expenditures in GDP for available years in 1960–90. Source:WBDB. |
| gfixcap | Share of gross fixed capital formation for consolidated government in GDP. Source: WBDB. |
| prodexp | Share of productive expenditures, including education, health, and economic and infrastructure services. Source: WBDB. |

Composite indices

| | |
|---|---|
| index1 | An index for incentives and stability based on average data for 1977–87 for seven variables: three measures of trade restriction (TPI, Cmpindex, Dollar) and measures of sectoral distortion (Total), real interest rate (Real), the PMP, and Inflation rate. Each variable enters in an ascending order from less to more stability (or large to small distortions). See text for the Borda ranking method. |
| index2 | An index for government intervention based on average data for 1977–87 for four variables: public sector investment (invpub), government fixed capital formation (gfixcap), productive expenditures (prodexp, including expenditures on education, health, and economic services), and the total government expenditures (gexptot), each as a share of GDP. |

*(continued)*

| | |
|---|---|
| index2sq | index2 squared. |
| index2k1 | = index2 if index2 $\leq$ 30, = 0 otherwise. |
| index2k2 | = index2 if index2 > 30, = 0 otherwise. |
| dindex2k2 | = 1 if index2k2 > 0, = 0 otherwise. |
| EA. | Interaction terms between East Asia and indexes. |
| Input variables | |
| zcapital (zkpn) | Instrumented growth of capital variable. Source: Bhalla-Lau 1991. For a description, see *World Development Report, 1991,* supplementary data (World Bank 1991). |
| zland | Growth rates of arable land in thousands of square kilometers. Source: WBDB. |
| zlabor | Growth rates of total labor force, interpolated. Source: WBDB. |
| edt | Estimated average years of education of the population of working age group (15–64). Based on UNESCO data on enrollment rates for the period 1960–88 and on mortality and birth statistics. Source: Lau, Jamison and Louat 1991. |
| edt60 | edt in 1960. |
| de03 | = first difference of edt if edt is between zero and three years, zero otherwise. |
| de39 | = first difference of edt if edt is between three and nine years, zero otherwise. |
| Regional Dummies | |
| Africa | = 1 if the country is located in sub-Saharan Africa, = 0 otherwise. |
| East Asia | = 1 if the country is under the East Asia and Pacific vice presidency (as defined in World Bank 1994), = 0 otherwise. |
| South Asia | = 1 if the country is under the South Asia vice presidency, = 0 otherwise. |
| EMENA | = 1 if the country is located in Europe, the Middle East, or North Africa, = 0 otherwise. |
| LAC | = 1 if the country is located in Latin America or the Caribbean, = 0 otherwise. |

## TABLE A9.2. Economies in the Analysis

| Economies | Value of INDEX1 | Value of INDEX2 | Economies | Value of INDEX1 | Value of INDEX2 |
|---|---|---|---|---|---|
| 1. Argentina | 26 | 13 | 35. Sri Lanka | 50 | 42 |
| 2. Burundi | 18 | na | 36. Morocco | 44 | 44 |
| 3. Benin | na | na | 37. Madagascar | 22 | na |
| 4. Bangladesh | 24 | 4 | 38. Mexico | 32 | 21 |
| 5. Bolivia | 2 | 9 | 39. Mali | 39 | 8 |
| 6. Brazil | 21 | 14 | 40. Malta | na | 40 |
| 7. Central African Republic | 40 | na | 41. Mauritania | 12 | na |
| 8. Chile | 53 | 22 | 42. Mauritius | 48 | 24 |
| 9. China | na | na | 43. Malawi | 19 | 43 |
| 10. Cote d'Ivoire | 42 | na | 44. Malaysia | 58 | 37 |
| 11. Cameroon | 36 | 26 | 45. Nigeria | 8 | na |
| 12. Congo | na | na | 46. Nicaragua | na | na |
| 13. Colombia | 51 | 17 | 47. Taiwan (China) | na | na |
| 14. Costa Rica | 27 | 23 | 48. Pakistan | 49 | 20 |
| 15. Algeria | 11 | na | 49. Panama | 46 | 29 |
| 16. Egypt | 33 | 39 | 50. Peru | 15 | 12 |
| 17. Spain | 52 | 15 | 51. Philippines | 47 | 6 |
| 18. Ethiopia | 20 | 28 | 52. Portugal | 43 | 36 |
| 19. Gabon | 38 | 49 | 53. Rwanda | 13 | 16 |
| 20. Ghana | 5 | 7 | 54. Sudan | 3 | na |
| 21. Greece | 30 | 35 | 55. Senegal | 37 | na |
| 22. Guatemala | 25 | 3 | 56. Singapore | 57 | 30 |
| 23. Hong Kong | 56 | na | 57. El Salvador | 6 | 5 |
| 24. Haiti | 29 | 2 | 58. Syria | 16 | 50 |
| 25. Hungary | na | 48 | 59. Togo | 54 | 47 |
| 26. Burkina Faso | 35 | 18 | 60. Thailand | 59 | 19 |
| 27. Indonesia | 45 | 31 | 61. Turkey | 34 | 34 |
| 28. India | 41 | na | 62. Tanzania | 7 | 41 |
| 29. Israel | 31 | na | 63. Uganda | 1 | 1 |
| 30. Jamaica | 23 | 27 | 64. Venezuela | 9 | 32 |
| 31. Japan | na | na | 65. Yugoslavia | 14 | 11 |
| 32. Kenya | 28 | 33 | 66. Zaire | 4 | 25 |
| 33. Korea, Rep. | 55 | 10 | 67. Zambia | 10 | 45 |
| 34. Liberia | na | 46 | 68. Zimbabwe | 17 | 38 |

*Source:* Author estimates.

*Note:* INDEX1 is constructed for 59 economies, INDEX2 for 50 economies. Those for which both indexes are not available due to missing policy variables are used only in the descriptive analysis and the estimation of Cobb-Douglas production functions.

**TABLE A9.3.   Total Factor Productivity Growth by Region and Economy: Estimated Cobb-Douglas Production Function Using the LSDV Approach**

Dependent variable: zgdpkd

| Variables | Regressions by Region | | Regressions by Individual Economy | |
|---|---|---|---|---|
| | Without Education (1) | With Education (2) | Without Education (3) | With Education (4) |
| zcapital | .3862 (17.8) | .3917 (18.0) | .3909 (17.1) | .3972 (17.3) |
| zlabor | .3137 (2.68) | .3643 (3.04) | .0978 (0.59) | .1677 (1.00) |
| zland | .0509 (1.57) | .0476 (1.47) | .0561 (1.68) | .0529 (1.59) |
| Education | | | | |
| de03 | | .0671 (2.48) | | .0906 (3.12) |
| de39 | | −.0020 (−.92) | | −.0031 (−1.4) |
| edt60 | | .0014 (1.60) | | .0009 (1.5) |

| Total Factor Productivity Growth | | | | | |
|---|---|---|---|---|---|
| By Region | TFPG1 | TFPG2 | By Economy[a] | TFPG1 | TFPG2 |
| Africa | .0012 (0.36) | −.0057 (−1.3) | China | .0271 (2.66) | .0188 (1.79) |
| | | | Hong Kong | .0466 (4.30) | .0396 (3.57) |
| East Asia | .0206 (4.43) | .0114 (1.66) | Indonesia | .0082 (0.82) | .0033 (.33) |
| | | | Japan | .0246 (2.54) | .0233 (2.40) |
| South Asia | .0075 (1.38) | −.0001 (−.02) | Korea | .0238 (2.26) | .0213 (2.02) |
| | | | Malaysia | .0221 (2.09) | .0195 (1.84) |
| EMENA | .0149 (4.12) | .0081 (1.56) | Taiwan (China) | .0388 (3.56) | .0363 (3.41) |
| | | | Philippines | .0102 (1.00) | .0081 (.80) |
| LAC | .0023 (0.57) | −.0046 (−.86) | Singapore | .0310 (2.90) | .0284 (2.65) |
| | | | Thailand | .0256 (2.48) | .0234 (2.26) |
| N | 1826 | 1826 | | 1826 | 1826 |
| Adjusted $R^2$ | .2032 | .2063 | | .2391 | .2440 |
| F value | 236.47 | 173.03 | | 28.11 | 27.63 |

*Source:* Author estimates.

*Note:* The least squares dummy variable approach is used here on data from 68 countries for the period of 1960–87; *t*-ratios are in parentheses.

[a] In equations 3 and 4, 68 dummies for economies are included; only 10 East Asian economies are presented.

REFERENCES

Amsden, Alice H. 1989. *Asia's Next Giant: South Korea and Late Industrialization.* New York: Oxford University Press.

Amsden, Alice H. 1991. "Diffusion of Development: The Late-Industrialization Model and Greater East Asia." *American Economic Review* 81 (May): 282–86.

Barro, Robert J. 1990. "Government Spending in a Simple Model of Endogenous Growth." *Journal of Political Economy* 98: S103–25.

Barro, Robert J. 1991. "Economic Growth in a Cross Section of Countries." *Quarterly Journal of Economics* 106: 407–33.

Barro, Robert J., and Jong-Wha Lee. 1992. "International Comparisons of Educational Attainment." Working Paper, World Bank. Mimeo.

Bhalla, Surjit, Lawrence Lau, and Frederic F. Louat. Forthcoming. "Human and Physical Capital Stock in Developing Countries: Construction of Data and Trends." Working Paper, World Bank. Mimeo.

Dasgupta, Partha. 1989. "Well-Being and the Extent of Its Realization in Developing Countries." *Economic Journal* 100, supplement, 1–32.

De Long, Bradford, and Lawrence H. Summers. 1992. "How Robust is the Growth-Machinery Nexus?" Working Paper, World Bank. Mimeo.

Dollar, David. 1992. "Outward Oriented Developing Countries Do Grow More Rapidly: Evidence from 95 LDCs, 1976–85." *Economic Development and Cultural Change* 40, no. 3 (April): 523–44.

Easterly, William, Robert King, Ross Levine, and Sergio Rebelo. 1991. "Do National Policies Affect Long-Run Growth? A Research Agenda." Working Paper, World Bank. Mimeo.

Easterly, William, Michael Kremer, Lant Pritchett, and Lawrence H. Summers. 1992. "Good Policy or Good Luck? Country Growth Performance and Temporary Shocks." Working Paper, World Bank. Mimeo.

Easterly, William, and Sergio Rebel. 1992. "Fiscal Policy and Economic Growth: An Empirical Investigation." Working Paper, World Bank, Mimeo.

Fine, B., and K. Fine. 1974. "Social Choice and Individual Rankings, I and II." *Review of Economic Studies* 41: 303–22 and 459–75.

Fischer, Stanley. 1992. "Macroeconomic Factors in Growth." Working Paper, World Bank. Mimeo.

Gastil, Raymond. 1989. *Freedom in the World.* New York: Freedom House.

Gelb, Alan H. 1989. "Financial Policies, Growth, and Efficiency." Working Paper, World Bank. Mimeo.

Goodman, L. A., and H. Markowitz. 1952. "Social Welfare Functions Based on Individual Rankings." *American Journal of Sociology* 58: 38–63.

Grossman, Gene M., and Elhanan Helpman. 1990. "Trade, Innovation, and Growth." *American Economic Review* 80: 86–91.

Harrison, Ann E. 1991. "Openness and Growth: A Cross-Country, Time Series Analysis for Developing Countries." In World Bank, *World Development Report, 1991.* New York: Oxford University Press.

International Currency Analysis, Inc. Various years. *World Currency Yearbook.* Brooklyn: International Currency Analysis.

Kaufmann, Daniel, and Yan Wang. 1995. "Macroeconomic Policies and Project Performance in the Social Sectors: A Model of Human Capital Production and Evidence from LDCs." *World Development* 23: 751–65.

King, Robert G., and Sergio Rebelo. 1990. "Public Policy and Economic Growth:Developing Neoclassical Implications." *Journal of Political Economy* 98:S126–44.

Krueger, Anne O. 1990. "Asian Trade and Growth Lessons." *American Economic Review* 80:108–12.

Krueger, Anne O., Maurice Schiff, and Alberto Valdes, 1991. *The Political Economy of Agricultural Pricing Policies.* Baltimore: Johns Hopkins University Press.

Lau, Lawrence, Dean T. Jamison, and Frederic F. Louat. 1991. "Education and Productivity in Developing Countries: An Aggregate Production Function Approach." PRE Working Papers No. 612, World Bank. Mimeo.

Lucas, Robert E., Jr. 1988. "On the Mechanics of Economic Development." *Journal of Monetary Economics* 22: 3–42.

Mankiw, N. Gregory, David Romer, and David N. Weil. 1992. "A Contribution to the Empirics of Economic Growth." *Quarterly Journal of Economics* (May): 407–37.

Nair, G., and A. Filippides. 1988. "How Much Do State-Owned Enterprises Contribute to Public Sector Deficits in Developing Countries—and Why." PPR Working Papers No. 45, World Bank. Mimeo.

Pack, Howard, and Larry E. Westphal. 1986. "Industrial Strategy and Technological Change." *Journal of Development Economics* 22: 87–128.

Papageorgiou, D., M. Michaely, and A. M. Choksi, 1990. *Liberalizing Foreign Trade in Developing Countries: Lessons of Experience.* Washington, D.C: World Bank.

Park, Yung Chul. 1991. "Liberalization in Korea and Taiwan (China)." In *Foreign Economic Liberalization: Transformations in Socialist and Market Economies*, edited by Andrès Koves and Paul Marer. Boulder: Westview Press.

Rebelo, Sergio. 1991. "Long-Run Policy Analysis and Long-Run Growth." *Journal of Political Economy* 99: 500–521.

Romer, Paul M. 1986. "Increasing Returns and Long-Run Growth." *Journal of Political Economy* 94: 1002–37.

Romer, Paul M. 1990. "Endogenous Technological Change." *Journal of Political Economy* 98: S71–102.

Smith, J. H. 1973. "Aggregation of Preferences with Variable Electorate." *Econometrica* 41: 1027–41.

Srinivasan, T. N. 1991. "Development Thought, Strategy, and Policy: Then and Now." Background paper for the *World Development Report, 1991*, World Bank. Mimeo.

Thomas, Vinod, Nadav Halevi, and Julie Stanton. 1991. "Does Policy Reform Improve Performance?" Background paper for the *World Development Report, 1991*, World Bank. Mimeo.

Thomas, Vinod, and John Nash, 1991. *Best Practices in Trade Policy Reform.* New York: Oxford University Press.

Wade, Robert. 1990. *Governing the Market: Economic Theory and the Role of Government in East Asian Industrialization* Princeton: Princeton University Press.

Westphal, Larry. 1990. "Industrial Policy in an Export-Propelled Economy: Lessons from South Korea's Experience." *Journal of Economic Perspectives* 4: 41–59.

World Bank. 1991. *World Development Report, 1991: The Challenge of Development.* New York: Oxford University Press.

World Bank. 1994. *World Development Report, 1994: Infrastructure for Development.* New York: Oxford University Press.

CHAPTER 10

# Foreign Direct Investment in East Asia

*Maxwell J. Fry*

## I. Introduction

Foreign capital inflows to developing countries constitute part of the world's saving. Over the past two decades, world saving as a proportion of world income has fallen. As world saving has shrunk, so the world real interest rate, has risen from .8 percent during the period 1971–78 to 4.8 percent in the period 1981–91 (*International Financial Statistics,* September 1994).[1] It is against this background that foreign direct investment (FDI) has appeared increasingly attractive to developing countries facing declining domestic investment and higher costs of foreign borrowing. Foreign direct investment seems an attractive form of capital inflow because it involves a risk-sharing relationship with the suppliers of this type of foreign capital. This kind of risk sharing does not exist in the formal contractual arrangements for foreign loans. Furthermore, as the World Bank (1993, 3) claims, there may be dynamic benefits: "Foreign direct investment is a large and growing source of finance that may help developing countries close the technology gap with high-income countries, upgrade managerial skills, and develop their export markets."

Globally, FDI has increased dramatically over the past decade. However, most of this increase has occurred in the industrial countries. In the developing world, FDI has been heavily concentrated among a small number of countries; over 90 percent of FDI inflows to developing countries in 1990 was received by only 18 countries. Half of this total flowed to eight East Asian developing market economies—Hong Kong, Indonesia, Korea, Malaysia, Philippines, Singapore, Taiwan, and Thailand. Given that neither Korea nor Taiwan has shown strong interest in attracting FDI, it may seem surprising that these economies feature in this group of developing countries. Their appearance in this list may

---

1. The world real interest rate is the London interbank offered rate on U.S. dollar deposits adjusted for the percentage change in the U.S. GDP deflator. During the period 1992–95, the world real interest rate averaged only 1.5 percent, but it has been rising rapidly since 1993 (*World Economic Outlook*, May 1994, 177).

support the view that explicit incentive packages are not the key determinants of FDI flows. Without doubt, a much more important determinant in these countries has been their superlative investment climates (Fry 1991).

Table 10.1 illustrates the changing distribution of FDI over the past two decades. In the 1973–76 period the Western Hemisphere was the recipient of the largest amount (over half) of FDI to developing countries. In the 1990s, this share had fallen to just over one-quarter. While the absolute dollar values of FDI inflows to Africa, the Middle East, and Europe have remained relatively constant since 1977, the inflow to Asia has accelerated dramatically; by the 1990s, Asia had received over half of the total inflows to developing countries. While the six East Asian countries—Indonesia, Korea, Malaysia, Philippines, Singapore, and Thailand—examined in this chapter received one-quarter of the total inflow of FDI to developing countries in the period 1973–76, they received one-third of this inflow in the 1990–93 period. The accelerating inflow of FDI to East Asia would be greatly increased with the addition of China to the six sample countries.

Table 10.2 shows the 10 developing countries receiving the largest inflows of FDI in the 1970s and 1980s. The first notable feature of this table is that FDI to developing countries increased threefold between the 1970s and the 1980s. The increases in 1992 and 1993 are spectacular, too, except in the cases of Brazil and Egypt. The second noteworthy observation from table 10.2 is the growing concentration of FDI to developing countries in East Asia. Figures 10.1 and 10.2 show how FDI as a percentage of GNP has fluctuated in six of these East Asian countries over the past two decades, while figures 10.3 and 10.4 show FDI in relation to total capital formation. Given above average rates of economic growth in these countries, rising ratios imply substantial FDI growth rates.

Although the East Asian developing market economies all pursue export-oriented development policies, their policies toward capital account liberalization differ substantially. Hong Kong, Singapore, and Malaysia have open

**TABLE 10.1.  Gross Foreign Direct Investment Inflows to Developing Countries (annual averages, U.S.$ billions)**

| Region | 1973–76 | 1977–82 | 1983–89 | 1990–93 |
|---|---|---|---|---|
| Developing countries | 4.0 | 12.2 | 16.7 | 44.3 |
| Africa | 1.2 | 1.1 | 1.2 | 1.5 |
| Asia | 1.4 | 2.9 | 7.8 | 27.7 |
| Six East Asian countries[a] | 1.1 | 2.3 | 4.7 | 14.2 |
| Middle East and Europe | −0.9 | 2.6 | 2.9 | 2.6 |
| Western Hemisphere | 2.3 | 5.5 | 4.7 | 12.3 |

Source: World Economic Outlook, International Monetary Fund, table 7, 0; International Monetary Fund 1994.

[a]Indonesia, Korea, Malaysia, Philippines, Singapore, and Thailand.

capital accounts, while Korea and Taiwan have liberalized slowly and reluctantly. Nevertheless, Hal Hill (1990, 24) detects a common trend:

> A key feature of East Asia has been an increasingly open and receptive policy environment during the 1980s for a variety of reasons: the need to recycle trade surpluses (in Korea and Taiwan); greater confidence in the competitive capacities of domestic business groups (these two states plus Thailand); economic imperatives, such as a deteriorating current account for all or part of the decade (Indonesia, Malaysia, and Philippines); and a perception that FDI may be preferable to local nonindigenous investment (as in Malaysia).

Less liberal capital account policies in Korea and Taiwan appear not to have been costly in terms of foregone growth. Indeed, Rudiger Dornbusch and Yung Chul Park (1987, 432–33) conclude:

> The overriding characteristic of private capital flows, without much exaggeration, is that capital tends to come when it is unnecessary and leave when it is least convenient. As a result it tends to increase the variability of real exchange rates and introduces avoidable macroeconomic instability. One cannot escape the impression that Korea, under the impact of abundant external capital, might lose its competitive exchange rate, overborrow, and ultimately become once again a problem debtor. Korea's investment ratio is more than 30 percent of GNP. There is little to suggest that capital imports are necessary because capital is in short supply.

**TABLE 10.2. Foreign Direct Investment Inflows to Selected Developing Countries (U.S.$ millions)**

| Country | 1970–80 | Country | 1981–91 | 1992 | 1993 |
|---|---|---|---|---|---|
| Brazil | 1,390 | Singapore | 2,287 | 6,730 | 6,829 |
| Mexico | 743 | Mexico | 2,148 | 4,393 | 4,389 |
| Singapore | 386 | China | 2,080 | 11,156 | 27,515 |
| Malaysia | 381 | Brazil | 1,663 | 1,580 | 802 |
| Nigeria | 219 | Malaysia | 1,374 | 5,183 | 5,206 |
| Egypt | 205 | Hong Kong | 1,278 | na | na |
| Indonesia | 194 | Argentina | 874 | 4,179 | 6,305 |
| Hong Kong | 162 | Thailand | 850 | 2,116 | 1,715 |
| Argentina | 121 | Egypt | 821 | 459 | 493 |
| Algeria | 120 | Taiwan | 650 | 1,461 | na |
| Percentage share of total flows to developing countries | 67% | | 66% | na | na |

*Sources:* United Nations 1993, annex table 4, 255; International Monetary Fund 1994.

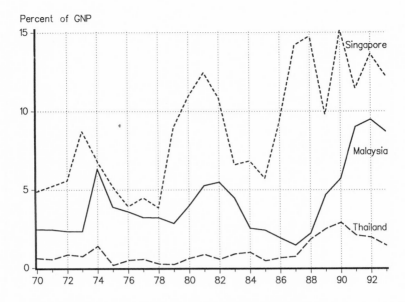

**Fig. 10.1.  Foreign direct investment in Malaysia, Singapore, and Thailand**

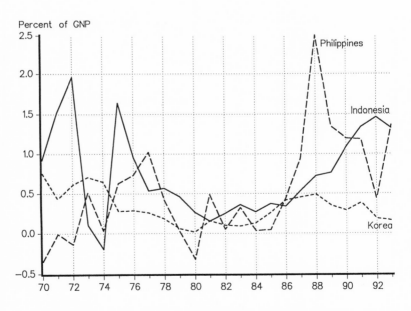

**Fig. 10.2.  Foreign direct investment in Indonesia, Korea, and the Philippines**

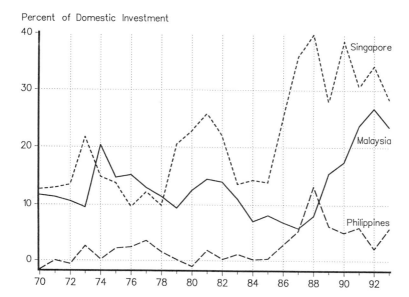

**Fig. 10.3. Foreign direct investment as a percentage of total investment in Malaysia, the Philippines, and Singapore**

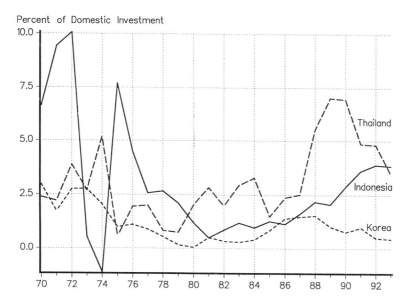

**Fig. 10.4. Foreign direct investment as a percentage of total investment in Indonesia, Korea, and Thailand**

This essay is concerned not with the determinants of FDI inflows to the East Asian developing countries but rather with their effects. The balance of payments accounts show that a current account deficit is financed by capital inflows or decreases in official reserves. One way of presenting this identity is[2]

$$CA + KA = \Delta R, \tag{1}$$

where CA is the current account, KA is the capital account, and $\Delta R$ is the change in official reserves. As an item in the balance of payments accounts, FDI is one of several capital flows. Other things being equal, therefore, an increase in FDI increases capital inflows. If the change in official reserves is unaffected, the increased capital inflow is matched by a smaller current account surplus or a larger current account deficit.

The current account itself can be defined as the difference between national saving $(S)$ and domestic investment $(I)$:

$$CA = S - I. \tag{2}$$

The most obvious link between FDI and the current account in equation 2 is through domestic investment. If FDI finances additional capital formation in the host country, it raises domestic investment $(I)$. Equation 2 shows that this worsens the current account as required by equation 1.

The current account can also be defined as the difference between exports of goods and services $(X)$ plus net factor income from abroad (NFI) and imports of goods and services (IM):

$$CA = X + NFI - IM \tag{3}$$

If FDI increases capital formation in the host country, the increased investment could involve increased imports of raw materials or capital equipment. Alternatively, it could reduce exports by diverting them into the additional investment. In either case, the current account must deteriorate in equation 3 by exactly the same amount as it does in equations 1 and 2.

If FDI finances additional capital formation, equation 2 demonstrates that the current account deteriorates to the same extent that FDI increases capital inflows provided that saving remains unchanged. In such a case, FDI cannot provide additional foreign exchange to finance a preexisting current account deficit. The extra foreign exchange is entirely absorbed in financing a larger current account deficit. However, an increase in FDI could provide additional finance for the balance of payments if it failed to result in additional capital formation in the host country. In undertaking any analysis of FDI, one must recognize that FDI data record financial flows that may or may not correspond to

---

2. This identity ignores errors and omissions.

changes in capital formation. Whether or not they do depends on the extent of crowding out of domestically financed investment and substitutability of this type of financial flow for other types of financial flows.

Suppose that capital inflows were used for new capital formation. If this capital formation would have taken place in any event, or if this capital formation deters an equal amount of domestically financed investment in other projects, then total domestic investment ($I$) remains unchanged. In such a case, FDI does not affect the current account unless it changes the level of national saving. If the current account and the change in official reserves remain the same, this FDI becomes one of the sources of finance for the preexisting current account deficit.

An inflow of FDI also provides balance of payments financing if it is not used for new capital formation. For example, privatization programs in a number of countries have produced capital inflows in the form of FDI. The privatization has resulted in foreign ownership of an existing company and its capital assets but not necessarily in any new capital formation. Typically, a capital inflow used to acquire ownership of an existing firm is recorded as FDI if it achieves ownership of 10 percent or more in the company. Again, this FDI is not accompanied by additional capital formation and so does not increase the current account deficit. It does, therefore, provide additional or alternative balance of payments financing.

Some of the literature on FDI suggests that FDI can serve two purposes, namely, increasing investment and relieving foreign exchange shortages. For example, Laurence Cockcroft and Roger Riddell (1991, 3) note:

> Two of the principal factors inhibiting higher levels of economic growth in Sub-Saharan Africa in the 1990s are low levels of investment and foreign exchange shortages. The first attraction of foreign investment lies in its potential to address both these constraints.

Unless it affects national saving, however, FDI can increase domestic investment or provide additional financing for a preexisting current account deficit or achieve some combination of the two, but these two effects must always sum to one. In other words, if $100 FDI increases capital formation by $75, it would provide $25 for additional current account financing.

By analyzing FDI to East Asian developing economies within a macroeconomic framework, this essay throws new light on various channels by which FDI influences the balance of payments on the current account through its effects on saving, investment, exports, imports, and economic growth. Section II derives this five-equation macroeconomic model and presents estimates for six developing market economies of East Asia—Indonesia, Korea, Malaysia, the Philippines, Singapore, and Thailand.

The regression method used here is iterative three-stage least squares, which is, asymptotically, full-information maximum likelihood (Johnston 1984, 486–92). I estimate the six individual-country equations as a system of equations with cross-equation equality restrictions on all coefficients except the intercept. Hence, the estimates apply to a representative East Asian developing market economy. The estimation technique corrects for heteroscedasticity across country equations and exploits contemporaneously correlated disturbances. The instruments are the exogenous explanatory variables plus the terms of trade index in natural logarithms, the world real interest rate, oil price inflation, and lagged endogenous variables. The estimation period is 1972–92.[3]

While section II examines the effects of inflows on domestic investment, national saving, exports, and imports, section III concentrates on both its direct and indirect effects on rates of economic growth. Section IV presents some policy implications by comparing the estimated effects of FDI in East Asia with estimated effects in a sample control group of 11 other developing countries. Since these comparisons show that the effects of differ widely from country to country, I also attempt to pinpoint the factors responsible for FDI's differential impacts.

## II.   Foreign Direct Investment in a Macroeconomic Model

Whether or not substitutability and fungibility are so high that flows provide no relevant economic information at all is an empirical question. Indeed, some recent estimates of current account financing requirement equations suggest that FDI is either a close substitute for at least one other type of capital flow or is autonomous in a sample of 16 developing countries (Fry 1993, 13, table 3). In an attempt to discriminate between these two possibilities, this section investigates whether or not FDI affects the ratio of gross domestic investment to GNP. To do this, I use FDI as an explanatory variable rather than as the dependent variable in a five-equation macroeconomic model. Since causation could run both ways and FDI could well be determined simultaneously with saving and investment, I treat it as an endogenous variable.

Table 10.3 presents the macroeconomic model derived in this section; hats denote the endogenous variables. The real exchange REXL adjusts to equate the export-import balance with the saving-investment balance, while the

---

3. Data availability restricts the estimation periods. For the investment and saving equations, the estimation period is 1972–91 for all countries except Indonesia. For the growth rate equation, the estimation period is 1972–92 for all countries except Singapore. All equations for Indonesia are estimated over the period 1972–92. Korea's export equation is estimated over the period 1972–92, but its import equation is estimated over the period 1972–91. Trade equations are estimated over the period 1972–91 for Malaysia and the Philippines and 1976–91 for Singapore. Singapore's growth rate equation is estimated over the period 1976–92.

change in domestic credit scaled by GNP is determined in a monetary policy reaction function specified and estimated elsewhere (Fry 1995, 248–52). The ratio of other capital flows to GNP (OKY) is treated as an endogenous variable for the same reason that FDI is.

## The Effect of Foreign Direct Investment on Domestic Investment

The investment function specified here in terms of the ratio of investment to GNP is based on the flexible accelerator model. Mario Blejer and Mohsin Khan

**TABLE 10.3.   A Macroeconomic Model of Foreign Direct Investment**

$$IY = b_{10} + \overset{+\ \wedge}{b_{11}FDIY} + \overset{+}{b_{12}FDIYL} + \overset{+\ \wedge}{b_{13}DDCY} + \overset{?}{b_{14}REXL} + \overset{\wedge}{b_{15}YG} + \overset{+}{b_{16}YG_{t-1}} + \overset{+}{b_{17}IY_{t-1}}. \qquad (4)$$

$$SNY = b_{20} + \overset{?\ \wedge}{b_{21}FDIY} + \overset{?}{b_{22}FDIYL} + \overset{+}{b_{23}YG} + \overset{\wedge}{b_{24}(YG \cdot FDIY)} + \overset{?}{b_{25}(YG \cdot FDIYL)} + \overset{+}{b_{26}SNY_{t-1}}. \qquad (5)$$

$$IMKY = b_{30} + \overset{+\ \wedge}{b_{31}FDIY} + \overset{?}{b_{32}FDIYL} + \overset{+}{b_{33}OKY} + \overset{+}{b_{34}REXL} + \overset{+\ \wedge}{b_{35}IKY} + \overset{+\ \wedge}{b_{36}XY} + \overset{+}{b_{37}IMKY_{t-1}}. \qquad (6)$$

$$XKY = b_{50} + \overset{?\ \wedge}{b_{51}FDIY} + \overset{?}{b_{52}FDIYL} + \overset{-\ \wedge}{b_{53}REXL} + \overset{+}{b_{54}XKY_{t-1}}. \qquad (7)$$

$$YG = \overset{?\ \wedge}{b_{61}FDII} + \overset{?}{b_{62}FDIIL} + \overset{+\ \wedge}{b_{63}IKY} + \overset{+}{b_{64}XKG} + \overset{+}{b_{65}WG} + \overset{+}{b_{66}YG_{t-1}}. \qquad (8)$$

Endogenous variables

| | |
|---|---|
| IY | Domestic investment/GNP (current prices) |
| FDIY | Inflow of foreign direct investment/GNP (dollar values converted to domestic currency, current prices) |
| DDCY | Change in domestic credit/GNP (current prices) |
| YG | Rate of growth in GNP (constant prices, continuously compounded) |
| SNY | National savings/GNP (current prices) |
| IMKY | Imports/GNP (constant prices) |
| REXL | Real exchange rate [(domestic GNP deflator/U.S. wholesale price index)/domestic currency per U.S. dollar] |
| IKY | Domestic investment/GNP (constant prices) |
| XY | Exports/GNP (current prices) |
| OKY | Other capital flows/GNP (dollar values converted to domestic curency, current prices) |
| XKY | Exports/GNP (constant prices) |
| FDII | Inflow of foreign direct investment/domestic investment (dollar values converted to domestic currency, current prices) |
| XKG | Rate of growth in exports (constant prices, continuously compounded) |

Exogenous of predetermined variables

| | |
|---|---|
| FRIYL | Average FDI over a period of five years |
| FDIIL | Average ratio of FDI to domestic investment over five years |
| WG | Real growth rate of OECD countries (continuously compounded) |

(1984, 382–83) describe some of the difficulties of estimating neoclassical investment functions for developing countries. Without data on the capital stock and the return to capital, there is little choice in practice but to use some version of the accelerator model.

The accelerator model has the desired capital stock $K^*$ proportional to real output $y$:

$$K^* = \alpha y. \tag{9}$$

This can be expressed in terms of a desired ratio of net investment to output $(I/Y)^*$

$$(I/Y)^* = \alpha\gamma, \tag{10}$$

where $\gamma$ is the rate of growth in real output (denoted $YG$ in the regression equation).

The partial adjustment mechanism specified for the investment *ratio* is somewhat more complicated than is the equivalent mechanism for the *level* of investment. Specifically, there could be a lag in achieving the same investment ratio this year as last year if output rose rapidly last year; this year's desired investment *level* will be higher than last year's, despite a constant desired *ratio* of investment to output. To incorporate this adjustment lag, last year's growth rate $\gamma_{t-1}$ can be included as an explanatory variable. In this case, however, the coefficient of $\gamma_{t-1}$ was insignificant; hence, $\gamma_{t-1}$ is omitted from the estimate.

The remaining adjustment mechanism allows the actual investment ratio to adjust partially in any one period to the difference between the desired investment ratio and the investment ratio in the previous period ($\lambda$ is the coefficient of adjustment):

$$\Delta(I/Y) = \lambda[(I/Y)^* - (I/Y)_{t-1}] \tag{11}$$

or

$$I/Y = \lambda(I/Y)^* + (1 - \lambda)(I/Y)_{t-1}. \tag{12}$$

The flexible accelerator model allows economic conditions to influence the adjustment coefficient $\lambda$. Specifically,

$$\lambda = \beta_0 + \left[ \frac{\beta_1 z_1 + \beta_2 z_2 + \beta_3 z_3 \cdots}{(I/Y)^* - (I/Y)_{t-1}} \right], \tag{13}$$

where $z_i$ are the variables that affect $\lambda$. Since one of these variables can be an intercept term for the depreciation rate, the flexible accelerator model can be estimated for the gross rather than the net investment ratio.

A simple specification search suggests that, for the six East Asian countries analyzed here, the speed of adjustment is determined by the ratio of FDI inflows to GNP FDIY, the real exchange rate index expressed in natural logarithms REXL,[4] and credit availability as measured by the change in domestic credit divided by GNP DDCY. I also include the FDI ratio over the preceding five years (FDIYL) as an explanatory variable in all the equations.

The price of intermediate imports may affect the profitability of investment projects. Hence, the real exchange rate expressed in natural logarithms REXL is included as a proxy for the price of nontradable goods in relation to import prices. I measure the real exchange rate REX as (domestic GNP deflator / U.S. wholesale price index) / domestic currency per U.S. dollar. Therefore, a higher value of REXL implies a lower relative price of imports. By appreciating the real exchange rate, capital inflows may stimulate investment. On the other hand, an appreciation in the real exchange rate prices exports out of world markets and may worsen the investment climate. Hence, its effect on investment is ambiguous.

Effective domestic costs of borrowing are extraordinarily difficult to measure in almost all developing countries because of selective credit policies and disequilibrium institutional interest rates; hence, the quantity rather than the price of credit is used here. The availability of institutional credit can be an important determinant of the investment ratio for the reasons discussed by Alan Blinder and Joseph Stiglitz (1983), Fry (1980), and Peter Keller (1980). Banks specialize in acquiring information on default risk. Such information is highly specific to each client and difficult to sell. Hence, the market for bank loans is a customer market in which borrowers and lenders are very imperfect substitutes. A credit squeeze rations out some bank borrowers who may be unable to find loans elsewhere and thus be unable to finance their investment projects (Blinder and Stiglitz 1983, 300). Here, therefore, the investment ratio is influenced by the change in total domestic credit scaled by GNP DDCY.

The dependent variable in equation 4 of table 10.3 is gross domestic investment divided by GNP at current prices IY. The three-stage iterative least-squares estimate of this equation for the six East Asian countries is (121 observations, *t*-statistics in parentheses)

$$IY = 0.745\hat{FDIY} - 0.148FDIYL + 0.400D\hat{D}CY + 0.063R\hat{E}XL$$
$$(3.675) \qquad (-0.484) \qquad (5.555) \qquad (3.796)$$

$$+ \quad 0.354\hat{YG} + .718IY_{t-1}$$
$$(4.934) \quad (13.253)$$

$$R^2 = 0.857. \tag{14}$$

---

4. The variable REXL is divided by 10 for scaling purposes.

Evidently, FDI increases capital formation in this sample of East Asian countries. Indeed, this estimate is consistent with the statement that FDI in East Asia corresponds to capital formation on a one-to-one basis, since the coefficient of FDIY is not significantly different from 1. This implies that FDI may not be a close substitute for other forms of capital inflow in these economies. Furthermore, it suggests that FDI does not crowd out or substitute for domestically financed investment. Ceteris paribus, it increases the current account deficit by the magnitude of the capital inflow. The conclusion that FDI is not a close substitute for other capital inflows in these East Asian countries corroborates the same conclusion reached by Pradumna Rana and Malcolm Dowling (1990, 92) for a similar sample of East Asian economies. As expected, the domestic investment ratio is also increased by greater credit availability, an appreciation in the exchange rate, and higher economic growth. It is not affected significantly by the FDI ratio over the preceding five years.

## The Effect of Foreign Direct Investment on Saving

So far, the analysis of the effect of FDI on investment is incomplete in that it ignores possible effects of FDI on national saving and the rate of economic growth. If FDI affects national saving directly or indirectly by influencing the rate of economic growth, its impact on the current account will not be identical to its impact on domestic investment. If it affects the rate of economic growth, FDI will also exert an indirect effect on domestic investment. In this and other ways, FDI could increase domestic investment by more than its own direct contribution.

My saving function SNY expressed as the ratio of national saving to GNP (both in current prices) is based on a life-cycle model (Mason 1987). The standard life-cycle saving model assumes that young, income-earning households save to finance consumption when they become old, nonearning households. Figure 10.5 illustrates these life-cycle patterns of income and consumption. Income $E(a)$ and consumption $C(a)$ of a household aged a are expressed as a fraction of lifetime income.

The simplest life-cycle model assumes that each household consumes all its resources over its lifetime. In such a case, the level of household consumption $L$ over its lifetime,

$$L = \int C(a)da, \tag{15}$$

is equal to 1. Even if no household saves over its lifetime, this life-cycle model shows that aggregate saving can still be positive provided that there is positive growth in aggregate real income. With positive growth, the lifetime resources

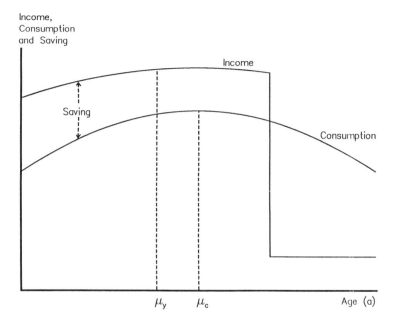

**Fig. 10.5.   Life-cycle patterns of income, consumption, and savings**

of young savers exceed those of old dissavers, and there will be positive aggregate saving. Because incomes of younger, earning households are higher than were incomes of older, nonearning households, saving exceeds dissaving in the society as a whole.

The aggregate saving ratio is determined by the age profile of the average household's saving $S(a) = E(a) - C(a)$ and by the lifetime resources that each age group can mobilize. If $V(a)$ is the ratio of lifetime resources of all households aged $a$ to aggregate real income, then $V(a)S(a)$ is the total saving of age group $a$ as a fraction of aggregate real income. The aggregate saving ratio $s$ is derived by summing across all age groups:

$$s = \int V(a)S(a)da. \tag{16}$$

With steady-state growth, $V(a)$ is independent of time and given by

$$V(a) = V(0)e^{-ga}, \tag{17}$$

where $V(0)$ is the ratio of lifetime resources of newly formed households to aggregate real income and $g$ is the rate of growth in aggregate real income. If $g$ is zero,

$$s = V(0)(1 - L) = 0. \tag{18}$$

All aggregate real income is consumed because $V(a)$ is a constant, $L$ equals 1, and $\int S(a)da$ is $1 - L$.

With positive growth in aggregate real income, the lifetime resources $V(a)$ of young savers exceed those of old dissavers, and there can be positive aggregate saving. This is the rate of growth effect. The rate of growth effect is itself determined by the relationship between income and consumption over the household's lifetime. Andrew Mason (1987) shows that the timing of household saving can be defined in terms of the mean ages of consumption $\mu_c$ and income $\mu_y$, as shown in figure 10.5. These are the average ages (weighted by the values of consumption expenditures and income at each age) at which half of a lifetime's consumption and income is reached.

The higher is the rate of economic growth, the richer is the current generation compared with the previous generation. The rate of growth effect can be positive only to the extent that households on average accumulate wealth when they are younger in order to dispose of these assets when they are older. In countries where households can borrow against future income, households may have spent more than they have earned, in cumulative terms, for a large part of their lifetimes. In this case, the rate of growth effect can be negative.

When the restrictive assumption of zero lifetime saving is discarded, the life-cycle model can incorporate both a level effect and the rate of growth effect. The level effect, which includes the bequest motive for saving, refers to the ratio of lifetime consumption to lifetime income. Any factor that increases this consumption ratio reduces the ratio of lifetime saving to lifetime income. It also reduces the ratio of current saving to current income.

The aggregate saving ratio can be represented approximately as a function of $g$, $L$, $\mu_c$, and $\mu_y$. All factors that influence the aggregate saving ratio must enter through one of these four variables (Fry and Mason 1982, 430):

$$s \approx -\log(L) + (\mu_c - \mu_y)g. \tag{19}$$

Equation 19 allows factors that influence the timing of consumption or income over the life cycle to enter the saving function interactively with the rate of growth in income.

The level of household consumption can be approximated by a log-linear function in a vector of independent variables $z$:

$$L = e^{-\alpha z}. \tag{20}$$

The difference between the mean ages of consumption and income is represented by a linear function in the same vector of independent variables $z$:

$$\mu_c - \mu_y = \beta z. \tag{21}$$

Substituting equations 20 and 21 into equation 19 gives

$$s \approx \alpha z + \beta zg. \tag{22}$$

Inflows of FDI could be accompanied by either an increase or a decrease in the measured national saving ratio. On the one hand, rising inflows of FDI may indicate a general increase in confidence in both the economic and political stability of this country. In such a case, residents may be more willing to hold their assets at home rather than remove them to safe havens abroad through overinvoicing imports and underinvoicing exports (Cuddington 1986, 38; Dooley 1986; Khan and Haque 1985; Watson et al. 1986).[5] This method of removing capital from a country reduces measured national saving, even if the true level of saving remains constant, because the national saving ratio is measured residually as the investment ratio plus the current account ratio (SNY $\equiv$ IY + CAY, where SNY is national saving divided by GNP, IY is domestic investment divided by GNP, and CAY is the current account divided by GNP. Hence, this saving function represents only that part of national saving available to finance domestic investment.

On the other hand, if some residents realize that terms and conditions for FDI are more favorable than they are for locally financed investment, they have an incentive to remove capital from their country and to bring it back again in the form of FDI. To the extent that these individuals wish to conceal the capital outflow, they will also overinvoice imports and underinvoice exports. In such case, an *increase* in FDI would be accompanied by a *reduction* in recorded national saving through this round-trip capital flow (Fry 1993, 41–44).

In effect, the saving function derived here is the private sector saving function Sng/Y to which the government saving ratio Sng/Y has been added; Snp is private national saving, Sng is government sector national saving, and Y is GNP. Unfortunately, disaggregated saving data are unavailable for most of the sample countries.[6] In any case, inflation badly distorts the measurement of disaggregated private and public saving because of the failure to account correctly for the inflation tax revenue. Fortunately, however, including components of public saving that are not substitutes for private saving affects only the intercept

5. An exporter submits an invoice for a smaller sum than that actually received for the exports when surrendering foreign exchange to the central bank; the difference can then be deposited in the exporter's bank account abroad. Conversely, an importer submits an invoice for an amount exceeding the true cost of the imports in order to siphon the difference into his foreign bank account.

6. Indeed, not even government deficit or government revenue and consumption expenditures data are available for some of the sample countries.

provided that they are independent of the explanatory variables (Fry and Mason 1982, 433).

The national saving function derived for estimation from this life-cycle model takes the form of equation 5 in table 10.3. The dependent variable SNY is national saving divided by GNP at current prices. The interactive terms were insignificant and so are omitted. The lagged dependent variable is included to incorporate any adjustment lag (121 observations):

$$SNY = 0.162\widehat{FDIY} + 0.330FDIYL + 0.438\widehat{YG} + 0.812SNY_{t-1}$$
$$(2.680) \qquad (2.575) \qquad (10.051) \quad (24.182)$$
$$R^2 = 0.904. \tag{23}$$

Evidently both current and lagged FDI ratios increase national saving ratios in this sample of East Asian countries.

### The Effect of Foreign Direct Investment on Exports and Imports

Equation 3 indicates that any deterioration in the current account must be accompanied by an increase in imports, a decrease in exports, or some combination of increased imports and decreased exports. To investigate the trade effects of FDI inflows, I estimate both an import demand and an export supply function.

The import demand equation IMKY is expressed as the ratio of imports to GNP (both in constant prices). I assume that all the sample developing countries face an infinitely elastic supply of imports. Hence, their import volume is determined solely by their own demands. These demands are affected by the real exchange rate in natural logarithms, REXL, as a proxy for the relative price of nontraded goods to imports. The income elasticity of import demand is unitary,[7] but the composition of GNP affects imports. Specifically, investment is more import intensive than is consumption. Hence, the ratio of imports to GNP is determined in part by the ratio of investment to GNP (both in constant prices) IKY.

Adjustment to the desired level of imports may be constrained by the availability of foreign exchange earned by exporters. Many developing countries impose quantitative restrictions on imports of consumer goods. Typically, licenses to import these restricted items are rationed not on the basis of total

---

7. This is supported by the fact that the logarithm of per capita real GNP, the reciprocal of the logarithm of per capita real GNP, and the rate of economic growth are all insignificant in both the import demand and export supply functions.

foreign exchange availability but rather on the availability of nonborrowed foreign exchange or foreign exchange earned by exporters. Hence, the ratio of nominal exports to nominal GNP XY is used to proxy rationing constraints.

Finally, IMKY may be influenced by FDI expressed as a ratio to GNP FDIY and by other capital inflows OKY also expressed as a ratio to GNP. In order to capture any delayed response to these capital inflows, I tested the effects of current and lagged values of both variables. The import equation derived for estimation purposes takes the form of equation 6 in table 10.3. Since the coefficient of lagged OKY was insignificant, it is omitted from the estimate reported here (117 observations):

$$\overset{\wedge}{IMKY} = 1.169\overset{\wedge}{FDIY} + 0.461FDIYL + 0.197\overset{\wedge}{OKY} + 0.121\overset{\wedge}{REXL}$$
$$\quad\quad (5.737) \quad\quad (1.101) \quad\quad (4.960) \quad\quad (12.491)$$
$$\quad + 0.322\overset{\wedge}{IKY} + 0.323\overset{\wedge}{XY} + 0.245IMKY_{t-1}$$
$$\quad\quad (11.073) \quad (9.495) \quad\quad (4.912)$$
$$R^2 = 0.982. \tag{24}$$

The signs of all coefficients agree with a priori expectations.

In this model, export supply XKY, expressed as the ratio of exports to GNP (both in constant prices), is determined by the relative prices of exports and nontraded goods REXL as well as by FDI inflows FDIY. Hence, the export equation estimated here takes the form of equation 7 in table 10.3 (122 observations):

$$XKY = -0.058\overset{\wedge}{FDIY} + 0.842FDIYL - 0.08\overset{\wedge}{REXL} + 1.075XKY_{t-1}.$$
$$\quad\quad (-0.259) \quad\quad (1.865) \quad\quad (-5.686) \quad\quad (50.829)$$
$$R^2 = 0.990. \tag{25}$$

While FDI worsens the current account balance in the short run by increasing imports, equation 25 shows that the FDI ratio over the preceding five years raises the export ratio. This suggests that FDI in East Asia has been concentrated in the export sectors of these economies.

## III.  The Effect of Foreign Direct Investment on Economic Growth

Before the overall effect of FDI on the current account can be determined, the effect of FDI on the rate of economic growth has to be analyzed because growth affects both the domestic investment and national saving ratios. Jung-soo Lee, Rana, and Yoshihiro Iwasaki (1986) estimate a simultaneous equation model of saving and growth for a sample of Asian developing countries. Of the

various capital inflow components included in their growth rate equation, FDI
has the greatest positive impact. The authors also find that FDI increases total
factor productivity. Ishrat Husain and Kwang Jun (1992, 16) use a similar approach and also detect a significantly positive effect of FDI on the rate of
economic growth for four ASEAN countries—Indonesia, Malaysia, the Philippines, and Thailand.

The growth function specified as equation 8 in table 10.3 has the rate of
growth in GNP at constant prices YG affected positively by the investment ratio
IKY and the rate of growth in exports XKG in constant prices. To determine
whether FDI exerts a different effect on growth from domestically financed
investment, I include the ratio of FDI to domestic investment FDII and also
the average ratio of FDI to domestic investment over the preceding five years
FDIIL.[8]

Gershon Feder (1982) argues that there are two channels—higher marginal productivities and externalities—through which rapid export growth can
affect the rate of economic growth in excess of the contribution of *net* export
growth to GNP. If exports effect the production of nonexports with a constant elasticity $\theta$, the rate of growth in *gross* exports at constant prices XKG
captures solely the externality effect, while the rate of growth in exports scaled
by the lagged export/GNP ratio XKGY picks up both the differential marginal
productivity $\delta$ and the externality effects (Feder 1982, 67):

$$YG = \alpha \times FDIY + [\delta / (1 + \delta) - \theta] \times XKGY + \theta \times XKG.$$

In fact, only XKG is significant for this country sample, implying that
$\delta / (1 + \delta) = \theta$.

The final explanatory variable is the growth rate in the OECD economies
WG, included to capture external demand effects on growth not picked up by
export growth (Callier 1984). The estimated growth rate function is (121 observations):

$$YG = \underset{(-0.952)}{-0.052\hat{FDII}} + \underset{(0.181)}{0.011FDIIL} + \underset{(3.290)}{0.084\hat{IKY}} + \underset{(3.671)}{0.120\hat{XKG}}$$

$$+ \underset{(3.724)}{0.628WG} + \underset{(3.949)}{0.303YG_{t-1}}$$

$$R^2 = 0.374. \tag{26}$$

Evidently, FDI does not have a significantly different effect from domestically
financed investment on growth in this sample of East Asian countries. Hence,

---

8. The variables FDII and FDIIL are used instead of FDIY and FDIYL to avoid multi-
collinearity with IKY.

its impact on growth is exerted indirectly through its effects on the investment ratio and the export growth rate.

Equations 14, 23, and an alternative version of 26 with FDII and FDIIL dropped from the estimate form a simulation model in which FDI affects economic growth through its effects on domestic investment. The result of this simulation using the average values for all the explanatory variables for the six East Asian countries over the period 1983–92 indicates that the short-run effects of FDI inflows into these East Asian economies were responsible for a 1.4 percentage point variation in growth rates among these six countries. The long-run effects produced when the lagged endogenous variables adjust to their steady-state levels indicate a 2.6 percentage point variation in growth rates between Singapore and Korea.[9] This is the same effect as that caused by an increase in FDI from zero to 10 percent of GNP.

In these simulations, the growth rate effects of FDI occur solely through higher investment ratios. One might therefore assume that FDI would worsen the current account. In fact, the simulations indicate that, while the current account does indeed deteriorate in the short run as FDI rises, it improves in the long run. An increase in FDI from zero to 10 percent of GNP worsens the current account from −0.6 to −6.4 percent of GNP in the short run but improves the current account to +7.6 percent of GNP in the long run.

There are two factors that explain this paradoxical outcome. The first is that higher growth increases the saving ratio by more than it increases the investment ratio. The second is that FDI stimulates saving directly, the more so in the medium and longer runs. While the current account is improving, export growth will be above its long-run rate, thus providing an extra growth enhancing impact. All in all, the recipients of FDI in East Asia appear to have been able to have their cakes and eat them too. As discussed in the next section, however, this serendipitous experience with FDI does not seem to have been replicated outside East Asia. Several specific features of these East Asian economies appear to act as prerequisites for such positive results.

## IV.  Some Policy Implications

Section I stresses the point that FDI can take different forms in different countries. Although FDI seems to augment capital formation in the six East Asian countries examined in section II, I find that it exerts the opposite effect in another sample of 11 developing countries outside East Asia—Argentina, Brazil, Chile, Egypt, India, Mexico, Nigeria, Pakistan, Sri Lanka, Turkey, and

9. Over the decade 1983–92, the ranking by average ratios of FDI to GDP is Singapore (0.109), Malaysia (0.042), Thailand (0.015), the Philippines (0.008), Indonesia (0.007), and Korea (0.003).

Venezuela—hereafter referred to as the control group. By producing a positive effect on the investment ratio in East Asia and a negative effect on the investment ratio elsewhere, FDI has opposite indirect effects on economic growth in these two country groups.

Econometric estimates presented elsewhere show that high black market exchange rate premiums and foreign debt ratios produce the negative associations between FDI and the domestic investment ratio detected in the 11 developing countries outside East Asia (Fry 1993, 40). If FDI constitutes a last-resort source of external financing during debt and balance of payments crises, it may well be associated with a reduction in investment productivity. In a direct test, I find that investment productivity does deteriorate as a country accumulates foreign debt (Fry 1989). In any event, only in an open economy with a low black market exchange rate premium (perhaps signifying open capital as well as current accounts) and a low foreign debt ratio is there a positive association between FDI and the domestic investment ratio.

Somewhat surprisingly, higher FDI is associated with lower national saving outside East Asia in contrast to the positive effect of FDI on national saving ratios in the East Asian countries. In examining the determinants of saving behavior, I find that a more open economy can anticipate a less negative or more positive effect of FDI on its national saving ratio. Hence, greater openness in the East Asian economies induces greater positive effects of FDI on both domestic investment and national saving ratios. An improved investment climate, as proxied by the average investment ratio over the preceding five years, also reduces the negative effect of FDI on national saving ratios (Fry 1993, 44).

An increasing body of evidence suggests that qualitative differences in investment are far more important than quantitative differences in explaining different rates of growth across countries (Fry 1995, chap. 8; King and Levine 1993a, 1993b; Roubini and Sala-i-Martin 1992). For example, the World Bank (1989, 29–31) states:

> Historically, the quality of investment has been at least as important for growth as the quantity. Although the fastest-growing countries had higher investment ratios than the others, empirical studies generally find that less than half the growth in output is attributable to increases in labor and capital. Higher productivity explains the rest. . . . Faster growth, more investment, and greater financial depth all come partly from higher saving. In its own right, however, greater financial depth also contributes to growth by improving the productivity of investment.

Several studies have traced productivity differentials to both financial repression and trade distortions imposed on the economy by government policy (Dollar 1992; Roubini and Sala-i-Martin 1991).

Referring to work by Guillermo Calvo and Fabrizio Coricelli (1992), José De Gregorio and Pablo Guidotti (1992, 11) claim that real interest rates are not a good indicator of financial repression or distortion. They suggest that the relationship between real interest rates and economic growth might resemble an inverted U curve:

> Very low (and negative) real interest rates tend to cause financial disintermediation and hence tend to reduce growth, as implied by the McKinnon-Shaw hypothesis. . . . On the other hand, very high real interest rates that do not reflect improved efficiency of investment, but rather a lack of credibility of economic policy or various forms of country risk, are likely to result in a lower level of investment as well as a concentration in excessively risky projects.

In other words, large negative and large positive real interest rates may well exert the same deleterious effect on economic growth. De Gregorio and Guidotti abandon real interest rates in favor of domestic credit to the private sector divided by GNP as a measure of financial development.

In a cross-country time-series estimate for 16 developing countries (the 11 countries outside East Asia combined with Indonesia, Korea, Malaysia, Philippines, and Thailand), I address this problem by using the square of the real deposit rate. This ensures that large positive and negative values exert the same effect, presumably negative, on economic growth. The iterative three-stage least-squares estimate is (297 observations):

$$YG = 0.582\hat{FDIY} + 0.093RD - 9.425(\hat{FDIY} \times RD)$$
$$(7.599) \quad (17.134) \quad (-12.621)$$
$$- 5.965(\hat{FDIY} \times RD^2) + 2.886(\hat{FDIY} \times RD^3) + 0.065X\hat{KG}$$
$$(-6.082) \quad (5.647) \quad (13.142)$$
$$R^2 = 0.161. \tag{27}$$

Evidently, the point made by Calvo and Coricelli (1992) and De Gregorio and Guidotti (1992) holds up well in this growth rate estimate. The estimated effect of changes in the real interest rate growth in equation 27 is illustrated in figure 10.6. This figure is produced using the mean values of all the explanatory variables with the exception of the real deposit rate of interest. The mean value of the real deposit rate is zero with a standard deviation of 23 percent. Its minimum value is –83 percent and its maximum value 221 percent. Figure 10.6 shows that the relationship between the real interest rate and growth does indeed resemble an inverted U. Low real interest rates reduce growth both directly and through the effects of such interest rates on FDI productivity.

The line $E_n$ denotes two standard deviations below the mean of all negative interest rates in the East Asian economies, $C_n$ denotes two standard deviations below the mean of all negative interest rates in the control group, $E_p$ denotes two standard deviations above the mean of all zero or positive interest rates in the East Asian economies, while $C_p$ denotes two standard deviations above the mean of all zero or positive interest rates in the control group. Evidently, real interest rates deviated from their growth maximizing level far more in the control group countries than they did in the East Asian economies. Indeed, the range of real deposit rates observed in the East Asian economies exerted virtually no negative effect on the rate of economic growth.

This result is comparable to other estimates of the effect of real interest rates of economic growth. For example, Jacques Polak (1989, 66–70) reports econometric estimates for a sample of 40 developing countries over the period 1965–85 in which an increase in a negative real interest rate by 10 percentage points raises the rate of economic growth by between 2 and 3 percentage points. He concludes that a reduction in the real interest rate below its equilibrium level by 1 percentage point requires an increase in the investment ratio by 1 percentage point in order to maintain a fixed rate of economic growth. I find similar relationships in various samples of Asian developing economies (Fry 1991, 1995).

Trade distortions manifest themselves in a set of relative prices that deviate substantially from relative prices in the world economy. As the World Bank (1991, 95) states, "direct foreign investment in an economy with highly distorted policies is likely to generate net losses for the host country instead of welfare gains." Indeed, the theory of immiserizing growth might well apply most forcefully in the case of FDI simply because FDI that produces negative value added at world prices can be accompanied by the removal of resources in the form of repatriated profits from the country. Seiji Naya (1990, 298) points out that

> the immiserization literature is of great significance because it illustrates how FDI and other capital flows can lead to suboptimal welfare levels, and even reduce welfare below pre-flow levels, when recipient industries are protected. In short, since protection will result in non-optimal investment decisions by foreign investors which in turn cause a misallocation of resources, the level of social welfare could easily be lower with foreign investment in a protected industry than without it.

The indicator used here is the black market foreign exchange premium $B$ because of its availability on an annual basis for all 16 sample countries (353 observations):

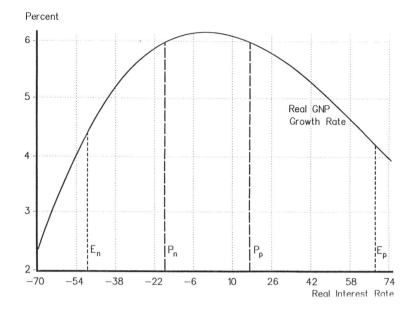

**Fig. 10.6.   Effect of real interest rate on economic growth rate**

$$YG = \overset{\wedge}{0.274}\text{FDIY} - \overset{\wedge}{1.331}(\text{FDIY} \times B^2) + \overset{\wedge}{0.029}\text{XKG}$$
$$(1.941) \qquad (-2.879) \qquad\qquad (2.410)$$
$$R^2 = 0.175. \tag{28}$$

The effect of a rise in the black market foreign exchange premium is illustrated in figure 10.7. The growth rate is reduced as the black market exchange rate premium rises through its effect on FDI productivity. The mean value of the black market exchange rate premium is 31 percent with a standard deviation of 63 percent. Its minimum value is −10 and its maximum value is 639 percent.

The line $E$ denotes two standard deviations above the mean of all zero or positive black market exchange rate premiums in the East Asian economies, while $C$ denotes two standard deviations above the mean of all zero or positive black market exchange rate premiums in the control group. Evidently, black market exchange rate premiums tended to be considerably higher in the control group than they were in the East Asian economies. Again, the range of black market exchange rate premiums in the East Asian economies exerted virtually no negative effect on the rate of economic growth.

## V. Conclusion

The overall conclusion of this chapter is that both the nature and the effects of FDI flows vary significantly between different regions of the developing world. Outside East Asia, FDI appears to have been used in large part as a substitute for other types of foreign flows; it has not increased aggregate domestic investment. When the control group countries attracted more inflows, national saving, domestic investment, and the rate of economic growth all declined. Hence, FDI appears to have been immiserizing in these countries. In contrast, the role of FDI in East Asia has been benign. In these economies, FDI financial flows have not been close substitutes for other types of foreign capital flows.

The superior efficiency of FDI in the East Asian economies reflects not only less distorted financial conditions than in other parts of the developing world but less distorted trading systems. The outward orientation of the East Asian economies ensures that relative prices cannot diverge too far from world market prices. Under these conditions, there are few possibilities for FDI to find high profits in protected markets.

The favorable investment climates in the developing economies of East Asia have ensured that FDI flows are readily available without the need for governments to discriminate in favor of this particular form of investment finance. Hence, these economies have avoided the two major pitfalls of FDI, namely, low or negative productivity caused by distortions in the economy and expensive discriminatory incentives provided in the mistaken belief that FDI brings externalities.[10]

Recently, Morris Goldstein, Donald Mathieson, and Timothy Lane (1991, 43) have noted the links between macroeconomic policies that promote domestic saving and capital repatriation, on the one hand, and a successful experience with FDI on the other.

> At a minimum, domestic fiscal, monetary, exchange rate, and financial policies must be designed to create stable domestic economic and financial market conditions, to provide domestic residents with clear incentives to hold their savings in domestic financial claims, and to ensure that available domestic and foreign savings are used to support productive investment. Stable economic conditions are also important for encouraging foreign direct investment.

It comes as no surprise, therefore, to find a strong positive correlation between the ratio of domestically financed investment to GNP and the ratio of FDI to GNP.

---

10. The Maxwell Stamp report (Maxwell Stamp 1991, 246) concludes that general economic conditions can outweigh various deterrents such as poor accounting standards: "foreign investors in Thailand do not appear to have been discouraged by these factors."

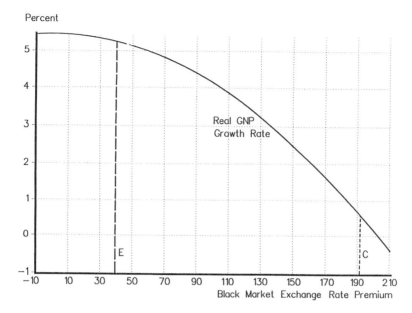

**Fig. 10.7.   Effect of black market exchange rate premium on economic growth rate**

Indeed, inflows of foreign direct and portfolio investment provide good indicators of development performance and potential. Policies aimed directly at stimulating these forms of capital inflows appear to be ineffective or to produce the opposite effects to those desired. The evidence suggests overwhelmingly that policies that promote domestic investment and growth are most likely to stimulate private sector capital inflows in all forms. In summarizing findings similar to those of Venkataraman Balasubramanyam (1984), Jamuna Agarwal, Andrea Gubitz, and Peter Nunnenkamp (1991, 128) conclude:

> the effectiveness of tax and tariff exemptions as well as related privileges for FDI, some of which are very costly for the host countries, is uncertain at best. They may even result in a vicious circle if privileges granted to foreign investors give rise to hostile feelings against FDI in the recipient countries. The consequences may be a new wave of regulations, intensified efforts to circumvent the restrictions, and finally the retreat of foreign investors. It appears more promising to adhere to the rule: "what is good policy for domestic investors is also good for foreign investors," by creating a stable and favorable general framework for investment. Ad hoc interventions should be kept to the minimum. It is not only the rules and regulations that matter, but also how they are applied in practice. The ap-

proval procedure should be fast and transparent as it is a crucial element in the investment decision of foreign companies.

The evidence presented in this chapter is certainly consistent with this conclusion.

The policy implications that might be derived from the East Asian experience with FDI are as follows.

Foreign direct investment can increase capital formation or provide additional balance of payments financing but cannot perform both functions at the same time. If FDI is attracted for privatization or debt-equity swap programs, it may provide additional or alternative balance of payments support, but it will not accelerate capital formation or economic growth.

Stimulating FDI through special incentive schemes may simply encourage round-trip capital flows from the host country. In such case, measured national saving may fall.

In the presence of financial and trade distortions, FDI can remove from the host country more than it contributes. In other words, it can be immiserizing.

The most efficacious way of encouraging FDI is to implement policies that generally improve the investment climate. Where domestically financed investment is booming, FDI will seek to participate. Nondiscrimination discourages round-trip capital flows and reduces the possibilities for immiserization.

Maximum benefit from FDI can be achieved in open economies that are free of domestic distortions such as financial repression and trade controls. Under such conditions, restrictions on the sectoral location of FDI reduce its growth enhancing impact.

REFERENCES

Agarwal, Jamuna P., Andrea Gubitz, and Peter Nunnenkamp. 1991. *Foreign Direct Investment in Developing Countries: The Case of Germany.* Kieler Studien No. 238. Tubingen: J. C. B. Mohr and Paul Siebeck.
Balasubramanyam, Venkataraman N. 1984. "Incentives and Disincentives for Foreign Direct Investment in Less Developed Countries." *Weltwirtschaftliches Archiv* 120: 720–35.
Blejer, Mario I., and Mohsin S. Khan. 1984. "Government Policy and Private Investment in Developing Countries." *International Monetary Fund Staff Papers* 31 (June): 379–403.
Blinder, Alan S., and Joseph E. Stiglitz. 1983. "Money, Credit Constraints, and Economic Activity." *American Economic Review* 73 (May): 297–302.

Callier, Philippe. 1984. "Growth of Developing Countries and World Interest Rates." *Journal of Macroeconomics* 6 (fall): 465–71.

Calvo, Guillermo A., and Fabrizio Coricelli. 1992. "Stagflationary Effects of Stabilization Programs in Reforming Socialist Countries: Enterprise-Side and Household-Side Factors." *World Bank Economic Review* 6 (January): 71–90.

Cockcroft, Laurence, and Roger C. Riddell. 1991. "Foreign Direct Investment in Sub-Saharan Africa." World Bank, International Economic Department, Working Paper 619.

Cuddington, John T. 1986. "Capital Flight: Estimates, Issues, and Explanations." *Princeton Studies in International Finance* 58: Princeton: Princeton University Economics Department.

De Gregorio, José, and Pablo E. Guidotti. 1992. "Financial Development and Economic Growth." *International Monetary Fund Staff Working Papers* (December).

Dollar, David. 1992. "Outward-Oriented Developing Economies Really Do Grow More Rapidly: Evidence from 95 LDCs, 1976–1985." *Economic Development and Cultural Change* 40 (April): 523–44.

Dooley, Michael P. 1986. "Country-Specific Risk Premiums, Capital Flight, and Net Investment Income Payments in Selected Developing Countries." International Monetary Fund, DM/86/17. Mimeo.

Dornbusch, Rudiger, and Yung Chul Park. 1987. "Korean Growth Policy." *Brookings Papers on Economic Activity* 2:389–444.

Feder, Gershon. 1982. "On Exports and Economic Growth." *Journal of Development Economics* 12 (February-April): 59–73.

Fry, Maxwell J. 1980. "Money, Interest, Inflation, and Growth in Turkey." *Journal of Monetary Economics* 6 (October): 535–45.

Fry, Maxwell J. 1989. "Foreign Debt Instability: An Analysis of National Saving and Domestic Investment Responses to Foreign Debt Accumulation in 28 Developing Countries." *Journal of International Money and Finance* 8 (September): 315–44.

Fry, Maxwell J. 1991. "Domestic Resource Mobilization in Developing Asia: Four Policy Issues." *Asian Development Review* 9:15–39.

Fry, Maxwell J. 1993. *Foreign Direct Investment in Southeast Asia: Differential Impacts.* Singapore: Institute of Southeast Asian Studies.

Fry, Maxwell J. 1995. *Money, Interest, and Banking in Economic Development.* 2nd ed. Baltimore: Johns Hopkins University Press.

Fry, Maxwell J., and Andrew Mason. 1982. "The Variable Rate-of-Growth Effect in the Life Cycle Saving Model: Children, Capital Inflows, Interest, and Growth in a New Specification of the Life-Cycle Model Applied to Seven Asian Developing Countries." *Economic Inquiry* 20 (July): 426–42.

Goldstein, Morris, Donald J. Mathieson, and Timothy Lane. 1991. "Determinants and Systemic Consequences of International Capital Flows." In *Determinants and Systemic Consequences of International Capital Flows,* edited by Research Department of the International Monetary Fund. Occasional Papers No. 77. Washington, D.C.: International Monetary Fund. Pp. 1–45.

Hill, Hal. 1990. "Foreign Investment and East Asian Economic Development." *Asian-Pacific Economic Literature* 4 (September): 21–58.

538     Lessons from East Asia

Husain, Ishrat, and Kwang W. Jun. 1992. "Capital Flows to South Asian and ASEAN Countries." *World Bank International Economics Department* WPS 842. Mimeo.

International Monetary Fund. [IMF]. 1994. *Balance of Payments Yearbook.* Washington, D.C.: IMF.

International Monetary Fund. [IMF]. Various years. *International Financial Statistics.* Washington, D.C.: IMF.

International Monetary Fund. [IMF]. Various issues. *World Economic Outlook.* Washington, D.C.: IMF.

Johnston, John. 1984. *Econometric Methods.* 3d ed., New York: McGraw-Hill.

Keller, Peter M. 1980. "Implications of Credit Policies for Output and the Balance of Payments." *International Monetary Fund Staff Papers* 27 (September): 451–77.

Khan, Mohsin S., and Nadeem Ul Haque. 1985. "Foreign Borrowing and Capital Flight: A Formal Analysis." *International Monetary Fund Staff Papers* 32 (December): 606–28.

King, Robert G., and Ross Levine. 1993a. "Finance and Growth: Schumpeter Might Be Right." Working Paper 1083. Washington, D.C.: World Bank.

King, Robert G., and Ross Levine. 1993b. "Finance, Entrepreneurship, and Growth: Theory and Evidence." *Journal of Monetary Economics* 32:

Lee, Jungsoo, Pradumna B. Rana, and Yoshihiro Iwasaki. 1986. "Effects of Foreign Capital Inflows on Developing Countries in Asia." Asian Development Bank Economic Staff Papers No. 30. Mimeo.

Mason, Andrew. 1987. "National Saving Rate and Population Growth: A New Model and New Evidence." In *Population Growth and Economic Development: Issues and Evidence,* edited by D. Gale Johnson and Ronald D. Lee. Madison: University of Wisconsin Press for the National Academy of Sciences. Pp. 523–60.

Maxwell Stamp Ltd.. 1991. *Regional Study of Resource Flows and Financial Intermediation.* London: Maxwell Stamp.

Naya, Seiji. 1990. "Direct Foreign Investment and Trade in East and Southeast Asia." In *The Political Economy of International Trade: Essays in Honor of Robert E. Baldwin,* edited by Ronald W. Jones and Anne O. Krueger. Cambridge: Basil Blackwell. Pp. 288–312.

Polak, Jacques J. 1989. *Financial Policies and Development.* Paris: Development Centre of the Organisation for Economic Co-operation and Development.

Rana, Pradumna B., and J. Malcolm Dowling. 1990. "Foreign Capital and Asian Economic Growth." *Asian Development Review* 8:77–102.

Roubini, Nouriel, and Xavier Sala-i-Martin. 1991. "Financial Development, the Trade Regime, and Economic Growth." National Bureau of Economic Research Working Papers No. 3876. Cambridge: NBER.

Roubini, Nouriel, and Xavier Sala-i-Martin. 1992. "Financial Repression and Economic Growth." *Journal of Development Economics* 39 (July). 5–30.

Watson, C. Maxwell, G. Russell Kincaid, Caroline Atkinson, Eliot Kalter, and David Folkerts-Landau. 1986. "International Capital Markets: Developments and Prospects." IMF Occasional Paper 43. Washington, D.C.: IMF.

United Nations. 1993. *World Investment Report 1993: Transnational Corporations and Integrate International Production.* New York: United Nations.

World Bank. 1989. *World Development Report, 1989.* New York: Oxford University Press for the World Bank.

World Bank. 1991. *World Development Report, 1991.* New York: Oxford University Press for the World Bank.

World Bank. 1993. *Global Economic Prospects and the Developing Countries.* Washington, D.C.: World Bank.

CHAPTER 11

# Common Foundations of East Asian Success

*Peter A. Petri*

## I. Introduction

East Asia is an ideal place to develop. Eight of the nine major market-oriented[1] economies of developing East Asia (China, Hong Kong, Indonesia, Korea, Malaysia, the Philippines, Singapore, Taiwan, and Thailand) were among the 12 most rapidly growing economies of the world during the 1965–90 period. Had growth rates been randomly distributed across all developing countries, there is only one chance in a million that success would have turned out so regionally concentrated. Whether this "coincidence" is due to common characteristics and strategies or interactions with fast growing neighbors, there is clearly something significant about being East Asian.

Empirical studies have shown that much of East Asian growth can be traced to large investments in human and physical capital.[2] But the region's total factor productivity (TFP) growth rates are also unusual. In a study of 87 countries, Page and Petri (1993) found that Hong Kong, Japan, Korea, Taiwan (China), and Thailand were within the top decile of all countries in terms of TFP growth rates and that Indonesia, Malaysia, and Singapore, though not as unusual, were also above developing country norms. In terms of Chenery, Robinson, and Syrquin's (1986) topology of growth, the East Asian economies look more like industrialized than developing countries since they derive nearly half of their output growth from TFP growth rather than accumulation (table 11.1).

The productivity issue has received much attention in the popular press recently due to Paul Krugman's article "The Myth of Asia's Miracle" (1994).

---

1. Whether China belongs in this category is debatable; it is included in this study because it followed market-oriented policies for a significant part of the study period. The probability calculation would change, of course, if China were excluded or planned economies such as North Korea included, but the fundamental point of the passage would not.

2. The literature on cross-country empirical tests of the sources of growth is examined more fully in Page and Petri 1993.

Building on research by Young (1992), Krugman argues that Soviet-style growth and East Asian development are similar because both were based on investment rather than productivity increases. He concludes that East Asian growth is "no more than what the most boringly conventional economic model would lead us to expect"[3] and "the future prospects for [rapid Asian] growth are more limited than almost anyone now imagines."[4]

Krugman's paper is so preoccupied with productivity—and specifically with the unusual case of Singapore—that it misses the uniqueness of the East Asian experience: there are no comparable examples of sustained and widespread growth anywhere else, now or in the past. That Singapore could invest as much as half of its output at times and still maintain productivity growth at above-average levels is remarkable in itself. Singapore's per capita income today is an order of magnitude larger than Russia's, and yet its growth remains very rapid. East Asian experience shows how accumulation can be accelerated and how large increases in inputs can be put to productive use. Of course, growth will slow as East Asian countries reach international frontiers of capital

**TABLE 11.1.   Sources of Growth**

| | Value Added Growth | TFP Growth | Capital Growth | Labor Growth | TFP/Value-Added Share (%) |
|---|---|---|---|---|---|
| Developed Economies | | | | | |
| 1947–73 | 5.4 | 2.7 | 2.0 | 0.7 | 49.0 |
| Developing Economies | | | | | |
| 1960–73 | 5.1 | 1.3 | 7.4 | 2.2 | 25.5 |
| 1973–87 | 3.5 | −0.2 | 7.1 | 2.4 | −5.7 |
| East Asia | | | | | |
| 1960–73 | 7.5 | 2.6 | 9.8 | 2.8 | 34.7 |
| 1973–87 | 6.5 | 1.3 | 10.7 | 2.6 | 20.0 |
| Hong Kong | | | | | |
| 1955–60 | 8.3 | 2.4 | 4.7 | 6.6 | 29.1 |
| 1960–70 | 9.1 | 4.3 | 7.6 | 3.0 | 47.0 |
| Korea | | | | | |
| 1955–60 | 4.2 | 2.0 | 2.2 | 2.3 | 47.4 |
| 1960–73 | 9.7 | 4.1 | 6.6 | 5.0 | 42.3 |
| Singapore | | | | | |
| 1972–80 | 8.0 | 0.0 | 9.5 | 5.5 | 0.0 |
| Taiwan | | | | | |
| 1955–60 | 5.2 | 3.1 | 2.7 | 1.8 | 59.5 |

*Sources:* World Bank 1991; Chenery, Robinson, and Syrquin 1986, table 2–2.

3. Krugman 1994, 78.
4. Ibid., 64.

intensity and productivity, but this does not make their examples any less important for other developing countries.

Another remarkable aspect of the East Asian experience is "hyperspeed" growth. While the background rate of growth of East Asian economies is high—seldom do growth rates fall below the 4 or 5 percent range—each has also experienced periods of exceptionally fast growth at rates reaching into double digits. These spurts often have been sustained over several years and sometimes decades (table 11.2). Each spurt seems to have been associated with a powerful and often unique "engine of growth." Each typically increased savings and strengthened international trade and technology linkages. Each also triggered massive changes in economic structure and large slides down the experience curves of major industries.

The daunting task of this paper is to identify the common elements of East Asian success: why did these countries invest so much, how did they use investments so efficiently, and what engines propelled such exceptional growth? In contrast to many previous studies, which limited their attention to subsets of East Asian countries,[5] this essay will consider the experiences of both the NIEs (Hong Kong, Korea, Singapore, and Taiwan [China]) and the next-tier miracles

**TABLE 11. 2.   Hyperspeed Growth**

| Country | Growth Spurt[a] | Years | Growth Rate | Possible Engines |
|---|---|---|---|---|
| Indonesia | 1970–73 | 4 | 8.8 | Recovery from Sukarno period |
| | 1976–79 | 4 | 7.5 | Oil investment |
| | 1989– | 3+ | 7.5 | Manufacturing, foreign investment |
| Korea | 1963–77 | 15 | 9.6 | Export promotion |
| | 1981– | 11+ | 9.3 | Chaebul dynamism |
| Malaysia | 1969–72 | 4 | 8.3 | Raw materials |
| | 1976–79 | 4 | 8.9 | Government investment, export processing zones |
| | 1987– | 5+ | 8.2 | Foreign investment boom |
| Singapore | 1965–73 | 9 | 12.1 | Foreign investment boom |
| | 1976–79 | 4 | 8.5 | Infrastructure investment |
| | 1986– | 6+ | 9.0 | Communications and finance |
| Thailand | 1962–69 | 8 | 8.4 | Investment promotion, war |
| | 1975–77 | 3 | 8.0 | Industrial promotion |
| | 1986– | 6+ | 9.9 | Manufacturing, foreign investment |

*Source:* Author and World Bank Data.

[a] Spurts are defined as periods during which the three-year moving average of real GDP growth remained higher than 7 percent.

5. In economic terminology, including too few countries "underidentifies" the problem, as several different explanations may be consistent with the relatively few data points available. Of course, including too many countries may "overidentify" the problem, making it difficult to find an explanation that fits the different stories that emerge from country experiences.

of East and Southeast Asia (Indonesia, Malaysia, and Thailand).[6] The strategies of these "latecomers" may well be more relevant for developing countries today than those of the NIEs decades ago.

The analytical scope of this study will be similarly inclusive. The alternative explanations considered will not be restricted to just the proximate determinants of East Asian success such as specific policies affecting trade, investment, and macroeconomic management. It is equally important to understand why East Asian economies consistently chose the "right" approaches and implemented them effectively.[7] This requires analysis of factors such as institutional capacity, the political framework of economic decisions, and societal attitudes toward government, education, and economic activity.

In searching for the common foundations of East Asian success, we will confront alternative theories with detailed country experience. Three groups of explanations—neoclassical, structuralist, and culturalist—will be examined in detail, and each will be shown to capture important aspects of East Asian development. A fourth, new explanation will be added, arguing that certain "contagion" effects helped to spread growth among the region's economies.

The most important finding is that none of the explanations fits the full range of East Asian case studies—there is no single "East Asian recipe" for rapid growth. In nearly every dimension analyzed, the region's success stories are too diverse to yield any single recipe. Rather, the East Asian experience illustrates Gerschenkron's (1962) finding of high elasticity and variability in the industrialization processes which are known from historical experience."

Nevertheless, some basic commonalities underlie East Asia's approaches to development. Three characteristics seem to be associated with each success story: (1) an economic environment that encouraged investment and enterprise, (2) powerful incentives that guided resources and initiative into efficient activities, and (3) some engine of growth that provided economic leadership. These requirements were met by diverse institutions and policies—both market oriented and interventionist. The details of economic management varied considerably across East Asia, with approaches adapted to domestic circumstances

---

6. China and the Philippines are potential candidates for inclusion in this analysis, but they are excluded because they were not part of the original detailed country studies conducted for this project. Japan is excluded because it had reached a high level of industrialization by the time of World War II.

7. The strategies pursued by many East Asian countries were initially advocated by Western advisers who were presumably dispensing similar recommendations throughout the world. For example, U.S. aid agencies played a critical role in formulating reforms in Korea, the United Nations in Singapore, and the consulting firms Stanford Research Institute and Arthur D. Little in Taiwan. Thus, the success of East Asian strategies cannot be attributed to special insights that were unavailable to other countries.

and the international environment through experiment and reform. The ability to innovate and adapt institutions to achieve these results is a hallmark of East Asian success.

## II.  Theories of the Miracle

There are at least four "deeper" explanations of the factors that cause accumulation and productivity to be so strong in East Asia. Neoclassical approaches have emphasized outward orientation and macroeconomic discipline. Structuralist theories have singled out government leadership in industrial policy. Culturalist explanations have focused on governance and societal characteristics. And, finally, East Asia's dynamism may be due to the contagion effects of success. These four theories will be described briefly. The next section confronts these theories with the actual experience of eight rapidly developing East Asian economies.

### Neoclassical Explanations: Right Fundamentals

> The neutrality and stability of the incentive system, together with limited government interventions, well-functioning labor and capital markets, and reliance on private capital . . . have been the main ingredients of successful economic performance in East Asia. (Balassa 1988, 288)

Early analyses of the East Asian miracles emphasized neoclassical causes by arguing that the NICs "got the fundamentals right" in several key policy areas. In this view, East Asian economies succeeded because they came closer than other developing countries to providing a stable macroeconomic environment and strong connections to global trade and technology. Modern versions of this approach place somewhat more emphasis on the government's market-friendly support of investment, especially in human capital (World Bank 1991). In this view, East Asia's miracle economies succeeded because

> *They adopted an outward oriented trade strategy* to build linkages with world markets and technology. They achieved this with policies ranging from broad liberalization to export promotion designed to offset protectionist biases favoring domestic industries.
>
> *They pursued conservative macroeconomic policies* to create a stable, predictable environment for investment and trade. Imbalances were addressed swiftly and decisively, keeping inflation low, exchange rates competitive, and debt affordable.
>
> *They invested vigorously in human capital* to develop an educated and technically competent labor force.

*They maintained competitive markets for factors* to facilitate the structural transformation from primary production to manufacturing and eventually to knowledge-intensive industries.

The empirical evidence summarized later confirms that East Asia performed better on these measures of accumulation and allocation than other developing countries did.

### Structuralist Explanations: Wrong Prices

[E]conomic expansion depends on state intervention to create price distortions that direct economic activity toward greater investment. State intervention is necessary in even the most plausible cases of comparative advantage, because the chief asset of backwardness—low wages—is counterbalanced by heavy liabilities. (Amsden 1989, 14)

Structuralist interpretations of East Asian success emphasize that policy regimes in many East Asian countries departed significantly from market-oriented norms. In the structuralist view, these interventions were necessary to develop infant industries and upgrade the industrial structure. In more sophisticated variants of the argument, interventions are seen as remedies for market failures in capital markets (Stiglitz 1989) and externalities in the development of new industries (Pack and Westphal 1986). To overcome these common problems of early industrialization, the East Asian economies:

*Targeted sectors that offered strong opportunities* for growth and productivity, based on the experiences of similar, more advanced economies (e.g., Japan)[8]

*Directed resources into targeted sectors* by "getting prices wrong" with selective trade restrictions, preferential access to credit and important inputs, and government investment

*Avoided big policy mistakes* by limiting the duration of government support and setting performance-oriented criteria, such as export success, for promoted firms

As we will see, several East Asian economies followed structuralist policies at one time or another. However, few sustained such policies for a significant length of time, and several intervened in ways that cannot be reconciled with structuralist models.

---

8. If market failures are systematically associated with early stages of development, it may be relatively easy to identify appropriate interventions and to choose sectoral "winners."

## Culturalist Explanations: Confucianism

> Four institutions and cultural practices rooted in the Confucian tradition but adapted to the needs of an industrial society—a meritocratic elite, an entrance exam system, the importance of the group, and the goal of self-improvement—have . . . ignited the greatest burst of sustained economic growth the world has yet seen. (Vogel 1991, 101)

This approach argues that East Asia's cultural traditions positively affected the behavior of individual economic agents and economic organizations and methods of governance. Confucian traditions may have been responsible for East Asia's unusually high propensities to save and educate and for its strong, publicly motivated bureaucracies. In this view, East Asian culture:

*Emphasized group over individual values,* giving rise to cohesive forms of political and business organizations.

*Developed meritocratic institutions,* creating incentives for learning and education and ensuring high-quality policy making

*Legitimized authoritarian rule,* leading to long-lived regimes and stable, consistent policies

The next section will show that the institutions highlighted by culturalist explanations have played an important role in some East Asian case histories. The viability of the culturalist explanation, however, is undermined by the region's cultural variety; Confucian traditions were not equally influential in all rapidly growing East Asian economies.

## Interaction Effects: Contagion

While most previous writing has focused on these three approaches, the most obvious common feature of the East Asian miracles is geography. East Asian development patterns are also more alike than they might have been, given only similarities in resource endowments. This suggests that East Asian economic growth may have been shaped by regional contacts—including flows of goods, investments, technologies, aspirations, and ideas about governance. Thus, individual East Asian economies might have been especially successful because they developed together rather than in isolation. The geographical proximity of East Asian countries may have:

*Encouraged the imitation of policies* by exposing policymakers to successes in similar, nearby economies

> *Promoted the imitation of technologies and business strategies* by expos-
> ing entrepreneurs to the achievements of similar, nearby companies
> *Facilitated direct investment and trade,* particularly by smaller firms,
> through cultural and ethnic ties based on history and migration

Empirical studies show that physical distance is an important correlate of economic integration, and East Asia is well integrated through trading, investment,
and migration relationships (Petri, forthcoming). But, while the contagion hypothesis appears to be important in explaining why East Asian growth was so
rapid, widely shared, and regionally concentrated, it does not ultimately point
to the root causes of East Asian growth.[9]

## III.  Causal Factors and Country Experience

Each of the approaches is derived from or linked to certain critical features of
East Asian experience. This section examines seven such features that often
have been identified as sources of East Asian success and places them in the
perspective of country and econometric evidence. One objective is to examine
how each feature influenced development in one or more countries of the East
Asian sample. Another is to test whether the feature was "common" in East
Asian development—that is, whether it was present and significant in most of
the miracles.

The evidence presented subsequently is primarily qualitative and draws
heavily on the country studies of this volume. But, in addition, some limited
quantitative evidence is developed along the lines of the regression approach pioneered by Syrquin and Chenery (1989).[10] This exercise seeks to identify what
characteristics East Asian countries have in common and whether the region is
an outlier (from international norms) in these characteristics. In other words,
how do East Asian countries differ from other developing countries in terms of
the factors theoretically associated with success?[11]

Each variable of interest was regressed on income and population across
the full cross section of low- and middle-income countries. In addition to these
controls, dummy variables were added for East Asia (all seven economies) and
then in separate regressions for each of the several East Asian economies. A
significant coefficient for a dummy variable indicates that East Asia (or a par-

---

9. The contagion hypothesis has points in common with the Japanese "flying geese"
model, which argues that latecomers follow the development patterns of economies in more advanced stages of growth (Akamatsu 1960).

10. The equation, before the addition of dummy variables, is $z = b_0 + b_1 y + b_2 y^2 + b_3 n + b_4 n^2$, where $y$ is log GDP and $n$ is log population.

11. This equation is quite different from that used in conventional production function studies that seek to decompose growth into the contributions of particular determinants.

ticular country) is an outlier in cross-country patterns. The results are presented in table 11.3.

As the table shows, and qualitative evidence confirms, some of the factors theoretically associated with success are much more pervasive in East Asian experience than others are. Also, due to the great variability of international experience, even these cannot be always statistically identified as unique to the region. Finally, in some dimensions the region's uniqueness emerged only in the latter period, casting doubt on its causal role in the region's success. For all these reasons, few factors will emerge from this analysis intact as potential candidates for a common theory of the miracles.

### Outward-Oriented Development Strategies

Trade played an important role in the development strategies of all East Asian economies (see, e.g., World Bank 1991, chap. 5). This is evident in table 11.3, where openness appears as the most consistently significant attribute of East Asian economies. Even allowing for their small size, Hong Kong, Malaysia, and Singapore had some of the world's highest export-GDP ratios as early as the 1960s and 1970s, and Korea, Taiwan, and Thailand rapidly surpassed international norms after switching to outward-oriented policies. These rankings reflect policy choices: Hong Kong and Singapore largely eliminated trade restrictions; Malaysia, Korea, and Taiwan shifted to export promotion by the 1960s; and Thailand and Indonesia have made considerable progress in the last decade.[12]

Several East Asian countries also created a hospitable environment for foreign investment—some at a time when other developing countries still favored nationalization. Investment incentives included tax concessions (Singapore between 1968 and 1973), export processing zones, or EPZs (Taiwan and Malaysia), and investment promotion (Thailand). Significant results were achieved in several countries: foreign investment in Malaysian EPZs reached 19 percent of GDP in 1975, and much of Singapore's industry is foreign owned. In Table 11.3, Thailand also appears as an outlier in its FDI-GDP ratio, and together these countries make East Asia as a whole a positive outlier in the 1990 data. In the early 1990s, Indonesia also experienced a major foreign investment boom. By this time nearly all East Asian countries were actively reforming economic policies to attract foreign investment, suggesting a virtuous interaction of external circumstances, policy experiments, and policy imitation.

The prevalence of outward orientation offers support for neoclassical interpretations of East Asian success. Balassa (1981), Krueger (1985), and other

---

12. To be sure, the regimes vary from relatively neutral policies to strategies that balanced high import barriers with intensive export protection.

**TABLE 11.3. East Asian Performance and International Norms**

| | Outward Orientation | | Macroeconomics | | | Government | | Investment | | Finance |
|---|---|---|---|---|---|---|---|---|---|---|
| | Exports/ GDP (%) | FDI/ GDP (%) | Inflation Rate (%) | Government Surplus/ GDP (%) | Debt/ Exp. (%) | Spending/ GDP (%) | Investment/ GDP (%) | Primary Enrollment (%) | Secondary Enrollment (%) | Money/ GDP (%) |
| **Mean Values** | | | | | | | | | | |
| **All low and middle income** | | | | | | | | | | |
| 1965 | 22.6 | 0.9 | 14.0 | -3.3 | 153.3 | 17.4 | 17.4 | 72.7 | 16.9 | 20.8 |
| 1990 | 30.1 | 0.7 | 34.8 | -2.6 | 335.4 | 20.7 | 20.3 | 90.1 | 38.1 | 34.4 |
| **East Asia** | | | | | | | | | | |
| 1965 | 44.3 | 1.0 | 13.0 | -3.7 | 91.6 | 18.6 | 20.2 | 91.5 | 27.2 | 23.9 |
| 1990 | 83.7 | 2.8 | 4.6 | 2.0 | 102.8 | 21.2 | 35.2 | 103.8 | 60.3 | 70.7 |
| **East Asia Dummy Variable** | | | | | | | | | | |
| **East Asia** | | | | | | | | | | |
| 1965 | 28.0[a] | 0.67 | -1.7 | -0.8 | -83.3[b] | 0.3 | 2.7 | 18.4[b] | 8.7[a] | 8.3[c] |
| 1990 | 49.1[a] | 2.10[a] | -30.3[a] | 5.5[a] | -119.9[b] | -5.6 | 15.8[a] | -2.6 | -5.9 | 29.6[a] |
| **Country Dummy Variables** | | | | | | | | | | |
| **Hong Kong** | | | | | | | | | | |
| 1965 | 45.3[a] | na | -11.8 | na | na | na | 14.2[a] | 6.2 | -0.4 | na |
| 1990 | 106.4[a] | na | -55.9[a] | na | na | na | 6.7 | -4.9 | -10.2 | na |
| **Indonesia** | | | | | | | | | | |
| 1965 | 2.1 | 0.83 | 24.4[a] | -0.5 | -69.3 | 2.6 | -6.2 | 30.2 | 1.6 | na |
| 1990 | 8.7 | 0.35 | -5.2 | 3.5 | -36.6 | 1.6 | 15.1[b] | 17.4 | 4.1 | na |
| **Korea** | | | | | | | | | | |
| 1965 | -2.3 | 0.66 | 7.2 | -2.2 | -61.8 | 3.3 | 1.2 | 48.0[a] | 25.0[a] | -8.1 |
| 1990 | 9.7 | -0.81 | -43.3[b] | 3.6 | -114.9 | -16.3[c] | 18.3[a] | -3.2 | 7.6 | na |
| **Malaysia** | | | | | | | | | | |
| 1965 | 21.5[a] | 0.96 | -11.2 | -6.2[c] | -123.9[c] | 5.4 | 1.7 | 7.4 | 6.7 | 1.5 |
| 1990 | 52.8[a] | 6.10[a] | -26.1 | 0.0 | -164.5[c] | 6.3 | 17.2[b] | -7.6 | 1.0 | |
| **Singapore** | | | | | | | | | | |
| 1965 | 92.5[a] | na | -11.3 | 6.8[b] | na | -9.6[c] | -0.1 | 5.6 | 18.0[b] | 36.4[a] |
| 1990 | 154.5[a] | na | -61.1[a] | 14.3[a] | na | -21.6[b] | 15.2 | -2.9 | -13.9 | |
| **Thailand** | | | | | | | | | | |
| 1965 | 3.0 | 0.21 | -5.9 | -2.3 | -75.5 | 1.0 | 4.8 | 14.6 | 0.6 | 1.6 |
| 1990 | 16.5[c] | 2.34[a] | -18.0 | 8.7[a] | -166.3[c] | -6.1 | 18.6 | -16.7 | -25.4 | |

*Source:* Author's estimates.

[a] Significant at the 5 percent level, [b] at 10 percent, and [c] at 20 percent.

*Note:* $Y = a + b_1 G + b_2 G^2 + b_3 N + b_4 N^2$, where $Y$ is the dependent variable indicated at the top of the column, $G$ is log GDP, and $N$ is log population.

neoclassical writers argue that openness to international trade has positively affected East Asian development through allocative gains associated with specialization as well as dynamic gains associated with competition and the acquisition of technology. Outward orientation also provides support for the contagion approach. And, finally, outward orientation is consistent with structuralist claims that countries like Korea and Taiwan "managed" international relationships strategically in order to build competence in desirable industries. Thus, while outward orientation appears to be common to most East Asian success stories, it does not by itself help to distinguish alternative explanations.

## Macroeconomic Discipline

East Asia has been generally successful on indicators of macroeconomic stability. Thomas and Wang (1992) show that inflation rates were only half as high, on average, as those in other low- and middle-income countries. Real interest rates averaged 4 percent, compared with a negative 3 percent in other developing countries, ensuring good returns on savings and the efficient use of capital. Real exchange rates were generally competitive and less variable than exchange rates elsewhere, and less debt was accumulated. East Asia appears unusually successful on most of the macroeconomic indicators analyzed in table 11.3. But the table also shows that several East Asian countries did not yet differ substantially from international norms in the 1960s.[13]

Stability was achieved partly by keeping public sector deficits below developing country averages (Thomas and Wang 1992). This was accomplished by a range of institutions: in Hong Kong, Taiwan, and Singapore, budget policy was left to conservative governments, and, in Thailand, Parliament could only reduce expenditures but not increase them (Christensen et al. 1996). In Indonesia, an open capital account imposed external discipline: when oil prices were high, the government limited borrowing to avoid revaluation, and, when oil prices fell, it switched to austerity to prevent capital flight (Bhattacharya and Pangestu 1996).

East Asian macroeconomic policies also aimed for realistic (and even undervalued) exchange rates. Several of the success stories began with exchange rate reforms—devaluations, unification, and commitment to competitive real rates. Taiwan in the 1960s and virtually all of the NICs in the 1980s kept their exchange rates undervalued in order to build export market shares (Petri 1989). When imbalances arose (Malaysia in the mid-1970s, Korea in the late 1970s, and Indonesia in the mid-1980s), governments generally responded with devaluations and retrenchments. While East Asian countries have not avoided

13. For example, both Indonesia and Korea had inflation rates well above international norms in 1965.

macroeconomic difficulties, they have reacted more quickly and adjusted less painfully than other developing countries have.

The prevalence of sound macroeconomic management is a second factor that favors neoclassical explanations of East Asian success. But the exact contribution of macroeconomic management to miracle growth is unclear. For one thing, the relationships could run from strong growth to macroeconomic performance: it is easier to avoid deficits when a country is growing rapidly. Indeed, the difference in macroeconomic performance between East Asia and other developing countries began to be significant only after East Asian growth started to accelerate. Finally, macroeconomic stability also may be a symptom of culturalist explanations, since the longevity and meritocratic character of East Asian governments surely contributed to stable macroeconomic management.

## Public Resource Mobilization and Investment

East Asian savings and investment rates are exceptional today, but not all of them were at the outset of rapid growth. Only in 1990 does table 11.3 show East Asian savings to be significantly above world norms. Three countries with high savings rates now—Indonesia, Korea, and Singapore—saved 10 percent or less in the 1960s and borrowed heavily abroad. In some cases, government was the catalyst in the mobilization of capital. The most striking example is Singapore, which at one time imposed a 50 percent wage tax on employers and employees through its Central Provident Fund. The state played a positive but more modest role in Korea and Taiwan, where private savings were channeled through state-controlled banks and postal savings systems (Dahlman and Sananikone 1993). Even Hong Kong relied somewhat on public savings, financed by the development of "crown land."

Public investments in human capital also have been widely credited with triggering growth. In table 11.3, the educational enrollment variables are the only factors that tend to be more significant in 1965 (when the miracles were getting under way) than in 1990. The relationship, to be sure, is still imperfect: educational attainment is high in East Asia's least successful market economy (the Philippines), and in some other developing countries, and is generally below international norms in such successful economies as Hong Kong and Thailand. Rather than being sufficient or necessary for rapid growth, public investments in education appear to have been a facilitating factor (say, in combination with openness). Moreover, educational attainment is not clearly "caused" by public investment. Thomas and Wang (1996) show that the public educational effort relative to GDP is not unusually large in East Asia—what is unusual is its quality and technical orientation. Society's general commitment to learning may have been as important as public investment.

Public investments in infrastructure have been visible and effective in East Asia, but there is little evidence that they led, rather than accommodated, rapid growth. The importance of public investments in other sectors has varied widely across East Asia. Singapore's government-linked companies accounted for 23 percent of the assets of larger firms in 1986 (Soon and Tan 1996) and are said to be as profitable as private companies. Other successful cases of public investment include Taiwan (steel, automobiles, shipbuilding, and petrochemicals) and Korea (steel, fertilizer, and machinery). Public enterprise produced mixed results in Indonesia, Malaysia, and Thailand. In general, the role of SOEs has been declining—in Taiwan, for example, the state-owned enterprise's (SOE) share of manufacturing output fell from 51 percent in 1955 to 19 percent in 1990 (Dahlman and Sananikone 1996).

Overall, the role of government in East Asian savings and investment is significant but uneven. In line with structuralist views, several (but certainly not all) East Asian governments went beyond neoclassical prescriptions to encourage saving and undertake investment. But the market's role in accumulation remained important, and over time it generally increased. The critical point is that East Asia's public investments were surprisingly profitable. It appears that East Asian governments exercised greater financial discipline in making such investments than is usually the case in developing countries. With the possible exception of Singapore, it would be hard to argue that public investments principally caused East Asian success, but clearly they also did not stand in its way.[14]

## Targeted Industrial Policies

Most East Asian governments launched some industrial policy scheme. Singapore attempted a "Second Industrial Revolution," Taiwan an "Industrial Escalation," Korea a "Heavy and Chemical Industry" (HCI) drive, Hong Kong an "Industrial Diversification" program, Malaysia a "Heavy Industrialization" push, and so on. Korea's HCI drive was the most ambitious and most thoroughly analyzed. But, as table 11.4 shows, the degree of bias in favor of domestic manufacturing was low in Korea, Taiwan, and Singapore compared with that of other developing countries.

Nevertheless, several observers have attached particular importance to the government's industrial policy efforts. Amsden (1989) credits Korean HCI policies with a major role in technological upgrading. The World Bank (1987) is more neutral, noting that the drive created dynamic industries as well as costly failures. Most other analyses are critical, arguing that the HCI drive diverted capital from efficient labor-intensive industries (Yoo 1990). The HCI

---

14. The excellent performance of many East Asian SOEs does provide models for operating such firms elsewhere. Successful firms have been operated with professional management, at arms length from government control, and with clear incentives for profitability.

push also weakened the Korean financial sector and led to increased concentration—problems that continue to plague Korean policy.

Elsewhere, industrial targeting was more constrained. Taiwan provided selective support for steel, petrochemicals, automobiles, and shipbuilding; the first two succeeded, while the second two failed (Dahlman and Sananikone 1993). Taiwan's most dynamic sectors (apparel, electronics, and computers) received little selective but considerable functional support through EPZs and research institutes. In Malaysia, a heavy industry push created a host of low-profit enterprises in cement, steel, automobiles, and motorcycles (Salleh, Leng, and Meyanathan 1996). Throughout the region, the most ambitious industrial policy initiatives (e.g., in Korea, Singapore, Malaysia, and Thailand) were scaled back or abandoned within 10 years after their start.

The coincidence of industrial policy and rapid industrial upgrading supports the structuralist view that such programs accelerated East Asian economic development (Amsden 1989; Pack and Westphal 1986; Wade 1990). But the collapse of these initiatives—and their absence in some countries—also supports the neoclassical view that governments were not effective at targeting. The most successful industrial policies were those that reinforced comparative advantage—for example, Korea's general export subsidies in the 1960s, Taiwan's industrial estates and export processing zones, and Singapore's investments in telecommunications. In some cases, industrial policies may have contributed to rapid development, but one cannot argue that they were necessary or even predominantly successful.

## Regulated Financial Markets

East Asia provides an interesting test case for the theory that mild financial repression (as implemented through interest rate regulations and state-owned banking) can improve the efficiency of financial intermediation (Stiglitz

**TABLE 11.4.   Incentives for Domestic Relative to Export Sales**

|           | Traditional Industry | Nontraditional Industry | Manufacturing Industry |
|-----------|:--------------------:|:-----------------------:|:----------------------:|
| Argentina | 1.02                 | 3.58                    | 3.53                   |
| Colombia  | 0.97                 | 0.87                    | 1.42                   |
| Israel    | 1.11                 | 1.39                    | 1.63                   |
| Korea     | 1.18                 | 1.09                    | 0.95                   |
| Singapore | —                    | 1.09                    | 1.06                   |
| Taiwan    | 1.11                 | 1.13                    | 1.34                   |

*Source:* Balassa 1982.

*Note:* The table shows the ratio of effective protection on sales in domestic markets plus one to effective protection in export markets and one in the late 1960s.

1989).[15] In practice, East Asia's mechanisms of financial intermediation have ranged from highly regulated, state-controlled banking systems to competitive private banking. In between, many countries operated dualistic systems, with regulated markets providing capital for large industry and unregulated curb markets financing small enterprise.

A novel, two-step, intermediation process emerged in Korea: credit was sold wholesale to conglomerates (at low, rationed rates), which then used internal markets to ration funds to subsidiaries across many industries (Lee 1992). In Taiwan, regulated government-owned banks coexisted with a large unregulated curb market. This market, legitimized by an unusual Negotiable Instruments Law, which required issuers to honor postdated checks, played a central role in financing Taiwan's important small-scale manufacturing sector (Dahlman and Sananikone 1996). At the other extreme, relatively unregulated domestic and foreign banks financed development in Malaysia, Hong Kong, Singapore, and Thailand. In Thailand, private banks even assumed a role in sectoral coordination by reconciling conflicts over protection (Christensen et al. 1996).

Given these varied institutions, it is hard to argue that either a laissez-faire or a structuralist approach in finance was the general cause of East Asian success. On average, the region's economies were highly monetized relative to international norms (table 11.3)—but this average includes very diverse positions, with Singapore far above international norms and Korea far below. The fact that such a wide range of intermediation systems existed in East Asia suggests that the "macro" structure of credit markets alone does not determine efficiency in the allocation of credit. Flexibility and profit orientation at the operational level of financial decisions may be more important than the formal organization of the intermediation system, and in East Asia both state- and market-controlled systems were concerned with economic results. Thus, both highly regulated public and relatively open private banking systems appear have been able to finance rapid growth.

## Sophisticated Bureaucracies

Several East Asian countries have been described as strong "developmental states," distinguished by high-level commitment to economic objectives from powerful leaders, mechanisms for sheltering economic decisions from the political process, and powerful and capable "elite" bureaucracies (Johnson 1982,

---

15. In the early stages of development, the lack of financial information undermines the operation of financial markets. In this setting interest rates can rise to very high levels to cover default risk, and credit becomes unavailable for low-risk projects. Interest rate ceilings solve the problem by motivating intermediaries to ration credit and develop information on borrowers.

1987). Such high-level leadership was especially important in Korea, Indonesia, Singapore, and Taiwan.

Small, elite agencies with authority over line ministries assumed major responsibilities in Korea (Economic Planning Board), Taiwan (Council for Economic Planning and Development and its precursors), and Singapore (Economic Development Board). Singapore's board, for example, was purposefully kept small by reassigning routine functions to other agencies (Soon and Tan 1996). These agencies typically attracted the most talented graduates and, at least by developing country standards, were unusually corruption free. Their control over other government divisions was often enhanced by budgetary authority.

But there were no superministries in Hong Kong or Indonesia, and the corresponding bodies in Malaysia (Economic Planning Unit) and Thailand (National Economic and Social Development Board) had little budgetary authority and made only broad, indicative plans. In Indonesia, the top technocrats were so concerned about their limited influence that they took preemptive measures—such as opening the capital account, contracting customs to a Swiss firm, and eventually liberalizing credit and trade—to limit discretion in other parts of the government.

Culturalist explanations of East Asian success emphasize government capabilities and attribute the high quality of East Asian bureaucracies to Confucian, meritocratic traditions. Such bureaucracies appear to have been important in the context of government-led growth strategies of, say, Korea and Taiwan. But they were not a factor in several East Asian success stories that did not rely on bureaucratic control.

## Favorable External Environment

The expanding and liberalizing markets of the 1960s and 1970s provided a favorable backdrop to rapid growth in East Asia. In this context, and because East Asia's market penetration rates were still modest in the 1970s, Korean, Taiwanese, and other producers were not penalized for export promotion and subsidy policies that would be unacceptable today. They could reverse engineer or cheaply license critical technologies, and they could enter standardized markets in textiles and steel without facing severe competition and regulation.

Countries developing today face quite different conditions, including tight textile quotas and stiff demands for the protection of intellectual property. But their environment is favorable in other respects. Certain types of know-how are now available from similar, nearby countries without the risks associated with pioneering investments. New entrants can also "plug into" marketing and sourcing networks established under earlier contacts between developed countries and East Asian suppliers. And some trade barriers erected against established exporters (e.g., quotas on Japanese or NIE products) can create special opportunities for new entrants (Petri 1988).

Then and now, East Asia's external environment provides valuable exposure to the policies and experiences of unusually successful neighbors. Korea, Singapore, Malaysia, and several other East Asian countries were conscious and successful imitators—initially of Japan and later of each other's outward-oriented policies. For example, Korea's general trading companies, patterned on Japan's, spearheaded the country's export drive in the 1970s and 1980s. Korea's duty drawback and export financing schemes in turn attracted attention in several ASEAN countries and eventually throughout the world. Taiwan's and Singapore's early innovations in export processing zones were also extensively replicated.

While these factors support the contagion theory of East Asian success, they also suggest limitations on the contagion model. In each of these cases, foreign models were used very selectively: Korea copied Japan's tilt toward international-scale companies without focusing on domestic markets; Malaysia invested in heavy industry but ran a relatively open trade regime; and Taiwan and Singapore encouraged knowledge-intensive industry without a heavy industry drive. The common target of imitation may have been the commitment to outward-oriented development; the region's technocrats ultimately developed different and unique institutions to implement the details of this strategy.

## IV.  Toward a Synthesis

The two factors that run consistently through the East Asian experience—outward orientation and macroeconomic discipline—are clearly important factors in the region's outstanding economic performance. But these factors are not consistently associated with rapid growth in time; in each country's most rapid growth period other factors also seem to play a role. Several other causal factors appear to have been important in particular countries at various times. So, in the end, no explanation fits the full diversity of regional experience. The lessons of the East Asian miracles must therefore admit multiple recipes for success. An alternative "multifactor" approach is needed to understand how success emerged from a variety of policies in a variety of institutional settings. In such an approach, the various policies pursued in different East Asian countries might be viewed as *substitute* strategies for accomplishing some basic developmental objective rather than alternative approaches that can be ranked according to effectiveness.

Since this synthesis offers not just a different model but a different way of approaching the problem of East Asian success, its main features are explained in formal terms in the appendix. In identifying structural differences among alternative explanations of East Asian success, the appendix shows that other recent, comprehensive models of economic development (proposed in World Bank 1991) have also tended to take a multifactor explanatory approach rather than the single-factor approaches typical in some of the academic literature on the subject.

## Multiple Solutions to Key Functions

Underneath the enormous range of East Asian policies and institutions, it is possible to converge on some important common aspects of economic management. For example, Korea and Singapore appear to have followed very different strategies with respect to ownership: Korean development was spearheaded by private, domestic firms, Singapore's by foreign subsidiaries and government-linked enterprises. But the end result was that both countries had dynamic entrepreneurial sectors suited to their particular environments.

Three fundamental objectives of development, in particular, appear to underlie the East Asian success stories. The road race provides an analogy for this synthesis: we will compare the requirements for growth to the need for a track, steering, and an engine. The concept of a smooth track represents the idea that the general economic environment needs to be stable and conducive to market-oriented decision making. The notion of efficient steering refers to mechanisms that guide the allocation of resources into productive industries instead of waste, speculation, and rent seeking. Finally, the concept of an engine refers to leadership from a vital economic sector or an entrepreneurial class. East Asia's miracle economies have had strong, albeit diverse, assets in each of these three areas.

*The Track.* East Asia's economic environment was generally conducive to market-oriented activity. Policies favored macroeconomic stability, competitive labor markets, relatively free entry into small-scale business, and vigorous investment in human and physical capital. To be sure, these favorable conditions did not always lead to rapid growth, and growth spurts sometimes occurred without all of them in place. The correlation between the economic environment and growth is strong enough to suggest an essential linkage but not so strong as to make the environment the single, sufficient cause of rapid growth.

The value of a market-oriented environment was enhanced in many East Asian economies by the exceptional flexibility of economic agents. Chau (1996) argues that Hong Kong's entrepreneurs were not committed to any particular business or technology but, true to merchant traditions, continuously floated to niches of profitable activity. Kim and Leipziger (1996) note similar tendencies in Korea's middle-sized firms, which spanned several industries and rapidly changed their product mix to exploit trends. More fundamentally, this flexibility may be the result of history: the collapse of the traditional power structure due to war, colonialism, and shifting political and economic ties.

Market-oriented macroeconomic environments evolved in East Asia under several different government institutions and philosophies. In Korea and Taiwan, strong governments maintained stable policies; in Indonesia and Thailand, stable policies resulted from self-imposed constraints on budgetary procedures and/or international financial commitments. Korea created competitive labor markets by suppressing unions, Singapore by inviting organized labor into governmental councils. Each "track" provided a favorable environment for markets but closely fitted the country's institutional framework.

*Steering.* East Asian economies excelled at channeling entrepreneurial and other resources into efficient activities. Because they were outward oriented, most of these economies used international competitiveness as a yardstick of economic success. Even state enterprises, though less exposed to market pressures, were often directed to become internationally competitive, and thus pursued economic rather than political goals.

International prices entered East Asia's domestic incentive systems in different ways. In Hong Kong, Singapore, and Malaysia, levels of protection were low, and all firms faced international prices. In Korea, the government used export performance to determine access to subsidized credit and other privileges. In Taiwan and several other countries, export-oriented firms were exempted from import duties and thus faced essentially international prices, while domestically oriented firms operated under conditions of intense competition.

State-owned enterprises were also typically accountable on economic criteria. In Korea, Singapore, and Taiwan, public companies were directed by professional managers isolated from political pressure. Public enterprises were often designed to export and had to meet international competitive standards. Over time, as their private sectors matured, East Asian economies also moved to reduce the role of public enterprises. Taiwan systematically divested its extensive industrial holdings. As more inefficiencies developed in the public sectors of Indonesia and Malaysia, these governments also embarked on privatization programs.

*Engines.* The engines of growth differed widely across East Asia. Hong Kong's miracle began with a large influx of capitalists from Shanghai. Experienced in textile manufacturing, these entrepreneurs diverted machinery and intermediate goods shipments bound for China and set up relatively large manufacturing operations. Four decades later, Hong Kong's own "merchant entrepreneurs" found a new niche as intermediaries between China and the world—incidentally also driving southern China's economic takeoff.

Korea's dynamism derived from a handful of large conglomerates financed by low-cost, government-controlled credit. Initially selected on the basis of personal connections, the list of promoted firms was constantly pruned according to economic performance. Government policies amplified market signals: successful firms not only earned profits but won access to fresh capital and lucrative investment opportunities (Petri 1990). By allocating capital across a wide range of business activities, these conglomerates also helped to mitigate inefficiencies in capital markets.

Singapore relied on foreign firms. The island's initial attraction was based on low-cost labor, tax concessions, and its location along major shipping lanes. As Singapore's advantages shifted to skilled labor, foreign investment also shifted to technologically advanced industries and services. Singapore dramatically upgraded its economic base with little control over its industry and minimal sectoral intervention.

The developmental engines of Malaysia, Indonesia, and Thailand were started in natural resource production—widespread improvements in rice farming in Indonesia and Thailand, intensive production of metals and oil crops in Malaysia—and have since shifted to manufacturing led by a major boom in foreign direct investment. Flexible labor markets, exchange rates, and foreign direct investment played an important role in these transitions.

The fit between these engines and their economic environments is remarkable. In the context of the relatively freewheeling economic systems of Malaysia and Thailand, for example, it would have been virtually impossible to implement effectively the kind of government intervention in business investment that was practiced in Korea. In the context of Korea's institutions, in turn, it would have been just as difficult to imagine the development of harmonious relationships between the bureaucracy and foreign firms, as occurred in Singapore.

## Fitting the Model to the Environment

A key implication of a multifactor approach to East Asian success is that policy options must be closely fitted to a country's circumstances. Necessity often played a role in forging the right fit. Korea and Taiwan both adopted equilibrium exchange rate policies and aggressive export promotion when their main source of foreign exchange—aid from the United States—suddenly slowed. Hong Kong and Singapore also had little choice but to emphasize trade when their historical entrepôt function was disrupted by political turmoil. Much later, the collapse of oil prices also pushed Indonesia toward realistic exchange rates and outward-oriented trade policies.

Other major policy choices resulted from experimentation, learning, and adjustment. East Asian policies have generally evolved through incremental adjustments, as in the case trade liberalization and investment incentive measures in Korea, Taiwan, and Thailand. East Asian economies have been also prompt in recognizing serious policy mistakes and adopting corrective measures. Important examples include the reversal of heavy industry initiatives in Korea, Malaysia, and Singapore.

Two characteristics of East Asian governance may explain their unusual ability to adapt. One is the longevity of East Asian governments. Facing indefinite tenures, governments are more willing to accept short-term sacrifice for long-term benefits. Second, in many East Asian countries, bureaucracies had considerable leeway in designing and executing policy. Finally, they generally kept in close contact with the private sector, helping to generate a continuous flow of information on the consequences of policy. The relationship between actual policies and certain underlying requirements of the development process helps to illuminate the common foundations of East Asian success.

## V.  Can East Asian Success Be Imitated?

The commonalities in East Asian development strategies are ultimately found not in specific policies but in functional aspects of economic management. Rapid development does not call for a particular policy recipe, but it does require a disciplined, balanced approach to policy making in order to achieve fundamental goals. Somehow, an economy must create an environment that encourages market-oriented investment, it must ensure that its dominant resource steering mechanisms are sensitive to economic efficiency, and it must "find" an engine of growth to generate dynamism and leadership.

How these objectives are best achieved in a particular economy depends on its own history as well as its external environment. World markets today will not tolerate large export subsidies, and many of the technologies required to participate aggressively in world markets cannot be acquired any more by copying or reverse engineering. This argues for more import and investment liberalization than was the case with the economies that based their development on export promotion in the 1960s.

The alternative approaches used in East Asia to meet the challenges of economic management differ quite substantially in their implications for government management capacity. Government-directed models of development are risky because their performance depends critically on the quality of leaders and bureaucracies. Although some countries have succeeded under government-directed models, many have done poorly. It is relatively unusual to have sophisticated, disciplined bureaucracies in an otherwise undeveloped economy; this happened to be the case for complex historical reasons in some East Asian countries. For most countries without such histories it will be unnecessary and inappropriate to choose strategies that require significant government involvement in microeconomic choices.

With regard to the issues raised at the outset, East Asian experience offers a range of models that differ considerably in degrees of government intervention, shares for private enterprise, and roles for accumulation and productivity. This makes the message of East Asian growth both more complex and more optimistic than single-factor analyses have suggested in the past. There is no single policy that can be copied to guarantee success, yet the fundamental elements of East Asian success have been achieved, in different countries and at different times, with a wide range of policies.

These findings have important implications for countries seeking to imitate the East Asian miracles. First, not one but several East Asian models need to be studied. The question is not "which is the best" but rather "which is the most relevant" to an imitator's initial conditions and environment. Second, although the elements of different models can be "mixed and matched," the development strategy must provide solutions to each of the three challenges of economic management. Third, the choices made at any given time must be closely monitored and modified if necessary. No new set of policies is likely to be right in all respects, nor will a set of effective policies remain so indefinitely. Close monitoring of economic performance, and flexibility in adapting policies to changing economic conditions at home and abroad, are essential for sustained success.

The availability of alternative strategies means that close attention must be paid to the task of matching policy approaches with institutional capacity and other aspects of an economy's environment. In East Asia, the match between policies and endowments was not usually the result of lucky or particularly insightful choices. Rather, over time, unsuccessful approaches were reformed or abandoned. A pattern of search, experimentation, and adjustment was essential to success and may itself have been the product of East Asia's unusual propensities for stability, pragmatism, and authoritarian leadership.

East Asia's experience shows that rapid catchup can be achieved in various ways. A market-oriented environment is a key ingredient, but interventionist approaches were also prominent. The range of policies compatible with rapid growth appears to be broader than neoclassical economics admits. But intervention was neither sufficient nor necessary for rapid progress—indeed, the region's most interventionist policies were generally unsuccessful and had to be abandoned. The real issue is not whether the policy environment is generally interventionist or laissez-faire but whether policies are properly structured to address the basic requirements of growth and whether they fit the economy's capacities and environment.

APPENDIX: THE FORMAL STRUCTURE OF
ALTERNATIVE EXPLANATIONS

Alternative explanations of the East Asian miracles can be best classified using simple, formal notation. Suppose that economic performance is explained by a "performance function" written in terms of a list of determinants:

$$g = f(x_1 \ldots x_k), \tag{1}$$

where $g$ = economic performance and $x_i$ = contribution of $i$ th determinant. Explanations will be classified in terms of the relationships they propose among different determinants and between the determinants and economic performance.

Single-factor explanations propose that only the $k$ th component is critical, so that the relationship is really $g = f(x_k)$.

Multifactor explanations recognize that several factors may be important.

Multifactor explanations can be further categorized as "independent" or "interdependent." An independent multifactor explanation assumes that each determinant makes a separate, additive contribution to performance. For example, such an approach may see success as the result of a combined list of factors such as outward orientation, macroeconomic stability, and appropriate cultural traditions. Different cases of success may thus be associated with different combinations of positive factors. Formally,

$$df / dx_i > 0 \qquad (2)$$

for several $i$, while independence implies that

$$d^2f / dx_i dx_j = 0 \qquad (3)$$

for all $i$ not equal to $j$.

Two recent studies have proposed interdependent multifactor explanations. The *World Development Report, 1991* (World Bank 1991) argued that there are positive interactions among four aspects of economic policy: outward orientation, human capital investment, macroeconomic stability, and domestic competition. In this context, East Asia's success is attributed to reinforcing feedbacks or, formally, positive interactions among policies:

$$d^2f / dx_i dx_j > 0 \qquad (4)$$

for $i$ not equal to $j$. No single variable needs to be perfectly correlated with success, but high values in several contributing dimensions will be very effective.

A similar model was proposed by *World Development Report, 1990* (World Bank 1990), which argued that success involves not getting any policies badly wrong. This implies that the weakest policy limits performance:

$$g = f(\min x_i) \qquad (5)$$

over all $i$ and focuses attention on "mistakes" or endowment gaps.

The synthesis proposed in this paper also follows an interdependent multifactor approach. In this framework, performance depends on how well the economy executes certain general functions (say, how well the economy steers resources into efficient uses). Success in these functions in turn depends on the extent to which any one of several substitute policies are implemented (say, domestic competition, foreign competition, or competitively assigned government rewards). Formally:

$$g = f(y_1, y_2, \ldots), \tag{6}$$

where $y_1 = h(x_{11}, x_{12}, \ldots)$, and so on. Successful economies will have high unit values for $y_1$, $y_2$, and so on (and perhaps for combinations of the $y$s if interactions are important), but these high values for intermediate functions could be the result of very different settings for specific policies $x_{ij}$.

The formal structure of an explanatory strategy has implications for testing. Single-factor approaches are the easiest to test; there either is or isn't a relationship between the presence of a policy and performance in the sample. Only a single relationship (or set of parameters) needs to be examined at a time. Independent multifactor explanations are the next easiest to test—the number of their parameters is proportional to the number of potential determinants. Interdependent multifactor approaches are the most difficult to test. The number of parameters required in such models is exponential in the number of determinants, since additional parameters are needed to fix the effects of interactions among policies.

REFERENCES

Akamatsu, K. 1960. "A Theory of Unbalanced Growth in the World Economy." *Weltwirtschaftliches Archiv* 86:2.
Amsden, Alice H. 1989. *Asia's Next Giant.* New York: Oxford University Press.
Aoki, Masahiko. 1990. "Toward and Economic Model of the Japanese Firm." *Journal of Economic Literature* 28 (March): 1–27.
Balassa, Bela. 1981. *The Newly Industrializing Economies in the World Economy.* New York: Pergamon Press.
———. 1982. *Development Strategies in Semi-industrializing Economies.* Baltimore: Johns Hopkins University Press.
———. 1988. "The Lessons of East Asian Development: An Overview." *Economic Development and Cultural Change* 36, no. 3 (April): S273–90.
Bhattacharya, Amar, and Mari Pangestu. 1996. "Indonesia: Development Transformation and the Role of Public Policy." This volume.
Chau, Leung Chuen. 1996. "Hong Kong: A Unique Case of Development." This volume.

Chen, Edward K. 1979. *Hypergrowth in Asian Economies: A Comparative Survey of Hong Kong, Japan, Korea, Singapore, and Taiwan.* London: Macmillan.

Chen, E. K. Y. 1988. "The Economics and Non-Economics of Asia's Four Little Dragons." *Supplement to the Gazette* (University of Hong Kong) 35, no. 1 (March 21).

Chenery, Hollis, Sherman Robinson, and Moshe Syrquin. 1986. *Industrialization and Growth: A Comparative Study.* New York: Oxford University Press for the World Bank.

Christensen, Scott R., David Dollar, Ammar Siamwalla, and Pakorn Vichyanond. 1996. "Thailand: The Institutional and Political Underpinnings of Growth." This volume.

Corbo, Vittorio, Anne O. Krueger, and Fernando Ossa. 1985. *Export-Oriented Development Strategies: The Success of Five Newly Industrializing Countries.* Boulder: Westview Press.

Dahlman, Carl J., and Ousa Sananikone. 1996. "Taiwan, China: Economic Policies and Institutions for the Rapid Growth." This volume.

Fry, Maxwell J. 1986. "National Saving, Financial Saving, and Interest Rate Policy in Asian Developing Countries." In United Nations, Department of International Economic and Social Affairs, *Savings for Development.* New York: United Nations Pp. 29–46.

———. 1988. *Money, Interest and Banking in Economic Development.* Baltimore: Johns Hopkins University Press.

Gerschenkron, Alexander. 1962. *Economic Backwardness in Historical Perspective.* Cambridge: Harvard University Press.

Hamilton, Gary, ed. 1991. *Business Networks and Economic Development in East and Southeast Asia.* Hong Kong: Hong Kong University Press.

Johnson, Chalmers. 1982. *MITI and the Japanese Miracle.* Stanford: Stanford University Press.

———. 1987. "Political Institutions and Economic Performance: The Government-Business Relationship in Japan, South Korea, and Taiwan." In *The Political Economy of the New Asian Industrialism,* edited by Frederic C. Deyo. Ithaca: Cornell University Press.

Jones, Leroy, and Il Sakong. 1980. *Government, Business, and Entrepreneurship in Economic Development: The Korean Case.* Cambridge: Harvard University Press.

Kim, Kihwan, and Danny M. Leipziger. 1996. "Korea: A Case of Government-Led Development." This volume.

Kreuger, Anne O. 1974. "The Political Economy of Rent Seeking Society." *American Economic Review* 64, no. 3: 291–303.

———. 1983. *Alternative Trade Strategies and Employment: Synthesis and Conclusions.* Chicago: University of Chicago Press.

———. 1985. "The Experience and Lessons of Asia's Super Exporters." In Vittorio Corbo, *Export-Oriented Development Strategies,* edited by Anne O. Krueger and Fernando Ossa. Boulder: Westview Press.

Krugman, Paul. 1994. "The Myth of Asia's Miracle." *Foreign Affairs* 73, no. 6 (November-December): 62–78.

Kuznets, Paul W. 1988. "An East Asian Model of Economic Development: Japan, Taiwan, and South Korea." *Economic Development and Cultural Change* 36, no. 6 (April): S11–S43.

Lee, Chung H. 1992. "The Government, Financial System, and Large Private Enterprises in the Economic Development of South Korea." *World Development* 20, no. 2: 187–97.

Leipziger, Danny M. 1993. "Industrial Restructuring in Korea." *World Development* 16, no. 1: 121–36.

Leipziger, Danny M., and Peter A. Petri. 1993. "Korean Industrial Policy: Legacies of the Past and Directions for the Future." World Bank Discussion Papers No. 197. Mimeo.

———. 1994. "Korean Industrial Policies: Legacies of the Past and Directions for the Future." In *Korea's Political Economy: An Institutional Perspective,* edited by Lee-Jay Cho and Yoon Hyung Kim. Boulder: Westview.

Moroshima, M. 1982. *Why Has Japan "Succeeded"? Western Technology and the Japanese Ethos.* Cambridge: Cambridge University Press.

Pack, Howard, and Larry E. Westphal. 1986. "Industrial Strategy and Technological Change: Theory vs. Reality." *Journal of Development Economics* 22:87–128.

Page, John M., and Peter A. Petri. 1993. "Productivity Change and Strategic Growth Policy in the Asian Miracle." World Bank working paper, Policy Research Department. Mimeo.

Pangestu, Mari, and Ahman D. Habir. 1989. "Trends and Prospects in Privatization and Deregulation in Indonesia." *ASEAN Economic Bulletin* 5, no. 3 (March): 224–41.

Petri, Peter A. 1988. "Korea's Export Niche: Origins and Prospects." *World Development* 16, no. 1: 47–63.

———. 1990. "Korean Trade as Outlier: An Economic Anatomy." In *Korean Economic Development,* edited by Jene K. Kwon. Westport: Greenwood Press. Pp. 53–78.

———. Forthcoming. "The East Asian Trading Bloc: An Analytical History." Forthcoming in a volume edited by Jeffrey Frankel and Miles Kahler. Chicago: University of Chicago Press.

Salleh, Ismail, Yeah Kim Leng, and Saha Meyanathan. 1996. "Malaysia: Growth, Equity, and Structural Transformation." This volume.

Scalapino, Robert, Seizaburo Sato, and Jusu Wanandi, eds. 1985. *Asian Economic Development: Present and Future.* Berkeley: Institute of East Asian Studies.

Soesastro, Hadi. 1985. "Japan 'Teacher'—ASEAN 'Pupils:' Can it Work?" In *Asian Economic Development: Present and Future,* edited by Robert A. Scalapino, Seizaburo Sato, and Jusuf Wanandi. Research Papers and Policy Studies No. 14. Berkeley: Institute of East Asian Studies.

Soon, Teck-Wong, and C. Suan Tan. 1996. "Singapore: Public Policy and Economic Development." This volume.

Stiglitz, J. E. 1989. "Markets, Market Failures, and Development." *American Economic Review* 79, no. 2 (May): 197–203.

Syrquin, Moshe, and Hollis B. Chenery. 1989. *Patterns of Development, 1950–1983.* Discussion Papers No. 41. Washington, D.C.: World Bank.

Thomas, Vinod, and Yan Wang. 1996. "Government Policies and Productivity Growth: Is East Asia an Exception?" This volume.

Vogel, Ezra. 1991. *The Four Little Dragons: The Spread of Industrialization in East Asia.* Cambridge: Harvard University Press.

Wade, Robert. 1990. *Governing the Market: Economic Theory and the Role of Government in East Asian Industrialization*. Princeton: Princeton University Press.

Weber, Max. 1951. "Confucianism and Taoism." In H. Gerth, ed. *The Religion of China*, Glencoe Ill: Free Press.

White, Gordon, ed. 1988. *Developmental States in East Asia*. London: Macmillan.

Wolf, Charles. 1988. *Markets or Governments: Choosing between Imperfect Alternatives*. Cambridge: MIT Press.

World Bank. 1987. *Korea: Managing the Industrial Transition*. Washington, D.C.: World Bank.

————. 1990. *World Development Report, 1990*. New York: Oxford University Press.

————. 1991. *World Development Report, 1991*. New York: Oxford University Press.

Yoo, Jung H. 1990. *The Industrial Policy of the 1970s and the Evolution of the Manufacturing Sector in Korea*. Working Papers No. 9017. Seoul: Korea Development Institute.

Yoshihara, Kunio. 1988. *The Rise of Ersatz Capitalism in Southeast Asia*. Oxford: Oxford University Press.

# Contributors

**Amar Bhattacharya** is Economic Advisor in the International Economics Department of the World Bank.

**Leung Chuen Chau** is Economics Professor at the University of Hong Kong.

**Scott R. Christensen** was Research Fellow at the Thailand Development Research Institute.

**Carl J. Dahlman** is currently the World Bank's Resident Representative in Mexico.

**David Dollar** is the Chief of the Macroeconomics and Growth Division of the World Bank.

**Maxwell John Fry** holds the Tokai Bank Chair in International Finance at the University of Birmingham.

**Homi J. Kharas** is Lead Economist and Chief of Operations for Brazil at the World Bank.

**Kim Kihwan** is Chairman of several policy advisory committees for the Korean Government, including the Trade Policy Advisory Committee and the Policy Advisory Committee for the Ministry of Unification.

**Danny M. Leipziger** is Divisional Manager for Private Sector Development, Regulation, and Public Sector Management at the Economic Development Institute of the World Bank.

**Saha Meyanathan** is Senior Industrial Economist with the Economic Development Institute of the World Bank.

**Mari Pangestu** is Head of the Economics Department at the Center for Strategic and International Studies in Jakarta.

**Peter Petri** is Dean and Carl Shapiro Professor of International Finance in the Graduate School of International Economics and Finance at Brandeis University.

**Ismail Salleh** is the CEO of L&G Twintech, Kuala Lumpur, Malaysia and the Director of the Centre for Policy Studies.

**Ousa Sananikone** is a Private Sector Development Specialist at the World Bank.

**Ammar Siamwalla** is a distinguished scholar and former President of the Thailand Research Institute.

**Teck-Wong Soon** is a Senior Lecturer in the Department of Economics and Statistics at the National University of Singapore.

**C. Suan Tan** was a Senior Economist at the World Bank.

**Vinod Thomas** is Director of the World Bank's Economic Development Institute.

**Pakorn Vichyanond** was Senior Fellow at the Thailand Development Research Institute.

**Yan Wang** is an Economist in the Office of the East Asia Regional Vice President at the World Bank.

# Index